Charlotte Huck's
Children's
Literature
Third Edition

A Brief Guide

Charlotte Huck's
Children's
Literature
Third Edition

Barbara Z. Kiefer
The Ohio State University

Cynthia A. Tyson
The Ohio State University

Bettie Parsons Barger
Winthrop University

Lisa Patrick
The Ohio State University

Erin Reilly-Sanders
Independent Scholar

CHARLOTTE HUCK'S CHILDREN'S LITERATURE

Published by McGraw-Hill Education, 2 Penn Plaza, New York, NY 10121. Copyright ©2019 by McGraw-Hill Education. All rights reserved. Printed in the United States of America. No part of this publication may be reproduced or distributed in any form or by any means, or stored in a database or retrieval system, without the prior written consent of McGraw-Hill Education, including, but not limited to, in any network or other electronic storage or transmission, or broadcast for distance learning.

Some ancillaries, including electronic and print components, may not be available to customers outside the United States.

This book is printed on acid-free paper.

1 2 3 4 5 6 7 8 9 LCR 21 20 19 18

ISBN 978-1-260-08552-5
MHID 1-260-08552-X

Cover and Interior Design Image: ©McGraw-Hill Education/Rafael López, Illustrator

mheducation.com/highered

Contents in Brief

Contents

Part One
Learning About Books and Children   1

Part Two
Exploring Genres in Children's Books   65

Part Three
The Literature Program Across the Curriculum   323

Preface

Charlotte Huck's Children's Literature continues to be the classic, comprehensive text for those involved in all aspects of the evaluation and selection of children's literature for preK through middle-school readers. Like no other book, it not only provides the classroom teacher, librarian, administrator, and parent with a thorough understanding of children's literature, but it also—like no other book—reflects the passion for children's literature that resonated with Charlotte Huck. A true pioneer in the field, it was apparent that Charlotte's goal was not for readers to simply learn the history, concepts, and evaluation criteria necessary to understand and select children's literature—but to jump headfirst into the joy and excitement that the literature of childhood can bring, and in turn to share this enthusiasm with the children they teach. As we continue with the tenets originated by Charlotte, who passed away in 2005, we keep that goal of passion and enthusiasm at the forefront of our writing.

Approach of This Text

This briefer version of the original text provides an introduction to the field of children's literature that primarily addresses the needs of preservice teachers by employing a multifaceted approach to the study of children's literature:

- By focusing on the core definitions, key examples, and essential evaluation guidelines, *Charlotte Huck's Children's Literature: A Brief Guide, third edition* provides a **launching point for further exploration of actual children's books** during the course setting.
- This text not only serves as a valuable resource by providing the most current reference lists from which to select books, but it also emphasizes the critical skills needed to search for and select literature—**researching, evaluating, and implementing quality books in the preK–8 classroom**—to give preservice teachers the tools they

need to evaluate books, create curriculum, and share the love of literature.
- Beyond the key understandings in children's literature, we also include **critical perspectives that teachers face in the twenty-first century.** The critical perspectives offered here, many of which explore the use of multicultural literature, are presented to the reader to assist in the process of evaluating children's literature through themes and issues of social and political nature that often find their way into today's classrooms. These discussions, along with the application of the Ten-Point Model for Teaching Controversial Issues, encourage higher levels of examination and will help facilitate critical-thinking skills in even their youngest students.
- We contend that the literature and accomplishments of all groups should be part of every subject taught. Thus, **multicultural literature—broadly defined—is infused throughout the entire text** and in each genre or subject area.

Organization

The three-part organization of *Charlotte Huck's Children's Literature: A Brief Guide* emphasizes the triple focus of the text: the reader, the book, and teaching. Part One focuses on the values and criteria for choosing and using literature with children at various stages in their development. Part Two provides an in-depth look at the various genres of children's literature and establishes evaluative criteria for each genre. Each of these chapters has been written with children at the center and includes references and resources for involving children in exploring books across the curriculum. Part Three explores this curricular strand in-depth by focusing on the teaching, planning, and evaluating of literature-based programs.

Features

As touched on previously, this text not only provides the core material necessary to understand children's literature, but it also provides a number of unique features and presentations:

- **Full-color throughout:** In order to truly show the visual impact of children's literature, the entire text is full-color, with approximately one hundred images of covers and illustrations from children's books presented throughout the chapters.
- **The art of Rafael López:** We are very fortunate to have Rafael López involved in this text. The multitalented and award-winning illustrator created a vibrant and exciting look for the book, developing unique artwork for the cover and interior features.
- **Thoroughly integrated multicultural literature and diversity topics:** Examples of multicultural literature and its applications in the classroom are provided throughout the entire text, ensuring that future teachers will have the skills to choose challenging and inspiring literature for all their students. Multicultural titles are called out by a margin icon as well as printed in blue in the children's literature lists at the end of each chapter.
- **The Ten-Point Model for Teaching Controversial Issues:** A unique framework for tackling controversial topics in and out of the classroom, the Ten-Point Model for Teaching Controversial Issues is presented in Chapter 1. Sample models for the genre chapters are provided within Connect®, as well as a template for creating models for specific issues.
- **Teaching Features:** Resource boxes throughout the text highlight the best examples of children's literature for each genre or topic.
- **Evaluating children's literature:** *Guidelines* boxes provide specific criteria and questions to consider when evaluating children's literature. Expanded forms are available within Connect®. These forms can be used as course activities or in practice when evaluating specific books.
- **Unique Challenging Perspectives discussions:** *Challenging Perspectives* sections appear in each genre chapter, outlining difficult or controversial social issues facing today's teacher (and children) and providing instruction on how to evaluate and select appropriate children's literature that will help address those topics. Many topics involve cultural issues, such as sensitivity to the use of color in different cultures and "slams" in poetry.
- **Applications to standards:** A restructured *Curriculum Connections* feature at the end of each genre chapter gives examples of how to use children's literature to fulfill state educational standards in a variety of course areas.
- **Children's literature selections:** Comprehensive, up-to-date lists of children's literature are provided at the end of each chapter, with more titles available in the searchable Children's Literature Database within Connect®.
- **Books to Read Aloud:** The endpapers serve as an introduction to the field of children's literature by providing a quick list of books to read aloud to different age groups.
- **Practical appendixes:** The book's appendixes—Children's Book Awards and Book Selection Aids—provide current resources to aid in text selection.

New to This Edition

This third edition has been thoroughly updated, including mention of hundreds of recently published children's books throughout the text and the updated **Teaching Resources** and **Children's Literature** lists. Illustrations from many of these new books are seen throughout the chapters. New images and suggested book titles have been chosen to emphasize the diversity of readers and their need to see themselves reflected in books.

Chapter-opening vignettes have been revised to focus on the faces of young readers and their enthusiastic responses to many different genres.

The **Curriculum Connections** feature has been restructured to reflect the newest educational standards and capitalize on cross-discipline opportunities.

Some of the additional changes you will find include:

Chapter 1: Knowing Children's Literature
- Many new titles are included as examples of personal and educational values and experiences.
- Teaching Feature 1.2: Selected Book Awards for Children includes new information on the Asian/Pacific American Award for Literature and the Charlotte Huck Award.

- A number of recent titles are included with descriptions on how to evaluate for plot, style, and point of view.

Chapter 2: Understanding Children's Responses to Literature
- New opening vignette shows the influence of literature on literacy fluency.
- The section "Developmental Patterns That Influence Response" emphasizes the sociocultural aspects of development. This concept extends our understanding of the development of children from diverse cultures, whose family beliefs and practices may be different from the children studied by Piaget and others.
- An updated Teaching Feature 2.1: Books for Ages and Stages includes more than 40 new suggested titles.

Chapter 3: Picturebooks
- New opening vignette shows how the art in picturebooks can inspire children's visual, mental, and verbal imaginations and how an integrated curriculum can be centered in picturebooks.
- An expanded section on graphica emphasizes the many different forms they can take.
- The inclusion of more nonfiction titles indicates that beautiful illustration and design is not limited to works of fiction.
- New, updated examples of recent picturebooks effectively illustrate the elements of design.
- Teaching Feature 3.2 includes many new examples of various media used in picturebooks.
- Teaching Feature 3.4: A Sampling of Picturebooks includes more than 30 new titles.
- A completely revised Curriculum Connections: Using Picturebooks to Address Standards highlights *They All Saw a Cat* by Brendan Wenzel (2016).
- A thoroughly updated Children's Literature list adds a new section devoted to graphica.

Chapter 4: Traditional Literature
- New opening vignette emphasizes the role family can play in establishing an early interest in reading.
- "Epic and Legendary Heroes" section has been streamlined to permit discussion of more heroes from a various cultures. It also acknowledges the absence of female heroes.

- Christian Bible stories previously discussed have been integrated into the appropriate tale types, along with sacred literature from other faiths.
- Myths have been expanded to respectfully include more variety of sacred stories while reducing the predominance of Greek and Norse mythology.
- Instructional Tales, or Parables, have been incorporated into the "Fables" section.
- Many new titles focusing on multicultural tales have been added throughout the chapter.
- Teaching Feature 4.1: A Cross-Cultural Study of Folktale Types includes new titles from India, Cuba, and Russia, among others.
- Teaching Feature 4.2: A Cross-Cultural Study of Folktale Motifs and Variants includes new titles from China and Mexico, among others.

Chapter 5: Modern Fantasy
- "Types of Fantasy" section has been clarified to improve readers' understanding.
- Many examples of recent series books appear throughout the chapter and updated Teaching Feature 5.1: Chronicles, Sagas, and Trilogies: Recent Fantasy Series for Children.
- Teaching Feature 5.2: Exploring Possible Futures: Science Fiction for Today's Youth includes new authors as well as new titles for previously published authors.
- A completely revised Curriculum Connections: Using Modern Fantasy to Address Standards highlights *The Girl Who Drank the Moon* by Kelly Barnhill (2016).

Chapter 6: Poetry
- The updated Teaching Features 6.1 and 6.2 contain recent poetry titles, including numerous multicultural publications.
- New sample poems offer fresh examples to illustrate the elements of poetry and reflect the current focus on the refugee crisis in the world.
- Resources specifically designed for classroom teachers by Sylvia Vardell and Janet Wong are included.
- A new Curriculum Connections: Using Poetry to Address Standards highlights *Echo Echo*, Marilyn Singer's newest book of reverso poems about Greek myths.

Chapter 7: Contemporary Realistic Fiction

- The updated Teaching Features 7.1 and 7.2 include texts that portray a variety of genders, family types, races, and cultures.
- Enhanced comparisons of historical and contemporary realistic fiction as well as magical realism, fantasy, and contemporary realism explore the blurred spaces between genre boundaries.
- New suggested books represent different races, abilities, sexual preferences, gender identities, religions, illnesses, and more aspects of diversity.
- Multiple formats, including novels in verse and graphica, have been included.
- A completely revised Curriculum Connections: Using Realistic Fiction to Address Standards highlights *Forever, or a Long, Long Time* by Caela Carter (2017).

Chapter 8: Historical Fiction

- New opening vignette emphasizes the connections between today and the past through fiction.
- The latest fiction, especially that which connects to contemporary issues such as race, immigration, oppression of laborers, and women in STEM, is discussed in detail.
- Teaching Feature 8.1: Historical Fiction and the Social Studies Sequence by Grade Level includes many new examples as well as a new section on the Civil Rights era in the United States.
- "The Challenging Perspectives on Historical Fiction" section expands on some of the touchier issues in American history, notably Japanese internment and Juneteenth, the celebration of the end of slavery.
- A completely revised Curriculum Connections: Using Historical Fiction to Address Standards highlights *The War That Saved My Life* by Kimberly Brubaker Bradley (2015).

Chapter 9: Nonfiction

- Comparisons between conflicting terminology has been replaced with clearer definitions, with emphasis on the variety within the genre.
- Current interest in social implications of scientific developments is featured in the discussions of several new titles.
- Teaching Feature 9.1: Types of Nonfiction has been updated with more than half new titles.

- Although a significant portion of new multicultural nonfiction is biography, many new titles have been included.
- A completely revised Curriculum Connections: Using Nonfiction to Address Standards highlights *Animals by the Numbers: A Book of Animal Infographics* by Steve Jenkins (2016).

Chapter 10: Biography

- Updated titles throughout the chapter reflect trends in recently published picturebook biographies for children, such as pioneering women in science.
- An updated Teaching Feature 10.1: Types of Biography includes an expanded section of picturebook biographies divided into various themes.
- A revised Curriculum Connections: Using Biography to Address Standards highlights Melissa Sweet's Caldecott Medal-winning *Some Writer!: The Story of E. B. White* by Melissa Sweet (2016).

Chapter 11: Planning the Literature Program

- The section on libraries includes the latest information and terminology.
- "Providing Time for the In-Depth Study of Books" section includes a new subsection: Extending Literature Through Technology.
- Teaching Feature 11.1: Fact and Fiction Books to Use Together has been revised to reflect current issues of social justice and to highlight an integrated curricular approach to addressing state standards.
- New examples of books to read aloud are provided, including an updated, handy reference on the inside covers of the text.

Connect: Teaching and Learning Resources

Charlotte Huck's Children's Literature: A Brief Guide, third edition is now available online with *Connect*®, McGraw-Hill Education's integrated assignment and assessment platform. *Connect*® also offers Smart-Book for the new edition, which is the first adaptive reading experience proven to improve grades and help students study more effectively. All of the title's website and ancillary content is also available through *Connect*®.

Resources for the Instructor:

- Downloadable PowerPoint presentations
- Instructor's manual, originally developed by Erika Thulin Dawes, Lesley University
- Test bank available as downloadable Word files and through EZ Test Online, which allows instructors to create and print a test or create and deliver an online and printed (Word or PDF) test

Resources for the Student:

- Downloadable PowerPoint presentations
- Self-grading multiple choice and true or false quizzes with feedback
- Chapter outlines, summaries, and learning objectives
- Annotated web links of useful resources
- Expanded evaluation guides
- Ten-Point Model examples for each genre
- Complete lists of major book awards
- Children's Literature Database. This extensive children's literature database of more than five thousand titles can be searched a number of ways. The books listed have been carefully evaluated and selected as excellent books for children.

McGraw-Hill Create.

Design your ideal course materials with McGraw-Hill's *Create* at www.mcgrawhillcreate.com. Rearrange or omit chapters, combine material from other sources, and/or upload your syllabus or any other content you have written to make the perfect resource for your students. Search thousands of leading McGraw-Hill textbooks to find the best content for your students, then arrange it to fit your teaching style. You can even personalize your book's appearance by selecting the cover and adding your name, school, and course information. When you order a *Create* book, you receive a complimentary review copy. Get a printed copy in three to five business days or an electronic copy (eComp) via e-mail in about an hour.

Acknowledgments

We want to personally thank and acknowledge the contributions of those educators who participated in course surveys and chapter reviews during development of the first three editions and provided excellent suggestions for revisions:

S. Miriam Blake, *St. Joseph's College*
Dawna Lisa Butterfield, *University of Central Missouri*
Margaret Deitrich, *Austin Peay State University*
Gail Ditchman, *Moraine Valley Community College*
Thomas Eaton, *Southeast Missouri State University*
Penny Garcia, *Eastern New Mexico University*
Carol Greene, *Ashland Community & Technical College*
Joyce Gulley, *University of Southern Indiana*
Nikola Hobbel, *Humboldt State University*
Michelle Hudgens, *Ozarks Technical Community College*
Leslie Jacoby, *San Jose State University*
Michael Jaynes, *University of Tennessee-Chattanooga*
Dawn Kolakoski, *Hudson Valley Community College*
Melanie D. Koss, *Northern Illinois University*
DeAnne Luck, *Middle Tennessee State University*
Emily Midkiff, *University of Minnesota*
Kathryn Moisant, *Middle Tennessee State University*
Ann Powell-Brown, *University of Central Missouri*
Randi Rezendes, *Bridgewater State University*
Elizabeth Robinson, *Texas A&M University*
Jennifer Sanders, *Oklahoma State University*
Lisa Sandoval, *Joliet Junior College*
Barbara Schneider, *Grand Valley State University*
Diane Carver Sekeres, *University of Alabama*
Marilyn M. Senter, *Johnson County Community College*
Anna Shakarian, *The Ohio State University*
Jan Myers Stevenson, *University of Minnesota-Duluth*
Barbara J. Thomas, *Illinois Central College*
Jennifer Volkers, *Muskegon Community College*
Barbara Ward, *Washington State University*

Alyson Paige Warren, *Columbia College-Chicago; Loyola University-Chicago*
Nancy White, *University of Northern Iowa*
Kathryn Whitmore, *University of Iowa*

We also must thank Susan Hepler and Janet Hickman, dear friends and colleagues whose involvement in earlier editions of *Charlotte Huck's Children's Literature* has surely made its way into the content—if not the soul—of this text as well.

Special thanks also go to Vicki Malinee of Van Brien & Associates for guiding our efforts through three editions of this text.

Finally, we hope that readers of this book will see it as a first step to understanding and appreciating the richness of offerings in children's literature and the complexity of its readership. Our desire is that as you gain insights into children's developmental needs and interests, the information provided here will simultaneously better prepare you to appropriately incorporate considerations from cultural points of view and the social contexts in which the deepest responses to literature can occur.

Barbara Z. Kiefer
Cynthia A. Tyson
Bettie Parsons Barger
Lisa Patrick
Erin Reilly-Sanders

Welcome to *Charlotte Huck's Children's Literature: A Brief Guide, third edition*. This text has been designed to launch your exploration of children's literature and to prepare you to evaluate and select books for your future students that will instill an interest and passion for literature.

- Approximately one hundred **full-color images** of covers and illustrations from children's books show the visual impact of children's literature.

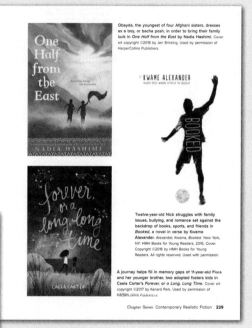

- **Teaching Feature** resource boxes throughout the text highlight the best examples of children's literature for each genre or topic.

- **Multicultural literature** is thoroughly integrated throughout, pointed out by an icon in the text as well as printed in blue in the children's literature lists.

Choosing Artistic Conventions

Artists may choose to borrow conventions or ways of depicting that we have come to associate with certain historical or cultural periods, such as Renaissance art or Impressionism, or art associated with a people, such as art of Tibetans or of the Northern Plains Indian tribes. Such choices often add authenticity to a story set "once upon a time" or one that originated in a particular society or culture.

A wonderful example of an homage to Impressionism can be found in the Monet-like paintings by Maurice Sendak for *Mr. Rabbit and the Lovely Present*, written by Charlotte Zolotow. In luscious shades of blues and greens, Sendak has created a dreamlike world where a very sophisticated rabbit and a little girl wander about the countryside looking for presents of red, yellow, green, and blue (her mother's favorite colors) for the little girl's mother. The dappled endpapers for this book are examples of Impressionistic techniques in themselves.

David Diaz's Mexican folk art motifs mirror Oaxacan ceramic figures and provide a culturally rich visual setting for Eve Bunting's *Going Home*. Jacket art copyright ©1996 by David Diaz. Text copyright ©1996 by Edward D. Bunting and Anne E. Bunting, Trustees of the Edward D. Bunting and Anne E. Bunting Family Trust. Used by permission of HarperCollins Publishers.

Many artists illustrating stories, folktales, or legends make use of the conventions found in art forms of their respective countries or cultures. David Diaz uses elements of Mexican folk art to tell contemporary stories set within Mexican and Mexican American cultures. In Eve Bunting's *Going Home*, the story of a farm family returning to Mexico for Christmas, Diaz creates endpapers that feature close-up photographs of brilliant "artesanias Mexicanas," decorative objects, figures, and other popular arts found in the marketplaces of Mexico. This "arté popular" then forms the background on which the paintings and type are placed. Folk art silhouettes outline these panels; they are also found on the title page and the final page, set against a brilliant presidential blue background. **Teaching Feature 3.3: Historical and Cultural Conventions in Picturebooks** summarizes other historical and cultural conventions and suggests art and picturebooks for further study.

Paul O. Zelinsky's *Rapunzel* pays homage to Renaissance artists, in this case to Raphael's painting, "Madonna of the Meadow." Illustrations from RAPUNZEL by Paul O. Zelinsky, copyright ©1997 by Paul O. Zelinsky. Used by permission of Dutton Children's Books, an imprint of Penguin Young Readers Group, a division of Penguin Random House LLC. All rights reserved.

78 Part 2 Exploring Genres in Children's Books

figure 1.1 The Ten-Point Model for Teaching Controversial Issues

The Ten-Point Model for Teaching Controversial Issues provides a framework for encouraging students to question, research, share, and evaluate information related to current, controversial topics.

Step

1. **Raise the initial question and have the children brainstorm all their initial responses.** Write them down. Don't discuss them, and accept all contributions. The teacher only asks questions, such as "What does that mean?" "Can you say any more about that?" "Does anyone else have anything to add to that information?" and (especially for erroneous or extremely one-sided information) "Where did you learn that?" or "Is that a fact or is it someone's opinion?"
2. **Begin a separate list of "Things to find out more about."** List as soon as undefined vocabulary words, vague concepts, and unanswered questions begin to emerge. These will serve as guidelines for the ongoing research, and some may even develop into separate topics to pursue later.
3. **Assign information-gathering homework.** Have children find out everything they can about the initial questions. Tell them to be prepared to share what they can in their own words. It is fine to read articles or watch the TV news, but the best source of information is interviewing parents, other relatives, or friends. Tell them not to copy down anyone else's words, but that it is a good idea to take notes.
4. **Share again responses to the initial question in a brainstorming session.** Again, children must share the information they gathered in their own words. Write down all responses. You can ask the same questions as in item 1, but offer no information and no "answers." Add to the list of "Things to find out more about" from item 2.
5. **Continue the process of gathering information.** Identify things to find out more about and continue to gather still more information for as long as the topic seems interesting. Encourage the children to listen to and learn from each other. They can begin to ask each other to explain what a new word means, to elaborate on a concept, to consider a new question, and to state their source of information. The teacher's role is an active one—facilitating, clarifying, and questioning—but the teacher doesn't impose information.
6. **If a concept emerges that sparks much interest or confusion, pose it as a new question about which to seek information.** Share and question until a satisfactory base of information has been established. More than one line of questioning can go on at the same time.
7. **Periodically give the children an individual written assignment in class to summarize their thoughts about a particular question.** The assignment can be worded as "What you know about X," "Things you don't understand about X," "Something X makes you think about," or any other way you can find to help crystallize children's individual thinking about the topic. Sharing these compositions aloud or posting them for all to read helps make all information public.
8. **As individual or group projects emerge, follow up on them.** The class may decide to write letters to a public figure; one or two children may decide to pursue a challenging research topic to report on to the group; or an outside resource may unexpectedly appear. Be flexible.
9. **Let others—parents, your colleagues, the media—know what you are doing.** Invite their participation. Encourage dialogue.
10. **End your project with something either public or permanent.** Ideas include a class presentation to the rest of the school about what they have learned, an article for the school paper or the local newspaper, a class book or individual books for the school library, or class participation in an event. It is important for children to feel that their learning is relevant and can lead to the ability to contribute to the larger world.

Source: Adapted from Kreidler, W. *Elementary Perspectives: Teaching Concepts of Peace and Conflict*. Copyright ©1990, Educators for Social Responsibility, Cambridge, MA. www.esrnational.org. Used by permission.

22 Part 1 Learning About Books and Children

- A unique framework for tackling controversial topics in and out of the classroom, the **Ten-Point Model for Teaching Controversial Issues** is presented in Chapter 1 with relevant examples for each genre provided within *Connect*®.

teaching **feature 8.1**

(continued)

Title (Author, Illustrator)	Place/Time (if specified)	Grade Level
GRADE 7: World History: The Middle Ages		
Adam of the Road (Gray, Lawson)	England, thirteenth century	3–5
Blood Red Horse (Grant)	The Crusades	4–6
Crispin: The Cross of Lead (Avi)	England, fourteenth century	4–6
Good Masters! Sweet Ladies! Voices from a Medieval Village (Schlitz Byrd)	English village, 1255	4–6
The Midwife's Apprentice (Cushman)	England	4–6
A Single Shard (Park)	Korea, twelfth century	4–6
The Door in the Wall (de Angeli)	England, fourteenth century	5 and up
Catherine, Called Birdy (Cushman)	England, 1290	6 and up
The King's Shadow (Alder)	England, 1053	7 and up
The Kite Rider (McCaughrean)	China, thirteenth century in the time of Genghis Kahn	7 and up

Source: National Council for the Social Studies Curriculum Standards.

Challenging Perspectives on Historical Fiction

When children are asked to name their least favorite school subject, the answer is often social studies. Anything to do with history, ancient or modern, seems to turn off young readers. The question for educators then becomes, "How can I pique the interest of my students in historical events? And especially those events that link the past experiences of people near and far to the lived experiences of contemporary times?"

Researchers and observant teachers have concluded that students' interest in social studies (history, political science, economics, religious studies, geography, psychology, anthropology, and civics) and their ability to learn, retain, and think critically about social studies content increases considerably when their instruction included literature.[7,8]

One efficient way to accomplish this is by integrating social studies education into the language arts curriculum using historical fiction. Students can integrate literacy skills with social studies content as they read historical fiction and informational texts.

Originally written in German, *My Family for the War* by Anne C. Voorhoeve presents a challenge to typical perspectives. When Ziska is taken out of Berlin in 1939 on a

258 Part 2 Exploring Genres in Children's Books

Evaluating Nonfiction Books

Guidelines

Go to Connect® to access study resources, practice quizzes, and additional materials.

Consider the following when evaluating nonfiction books for children:

Accuracy and Authenticity
- Is the author qualified to write about this topic?
- Has the manuscript been checked by authorities in the field?
- Are the facts accurate according to other sources?
- Is the information up-to-date?
- Are all the significant facts included?
- Do text and illustrations reveal diversity and avoid stereotypes?
- Are generalizations supported by facts?
- Is there a clear distinction between fact and theory?
- Are the text and illustrations free of anthropomorphism or philosophical explanations?

Content and Perspective
- For what purpose was the book designed?
- Is the book within the comprehension and interest range of its intended audience?
- Is the subject adequately covered?
- Are different viewpoints presented?
- Does the book lead to an understanding of the scientific method?
- Does it foster the spirit of inquiry?
- Does the book show interrelationships?
- If it is a science book, does it indicate related social issues?

Style
- Is information presented clearly and directly?
- Is the text appropriate for the intended audience?
- Does the style create the feeling of reader involvement?
- Is the language vivid and interesting?

Organization
- Is the information structured clearly, with appropriate subheadings?
- Does the book have reference aids that are clear and easy to use, such as a table of contents, index, bibliography, glossary, and appendix?

Illustrations and Format
- Do illustrations clarify and extend the text or speak plainly for themselves?
- Are size relationships made clear?
- Are media suitable to the purposes for which they are used?
- Are illustrations explained by captions or labels where needed?
- Does the total format contribute to the clarity and attractiveness of the book?

proven their integrity with facts—Penny Colman, Candace Fleming, Marc Aronson, Philip Hoose, Laurence Pringle, and Seymour Simon, among others. But authorship, while it may be a valuable rule of thumb, is a dangerous final criterion. Each book must be evaluated on its own merits.

Factual Accuracy Fortunately, many of the errors of fact in children's nonfiction books are often minor. Children who have access to a variety of books on one topic should be encouraged to notice discrepancies and pursue the correct answer, a valuable exercise in critical reading.

270 Part 2 Exploring Genres in Children's Books

- **Guidelines** boxes provide specific criteria and questions to consider when evaluating children's literature.

- **Challenging Perspectives** discussions appear in each genre chapter, outlining difficult or controversial social issues and providing instruction on how to evaluate and select appropriate children's literature that will help address those topics.

A restructured **Curriculum Connections** feature at the end of each genre chapter gives examples of how to use children's literature to fulfill educational standards in a variety of course areas.

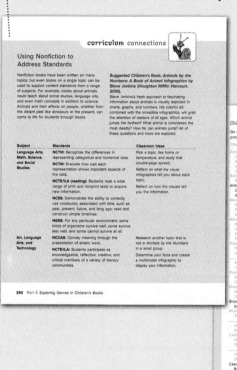

Comprehensive, up-to-date **lists of children's literature** are provided at the end of each chapter, with multicultural titles printed in blue. More titles are available in the searchable Children's Literature Database.

Accessible within Connect®, the **Children's Literature Database** is a searchable database listing more than 5,500 carefully selected children's books, including major award winners and the hundreds of titles referenced in this text.

In Memoriam

Charlotte S. Huck 1923–2005

Courtesy Charlotte Huck

Born in Evanston, Illinois, Charlotte Huck attended Wellesley College in Massachusetts, then graduated from Northwestern University, where she earned master's and doctoral degrees. After teaching in elementary schools in Missouri and Illinois, followed by a teaching position at Northwestern, Dr. Huck joined the faculty of The Ohio State University (OSU) in 1955, where she created and led the first-ever graduate program in children's literature for thirty years. She believed that stories are what motivate children to want to read, and she encouraged teachers to use children's literature in reading lessons, emphasizing her concept of "webbing," in which every subject taught to a child is supported by reading.

Charlotte Huck established an annual OSU children's literature conference that attracted thousands of teachers, librarians, and book enthusiasts from 1982 to 2004. After she retired and moved to California, she started a similar conference at the University of Redlands. She continued to write professionally and remained active in community and school-based literacy programs.

Besides authoring the classic *Children's Literature in the Elementary School* (originally published in 1961), she also wrote books for children. With Anita Lobel, she published *Princess Furball* (1994), *Toads and Diamonds* (1995), and *The Black Bull of Norroway* (2001). These and her other books, *Secret Places* (1993) and *A Creepy Countdown* (1999), were published by Greenwillow Books.

Dr. Huck served on both the Newbery and Caldecott Medal committees and was a president of the National Council of Teachers of English. The numerous awards and honors she received included OSU's Distinguished Teaching Award, the Landau Award for Distinguished Service in Teaching Children's Literature, and the Arbuthnot Award, given annually by the International Reading Association to an outstanding professor of children's literature. In 1997, she was presented with the Outstanding Educator in the English Language Arts Award by the National Council of Teachers of English (NCTE) Elementary Section.

Charlotte Huck was honored in 1987 with the NCTE Distinguished Service Award for her service to the English teaching profession and to NCTE. The 1988 NCTE President Julie Jensen made the award presentation, commending Huck for her service "to The Ohio State University, to the state of Ohio, and most of all, to language learners and teachers everywhere. They are the beneficiaries of her knowledge and enthusiasm for the literature of childhood, and of her unyielding conviction that readers are made by those who have themselves discovered the joys of reading."

Charlotte Huck was considered one of the foremost experts on children's literature and its uses. In 1996, OSU established in her name the first endowed professorship in children's literature in the United States. In her career at OSU, she mentored Ph.D. students, teachers, and library media specialists who continue her beliefs and enthusiasm as new programs in children's literature are launched across the country.

About the Authors

Courtesy Barbara Kiefer

Barbara Z. Kiefer

Barbara Kiefer is the Charlotte S. Huck Professor of Children's Literature at The Ohio State University. She was formerly Robinson Professor of Children's Literature at Teachers College, Columbia University. Originally trained in art education, she taught grades one, two, four, and five in several regions of the United States and in overseas schools. She served as the elected chair of the year 2000 Caldecott Award Committee of the American Library Association and was a member of the 1988 Caldecott Award Committee. She has also served as chair of the Elementary Section Committee of the National Council of Teachers of English (NCTE) and as a member of the NCTE Executive Board. She is currently a coeditor of *Language Arts,* a journal of the NCTE, and a board member of NCTE's Children's Literature Assembly. She has published numerous articles and book chapters about reading and children's literature and is author of *The Potential of Picturebooks: From Visual Literacy to Aesthetic Understanding,* and the coauthor of *An Integrated Language Perspective in the Elementary School: Theory into Action,* 4th edition, with Christine Pappas and Linda Levstik.

Courtesy Cynthia Tyson

Cynthia A. Tyson

Cynthia A. Tyson, Ph.D., MSW, LSW, is a professor in the School of Teaching and Learning at The Ohio State University (OSU), where she teaches courses in Multicultural and Equity Studies in Education, Early Childhood Social Studies, and Multicultural Children's Literature. Her research interests include inquiry into the social, historical, cultural, and global intersections of teaching, learning, and educational research. Her teaching, research, and service commitments are deeply rooted in these concepts as interrelated, mutually reinforcing, and fundamental to the study of multiculturalism and teaching for social justice. She has presented numerous research papers at national and international meetings and conferences. She has published articles in *Educational Researcher, Theory and Research in Social Education, International Journal of Qualitative Research in Education, Journal of Literacy Research*, and other books and journals. She is also the coauthor of two books: *Handbook of Social Studies Research* and the American Educational Research Association volume, *Studying Diversity in Teacher Education.* She has won several awards over her career, including The Social Science Educators' Young Scholar Award, OSU's Diversity Enhancement Award, and The American Educational Research Association's Mid-Career Award for her contributions to Teaching and Teacher Education. She has worked in a consulting capacity with universities, school districts, and learning communities across the United States, the United Kingdom, Mali, Ghana, and South Africa.

Bettie Parsons Barger

©Rachel Cobb

Bettie Parsons Barger is a professor in the Richard W. Riley College of Education at Winthrop University, where she teaches courses in children's literature and elementary education. She completed her doctorate in Literature for Children and Young Adults at The Ohio State University. Prior to completing her doctorate, she taught second and third grades and worked as an academic technology integrator, helping teachers enhance the curriculum by utilizing technology. Her dissertation, *The eBook Hook*, explored teacher and student perceptions of integrating eBooks into Language Arts and Science curricula. Dr. Barger has published in *Science & Children, Reading Horizons,* and *Creating Books for the Young in the New South Africa.* She has published reviews in *Bookbird* and *Language Arts.* She is active in the National Council of Teachers of English (NCTE), Children's Literature Assembly, and the United States Board of Books for Young People. Currently, she is serving on NCTE's Charlotte Huck Award for Outstanding Fiction for Children. Dr. Barger avidly reads children's literature and has traveled, nationally and internationally, in pursuit of incredible works, and the authors and illustrators who create them.

Lisa Patrick

©Jonathan Bailey

Lisa Patrick, Ph.D., works as a Literacy Collaborative and Reading Recovery Trainer at The Ohio State University (OSU). She also works as Senior Lecturer in the College of Education and Human Ecology at OSU at Marion. She completed her doctorate in Literature for Children and Young Adults at OSU in 2013. Her university teaching experience includes four years at Ohio Wesleyan University's Department of Education and six years in the Master of Education program at Ashland University's Columbus Center. She also works as a private literacy education consultant. Dr. Patrick has published in *Literacy Research: Theory, Method, and Practice*; *Language Arts*; and the *New England Reading Association Journal.* She has also published online children's book reviews in the International Literacy Association's *Literacy Daily*, the Assembly on Literature for Adolescents' *ALAN Picks*, and the University of Arizona's *Worlds of Words.* Her research interests reside at the intersection of found poetry and readers' transactional relationships with texts. Dr. Patrick serves on USBBY's (the United States Board on Books for Young People) 2018 Hans Christian Andersen Award Jury, as well as the National Council of Teachers of English Award for Excellence in Poetry for Children Committee. She also serves on the board of directors of the International Literacy Association's Children's Literature and Reading Special Interest Group and the Buckeye Children's and Teen Book Award Council. She is the chair of the Children's Literature Strand Committee for the annual National Reading Recovery & K–6 Literacy Conference and presents on a range of literacy topics at national and local conferences. She is an avid reader and can usually be found putting books in the hands of children and teachers.

©Erin Reilly-Sanders

Erin Reilly-Sanders

Erin F. Reilly-Sanders, Ph.D., AIA, is an independent scholar of children's literature. She completed her doctorate at The Ohio State University through the Literature for Children and Young Adults program in the School of Teaching and Learning. Her background includes six years of youth service at the Columbus Metropolitan Library system. Also a registered architect, Dr. Reilly-Sanders's research often focuses on the visual aspects of literature such as in her dissertation, "Drawing Outside the Bounds: Tradition and Innovation in Depictions of the House in Children's Picturebooks," advised by Dr. Kiefer. She has published in *The ALAN Review, Children and Libraries*, International Reading Association's *Reading Today* Online, and *Creating Books for the Young in the New South Africa*. Currently, she is a member of YALSA's Journal of Research on Libraries and Young Adults Advisory Board and the Kent State University's Marantz Picturebook Research Symposium Advisory Board. She served on the Association for Library Service to Children's 2013 Mildred L. Batchelder Award Committee. Over the years, Dr. Reilly-Sanders has been active in the American Library Association, National Council of Teachers of English, and the Children's Literature Association.

About the Illustrator

Courtesy Rafael López

Rafael López

The work of Rafael López is a fusion of strong graphic style and magical symbolism. López grew up in Mexico City, where he was immersed in the city's rich cultural heritage and in the native color of its street life. Influenced by Mexican surrealism, *dichos* (proverbs), and myths, he developed a style with roots in these traditions.

His many international clients include Amnesty International, Apple, Chicago Tribune, HarperCollins, IBM, Intel, *Los Angeles Times*, the Grammy Awards, and World Wildlife Fund. His work has been selected into multiple juried shows and his children's books have won two Americas Awards and a Pura Belpré Honor for *My Name Is Celia/ Me llamo Celia: The Life of Celia Cruz/La vida de Celia Cruz* (2004) by Monica Brown. His 2008 poster "Voz Unida" was selected by the Obama/Biden campaign as an official poster at Artists for Obama. The Latino dance stamp he created for the United States Postal Services (U.S.P.S) was featured on the cover of the commemorative stamp yearbook in 2006 and at a special exhibition at the Smithsonian entitled "Trendsetters." His 2007 U.S.P.S. stamp celebrated *Mendez vs. Westminster,* an important legal case in equality of education.

López envisioned and led the Urban Art Trail Project that transformed San Diego's blighted East Village with colorful murals, sculptures, and art installations that serves as a model of urban renewal that has been implemented in cities around the nation.

He divides his time between his studios in the colonial town of San Miguel de Allende, Mexico, and a loft in downtown San Diego, where he works and lives with his wife and son.

Part One

Learning About Books and Children

Chapter One

Knowing Children's Literature

Chapter Outline

A toddler's first response when introduced to the wonderful world of reading is typically an excited, "Read it again!" A three-year-old carries a copy of Martin Waddell's *Can't You Sleep, Little Bear?* for a week, hugging it as tightly and lovingly as a stuffed bear. Seven-year-old twins close the cover of Jessica Scott Kerrin's *Martin Bridge: In High Gear,* saying proudly, "We read the whole book." Five 10-year-olds joyfully page through Louis Sachar's *Holes* looking for clues and connections in the intertwining stories. A 12-year-old

©Sara Dashner Photography, Gahanna, Ohio

holds up a copy of Mildred Taylor's *Roll of Thunder, Hear My Cry* and states emphatically, "This is the best book I've ever read." All of these children have had some deep and intensely personal response to a work of children's literature. Surely, it is such responses that may lead them to become lifelong lovers of literature.

Children's Literature Defined

There are many ways of defining children's literature. Our ideas about what should be included have changed over time, and definitions vary a bit from culture to culture, critic to critic, and reader to reader. In this book, we think of literature as *the imaginative shaping of life and thought into the forms and structures of language.* We consider fiction as well as nonfiction, books with pictures as well as those with words, and ask how different genres work to produce an aesthetic experience. How do they help the reader perceive pattern, relationships, and feelings that produce an inner experience of art? This aesthetic experience might be a vivid reconstruction of past experience, an extension of a recent experience, or the creation of a new experience.

We all have memories of certain books that changed us in some way—by disturbing us, by affirming some emotion we knew but could never shape in words, or by revealing to us something about human nature. The province of literature is the human condition and it encompasses all such feelings and experiences. Perhaps our memories of books are strong because they help illuminate life by shaping our insights.

What Is Children's Literature?

The experience of literature always involves both the book and the reader. Try as we might to set objective criteria, judgments about the quality of literature must always be tempered by an awareness of its audience. The audience we address in this text is the group of children from birth to 14. Therefore, we will want to ask if and how children's literature is different from literature for adults. We could say that a child's book is a book a child is reading, and an adult book is a book occupying the attention of an adult. Before the nineteenth century, only a few books were written specifically for the enjoyment of children. Children read books written for adults, taking from them what they could understand. Today, children continue to read some books intended for adults, such as the works of Stephen King and Mary Higgins Clark. And yet some books first written for children—such as Margery Williams's *The Velveteen Rabbit,* A. A. Milne's *Winnie the Pooh,* J. R. R. Tolkien's *The Hobbit,* and J. K. Rowling's Harry Potter stories—have been claimed as their own by adults.

Books about children might not necessarily be for them. Richard Hughes's adult classic *A High Wind in Jamaica* shows the "innocent" depravity of children in contrast to the group of pirates who had captured them. Yet in Harper Lee's novel *To Kill a Mockingbird,* also written for adults, 8-year-old Scout Finch reveals a more finely developed conscience than is common in the small Southern town in which she is raised. The presence of a child protagonist, then, does not assure that the book is for children. Obviously, the line between children's literature and adult literature is blurred.

Children today appear to be more sophisticated and knowledgeable about certain life experiences than children of any previous generation were. They spend a great deal of time with electronic devices. The television shows them actual views of war while they eat their dinners. They have witnessed acts of terror, assassinations, and starvation. Though most modern children are separated from first-hand knowledge of birth, death, and senility, the mass media bring the daily experiences of crime, poverty, war, death, and depravity into the living rooms of virtually all American homes. In addition, today's children are exposed to violence purely in the name of entertainment. Such exposure has forced adults to reconsider what seems appropriate for children's literature. Today it is difficult to believe that Madeleine L'Engle's *Meet the Austins* was rejected by several publishers because it began with a death or that some reviewers were shocked by a mild "damn" in *Harriet the Spy* by Louise Fitzhugh. Such publishing taboos have long since disappeared. Children's books are generally less frank than adult books, but contemporary children's literature does reflect the problems of today, the ones children read about in the newspapers, see on television and in the movies, and experience at home or in their communities.

There are some limits to the content of children's literature, however. These limits are set by children's experience and understanding. Certain emotional and psychological responses seem outside the realms of childhood and are therefore unlikely in children's literature. For example, nostalgia is an adult emotion that is foreign to most boys and girls. Children seldom look back on their childhood, but always forward. Also, stories that portray children as "sweet" or that romanticize childhood, like the Holly Hobbie books that go with cards and gift products, often have more appeal for adults than for children. The late Dr. Seuss (Theodor S. Geisel) also took an adult perspective in his later books such as *Oh, the Places You'll Go.* His enduring place in children's literature rests on earlier titles such as *And to Think That I Saw It on Mulberry Street* and *The Cat in the Hat,* books that are filled with childlike imagination and joyful exuberance.

Cynicism and despair are not childlike emotions and should not figure prominently in a child's book. Even though children are quick to pick up a veneer of sophistication, of disillusionment with adults and authority, they still expect good things to happen in life. And although many children do live in desperate circumstances, few react to these with real despair. They may have endured pain, sorrow, or horror; they may be in what we would consider hopeless situations; but they are not without hope. In Glenn Ringtveld's Batchelder award-winning *Cry, Heart, But Never Break,* when children try to prevent Death from taking their beloved grandmother, they come to accept that grief and joy are both a part of life. This demonstrates that not all stories for children must have happy endings; many today do not. It is only to say that when you close the door on hope, you have left the realm of childhood.

The only limitations, then, that seem binding on literature for children are those that appropriately reflect the emotions and experiences of children today. Children's books are books that have the child's eye at the center.

Writing for Children

Editor William Zinsser says:

> No kind of writing lodges itself so deeply in our memory, echoing there for the rest of our lives, as the books that we met in our childhood. . . . To enter and hold the mind of a child or a young person is one of the hardest of all writers' tasks.[1]

The skilled author does not write differently or less carefully for children just because she thinks they will not be aware of style or language. E. B. White asserts:

> Anyone who writes down to children is simply wasting his time. You have to write up, not down. . . . Some writers for children deliberately avoid using words they think a child doesn't know. This emasculates the prose and . . . bores the reader. . . . Children love words that give them a hard time, provided they are in a context that absorbs their attention.[2]

Authors of children's literature and those who write for adults should receive equal admiration. C. S. Lewis maintained that he wrote a children's story because a children's story was the best art form for what he had to say.[3] Lewis wrote for both adults and children, as have Madeleine L'Engle, Paula Fox, E. B. White, Isaac Bashevis Singer, Amy Krouse Rosenthal, and many other well-known authors.

The uniqueness of children's literature, then, lies in the audience that it addresses. Authors of children's books are circumscribed only by the experiences of childhood, but these are vast and complex. Children think and feel; they wonder and they dream. Much is known, but little is explained.

Children are curious about life and adult activities. They live in the midst of tensions—balances of love and hate within the family and the neighborhood. The author who can bring imagination and insight into these experiences, give them literary shape and structure, and communicate them to children is writing children's literature.

Valuing Literature for Children

Because children naturally take such delight in books, we sometimes need to remind ourselves that books can do more for children than entertaining

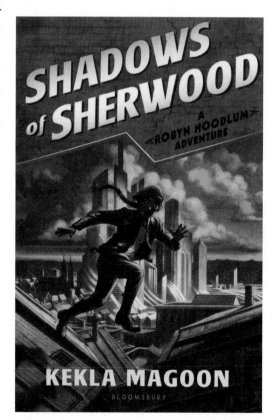

In the first book of a new series, Robyn Loxley finds herself in a thrilling mystery centered on the disappearance of her parents in *Shadows of Sherwood: A Robyn Hoodlum Adventure*. ©Kekla Magoon, 2015, *Shadows of Sherwood: A Robin Hoodlum Adventure*, Bloomsbury Publishing Inc.

them. Values inherent in sharing literature with children include personal qualities that might be difficult to measure as well as qualities that result in important educational understandings.

Personal Values

Literature should be valued in our homes and schools for the enrichment it gives to the personal lives of children, as well as for its proven educational contributions. We will consider these affective values of literature before we discuss the more obvious educational ones.

Enjoyment   First and foremost, literature provides delight and enjoyment. Children need to discover delight in books before they are asked to master the skills of reading. Then learning to read makes as much sense as learning to ride a bike; they know that eventually it will be fun. Four- and 5-year-olds who have laughed out loud at Jules Feiffer's *Bark, George* can hardly wait to read it themselves. Six- and 7-year-olds giggle at the silly antics in Arnold Lobel's Frog and Toad books. Many older children revel in tales of mystery and suspense such as Shelia Turnage's Tupelo Landing mystery series, which includes *Three Times Lucky,* Anne Nesbet's *Cloud and Wallfish,* and Adam Gidwitz's *The Inquisitor's Tale.* Sad books also bring a kind of enjoyment, as the children who have read *Bridge to Terabithia* by Katherine Paterson or *Stone Fox* by John Reynolds Gardiner will tell you. The list of books that children enjoy can go on and on. There are so many fine ones—and so many that children won't find unless teachers, librarians, and parents share them with children. A love of reading and a taste for literature are the finest gifts we can give to our children, for we will have started them on the path of a lifetime of pleasure with books.

Imagination   Literature develops children's imagination and helps them consider people, experiences, or ideas in new ways. Books such as David Ezra Stein's *Interrupting Chicken,* Andrea Beaty's *Ada Twist, Scientist,* and Bob Raczka's *Niko Draws a Feeling* celebrate characters who see the world differently and make the most of their imagination. Nonfiction books such as *Penguin Day: A Family Story* by Nic Bishop or *The Case of the Vanishing Golden Frogs: A Scientific Mystery* by Sandra Markle can spark children's scientific imagination.

Today, visual and digital technologies have made everything so explicit that children are not developing their power to visualize. Teachers need to help them see with their inner eye to develop a country of the mind. Natalie Babbitt's prose in *Tuck Everlasting* functions as paintbrushes as well as text. Mollie Hunter, whose books such as *A Stranger Came Ashore* and *Mermaid Summer* have this power to create the visual image in the mind of the reader and to stretch the imagination, says that the whole reward of reading is:

> to have one's imagination carried soaring on the wings of another's imagination, to be made more aware of the possibilities of one's mind . . . ; to be thrilled, amazed, amused, awed, enchanted in worlds unknown until discovered through the medium of language, and to find in those worlds one's own petty horizons growing ever wider, ever higher.[4]

Vicarious Experience Their experiences with literature give children new perspectives on the world. Good writing can transport readers to other places and other times and expand their life space. Readers feel connected to the lives of others as they enter an imagined situation with their emotions tuned to those of the story. One 10-year-old boy, sharing his love of Jean Craighead George's survival story *My Side of the Mountain,* said, "You know, I've always secretly felt I could do it myself." This boy had vicariously shared Sam Gribley's adventure of "living off the land" in his tree home in the Catskill Mountains. Sam's experiment in self-sufficiency had strengthened the conviction of a 10-year-old that he, too, could take care of himself.

Insight into Human Behavior Literature reflects life, yet no book can contain all of living. By its very organizing properties, literature has the power to shape and give coherence to human experience. It might focus on one aspect of life, one period of time in an individual's life, and so enable a reader to see and understand relationships that he had never considered. In *Wish* by Barbara O'Connor, a young girl is uprooted and sent to live with her aunt and uncle in the Blue Ridge Mountains. Creating new ties with a stray dog, a neighbor boy, and extended family helps her develop a new idea of home. *Little Dog, Lost,* Marion Dane Bauer's novel in verse, is a story about longing and belonging. A boy needs a dog, a dog needs a boy, and an elderly neighbor needs a community. When these three cross paths during a thunderstorm one summer, each finds what he needs.

So much of what we teach in school is concerned with facts. Literature is concerned with feelings and the quality of life. It can educate the heart as well as the mind. As children gain increased awareness of the lives of others, as they vicariously try out other roles, they may develop a better understanding of themselves and those around them. Through wide reading as well as living, they acquire their perceptions of literature and life.

Universality of Experience Literature continues to ask universal questions about the meaning of life and our relationships with nature and other people. Every book provides a point of comparison for our own lives. In the picturebook *Black Dog* by Levi Pinfold, the youngest child ventures outside the house to confront her fears, while the rest of her family cowers inside. Are we as courageous as the tiny mouse who must take responsibility for her family in Avi's *Poppy,* or as Delly, who tries to save her friend from an abusive situation in Katherine Hannigan's *True (. . . Sort Of)*? Would we have the tenacity and resilience of August Pullman in R. J. Palacio's *Wonder*?

We also learn to understand the common bonds of humanity by comparing one story with another. The story of Max leaving home to go to the island in Maurice Sendak's *Where the Wild Things Are* follows the ancient pattern of Homer's *Iliad* and *Odyssey.* This pattern is repeated again and again in myth and legend and seen in such widely divergent stories as Cynthia Voigt's *Homecoming* and Kathi Appelt's *The Underneath.* These are all stories of a journey through trials and hardship and the eventual return home. The pattern reflects everyone's journey through life.

Books can also highlight human compassion in the midst of inhumanity. *Number the Stars* by Lois Lowry and *An Elephant in the Garden* by Michael Morpurgo both tell of the uncommon bravery of common people to do what they can to right a wrong.

Literature illumines all of life; it casts its light on all that is good, but it can also spotlight what is dark and debasing in the human experience. Literature enables us to live many lives, good and bad, and to begin to see the universality of human experience.

Educational Values

The intrinsic values of literature should be sufficient to give it a major place in the school curriculum. Happily, there is research to show that literature plays a significant role in developing oral, language, reading, and writing abilities and should play a central part in the school curriculum. Books such as *LMNO Peas* by Keith Baker engage young children in language play that can help them develop the phonological understanding so necessary to learning letter-sound relationships. In Jim Averbeck's *One Word from Sophie,* Sophie uses too many words when one word will do. The playful text draws attention to complex vocabulary. Kate DiCamillo and Alison McGhee's Bink and Gollie books or Jane O'Connor's Fancy Nancy books intrigue young children with multisyllable words. Older children will find models for writing in Katrina Goldsaito's *The Sound of Silence* and Steve Jenkins's *Deadliest!: 20 Dangerous Animals.* They will make personal connections to the environment in Jane Thompson's *Faraway Fox* or discover mathematical concepts in *Bugs by the Numbers* by Sharon Werner and Sarah Forss.

Reviews of research found in such books as *Handbook of Early Literacy Research,* edited by Susan B. Neuman and David K. Dickinson (2011); *On Reading Books to Children: Parents and Teachers,* edited by Anne Van Kleeck, Steven A. Stahl, and Eurydice B. Bauer (2003); and *Handbook of Research on Children's and Young Adult Literature,* edited by Shelby A. Wolf, Karen Coats, Patricia Enciso, and Christine A. Jenkins (2011), summarize research conducted over the past 50 years that supports the importance of literary experiences both before and after children come to school. **Teaching Feature 1.1: Books at the Center** highlights classic research studies that began the support for literature across the curriculum.

Picturebooks, such as Sharon Werner and Sarah Forss's *Bugs by the Numbers,* entice children to learn in various content areas, such as math and science. Cover of *Bugs by the Numbers* by Sharon Werner and Sarah Forss. Reprinted by permission of Blue Apple Books.

Books at the Center

In the Home

Phonological Development	Toddlers who were read to at home produced more sounds and vocalized more often than those who were not read to. (Irwin, 1960; National Literacy Panel, 2008)
Syntactic Development	Three- to 4-year-olds who interact with adults around book readings have more complex sentence structure. (Cazden, 1966; Pullen and Justice, 2003)
Lexical Development	Reading to young children supports their acquisition of vocabulary. (Ninio and Bruner, 1978; Richman and Colombo, 2007)
Interactional Patterns	Children learn discourse patterns in the context of picturebook reading. (Snow and Goldfield, 1983; Crowe, Norris, and Hoffman, 2003)
Text Patterns	Children who are read to form understandings of how stories and characters work. (Applebee, 1978; Stadler and Ward, 2005)
Correlated with Early Reading	Access to books and being read to were significant factors in children's learning to read before they came to school. (Durkin, 1966; Strickland, Morrow, Neuman, Roskos, Schickedanz, and Vukelich, 2004)

In the School

Correlated with Successful Reading	Reading aloud in the home was significantly associated with later reading comprehension test scores. (Wells, 1986; Jacobs, Morrison, and Swinyard, 2000)
Knowledge of Textual Characteristics	Children acquired understandings of text patterns and characteristics of fiction and nonfiction genres when books were shared regularly. (Pappas and Brown, 1989; Maloch, 2008)
Correlated with Attitude	Sixth graders with positive attitudes toward reading had been read to as children. (Sostaritch, 1974; Fox, 2008)
Recreational Reading	Reading outside of school was related to improved comprehension, vocabulary, and fluency scores. (Anderson, Wilson, and Fielding, 1986; Cunningham and Stanovich, 2001)
Literature Across the Curriculum	Literature positively affected understanding of written language. (Purcell, et al., 1995; Duke, 2003) Literature positively affected science and social studies learning. (Smith, 1993; Pappas, 2006)

Evaluating Children's Literature

What makes a good children's book? Who will read it? Why? Whose purposes will it serve? All of these are important considerations to be taken up in later sections of this chapter and throughout the book. The primary concern of evaluation, however, is a book's literary and aesthetic qualities. Children show what they think of books through their responses, but they are not born critics in the conventional sense. Teachers and librarians need to value children's own interests, interpretations, and judgments. At the same time, they need to help children discover what practiced readers look for in a well-written book. Each genre or type of literature (picturebooks, traditional literature, fantasy, poetry, contemporary realistic fiction, historical fiction, and nonfiction) has criteria that relate to that form. For example, in picturebooks, it is important that the verbal text and illustrations act harmoniously. Nonfiction books should be accurate and unbiased. All books need to be evaluated from a multicultural perspective. It is important for readers to identify the kind of book they are reading in order to apply the appropriate criteria for evaluation. As we discuss specific genres in Chapters 3 through 9, we will highlight criteria that apply to these particular types of literature. In general, the traditional categories of literary analysis can be applied to all genres of children's literature. For example, authors of both fiction and nonfiction can involve us in a compelling narrative, establish a vivid setting, bring characters to life, and engage us with important themes. They can write with poetic style, and their point of view can link us more intimately with the subject matter and place us as active observers of events.

Plot

Of prime importance in any work of fiction for children is the plot. Children ask first, "What happens? Is it a good story?" The plot is the plan of action; it tells what the characters do and what happens to them. In *Blizzard of Glass*, the thrilling nonfiction story of the explosion in Halifax Harbor in 1917, author Sally M. Walker builds suspense by relating the minute-by-minute accounts of what real people were experiencing on the days leading up to the blast. Plot is the thread that holds the fabric of the narrative together and makes the reader want to continue reading.

A well-constructed plot is organic and interrelated. It grows logically and naturally from the action and the decisions of the characters in given situations. The plot should be credible and ring true rather than depend on coincidence and contrivance. It should be original and fresh rather than trite, tired, and predictable.

In books that have substance, obstacles are not easily overcome and choices are not always clear-cut. Louis Sachar's *Fuzzy Mud* is an exciting survival tale. In addition to being a compelling read, the plot is complicated by the ethical choices characters must make.

Setting

The structure of a story includes both the construction of the plot and its setting. The setting may be in the past, the present, or the future. The story may take place in a specific locale, or the setting may be deliberately vague to convey the universal feeling of all suburbs, all large cities, or all rural communities.

The setting for Karen Hesse's *Out of the Dust* is so well developed that readers can almost feel the grit of dirt between their teeth. Hesse's use of free verse conveys the essence of Billie Jo's terrible experiences during the Oklahoma dustbowl.

> On Sunday winds came, Bringing a red dust Like prairie fire, Hot and peppery, searing the inside of my nose, and the whites of my eyes.[5]

Just as the wind tore away layers of sod to lay bare the land, Hesse dispenses with flowery rhetoric for words and rhythms that reveal the depths of human courage and the heart of human love.

Theme

A third point in the evaluation of any story is its overarching theme, or themes, the larger meanings that lie beneath the story's surface. Most well-written books can be read for several layers of meaning—plot, theme, or metaphor. On one level, the story of *Charlotte's Web* by E. B. White is simply an absurd but amusing tale of how a spider saves the life of a pig; on another level, it reveals the meaning of loneliness and the obligations of friendship. A third layer of significance can be seen in the acceptance of death as a natural part of the cycle of life. Finally, E. B. White himself wrote that it was "an appreciative story. . . . It celebrates life, the seasons, the goodness of the barn, the beauty of the world, the glory of everything."[6]

The theme of a book reveals something of the author's purpose in writing the story and provides a dimension to the story that goes beyond the action of the plot. The theme of a book might be the acceptance of self or others, growing up, the overcoming of fear or prejudice. This theme should be worth imparting to young people and be based on justice and integrity. Sound moral and ethical principles should prevail. However, one danger in writing books for children is that the theme will override the plot. Authors might be so intent on conveying a message that they neglect story or characterization. Didacticism, the attempt by an author to preach a moral lesson, is still alive and well in the twenty-first century. However, the best books don't *teach* children, they *reach* children. Or, as Roger Sutton emphasized, "If you want to convince children of the power of books don't tell them stories are good, tell them good stories."[7]

Characterization

True characterization is another hallmark of fine writing. The people portrayed in children's books should be as convincingly real and lifelike as our next-door neighbors. Many of the animal characters in modern fantasy also have human personalities. The credibility of characters depends on the author's ability to show their true natures, their strengths, and their weaknesses. Delphine, the narrator of Rita Williams-Garcia's *One Crazy Summer,* is a vivid and dynamic character, one that readers will not soon forget. Authors Jean Fritz, Jen Bryant, Melissa Sweet, and Doreen Rappaport bring characters to life in their many picturebook biographies by using quotes from primary sources.

Just as it takes time to know a new friend in all her various dimensions, so too does an author try to present the many facets of a character bit by bit. In revealing character, an author might tell about the person through narration, record the character's conversation with others, describe the thoughts of the character, show the thoughts of others about the character, or show the character in action. A character who is revealed in only one way is apt to lack depth. If a single dimension of character is presented, or one trait overemphasized, the result is likely to be stereotyped and wooden. One-dimensional characters are the norm in folk and fairy tales, where witches are prototypes of evil and youngest children are deserving and good. However, modern fiction requires multidimensional characters whose actions and feelings grow out of the circumstances of the story.

Style

An author's style of writing is simply selection and arrangement of words in presenting the story. Good writing style is appropriate to the plot, theme, and characters, both creating and reflecting the mood of the story. Most children do not enjoy a story that is too descriptive, but they can appreciate figurative language, especially when the comparisons are within their background of understanding. Natalie Babbitt's vivid prologue to *Tuck Everlasting* invites children to visualize the intense images by describing the month of August as curiously silent "with blank white dawns and glaring noons and sunsets smeared with too much color."[8]

There is no one style or set of language patterns that is more appropriate than others for a children's book. Yet children's tastes do place some demands on the writer. Because young readers tend to prefer action over description or introspection, those elements must be handled with special skill. Children crave dialogue, like readers of all ages. Masters at writing dialogue that sounds natural and amusing include Sara Pennypacker's Clementine series and Waylon series. Writing the dialogue for a book of contemporary realistic fiction is particularly difficult because slang and popular expressions are quickly dated. Barbara Wright captures African American cultural nuances in *The Crow*. Anne Ursu writes dialogue that adds veracity to her fantasies, such as *The Real Boy* and *Breadcrumbs*.

The best test of an author's style is probably oral reading. Does the story read smoothly? Does the conversation flow naturally? Does the author provide variety in sentence patterns, vocabulary, and use of stylistic devices?

Point of View

The term *point of view* is often used to indicate the author's choice of narrator(s) and the way the narrator reveals the story. Whose story is it? Who tells it? A storyteller's voice is often used in modern fiction, for books in which the author reports the comings and goings, the conversations, and the feelings of all the characters, villains as well as heroes. We say that such stories have an omniscient, or all-knowing, narrator.

Many children's books take a point of view that also uses the third person but gives the author less freedom. This limited-omniscient, or concealed, narrator view does, however, provide closer identification with a single character. The author chooses to stand behind one character, so to speak, and tell the story from over his or her shoulder. The story is then limited to what that character can see, hear, believe, feel, and understand. Katherine Paterson has told the story *The Great Gilly Hopkins* from this perspective.

The more direct narrative voice of the first person is quite common today in both fiction and nonfiction. In contemporary realism, it is almost the norm. The advantage of using first-person narrative is that it can make for easy reading. It attempts to invite its audience by taking a stance that says, "Look—we speak the same language."

At times, authors counter the limitations of a single point of view by alternating the presentation of several views within the same story or changing points of view. E. L. Konigsburg's multiple narratives in *The View from Saturday* add great richness to the textual tapestry. John David Anderson's three characters in *Ms. Bixby's Last Day* have very different personalities (and quirks) that are reflected in their retelling of their sixth-grade year.

The author's own personal and cultural experience is reflected in more subtle ways in every book's point of view. For example, Deborah Wiles is not African American, but in *Revolution,* she has told a moving story of life in the Jim Crow South based in part on her own experiences. Her point of view is no substitute for those of an author who has lived those cultural experiences from birth. Mildred Taylor's *Roll of Thunder, Hear My Cry* is based on her own history as an African American, and Margarita Engle's *All the Way to Havana* is based on her own family experiences in 1950s Cuba. These books show how an author of color has a unique opportunity to illuminate those nuances of culture that outsiders can never capture.

Additional Considerations

Presentation The books we think of as truly excellent have significant content and, if illustrated, fine illustrations. Their total design, from the front cover to the final endpaper, creates a unified look that seems in character with the content and invites the reader to proceed. Today, we have so many picture storybooks and so many beautifully illustrated books of poetry, nonfiction, and other genres that any attempt to evaluate children's literature should consider both the role of illustration and the format or physical characteristics of the book. We will discuss these criteria in greater depth in the subsequent genre chapters of this book. In general, however, we should consider the format of a book—its size, shape, page design, illustrations, typography, paper quality, and binding. Frequently, some small aspect of the format, such as the book jacket, will be an important factor in a child's decision to read a story. All varieties of books—novels, picturebooks, poetry, biography, nonfiction books—should be well designed and well made. The typeface/font should be large enough for easy reading by children at the age level for which the book is intended. At the same time, if the type is too large, children might see the book as "babyish." Space between the lines (leading) should be sufficient to make the text clear. The paper should be of high quality, heavy enough to prevent any penetration of ink. In longer works written for older children, this means off-white with a dull finish to prevent glare, although other surfaces are used for special purposes. The binding should be durable and practical, able to withstand hard use.

Cultural Implications In addition, we should consider evaluating the many aspects of cultural authenticity and cultural consciousness in children's books. It is important that children's books show people from diverse groups playing and working together, solving problems, and overcoming obstacles. Multicultural children's literature helps children understand that despite our many differences, people share some common as well as unique perspectives.[9]

In recent years, we have seen an increase in the number of books for children that highlight or include diverse material. However, this does not mean that all multicultural books are created equal. When you are looking for Native American books, for example, are the characters depicted as a universal or generic group of people? Or are the sovereign nations (Navajo, Cherokee, Seminole, for example) of the American Indian or Alaska Native tribal entities portrayed? Dietrich and Ralph discussed the vital role of the teacher:

> When multicultural literature becomes an integral part of the curriculum and teachers act as models and guides, classrooms can become arenas for open exchange. Literature and the ensuing discussion permit students to read, think, and become actively engaged with the texts. As a consequence, it should be easier for a student to cross cultural borders.[10]

Summer Edward, a student scholar, freelance reviewer of multicultural children's books, and Caribbean children's books specialist, reviewed the literature and the views of several authors and illustrators of multicultural children's books (Joseph Bruchac, Gary Soto, Floyd Cooper, Patricia Polacco, and Yumi Heo) to answer the question: *How do you know if a children's book you're thinking of sharing with your students accurately and authentically portrays the culture of its characters?* Edward synthesized this information and developed the following Ten Tips for Selecting Multicultural Children's Literature:[11]

1. **The book avoids offensive expressions, negative attitudes, or stereotypical representations.** You'll know a racist, sexist, or other offensive stereotype when you see it;

trust your instincts. If you feel that you have no instincts in this area, then do some research. Historically, what are some of the negative stereotypes that have been associated with a particular culture? Once you know what the stereotypes are, look at both the pictures and the text of a book for the presence or absence of such depictions.

2. **The author of the book is from the culture being depicted.** If not, be wary. A cultural insider is more likely to get it right. A good sign to look for is a biography explaining the author's connection to the culture or an author's/illustrator's note explaining the sources of information the author and illustrator drew upon in writing and illustrating the book.

3. **The events, situations, and objects depicted are historically accurate.** In a work of fiction, the events, situations, or objects described are plausible within the historical context of the setting and time period.

4. **The book exemplifies good storytelling.** Donna Ford and colleagues suggest that good children's literature inspires, amuses, and tackles larger themes relevant to children, like coming of age or coming to terms with the past. The plot is accessible, interesting, and makes sense. The characters are well-developed, convincing, and memorable. The story should be worth revisiting again and again. Social justice books have their place in the classroom, but too often, books depicting minority or "parallel" cultures adopt a patronizing, "poor them" tone. In fact, children's author Gary Soto says, "If the author is not dealing with social issues, that's a good sign."

5. **The book avoids any suggestion that there is a single cause or simple answer to the socio-historical dilemmas of the culture being represented.** Ford and colleagues recommend that when issues of human rights and oppression are central to a story, the book should address those issues in a way that emphasizes the dignity and resilience of people living under oppressive conditions. They also note that "children should perceive the characters as competent problem-solvers, responding in positive ways to the challenges they confront."

6. **The story includes words and phrases from the culture being depicted.** The inclusion of Spanish words in a book about a Mexican family, for example, provides realism and shows respect for the culture. Give extra points if the book comes with a glossary at the back and a pronunciation guide.

7. **The book is explicit and precise about the cultural roots of the group being depicted.** For example, for books depicting Caribbean characters, the author avoids vague references to "island people" and "island culture" and, rather, names and accurately represents the specific Caribbean country the character(s) comes from. Abenaki Indian author and storyteller Joseph Bruchac warns that for Native American children's books, the book should depict characters from a specified native nation, as opposed to generic Indians, and the descriptions and illustrations in the book should show an awareness of the particular customs, history, dress, and ways of speaking of the particular Native American nation. Although books about immigrant cultures in America are valuable, assign extra points if the book is set in or touches upon experiences in another country.

8. **The book does not set different cultures or groups in opposition to each other.** For example, for a book depicting Native Americans, the story avoids what children's author Joseph Bruchac refers to as "The Dances with Wolves Syndrome"—books in which all Indians are noble and all white people are bad.

9. **The story accurately reflects the values inherent to the culture being depicted.**
Serious consideration should be given to the ideals, principles, or beliefs that a cultural group considers to be important. For example, a book depicting Asian Americans might reflect the values of cooperation and a respect for family and tradition.

10. **The story acknowledges the diversity of experiences within a particular cultural group.** For example, as Ford and colleagues remind us, the experiences of African Americans in the South do not necessarily resemble those of the North, and inner-city situations do not parallel experiences in rural settings. A good multicultural book shows an awareness of such differences.

These "tips" for evaluating and selecting multicultural children's books are not meant to be an exhaustive checklist. In addition to these Ten Tips, consult with colleagues, parents/caregivers, and local diverse community members, drawing upon their specialized knowledge, unique perspectives, and lived experiences to help you when selecting books.

As children read and respond to books, we ask them to connect their lived experiences. If the books are not carefully selected, it may be impossible for some students to do so. Sims Bishop stated, "Books are sometimes windows, offering views of worlds that may be real or imagined, familiar or strange. These windows are also sliding glass doors, and readers have only to walk through in imagination to become part of whatever world has been created or recreated by the author. When lighting conditions are just right, however, a window can also be a mirror. Literature transforms human experience and reflects it back to us, and in that reflection we can see our own lives and experiences as part of the larger human experience. Reading, then, becomes a means of self-affirmation, and readers often seek their mirrors in books."[12]

If readers are going to look into the "windows," walk through the "sliding glass doors," or see themselves in the "mirrors" with children's books, it is very important that the evaluation and selection of books with diverse and multicultural themes be thoughtfully conducted.

Guidelines: Evaluating Children's Fiction lists criteria by which we have traditionally evaluated a work of literature. These criteria relate to elements as plot, setting, theme, characterization, style, point of view, and format and form a foundation on which to examine each of the genres described in subsequent chapters.

Developing Sources to Help Choose Books

There are many professional resources to help teachers as they go about choosing books for their students. Book review journals such as *School Library Journal, The Horn Book Magazine,* and *Booklist Magazine* and reviews in other professional journals such as *Language Arts and the Reading Teacher* provide guidance and often single out titles with exceptional strengths. Book award lists are another source to help busy teachers single out books of note. Three of the most coveted awards in children's literature in the United States are the Newbery, Caldecott, and Sibert medals. Winners are chosen every year by two committees of the Association for Library Service to Children, a division of the American Library Association. The International Board on Books for Young People awards the Hans Christian Andersen Medal every two years to an artist and author for a "substantial and lasting contribution to children's literature." The Children's Book Council publishes a list called "Awards and Prizes for Children's Books," which includes more than 321 awards in English. We have named a few of these awards in **Teaching Feature 1.2: Selected Book Awards for Children.** See Appendix A for recent winners of the most prominent awards.

Evaluating Children's Fiction

Go to **Connect**® *to access study resources, practice quizzes, and additional materials.*

Before Reading

- What kind of book is this?
- What does the reader anticipate from the title?
- Dust jacket illustration? Size of print? Illustrations? Chapter headings? Opening page?
- For what age range is this book intended?

Plot

- Does the book tell a good story?
- Will children enjoy it? Is there action?
- Does the story move?
- Is the plot original and fresh?
- Is it plausible and credible?
- Is there preparation for the events?
- Is there a logical series of happenings?
- Is there a basis of cause and effect in the happenings?
- Is there an identifiable climax? How do events build to a climax?
- Is the plot well constructed?
- Will the children learn to respect their own cultural groups? And other groups that they may not meet in their daily lives?

Setting

- Where does the story take place?
- How does the author indicate the time?
- How does the setting affect the action, characters, or theme?
- Does the story transcend the setting and have universal implications?

Theme

- Does the story have a theme?
- Is the theme worth imparting to children?

- Does the theme emerge naturally from the story, or is it stated too obviously?
- Does the theme overpower the story?
- Does it avoid moralizing?
- How does the author use motifs or symbols to intensify meaning?
- Does the story have pluralistic themes to foster value in cultural diversity?

Characterization

- How does the author reveal characters? Through narration? In conversation? By thoughts of others?
- Are the characters convincing and credible?
- Do we see their strengths and their weaknesses?
- Does the author avoid stereotyping? Bias?
- Is the behavior of the characters consistent with their ages and background?
- Is there any character development or growth?
- Has the author shown the causes of character behavior or development?
- How does the author present diverse groups of people?

Style

- Is the style of writing appropriate to the subject?
- Is the style straightforward or figurative?
- Is the dialogue natural and suited to the characters?
- How did the author create a mood? Is the overall impression one of mystery? Gloom? Evil? Joy? Security?
- Are there derogatory overtones to the words used to describe the characters and culture?

Guidelines

Point of View

- Is the point of view from which the story is told appropriate to the purpose of the book? Does the point of view change?
- Does the point of view limit the reader's horizon, or enlarge it?
- Why did the author choose this particular point of view?
- Are cultural perspectives highlighted in multiple points of view?

Additional Considerations

- Do the illustrations enhance or extend the story?
- Are the pictures aesthetically satisfying?

- How well designed is the book?
- Is the format of the book related to the text?
- What is the quality of the paper? How sturdy is the binding?
- How does the book compare with other books on the same subject?
- How does the book compare with other books written by the same author?
- How have other reviewers evaluated this book?
- What age range would most appreciate this story?
- Is there anything in the story that would embarrass or offend a child whose culture is being portrayed?

No one but the most interested follower of children's literature would want to remember all the awards that are given for children's books. And certainly no one should assume that the award winners are the only children's books worth reading. Like the coveted Oscars of the motion picture industry and the Emmys of television, the awards in children's literature focus attention not only on the winners of the year but also on the entire field of endeavor. They recognize and honor excellence and also point the way to improved writing, illustrating, and producing of worthwhile and attractive books for children.

Rafael López won the 2016 Pura Belpré Award for illustration for *Drum Dream Girl: How One Girl's Courage Changed Music*, by Margarita Engle. Engle, Margarita, *Drum Dream Girl: How One Girl's Courage Changed Music*. Illustrated by Rafael López. New York, NY: HMH Books for Young Readers, 2015, Cover. Copyright ©2015 by HMH Books for Young Readers. All rights reserved. Used with permission.

Selected Book Awards for Children

Go to **Connect®** *to access study resources, practice quizzes, and additional materials.*

Award	Given by	Description	More Information
Caldecott Medal	Association for Library Service to Children (ALSC)	Awarded annually to the artist of the most distinguished American picturebook for children.	http://www.ala.org/alsc/ awardsgrants/bookmedia/ caldecottmedal/ caldecottmedal
Newbery Medal	Association for Library Service to Children (ALSC)	Awarded annually to the author of the most distinguished contribution to American literature for children.	http://www.ala.org/alsc/ awardsgrants/bookmedia/ newberymedal/ newberymedal
Robert F. Sibert Informational Book Medal	Association for Library Service to Children (ALSC)	Awarded annually to the author and illustrator of the most distinguished informational book published in English.	http://www.ala.org/alsc/ awardsgrants/bookmedia/ sibertmedal
Charlotte Huck Award	National Council of Teachers of English (NCTE)	Given annually for fiction that has the power to transform children's lives.	www.ncte.org/awards/ charlotte-huck
Orbis Pictus Award	National Council of Teachers of English (NCTE)	Promotes and recognizes excellence in the writing of nonfiction for children.	www.ncte.org/awards/ orbispictus
Pura Belpré Medal	Association for Library Service to Children (ALSC) and REFORMA	Presented to a Latino/Latina writer and illustrator whose work best portrays, affirms, and celebrates the Latino cultural experience in a work of literature for children and youth.	http://www.ala.org/alsc/ awardsgrants/bookmedia/ belpremedal
Asian/Pacific American Award for Literature	Asian/Pacific American Librarians (APALA)	Recognizes and honors individual work about Asian Americans and their heritage.	www.apalaweb.org/ awards/literature-awards/
Mildred L. Batchelder Award	Association for Library Service to Children (ALSC)	Awarded to an American publisher for a children's book considered to be the most outstanding of those books originally published in a foreign language in a foreign country.	http://www.ala.org/alsc/ awardsgrants/bookmedia/ batchelderaward

teaching feature 1.2

Award	Given by	Description	More Information
Coretta Scott King Book Award	Ethnic Multicultural Information Exchange Round Table of the American Library Association (EMIERT)	Recognizes an African American author and illustrator of outstanding books for children and young adults.	www.ala.org/emiert/cskbookawards
Hans Christian Andersen Award	International Board on Books for Young People	Presented every other year to a living author and illustrator of children's books whose complete works have made a lasting contribution to children's literature.	www.ibby.org
Carter G. Woodson Award	National Council for the Social Studies	Awarded to the most distinguished social science books appropriate for young readers that depict ethnicity in the United States.	www.socialstudies.org/awards/woodson/winners

Challenging Perspectives

"Each of the children had completed the text for their 32-page picture book on spiders.
The only task left to complete was the illustrations. The children were instructed to select a medium for their art. They were familiar with the variety that they could choose from. Some chose collage, some chose pen and ink, some chose photo essay. Each of the children was also aware that a panel of fifth-grade judges would select an 'award winner' and an 'honor book.' After two days of work, Eric brought his book up to my desk saying that he had completed his task. Upon opening the book, I saw that the pages were blank. I asked Eric where his illustrations were, and he answered, 'They are right there!' When I asked where the spider was in his story, he said that as soon as you turn the page, it crawls away and you don't see it anymore. I told him that while this was a clever and different perspective, I wasn't sure if the judges would 'get it.' His response was, 'Then we need a new panel of judges!'"
—First-grade teacher

This teacher's story recounts a student's display of imagination, creativity, and alternative art form or expression. The challenge for the fifth-grade panel of judges would be to look at the aesthetic representation of spiders in Eric's story and use criteria to judge and later award a prize. Unfortunately, criteria for such awards often fall short when juxtaposed with new perspectives. In the picturebook world, the emergence of new and challenging perspectives in picturebook illustrations was often met by award committees as not deserving an honorable mention. Neither did these award committees respond to the racial and cultural stereotypes found in picturebooks. Often the stereotypes were oversimplifications and generalizations about a particular group, which carried derogatory implications. Some of the stereotypes were blatant, others more subtle. These committees, historically, did little to check for depictions that demeaned or ridiculed characters because of their race, gender, age, ability, appearance, size, religion, sexual orientation, socioeconomic class, or indigenous language. For example, *Tikki Tikki Tembo,* a book that depicts a Chinese protagonist, has been at the seat of controversy related to language, culture, and authenticity. Though the book has a delightful repetitive pattern that many children enjoy, the text and illustrations are inaccurate depictions of Chinese people and culture. In the text, the first and most honored son had the grand long name of "Tikki tikki tembo-no sa rembo-chari bari ruchi-pip peri pembo," which sends a false and less-than-flattering message about Chinese names.

With so few books historically and in contemporary times portraying underrepresented groups as protagonists or serving as the center of picturebook illustrations, it is no wonder that when judged in a larger pool, the illustrators of non-mainstream subjects often continued to be marginalized or excluded. This gave rise to the creation of new awards to bring a new lens to the artistic and sometimes alternative formats in picturebooks.

One example is the Coretta Scott King Book Award that is presented annually by the Coretta Scott King Committee of the American Library Association's Ethnic Multicultural Information Exchange Round Table (EMIERT) and is awarded to an African American author and African American illustrator for an outstandingly inspirational and educational contribution. These books should promote "understanding and appreciation of the culture of all peoples and their contribution to the realization of the American dream and commemorate the life and works of Dr. Martin Luther King, Jr. and to honor Mrs. Coretta Scott King for her courage and determination to continue the work for peace and world brotherhood."

These new awards at their inception were not seen as "the awards." The Caldecott Medal is still viewed by some as the top medal awarded for illustrations in picturebooks. However, librarians and independent bookstore owners that serve diverse constituencies use other award winners to help make selections for stocking the shelves. It is not unusual, for example, for some libraries to feature Pura Belpré Medal and Coretta Scott King winners alongside Caldecott winners.

The challenge for those of us who use award-winning book lists to make decisions about books we use in classrooms or how we use our resources to purchase books for classrooms or libraries is to not depend *only* on the books that make the best-seller list but to look for lists of award winners that represent diverse children, families, and communities. Often as teachers, you will receive a list of chosen titles to support standards and objectives outlined in your curriculum, which will likely include award winners from current or previous years. Seldom will these lists include books from smaller presses or other awards that don't receive the same spotlight of recognition from the American Library Association or the *New York Times* best-seller list. This is not to suggest that award criteria, evaluation, and subsequent lists do not have a useful place in the criteria and selection of books used in classroom settings. It does suggest, however, that as diverse as our lived experiences are, so should be the list from which we select books to use in classrooms with children.

Throughout this text, we will explore the issues you will encounter as you strive to develop an effective reading curriculum for your students. Instilling a passion for reading often takes a backseat to the challenges you will face in today's sociocultural and political climate. The Ten-Point Model, introduced in the next section, has been developed and adapted to serve as a tool to help you address challenging and controversial situations and issues.

Teaching Controversial Issues: The Ten-Point Model

Everyday life is full of controversies. Children's literature is not immune to it. Issues such as censorship, gender stereotypes, the struggle for freedom and equality, cultural authenticity, ethical heroes, violence, sexuality, the partnership of classroom teacher and librarian, and the current trends in buying, selling, publishing, and using children's books all cause or contribute to controversy.

Exploring controversial issues helps children develop a comprehensive, more critical understanding of the world they live in and is an important part of helping them become critically reflective thinkers. Teaching controversial issues allows for content across the curriculum to be related in authentic ways to children's lives, providing an opportunity for children and teachers to reflect, analyze, and critically comprehend more deeply. The goal can be summed up in a quote from Dr. Martin Luther King, Jr.: "The ultimate measure of a man is not where he stands in moments of comfort and convenience, but where he stands at times of challenge and controversy." Teaching about controversial issues related to books written for children, when it is well planned, can help children gain the necessary confidence and skills to "take a stand."

Teaching controversial issues is multifaceted and complex. It challenges the student's as well as the parent's personally held values, beliefs, and worldviews, and it requires achieving a balance between taking a stance and coercion or indoctrination. This can be confusing to students and may cause some children and their parents and communities considerable concern.

It is important to plan thoroughly for issues-related teaching. The Ten-Point Model for Teaching Controversial Issues,[13] developed by Susan Jones (a Boston educator and member of Educators for Social Responsibility), is a framework for teaching controversial and difficult issues (**Figure 1.1**). In this approach, students begin by pooling what they know and what they think they know about an issue. They also develop a list of questions. This is followed by an information-gathering period during which students search for answers to the questions.

Next, using information they have collected, students correct any misinformation previously listed and develop more questions. This process continues until some type of culminating activity emerges from the information.

This model can be easily adapted to various topics across the curriculum to assist in teaching about controversial issues. For example, consider using the Ten-Point Model in figure 1.1

The Ten-Point Model for Teaching Controversial Issues

The Ten-Point Model for Teaching Controversial Issues provides a framework for encouraging students to question, research, share, and evaluate information related to current, controversial topics.

Step

1. **Raise the initial question and have the children brainstorm all their initial responses.** Write them down. Don't discuss them, and accept all contributions. The teacher only asks questions, such as "What does that mean?" "Can you say any more about that?" "Does anyone else have anything to add to that information?" and (especially for erroneous or extremely one-sided information) "Where did you learn that?" or "Is that a fact or is it someone's opinion?"

2. **Begin a separate list of "Things to find out more about."** List as soon as undefined vocabulary words, vague concepts, and unanswered questions begin to emerge. These will serve as guidelines for the ongoing research, and some may even develop into separate topics to pursue later.

3. **Assign information-gathering homework.** Have children find out everything they can about the initial questions. Tell them to be prepared to share what they can in their own words. It is fine to read articles or watch the TV news, but the best source of information is interviewing parents, other relatives, or friends. Tell them not to copy down anyone else's words, but that it is a good idea to take notes.

4. **Share again responses to the initial question in a brainstorming session.** Again, children must share the information they gathered in their own words. Write down all responses. You can ask the same questions as in item 1, but offer no information and no "answers." Add to the list of "Things to find out more about" from item 2.

5. **Continue the process of gathering information.** Identify things to find out more about and continue to gather still more information for as long as the topic seems interesting. Encourage the children to listen to and learn from each other. They can begin to ask each other to explain what a new word means, to elaborate on a concept, to consider a new question, and to state their source of information. The teacher's role is an active one—facilitating, clarifying, and questioning—but the teacher doesn't impose information.

6. **If a concept emerges that sparks much interest or confusion, pose it as a new question about which to seek information.** Share and question until a satisfactory base of information has been established. More than one line of questioning can go on at the same time.

7. **Periodically give the children an individual written assignment in class to summarize their thoughts about a particular question.** The assignment can be worded as "What you know about X," "Things you don't understand about X," "Something X makes you think about," or any other way you can find to help crystallize children's individual thinking about the topic. Sharing these compositions aloud or posting them for all to read helps make all information public.

8. **As individual or group projects emerge, follow up on them.** The class may decide to write letters to a public figure; one or two children may decide to pursue a challenging research topic to report on to the group; or an outside resource may unexpectedly appear. Be flexible.

9. **Let others—parents, your colleagues, the media—know what you are doing.** Invite their participation. Encourage dialogue.

10. **End your project with something either public or permanent.** Ideas include a class presentation to the rest of the school about what they have learned, an article for the school paper or the local newspaper, a class book or individual books for the school library, or class participation in an event. It is important for children to feel that their learning is relevant and can lead to the ability to contribute to the larger world.

Source: Adapted from Kreidler, W. *Elementary Perspectives: Teaching Concepts of Peace and Conflict.* Copyright ©1990, Educators for Social Responsibility, Cambridge, MA. www.esrnational.org. Used by permission.

a discussion of global warming, a very timely topic that can elicit a variety of responses and may be controversial. The following is a possible approach to such a discussion:

1. **Raise the initial question and have the children brainstorm all their initial responses.** *Does global warming really exist?* Ground rules should be created to enable the free flow of ideas in a safe, nonthreatening environment, with the goal of having students think about and question their assumptions and listen to others' ideas.

2. **Begin a separate list of "Things about global warming to find out more about."** Students should create a list of what they know about the issue and what they want to learn about the issue.

3. **Assign information-gathering homework.** For homework, ask children to research information from different sides of the debate. For example, some believe the scientific evidence argues against the existence of a greenhouse crisis, or against the notion that realistic policies could achieve any meaningful climatic impact, or against the claim that we must act now if we are to reduce the greenhouse threat. Others believe the evidence is overwhelming and undeniable that global warming is real, is a serious concern, and is the result of our activities and not a natural occurrence. Children can use research skills to explore opposite views using children's literature, such as *The Down-to-Earth Guide to Global Warming,* co-authored by activists Laurie David and Cambria Gordon, and *The Sky's Not Falling! Why It's OK to Chill About Global Warming* by Holly Fretwell, resource economist and a senior research fellow at the Property and Environment Research Center (PERC). The two books sharply disagree on whether humans are causing global warming.

    Students could research organizations that have information representative of both sides. Following are examples of websites that have resources geared for students, parents, and teachers:

    - *NASA Climate Kids* <https://climatekids.nasa.gov>. Sponsored by NASA, this easy-to-navigate, interactive site offers activities, videos, articles, and games for elementary students. It is organized by Big Questions, Weather & Climate, Atmosphere, Water, Energy, and Plants & Animals. A companion site for teachers at <https://climatekids.nasa.gov/menu/teach/> includes step-by-step experiment directions, lesson plan activities, and more resources.
    - *Interesting Information About Global Warming Every Kid Should Have* <https://helpsavenature.com/global-warming-for-kids>. This site features engaging articles to help students learn about climate change, conservation, and the environment. These articles are short and direct and are peppered with visuals to enhance learning. Each article is broken down into smaller portions of text with links to additional articles on a sidebar.
    - *NeoK12: Global Warming for Kids* <https://www.neok12.com/Global-Warming.htm>. This site provides videos for students in grades 3 and up. These videos, from sources like NASA and National Geographic, are curated and approved by teachers. There are also extended subscription-based resources for teachers.
    - *The Why Files: Global Warming* <www.whyfiles.org/080global_warm/index.html>. Designed for teachers, students, and the lay public, this site provides a fairly detailed explanation of global-warming issues. Articles include graphs from NASA and hyperlinks to original data and articles, with additional internal links to related topics such as overpopulation, the greenhouse effect, and biodiversity.

4. **Share again responses to the initial question in a brainstorming session.** Return to the brainstorming session questions and, given the information they have gathered, have students determine if they can now answer questions raised using inquiry and information-gathering skills: searching for relevant information, determining the reliability of the source, and evaluating the information.

5. **Continue the process of gathering information.** Students can use the school and local library to look for print and multimedia resources that have information about global warming. They could brainstorm lists of keywords to use in their searches to answer questions about climate, greenhouse gas emissions, extreme weather, glacier retreat, extinctions of flora and fauna, and so on.

6. **If a concept emerges that sparks much interest or confusion, pose it as a new question about which to seek information.** For example, the teacher may pose the questions, "What is the debate or dispute regarding global warming?" "What do scientists say about the causes of increased global average air temperature?" Students can then discuss the disputes concerning the estimates of climate sensitivity, predictions of additional warming, what the consequences are, and what action should be taken (if any). While differences of opinion related to global warming will arise, students can take a stand using supporting evidence from their research.

7. **Periodically give the children an individual written assignment in class to summarize their thoughts about a particular question.** As the conversations ensue, use whole-class discussion, small-group discussions, journaling, and other forms of writing to help students create outlines or other formats to summarize the information they have gathered.

8. **As individual or group projects emerge, follow up on them.** Some students may wish to contact organizations that provide guest speakers that present both sides of the issue. Students can generate a list of people from the popular media, on the policy level (local politicians and environmental protection agencies), with individuals in the community (local scientists or professors), and corporations (oil or automobile manufacturers) to speak to the class. The availability of speakers may be limited to the location of the school; however, using technology, such as video conferencing (Skype, for example), may enable you to bring in speakers from outside the geographical location of the school.

9. **Let others—parents, your colleagues, the media—know what you are doing.** Parents may express their dismay or delight with the discussion of the topic depending on where they stand. If you live in an area where logging, mining, hunting, or fishing contribute significantly to the local economy or recreation, reading children's literature that highlights preservation and conservation by curtailing these activities may not be well received. Keep them informed of your goal: to create open-ended dialogue from multiple points of view and to create a space for debate and discussion, so that once students have gathered information they can make their own decisions.

10. **End your project with something either public or permanent.** Depending on where students stand, they may choose to work with organizations on either side of the issue or conduct a debate with other students to evaluate the reliability and credibility of information gathered. Students may also advocate for the inclusion of a particular book in the school library to expand the information available for other students to read, analyze, and evaluate related to this issue.

There are several benefits to the Ten-Point Model. The model starts where students are and is very respectful of children's knowledge. The process of correcting misinformation is empowering, not punitive. Because students spend time going from whole group to small group and back again, the process encourages community building and lets all students participate at their own level.

The Ten-Point Model requires that elementary students make use of some sophisticated reference and study skills. However, there can be an aimless quality to the procedure if the teacher doesn't present students with some boundaries to their explorations. Even though one purpose of the procedure is to demonstrate the open-ended nature of inquiry, the teacher often needs to structure a clear culminating activity so that the process doesn't just drift off into an anticlimactic and unsatisfying ending.

There are concerns that delving into issues that cause children to use their ethical and moral reasoning is like opening a metaphorical Pandora's box. While there is a variety of versions of the legend of Prometheus and Pandora's box, one component that finds its way into every story is that Pandora was inquisitive, curious, and a risk taker—after all, she did open the box! That being said, it is the inherent nature of what makes an issue controversial: the competing values, people strongly disagreeing with statements, the political sensitivity, the evoked strong emotions that is fodder for increased student engagement, culturally relevant teaching, service learning, authentic assessments, and ultimately children that grow up to be participants in our constitutional democracy.

For each of the genre chapters (Chapters 3 through 9), a sample of how to use the Ten-Point Model to teach controversial issues related to each chapter's content is provided within Connect®. For example, when discussing picturebooks in Chapter 3, you can determine how culture may influence our perceptions and use of color and how to encourage children to create meaning that enhances and extends stories using their lived experiences.

Additionally, each of the genre chapters in the text includes a **Curriculum Connections** feature. Using a suggested children's book as an example, this feature demonstrates how children's literature can be integrated into a variety of disciplines to accomplish meeting educational standards.

Notes

1. William Zinsser, ed., *Worlds of Childhood: The Art and Craft of Writing for Children* (Boston, Mass.: Houghton Mifflin, 1990), p. 3.
2. E. B. White, "On Writing for Children," quoted in *Children and Literature: Views and Reviews,* ed. Virginia Haviland (Glenview, Ill.: Scott, Foresman, 1973), p. 140.
3. C. S. Lewis, "On Three Ways of Writing for Children," *Horn Book Magazine* 39 (October 1963): 460.
4. Mollie Hunter, *The Pied Piper Syndrome* (New York: HarperCollins, 1992), p. 92.
5. Karen Hesse, *Out of the Dust* (New York: Scholastic, 1997), p. 46.
6. Dorothy L. Guth, ed., *Letters of E. B. White* (New York: Harper & Row, 1976), p. 613.
7. Roger Sutton, "Because It's Good for You," *New York Times Book Review* (11 May 2008): 25.
8. Natalie Babbitt, *Tuck Everlasting* (New York: Farrar, Straus & Giroux, 1975), p. 62.
9. Rudine Sims, *Shadow and Substance: Afro-American Experience in Contemporary Children's Fiction* (Urbana, Ill.: National Council of Teachers, 1982).
10. D. Dietrich and K. S. Ralph, "Crossing Borders: Multicultural Literature in the Classroom," *The Journal of Educational Issues of Language Minority Students* 5 (Winter 1995).

11. Reproduced by permission of Summer K. Edward.
12. Rudine Sims Bishop, "Mirrors, Windows, and Sliding Glass Doors," in *Perspectives: Choosing and Using Books for the Classroom* 6, no. 3 (Summer 1990).
13. Adapted from Kreidler, W. *Elementary Perspectives: Teaching Concepts of Peace and Conflict*. Copyright ©1990, Engaging Schools, Cambridge, MA. www.engagingschools.org. Used by permission.

Children's Literature

Go to **Connect**® *to access the Children's Literature Database. The following includes some of the titles you will find in the database.*

Titles in blue = multicultural titles

Anderson, John David. *Ms. Bixby's Last Day*. Walden Pond, 2016.

Appelt, Kathi. *The Underneath*. Illustrated by David Small. Atheneum, 2010.

Averbeck, Jim. *One Word from Sophia*. Illustrated by Yasmeen Ismail. Simon, 2015.

Babbitt, Natalie. *Tuck Everlasting*. Farrar, 1985.

Baker, Keith. *LMNO Peas*. Beach Lane, 2010.

Bauer, Marion Dane. *Little Dog, Lost*. Antheneum, 2012.

Beatty, Andrea. *Ada Twist, Scientist*. Illustrated by David Roberts. Abrams, 2016.

Burg, Shana. *A Thousand Never Evers*. Delacorte, 2008.

Carle, Eric. *The Artist Who Painted a Blue Horse*. Philomel, 2011.

Curtis, Christopher Paul. *Bucking the Sarge*. Random, 2004.

Dicamillo, Kate, and Alison McGhee. *Bink and Gollie*. Illustrated by Tony Fucile. Candlewick, 2012.

Drummond, Allan. *Energy Island: How One Community Harnessed the Wind and Changed Their World*. Farrar, 2011.

Engle, Margarita. *Drum Dream Girl: How One Girl's Courage Changed Music*. Illustrated by Rafael López. Houghton, 2015.

Feiffer, Jules. *Bark, George*. Harper, 1999.

Fitzhugh, Louise. *Harriet the Spy*. Harper, 1964.

Fritz, Jean. *And Then What Happened, Paul Revere?* Illustrated by Margot Tomes. Puffin, 1996.

Gardiner, John Reynolds. *Stone Fox*. Illustrated by Marcia Sewall. Crowell, 1980.

Garza, Carmen Lomas. *Family Pictures, 15th Anniversary Edition*. Children's Book Press, 2005.

_____. *In My Family*. Children's Book Press, 2000.

George, Jean Craighead. *My Side of the Mountain*. Dutton, 1988 [1959].

Gibbs, Edward. *I Spy with My Little Eye*. Templar, 2011.

Giddwitz, Adam. *The Inquisitor's Tale: Or, The Three Magical Children and Their Holy Dog*. Illustrated by Hatem Aly. Dutton, 2016.

Goldsaito, Katrina. *The Sound of Silence*. Illustrated by Julia Kuo. Little, 2016.

Hannigan, Katherine. *True (. . . Sort Of)*. Greenwillow, 2012.

Henkes, Kevin. *Bird Lake Moon*. Greenwillow, 2008.

_____. *Olive's Ocean*. Greenwillow, 2003.

Hesse, Karen. *Out of the Dust*. Scholastic, 1997.

Hughes, Richard. *A High Wind in Jamaica*. Harper, 1989 [1929].

Hunter, Mollie. *Mermaid Summer*. Harper, 1988.

_____. *A Stranger Came Ashore*. Harper, 1975.

Jenkins, Steve. *Deadliest!: 20 Dangerous Animals*. HMH, 2017.

Kerrin, Jessica Scott. *Martin Bridge: In High Gear*. Illustrated by Joseph Kelly. Kids Can, 2008.

Konigsburg, E. L. *The View from Saturday*. Atheneum, 1996.

Lee, Harper. *To Kill a Mockingbird*. HarperCollins, 1995 [1960].

L'Engle, Madeleine. *Meet the Austins*. Vanguard, 1960.

Lowry, Lois. *Number the Stars*. Houghton, 1989.

Magoon, Kekla. *Shadows of Sherwood: A Robyn Hoodlum Adventure*. Bloomsbury, 2016.

Marino, Gianna. *Meet Me at the Moon*. Viking, 2012.

Markle, Sandra. *The Case of the Vanishing Golden Frogs: A Scientific Mystery*. Millbrook, 2011.

Messner, Kate. *Capture the Flag*. Scholastic, 2012.

Morpurgo, Michael. *An Elephant in the Garden*. Feiwel & Friends, 2011.

Mosel, Arlene. *Tikki Tikki Tembo*. Illustrated by Blair Lent. Holt, 1968.

Nesbet, Anne. *Cloud and Wallfish*. Candlewick, 2017.

O'Connor, Jane. *Fancy Nancy: Bonjour Butterfly*. Illustrated by Robin Preiss Glasser. HarperCollins, 2008.

_____. *Fancy Nancy*. Illustrated by Robin Preiss Glasser. HarperCollins, 2005.

Palacio, R. J. *Wonder.* Knopf, 2012.

Paterson, Katherine. *Bridge to Terabithia.* Illustrated by Donna Diamond. Crowell, 1977.

Pennypacker, Sara. *The Great Gilly Hopkins.* Crowell, 1978.

——. *Waylon! One Awesome Thing.* Illustrated by Marla Frazee. Disney, 2017.

Pinfold, Levi. *Black Dog.* Candlewick, 2012.

Raczka, Bob. *Nico Draws a Feeling.* Illustrated by Simone Shin. 21st Century, 2017.

Ringtved, Glenn. *Cry, Heart, But Never Break.* Illustrated by Charlotte Pardi. Enchanted Lion, 2016.

Rosoff, Meg. *Jumpy Jack and Googily.* Illustrated by Sophie Blackall. Holt, 2008.

Rowling, J. K. *Harry Potter and the Deathly Hallows.* Scholastic, 2007.

Sachar, Louis. *Fuzzy Mud.* Delacorte, 2015.

——. *Holes.* Farrar, 1998.

Sendak, Maurice. *Where the Wild Things Are.* HarperCollins, 1963.

Seuss, Dr. [Theodor S. Geisel]. *The Cat in the Hat.* Random, 1966 [1957].

——. *Oh, the Places You'll Go!* Random, 1990.

——. *And to Think That I Saw It on Mulberry Street.* Random, 1989 [1937].

Solheim, James. *Born Yesterday.* Illustrated by Simon James. Philomel, 2010.

Spinelli, Jerry. *Wringer.* HarperCollins, 1997.

Stead, Rebecca. *Liar & Spy.* Random, 2012.

Stein, David Ezra. *Interrupting Chicken.* Candlewick, 2010.

Taylor, Mildred. *Roll of Thunder, Hear My Cry.* Dial, 1976.

Thompson, Jolene. *Faraway Fox.* Illustrated by Justin K. Thompson. Houghton, 2016.

Tolkien, J. R. R. *The Hobbit.* Houghton, 1938.

Ursu, Anne. *Breadcrumbs.* Illustrated by Erin McGuire. Walden Pond, 2013.

——. *The Real Boy.* Illustrated by Erin McGuire. Walden Pond, 2015.

Vanderpool, Clare. *Moon Over Manifest.* Yearling, 2011.

Voigt, Cynthia. *Homecoming.* Atheneum, 1981.

Waddell, Martin. *Can't You Sleep, Little Bear?* Illustrated by Barbara Firth. Candlewick, 1992.

Walker, Sally M. *Blizzard of Glass: The Halifax Explosion of 1917.* Henry Holt, 2011.

Werner, Sharon, and Sarah Forss. *Bugs by the Numbers.* Blue Apple, 2011.

White, E. B. *Charlotte's Web.* Illustrated by Garth Williams. Harper, 1952.

Williams, Margery. *The Velveteen Rabbit.* Illustrated by William Nicholson. Doubleday, 1969 [1922].

Williams-Garcia, Rita. *One Crazy Summer.* Amistad, 2011.

Wright, Barbara. *Crow.* Random House, 2012.

Chapter Two

Understanding Children's Responses to Literature

Chapter Outline

The following story, written by a second grader, clearly shows the influence of literature on his literacy development.

The Lonesome Egg

Once there lived a Lonesome Egg. [*The Golden Egg Book* (Brown)]

And nobody liked him because he was ugly. And there was an ugly duck too, but they didn't like each other. [*The Ugly Duckling* (Andersen)]

One day while the Lonesome Egg was walking, he met the Ugly duck. And the Egg said to the Duck, "Will you be my friend?" [*Do You Want to Be My Friend?* (Carle)]

"Well, O.K."

"Oh, thank you."

"Now let's go to your house, Duck."

"No let's go to your house."

"No we'll go to your house first and my house too."

"O.K." [Dialogue from the *Frog and Toad* series (Lobel)]

And then while they were walking, they met a baby Panda Bear and they picked it up and took it to Duck's house.

And then the baby Panda Bear said, "I'm tired of walking." So they rested.

And soon came a tiger. And the tiger ate them up, except for Duck. [*The Fat Cat* (Kent)]

And right as he saw that, he ran as fast as he could until he saw a woodcutter and he told the woodcutter to come very quickly. [*The Gingerbread Boy* (Galdone)]

And when they got there, the tiger was asleep. So, the woodcutter cut open the tiger [*Little Red Riding Hood* (Grimm Brothers)]

And out came Egg and baby Panda Bear.

And they ate the tiger and lived happily ever after.[1]

This child's story shows how books influence children's intellectual and emotional lives. As teachers, we hope to provide children with books that deeply engage their intellect and emotions—books that will help them to decide to become life-long readers. The phrase "response to literature" has been used in a variety of ways. Theoretically, response refers to any outward sign of that inner activity, something said or done that reveals a reader's thoughts and feelings about literature. A 6-year-old's drawing of a favorite character and a book review in the *New York Times* are both responses in this sense. Teachers or librarians who predict that a book will bring "a good response" use the term in a different way, focusing on the likelihood that children will find a book appealing and will be eager to read, talk about it, and transform it through writing and other art forms. In order to choose books that will satisfy individual readers and to plan for satisfying responses to literature in elementary classrooms, teachers may gain insight through studying research on children's reading interests and preferences, research about children's developmental patterns of growth, and research into classroom-based studies of responses to literature.

Reading Interests and Preferences

Children's desire to read is a major concern for adults in this multimedia age. Happily, the *2017 Kids & Family Reading Report* indicated that there is still great enthusiasm for reading for enjoyment, although the percentage of children who read for pleasure drops as children get older.[2] If we are to reverse this trend, teachers, librarians, parents, publishers, and booksellers who select children's books can make better choices by knowing which books are likely to have immediate appeal for many children and which ones might require introduction or encouragement along the way.

Studies of reading interests over the years have consistently identified certain topics and elements of content that have wide appeal.[3] Researchers have found that animals and humor, for instance, are generally popular across age levels. Among other elements that are frequently mentioned for reader appeal are action, suspense, and surprise. Sales figures, too, can reflect children's reading interests. Best-seller lists in *Publishers Weekly* magazine show that tie-ins to popular movies or television shows and series books were among the best-selling children's books. The *Kids & Family Reading Report* found that readers ages 6 to 17 like good story lines and books that make them laugh. They also prefer to read about "smart, brave, and kind" characters that overcome challenges set before them.[4] In 2017, trends in children's reading included funny books, the re-introduction of classics, a focus on kindness, and twists.[5]

Even though we can identify commonly chosen topics and story features that have wide general appeal, it is still impossible to concoct a formula for books that would have

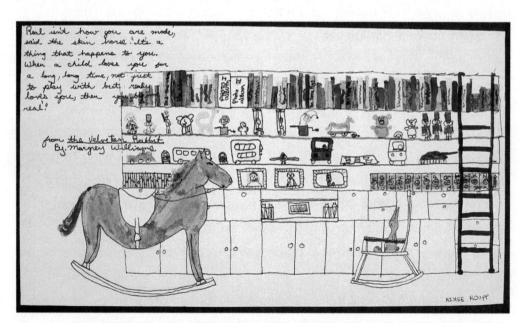

Choosing favorites and interpreting them are both a part of response to literature. Notice how the details of the modern playroom setting in this child's illustration of *The Velveteen Rabbit* provide a glimpse of her unique personal perspective on the book. Martin Luther King, Jr., Laboratory School, Evanston Public Schools, Evanston, Illinois.

unfailing popularity with all children. Teachers and librarians need to be sensitive to children's individual tastes, which often are unique and very particular. Nevertheless, the variations in interests among different groups of children seem to be linked to age, gender, and certain other influences.

Age and Gender Differences

The most obvious change in children's interest patterns occurs with age, as children take on more complex material and new areas of concern. Good book choices for first and sixth graders seldom overlap, even when the general topic is the same. Robert McCloskey's picturebook *Make Way for Ducklings* is a favorite animal story among 4- and 5-year-olds; 12-year-olds prefer their animal characters to be part of something more dramatic, as in Cynthia Lord's *A Handful of Stars* or Katherine Applegate's *The One and Only Ivan.* Seven-year-olds laugh at Peggy Parish's *Amelia Bedelia* and her literal interpretation of instructions such as "Draw the drapes" and "Dress the chicken." Eleven-year-olds like "funny" books, too, but prefer a different brand of humor, such as the comic situations in Roald Dahl's *The BFG* or the deadpan humor of Louis Sachar's *Holes.*

Previous studies have found that interests of children vary according to age and grade level and that girls read more than boys, but boys had a wider interest range and read a greater variety. Girls showed an earlier interest in adult romantic fiction than boys, whereas boys tended to prefer nonfiction from an early age. Boys seldom showed preference for a "girl's" book, but girls read a "boy's" book more often.[6] A 1995 study done in England with close to eight thousand 10-, 12-, and 14-year-olds found a swing away from book reading as children grow older, particularly among 14-year-old boys. The survey found that although "boys' predilection for non-narrative remains, . . . its significance in boys' reading diet is somewhat overstated."[7] The 2011 National Literacy Trust report, also conducted in Great Britain with eight thousand primary and secondary school students, stated that when it came to reading fiction, both boys' and girls' most popular topics were adventure, comedy, and horror or ghost stories. Least favorite topics for boys were poetry and romance/relationships, while girls' least favorites were sports related and war/spy titles.[8] A study that looked at sixth graders' preferences for media such as magazines and comics in addition to books found that boys' and girls' top choice was scary stories. For boys, comics and sports stories were next, while girls chose magazines and comics.[9]

The influence of gender on reading interests is thus not entirely clear. What we do not know about gender differences in children's choices is whether they reflect a natural interest or conformity to cultural expectations. Research that further updates preference studies in our postmodern age is certainly important. We can assume, however, that in school and home settings where traditional sexual stereotypes are downplayed, boys and girls share enthusiasm for many common favorites. It is important to give children many options for book choice so that girls and boys can have a chance to explore each other's perspectives. It is just as unfortunate for girls to miss the excellent nonfiction being published today as it is for boys to turn away from fine fiction that offers insight into human relationships.

Other Determinants of Interest

Many factors other than age and gender have been investigated in relation to children's reading interests. At one time, the influence of mental age vs. chronological age as measured by standardized tests received considerable attention. Now, however, we believe that children of varying academic abilities still are more alike than different in the character of their reading interests. It is more likely that the quantity of books involved and the rate at which interests develop will vary widely.

Illustrations, color, format, length, and type of print can also influence children's choices. It would be unwise to oversimplify the effect of these factors on children's book choices, especially because so much of the research has been done outside the context of normal reading and choosing situations. When children choose and use books in their own classrooms, their reactions to books are more complex than controlled experiments or surveys could reveal.

Social and environmental influences also affect children's book choices and reading interests. Many teachers and librarians feel that cultural and ethnic factors impact reading interests. One of the arguments for providing culturally authentic picturebooks and novels about Asian, Hispanic, African American, and Native American children is that readers from a particular culture will find material drawn from their own culture more interesting. The relationship between interests and culture is not simple, and unfortunately there is not yet enough research to clarify this point.

Although interests do not seem to vary greatly according to geographical location, the impact of the immediate environment—particularly the availability and accessibility of reading materials in the home, classroom, and public and school libraries—can be very strong. Children in classrooms where books are regularly discussed, enjoyed, and given high value tend to show livelier interest in a wider range of literature than do children from situations where books are given less attention. It is hard to tell how much of this effect is due to contact with the books and how much is social. Teachers' favorite books are often mentioned by children as their own favorites, perhaps because these are the stories closest at hand or have positive associations with the teacher.

Children influence each other in their choice of books. In the culture of the classroom, a title, author, or topic may rise to celebrity status for a time. Brian Selznick's *Wonderstruck* might be "the book" to read in one group of third graders, or children might make their own sign-up sheets to read the classroom's only copy of the latest from the Voyagers series. Younger children might spend time studying bears and long afterward point out "bear stories" to each other.

Peer recommendations are especially important to middle graders in choosing what to read. Some fifth and sixth graders are very candid:

"Everyone else in the class read it, so I figured I ought to, too."
"I usually read what Tammy reads."
"Most of my friends just like the same type of book I like. So, if they find a book, I'll believe them and I'll try it."[10]

Explaining Children's Choices

How can children influence each other's book choices so readily? Part of the answer may be simply that age-mates are likely to enjoy the same kinds of stories because they share many developmental characteristics. As children grow and learn, their levels of understanding change, and so do their favorites in literature. A few thought-provoking studies have suggested that children prefer those stories that best represent their own way of looking at the world—stories that mirror their experiences, needs, fears, and desires at a given age.[11]

There are many things to consider in explaining children's book choices. One of the most important is prior experiences with literature. Some children have heard many stories read aloud at home or have been introduced by their teachers to many different authors and genres. These children are likely to have tastes and preferences that seem advanced compared with those of children of their age who have had less exposure to books. Children's personal experiences influence their interests in ways that teachers and librarians might never be able to discover. And sometimes apparent interests are only the product of which books are available and which are not. We must be careful not to oversimplify the reasons for children's book choices. Even so, it is important not to underestimate a developmental perspective that takes into account both experience and growth. This is a powerful tool for predicting reading interests and for understanding other ways in which children respond.

Developmental Patterns That Influence Response

The child-development point of view begins with recognizing and accepting the uniqueness of childhood. Children are not miniature adults but individuals with their own needs, interests, and capabilities, all of which change over time and at varying rates.

In the early decades of child study, emphasis was placed on discovery of so-called normal behavior patterns for each age. Growth studies revealed similarities in patterns of physical, mental, and emotional growth. Later, longitudinal studies showed wide variations in individual rates of growth. One child's growth might be uneven, and a spurt in one aspect of development might precede a spurt in another. In 1992, Luis Moll called attention to "family funds of knowledge," which emphasized the sociocultural aspects of development. This concept extends our understanding of the development of children from diverse cultures, whose family beliefs and practices may be different from the children studied by Piaget and others.[12] Age trends continue to be useful in understanding the child, but by the 1960s, research began to be concerned with the interaction of biological and cultural forces with life experience. Researchers recognized that development is not simply the result of the maturation of neural cells but evolves with each new experience. Thus, the interaction of the individual with his or her environment, especially the social and cultural aspects of that environment, affects the age at which development appears.

Studies in children's cognitive and language growth, as well as in other areas of human development, can be very helpful in the choice of appropriate books and the understanding of children's responses. Although in this text we can highlight only a few findings, it should alert you to the importance of such information.

Physical Development

Children's experiences with literature can begin at a very early age. Even before they can talk, babies enjoy the sounds of the human voice reading stories and poetry. Their eyes are increasingly able to focus on color and shape, and by the time they are beginning to talk, their visual perception has developed to the point where they show fascination with small details in illustrations and often enjoy searching for specific objects in pictures.

Children's attention spans generally increase with age. In their first school experiences, some young children have trouble sitting quietly for even a twenty-minute story. It is better to have several short story times for these children than to demand their attention for longer periods and so lose their interest. Some kindergarten and primary teachers provide many opportunities for children to listen to stories in small groups of two or three by using the listening center or asking parent aides or student teachers to read to as few as one or two children.

Physical development influences children's interests as well as their attention spans. Growth in size, muscularity, and coordination is often reflected in a child's choice of a book in which characters share their own newly acquired traits or abilities. *Ben Rides On* by Matt Davies, for example, will be most enjoyed by children who have just learned to ride a bicycle. The demand for sports books increases as girls and boys gain the skills necessary for successful participation.

Children are growing up faster, both physically and psychologically, than they ever have before. The age of onset of puberty figures prominently in an early adolescents' self-concept and influences book choices. Both physical maturity and social forces have led to the development of sexual interests at a younger age. Girls are still reading Judy Blume's *Are You There, God? It's Me, Margaret* (1970) because it reflects their own concerns about menstruation. Robie Harris's nonfiction books such as *Who Has What?: All About Girls' Bodies and Boys' Bodies* (2011) are popular with elementary-age children whose parents may feel squeamish about the book's frank discussions about physical maturation and human reproduction, while today's children seem to take such books in stride.

Cognitive Development

The work of the Swiss psychologist Jean Piaget has had a great influence on educators' understanding of children's intellectual development.[13] Piaget proposed that intelligence develops as a result of the interaction of environment and the maturation of the child. In his view, children are active participants in their own learning. Piaget's observations led him to conclude that there are distinct stages in the development of logical thinking. According to his theory, all children go through these stages in the same progression but not necessarily at the same age. He identified these stages as the sensory-motor period, from infancy to about 2 years of age; the preoperational period, from approximately 2 to 7 years; the concrete operational period, from about 7 to 11 years; and a two-phase development of formal operations, which begins around age 11 and continues throughout adult life.

In recent years, the validity of Piaget's stage theory has been called into question by many researchers who express concerns about its interpretation. Researchers have suggested that children's social and cultural backgrounds and their familiarity with a task or situation might influence their thinking.[14] Some psychologists feel that stage theory fails to describe the intricacy and complexity of children's thinking and might lead adults to focus on what children are supposedly not able to do, thus falsely lowering expectations. We need to keep these cautions in mind if we look to Piagetian theory for guidance in selecting books for children and planning literature experiences.

Piaget's main contribution to our understanding of cognitive development was his recognition of the child as a meaning maker. Piaget's work and the work of cognitive psychologists since the mid-1900s have helped us view children as individuals. We can expect them to think about their experiences differently as they develop, and we can expect that thinking to change as they move toward adulthood. Thus, it is still useful for us to look at some of the characteristics of children's thinking described by Piaget and to compare them with those of the children with whom we work. Then we can consider how children's thinking patterns are related to the books they like and to their responses to literature.

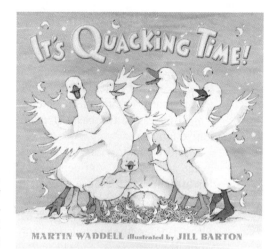

Author Martin Waddell is a master at telling engaging, predictable stories for toddlers, such as *It's Quacking Time!* IT'S QUACKING TIME! Text copyright ©2005 by Martin Waddell. Illustrations copyright ©2005 by Jill Barton. Reproduced by permission of Candlewick Press, on behalf of Walker Books Ltd., London.

MARTIN WADDELL illustrated by JILL BARTON

During the preschool and kindergarten years, children learn to represent the world symbolically through language, play, and drawing. Their thinking seems to be based on direct experience and perception of the present moment. Many of the particular features ascribed to this stage of thought seem to be reflected in young children's response to literature. During these years, children have a hard time holding an image in mind as it changes form or shape. They enjoy predictable stories like *Owl Babies, Tiny's Big Adventure,* or *It's Quacking Time!* by Martin Waddell. The built-in repetition in these stories carries the sequence of the action along from page to page. Older children who are able to follow the more complex logic of stories can remember the events without aid and often say that the repetitious language is boring.

Most children of elementary-school age would be described as being in the concrete operational stage according to Piaget's theory. Classifying and arranging objects in series are important abilities within children's command during this period, making them more systematic and orderly thinkers. Their thought also becomes flexible and reversible, allowing them to unravel and rearrange a sequence of events. It is no surprise, then, that elementary-age children begin to like mysteries and to understand stories with more complex plot features such as flashbacks or a story within a story. Older elementary-age children also seem to identify more spontaneously with different points of view. Books like *Me and You* by Anthony Browne or *The True Story of the 3 Little Pigs!* by Jon Scieszka suit this developmental level well because readers understand what the author has done with the structure of a familiar tale and can also begin to see the events through the eyes of a new narrator or a new culture.

As students begin the transitional period that corresponds roughly to the middle-school years, they begin to develop abstract theoretical thought; they are no longer dependent on concrete evidence but can reason from hypotheses to logical conclusions. This allows them to think of possibilities for their lives that are contrary to their prior experience and enables them to see the future in new ways. Complex novels and science fiction in particular begin to have appeal for students at this level. Also, students gain an understanding of the use of symbols, such as letters for numbers in algebra or symbolic meanings in literature. While they have understood the use of obvious symbols like the illustrator's use of light in Shane W. Evan's *Underground,* they can now deal with the layers of meaning found in some poetry and complex stories like Lois Lowry's *The Giver.*

However we look at cognitive development, we need to remember that it is only one part of a much larger picture of growth patterns that influence interests and responses.

Language Development

The pattern of language learning moves from an infant babbling and cooing to the use of single words, to simple sentences and transformations such as questions and negatives. Language development proceeds at a phenomenal pace during the pre-school years. By the end of that time, children will have learned to express their thoughts in longer sentences that combine ideas or embed one idea within another. In short, they will have gained access to the basic structure of grammar—all this by about age 4, whatever their native language.[15]

Children improvise and explore words as they learn, chanting and playing with language as they gain confidence. Rhythmic rhymes and nonsense verses are natural choices for preschoolers because they fit this pattern so well. However, children's fun in playing with language as various forms are mastered is not limited to the very young. Middle-grade children, with their wider range of language competence, are fascinated by the variety of jokes, riddles, tongue twisters, and folklore miscellany offered by Bob Raczka in collections like *Lemonade: And Other Poems Squeezed from a Single Word*. They are also intrigued by ingenious uses of language in a story context, as in Pamela Edwards's *Some Smug Slug*, Norton Juster's *The Phantom Tollbooth,* or Maryrose Wood's The Incorrigible Children of Ashton Place books.

We know that children's language growth continues through the elementary grades and beyond, although the rate is never again as dramatic as during the preschool years. The average length and complexity of their statements, both oral and written, increase as children progress through school.[16] We also know, however, that children's capacity to produce language consistently lags behind their ability to understand it. This suggests that we owe students of all ages the opportunity to read and hear good writing that is beyond the level of their own conversation. Seven-year-olds, for instance, cannot speak with the eloquence and humor that characterize William Steig's picturebooks, such as *The Amazing Bone* or *Doctor De Soto*. Still, they can understand the language in its story context, and hearing it will add to their knowledge of how language sounds and works. Books by Virginia Hamilton or E. L. Konigsburg might serve the same function for older students. Unlike novels that do little more than mirror contemporary speech, the work of these and other fine writers can give children a chance to consider the power of language used with precision and imagination. *interesting contrast*

Moral Development

Piaget's extensive studies of children included special attention to their developing ideas about fairness and justice. According to Piaget, the difference between younger and older children's concepts is so pronounced that there are really "two moralities" in childhood.[17] Other researchers such as Lawrence Kohlberg[18] and Carol Gilligan have contributed to our understanding of moral development in children.

According to both Piaget's and Kohlberg's descriptions of the general direction of elementary-age children's development, as children grow in intellect and experience, they move away from ideas of morality based on authority and adult constraint and toward morality based on the influence of group cooperation and independent thinking. To the later stages of this development, Gilligan adds a dimension based on gender.[19] She suggests that as girls mature, their sense of their identity is influenced by interconnections with others to a greater degree than for boys. Consequently, their moral judgment develops along lines of an enhanced sense of responsibility and caring for others. Girls might seem less decisive than boys in discussing moral dilemmas because they are trying to take into account a whole network of people who could be affected by a choice. This concern for others is present in boys' thinking as well but seldom takes precedence over their ideas about what is "fair."

Some of the contrasts between the moral judgment of younger and older children are as follows:

- Young children judge the goodness or badness of an act according to its likelihood of bringing punishment or reward from adults; in other words, they are constrained by the rules that adults have made. Older elementary-age children usually understand that there are group standards for judging what is good or bad and by then are very conscious of situations where they can make their own rules.

- In a young child's eyes, behavior is totally right or totally wrong, with no allowance for an alternate point of view. More-mature children are willing to consider the possibility that circumstances and situations make for legitimate differences of opinion.

- Young children tend to judge an act by its consequences, regardless of the actor's intent. By third or fourth grade, most children have switched to considering motivation rather than consequences alone in deciding what degree of guilt is appropriate.

- Young children believe that bad behavior and punishment go together; the more serious the deed, the more severe the punishment they would prescribe. Its form would not necessarily be related to the offense, but it would automatically erase the offender's guilt. Older children are not so quick to suggest all-purpose pain. They are more interested in finding a "fair" punishment, one that somehow fits the crime and will help bring the wrongdoer back within the rules of the group.

These developmental differences are apparent in the responses of two groups of children to Taro Yashima's *Crow Boy.* When asked what the teacher in the story should do about shy Chibi, who hid under the schoolhouse on the first day, many first graders said "Spank him!" Nine- and 10-year-olds, however, suggested explaining to him that there was nothing to be afraid of or introducing him to classmates so he wouldn't be shy. Many stories for children present different levels of moral complexity that have the potential for stimulating rich discussions among children. In *The Teddy Bear,* David McPhail provides younger children with a chance to consider the impulse to help others over their own wants and desires. *Breaking Stalin's Nose* by Eugene Yelchin provides older readers with a chance to discuss the complexities of a tragic personal experience.

Working through dilemmas, the experts suggest, allows us to move from one level of moral judgment toward another. Literature provides a means by which children can rehearse and negotiate situations of conflict without risk, trying out alternative stances to problems as they step into the lives and thoughts of different characters.

Personality Development

Every aspect of a child's growth is intertwined with every other. All learning is a meshing of cognitive dimensions, affective or emotional responses, social relationships, and value orientation. This is the matrix in which personality develops. The process of "becoming" is a highly complex one indeed. For children to become "fully functioning" persons, their basic needs must be met. They need to feel they are loved and understood; they must feel they are members of a group significant to them; they must feel they are achieving and growing toward independence. Psychologist Abraham Maslow's research suggests

that a person develops through a "hierarchy of needs," from basic animal-survival necessities to the "higher" needs that are more uniquely human and spiritual.[20] Self-actualization might take a lifetime, or it might never be achieved. But the concept that the individual is continually "becoming" is a more positive view than the notion that little change can take place in personality.

Literature can provide opportunities for people of all ages to satisfy higher-level needs, but it is important to remember that books alone cannot meet children's basic needs.

Psychologist Erik Erikson sees human emotional and social development as a passage through a series of stages.[21] Each stage centers around the individual's meeting a particular goal or concern associated with that stage. Erikson theorized that accomplishments at later stages depend on how well the individual was able to meet the goals of preceding stages. According to this theory, a sense of trust must be gained during the first year; a sense of autonomy should be realized by age 3; between 3 and 6 years, the sense of initiative is developed; and a sense of duty and accomplishment or industry occupies the period of childhood from 6 to 12 years. In adolescence, a sense of identity is built. A sense of intimacy, a parental sense of productivity, and a sense of integrity are among the tasks of adulthood.

The audience for children's books can be grouped according to their orientations toward achieving initiative, accomplishment, and identity. Preschool and early primary children can be described as preoccupied with first ventures outside the circle of familiar authority. Most elementary-age children are caught up in the period of industry, or "task orientation," proud of their ability to use skills and

GARY D. SCHMIDT

Winner of a Newbery Honor for THE WEDNESDAY WARS

OKAY FOR NOW

tools, to plan projects, and to work toward finished products. Middle-school students are more concerned with defining values and personal roles. Writers of children's books sometimes suggest a natural audience for their work by bringing one of these orientations into the foreground. In Beatrix Potter's *The Tale of Peter Rabbit,* Peter's adventures demonstrate a developing sense of initiative like that of the preschoolers listening to the story. The fearsome aspects of taking those first steps away from one's mother are reflected in Phyllis Root's *Oliver Finds His Way. Okay for Now* by Gary D. Scmidt speaks to the adolescent's struggle for identity and independence.

Guides for Ages and Stages

Adults who are responsible for children's reading need to be aware of child development and learning theory and of children's interests. They must keep in mind characteristics and needs of children at different ages and stages of development. At the same time, it is important to remember that each child has a unique pattern of growth. **Teaching Feature 2.1: Books for Ages and Stages** summarizes some characteristic growth patterns, suggests implications for selection and use of books, and provides examples of suitable books for a particular stage of development. Remember that the age levels indicated are only approximates. Also, books suggested as appropriate for one category might fit several other categories.

teaching feature 2.1

Books for Ages and Stages

Characteristics	Implications	Examples
Preschool and Kindergarten: Ages 3, 4, and 5		
Rapid development of language.	Interested in words. Enjoys rhymes, nonsense, repetition, and cumulative tales. Enjoys retelling simple folktales and "reading" stories from books without words.	*The Three Bears* (Galdone) *A Hole in the Bottom of the Sea* (Law) *Mangrove Tree* (Roth and Trumbore) *Demolition* (Sutton) *The Cazuela That the Farm Maiden Stirred* (Vamos)
Very active, short attention span.	Requires books that can be completed in one sitting. Enjoys participation such as naming, pointing, singing, and identifying hidden pictures. Should have a chance to hear stories several times each day.	*Anywhere Farm* (Root) *Press Here* (Tullet) *The Wheels on the Bus* (Cabrera) *Each Peach Pear Plum* (Ahlberg) *The Very Hungry Caterpillar* (Carle)

(continued)

teaching feature 2.1

Characteristics	Implications	Examples
Child is center of own world. Interest, behavior, and thinking are egocentric.	Likes characters that are easy to identify with. Normally sees only one point of view.	*The Animals' Ark* (Dubuc) *Here Is the Baby* (Kanevsky) *Say Hello, Sophie!* (Wells) *Hoot and Peep* (Judge) *Leonardo, the Terrible Monster* (Willems) *No, David!* (Shannon) *Bunny Cakes* (Wells) *Big Red Lollipop* (Khan)
Curious about own world.	Enjoys stories about everyday experiences, pets, playthings, home, and people in the immediate environment.	*Maggie and Michael Get Dressed* (Fleming) *The Best Days Are Dog Days* (Meshon) *My Big Barefoot Book of Spanish and English Words* (Fatus) *When You Were Born* (Aston) *And Then It's Spring* (Fogliano) *Pecan Pie Baby* (Woodson)
Beginning interest in how things work and the wider world.	Books feed curiosity and introduce new topics.	*I'm New Here* (O'Brien) *Explorers of the Wild* (Atkinson) *Fabulous Frogs* (Jenkins) *Time to Eat* (Jenkins and Page) *Back of the Bus* (Reynolds)
Building concepts through many first-hand experiences.	Books extend and reinforce child's developing concepts.	*Billions of Bricks* (Cyrus) *Swirl by Swirl* (Sidman) *My Car* (Barton) *Eating the Alphabet* (Ehlert)
Has little sense of time. Time is "before now," "now," and "not yet."	Books can help children begin to understand the sequence of time.	*This House, Once* (Freedman) *Hickory Dickory Dock* (Baker) *Clocks and More Clocks* (P. Hutchins) *A Second Is a Hiccup* (H. Hutchins) *April and Esme, Tooth Fairies* (Graham) *City Dog, Country Frog* (Willems) *About Time* (Koscielniak)
Learns through imaginative play; make-believe world of talking animals and magic seems very real.	Enjoys stories that involve imaginative play. Likes personification of toys and animals.	*Piggy Bunny* (Vail) *When an Elephant Comes to School* (Ormerod) *Corduroy* (Freeman) *We're Going on a Bear Hunt* (Rosen)

Characteristics	Implications	Examples
Seeks warmth and security in relationships with family and others.	Likes to hear stories that provide reassurance. Bedtime stories and other read-aloud rituals provide positive literature experiences.	*The Moon Inside* (Feder) *Tuck Me In!* (Hacohen) *Bedtime for Bear* (Helquist) *The Helpful Puppy* (Zarins) *Little Bear* (Minarik)
Beginning to assert independence. Takes delight in own accomplishments.	Books can reflect emotions. Enjoys stories where small characters show initiative.	*Bink & Gollie* (DiCamillo) *Alfie Gets in First* (Hughes) *The Dark* (Snicket) *Will I Have a Friend?* (Cohen) *Charlotte Jane Battles Bedtime* (Wolfe)
Makes absolute judgments about right and wrong.	Expects bad behavior to be punished and good behavior to be rewarded. Requires poetic justice and happy endings.	*Extra Yarn* (Barnett) *The Little Red Hen* (Barton) *The Gingerbread Man* (Aylesworth) *The Tale of Peter Rabbit* (Potter) *One of a Kind* (Winter)

Early Primary: Ages 6 and 7

Characteristics	Implications	Examples
Continued development and expansion of language.	Frequent story times during the day provide opportunity to hear the rich and varied language of literature. Wordless books and simple tales encourage storytelling.	*Last Stop on Market Street* (de la Peña) *Rainstorm* (Lehman) *Sylvester and the Magic Pebble* (Steig) *The Boy Who Loved Words* (Schotter) *The Adventures of the Dish and the Spoon* (Grey) *Diary of a Worm: Teacher's Pet* (Cronin) *Chalk* (Thomson)
Attention span increasing.	Prefers short stories; may enjoy a continued story provided each chapter is a complete episode.	*Tales from the Waterhole* (Graham) *Zelda and Ivy: The Runaways* (Kvasnosky) *Library Lion* (Knudsen) *Aggie and Ben: Three Stories* (Ries) *Rubia and the Three Osos* (Elya) *Flappy and Scrappy* (Yorinks)

(continued)

teaching **feature** 2.1

Characteristics	Implications	Examples
Striving to accomplish skills expected by adults.	Proud of accomplishments in reading and writing. Needs reassurance that everyone progresses at own rate. First reading experiences should be enjoyable, using familiar or predictable stories.	*Duck, Duck, Goose!* (Beaumont) *A Splendid Friend, Indeed* (Bloom) *The Day of Ahmed's Secret* (Heide and Gilliland) *You Read to Me, I'll Read to You* (Hoberman) *Except If* (Averbeck)
Learning still based on immediate perception and direct experiences.	Uses information books to verify as well as extend experience. Much value in watching guinea pigs or tadpoles before using a book.	*Whose Poop Is That?* (Lunde) *Actual Size* (Jenkins) *On the Way to the Beach* (H. Cole) *My Puppy Is Born* (J. Cole) *Chameleon, Chameleon* (Cowley) *Yucky Worms: Read and Wonder* (French)
Continued interest in own world; more curious about a wider range of things. Still sees world from an egocentric point of view.	Needs a wide variety of books. TV has expanded interests beyond home and neighborhood.	*Lost and Found Cat* (Kuntz and Shrodes) *Bee-Bim Bop!* (Park) *Bebé Goes Shopping* (Elya) *I Live in Tokyo* (Takabayashi) *Castle: How It Works* (Macaulay) *The True Story of Stellina* (Pericoli)
Vague concepts of time.	Needs to learn basics of telling time and the calendar. Simple biographies and historical fiction may give a feeling for the past, but accurate understanding of chronology is beyond this age group.	*Little Tree* (Long) *Mimmy and Sophie, All Around the Town* (Cohen) *The House on Maple Street* (Pryor) *Ox-Cart Man* (Hall) *When I Was Young in the Mountains* (Rylant)
More able to separate fantasy from reality; more aware of own imagination.	Enjoys fantasy. Likes to dramatize simple stories or use feltboard, puppets, etc.	*Ker-splash!* (O'Connor) *Traction Man Is Here!* (Grey) *Where the Wild Things Are* (Sendak) *There Was an Old Lady Who Swallowed a Fly* (Taback)
Beginning to develop empathy for others.	Adults can ask such questions as "What would you have done?" "How would you have felt?"	*Strictly No Elephants* (Mantchev) *Rickie and Henri* (Goodall) *Crow Boy* (Yashima) *The Teddy Bear* (McPhail) *Fly Away Home* (Bunting) *Little Dog, Lost* (Carnesi)

teaching feature 2.1

Characteristics	Implications	Examples
Has a growing sense of justice. Demands application of rules, regardless of circumstances.	Expects poetic justice in books.	*Wolf Won't Bite!* (Gravett) *Flossie and the Fox* (McKissack) *Too Many Tamales* (Soto) *All For Me and None for All* (Lester)
Humor is developing.	Needs to hear many books read aloud for pure fun. Enjoys books and poems that have surprise endings, plays on words, incongruous situations, and slapstick comedy. Likes to be in on the joke.	*Once Upon a Banana* (Armstrong) *Meet Wild Boars* (Rosoff) *My Little Sister Hugged an Ape* (Grossman) *Bad Kitty Meets the Baby* (Bruel) *Substitute Creacher* (Gall) *Frog and Fly* (Mack)
Shows curiosity about gender differences and reproduction.	Teachers need to accept and be ready to answer children's questions about sex.	*Heather Has Two Mommies* (Newman) *The Baby Tree* (Blackall) *Donovan's Big Day* (Newman) *My Mom's Having a Baby!* (Butler) *How You Were Born* (Cole)
Physical contour of the body is changing; permanent teeth appear; learning to whistle and developing other fine motor skills.	Books can help the child accept physical changes in self and differences in others.	*Take Me Out to the Yakyu* (Meshon) *My Bike* (Barton) *Body Actions* (Rotner) *You'll Soon Grow into Them, Titch* (P. Hutchins)
Continues to seek independence from adults and to develop initiative.	Needs opportunities to select own books and activities. Enjoys stories of responsibility and successful ventures.	*Go, Otto, Go!* (Milgrim) *Elena's Serenade* (Geeslin) *My Rows and Piles of Coins* (Mollel) *Adèle & Simon* (McClintock) *Ira Sleeps Over* (Waber)
Continues to need warmth and security in family relationships.	Books may emphasize universal human characteristics in a variety of lifestyles.	*A Family Is a Family Is a Family* (O'Leary) *For You Are a Kenyan Child* (Cunnane) *A Bear for Miguel* (Alphin) *Henry's First-Moon Birthday* (Look) *Mirror* (Baker)

(continued)

teaching feature 2.1

Characteristics	Implications	Examples
Middle Elementary: Ages 8 and 9		
Attaining independence in reading skill. May read with complete absorption, or may still be having difficulty learning to read. Wide variation in ability and interest.	Discovers reading as an enjoyable activity. Prefers an uninterrupted block of time for independent reading. During this period, many children become avid readers.	*Juana & Lucas* (Medina) *Ruby Lu, Star of the Show* (Look) *Judy Moody; Stink* (McDonald) *Shredderman: Attack of the Tagger* (Van Draanen) *Martin Bridge: Onwards and Upwards* (Kerrin) *Ivy + Bean* (Barrows)
Reading level may still be below appreciation level.	It is essential to read aloud to children each day in order to extend interests, develop appreciation, and provide balance.	*The Wild Robot* (Brown) *Remarkable* (Foley) *The Pepins and Their Problems* (Horvath) *Mr. and Mrs. Bunny—Detectives Extraordinaire!* (Horvath)
Peer-group acceptance becomes increasingly important.	Children need opportunities to recommend and discuss books. Sharing favorites builds a sense that reading is fun and has group approval. Popular books may provide status and be much in demand.	*Recess Is a Jungle* (Chabert) *Mercy Watson: Princess in Disguise* (DiCamillo) *Clementine's Letter* (Pennypacker)
Developing standards of right and wrong. Begins to see viewpoints of others.	Books provide opportunities to relate to several points of view.	*Honeysuckle House* (Cheng) *My Heart Will Not Sit Down* (Rockliff) *Freedom on the Menu* (Weatherford) *Through My Eyes* (Bridges)
Less egocentric; developing empathy for others. Questioning death.	Accepts some books with a less-than-happy ending. Discussion helps children explore their feelings for others.	*Cry, Heart, But Never Break* (Ringtved) *Each Little Bird That Sings* (Wiles) *Michael Rosen's Sad Book* (Rosen) *The Cat with the Yellow Star* (Rubin) *Stone Fox* (Gardiner) *Ninth Ward* (Rhodes)
Time concepts and spatial relationships developing. This age level is characterized by thought that is flexible and reversible.	Interested in biographies, life in the past, in other lands, and the future. Prefers fast-moving, exciting stories.	*I Dissent: Ruth Bader Ginsburg Makes Her Mark* (Levy) *Maritcha: A Nineteenth-Century American Girl* (Bolden) *Sequoyah* (Rumford) *Being Teddy Roosevelt* (Mills) *The Green Book* (Walsh)

teaching feature 2.1

Characteristics	Implications	Examples
Enjoys tall tales and slapstick humor in everyday situations. Appreciates imaginary adventure.	Teachers need to recognize the importance of literature for laughter, releasing tension, and providing enjoyment.	*The Golden Goose* (King-Smith) *Oh, No! Where Are My Pants?* (Hopkins) *Friends: Snake and Lizard* (Cowley) *Wake the Dead* (Harris) *The Dunderheads Behind Bars* (Fleischman)
Cognitive growth and language development increase capacity for problem solving and word play.	Likes the challenge of solving puzzles and mysteries. High interest in twists of plot, secret codes, riddles, and other language play.	*Pieces and Players* (Balliett) *Can You See What I See?* (Wick) *Math Potatoes* (Tang) *Cam Jansen and the New Girl Mystery* (Adler) *Ten Rules for Living with My Sister* (Martin) *The Amber Cat* (McKay)
Improved coordination makes proficiency in sports and games possible and encourages interest in crafts and hobbies.	Interested in sports books; wants specific knowledge about sports. Enjoys how-to-do-it books.	*The Jumbo Book of Needlecrafts* (Sadler, et al.) *National Geographic Photography Guide for Kids* (Johnson) *The Visual Dictionary of Baseball* (Buckley, Jr.) *ABC's of Baseball* (Golenbock)
Sees categories and classifications with new clarity; interest in collecting is high.	Likes to collect and trade paperback books. Begins to look for books of one author or series books.	*Dinkin Dings and the Frightening Things* (Bass) *A Crazy Day with Cobras* (Osborne) *Meet Addy: The American Girl Collection* (Porter)
Seeks specific information to answer questions; may go to books beyond own reading ability to search for answers.	Enjoys nonfiction and identification books that collect facts. Requires guidance in locating information within a book and in using the library.	*Rivers of Sunlight* (Bang and Chisholm) *A Black Hole Is NOT a Hole* (DeCristofano) *Billions of Years, Amazing Changes* (Pringle) *New Beginnings: Jamestown and the Virginia Colony 1607–1699* (Rosen)

(continued)

teaching feature 2.1

Characteristics	Implications	Examples
Later Elementary: Ages 10 and 11		
Rate of physical development varies widely. Rapid growth precedes beginning of puberty. Girls are about 2 years ahead of boys in development. Both are increasingly curious about all aspects of sex.	Books guide understanding of the growth process and help children address personal problems. Continued differentiation in reading preferences of boys and girls.	*Are You There, God? It's Me, Margaret* (Blume) *What's the Big Secret? Talking About Sex with Girls and Boys* (Brown) *The Period Book* (Gravelle)
Understanding of sex role is developing; boys and girls form ideas about their own and each other's identity.	Books may provide identification with gender roles and impetus for discussion of stereotypes.	*The Other Boy* (Hennessey) *One Half From the East* (Hashimi) *Warp Speed* (Yee) *Project Mulberry* (Park) *Guys Write for Guys Read* (Scieszka)
Increased emphasis on peer group and sense of belonging.	Book choices often influenced by peer group. Books can highlight problems with peer pressure.	*Save Me a Seat* (Weeks and Varadarajan) *Ms. Bixby's Last Day* (Anderson) *Love of the Game* (Coy) *Some Friend* (Bradby) *No Talking* (Clements) *Wringer* (Spinelli)
Deliberate exclusion of others; some expressions of prejudice.	Books can emphasize unique contributions of all. Discussion can be used to clarify values.	*Stella by Starlight* (Draper) *Days of Tears* (Lester) *A Long Walk to Water* (Park) *Roll of Thunder, Hear My Cry* (Taylor) *Lizzie Bright and the Buckminster Boy* (Schmidt) *Each Kindness* (Woodson)
Family patterns changing; may challenge parents' authority. Highly critical of siblings.	Books may provide some insight into these changing relationships.	*The Great Wall of Lucy Wu* (Shang) *Millions* (Boyce) *Al Capone Does My Homework* (Choldenko) *Rules* (Lord) *The Detention Club* (Yoo)

teaching feature 2.1

Characteristics	Implications	Examples
Begins to have models other than parents drawn from TV, movies, sports figures, books. Beginning interest in future vocation.	Biographies may provide models. Career books broaden interests and provide useful information.	*Nelson Mandela* (Kramer) *When Marian Sang* (Ryan) *What to Do About Alice?* (Kerley) *Freedom Walkers* (Freedman)
Sustained, intense interest in specific activities.	Seeks book about hobbies and other interests.	*Catch the Wind, Harness the Sun* (Caduto) *Galileo for Kids* (Panchyk) *Faces from the Past: Forgotten People of North America* (Deem) *Inkblot: Drip, Splat, and Squish Your Way to Creativity* (Peot)
A peak time for voluntary reading.	Avid readers welcome challenges and repeated contact with authors, genres.	*Lowriders to the Center of the Earth* (Camper) *Ghost* (Reynolds) *Harry Potter and the Half-Blood Prince* (Rowling) *Caddy's World* (McKay) *Kingdom Keepers* (Pearson) *The Secret of the Fortune Wookiee* (Angleberger)
Seeks to test own skills and abilities; looks ahead to a time of complete independence.	Enjoys stories of survival and "going it alone."	*Fish* (Matthews) *Take Me to the River* (Hobbs) *Hatchet* (Paulsen) *I Don't Believe It, Archie!* (Norriss) *Small as an Elephant* (Jacobson)
Increased cognitive skill can be used to serve the imagination.	Tackles complex and puzzling plots in mysteries, science fiction, fantasy. Can appreciate more subtlety in humor.	*The Inquisitor's Tale* (Gidwitz) *The Calder Game* (Balliett) *In a Glass Grimmly* (Gidwitz) *Framed* (Boyce) *The Clue of the Linoleum Lederhosen* (Anderson) *The Extraordinary Education of Nicholas Benedict* (Stewart)

(continued)

teaching feature 2.1

Characteristics	Implications	Examples
Increased understanding of the chronology of past events; developing sense of own place in time. Begins to see many dimensions of a problem.	Literature provides opportunities to examine issues from different viewpoints. Guidance needed for recognizing biased presentations.	*El Deafo* (Bell) *Wolf Hollow* (Wolk) *A Dream of Freedom* (McWhorter) *Adam Canfield of the Slash* (Winerip) *The Elephant in the Garden* (Morpurgo) *Emil and Karl* (Glatshteyn)
Highly developed sense of justice and concern for others.	Willing to discuss many aspects of right and wrong; likes "sad stories"; shows empathy for victims of suffering and injustice.	*Tiger Boy* (Perkins) *Gentle's Holler* (Madden) *Crow* (Wright) *Bud, Not Buddy* (Curtis)
Searching for values; interested in problems of the world. Can deal with abstract relationships; becoming more analytical.	Valuable discussions may grow out of teacher's reading aloud prose and poetry to this age group. Questions may help students gain insight into both the content and the literary structure of a book.	*The Other Side of Truth* (Naidoo) *Under the Persimmon Tree* (Staples) *I Am Thomas* (Gleeson) *The View from Saturday* (Konigsburg) *The Five Lives of Our Cat Zook* (Rocklin) *One Last Word* (Grimes)

Middle School—Ages 12, 13, and 14

Characteristics	Implications	Examples
Wide variation in physical development; both boys and girls reach puberty by age 14. Developing sex drive; intense interest in sexuality and world of older teens.	Books provide insight into feelings, concerns. Guidance needed to balance students' desire for frank content with lack of life experience.	*It's Perfectly Normal* (Harris) *Am I Blue?* (Bauer) *Will Grayson, Will Grayson* (Green and Levithan) *There Is No Dog* (Rosoff)
Self-concept continues to grow. Developing a sense of identity is important.	Books help students explore roles, rehearse journey to identity. Many stories based on myth of the hero.	*A Wizard of Earthsea* (Le Guin) *The Hero and the Crown* (McKinley) *Shadows on the Stars* (Barron) *Absolute Brightness* (Lecesne) *Jefferson's Sons* (Bradley)
Peer group becomes increasingly influential; relationships with family are changing.	Concerns about friends and families reflected in books. School should provide chance to share books and responses with peer group.	*Amina's Voice* (Khan) *A Dog Like Sam* (van de Vendel) *Breaking Through* (Jiménez) *A Step from Heaven* (Na) *Criss Cross* (Perkins)

teaching feature 2.1

Characteristics	Implications	Examples
New aspects of egocentrism lead to imagining self as center of others' attention and feeling one's own problems are unique.	Students begin to enjoy introspection; may identify with characters who are intense or self-absorbed.	*The Best Man* (Peck) *The Crossover* (Alexander) *The Absolutely True Diary of a Part-Time Indian* (Alexie) *Between Shades of Gray* (Sepetys) *Jacob Have I Loved* (Paterson) *My Name Is Not Easy* (Edwardson) *The Fault in Our Stars* (Green)
Cognitive abilities are increasingly abstract and flexible, but not consistently. New capacity to reason from imaginary premises, manipulate symbolic language, and make hypothetical judgments.	Students read more complex stories, mysteries, and high fantasy that call for complex logic; enjoy science fiction and high adventure. Metaphor, symbols, and imagery are understood at a different level.	*Magnus Chase and the Gods of Asgard* (Riordan) *The Land of the Silver Apples* (Farmer) *The Year of the Beasts* (Castellucci) *The Hunger Games* (Collins) *The Scorpio Races* (Stiefvater)
Able to apply ideas of relativity to questions of values; girls might see moral issues differently than boys do.	Students need discussion time to negotiate meanings in stories that pose moral dilemmas.	*Shabanu* (Staples) *The Giver* (Lowry) *Keeping Corner* (Sheth) *The Diary of Pelly D* (Adlington) *Breaking Stalin's Nose* (Yelchin)
Sensitive to great complexity in human feelings and relationships.	Students seek richer and more complex stories.	*Ashes* (Anderson) *Tamar* (Peet) *Copper Sun* (Draper) *Sunrise Over Fallujah* (Myers)
Cumulative effects of development and life experience produce wide variation among individuals in abilities and interests.	Reading ability and interests in one class may range from early elementary to adult.	*The Hobbit* (Tolkien) *Honeybee* (Nye) *The Bird King* (Tan) *The Mark of Athena* (Riordan) *Where Things Come Back* (Whaley) *Cold Kiss* (Garvey)

Response in the Classroom

Understanding children's responses to literature would be much easier if it were possible to peer inside children's heads. Instead, teachers must be satisfied with secondary evidence. Children's perceptions and understandings are revealed in many different ways—as the children choose and talk about books and as they write, paint, play, or take part in other classroom activities.

Classroom responses can be obvious and direct (primary children have been known to kiss a favorite book) or hidden within a situation that appears to have little to do with literature (e.g., block corner play). Many responses are verbal, many come without words. Some are spontaneous, bubbling up out of children too delighted to be still, or shyly offered in confidence. Other responses would not be expressed at all without the direct invitation of teachers who plan extension activities or discussions (see Chapter 11) to generate thoughtful reaction to literature. To understand any of these observed responses, it is helpful to be acquainted with a few basic theoretical perspectives.

Theories of Response

What really goes on between a reader and a story or poem is a complex question with many answers. Theories about reader response draw from many disciplines, including psychology, linguistics, aesthetics, and, of course, literature and education.

Some theories focus on what is read; others focus on the reader. For instance, some researchers have examined in careful detail the structure of stories, noting the precise arrangement of words and sequence of ideas. These patterns are called "story grammars," and studies indicate that they can affect the way readers understand and recall a story.[22] Other theorists are more concerned with individual readers and how their personalities can influence their ideas about what they read.[23] Still other researchers emphasize the cultural or social aspects of response. According to Richard Beach, "While all these theoretical perspectives rest on different assumptions about meaning, they ultimately intersect and overlap. The local—the focus on readers' textual knowledge and experience—is embedded within the global, larger social and cultural contexts." All categories of reader response research focus on the reader's textual knowledge and experience, but they are embedded within larger social and cultural contexts.[24]

One important point on which scholars agree is that the process of reading and responding is active rather than passive. The words and ideas in the book are not transferred automatically from the page to the reader. Rather, as Louise Rosenblatt has argued:

> The literary work exists in the live circuit set up between reader and text: the reader infuses intellectual and emotional meanings into the pattern of verbal symbols, and those symbols channel his thoughts and feelings.[25]

Response is dynamic and open to continuous change as readers anticipate, infer, remember, reflect, interpret, and connect. The "meaning" and significance of stories like Kathi Appelt's *The Underneath* or Lois Lowry's *The Giver* will vary from reader to reader, depending on age and personal experience as well as experience with literature. However, each reader's response will also change, given time for reflection, discussion, or repeated readings.

Reader response theory also points out that readers approach works of literature in special ways. James Britton proposes that in all our uses of language we can be either *participants* or *spectators*.[26] In the participant role, we read in order to accomplish something in the real world, as in following a recipe. In the spectator role, we focus on what the language says as an end in itself, attending to its forms and patterns, as we do in enjoying poetry.

Rosenblatt suggests that reading usually involves two roles, or stances, and that we shift our emphasis from one to the other according to the material and our purposes for reading it.[27] In the *efferent* stance, we are most concerned with what information can be learned from the reading. In the *aesthetic* stance, our concern is for the experience of the reading itself, the feelings and images that come and go with the flow of the words. Most readers, of course, find themselves switching back and forth from one of these stances to the other as they read. One thing teachers can do to help children share the world the author has created is to help them find an appropriate stance as they begin to read.

Types of Response

Teachers who are familiar with reader response theories and who study children's responses to literature will discover that they provide a basis for deepening children's satisfaction with books and for supporting children's growth in interpretation.

The most common expressions of response to literature are statements, oral or written. In their most polished form, such responses are known as literary criticism, and for many years research in literature involved measuring young people's statements against a standard of mature critical ability.

Where children are concerned, it is important to remember that direct comment is only one of many ways of revealing what goes on between the book and its audience. Language used in other ways—to tell or write stories based on other stories, for instance— often provides good clues about a child's feelings and understandings about the original. Parents and teachers of young children also recognize nonverbal behaviors as signs of response. For instance, young listeners almost always show their involvement, or lack of it, in body postures and facial expressions. Children's artwork, informal drama, and other book extension activities (see Chapter 11) also provide windows on response.

Interpreting Children's Responses

Previous research in response to literature provides teachers and librarians with a framework for interpreting their students' reactions to books. This classroom-based research can give us a deeper understanding of children's responses.

Recognizing Patterns of Change Teachers and researchers alike have observed that when children at different grade levels read and respond in ways that are comfortable for them, their responses will be alike in some ways and different in others. What might teachers expect to see in a fourth-grade classroom? What are typical first-grade responses? No one can answer these questions with exactness, for every child is a unique reader and every classroom represents a different composite of experiences with literature and with the world. Even so, it is helpful to know what researchers and teachers have discovered about the responses of their students at various grade levels. This section outlines some of these findings to provide information on the patterns of change in responses that usually take place as children have experiences with literature in the elementary school.[28] Although these findings are presented in an age-level sequence, any of these characteristics can be seen at other ages, depending on the child, the situation, and the challenge presented by the material. Like the Teaching Feature 2.1: Books for Ages and Stages chart, this guide is more useful for making predictions about a class than for making predictions about an individual child.

Younger Children (Preschool to Primary) Younger children are motor oriented. As listeners, they respond with their whole selves, chiming in on refrains or talking back to the story. They lean closer to the book, point at pictures, clap their hands, etc. They use body movements to try out some of the story's action, "hammering" along with *Press Here* by Hervé Tullet or making wild faces to match the illustrations in Maurice Sendak's *Where the Wild Things Are*. Actions to demonstrate meaning ("Like this") might be given as answers to a teacher's questions. These easily observable responses go undercover as children mature; older children reveal feelings through subtle changes of expression and posture.

At this age, children spontaneously act out stories or bits of stories using actions, roles, and conventions of literature in their dramatic play. Witches, kings, "wild things," and other well-defined character types appear naturally, showing how well children have assimilated elements of favorite tales. Examples of story language ("We lived happily ever after") are sometimes incorporated. Spontaneous dramatic play disappears from the classroom early in the primary years (although it persists out of school with some children) and is replaced by more structured drama of various kinds. Older children are usually much more conscious of their own references to literature.

These children respond to stories piecemeal. Their responses deal with parts rather than wholes. A detail of text or illustration might prompt more comment than the story itself, as children make quick associations with their own experience: "I saw a bird like that once" or "My sister has bunk beds just like those." This part-by-part organization can also be seen in very young children's art, where the pictures show individual story items without any indication of relationship ("This is the baby bear's chair, and this is Goldilocks, and this is the house the bears lived in, and here is the bed."). This is the same sort of itemization or cataloging of characters, objects, and events that children sometimes use when asked to tell something about a story. Young children are more likely to respond to the story as a whole if they have heard it many times or if an adult provides that focus by asking good questions.

Children at this age use embedded language in answering direct questions about stories. Because young children see the world in literal, concrete terms, their answers are likely to be couched in terms of the characters, events, and objects found in the story. One first grader made a good attempt to generalize the lesson of "The Little Red Hen" but couldn't manage without some reference to the tale: "When someone already baked the cake and you haven't helped, they're probably just gonna say 'No'!" A teacher or other adult who shares the child's context—who knows the story, has heard or read it with the child, and knows what other comments have been made—will understand the intent of such a statement more readily than a casual observer will.

Children in Transition (Primary to Middle Grades) Children in transition from the primary to the middle grades develop from being listeners to becoming readers. They go through a period of focus on the accomplishment of independent reading. They make many comments about quantity—number of pages read, the length of a book, or the number of books read. Conventions of print and of bookmaking might draw their attention. One third grader refused to read any of the poems from Shel Silverstein's *Where the Sidewalk Ends* without locating them in the index first; a classmate was fascinated with the book's variety of word and line arrangements for poetry. Another child studied the front matter of a picturebook and pronounced it "a dedicated book." So-called independent reading may be more sociable than it sounds because many children like to have a listener or reading partner and begin to rely on peers as sounding boards for their response.

At this age, children become more adept at summarizing in place of straight re-telling when asked to talk about stories. This is a skill that facilitates discussion and becomes more useful as it is developed. Summarizing is one of the techniques that undergirds critical commentary, but adults use it more deliberately and precisely than children do.

These children classify or categorize stories in some of the same ways that adults do. Middle graders who are asked to sort out a random pile of books use categories like "mysteries," "humorous books," "make-believe," and "fantasy." If you ask kindergartners to do the same, they are more likely to classify the books by their physical properties ("fat books," "books with pretty covers," "red books") than by content. Children at this age *attribute personal reactions to the story* itself. A book that bores an 8-year-old will be thought of as a "boring book," as if "boring" were as much a property of the story as its number of pages or its first-person point of view. Children judge a story on the basis of their response to it, regardless of its qualities as literature or its appeal to anyone else. This is a very persistent element in response; it affects the judgment of students of children's literature and of professional book reviewers as well as children in elementary school. Personal response can never be totally eliminated from critical evaluation; but with experience, readers can develop more objectivity in separating a book's literary characteristics from its personal appeal.

These children also use borrowed characters, events, themes, and patterns from literature in their writing, just as younger children do in dramatic play. In the earliest stages, much of this is unconscious and spontaneous. One example is a 7-year-old who was convinced that her story about a fish with paint-splashed insides was "made up out of my own head," even when reminded that the class had just heard Robert McCloskey's *Burt Dow, Deep Water Man.* A 9-year-old spontaneously combined a favorite character with a field-trip experience in his story "Paddington Bear Goes to Franklin Park Conservatory," but he was aware of his idea sources. Other children produce their own examples of patterns, forms, or genres. The direction of growth is toward more conscious realization of the uses of literature in writing.

Older Children (Middle Grades to Middle School) Older children express stronger preferences, especially for personal reading. Younger children seem to enjoy almost everything that is reasonably appropriate, but older ones do not hesitate to reject books they do not like. Some children show particular devotion to certain authors or genres or series at this time. Some children also become more intense and protective about some of their reactions, and they should not be pressed to share those feelings that demand privacy.

At this age, children are more skillful with language and more able to deal with abstractions. They can deduce ideas from a story and put them in more generalized terms, as in stating a universal moral for a particular fable.

These children also begin to see (but not consistently) that their feelings about a book are related to identifiable aspects of the writing. Responses like "I love this book because it's great" develop into "I love this book because the characters say such funny things" or "*Strider* [by Cleary] is my favorite because Leigh is a lot like me."

Older children go beyond categorizing stories toward a more analytical perception of why characters behave as they do, how the story is put together, or what the author is trying to say. They begin to test fiction against real life and understand it better through the comparison. They use some critical terminology, although their understanding of terms may be incomplete. In talk and writing, children who are encouraged to express ideas freely begin to stand back from their own involvement and take an evaluative look at literature. One sixth grader had this to say about *A Taste of Blackberries* by Doris Buchanan Smith:

> I thought the author could have put more into it. I really didn't know much about the kid who died. I mean, it really happened fast in the book. It started out pretty soon and told about how sad he was and what they used to do. All the fun things they used to do together. I wished at the beginning they would have had all the things that he talked about and then have him thinking about what a good friend he is and then all of a sudden he dies—a little closer to the end. Because when he died, you didn't much care cause you didn't really know him. But I guess the author wanted to talk about how it would be, or how people feel, or maybe what happened to her—how it felt when one of her friends died like that.[29]

In general, children's responses move toward this sort of conscious comment. Young children sometimes make stunningly perceptive observations about stories, but they are not usually able to step back and see the importance of what they have said. Older children begin to have a deeper understanding of their observations and can then take command of it. This allows them to layer mature appreciation on top of the beginner's natural delight.

However, older children's increasing capacity for abstraction, generalization, and analysis should *not* be interpreted as a need for programs of formal literary analysis or highly structured study procedures. Opportunities to read, hear, and talk about well-chosen books under the guidance of an interested and informed teacher will allow elementary school children to develop their responses to their full potential.

Children, no matter what their age, will respond to a story on their own terms of understanding. It does little good (and can be destructive to the enjoyment of literature) if younger children are pushed to try to formulate the abstractions achieved by more mature children. However, James Britton maintains that teachers may refine and develop the responses that children are already making by gradually exposing them to stories with increasingly complex patterns of events.[30]

Collecting Children's Responses

Finding out how children understand literature and which books they like is such essential information for elementary teachers and librarians that it should not be left to chance. Techniques for discovering responses that are simple and fit naturally into the ongoing business of classrooms and library media centers are discussed in the context of planning the school literature program in Chapter 11.

As elementary teachers become aware of the way they can tune in to children's responses to literature, they will see the value of examining the nature of children's thinking about it. We all believe that literature is important for children, but we do not truly know what difference it makes in a child's life, if any. An in-depth study of children's responses to books is just as important as, if not more important than, the studies of children's interests in books. We should explore the developmental nature of response and conduct longitudinal studies of a child's responses over the years. As teachers and librarians, we need to listen to what the children are telling us about their involvement with books and what it means to them.

When asked to replicate Leo Lionni's story of *The Biggest House in the World* using a new main character, two children demonstrated different levels in their understanding of the theme. The 8-year-old (left picture) showed a bird growing more elaborate; the 10-year-old (right picture) portrayed a change leading to the bird's self-destruction. Tremont Elementary School, Upper Arlington Public Schools, Upper Arlington, Ohio. Jill Boyd, teacher.

Notes

1. Martha L. King and Victor Rentel, co-researchers, "Study of Cohesive Elements on Three Modes of Discourse," NIE research project, Ohio State University, 1982.
2. *2017 Kids & Family Reading Report: What Kids & Parents Want in Children's Books,* Scholastic, Inc. Retrieved from http://www.scholastic.com/readingreport/what-parents-and-kids-want.htm.
3. See, for example, Christina Clark and Amelia Foster, *Children's and Young People's Reading Habits and Preferences: The Who, What, Why, Where and When,* National Literacy Trust (December 2005); Mary-Jo Fresch, "Self-Selection Strategies of Early Literacy Learners," *Reading Teacher 49* (November 1995): 220–27; Alan Purves and Richard Beach, *Literature and the Reader: Research in Response to Literature, Reading Interests, and the Teaching of Literature* (Urbana, Ill.: National Council of Teachers of English, 1972), pp. 69–71.
4. *2017 Kids & Family Reading Report: What Kids & Parents Want in Children's Books,* Scholastic, Inc. Retrieved from http://www.scholastic.com/readingreport/what-parents-and-kids-want.htm.
5. Michael Barrett, "Top Trends in Children's Books for 2017." Scholastic, Inc. (December 20, 2016). Retrieved from http://oomscholasticblog.com/post/top-trends-childrens-books-2017.
6. Glenda Childress, "Gender Gap in the Library: Different Choices for Boys and Girls," *Top of the News* 42 (fall, 1985): 69–73; Helen Huus, "Interpreting Research in Children's Literature," in *Children, Books and Reading* (Newark, Del.: International Reading Association, 1964), p. 125.
7. Christine Hall and Martin Coles, *Children's Reading Choices* (London: Routledge, 1999), p. 136.
8. Christina Clark, *Children's and Young People's Reading Today: Findings from the 2011 National Literacy Trust's Annual Survey* (London: National Literacy Trust, 2012). Retrieved from http://www.literacytrust.org.uk/research/nlt_research.
9. Jo Worthy, Megan Moorman, and Margo Turner, "What Johnny Likes to Read Is Hard to Find in School," *Reading Research Quarterly* 34.1 (1999): 20.
10. Susan I. Hepler and Janet Hickman, "'The Book Was Okay. I Love You'—Social Aspects of Response to Literature," *Theory into Practice* 21 (autumn, 1982): 279.
11. See Andre Favat, *Child and Tale: The Origins of Interest* (Urbana, Ill.: National Council of Teachers of English, 1977), and Norma Marian Schlager, "Developmental Factors Influencing Children's Responses to Literature" (Ph.D. dissertation, Claremont Graduate School, 1974).
12. Luis C. Moll, et al., "Funds of knowledge for teaching: Using a Qualitative Approach to Connect Homes and Schools," *Theory into Practice*, V XXXL 132–141, 2009.

13. Barbel Inhelder and Jean Piaget, *The Growth of Logical Thinking* (New York: Basic Books, 1962); Barry J. Wadsworth, *Piaget's Theory of Cognitive and Affective Development* (Reading, Mass.: Addison-Wesley, 1996).
14. Margaret Donaldson, *Children's Minds* (New York: Norton, 1979), chap. 2.
15. Dan I. Sobin, "Children and Language: They Learn the Same Way All around the World," in *Contemporary Readings in Child Psychology*, 2nd ed., eds. E. Mavis Hetherington and Ross D. Parke (New York: McGraw-Hill, 1981), pp. 122–26.
16. Walter Loban, *Language Development: Kindergarten Through Grade Twelve* (Urbana, Ill.: National Council of Teachers of English, 1976).
17. Jean Piaget, *The Moral Judgment of the Child*, trans. M. Gabain (New York: Free Press, 1965).
18. Lawrence Kohlberg, *The Meaning and Measurement of Moral Development* (Worcester, Mass.: Clark University Heinz Wemer Institute, 1981).
19. Carol Gilligan, *In a Different Voice: Psychological Theory and Women's Development* (Cambridge, Mass.: Harvard University Press, 1982).
20. Abraham H. Maslow, *Motivation and Personality*, rev. ed. (Reading, Mass.: Addison-Wesley, 1987).
21. Erik H. Erikson, *Childhood and Society*, rev. ed. (New York: Norton, 1993).
22. Dorothy S. Strickland and Joan Feeley, "Development in the Elementary School Years," *Handbook of Research on Teaching the English Language Arts*, eds. James Flood, Julie Jensen, Diane Lapp, and James Squire (New York: Macmillan, 1991), pp. 386–402.
23. Norman H. Holland, *Five Readers Reading* (New Haven, Conn.: Yale University Press, 1975).
24. Richard Beach, *A Teacher's Introduction to Reader-Response Theories* (Urbana, Ill.: National Council of Teachers of English, 1993), p. 9.
25. Louise M. Rosenblatt, *Literature as Exploration*, 5th ed. (New York: Modern Language Association, 1996), p. 25.
26. James Britton, et al., *The Development of Writing Abilities (11–18)*, Schools Council Research Studies (London: Macmillan Education Limited, 1975).
27. Louise M. Rosenblatt, *The Reader, the Text, the Poem: The Transactional Theory of the Literary Work* (Carbondale: Southern Illinois University Press, 1994).
28. This section is based on observations with reference to the work of Arthur Applebee, *The Child's Concept of Story* (Chicago, Ill.: University of Chicago Press, 1978), pp. 123–25; and others.
29. Recorded in the classroom of Lois Monaghan, teacher, Barrington School, Upper Arlington, Ohio.
30. James Britton, in *Response to Literature*, ed. James R. Squire (Champaign, Ill.: National Council of Teachers of English, 1968), p. 4.

Children's Literature

Go to **Connect**® *to access the Children's Literature Database. The following includes some of the titles you will find in the database.*

Titles in blue = multicultural titles

Adler, David A. *Young Cam Jansen and the New Girl Mystery*. Viking, 2004.

Adlington, L. J. *The Diary of Pelly D.* Greenwillow, 2005.

Ahlberg, Janet, and Allan Ahlberg. *Each Peach Pear Plum*. Viking, 1978.

Alexander, Kwame. *The Crossover*. Houghton, 2014.

Alexie, Sherman. *The Absolutely True Diary of a Part-Time Indian*. Little, 2007.

Alphin, Elaine Marie. *A Bear for Miguel*. Illustrated by Joan Sanders. HarperCollins, 1996.

Anderson, John David. *Ms. Bixby's Last Day*. Walden Pond, 2016.

Anderson, Laurie Halse. *Ashes*. Atheneum, 2016.

Anderson, M. T. *The Clue of the Linoleum Lederhosen*. Harcourt, 2006.

Angleberger, Tom. *The Secret of the Fortune Wookiee*. Amulet, 2012.

Appelt, Kathi. *The Underneath*. Illustrated by David Small. Atheneum, 2010.

Applegate, Katherine. *The One and Only Ivan*. Illustrated by Patricia Castelo. Harper, 2013.

Argueta, Jorge. *Somos como los nubes/We Are Like the clouds*. Illustrated by Alfonso Ruano. Groundwood, 2016.

Aston, Dianna Hutts. *When You Were Born*. Illustrated by E. B. Lewis. Candlewick, 2004.

Atkinson, Cale. *Explorers of the Wild*. Disney, 2016.

Austrian, J.J. *Worm Loves Worm*. Illustrated by Mike Curato. Balzer and Bray, 2016.

Averbeck, Jim. *Except If*. Atheneum, 2011.

Aylesworth, Jim. *The Gingerbread Man*. Illustrated by Barbara McClintock. Scholastic, 1998.

Bahk, Jane. *Juna's Jar*. Illustrated by Felicia Hoshimo. Lee & Lows, 2016.

Baker, Jeannie. *Mirror*. Candlewick, 2011.

Baker, Keith. *Hickory Dickory Dock*. Harcourt, 2007.

Balliett, Blue. *The Calder Game*. Scholastic, 2008.

_____. *Pieces and Players*. Holt, 2016.

Bang, Molly, and Penny Chisholm. *Rivers of Sunlight: How the Sun Moves Water Around the World*. Illustrated by Molly Bang. Scholastic, 2017.

Barnett, Mac. *Extra Yarn*. Illustrated by Jon Klassen. Balzer + Bray, 2012.

Barnhill, Kelly. *The Girl Who Drank the Moon*. Algonquin Young Readers, 2016.

Barron, T. A. *The Great Tree of Avalon: Shadows on the Stars*. Philomel, 2005.

Barrows, Ivy. *Bean: No News Is Good News*. Chronicle, 2011.

Barton, Byron. *The Little Red Hen*. HarperCollins, 1993.

_____. *My Car*. HarperCollins, 2001.

Bass, Guy. *Dinkin Dings and the Frightening Things*. Illustrated by Pete Williams. Grosset, 2011.

Bauer, Marion Dane. *Am I Blue? Coming Out from the Silence*. HarperCollins, 1994.

_____. *On My Honor*. Clarion, 1986.

Beaumont, Karen. *Duck, Duck, Goose!* Illustrated by Jose Aruego and Ariane Dewey. HarperCollins, 2004.

Bell, Cece. *El Deafo*. Abrams, 2014.

Blackall, Sophie. *The Baby Tree*. Penguin, 2014.

Bloom, Suzanne. *A Splendid Friend, Indeed*. Boyds Mills, 2005.

Blume, Judy. *Are You There, God? It's Me, Margaret*. Bradbury, 1970.

Bolden, Tonya. *Maritcha: A Nineteenth-Century American Girl*. Abrams, 2005.

Bond, Michael. *A Bear Called Paddington*. Illustrated by Peggy Fortnum. Houghton, 1998.

Bondoux, Anne-Laure. *The Killer's Tears*. Translated from the French by Y. Maudet. Delacorte, 2006.

Boyce, Frank Cottrell. *Framed*. HarperCollins, 2006.

_____. *Millions*. HarperCollins, 2004.

Bradby, Marie. *Some Friend*. Atheneum, 2004.

Bray, Libba. *Beauty Queens*. Scholastic, 2011.

Bridges, Ruby. *Through My Eyes*. Scholastic, 1999.

Broach, Elise. *Wolf Keepers*. Holt, 2016.

Brown, Laurene Krasny, and Marc Brown. *What's the Big Secret? Talking About Sex with Girls and Boys*. Little, 1997.

Brown, Peter. *The Wild Robot*. Little, Brown, 2016.

Browne, Anthony. *Me and You*. Farrar, 2010.

Bryan, Ashley. *Freedom Over Me*. Atheneum, 2016.

Bryant, Sarah Cone. *The Burning Rice Fields*. Illustrated by M. Funai. Holt, 1963.

Buckley Jr., James. *The Visual Dictionary of Baseball*. DK, 2001.

Buell, Nick. *Bad Kitty Meets the Baby*. Roaring Brook, 2011.

Bunting, Eve. *Fly Away Home*. Illustrated by Ron Himler. Clarion, 1991.

Cabrera, Jane. *The Wheels on the Bus*. Holiday, 2011.

Caduto, Michael J. *Catch the Wind, Harness the Sun: 22 Super-Charged Science Projects for Kids*. Storey, 2011.

Campbell, Geeslin. *Elena's Serenade*. Illustrated by Ana Juan. Atheneum, 2004.

Camper, Cathy. *Lowriders to the Center of the Earth*. Illustrated by Raul the Third. Chronicle, 2016.

Carle, Eric. *The Very Hungry Caterpillar*. Philomel, 1969.

Carnesi, Monica. *Little Dog, Lost*. Penguin Paulson, 2012.

Castelluci, Cecil. *Year of the Beasts*. Illustrated by Nate Powell. Roaring Brook, 2012.

Chabert, Jack. *Recess Is a Jungle*. Illustrated by Sam Rocks. Scholastic, 2016.

Cheng, Andrea. *Honeysuckle House*. Front St., 2004.

Choldenko, Gennifer. *Notes from a Liar and Her Dog*. Putnam, 2001.

_____. *Al Capone Does My Homework*. Dial, 2013.

Cleary, Beverly. *Strider*. Illustrated by Paul O. Zelinsky. HarperCollins, 2001.

Clements, Andrew. *No Talking*. Simon. 2007.

Cohen, Miriam. *Mimmy and Sophie, All Around the Town*. Illustrated by Thomas F. Yezerski. Farrar, 2004.

_____. *Will I Have a Friend?* Illustrated by Lillian Hoban. Macmillan, 1971.

Cole, Henry. *On the Way to the Beach*. Greenwillow, 2003.

Cole, Joanna. *How You Were Born*. Morrow, 1984.

_____. *My Puppy Is Born*. Photographs by Margaret Miller. Morrow, 1990.

Collard III, Sneed B. *Making Animal Babies*. Illustrated by Steve Jenkins. Houghton, 2000.

Collins, Suzanne. *The Hunger Games*. Scholastic, 2008.

Cowley, Joy. *Chameleon, Chameleon*. Photographs by Nic Bishop. Scholastic, 2005.

Coy, John. *Love of the Game.* Feiwel & Friends, 2011.

Cronin, Doreen. *Diary of a Worm: Teacher's Pet.* Illustrated by Harry Bliss. Harper, 2013.

Croze, Henry. *Africa for Kids.* Chicago Review, 2006.

Cunnane, Kelly. *For You Are a Kenyan Child.* Illustrated by Ana Juan. Atheneum, 2006.

Curtis, Christopher Paul. *Bud, Not Buddy.* Delacorte, 1999.

———. *Mr. Chickee's Funny Money.* Lamb/Random, 2005.

Cynes, Kurt. *Billions of Bricks.* Holt, 2016.

Dahl, Roald. *The BFG.* Illustrated by Quentin Blake. Farrar, 1982.

Dane, Larry. *The Littlest Wolf.* Illustrated by Jose Aruego and Ariane Dewey. HarperCollins, 2000.

Davies, Matt. *Ben Rides On: A Picture Book.* Roaring Brook, 2013.

DeCristofano, Carolyn Cinami. *A Black Hole Is NOT a Hole.* Illustrated Michael Carroll. Charlesbridge, 2012.

Deem, James M. *Faces from the Past: Forgotten People of North America.* Houghton, 2012.

de la Peña, Matt. *Last Stop on Market Street.* Illustrated by Christian Robinson. Putnam, 2015.

De Pucchio, Kelly. *Antoinette.* Atheneum, 2016.

DiCamillo, Kate. *Bink & Gollie.* Candlewick, 2010.

———. *Mercy Watson: Princess in Disguise.* Candlewick, 2007.

Doyle, Roddy. *A Greyhound of a Girl.* Amulet, 2012.

Draper, Sharon. *Copper Sun.* Atheneum, 2006.

Dubuc, Marianne. *The Animal's Ark.* Kid's Can, 2016.

Edwards, Pamela Duncan. *Some Smug Slug.* Illustrated by Henry Cole. HarperCollins, 1996.

Edwardson, Debby Dahl. *My Name Is Not Easy.* Marshall Cavendish, 2011.

Ehlert, Lois. *Eating the Alphabet.* Harper, 1989.

Elya, Susan Middleton. *Bebé Goes Shopping.* Illustrated by Steven Salerno. Harcourt, 2006.

———. *Rubia and the Three Osos.* Illustrated by Melissa Sweet. Hyperion, 2010.

Evans, Shane W. *Underground.* Roaring Brook Press, 2011.

Farish, Terry. *Luis Paints the World.* Illustrated by Oliver Dominguez. Lerner, 2016.

Fatus, Sophie. *My Big Barefoot Book of Spanish and English Words.* Barefoot, 2016.

Feder, Sarah. *The Moon Inside.* Illustrated by Aimée Sicuro. Groundwood, 2016.

Farmer, Nancy. *The Land of the Silver Apples.* Atheneum, 2007.

Fitzgerald, Joanna. *This Is Me and Where I Am.* Fitzhenry and Whiteside, 2004.

Fleischman, Paul. *The Dunderheads Behind Bars.* David Roberts. Candlewick, 2012.

Fleming, Denise. *Maggie and Michael Get Dressed.* Holt, 2016.

Fogliano, Julie. *And Then It's Spring.* Illustrated by Erin E. Stead. Roaring Brook, 2012.

Foley, Lizzie K. *Remarkable.* Dial, 2012.

Freedman, Deborah. *This House, Once.* Atheneum, 2017.

Freedman, Russell. *Freedom Walkers: The Story of the Montgomery Bus Boycott.* Holiday, 2006.

———. *The Voice That Challenged a Nation: Marian Anderson and the Struggle for Civil Rights.* Clarion, 2004.

Freeman, Don. *Corduroy.* Viking, 1968.

French, Vivian. *Yucky Worms.* Illustrated by Jessica Ahlberg. Candlewick, 2012.

Gall, Chris. *Substitute Creacher.* Little, 2011.

Garden, Nancy. *Molly's Family.* Illustrated by Sharon Wooding. Farrar, 2004.

Gardiner, John Reynolds. *Stone Fox.* Illustrated by Greg Hargreaves. HarperCollins, 1992.

Garvey, Amy. *Cold Kiss.* Harper, 2011.

Gidwitz, Adam. *In a Glass Grimmly.* Illustrated by Hugh D'Andrade. Dutton, 2012.

———. *The Inquisitor's Tale: Or, the Three Magical Children and Their Holy Dog.* Illustrated by Hatem Aly. Dutton, 2016.

Glatshteyn, Yankev. *Emil and Karl.* Translated by Jeffrey Shandler. Roaring Brook, 2006.

Gleeson, Libby. *I Am Thomas.* Illustrated by Armin Greder. Allen & Unwin, 2011.

Golenbock, Peter, and Dan Andreasen. *The ABC's of Baseball.* Dial, 2012.

Graham, Bob. *April and Esme, Tooth Fairies.* Candlewick, 2010.

———. *Tales from the Waterhole.* Candlewick, 2004.

Gravelle, Karen, and Jennifer Gravelle. *The Period Book: Everything You Don't Want to Ask (But Need to Know).* Walker, 2006.

Gravett, Emily. *Wolf Won't Bite!* Simon, 2012.

Green, John, and David Levithan. *Will Grayson, Will Grayson.* Dutton, 2010.

Grey, Mini. *Traction Man Is Here!* Knopf, 2005.

Grimes, Nikki. *One Last Word: Wisdom From the Harlem Renaissance.* Illustrated by various illustrators. Bloomsbury, 2017.

Grossman, Bill. *My Little Sister Hugged an Ape.* Illustrated by Kevin Hawkes. Knopf, 2004.

Hacohen, Dean, and Sherry Scharschmidt. *Tuck Me In.* Candlewick, 2010.

Hall, Donald. *Ox-Cart Man.* Illustrated by Barbara Cooney. Viking, 1979.

Harris, Monica A. *Wake the Dead.* Illustrated by Susan Estelle Kwas. Walker, 2004.

Harris, Robie H. *It's Perfectly Normal: A Book About Changing Bodies, Growing Up, Sex, and Sexual Health.* Illustrated by Michael Emberley. Candlewick, 1994.

_____. *Who Has What?: All About Girl's Bodies and Boy's Bodies (Let's Talk About You and Me).* Illustrated by Nadine Bernard Westcott. Candlewick, 2011.

Hashimi, Nadia. *One Half from the East.* Atheneum, 2016.

Heide, Florence Parry, and Judith Heide Gilliland. *The Day of Ahmed's Secret.* Illustrated by Ted Lewin. Lothrop, 1990.

Helquist, Brett. *Bedtime for Bear.* HarperCollins, 2011.

Hennesey, M. G. *The Other Boy.* Illustrated by Sfe R. Monster. Harper, 2016.

Hobbs, Will. *Take Me to the River.* Harper, 2011.

Hoberman, Mary Ann. *You Read to Me, I'll Read to You: Very Short Stories to Read Together.* Illustrated by Michael Emberley. Little, 2001.

Hodges, Margaret. *The Wave.* Illustrated by Blair Lent. Houghton, 1964.

Hoffman, Sarah. *Jacob's New Dress.* Illustrated by Ian Hoffman. Whitman, 2014.

Hopkins, Lee Bennett. *Oh, No! Where Are My Pants? and Other Disasters: Poems.* Illustrated by Wolf Erlbruch. HarperCollins, 2005.

Hopkinson, Deborah. *A Bandit's Tale: The Muddled Misadventures of a Pickpocket.* Knopf, 2016.

Horvath, Polly. *Mr. and Mrs. Bunny—Detectives Extraordinaire.* Illustrated by Sophie Blackall. Swartz and Wade, 2012.

_____. *The Pepins and Their Problems.* Farrar, 2004.

Hughes, Shirley. *Alfie Gets in First.* Lothrop, 1981.

Hurwitz, Joanna. *Llama in the Library.* Morrow, 1999.

Hutchins, Hazel. *A Second Is a Hiccup.* Scholastic, 2007.

Hutchins, Pat. *Clocks and More Clocks.* Macmillan, 1994 [1970].

_____. *You'll Soon Grow into Them, Titch.* Greenwillow, 1983.

Jacobson, Jennifer Richard. *Small as an Elephant.* Candlewick, 2011.

Jenkins, Martin. *Fabulous Frogs.* Candlewick, 2016.

Jenkins, Stephen, and Robin Page. *Time to Eat.* Houghton Mifflin, 2011.

Jenkins, Steve. *Actual Size.* Houghton, 2004.

Jiménez, Francisco. *Breaking Through.* Houghton, 2001.

Johnson, Neil. *National Geographic Photography Guide for Kids.* National Geographic, 2001.

Judge, Lita. *Hoot and Peep.* Dial Books, 2016.

Juster, Norton. *The Phantom Tollbooth.* Random, 1961.

Kanevsky, Polly. *Here Is the Baby.* Illustrated by Taseum Yoo. Random, 2014.

Kerley, Barbara. *What to Do About Alice? How Alice Roosevelt Broke the Rules, Charmed the World, and Drove Her Father Teddy Crazy.* Illustrated by Edwin Fotheringham. Scholastic, 2008.

Kerrin, Jessica Scott. *Martin Bridge: Onwards and Upwards!* Illustrated by Joseph Kelly. Kids Can, 2009.

_____. *Martin Bridge: Sound the Alarm!* Illustrated by Joseph Kelly. Kids Can, 2007.

Khan, Hena. *Amina's Voice.* Simon, 2017.

Khan, Rukhsana. *Big Red Lollipop.* Illustrated by Sophie Blackall. Viking, 2010.

King-Smith, Dick. *The Golden Goose.* Illustrated by Ann Kronheimer. Knopf, 2005.

Knudsen, Michelle. *Library Lion.* Illustrated by Kevin Hawkes. Candlewick, 2006.

Konigsburg, E. L. *The View from Saturday.* Atheneum, 1996.

Koscielniak, Bruce. *About Time.* Houghton, 2013.

Kramer, Ann. *Nelson Mandela: The Tribal Prince Who Grew Up to Be President.* National Geographic, 2005.

Kraus, Ruth. *Bears.* Illustrated by Maurice Sendak. HarperCollins, 2005.

Kuntz, Doug. *Lost and Found Cat: The True Story of Kunkush's Incredible Journey.* Illustrated by Amy Stokes. Crown, 2017.

Kvasnosky, Laura McGee. *Zelda and Ivy: The Big Picture.* Candlewick, 2010.

_____. *Zelda and Ivy: The Runaways.* Candlewick, 2006.

Law, Jessica. *A Hole in the Bottom of the Sea.* Illustrated by Jill McDonald. Barefoot, 2013.

Lecesne, James. *Absolute Brightness.* Harper, 2008.

Le Guin, Ursula K. *A Wizard of Earthsea.* Illustrated by Ruth Robbins. Parnassus, 1968.

Lehman, Barbara. *Rainstorm.* Houghton, 2007.

Lester, Helen. *All For Me and None at All.* Illustrated by Lynn Munsinger. Houghton Mifflin Books for Children, 2012.

Lester, Julius. *Days of Tears: A Novel in Dialogue.* Hyperion, 2005.

———. *John Henry.* Illustrated by Brian Pinkney. Dial, 1994.

Levy, Debbie. *I Dissent: Ruth Bader Ginsburg Makes Her Mark.* Illustrated by Elizabeth Baddeley. Simon, 2016.

Lionni, Leo. *The Biggest House in the World.* Dragonfly, 1973.

Long, Loren. *Little Tree.* Philomel, 2015.

Look, Lenore. *Henry's First Moon Birthday.* Illustrated by Yumi Heo. Atheneum, 2001.

———. *Ruby Lu, Brave and True.* Illustrated by Anne Wilsdorf. Simon, 2004.

———. *Ruby Lu, Empress of Everything.* Illustrated by Anne Wilsdorf. Simon, 2006.

———. *Ruby Lu, Star of the Show.* Illustrated by Stef Choi. Atheneum, 2011.

Lord, Cynthia. *Rules.* Scholastic, 2006.

Lowry, Lois. *The Giver.* Houghton, 1993.

Lunde, Darrin. *Whose Poop Is That?* Illustrated by Kelsey Oseid. Charlesbridge, 2017.

Macaulay, David, and Sheila Keenan. *Castle: How It Works.* David Macaulay Studio, 2012.

Mack, Jeff. *Frog and Fly.* Philomel, 2012.

Madden, Kerry. *Gentle's Holler.* Viking, 2005.

Magoon, Kekla. *Shadows of Sherwood.* Bloomsbury, 2015.

Marcantonio, Patricia Santos. *Red Ridin' in the Hood and Other Cuentos.* Illustrated by Ranato Alarcão. Farrar, 2005.

Marino, Gianna. *Meet Me at the Moon.* Viking, 2012.

Marsden, Carolyn. *Moon Runner.* Candlewick, 2005.

Martin, Ann M. *A Dog's Life: The Autobiography of a Stray.* Scholastic, 2005.

———. *Ten Rules for Living with My Sister.* Feiwel, 2011.

McCaughrean, Geraldine. *White Darkness.* HarperCollins, 2007.

McClintock, Barbara. *Adèle & Simon.* Farrar, 2006.

McCloskey, Robert. *Burt Dow, Deep Water Man.* Viking, 1963.

———. *Make Way for Ducklings.* Puffin, 2010.

McCully, Emily. *Four Hungry Kittens.* Dial, 2001.

McDonald, Megan. *Judy Moody and Stink!: The Mad Mad Mad Mad Treasure Hunt.* Illustrated by Peter F. Reynolds, Candlewick, 2010.

———. *Judy Moody Declares Independence.* Candlewick, 2005.

McKay, Hilary. *Permanent Rose.* Simon, 2005.

McKinley, Robin. *The Hero and the Crown.* Greenwillow, 1984.

McKissack, Patricia C. *Flossie and the Fox.* Illustrated by Rachel Isadora. Dial, 1986.

McNaughton, Janet. *The Secret Under My Skin.* HarperCollins, 2005.

McPhail, David. *The Teddy Bear.* Holt, 2002.

McWhorter, Diane. *A Dream of Freedom: The Civil Rights Movement from 1954–1968.* Scholastic, 2004.

Medina, Meg. *Juana and Lucas.* Candlewick, 2016.

Mershon, Aaron. *Take Me Out to the Yakyu.* Atheneum, 2013.

———. *The Best Days Are Dog Days.* Dial, 2016.

Milgrim, David. *Go, Otto, Go!* Simon, 2016.

Mills, Claudia. *Being Teddy Roosevelt.* Illustrated by R. W. Alley. Farrar, 2007.

Minarik, Else Holmelund. *Little Bear.* Illustrated by Maurice Sendak. Harper, 1957.

Mollel, Tolowa. *My Rows and Piles of Coins.* Illustrated by E. B. Lewis. Clarion, 1999.

Myers, Walter Dean. *Darius and Twig.* Amistad/Harper, 2013.

———. *Sunrise Over Fallujah.* Scholastic, 2008.

Na, An. *A Step from Heaven.* Front St., 2001.

Naidoo, Beverley. *The Other Side of Truth.* HarperCollins, 2001.

Newman, Leslea. *Donovan's Big Day.* Tricycle, 2011.

———. *Heather Has Two Mommies.* Candlewick, 2015 (1995).

Norris, Andrew. *I Don't Believe It, Archie!* Illustrated by Hannah Shaw. Random, 2012.

Novak, B. J. *The Book with No Pictures.* Dial, 2016.

O'Brien, Anne Sibbley. *I'm New Here.* Charlesbridge, 2015.

O'Leary, Sara. *A Family Is a Family Is a Family.* Illustrated by Qin, Leng. Groundwood, 2016.

O'Connor, George. *Ker-splash!* Simon, 2005.

Ormerod, Jan, and Freya Blackwood. *Maudie and the Bear.* Putnam, 2012.

Ormerod, Jan. *When an Elephant Comes to School.* Orchard, 2005.

Osborne, Mary Pope. *A Crazy Day with Cobras.* Illustrated by Sal Murdocca. Random House, 2011.

———. *Dragon of the Red Dawn.* Illustrated by Sal Murdocca. Random, 2007.

Parish, Peggy. *Amelia Bedelia.* Illustrated by Fritz Siebel. Harper, 1963.

Park, Linda Sue. *A Long Walk to Water: Based on a True Story*. Clarion, 2010.

____. *Bee-Bim Bop!* Illustrated by Ho Baek Lee. Clarion, 2005.

____. *Project Mulberry*. Clarion, 2005.

Paterson, Katherine. *Jacob Have I Loved*. Crowell, 1980.

Paulsen, Gary. *Hatchet*. Bradbury, 1987.

Pearson, Ridley. *Kingdom Keepers*. Hyperion, 2013.

Peck, Richard. *The Best Man*. Dial, 2016.

Peet, Mal. *Tamar*. Candlewick, 2007.

Pennypacker, Sara. *Clementine, Friend of the Week*. Hyperion/Disney, 2010.

____. *Waylon! One Awesome Thing*. Illustrated by Marla Frazee. Disney, 2017.

Peot, Margaret. *Inkblot: Drip, Splat and Squish Your Way to Creativity*. Boyds Mills, 2011.

Pericoli, Matteo. *The True Story of Stellina*. Knopf, 2006.

Perkins, Lynne Rae. *Criss Cross*. Greenwillow, 2005.

Perkins, Mitali. *Tiger Boy*. Illustrated by Jamie Hogan. Charlesbridge, 2015.

Piafold, Len. *Black Dog*. Candlewick, 2012.

Porter, Connie. *Meet Addy* (the American Girl collection). Illustrated by Nancy Niles. Pleasant, 1990.

Potter, Beatrix. *The Tale of Peter Rabbit*. Warne, 1902.

Pringle, Laurence. *Billions of Years, Amazing Changes: The Story of Evolution*. Illustrated by Steve Jenkins. Boyds Mills, 2011.

Pryor, Bonnie. *The House on Maple Street*. Illustrated by Beth Peck. Morrow, 1987.

Raczka, Bob. *A Mix of Concrete Poems*. Roaring Brook, 2016.

____. *Lemonade: and Other Poems Squeezed from a Single Word*. Roaring Brook Press, 2011.

Ramsey, Calvin Alexander. *Ruth and the Green Book*. Illustrated by Floyd Cooper. Carolrhoda, 2010.

Reynolds, Aaron. *Back of the Bus*. Illustrated by Floyd Cooper. Philomel, 2010.

Reynolds, Jason. *Ghost*. Atheneum, 2016.

Rhodes, Jewell Parker. *Ninth Ward*. Little, 2010.

Ringtveld, Glenn. *Cry, Heart, But Never Break*. Illustrated by Charlotte Pardi. Enchanted Lion, 2016.

Riordan, Rick. *Magnus Chase: The Gods of Asgard*. Disney, 2016.

____. *The Mark of Athena*. Hyperion/Disney, 2012.

Richardson, Justin, and Peter Parnell. *And Tango Makes Three*. Illustrated by Henry Cole. Simon, 2005.

Rockliff, Mara. *My Heart Will Not Sit Down*. Illustrated by Ann Tanksley. Knopf, 2012.

Rocklin, Joann. *The Five Lives of Our Cat Zook*. Amulet, 2012.

Rosoff, Meg. *There Is No Dog*. Putnam, 2012.

Rockwell, Anne. *The Three Bears and Fifteen Other Stories*. Crowell, 1975.

Rodman, Mary Ann. *Yankee Girl*. Farrar, 2004.

Root, Phyllis. Anywhere Farm. Illustrated by G. Brian Karas. Candelwick, 2017.

____. *Oliver Finds His Way*. Illustrated by Christopher Denise. Candlewick, 2002.

____. *What Baby Wants*. Illustrated by Jill Barton. Candlewick, 1998.

Rosen, Daniel. *New Beginnings: Jamestown and the Virginia Colony*, 1607–1699. National Geographic, 2005.

Rosen, Michael. *Michael Rosen's Sad Book*. Candlewick, 2005.

____. *We're Going on a Bear Hunt*. Illustrated by Helen Oxenbury. McElderry, 1989.

Rosoff, Meg. *Meet Wild Boars*. Illustrated by Sophie Blackall. Holt, 2005.

Roth, Susan L., and Cindy Trumbore. *The Mangrove Tree: Planting Trees to Feed Families*. Lee & Low, 2011.

Rotner, Shelley. *Body Actions*. Illustrated by David A. White. Holiday, 2012.

Rowling, J. K. *Harry Potter and the Half-Blood Prince*. Scholastic, 2005.

Rubin, Susan Goldman. *The Cat with the Yellow Star: Coming of Age in Terezin*. Holiday House, 2006.

Rumford, James. *Sequoyah. The Cherokee Man Who Gave His People Writing*. Translated by Anna Sixkiller Huckaby. Houghton, 2004.

Ruurs, Margriet. *Stepping Stones: A Refugee Family's Journey*. Illustrated by Nizar Ali Badr. Orca, 2016.

Ryan, Pam Muñoz. *When Marian Sang*. Illustrated by Brian Selznick. Scholastic, 2002.

Rylant, Cynthia. *When I Was Young in the Mountains*. Illustrated by Diane Goode. Dutton, 1982.

Sachar, Louis. *Fuzzy Mud*. Delacorte, 2015.

____. *Holes*. Farrar, 1998.

Sadler, Judy Ann. *The Jumbo Book of Needlecrafts*. Kids Can, 2005.

Sanna. Francesca. *The Journey*. Flying Eye, 2016.

Schmidt, Gary D. *Lizzie Bright and the Buckminster Boy*. Clarion, 2004.

____. *Okay for Now*. Clarion Books, 2011.

Schotter, Roni. *The Boy Who Loved Words.* Illustrated by Giselle Potter. Random, 2006.

Scieszka, Jon, ed. *Guys Write for Guys Who Read: Boys' Favorite Authors Write About Being Boys.* Viking, 2005.

_____. *The True Story of the Three Little Pigs.* Illustrated by Lane Smith. Puffin, 1996.

Sciurba, Katie. *Oye, Celia! A Song for Celia Cruz.* Illustrated by Edel Rodriguez. Holt, 2007.

Selznick, Brian. *Wonderstruck.* Scholastic, 2011.

Sendak, Maurice. *Where the Wild Things Are.* Harper, 1963.

Sepetys, Ruta. *Between Shades of Grey.* Philomel, 2011.

Shang, Wendy Wan-Long. *The Great Wall of Lucy Wu.* Scholastic, 2011.

Shannon, David. *No David!* Scholastic, 1998.

Sheth, Kashmira. *Keeping Corner.* Hyperion, 2009.

Sidman, Joyce. *Swirl by Swirl.* Illustrated by Beth Krommes. Houghton, 2011.

Silverstein, Shel. *Where the Sidewalk Ends.* Harper, 1963.

Smith, Doris Buchanan. *A Taste of Blackberries.* Illustrated by Charles Robinson. Crowell, 1973.

Snicket, Lemony. *The Dark.* Illustrated by Jon Klassen. Little, 2013.

Soto, Gary. *Too Many Tamales.* Illustrated by Ed Martinez. Putnam, 1993.

Spinelli, Jerry. *Maniac Magee.* Little, 1990.

_____. *Wringer.* HarperCollins, 1997.

Staples, Suzanne Fisher. *Shabanu: Daughter of the Wind.* Knopf, 1989.

_____. *Under the Persimmon Tree.* Farrar, 2005.

Steig, William. *The Amazing Bone.* Square Fish, 2011.

_____. *Doctor De Soto.* Farrar, 1982.

_____. *Sylvester and the Magic Pebble.* Simon, 1969.

_____. *Zeke Pippin.* HarperCollins, 1994.

Stewart, Trenton Lee. *The Extraordinary Education of Nicholas Benedict.* Little, 2012.

Stiefvater, Maggie. *The Scorpio Races.* Scholastic, 2011.

Sutton, Sally. *Demolition.* Illustrated by Brian Lovelock. Candlewick, 2012.

Taback, Sims. *I Know an Old Lady.* Dial, 1997.

Takabayashi, Mari. *I Live in Tokyo.* Houghton, 2001.

Tan, Shaun. *The Bird King.* Scholastic, 2012.

Tang, Greg. *Math Potatoes.* Illustrated by Harry Briggs. Scholastic, 2005.

Taylor, Mildred. *Roll of Thunder, Hear My Cry.* Dial, 1976.

Thomson, Bill. *Chalk.* Marshall Cavendish, 2010.

Tolkien, J. R. R. *The Hobbit.* Illustrated by Michael Hague. Houghton, 1989 [1938].

Tullet, Herve. *Press Here.* Chronicle, 2011.

Ursu, Anne. *The Real Boy.* Walden Pond, 2015.

Vail, Rachel. *Piggy Bunny.* Illustrated by Jeremy Tankard. Feiwel, 2012.

Vamos, Samantha R. *The Cazuela That the Farm Maiden Stirred.* Illustrated by Rafael López. Charlesbridge, 2011.

van de Vendel, Edward. *A Dog Like Sam.* Illustrated by Philip Hopman. Eerdman's, 2017.

Van Draanen, Wendelin. *Shredderman: Attack of the Tagger.* Knopf, 2004.

Waber, Bernard. *Ira Sleeps Over.* Houghton, 1973.

Waddell, Martin. *It's Quacking Time!* Illustrated by Jill Barton. Candlewick, 2005.

_____. *Owl Babies.* Illustrated by Patrick Benson. Candlewick, 2010.

_____. *Tiny's Big Adventure.* Illustrated by John Lawrence. Candlewick, 2008.

Wallace, John Corey. *When Things Come Back.* Simon, 2011.

Walsh, Jill Paton. *The Green Book.* Illustrated by Lloyd Bloom. Farrar, 1982.

Weatherford, Carole Boston. *Freedom on the Menu: The Greensboro Sit-Ins.* Illustrated by Jerome Lagarrigue. Dial, 2005.

Weeks, Sarah. *Save Me a Seat.* Scholastic, 2016.

Wells, Rosemary. *Bunny Cakes.* Dial, 1998.

_____. *Say Hello, Sophie!* Dial, 2017.

Westerfeld, Scott. *Horizon.* Scholastic, 2016.

White, Ruth. *The Search for Belle Prater.* Farrar, 2005.

Wick, Walter. *Can You See What I See? Picture Puzzles to Search and Solve.* Scholastic, 2002.

Wiles, Deborah. *Each Little Bird That Sings.* Harcourt, 2005.

Willems, Mo. *City Dog, Country Frog.* Illustrated by Jon Muth. Hyperion, 2011.

_____. *Leonardo, the Terrible Monster.* Hyperion, 2004.

Williams, Vera B. *Home at Last.* Illustrated by Vera B. Williams and Chris Raschka. Greenwillow, 2016.

Williams-Garcia, Rita. *Like Sisters on the Home Front.* Dutton, 1995.

Winerip, Michael. *Adam Canfield of the Slash.* Candlewick, 2005.

Winter, Ariel S. *One of a Kind.* Illustrated by David Hitch. Aladdin, 2012.

Wolfe, Myra. *Charlotte Jane Battles Bedtime.* Illustrated by Maria Monescillo. Harcourt, 2011.

Wolk, Lauren. *Wolf Hollow.* Dutton, 2016.

Wood, Maryrose. *The Incorrigible Children of Ashton Place: Book I: The Mysterious Howling.* Illustrated by Jon Klassen. Balzer + Bray, 2011.

Woodson, Jacqueline. *Each Kindness.* E. B. Lewis. Penguin, 2012.

Woodson, Jacqueline. *Pecan Pie Baby.* Illustrated by Sophie Blackall. Putnam, 2010.

Yashima, Taro. *Crow Boy.* Viking, 1955.

Yee, Lisa. *Stanford Wong Flunks Big-Time.* Scholastic, 2005.

Yelchin, Eugene. *Breaking Stalin's Nose.* Holt, 2011.

Yorinks, Arthur. *Flappy and Scrappy.* Illustrated by Alekzey and Olga Ivanov. Harper, 2011.

Part Two

Exploring Genres in Children's Books

Picturebooks

Chapter Outline

There is a buzz in this fourth-grade classroom. Low, hushed voices can be heard and the occasional exclamation of excitement or roar. It's group reading time on the carpet. These students are reading Jerry Pinkney's *The Lion & the Mouse*. The interesting thing about this particular book selection is that Pinkney's version is wordless. They are working on comparing versions of the

©Bettie Parsons Barger.

same story. Last week, they spent time pouring over Rand and Nancy Berkert's *Mouse and Lion.*

Salma's group notices the change in perspective. They talk about how things get bigger or smaller, depending on the page. Tyler's group details the events in the story, noting how it seems that each character is equally important because of the way Mr. Pinkney uses the pages and sizes. Nadia's group talks about Pinkney's use of gold and orange, noting how important color is to the telling of this story. Brian's group starts the comparison right away, discussing the subtle differences in the way each picturebook told the story.

After the fourth graders have time to read and discuss the story, they come together to share their findings. These careful readers notice the elements of design, particularly shape, color, value, and perspective, in each version. They are fully aware of the impact a well-designed picturebook can have on a reader. The experience began with a month-long class on Aesop and his fables, including the mysteries surrounding Aesop's life and the many ways artists have interpreted his tales over the centuries.

Their enthusiasm shows how the art in picturebooks can inspire children's visual, mental, and verbal imaginations and how an integrated curriculum can be centered in picturebooks.

The Picturebook Defined

Picturebooks are those books in which images and ideas join to form a unique whole. In the best picturebooks, the illustrations are as much a part of our experience with the book as the written text (if there is one). A picturebook provides the reader with an aesthetic experience that is more than the sum of the book's parts. (See **Teaching Feature 3.1: A Brief History of the Picturebook**.)

A picturebook might be a wordless book, an alphabet book, a counting book, a concept book, a graphic novel, or a picture storybook. The illustrations for a concept book or an alphabet book can depict a different object or an animal on each page, providing for much variety in the pictures. In a nonfiction book (discussed in Chapter 9), the illustrations can help support important concepts and clarify ideas. They can also emphasize themes and understandings that the author is trying to convey.

A Brief History of the Picturebook

The picturebooks we know today have roots that we might trace back to cave paintings of the prehistoric era. An African (Egyptian) papyrus that dates from approximately 1295 B.C. depicts a humorous tale that includes an antelope and a lion seated on chairs engaged in a board game. Books as we know them today—folded leaves bound between hard covers—date from the first century C.E., and many of these included images as well as words. Such books would blossom into incredibly beautiful works of art by the fourteenth century.

With the invention of a printing press with movable type in the 1450s, the images in books began to take a back seat to the convenience of mass production. Full-color, hand-painted, and hand-written books were replaced with black-and-white wood engravings or black prints. However, images in books were still highly popular with the reading audience. That audience might have included children, but until the 1600s books were not usually created for an audience of children. As society began to place more emphasis on a culture of childhood and the need to educate children in religious as well as secular matters, picturebooks were created to meet these needs. Many of these educational books were emblem books that followed a pictorial format in which a verse or couplet was illustrated with a small picture. Johann Amos Comenius's *Orbis Pictus* (The World in Pictures) was translated into English in 1659 and published with many woodcuts illustrating everyday objects. It is often referred to as the first picturebook for children.

In 1744, John Newbery published *A Little Pretty Pocket-Book,* which was meant to entertain as well as educate children, and modern children's book publishing was born. Many of the books written for children in the eighteenth and nineteenth centuries included illustrations, but they were still most often printed in black and white. In the late 1800s, a printer named Edmund Evans perfected a method of color printing that ushered in the golden age of children's picturebooks. Evans's extraordinary talent as an engraver and his important improvements in color printing techniques were responsible for dramatic changes in picturebooks for children. Evans recruited artists who would become the best-known illustrators of the nineteenth century— Walter Crane, Randolph Caldecott, and Kate Greenaway. The success of their many books opened the door to other illustrators of the twentieth century such as Beatrix Potter, Ernest Shepard, and Arthur Rackham.

Printing techniques continued to be refined over the rest of the twentieth century until computer scanning and laser reproduction removed some of the tedious technical tasks from the artist and allowed almost any artistic medium to be reproduced. At the same time, the audience for picturebooks expanded beyond the very young to children of all ages. The picturebook will likely continue to be printed on paper for the foreseeable future. These printed books cannot be transferred into e-books, as the aesthetic experience with such printed books depends as much on size of the book, the compositions we see on each double-page spread, and the tactile experience of holding the book and turning the pages. It is likely, however that as they have for centuries, illustrators will find a new way to convey image and idea through the unique attributes of e-books and other electronic platforms.

In a picture storybook, the message is conveyed equally through picture and word. In a well-designed book in which the total format reflects the meaning of the story, both the illustrations and the text must bear the burden of narration. The pictures help tell the story, showing the action and expressions of the characters, the changing settings, and the development of the plot.

Maurice Sendak's *Where the Wild Things Are* shows how pictures and words work together to create passionate responses to books. The cover shows an intriguing and gigantic creature, asleep beside an empty boat. The child reader is immediately invited to co-construct this story by asking such questions as "Who is in the boat?" "Is this monster scary?" The bold black letters of the title and author's name seem to offer stability and a reassuring answer. In addition, the monster is captured within the lines of type and by the white space of the borders. This monster is not likely to enter the child's world, just the imagination. The shape of the book is horizontal rather than vertical and implies movement over a broad landscape. The endpapers, full of lush leaves seen through a screen of cross-hatching lines, burst with energy and invite entry into the book. These plants are not the vegetation of the everyday world, however; they convey an unfamiliar world and imply that something magical may be at work. Sendak's use of soft, muted watercolor washes over delicate line drawings evokes a sense of unreality or mystery throughout the book. Sendak also creates cross-hatched lines that set up emotional tensions that ebb and flow across the pages. He uses curving shapes to create movement within each picture and to move our eyes across each page. The layout or composition of each double-page spread creates a rhythm as we proceed through the book. The small size of the early illustrations reflects the disciplinary reins placed on Max by his mother. As he sets off on his imaginary journey, those pictures break out of their rectangular white borders and grow out to the edges of the single page. They then begin to grow across the double-page spread until Max arrives upon his island. When the "wild rumpus" starts, there is no longer a need for white space or words at all. The three double-page spreads create a visual equivalent of three booming drumbeats, and the pictures fill the space just as sounds of the wild rumpus must fill the air. We know the book has reached a climax of excitement here because on the next double-page spread the picture begins to shrink and white space and words reappear. Max returns home to his room on the last page, but he is not the same child. Sendak removes the white border and sharp edge that began Max's adventure and leaves him on the right-hand page in a full bleed (i.e., the picture extends to the edge of the page). *Where the Wild Things Are* represents the type of real marriage between pictures and text that we hope to find in good picturebooks.

Creating Meaning in Picturebooks

A picturebook, then, must be a seamless whole conveying meaning through both the art and the text. Moreover, in a picturebook that tells a story, the illustration does not merely reflect the idea or action on a single page but shares in moving a story forward and in engaging the reader with the narrative on both an intellectual and an emotional level. Throughout the narration the pictures should convey, enhance, and extend the meaning behind the story.

The Elements of Design

Crucial to the visual meaning in a picturebook are the choices artists make about certain elements of design, particularly the use of line, shape, color, and space, as they decide what to illustrate in the story and how best to do it. Just as words can convey meaning on several levels, the elements of art have the capacity to convey meaning and evoke emotion.

Line and Shape Line is so inherently a part of every illustration that we forget that this element, too, can convey meaning. A horizontal line suggests repose and peace, a vertical line gives stability, and a diagonal line suggests action and movement. In *Stevie,* John Steptoe uses a heavy black outline for his figures to emphasize Robert's resentment of Stevie, the little boy his mother takes care of during the day. The tiny, sketchy lines in Marcia Brown's version of Perrault's *Cinderella* suggest the somewhat fussy elegance of the story's sixteenth-century French setting. Chris Raschka uses the element of line to great effect in books like *A Ball for Daisy*. Rather than detailing each shape with careful lines, Raschka paints quickly using thick "brushy" strokes that give shape to the dog's body while suggesting the texture of fur and adding energy to the story.

A line that encloses space creates shape, and this element is equally evocative of meaning. Illustrations comprise shapes with sharp edges and corners, like in Jon Klassen's illustrations for Mac Barnett's *Extra Yarn,* have an edginess that can show the viewer the brittle bleakness of a winter setting. On the other hand, when shapes have nongeometric curving forms found in nature, they can breathe a sense of life into illustrations, as we see in Suzanne Bloom's simple, rounded shapes in the pages of *A Splendid Friend, Indeed.*

Color Colors can evoke strong emotional connections in readers. Many classic picture-books did not use color in the illustrations, such as the sepia pictures of Robert McCloskey's *Make Way for Ducklings* and the well-loved black-and-white illustrations for *Millions of Cats* by Wanda Gág. Modern publishing techniques make it much easier and less expensive to publish full-color books, but many illustrators are still using black-and-white graphics to create exciting picturebooks.

The choice of colors should depend on the theme of the book. *The Rooster Who Would Not Be Quiet!* by Carmen Agra Deedy is a story about a vibrant and very exciting community, although very noisy. When a new mayor outlaws *all* noise—especially no singing any-where—a raucous rooster returns the city to its former effervescence. Illustrator Eugene Yelchin depicts the noisy town-scapes in brilliant full color. He portrays the mayor, however, in a monotone blue-gray (except for his red nose), underscoring the wonderful contrast between too much community and too much control. Molly Bang's *When Sophie Gets Angry—Really, Really Angry . . .* is a fine example of judicious use of color. Sophie, a ram-bunctious preschooler, is infuriated by an older sister who grabs her favorite toy. Sophie gets so angry, "she kicks, she screams, she wants to smash the world to smithereens." Bang's intense reds and oranges represent Sophie's rage perfectly. As she runs outside into the wider world and her anger diminishes, the colors turn to cool greens and blues, which follow her back home to the embrace of her now peaceful family. The final page is a pleas-ing family scene done in a full-color palette that provides a reassuring message that har-mony and balance have returned.

Value The element of value can be defined as the amount of light and dark in a pic-ture. Illustrator Chris Van Allsburg uses the element of value to create a dramatic three-dimensional effect for all his books. His masterful depiction of light and dark in books like *The Polar Express, Jumanji,* and *Queen of the Falls* suggests that the fig-ures and objects might leap off the page at any moment. On the other hand, the values in Erin E. Stead's pencil and woodblock prints for Philip C. Stead's Caldecott Medal-winning *A Sick Day for Amos McGee* are uniformly soft and muted. Thus, the illustra-tions are imbued with the tender caring that Amos and his animal friends at the zoo exhibit toward each other.

Space The illustrations in a picturebook exist on a two-dimensional plane. How-ever, artists can choose to use elements

David Wiesner's *The Three Pigs* breaks picturebook traditions when the pigs break out of their traditional story to write a new ending. Illustration from *The Three Pigs* by David Wiesner. Copyright ©2001 by David Wiesner. Reprinted by permission of Clarion Books, an imprint of Houghton Mifflin Harcourt Publishing Company. All rights reserved.

such as color, value, or line to create a feeling of realism and depth, as in Jeannie Bakers's *Circle*, a nonfiction picturebook about the migration of Godwits—birds with the longest known record of migration miles. Baker's illustrations use the elements of space and point of view to depict the majestic journey of this extraordinary species. The creative use of space can also enhance the underlying themes in a picturebook, as seen in *Little Black Crow*, Chris Raschka's story about the questions a young boy asks of a little bird. Raschka's use of space effectively emphasizes the contrast between the aerial realm the crow inhabits with the boy far below on the ground by pushing the black figure of the crow and focal point of the picture up against the upper edge of the paper. In *The Three Pigs*, David Wiesner violates the traditional use of space in picturebooks. When the three pigs step out of their familiar story, Wiesner emphasizes the pure white space of the page instead of filling up the double-page spread with images. This reinforces the feeling that we are entering a new world, one beyond our expectations.

Perspective or Point of View Just as an author decides what would be the best voice in which to tell a story, so too does an artist think about point of view. One way to obtain action in what might otherwise be a static series of pictures is to change the focus, just as a movie camera changes perspective or shows close-ups and then moves back to pan the whole scene. Part of the perfection of Donna Jo Napoli's poetic *Mama Miti: Wangari Maathai and the Trees of Kenya* is that illustrator Kadir Nelson uses shifting perspectives to portray the contrast between portraits of the first African American woman to win the Nobel Peace Prize and the strong hands of the Kenyan women and children who planted trees for peace. The perspective in Jon Klassen's illustrations for Ted Kooser's *House Held Up by Trees* shifts throughout the story, allowing the reader to view the changing house from many different angles. Bill Thomson gives us highly dramatic points of view in Carol Nevius's *Baseball Hour* as well as in his picturebooks, *Chalk*, *Fossil*, and *The Typewriter*, often looking down from high above or taking a "worm's eye" view from beneath the characters. Not all artists work with changing perspectives, but when they do, it is interesting to ask why and look to see how this adds to the meaning of the story.

Composition In good picturebooks, no single element of art exists apart from the others. Rather, the illustrator uses principles of composition to unify elements on each page and on each succeeding page. By arranging the elements on each page, including the printed type, the artist tries to obtain an effective balance between unity and variety, and creates certain visual patterns that may be carried from page to page. Illustrators try to ensure that the eye moves from one part of each double-page spread to another through elements within the picture that tie the picture to the printed text. This in turn sets up a subtle rhythm that can be carried throughout the book. All of these choices contribute to a whole that is greater than the sum of its parts. We have discussed how effective Sendak's choices in composition are in *Where the Wild Things Are*. Adam Rex's comical *Pssst!* tells of a child's visit to the zoo. As she makes her way around the exhibits, each animal catches her attention with "Pssst!" and asks for one unlikely object after another. The increasingly perplexed child does her best to accommodate the animals. The page layouts vary rhythmically. One double-page spread shows a drawing of the zoo landscape. On the next page, we see small rectangular vignettes of animal and child on the left-hand page, followed by a full-color picture of the child on an otherwise blank space on the right-hand page. This pattern continues throughout the book until the climactic

Bill Thomson uses unusual points of view for dramatic effect in *Fossil*. Excerpt from FOSSIL by Bill Thomson, reprinted under a license arrangement originating with Amazon Publishing, www.apub.com

Adam Rex creates interesting compositions on each double-page spread and throughout the pages of his amusing *Pssst!* Illustrations from *Pssst!* Copyright ©2007 by Adam Rex. Reprinted by permission of Harcourt Children's Books, an imprint of Houghton Mifflin Harcourt Publishing Company. All rights reserved.

double-page spread shows a full-color picture of what it was the animals wanted all those objects for. *Happy Dreamer* by Peter H. Reynolds is a story of an irrepressible boy whose dreams simply can't be contained. When he tries to stop dreaming, he is shown alone on a double-page spread. When he's off on another dream, he literally dances across the pages.

The Artist's Choice of Media

Children accept and enjoy a variety of art-making media in the illustrations of their picturebooks. The illustrator's choice of original media can be as important to the meaning of the book as the choice of the elements of design. Many artists today are using the picturebook as a vehicle for experimentation with new and interesting media and formats. For example, Melissa Sweet's mixed-media collages for *Balloons Over Broadway: The True Story of the Puppeteer of Macy's Parade*, winner of the 2012 Sibert and Orbis Pictus awards, are created using a combination of watercolors, papier-mâché puppets, and found objects and fabrics. In the "Author's Note" found at the end of the book, Sweet notes that she began the project by playing with a variety of materials to make toys and puppets, working to honor puppeteer Tony Sarg's legacy of play.

In today's creative experimentation with picturebooks, the medium the artist uses is not nearly as important as the appropriateness of the medium choice for a particular book and how effectively the artist uses it. Nevertheless, teachers and children are fascinated with the various aspects of illustrating and always ask what medium is used. This is becoming increasingly difficult to answer, as artists these days use a combination of media and printing techniques to achieve a particular effect. Some publishing houses provide information on the art techniques of some of their outstanding books. This might be found in a foreword, on the copyright page, or on a jacket flap. It is a service that teachers and librarians hope more companies will provide. **Teaching Feature 3.2** gives a brief overview of some of the media choices open to the artist.

teaching feature 3.2

The Artist's Media Choices

Medium	Description	Examples*
Printmaking	The process of cutting into metal or wood, applying ink to the surface, and pressing on paper.	Mary Azarian: *Snowflake Bentley* (Jacqueline Briggs Martin) Holly Meade: *In the Sea* (David Elliott) Ashley Wolff: *In the Canyon* (Liz Garton Scanlon) Erin E. Stead: *Tony* (Ed Galing)
Collage and Construction	Pictures are created by building up a variety of materials and textures onto a surface.	Cathryn Falwell: *The Nesting Quilt* David Diaz: *Smoky Night* (Eve Bunting) Ed Young: *Twenty Heartbeats* (Dennis Haseley) Eric Carle: *The Artist Who Painted a Blue Horse* Steve Jenkins: *My First Day* (Robin Page) Elly MacKay: *Butterfly Park*

teaching feature 3.2

Medium	Description	Examples*
Stitchery and Cloth	Pieces of cloth and sewn threads or yarns are used to create pictures.	Anna Grossnickle Hines: *1, 2, Buckle My Shoe* and *Peaceful Pieces: Poems and Quilts About Peace* María Hernández de la Cruz and Casimiro de la Cruz López: *The Journey of Tunuri and the Blue Deer* (James Endredy) Michele Wood: *I Lay My Stitches Down: Poems of American Slavery* (Cynthia Grady)
Paints, Pen, and Ink	Applying pigments mixed with a binder and medium such as water or oil to a surface.	Meilo So: *Follow the Moon Home* (Philippe Cousteau and Deborah Hopkinson) Marjorie Priceman: *Jazz Age Josephine* (Jonah Winter) Eric Velasquez: *As Fast as Words Could Fly* (Pamela Tuck) Jeanette Winter: *Nanuk the Ice Bear* Christopher Myers: *My Pen*
Drawing Materials	Process of making marks on a surface; includes materials such as crayon, charcoal, pastel chalks, and scratchboard.	Beth Krommes: *Before Morning* (Joyce Sidman) Kurt Cyrus: *Mammoths on the Move* (Lisa Wheeler) Chris Van Allsburg: *Queen of the Falls*
Computer-Generated Art	Use of computer applications to create illustrations.	Bob Staake: *The Book of Gold* Stian Hole: *Night Guard* (Synne Lea) Pamela Zagarenski: *Henry & Leo* Duncan Tonatiuh: *Funny Bones: Posada and His Day of the Dead Calaveras*
Mixed Media	Combinations of paint, drawing, collage, and other media.	Simms Taback: *Joseph Had a Little Overcoat* Adam Rex: *Chloe and the Lion* (Mac Barnett) David Ezra Stein: *Interrupting Chicken* Taeeun Yoo: *You Are a Lion!* Melissa Sweet: *Cricket in the Thicket: Poems About Bugs* (Carol Murray) Will Terry: *There Once Was a Cowpoke Who Swallowed an Ant* (Helen Ketteman) Javaka Steptoe: *Radiant Child: The Story of Young Artist Jean-Michel Basquiat*

*Book's author is in parentheses, if other than illustrator.

Mary Azarian's Caldecott Medal–winning woodcuts for Jacqueline Briggs Martin's *Snowflake Bentley* evoke the time and place of nineteenth-century Vermont. Illustration from *Snowflake Bentley* by Jacqueline Briggs Martin, illustrated by Mary Azarian. Illustrations copyright ©1998 by Mary Azarian. Reprinted by permission of Houghton MIfflin Harcourt Publishing Company. All rights reserved.

Beth Krommes's scratchboard drawings bring the glow of an early dawn to sky to life in Joyce Sidman's *Before Morning*. Sidman, Joyce, *Before Morning*. New York, NY: HMH Books for Young Readers, 2016, Cover. Copyright ©2016 by HMH Books for Young Readers. All rights reserved. Used with permission.

Each page of Anna Grossnickle Hines's *1, 2, Buckle My Shoe* is part of a larger handmade quilt. Illustration from *1, 2 Buckle My Shoe*, copyright ©2008 by Anna Grossnickle Hines, reproduced by permission of Houghton Mifflin Harcourt Publishing Company.

Sophie is a volcano,
ready to explode.

And when Sophie
gets angry—
really, really angry...

In Molly Bang's *When Sophie Gets Angry—Really, Really Angry.* . . . a young child finds space for a tantrum and room to calm down again. From *When Sophie Gets Angry—Really, Really Angry* . . . by Molly Bang. Scholastic Inc./The Blue Sky Press. Copyright ©1999 by Molly Bang. Reprinted by permission.

Two-time Caldecott Honor winner Pamela Zagarenski uses mixed-media—acrylic paints, color pencils, collage, and digital graphics—on wood to create her stunning illustration. Zagarenski, Paula, *Henry & Leo.* New York, NY: HMH Books for Young Readers, 2016, Cover. Copyright ©2016 by HMH Books for Young Readers. All rights reserved. Used with permission.

Choosing Artistic Conventions

Artists may choose to borrow conventions or ways of depicting that we have come to associate with certain historical or cultural periods, such as Renaissance art or Impressionism, or art associated with a people, such as art of Tibetans or of the Northern Plains Indian tribes. Such choices often add authenticity to a story set "once upon a time" or one that originated in a particular society or culture.

A wonderful example of an homage to Impressionism can be found in the Monet-like paintings by Maurice Sendak for *Mr. Rabbit and the Lovely Present*, written by Charlotte Zolotow. In luscious shades of blues and greens, Sendak has created a dreamlike world where a very sophisticated rabbit and a little girl wander about the countryside looking for presents of red, yellow, green, and blue (her mother's favorite colors) for the little girl's mother. The dappled endpapers for this book are examples of Impressionistic techniques in themselves.

David Diaz's Mexican folk art motifs mirror Oaxacan ceramic figures and provide a culturally rich visual setting for Eve Bunting's *Going Home*. Jacket art copyright ©1996 by David Diaz. Text copyright ©1996 by Edward D. Bunting and Anne E. Bunting, Trustees of the Edward D. Bunting and Anne E. Bunting Family Trust. Used by permission of HarperCollins Publishers.

Many artists illustrating stories, folktales, or legends make use of the conventions found in art forms of their respective countries or cultures. David Diaz uses elements of Mexican folk art to tell contemporary stories set within Mexican and Mexican American cultures. In Eve Bunting's *Going Home*, the story of a farm family returning to Mexico for Christmas, Diaz creates endpapers that feature close-up photographs of brilliant "artesanias Mexicanas," decorative objects, figures, and other popular arts found in the marketplaces of Mexico. This "arté popular" then forms the background on which the paintings and type are placed. Folk art silhouettes outline these panels; they are also found on the title page and the final page, set against a brilliant presidential blue background. **Teaching Feature 3.3: Historical and Cultural Conventions in Picturebooks** summarizes other historical and cultural conventions and suggests art and picturebooks for further study.

Paul O. Zelinsky's *Rapunzel* pays homage to Renaissance artists, in this case to Raphael's painting, "Madonna of the Meadow." Illustrations from RAPUNZEL by Paul O. Zelinsky, copyright ©1997 by Paul O. Zelinsky. Used by permission of Dutton Children's Books, an imprint of Penguin Young Readers Group, a division of Penguin Random House LLC. All rights reserved.

teaching feature 3.3

Historical and Cultural Conventions in Picturebooks

Go to Connect® to access study resources, practice quizzes, and additional materials.

Historical Style and Description	Example in Painting	Example in Picturebooks*
Historical Conventions		
Early Christian Art/Near Eastern Art: A clear uniform message was desired. Dramatic form was subdued for repetition of motifs and conventional symbols. This style can be found in Middle Eastern and Russian art today.	Sultan Mohammed, *Shahnama*	Demi: *The Hungry Coat*
Gothic: A style that began with architecture and sculpture; showed a movement toward more natural although still decorative depiction of religious subjects.	Giotto, *The Death of St. Francis*	Tomie dePaola: *The Clown of God*
Late Gothic: A movement away from stylized, two-dimensional depictions toward a renewed interest in realism. Symbolism survives but in increasingly realistic form.	Jan van Eyck, *The Marriage of Giovanni Arnolfini*	Nancy Ekholm Burkert: *Snow-White and the Seven Dwarfs* (Grimm)
Renaissance: A move toward realism; an emphasis on forms, proportioning of space, and dramatic lighting.	Raphael, *Madonna of the Meadow*	Paul O. Zelinsky: *Rapunzel* (Grimm)
Rococo Art: Centered in France with a move to genre scenes or mythology set in idealized park settings. Characterized by highly decorated, almost fussy use of curving lines, flowing forms, and lightened colors.	Jean-Honoré Fragonard, *The Swing*	Barbara McClintock: *Cinderella* (Perrault)
Romanticism: Late eighteenth to mid-nineteenth century movement influenced by romantic literature of Goethe and Byron. Nostalgic identification with nature and the past. Often focused on melancholy, emotional subjects.	Caspar David Friedrich, *Moonrise over the Sea*	Chris Van Allsburg: *The Polar Express, The Wreck of the Zephyr*
Impressionism: Concerned with a momentary and spontaneous view of a scene; characterized by broken color, softened contours.	Claude Monet, *Woman Seated Under the Willows*	Maurice Sendak: *Mr. Rabbit and the Lovely Present* (Zolotow)
Expressionism: Emotionally rooted, intense themes, characterized by brilliant, shocking colors, and rough, rapid brush work.	Georges Rouault, *The Old King*	John Steptoe: *Stevie* Susan Guevera: *Chato's Kitchen* (Soto)
Surrealism: Acknowledged the irrational and the power of imagination. Mixed a realistic style with bizarre, dislocated imagery.	René Magritte, *Time Transfixed*	Anthony Browne: *Changes* D. B. Johnson: *Magritte's Marvelous Hat*

(continued)

teaching feature 3.3

Historical Style and Description Cultural Conventions	Example in Painting	Example in Picturebooks*
African Art: A broad and diverse category that is often characterized by simplified forms and/or bright colors, with an emphasis on form and decoration rather than realism.	Angola, Chokwe peoples, *Chibinda Ilunga Figure*	Gail E. Haley: *A Story, A Story*
Folk Art: A term applied to crafts (more often than to painting) that use traditional designs. Often produced in rural communities these are typified by Tibetan, Indian, and Central and South American embroideries.	Oaxacan ceramic figures Gansevoort Limner, *Susanna Truax*	David Diaz: *Going Home* (Bunting) Barbara Cooney: *Ox-Cart Man* (Hall)
Asian Art: A method of painting using silk, fine papers, and inks that promoted exploration of linear and spatial effects. The style is rooted in calligraphy and involves controlled handling of the brush.	Guo Xi, *Early Spring*	Ed Young: *The Sons of the Dragon King* Demi: *Genghis Khan*
Japanese Prints: Woodblock prints of the seventeenth through nineteenth centuries were characterized by flattened forms, large areas of color, and decorative tensions created by use of line and shape.	Hokusai, *Tokaido Yoshida*	Leo and Diane Dillon: *The Tale of the Mandarin Ducks* (Paterson)

*Book's author is in parentheses, if other than illustrator.

Simms Taback's Caldecott Medal–winning *Joseph Had a Little Overcoat* is illustrated in Taback's signature collage style. Cover image from *Joseph Had a Little Overcoat* by Simms Taback, copyright ©1999 by Simms Taback, illustrations. Used by permission of Penguin Group (USA) Inc. All rights reserved.

An Artist's Personal Style

Few picturebook artists use only one style of art; they adapt their work to meet the requirements of a particular story. At the same time, many of them do develop a recognizable personal style that can be identified by their preference for a particular pictorial style of art, use of medium, or even choice of content. For example, we have come to associate the use of collage with Ed Young, Steve Jenkins, Elly MacKay, Simms Taback, and Eric Carle, even though they differ in how they use it. The amusing animals in the stories by Pat Hutchins are frequently stylized with patterned fur and feathers. Her birds and animals in *We're Going on a Picnic, What Game Shall We Play?* and that self-assured hen in *Rosie's Walk* and *Oh, Where Is Rosie's Chick?* are vintage Hutchins.

Style, then, is an elusive quality of the artist, which changes and varies over the years and with the particular demands of the work. Today, there is more freedom to experiment in illustrating children's picturebooks. Many artists are taking advantage of this new freedom and producing fresh and original art. Exposure to a variety of art styles through fine picturebooks can help children develop visual maturity and appreciation. Certainly, there is no one style that is appropriate for children or preferred by children. The major consideration in evaluating style is how well it conveys and enhances meaning.

The Format of the Book

A picturebook is not made up of single illustrated pictures but conveys its message through a series of images. The impact of the total format of the book is what creates the art object known as the picturebook. Book size and shape are often decisions made jointly by the illustrator and the art director of the publishing house. They might search for a size that will enhance the theme of the story. The horizontal size of *My Snake Blake* by Randy Siegel is long and narrow, mimicking the shape of illustrator Serge Bloch's thin green snake. Oliver Dunrea's Gossie books, about a tiny gosling and her circle of friends, are small in size, just right for its preschool audience. The shape of some books suggests their content. The shape of *Fish Eyes* by Lois Ehlert is long and narrow like a fish or small aquarium. In Mac Barnett and Jon Klassen's *Triangle*, the actual trim size (measurements of the book) gives away the book's ending.

Both the cover and dust jacket of a book should receive careful attention. The primary purpose of the jacket is to call attention to the book. The cover of Doreen Rappaport's *Eleanor, Quiet No More* needs no words. Gary Kelley's elegant, almost life-size, close-up of Eleanor Roosevelt's face is instantly recognizable. Publishers are increasingly duplicating the image from the dust jacket on the book's cover rather than preparing a separate cloth cover that few people ever see. However, a peek beneath a dust jacket can still reveal pleasant surprises. David Wiesner's books such as *Flotsam* and *The Three Pigs* have lovely embossed designs on their cloth covers.

The endpapers of a hardcover picturebook can also add to its attractiveness. These are the first and last pages of the book; one half of each is glued to the inside of the cover, while the other is not pasted down. Endpapers are usually of stronger paper than printed pages. In picturebooks, endpapers are often of a color that harmonizes with the cover or other pictures in the book, and frequently they are illustrated. Decorated endpapers can reflect the setting, the theme, or the content of the book and serve as a special invitation into the book. Jerry Pinkney's exquisitely painted endpapers for Hans Christian Andersen's *The Ugly Duckling* are as much a part of the storytelling as the other pages in the book. The opening endpapers give an overview of the setting with a family of ducks swimming in the stream. At the book's end, a glorious two-page spread shows the beautiful swan "with pure joy in his heart."

Even the copyright page of a picturebook can be beautiful, informative, and symbolic. The copyright page of *A Home for Bird* by Philip C. Stead provides the clue to the reason Bird lost his home, with a picture showing him being flung out of a cuckoo clock as it bounces along in the back of a moving truck. In Bob Graham's *"Let's Get a Pup!" Said Kate*, the story actually begins on the title page when Kate, missing her dead cat, leaps

Jerry Pinkney's exquisitely painted endpapers for Hans Christian Andersen's *The Ugly Duckling* reflect thoughtful care in book design. Illustration from *The Ugly Duckling* by Hans Christian Andersen, illustrations ©1999 by Jerry Pinkney. First published by Morrow Junior Books. All rights reserved. Used with permission of the Sheldon Fogelman Agency and HarperCollins Publishers.

out of bed and shouts, "Let's get a pup!" In Mac Barnett and Adam Rex's humorous postmodern picturebook, *Chloe and the Lion*, the author and illustrator are actual characters who get into a fight over the telling and illustrating of the story. Readers are introduced to the characters in the front matter of the book. We first see the author as he peeks into the book before the title page, and we first see the illustrator as he signs his initials on the dedication page.

All aspects of a book's design can reinforce or extend the meaning of the story. The composition (layout) of pictures and text on each double-page spread and on succeeding pages can have an important impact on the meaning and movement of a story. Full-size pictures might be interspersed with smaller ones, or a page might show a sequence of pictures. This visual pattern can set up a rhythm akin to a musical refrain. The spacing of the text on the page, the choice of margins, and the white space within a book contribute to the making of a quality picturebook. In Virginia Lee Burton's *The Little House*, the arrangement of the text on the page suggests the curve of the road in the opposite picture.

Appropriate typeface is also a matter for consideration. Type is the name given to all printed letters, and typeface refers to the thousands of letter styles available today. Before the advent of computer-created fonts, printers chose from some 6,000 different styles then available. Now the computer allows artists much more freedom. David Diaz designed the fonts for Eve Bunting's *Going Home* to resemble the linear forms of the Mexican folk art that fills the book. Whether they are traditional or computer-created, typefaces, or fonts, vary in legibility and the feeling they create. Some seem bold, others delicate and graceful, some crisp and businesslike. The type should enhance or extend the overall design of the book.

In sum, no single element creates an outstanding picturebook. All elements work together to create a cohesive whole that pleases the eye and delights the imagination.

Graphica and the Graphic Novel

Although a different media from traditional picturebooks, it seems appropriate to group graphica under the umbrella of "picturebook." They can be evaluated by using the same criteria that consider the contributions of words and images to a reader's response. We have elected to use the term *graphica* to include all graphic novels, comics, manga, graphic biographies, graphic nonfiction, graphic memoirs, and so on.

Graphica often have multiple images on one page that are separated into panels; the panels are divided by frames, which are typically thin black lines with white space between. Some graphica like *Binky: License to Scratch* (Binky Series Book 5) by Ashley Spires have different colored backgrounds. In this case, the gray frames lend a faux air of solemnity to the humorous tale of an overly serious cat. Within these panels, the text for the story, if any, is written in speech balloons (also known as word balloons or speech bubbles) that can contain a character's dialog or thoughts. Narration can be included in captions and often include information about the setting like time and place that are not easily conveyed with dialog. With a number of panels and speech balloons on a page, some readers have difficulty determining which to read first. The rule of thumb is to start in the upper left corner and read everything within the panel from left to right, top to bottom, before moving on to the next panel. Finish the entire left-hand page before moving to the right-hand page unless the panels extend over the gutter. Depending on what culture the piece of graphica is from, various different symbols may be used to indicate emotions and onomatopoeia. Motion lines are often used to indicate movement or impact, moving a lot of the plot line from the text into the pictures.

Graphica are often produced as a team effort similar to an animated movie. An author will write the story, including the dialog; then the artist lays out the visual aspects by creating a storyboard. The creation of the art can be broken down into separate tasks sometimes done by people or studios thousands of miles apart. The lead artist creates the drawings using pencil that is gone over by an inker with a nice dark line. The illustrations are then colored by a colorist, often using computer programs like Adobe Photoshop. Then the pages are given to a letterer who draws in the speech balloons and captions and either hand writes or types in the text. These things can all be done by the same person; Shaun Tan does all of the artwork in his wordless work of graphica about immigrant experience set in a fantasy world, *The Arrival*, but most graphic novels—such as *Real Friends* by Shannon Hale and LeUyen Pham, a contemporary realistic fiction book about friendship, and *The Emerald City of Oz* (Marvel's Oz Comics series #6) by Eric Shanower and Skottie Young, a retelling of L. Frank Baum's classic—have a substantial list of credits.

While combining pictures and words to make sequential art dates back to early civilizations,[2] modern graphica has typically focused on humor and superhero stories. An example of a child-appropriate superhero narrative can be seen in Justin LaRocca Hansen's *In the Trenches*. Graphica is very adept at communicating humor and action through the use of pictures as can be seen in Caludette's fantasy adventure, *Dragons Beware* by Jorge Aguirre and Rafael Rosado or the Mexican-inspired exploits of a trio of friends and their car in the Lowriders in Space series by Cathy Camper. Because there are typically many pictures to the page, it is easy for artists to show several steps that depict the physicality of the characters' movements. The focus on dialog in graphica also promotes the use of witty banter between characters and can be used to insert jokes without interrupting the story line which is carried primarily by the pictures.

While humor and fantasy remain the most popular subjects, other artists are using the conventions of the graphic novel for more serious subjects. *Little White Duck* by Na Liu and Andrés Vera Martínez chronicles eight stories from Liu's childhood in communist China and provides a valuable glimpse into another culture and time period. Raina Telgemeier creates poignant but funny graphic novels like *Smile* and *Sisters* that speak to everyday middle-school life by focusing on stories about being in Girl Scouts or going on a family road trip, respectively. Gene Yang's *American Born Chinese* even impressed critics to the extent that it has won several notable awards, including the 2007 Printz Award. A rich trilogy of interrelated stories, *American Born Chinese* weaves together Chinese mythology and a school story that addresses issues of multiculturalism. It also sparked some controversy over whether or not it should be considered a book when it was nominated as a National Book Award Finalist. *This One Summer* by Mariko Tamaki and Jillian Tamaki broke further ground in 2015 when it was the first graphic novel to be awarded a Caldecott Honor as well as a Printz Honor as a book for teens.

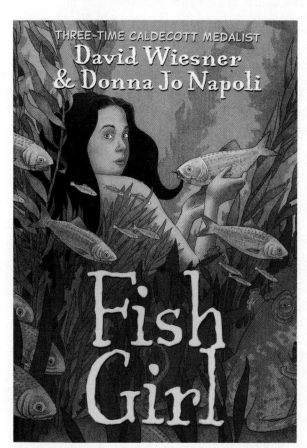

Graphica can dip into nonfiction as well. Nathan Hale's Hazardous Tales series revisits events in American history, such as the World War II Doolittle Raid in *A Raid of No Return*, and the often humorous perspective of the Revolutionary War Era spy, Nathan Hale, the British soldier, and his hangman. Graphic biographies and memoir make up the bulk of nonfiction graphica and vary in the amount of creative license. Ink wash and pencil softens the grittiness of life at the disintegration of the Soviet Union in *A Year Without Mom* by Dasha Tolstikova. Cece Bell portrays her childhood friends and family as rabbits in *El Deafo* as she struggles with hearing loss in a memoir that reads almost as fiction. At the other extreme, a biography can be so close to fact that the text is taken from actual letters and speeches by the subject, as in *Annie Sullivan and the Trials of Helen Keller* by Joe Lambert. Graphic memoir seems to welcome a wide variety of experiences, including the civil rights work of Representative John Lewis in his widely acclaimed March trilogy that targets slightly older readers.

Manga typically focuses on action stories like *Dragon Ball Full Color: Freeza Arc #5* by Akira Toriyama (grades 4 to 6) which is about a boy training in martial arts who goes on a quest to find the mystical orbs known as Dragon Balls. The manga spin-offs of the Pokemon video game, including Pokemon Adventures: Black 2 & White 2, are currently quite popular as well. With a different feel, *Yotsuba&!* by Kiyohiko Azuma, is a more playful look at an exuberant 5-year-old's funny misunderstandings of the world. Manga series like these are often adapted into animated television shows called anime.

The typical subjects and attributes of graphica tend to give the idea that it is less academic than other forms of children's literature and thus less valuable in a classroom. Gene Yang[3] makes a case for using graphica in educational settings because they re-invite students to discuss the visual after moving past picturebooks, and they give control of the speed of the information to the reader. The pictures are also thought to help struggling readers with decoding the text, and the combination of illustrations and words are thought to entice reluctant readers. Sean Connors[4] observes that while graphica is often stigmatized, it can promote critical thinking through evaluation of the visual aspects that is of value to gifted students as well as remedial students.

The Language of Picturebooks

The words of picturebooks are as important as the illustrations; they can help children develop an early sensitivity to the imaginative use of language and add to their overall experience with a picturebook. Because many of these books are read to children rather than by them, there is no reason to oversimplify or write down to today's knowledgeable and sophisticated child. Beatrix Potter knew that, given the context of *The Tale of Peter Rabbit* and the picture of Peter caught in the gooseberry net, most children would comprehend the words "his sobs were overheard by some friendly sparrows, who flew to him in great excitement, and implored him to exert himself" (p. 45). This is the way children increase their vocabularies—by hearing or reading words they do not know but in a context that provides a general sense of the meaning.

In evaluating picture storybooks, it is important to remember that a story should be told quickly because the action must be contained within a 32- to 64-page book. Even with this limitation, the criteria developed in Chapter 1 for all fiction apply equally well to picturebooks that tell stories. Both text and illustrations should be evaluated. The artistry of the words should be equal to the beauty of the illustrations. See **Guidelines: Evaluating Picturebooks** for some questions that can help you evaluate picturebooks.

The Content of Picturebooks

The content of picturebooks is as rich and varied as today's world. Picturebooks are not just for younger children; they are increasingly addressed to children in the middle grades and older. This seems appropriate for today's visually minded child. However, as the age range for picturebooks increases, it becomes imperative to evaluate the appropriateness of the content for the age level of its intended audience. You do not want to share *I Am Thomas* by Libby Gleeson and Armin Greder, *Duck, Death and the Tulip* by Wolf Erlbruch, or *And the Soldiers Sang* by J. Patrick Lewis, illustrated by Gary Kelley, with young children any more than you would read *Goodnight Moon* by Margaret Wise Brown to older children. There are books, such as *Grandfather's Island* by Benji Davies and *Cry, Heart, But Never Break* by Glenn Ringtved, that deal with difficult topics in ways that *are* appropriate for younger children.

Additional aspects regarding the quality of picturebooks need to be examined. For example, does the book avoid race, gender, and age stereotyping? Gender stereotyping

Evaluating Picturebooks

Go to Connect® to access study resources, practice quizzes, and additional materials.

The following questions are meant to help determine the strengths of the book. Not every question is appropriate for every book.

Content

- How appropriate is the content of the book for its intended age level?
- Is this a book that will appeal to children, or is it really written for adults?
- When and where does it take place? How has the artist portrayed this?
- Are the characters well delineated and developed?
- Are stereotypes regarding race, gender, and others avoided?
- What is the quality of the language of the text?
- How is the theme developed through text and illustrations?

Illustrations

- In what ways do the illustrations help create the meaning of the text?
- How are pictures made an integral part of the text?
- Do the illustrations extend the text in any way? Do they provide clues to the action of the story?
- Are the pictures accurate and consistent with the text?
- Where the setting calls for it, are the illustrations authentic in detail?

Medium and Style of Illustrations

- What medium has the illustrator chosen to use? Is it appropriate for the mood of the story?
- How has the illustrator used line, shape, and color to extend the meaning of the story?
- How would you describe the style of the illustrations? Is the style appropriate for the story?
- How has the illustrator varied the style and technique? What techniques seem to create rhythm and movement?
- How has the illustrator created balance in composition?

Format

- Does the size of the book seem appropriate to the content?
- Does the jacket design express the theme of the book?
- Do the cover design and endpapers convey the spirit of the book?
- In what way does the title page anticipate the story to come?
- Is the type design well chosen for the theme and purpose of the book?
- What is the quality of the paper?
- How durable is the binding?

Overall Evaluation

- How is this work similar to or different from other works by this author and/or illustrator?
- How is this story similar to or different from other books with the same subject or theme?
- What comments have reviewers made about this book? Do you agree or disagree with them?
- What has the artist said about her or his work?
- Will this book make a contribution to the growing body of children's literature? How lasting do you think it will be?

begins early. Examples can be found in pictures as well as in text. In the imaginative story *Can I Keep Him?* by Steven Kellogg, Albert asks his mother if he can keep one pet after another, ranging from real to imaginary to human. His distraught mother is always pictured attending to such household chores as scrubbing, ironing, and cleaning the toilet bowl. She explains in very literal terms why Albert cannot keep his pets; for example, a snake's scales could clog the vacuum. While the contrast between Albert's highly original ideas and his mother's mundane preoccupation with household duties is funny, it is also a stereotyped image of the traditional housewife.

Books that counteract gender stereotyping are not as hard to find as they were when *William's Doll*, by Charlotte Zolotow, was published in 1972. William is a little boy who desperately wants a doll but is misunderstood by family and teased by friends. Only his grandmother understands how he feels, and so she brings him a baby doll "to hug . . . so that when he's a father . . . he'll know how to care for his baby." More and more books portray characters who are willing to step outside of traditional roles to have fulfilling lives. *José! Born to Dance: The Story of José Limon*, written by Susanna Reich and illustrated by Raúl Colón, tells the life story of a boy who dreamed of giving a gift to the world—and found that gift in dance. Winner of the 2006 Tomás Rivera Children's Book Award, this picturebook biography introduces readers to a pioneer in modern dance and choreography. *Jacob's New Dress* by Sarah Hoffman deals with gender identity in a completely matter of fact way.

We have picturebooks that portray the experiences of more diverse cultures than ever before, although the total number of multicultural books is still small compared with the proportion of ethnic and racial groups in the population. Many people from parallel cultures are now represented in stories about contemporary children as well as in folktales. In *The Christmas Coat: Memories of My Sioux Childhood*, written by Virginia Driving Hawk Sneve and illustrated by Ellen Beier, the author shares a poignant memory from her childhood. This winner of the 2012 American Indian Youth Literature Award tells the story of a young girl's sacrifice and subsequent reward for her act of kindness. *Little You* by Richard Van Camp is a delightful board book that won the award in 2016.

The past few decades have seen an increase in books about Latino and Asian cultures, in bilingual books, and in translated books. Monica Brown's *Marisol McDonald Doesn't Match* is a story about a multiracial girl who feels mismatched to life. From the color of her hair and skin to the food she eats and the clothes she wears, Marisol exhibits a creative flair, one that makes perfect sense to her. However, tired of hearing other kids point out her eccentricity, Marisol decides to try to fit in. In the end, though, she decides to embrace her unique self. Sara Palacios's acrylic illustrations bring Marisol's engaging character to life. This bilingual 2012 Pura Belpré Illustrator Honor book is told in both English and Spanish.

In *Juna's Jar*, written by Jane Bahk and illustrated by Felicia Hoshino, Juna is a young Korean girl who uses an empty kimchi jar to collect interesting creatures with her friend, Hector. They love to study them before letting them go. When Hector moves away, the jar brings them back together, if only in Juna's imagination. *Juna's Jar* won the Asian Pacific American Culture Award in 2015. Yu Li-Qiong won the prestigious Feng Zikai Chinese Children's Picture Book Award for *A New Year's Reunion*. Little Maomao looks forward to her family's Chinese New Year celebrations, which mark her father's annual visit home. Maomao finds the coin that Papa hides in one of the sticky rice balls, which brings her good luck. When he has to leave, Maomao gives her coin to Papa for safekeeping until the next year's celebrations. Zhu Cheng-Liang's colorful gouache illustrations show the family engaged in their treasured family traditions.

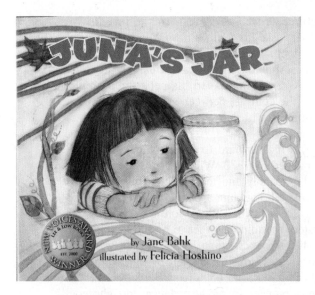

Though there are now more books about older people than ever before, we can find stereotypes among these, too. One young-appearing grandfather went to a bookstore recently and said he wanted "a book about a grandfather in which the main character doesn't die." Many grandparents today in their sixties and seventies are vigorous and healthy; we might well ask if they are being portrayed this way. Author Tony Johnston and illustrator Yuyi Morales celebrate the vitality of the older generation in *My Abuelita*, showing an energetic and loud grandmother who delights in caring for her grandson and telling stories. Morales earned a 2010 Pura Belpré Illustrator Honor for her illustrations, which she created by digitally manipulating photographs of characters and objects made from a variety of materials, such as clay, fabrics, paints, and Mexican crafts.

Picturebooks frequently give children their first impressions of various ethnic and racial groups. Only when our books portray characters of both sexes, all ages, and all ethnic and racial groups in a wide range of occupations and from a great variety of socioeconomic backgrounds and settings will we have moved away from stereotyping to a more honest portrayal of the world for children. **Teaching Feature 3.4: A Sampling of Picturebooks** provides an introduction to the many topics found in today's picturebooks.

teaching **feature 3.4**

A Sampling of Picturebooks

Following is an introduction to the many topics found in today's picturebooks.

Title (Author, Illustrator)	Grade Level	Description
ABC and Counting Books		
One Family (Shannon, Gomez)	PreK	Concepts about numbers are shown through counting diverse family groups.
Eating the Alphabet (Ehlert)	PreK–1	Fruits and vegetables are shown for every letter of the alphabet.
10 (Bataille)	PreK–1	A pop-up counting book.

Title (Author, Illustrator)	Grade Level	Description
LMNO Peas (Baker)	PreK–1	Activities of the peas are shown for every letter of the alphabet.
The Sleepy Little Alphabet: A Bedtime Story From Alphabet Town (Sierra, Sweet)	PreK–1	These letters have a lot to do before they can go to bed!
Feast for 10 (Falwell)	PreK–2	Beginning with one grocery cart, these textured collages show an African American family preparing a family feast.
Billions of Bricks (Cyrus)	PreK–2	A construction site introduces skip counting and engineering designs.
7 Ate 9: The Untold Story (Lazar, MacDonald)	PreK–3	This humorous detective story includes a cast of numerals and letters.
Z Is for Moose (Bingham, Zelinsky)	K–3	When Moose is cut from Zebra's alphabet, he tries to make an appearance in other letters.
Ashanti to Zulu: African Traditions (Musgrove, Dillon and Dillon)	2–5	Illustrations feature the people, their homes, and an artifact from twenty-six African tribes.

Wordless Books

Title (Author, Illustrator)	Grade Level	Description
A Ball for Daisy (Raschka)	PreK	While on an outing to the park, Daisy's beloved red ball is popped by another dog.
Little Fox in the Forest (Graegin)	PreK–3	A young girl searches for her stuffed fox in the forest.
Rainstorm (Lehman)	PreK–3	A rainy day inspires an imaginative adventure.
Flotsam (Wiesner)	PreK–8	A boy finds an unusual camera while at the beach.
The Lion and the Mouse (Pinkney)	K–3	Pinkney won the Caldecott Medal for his brilliant illustrations of Aesop's fable.
Mirror (Baker)	K–3	A wordless picturebook showing a boy in Australia and a boy in Morocco doing the same thing.
Fossil (Thomson)	K–3	A boy walking on a beach discovers magic fossils.
Chalk (Thomson)	K–3	Sidewalk chalk offers plenty of entertainment!
The Arrival (Tan)	4–8	A man must flee his family and country and adjust to a totally new place and culture.

Family Stories

Title (Author, Illustrator)	Grade Level	Description
Kitchen Dance (Manning)	PreK–1	Children wake to find their Mama and Papa dancing in the kitchen.

(continued)

teaching feature 3.4

Title (Author, Illustrator)	Grade Level	Description
My Dad Is Big and Strong, BUT . . . A Bedtime Story (Saudo, Di Giacomo)	PreK–2	Hilarious story of a child trying to put his father to bed.
Bee-Bim Bop! (Park, Lee)	PreK–2	A Korean American girl looks forward to eating "mix, mix rice" with her family.
All the Way to Havana (Engle, Curato)	K–3	A family takes a joyous trip to Havana in their old car.
Sona and the Wedding Game (Sheth, Jaeggi)	K–3	Sona and her cousin have a job to do at a family wedding.
Home at Last (Williams, Raschka)	1–3	A foster child finds a loving home with gay dads.
The Ring Bearer (Cooper)	1–3	A young boy serves as ring bearer in his mother's wedding.

Relatives

Title (Author, Illustrator)	Grade Level	Description
Grandfather Counts (Cheng, Zhang)	K–3	Helen and her Chinese grandfather learn to speak each other's language.
Malaika's Costume (Hohn, Luxbacher)	K–3	Malaika and her grandmother create a costume for Carnival in her Caribbean community.
Mango, Abuela, and Me (Medina, Dominguez)	K–3	Mia's Spanish-speaking grandmother comes to live with her and the two find ways to communicate.
Tia Isa Wants a Car (Medina, Muñoz)	K–3	Young girl who lives with her aunt and uncle helps with plans to buy a car.
Aunt Flossie's Hats (and Crab Cakes Later) (Howard, Ransome)	1–4	Two sisters listen to the stories of their great-great aunt's many hats.

Family History

Title (Author, Illustrator)	Grade Level	Description
Ice Cream Summer (Sis)	K–3	A boy and his grandfather discover the history of ice cream.
Brothers at Bat: The True Story of an Amazing All-Brother Baseball Team (Vernick, Salerno)	K–3	The story of thirteen brothers who played on an all-brother baseball team.
All the Way to America: The Story of a Big Italian Family and a Little Shovel (Yaccarino)	K–3	A family history that begins with the author's great grandfather.

Title (Author, Illustrator)	Grade Level	Description
Coming on Home Soon (Woodson, Lewis)	2–5	A young girl and her grandmother are separated from Mama when she moves north to work during World War II.
How I Learned Geography (Shulevitz)	2–6	Shulevitz looks back on his childhood as a refugee in a far-off land.

Familiar Experiences

Mom, It's My First Day of Kindergarten! (Yum)	PreK–1	This is a sweet story of a child telling his mother it is OK for him to go to kindergarten.
A Couple of Boys Have the Best Week Ever (Frazee)	PreK–2	Two best friends spend a happy week at the beach.
Small Bunny's Blue Blanket (Feeney)	PreK–2	When Bunny gets a bath and Blue Blanket gets a wash, Bunny is sad until Blue Blanket is back to normal.
Music, Music for Everyone (Williams)	K–3	Rosa uses her birthday accordion to earn money to help pay the bills.
Crafty Chloe (DiPucchio, Ross)	K–3	Chloe wants to make something very special for Emma's birthday.
Ada Twist, Scientist (Beaty, Roberts)	K–3	An inquisitive child is determined to be a scientist.
Windows (Denos, Goodale)	K–3	While walking his dog in the evening, a child watches the lights come on in his neighbors' houses.

Children Around the World

Little Treasures: Endearments from Around the World (Ogburn, Raschka)	PreK–2	Terms of endearment are gathered from around the world with expressions in English, native languages of each country, and a pronunciation guide for each term.
Baby Goes to Market (Atinuke, Brooksbank)	PreK–2	As Mother takes baby to market in Nigeria, he collects his own treats from sellers.
Over the Ocean (Gomi)	PreK–3	A young girl dreams about what lies in the rest of the world.
Stepping Stones: A Refugee Family's Journey (Ruurs, Badr)	1–4	Unique illustrations relay the story of a refugee family escaping war.
Same, Same but Different (Kostecki-Shaw)	1–4	Pen pals from the United States and India compare similarities and differences.
Four Feet, Two Sandals (Williams, Mohammed)	3–6	Two girls in a Pakistani refugee camp agree to share the pair of sandals they find.

(continued)

teaching **feature** 3.4

Title (Author, Illustrator)	Grade Level	Description
Social and Environmental Concerns		
Outside Your Window: A First Book of Nature (Davies, Hearld)	PreK–2	Beautifully illustrated poems about nature are organized by seasons.
Peace (Halperin)	PreK–3	A lovely plea for peace that can begin with each one of us.
Where's the Elephant? (Barroux)	PreK–3	Natural habitats are destroyed, leaving animals only in the zoo for a home.
Buried Sunlight: How Fossil Fuels Have Changed the Earth (Bang, Chisholm)	K–4	Vivid illustrations show the effects of climate change.
Jacob's New Dress (Hoffman and Hoffman, Case)	1–3	Jacob wears a "towel thing" to school to show he really wants to wear a dress.
My Beautiful Birds (Del Rizzo)	1–3	A young Syrian boy is traumatized by having to flee from his family's home and leave his beloved pigeons behind.
Home (Baker)	1–4	A wordless picturebook shows a neighborhood changing over time.
Fly Away Home (Bunting, Himler)	1–4	A young boy and his father must live in an airport concourse.
One Hen (Milway, Fernandes)	2–5	An Ashanti boy receives a micro loan and buys a hen to begin a thriving business.
Animals as People		
A Visitor for Bear (Becker, Denton)	PreK–1	An insistent mouse finally convinces reclusive Bear that friends are nice to have.
Leo the Late Bloomer (Kraus, Aruego)	PreK–2	Leo, a baby tiger, can't do anything right until he's ready to.
Boot & Shoe (Frazee)	PreK–3	Twin puppies share everything except their daytime habits.
Detective Gordon: The First Case (Nilsson, Spee)	K–3	A toad detective helps recover a squirrel's missing nuts.
If You Plant a Seed (Nelson)	K–3	Rabbit and Mouse lovingly tend garden until birds want to share.
Diary of a Spider (Cronin, Bliss) *Diary of a Worm* (Cronin, Bliss)	1–4	The world as seen through the eyes (and words) of a young spider and a worm.

teaching feature 3.4

Title (Author, Illustrator)	Grade Level	Description
Modern Folktale Style		
Huff & Puff: Can You Blow Down the Houses of the Three Little Pigs? (Rueda)	PreK–2	A simple spin on the traditional tale.
Lady Hahn and Her Seven Friends (Heo)	K–3	Seven friends debate which one is most important to Lady Hahn until they decide that they are all important.
The Cloud Spinner (Catchpool, Jay)	K–3	When a boy weaves beautiful fabric from the clouds, he realizes enough is enough. However, the King demands more and more until there are no more clouds.
Goldilocks and the Three Dinosaurs (Willems)	K–3	Goldilocks is lured into the dinosaurs' lair to be served as the dessert to the main course.
Noodleheads See the Future (Arnold, Weiss, and Hamilton)	K–3	Two wacky characters have adventures in the tradition of folktale fools.
The Midsummer Tomte and the Little Rabbits (Stark, Eriksson)	K–3	A gnome helps rescue forest animals during a flood.
A Well-Mannered Young Wolf (Leroy, Maudet)	K–3	A wolf has an unusual code of ethics.
Princess and the Peas (Himes)	1–4	This take on the traditional *Princess and the Pea* is set in Charleston County, South Carolina, with African American characters.
Humorous Picturebooks		
RRRalph (Ehlert)	PreK–2	Ralph, the dog, can answer questions.
Baabwaa & Wooliam (Elliott, Sweet)	PreK–3	Sheep friends with special talents try to outsmart a wolf in sheep's clothing.
Chloe and the Lion (Barnett, Rex)	K–2	Barnett, the author, interrupts the story to correct Rex for drawing a dragon instead of a lion. Chloe tries to make peace between the author and illustrator.
George and Martha (Marshall)	K–3	Brief stories about the adventures of two hippo friends are both poignant and hysterical.
I Want My Hat Back (Klassen)	K–3	Bear searches for his hat, even though it's right under his nose.
Triangle (Barnett, Klassen)	K–3	Triangle tries to put Square in this place.
Life on Mars (Agee)	K–3	An astronaut is oblivious to the alien spying on him as he explores a planet.

(continued)

teaching feature 3.4

Title (Author, Illustrator)	Grade Level	Description
The Wolf, the Duck, and the Mouse (Barnett, Klassen)	K–3	Duck and Mouse are swallowed by a wolf, but they experience cushy living quarters.
Perfectly Martha (Meddaugh)	1–4	Martha the Talking Dog copes with a crooked dog training scam.
Fantasy		
Friday My Radio Flyer Flew (Pullen)	PreK–2	A boy discovers his father's radio flyer wagon and eventually takes off!
Baby Bear Sees Blue (Wolff)	PreK–2	Baby bear sees the world for the first time, wide-eyed with curiosity.
Extra Yarn (Barnett, Klassen)	K–3	An enchanting box of yarn transforms a city.
Wolf Won't Bite! (Gravett)	K–3	The three little pigs make a circus show around wolf, guaranteeing that he won't bite.
April and Esme, Tooth Fairies (Graham)	K–3	April and Esme make their first run for a tooth!
City Dog, Country Frog (Willems, Muth)	K–3	A friendship blossoms between a city dog and a country frog.
The Adventures of Beekle: The Unimaginary Friend (Santat)	K–3	An imaginary friend goes looking for his human.
Go, Otto, Go! (Milgrim)	K–3	Robot builds a spaceship to take him home.
Graphica		
Benny and Penny series (Hayes)	K–2	In some of the most popular Toon Books-graphica for younger readers, Benny and his sister Penny have fun backyard adventures.
Squish series (Holm, Holm)	2–4	Squish the amoeba has to navigate real life issues while finding inspiration from his favorite superhero.
Lunch Lady series (Krosoczka)	2–4	The school Lunch Lady is secretly a super hero, saving the school children from a never-ending wave of various dangers with her silly techno-gadgets.
Storm in the Barn (Phelan)	2–4	During a Depression-era drought, a young boy is trapped in a barn by a mysterious figure.
Fish Girl (Wiesner and Napoli)	3–5	A carnival mermaid yearns to be a real girl.
Real Friends (Hale, Pham)	3–5	Peer pressure affects two best friends.
Amulet series (Kibuishi)	4+	Emily and her brother must venture into a strange alternate world to save their mother.

In Stephanie Graegin's *Little Fox in the Forest*, a little girl, her stuffed fox, and a real fox take a wordless journey. Illustrations from LITTLE FOX IN THE FOREST by Stephanie Graegin, copyright ©2017 by Stephanie Graegin. Used by permission of Schwartz & Wade Books, an imprint of Random House Children's Books, a division of Penguin Random House LLC. All rights reserved.

Maurie J. Manning's *Kitchen Dance* is a warm family story and a perfect goodnight book. Illustration from *Kitchen Dance* by Maurie J. Manning. Copyright ©2008 by Maurie J. Manning. Reprinted by permission of Houghton Mifflin Harcourt Publishing Company. All rights reserved.

Francesca Sanna's *The Journey* relates the story of a refugee family's journey to escape a brutal war.

Chris Haughton creates wonderfully funny illustrations for *Oh No, George!*

Katie Smith Milway's *One Hen,* illustrated by Eugenie Fernandes, shows how the gift of an animal can change the lives of poor people in dramatic ways.

Challenging Perspectives on Picturebooks

We have explored some qualities of picturebooks that affect children's emotional and intellectual responses to books, which we hope will lead to a lifelong appreciation of literature and art. The illustrations in picturebooks can help teach any number of pre-reading and independent reading skills that fall under the rubric of higher-level critical thinking (such as formulating questions about the material you are reading—especially questions that analyze, hypothesize, or evaluate). Understanding the concept of "book" is an important milestone on the road to literacy. Children with prior book experience may already know some concepts about how printed materials work, such as turning pages, recognizing the differences between print and pictures. It is at the next skill level that children are reaching benchmarks related to inference (a conclusion drawn from evidence or reasoning) and making meaning in literacy learning.

When young children look at pictures in texts, how are their inferences culturally bound? How can a teacher's understanding of the cultural context of aesthetic responses support or get in the way of how he or she introduces, discusses, and assesses picturebooks with children?

Earlier in this chapter, we discussed how color, as one of the elements of design, can elicit strong emotions that affect a viewer's response to a book. Colors, for example, can be full of symbolism. Cultural referents can be linked to geography, parental preferences, and any other number of things related to the culture in which one was raised. Brides in some countries, such as China, may traditionally wear red, while brides in other countries, such as Italy, may wear white. **Table 3.1** lists other color connections to consider.

Market researchers work hard to determine what consumers will like or dislike. The use of color in marketing, for example, is not random. They use many markers of difference (race, gender, social class, geography, sexuality, age, religion, physical ability, education, life experience) and trends are used to determine what the logos and marketing layouts for their products will be. Given the attention to color and style, the illustrators of children's books realize that the colors and mediums they choose are more than tangential to the creation of a picturebook. They are aware that very young children tend to prefer brighter colors, and thus use modern publishing techniques to create exciting, full-color picturebooks.

Again the choice of colors should depend on the theme of the book. However, as teachers encourage aesthetic responses, a discussion of color can be put in the cultural context of children's lived experiences. Using the example of Molly Bang's *When Sophie Gets Angry—Really, Really Angry,* we find Bang's intense reds and oranges represent Sophie's rage. As she runs outside into the wider world and her anger diminishes, the colors turn to cool greens and blues, which follow her back home to the embrace of her now peaceful family. Teachers using this book might ask if red denotes anger and intensity in every culture. Can the use of red have a cultural referent that would cause a student to think something else is going on with the protagonist? For example, in some African communities, red is used as a symbol of mourning.

The response to literature that includes the aesthetic response is a critical part of the enjoyment of reading. However, we know that in the art world, artistic works can be labeled controversial and political. Few book lists of criteria for the selection of a picturebook to read with children includes evaluation for the social-political construction of

table 3.1	Color Around the World	

Color	Country/Ethnicity/Culture	Meaning
Red	Eastern hemisphere	Worn by brides
	Western hemisphere	Excitement, danger, love, passion, stop, Christmas (with green)
	China	Good luck, celebration, summoning
	India	Purity
	Russia	Communism
	South Africa	Color of mourning
	Cherokee	Success, triumph
Orange	Western hemisphere	Halloween (with black), creativity, autumn
	Ireland	Religious (Protestants)
Yellow	Western hemisphere	Hope, hazards, coward
	China	Nourishing
	Egypt	Color of mourning
	India	Merchants
	Japan	Courage
Green	Western hemisphere	Spring, new birth, go, St. Patrick's Day, Christmas (with red)
	China	Green hats indicate a man's wife is cheating on him; exorcism
	India	Islam
	Ireland	Symbol of the entire country
Blue	Western hemisphere	Depression, sadness, conservative, corporate, "something blue" bridal tradition
	Iran	Heaven, spirituality
	Cherokee	Defeat, trouble
Purple	Western hemisphere	Royalty
	Thailand	Color of mourning (widows)
White	Eastern hemisphere	Funerals
	Western hemisphere	Brides, angels, "good guys," hospitals, doctors, peace (white dove)
	Japan	White carnation symbolizes death
Black	Western hemisphere	Funerals, death, Halloween (with orange), "bad guys," rebellion
	China	Color for young boys

what is art and how that may affect children's aesthetic responses. Conversely, what are the controversies in the art world that may have some impact on what shows up in illustrator's choices of artistic form in children's books? Children can participate in topics of conversations that include controversy. They can be taught the evaluative language of art, the explanations of artistic elements, and the principles of design to help them express their ideas and aesthetic responses.

We can help children have deeper understandings of how the use of various artistic elements represents different things to different people. For example, an important aspect of literacy instruction is reading comprehension. When reading a picturebook with a child, we often facilitate the development of comprehension with a series of questions. These questions ask students to go beyond immediately available information in the text. Through careful questioning and discussion, students realize the illustration contains hints that imply a whole network of information: clues to deeper understanding of the story. To push beyond what is written in the text, ask children to find clues within the illustrations, examine them, and discuss what inferences (meanings) are justified. This enhances reading comprehension through inference.

The question then becomes, *"How can we increase their understandings of cultural perspectives?"* For example, in Jo S. Kittinger's *The House on Dirty-Third Street* with illustrations by Thomas Gonzalez, the protagonists are a young girl and her mother who move to a rundown house on Third Street. The entire neighborhood appears somewhat rundown, but their house is the worst. The book begins with grays, dark blues, tans, and washed-out yellows. But as the story progresses, the colors soon change to bright yellows, bright blues, greens, and reds. The storyline of the book is presented through the changes in the coloration as the little girl's faith in her community is brought to life by the help of neighbors and new friends.

After reading the first pages of this story, the classroom teachers can engage children in a conversation about the use of color in the story, asking, "What colors do you see?" "Why do you think the illustrator used grays, dark blues, tans, and washed-out tones in the beginning and bright, bold colors by the end of the story?" "Do you know if using dark colors mean anything in other countries?" "Does it mean anything in your home or community?"

As students participate in a discussion of this type, they will share their cultural referents to color, those that are both positive and negative to their lived experiences. Helping students understand the variety of viewpoints related to the use of color can open a space for understanding the multiple perspectives of people around the globe in the arts and other content areas. An example of this can be seen in *Golden Domes and Silver Lantern: A Muslim Book of Colors* by Hena Khan, illustrated by Mehrdokht Amini. This book could be shared with children and young adults to learn about traditional and contemporary Islamic culture through the universal concept of color. A critical analysis of the text and the illustrations will help them to engage in conversations and provide reflective responses to what they read or what is read to them.

Picturebooks are for all ages, and they can be about all subjects. They can enrich children's lives, stretch their imaginations, and increase their sensitivities. The growth of beautiful picturebooks for children of all ages is an outstanding accomplishment of the past 50 years of publishing. Children do not always recognize the beauty of these books, but early impressions do influence the development of children's permanent tastes as they grow up. The challenge for teachers will be to change the lens through which the art of the picturebook is traditionally seen for one that offers critique and inclusion of multiple perspectives and cultural referents.

In this touching story, Kittinger describes the many benefits of reaching out to one's community members to help make a run-down, dirty house into a home.

First published in the United States under the title *The House on Dirty-Third Street* by Jo S. Kittinger, illustrated by Tom Gonzalez. Text Copyright ©2012 by Jo S. Kittinger. Illustrations Copyright ©2012 Tom Gonzalez. Published by arrangement with Peachtree Publishers.

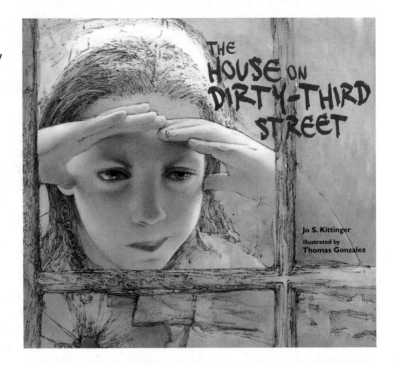

Go to **Connect®** for an example of how to use the Ten-Point Model to address perceptions and controversial issues related to picturebooks.

curriculum connections

Using Picturebooks to Address Standards

Using enchanting stories and visual creativity, picturebooks spark ideas in the imagination of students, help them see themselves reflected in the characters, and introduce readers to times, events, and places that give them insight into their past and hope for their future. The variety of styles and stories that encompass the genre of picturebooks offer a starting point for implementing curriculum standards in the classroom.

Suggested Children's Book: *They All Saw a Cat* by Brendan Wenzel (Chronicle, 2016). In this Caldecott Honor winner, Brendan Wenzel brings multiple perspectives to light through his creative use of style, media, scale, and point of view. As a cat goes out for a walk, a child sees it as one normally pictures a cat. However, the skunk sees it in black and white. It is a giant to the flea and blurry to the fish. The subtle theme of the book is that our identity is created by the interactions we have with the people we meet in our lives.

curriculum connections

Subject	Standard	Classroom Ideas
Science, Language Arts, Art, and Technology	**NGSS:** The environment affects the traits that an organism develops. **NCTE/ILA:** Students conduct research on issues and interests by generating ideas and questions and by posing problems. They gather, evaluate, and synthesize data from a variety of sources (e.g., print and non-print texts, artifacts, people) to communicate their discoveries in ways that suit their purpose and audience. **ISTE:** Students build knowledge by actively exploring real-world issues and problems, developing ideas and theories and pursuing answers and solutions. **NCCAS:** Convey meaning through the presentation of artistic work.	Investigate information about the sight of each animal in the book. For example, why do some snakes see in infrared? Then, investigate other animals' sense of sight. Write extensions of the text, using this information, and create additional images of the cat that could be used to extend the book. Report the reasons animals have differences in sight.
Language Arts, Social Studies, and Math	**NCTE/ILA (Writing):** Students use spoken, written, and visual language to accomplish their own purposes (e.g., for learning, enjoyment, persuasion, and the exchange of information). **NCSS:** Analyze a particular event to identify reasons individuals might respond to it in different ways. **NCTM:** Select and use various types of reasoning and methods of proof.	Describe the differences in each animal's reaction to the cat in the text. Provide reasons why you think each animal would respond as it did.
Textual Connections	*Glow: Animals with Their Own Night-Lights* (Beck); *Good Trick, Walking Stick!* (Bestor); *Masters of Disguise: Amazing Animal Tricksters* (Johnson)	
Other Books by Wenzel	Illustrated by Wenzel: *Some Pets*; *One Day in the Eucalyptus, Eucalyptus Tree*; *Beastly Babies*; and *Some Bug*	
Author's Website	https://brendanwenzel.info	

Sources: International Society for Technology in Education (ITSE); National Coalition for Core Arts Standards (NCCAS); National Council of Teachers of English (NCTE)/International Literacy Association (ILA); National Council for Teachers of Mathematics (NCTM); National Council for Social Studies Curriculum Standards (NCSS); and Next Generation Science Standards (NGSS).

Notes

1. Personal communication, April 2, 2017.
2. Scott McCloud, *Understanding Comics: The Invisible Art* (New York, NY: Morrow, 1994), pp. 10–15.
3. Gene Yang, "Graphic Novels in the Classroom," *Language Arts* (Urbana, Ill: National Council of Teachers of English, 2008), Vol. 85, No. 3.
4. Sean P. Connors, "The Best of Both Worlds: Rethinking the Literary Merit of Graphic Novels" (Blacksburg, VA: The Alan Review, 2010), Vol. 37. No. 3.

Children's Literature

Go to Connect® to access study resources, practice quizzes, and additional materials.

Titles in blue = multicultural titles

Picturebooks

Agee, Jon. *Life on Mars*. Dial, 2017.

Atinuke. *Baby Goes to Market*. Illustrated by Angela Brookbank. Candlewick, 2017.

Bahk, Jane. *Juna's Jar*. Illustrated by Felicia Hoshino. Lee & Low, 2015.

Baker, Jeannie. *Circle*. Candlewick, 2016.

_____. *Home*. Greenwillow, 2004.

_____. *Mirror*. Candlewick, 2011.

Baker, Keith. *LMNO Peas*. Beach Lane Books, 2010.

Bang, Molly. *When Sophie Gets Angry—Really, Really Angry*. Scholastic, 1999.

Bang, Molly, and Penny Chisholm. *Buried Sunlight: How Fossil Fuels Have Changed the Earth*. Illustrated by Molly Bang. Scholastic, 2014.

Barnett, Mac. *Chloe and the Lion*. Illustrated by Adam Rex. Hyperion/Disney, 2012.

_____. *Extra Yarn*. Illustrated by Jon Klassen. Balzer and Bray, 2012.

_____. *Triangle*. Illustrated by Jon Klassen. Candlewick, 2017.

_____. *The Wolf, the Duck, and the Mouse*. Illustrated by Jon Klassen. Candlewick, 2017.

Barroux. *Where's the Elephant?* Candlewick, 2016.

Bataille, Marion. *10*. Roaring Brook Press, 2011.

Beaty, Andrea. *Ada Twist Scientist*. Illustrated by David Roberts. Abrams, 2016.

Becker, Bonny. *A Visitor for Bear*. Illustrated by Kady MacDonald Denton. Candlewick, 2008.

Bingham, Kelly. *Z Is for Moose*. Illustrated by Paul Zelinsky. Greenwillow, 2012.

Bloom, Suzanne. *A Splendid Friend, Indeed*. Boyds Mills, 2005.

Brown, Margaret Wise. *Goodnight Moon*. Illustrated by Clement Hurd. Harper, 1975 [1947].

Browne, Anthony. *Changes*. Knopf, 1986.

Bunting, Eve. *Fly Away Home*. Illustrated by Ronald Himler. Clarion, 1991.

_____. *Going Home*. Illustrated by David Diaz. HarperCollins, 1996.

_____. *Smoky Night*. Illustrated by David Diaz. Sandpiper, 1999.

Catchpool, Michael. *The Cloud Spinner*. Illustrated by Allison Jay. Knopf, 2012.

Coerr, Eleanor. *Sadako*. Illustrated by Ed Young. Putnam, 1993.

Coombs, Kate. *Water Sings So Blue*. Illustrated by Meilo So. Chronicle, 2012.

Cooper, Floyd. *The Ring Bearer*. Philomel, 2017.

Coudray, Jean-Luc, and Phillipe Coudray. *A Goofy Guide to Penguins*. Toon, 2016.

Cousteau, Philippe, and Deborah Hopkinson. *Follow the Moon Home*. Illustrated by Meilo So. Chronicle, 2016.

Cronin, Doreen. *Diary of a Spider*. Illustrated by Harry Bliss. HarperCollins, 2006.

_____. *Diary of a Worm*. Illustrated by Harry Bliss. HarperCollins, 2005.

Cummins, Lucy Ruth. *A Hungry Lion; or, A Dwindling Assortment of Animals*. Atheneum, 2016.

Cyrus, Kurt. *Billions of Bricks*. Holt, 2016.

Davies, Benji. *Grandfather's Island*. Candlewick, 2016.

Davies, Nicola. *Outside Your Window: A First Book of Nature*. Illustrated by Mark Hearld. Candlewick, 2012.

Deedy, Carmen Agra. *The Rooster Who Would Not Be Quiet*! Illustrated by Eugene Yelchin. Scholastic, 2017.

Del Rizzio, Suzanne. *My Beautiful Birds*. Pajama Press, 2017.

Demi. *Chingis Khan*. Holt, 1991.

_____. *The Hungry Coat*. Simon, 2004.

Denos, Julia. *Windows*. Illustrated by B. Goodale. Candlewick, 2017.

dePaola, Tomie. *The Clown of God*. Harcourt, 1978.

DiPucchio, Kelly. *Crafty Chloe*. Illustrated by Heather Ross. Atheneum, 2012.

Dunrea, Olivier. *Gossie*. Houghton, 2002.

Ehlert, Lois. *Eating the Alphabet*. Harcourt, 1989.

_____. *Fish Eyes: A Book You Can Count On*. Harcourt, 1990.

_____. *RRRalph*. Beach Lane Books/Simon, 2011.

Elliott, David. *Baabwaa & Wooliam*. Illustrated by Melissa Sweet. Candlewick, 2017.

_____. *In the Sea*. Illustrated by Holly Meade. Candlewick, 2014.

_____. *On the Farm*. Illustrated by Holly Meade. Candlewick, 2008.

Ellis, Carson. *Du Iz Tak?* Candlewick, 2016.

Elya, Susan Middleton. *Rubia and the Three Osos*. Illustrated by Mellissa Sweet. Hyperion, 2010.

Endredy, James. *The Journey of Tunuri and the Blue Deer: A Huichol Indian Story*. Illustrated by María Hernández de la Cruz and Casimiro de la Cruz López. Bear Cub Books, 2003.

Engle, Margarita. *All the Way to Havana*. Illustrated by Mike Curato. Holt, 2017.

English, Karen. *The Baby on the Way*. Illustrated by Sean Qualls. Farrar, 2005.

Falwell, Cathryn. *Feast for Ten*. Clarion, 1993.

_____. *The Nesting Quilt*. Tilbury House, 2015.

_____. *Scoot!* HarperCollins, 2008.

Feeney, Tatyana. *Small Bunny's Blue Blanket*. Knopf, 2012.

Fogliano, Julie. *And Then It's Spring*. Illustrated by Erin E. Stead. Roaring Book Press, 2012.

Foreman, Michael. *A Child's Garden of Hope*. Candlewick, 2009.

Frazee, Marla. *A Couple of Boys Have the Best Week Ever*. Harcourt, 2008.

_____. *Boot and Shoe*. Simon, 2012.

Frazier, Craig. *Stanley Goes Fishing*. Chronicle, 2006.

Gág, Wanda. *Millions of Cats*. Coward-McCann, 1928.

Galing, Ed. *Tony*. Illustrated by Erin Stead. Roaring Brook, 2017.

Garden, Nancy. *Molly's Family*. Illustrated by Sharon Wooding. Farrar, 2004.

Gomi, Taro. *Over the Ocean*. Chronicle, 2016.

Gower, Catherine, and He Zhihong. *Long-Long's New Year*. Tuttle, 2005.

Graegin, Stephanie. *Little Fox in the Forest*. Schwartz & Wade, 2017.

Graham, Bob. *"Let's Get a Pup!" Said Kate*. Candlewick, 2003.

Gravett, Emily. *Little Mouse's Big Book of Fears*. Macmillan, 2007.

Grimm brothers. *Snow White and the Seven Dwarfs*. Translated by Randall Jarrell. Illustrated by Nancy Ekholm Burkert. Farrar, 1972.

Haley, Gail. *A Story, a Story*. Atheneum, 1970.

Hall, Donald. *The Ox-Cart Man*. Illustrated by Barbara Cooney. Viking, 1979.

Halperin, Wendy Anderson. *Peace*. Atheneum, 2013.

Harris, Robie H. *Mail Harry to the Moon!* Illustrated by Michael Emberley. Little, 2008.

Hayes, Geoffrey. *Benny and Penny: Lights Out*. Toon, 2012.

Heide, Florence Parry, and Judith Heide Gilliland. *Sami and the Time of the Troubles*. Illustrated by Ted Lewin. Clarion, 1992.

Heo, Yumi. *Lady Hahn and Her Seven Friends*. Holt, 2012.

Himes, Rachel. *Princess and the Peas*. Charlesbridge, 2017.

Hines, Anna Grossnickle. *1, 2, Buckle My Shoe*. Harcourt, 2008.

_____. *Peaceful Pieces: Poems and Quilts About Peace*. Holt, 2011.

Hoffman, Sarah. *Jacob's New Dress*. Illustrated by Ian Hoffman. Whitman, 2014.

Hohn, Nadia. L. *Malaika's Costume*. Illustrated by Irene Luxbacher. Groundwood, 2016.

Hole, Stian. *Garmann's Summer*. Translated by Don Bartlett. Eerdmans, 2008.

Holm, Jennifer, and Matt Holm. *Squish #4: Captain Disaster*. Random, 2012.

Howard, Elizabeth Fitzgerald. *Aunt Flossie's Hats (and Crab Cakes Later)*. Illustrated by James Ransome. Houghton, 1991.

Hutchins, Pat. *Rosie's Walk*. Macmillan, 1968.

_____. *We're Going on a Picnic!* Greenwillow, 2002.

_____. *What Game Shall We Play?* Greenwillow, 1990.

Jenkins, Steve. *Animals by the Numbers*. Houghton, 2016.

Jenkins, Steve, and Robin Paige. *My First Day*. Houghton, 2012.

Johnson, D. B. *Magritte's Marvelous Hat*. Houghton, 2012.

Kellogg, Steven. *Can I Keep Him?* Dial, 1971.

Ketteman, Helen. *There Once Was a Cowpoke Who Swallowed an Ant*. Illustrated by Will Terry. Whitman, 2014.

Khan, Hena. *Golden Domes and Silver Lanterns: A Muslim Book of Colors*. Illustrated by Mehrdokht Amini. Chronicle Books, 2012.

Kibuishi, Kazu. *Amulet #5: Prince of Elves*. Graphix, 2012.

Kittinger, Jo S. *The House on Dirty-Third Street.* Illustrated by Thomas Gonzalez. Peachtree, 2012.

Klassen, Jon. *I Want My Hat Back.* Candlewick, 2011.

Kostecki-Shaw, Jenny Sue. *Same, Same but Different.* Holt, 2011.

Kraus, Robert. *Leo the Late Bloomer.* Illustrated by José Aruego. Crowell, 1971.

Krosoczka, Jarrett J. *Lunch Lady and the Picture Day Peril.* Knopf, 2012.

____. *Lunch Lady and the Video Game Villain.* Knopf, 2013.

Lazar, Tara. *7 Ate 9: The Untold Story.* Illustrated by Ross MacDonald. Hyperion, 2017.

Lehman, Barbara. *Rainstorm.* Houghton, 2007.

Leroy, Jean. *A Well-Mannered Young Wolf.* Illustrated by Matthieu Maudet. Eerdmans, 2016.

Look, Leonore, and Yumi Heo. *Uncle Peter's Amazing Chinese Wedding.* Atheneum, 2006.

Lord, Cynthia. *I Lay My Stitches Down: Poems of American Slavery.* Illustrated by Michelle Wood. Eerdmans, 2012.

Mackay, Elly. *Butterfly Park.* Running Press, 2015.

Manning, Maurie J. *Kitchen Dance.* Houghton, 2008.

Marshall, James. *George and Martha: The Complete Stories of Two Best Friends.* Houghton, 1997.

Martin, Jacqueline Briggs. *Snowflake Bentley.* Illustrated by Mary Azarian. Houghton, 1998.

McCloskey, Robert. *Make Way for Ducklings.* Viking, 1941.

Meddaugh, Susan. *Perfectly Martha.* Houghton, 2004.

Medina, Meg. *Mango, Abuela, and Me.* Illustrated by Angela Dominguez. Candlewick, 2015.

____. *Tía Isa Wants a Car.* Illustrated by Claudio Muñoz. Candlewick, 2011.

Milgrim, David. *Go, Otto, Go!* Simon, 2016.

Milway, Katie Smith. *One Hen.* Illustrated by Eugenie Fernandes. Kids Can, 2008.

Mitchell, Margaree King. *Uncle Jed's Barbershop.* Illustrated by James Ransome. Simon, 1993.

Mollel, Tololwa. *My Rows and Piles of Coins.* Illustrated by E. B. Lewis. Clarion, 1999.

Mora, Pat. *Doña Flor: A Tall Tale About a Woman with a Big Heart.* Illustrated by Raúl Colón. Knopf, 2005.

Morgan, Emily, *Next Time You See the Moon.* NSTA Kids, 2014.

Murray, Carol. *Cricket in the Thicket.* Illustrated by Melissa Sweet. Holt, 2017.

Musgrove, Margaret. *Ashanti to Zulu: African Traditions.* Illustrated by Leo Dillon and Diane Dillon. Dial, 1976.

Myers, Christopher. *My Pen.* Disney, 2015.

Myers, Walter Dean. *Jazz.* Illustrated by Christopher Myers. Holiday, 2006.

Nelson, Kadir. *If You Plant a Seed.* Harper, 2015.

Nevius, Carol. *Baseball Hour.* Illustrated by Bill Thomson. Marshall Cavendish, 2008.

Nilsson, Ulf. *Detective Gordon: The First Case.* Translated by Julia Marshall. Illustrated by Gitte Spree. Gecko, 2015.

Ogburn, Jacqueline K. *Little Treasures: Endearments from Around the World.* Illustrated by Chris Raschka. Houghton Harcourt, 2012.

Park, Linda Sue. *Bee-Bim Bop!* Illustrated by Ho Baek Lee. Clarion, 2005.

Paterson, Katherine. *The Tale of the Mandarin Ducks.* Illustrated by Leo and Diane Dillon. Dutton, 1990.

Perrault, Charles. *Cinderella.* Illustrated by Marcia Brown. Macmillan, 1954.

____. *Cinderella.* Illustrated by Barbara McClintock. Scholastic, 2005.

Phelan, Matt. *The Storm in the Barn.* Candlewick, 2009.

Pinkney, Jerry. *The Lion and the Mouse.* Little, 2009.

Potter, Beatrix. *The Tale of Peter Rabbit.* Warne, 1902.

Pullen, Zachary. *Friday My Radio Flyer Flew.* Simon, 2008.

Rappaport, Doreen. *Eleanor, Quiet No More.* Illustrated by Gary Kelley. Hyperion, 2009.

Raschka, Chris. *A Ball for Daisy.* Random/Schwartz & Wade, 2011.

Reynolds, Peter H. *Happy Dreamer.* Orchard, 2017.

Rockliff, Mara. *My Heart Will Not Sit Down.* Illustrated by Ann Tanksley. Knopf, 2012.

Rodriguez, Edel. *Sergio Makes a Splash!* Little, 2008.

Rogers, Gregory. *Midsummer Knight.* Roaring Brook Press, 2007.

Rosoff, Meg. *Meet Wild Boars.* Illustrated by Sophie Blackall. Holt, 2005.

____. *Wild Boars Cook.* Illustrated by Sophie Blackall. Holt, 2008.

Roth, Susan L., and Cindy Trumbore. *The Mangrove Tree: Planting Trees to Feed Families.* Lee & Low, 2011.

Rueda, Claudia. *Huff & Puff: Can You Blow Down the Houses of the Three Little Pigs?* Abrams, 2012.

Ruurs, Margriet. *Stepping Stones: A Refugee Family's Journey.* Illustrated by Nizar Ali Badr. Orca, 2016.

Sanna, Francesca. *The Journey*. Flying Eye Books, 2016.

Santat, Dan. *The Adventures of Beekle: The Unimaginary Friend*. Little, 2014.

Saudo, Coralie. *My Dad Is Big and Strong, BUT . . . A Bedtime Story*. Illustrated by Chris Di Giacomo. Enchanted Lion, 2012.

Savage, Stephen. *Where's Walrus?* Scholastic, 2011.

Scanlon, Liz. *In the Canyon*. Illustrated by Ashley Wolff. Beach Lane, 2015.

Schaefer, Carole Lexa. *Kids Like Us*. Illustrated by Pierr Morgan. Viking, 2008.

Sendak, Maurice. *Where the Wild Things Are*. Harper, 1963.

Shannon, George. *One Family*. Illustrated by Bianca Gomez. Farrar, 2015.

Sheth, Kashmira. *Sona and the Wedding Game*. Illustrated by Yoshiko Jaeggi. Peachtree, 2015.

Shulevitz, Uri. *How I Learned Geography*. Farrar, 2008.

Sidman, Joyce. *Before Morning*. Illustrated by Beth Krommes. Houghton, 2016.

_____. *Swirl by Swirl*. Illustrated by Beth Krommes. Houghton, 2011.

Sierra, Judy. *The Sleepy Little Alphabet: A Bedtime Story from Alphabet Town*. Illustrated by Melissa Sweet. Knopf, 2012.

Simmons, Jane. *Come Along, Daisy!* Little, 1998.

Sis, Peter. *Ice Cream Summer*. Scholastic, 2015.

Soto, Gary, and Susan Guevara. *Chato's Kitchen*. Putnam, 1997.

Staake, Bob. *The Book of Gold*. Swartz & Wade, 2017.

Stanley, Diane. *The Giant and the Beanstalk*. HarperCollins, 2004.

Stark, Ulf. *The Midsummer Tomte and the Little Rabbits*. Illustrated by Eva Eriksson. Floris, 2016.

Stein, David Ezra. *Interrupting Chicken*. Candlewick, 2010.

Steptoe, Javaka. *The Jones Family Express*. Lee, 2003.

_____. *Radiant Child: The Story of Young Artist Jean-Michel Basquiat*. Little, 2016.

Steptoe, John. *Stevie*. Harper, 1969.

Swanson, Susan Marie. *The House in the Night*. Illustrated by Beth Krommes. Houghton, 2008.

Sweet, Melissa. *Some Writer! The Story of E. B. White*. Houghton, 2016.

Synne, Lea. *Night Guard*. Illustrated by Stian Hole. Eerdmans, 2016.

Taback, Simms. *Joseph Had a Little Overcoat*. Viking, 1999.

Thomson, Bill. *Chalk*. Marshall Cavendish, 2010.

_____. *Fossil*. Two Lions, 2013.

_____. *The Typewriter*. Two Lions, 2016.

Tonatiuh, Duncan. *Funny Bones: Posada and the Day of the Dead Calaveras*. Abrams, 2016.

Tuck, Pamela. *As Fast as Words Could Fly*. Illustrated by Eric Vasquez. Lee & Low, 2013.

Turkle, Brinton. *Deep in the Forest*. Dutton, 1976.

Udry, Janice May. *A Tree Is Nice*. Illustrated by Marc Simont. Harper, 1956.

Van Allsburg, Chris. *Jumanji*. Houghton, 2011. (1981).

_____. *The Polar Express*. Houghton, 1985.

_____. *The Wreck of the Zephyr*. Houghton, 1983.

Van Camp, Richard. *Little You*. Illustrated by Julie Flett. Orca, 2013.

Vernick, Audrey. *Brothers at Bat: The True Story of an Amazing All-Brother Baseball Team*. Illustrated by Steven Salerno. Clarion, 2012.

Viva, Frank. *Sea Change*. Toon Graphic, 2016.

Weiss, Mitch and Martha Hamilton. *Noodleheads See the Future*. Illustrated by Ted Arnold. Holiday House, 2017.

Wheeler, Lisa. *Mammoths on the Move*. Illustrated by Kurt Cyrus. Harcourt, 2006.

Wiesner, David. *Flotsam*. Clarion, 2006.

_____. *The Three Pigs*. Clarion, 2001.

Wiesner, David, and Donna Jo Napoli. *Fish Girl*. Clarion, 2017.

Willems, Mo. *City Dog, Country Frog*. Illustrated by Jon J. Muth. Hyperion, 2010.

_____. *Goldilocks and the Three Dinosaurs*. Harper, 2012.

Williams, Karen Lynn. *Galimoto*. Illustrated by Catherine Stock. Lothrop, 1990.

Williams, Karen Lynn, and Khadra Mohammed. *Four Feet, Two Sandals*. Illustrated by Doug Chayka. Eerdmans, 2007.

Williams, Vera B. *Home at Last*. Illustrated by Chris Raschka. Greenwillow, 2016.

_____. *Music, Music for Everyone*. Greenwillow, 1984.

Winter, Jeanette. *Nanuk the Ice Bear*. Beach Lane, 2016.

Winter, Jonah. *Jazz Age Josephine*. Illustrated by Marjorie Priceman. Atheneum, 2012.

Wolff, Ashley. *Baby Bear Sees Blue*. Beach Lane, 2012.

_____. *In the Canyon*. Beach Lane, 2015.

Wood, Michele. *I Lay My Stitches Down: Poems of American Slavery*. Illustrated by Cynthia Grady. Eerdmans, 2011.

Woodson, Jacqueline. *Coming on Home Soon*. Illustrated by E. B. Lewis. Putnam, 2004.

_____. *Each Kindness*. Illustrated by E. B. Lewis. Penguin, 2012.

Yaccarino, Dan. *All the Way to America: The Story of a Big Italian Family and a Little Shovel*. Knopf, 2011.

Yang, Belle. *Hannah Is My Name*. Candlewick, 2004.

Yoo, Taeeun. *You Are a Lion! And Other Fun Yoga Poses*. Penguin, 2012.

Young, Ed. *The Cat from Hunger Mountain*. Philomel, 2016.

_____. *The Sons of the Dragon King*. Atheneum, 2004.

Yum, Hyewon. *Mom, It's My First Day of Kindergarten!* Foster/Farrar, 2012.

Zagorinski, Pamela. *Henry and Leo*. Houghton, 2016.

Zelinsky, Paul. *Rapunzel*. Dutton, 1997.

Zolotow, Charlotte. *Mr. Rabbit and the Lovely Present*. Illustrated by Maurice Sendak. Harper, 1962.

_____. *William's Doll*. Illustrated by William Pène Du Bois. HarperCollins, 1972.

Graphica

Aguirre, Jorge. *Dragons Beware*. Illustrated by Rafael Rosado. First Second, 2015.

Azuma, Kiyohiko. *Yotsuba&!* (Book 13). Yen Press, 2016.

Bell, Cece. *El Deafo*. Amulet, 2014.

Camper, Cathy. *Lowriders to the Center of the Earth*. Illustrated by Raúl the Third. Chronicle, 2016.

Hale, Nathan. *Raid of No Return* (Hazardous Tales #7). Abrams, 2017.

Hale, Shannon. *Real Friends*. Illustrated by LeUyen Phan. First Second, 2017.

Hansen, Justin LaRocca. *In the Trenches* (Secondhand Heroes #2). Dial Books for Young Readers, 2017.

Kusaka, Hidenori. *Pokemon Adventures: Black 2 & White 2 (Volume 1)*. Illustrated by Satoshi Yamamoto. VIZ, 2017.

Lewis, John, and Andrew Aydin. *March: Book Three*. Illustrated by Nate Powell. Top Shelf Productions, 2016.

Liu, Na, and Andrés Vera Martínez. *Little White Duck: A Childhood in China*. Graphic Universe, 2012.

Shanower, Eric. *The Emerald City of Oz* (Oz Comics series #6). Illustrated by Scottie Young. Marvel, 2014.

Spires, Ashley. *Binky: A License to Scratch* (A Binky Adventure #5). Kids Can Press, 2013.

Tamaki, Mariko. *This One Summer*. Illustrated by Jillian Tamaki. First Second, 2014.

Tan, Shaun. *The Arrival*. Scholastic, 2007.

Telgemeier, Raina. *Sisters*. Graphix, 2014.

_____. *Smile*. Graphix, 2010.

Tolstikova, Dasha. *A Year Without Mom*. Groundwood, 2015.

Toriyama, Akira. *Dragon Ball Full Color: Freeza Arc #5*. VIZ, 2017.

Yang, Gene. *American Born Chinese*. First Second, 2006.

Traditional Literature

Chapter Outline

Elora's PopPop is considered quite the storyteller, having even kissed the Blarney Stone of Irish lore. This particular bedtime he sat down with a retelling of the Stone Soup story, called *Fandango Stew* by David Davis. In the traditional folktale, two hungry travelers trick selfish townspeople into contributing ingredients to make soup from water and

©Erin Reilly-Sanders.

a stone. *Fandango Stew* sets the story in a Wild West town called Skinflint, complete with appropriate trappings and a single bean for the stone. The integrated Spanish and other period dialects provided good inspiration for various southwestern accents.

As PopPop read aloud, he improvised a tune for the refrain of the book as each character added another ingredient to the communal pot, "Chili's good, so is barbecue, but nothing's FINER than FANDANGO STEW!" Aunt A.J. joined in on the third rendition, inviting Elora to chime in on the fourth, creating a tuneless chorus. Overhearing the story, Elora's Mamma and Grammie couldn't be kept out of the raucous fun either. Finally, as Luis and his grandfather rode off into the sunset with full bellies, a sweetly mournful chorus finally harmonized.

As one of Aesop's fables might conclude,

Timeworn stories combine the voices of many anew.

A Perspective on Traditional Literature

Traditional literature refers to all of the stories born of the oral tradition, the stories most often labeled "folklore," "folk literature," or "mythology." Generally, we say that myths are about gods and the creation or ways of things; legends are about heroes and their mighty deeds before the time of recorded history; and folktales, fairy tales, and fables are simple stories about talking beasts, woodcutters, and princesses who reveal human behavior and beliefs while playing out their roles in a world of wonder and magic.

When brothers Jacob and Wilhelm Grimm published the first volume of their *House-hold Stories* in 1812, they did not intend it for children. These early philologists were studying the language and grammar of such traditional tales. Today anthropologists study folklore in order to understand the inherent values and beliefs of a culture. Psychologists look at folktales and myths to learn about human motivation and feelings. Folklorists collect and categorize various stories, types, and motifs from around the world. These are all adult scholars of folk literature, which itself was first created by adults and usually told to an adult community. How, then, did folk literature become associated with children's literature, and what value does this kind of literature have for children?

Originally, folklore was the literature of the people; stories were told to young and old alike. Families or tribes would gather to hear an accomplished storyteller in much the same way that an entire family today will watch their favorite television program together. With the advances of science and technology, these stories were relegated to the nursery, often kept alive by resourceful nursemaids or grandmothers, much to the delight of children.

Children today still enjoy these tales because they are good stories. Born of the oral tradition, these stories usually are short and have fast-moving plots. They frequently are humorous and almost always end happily. Poetic justice prevails; the good and the just are eventually rewarded; the evil are punished. This particularly appeals to children's sense of justice and their moral judgment. Wishes come true but usually not without the fulfillment of a task or trial. The littlest child, the youngest child, or the smallest animal succeeds; the oldest or the largest is frequently defeated. Youngsters, who are the little people of their world, thrive on such turns of events.

Beyond the function of pure entertainment, folktales can kindle the child's imagination. Behind every great author, poet, architect, mathematician, or diplomat are that person's dreams of what she or he hopes to achieve. These dreams or ideals have been created by the power of imagination. If we always give children stories of "what is"—stories that only mirror the living of today—then we have not helped them to imagine "what might have been" or "what might be."

Our speech and vocabulary reflect many contributions from traditional literature. Think of the figures of speech that come from Aesop's fables: "sour grapes," "dog in the manger," "boy who cried wolf." Our language is also replete with words and phrases from the myths—*narcissistic, cereal, labyrinth, siren,* and many more.

Traditional literature is a rightful part of a child's literary heritage and lays the groundwork for greater understanding of literature and culture. Poetry and modern stories allude to traditional literature, particularly the Greek myths, Aesop's fables, and Bible stories. As you meet recurring patterns or symbols in mythlike floods, savior heroes, cruel stepmothers, the seasonal cycle of the year, and the cycle of a human life, you begin to build a framework for interpreting literature. Poetry, prose, and drama become more emotionally significant as you respond to these recurring archetypes.

This chapter discusses children's literature that comes from the oral tradition. Although traditional literature can be classified in a number of overlapping categories, we focus on folktales, fables, legendary heroes, and myths. Modern parodies, which are sometimes satirical imitations of traditional tales, are discussed with picturebooks in Chapter 3 and modern literary fairy tales, which are written by known authors and sometimes borrow from the motifs of traditional tales, are discussed with the fantasy genre in Chapter 5.

Folktales

Folktale is a broad term that encompasses a wide variety of traditional narratives. They typically have relatively brief stories with simple plots, sometimes simplistic characters, and generally happy endings.

Questions often arise about which of the available print versions of a tale is the "correct" or authentic text. From a folklorist's point of view, a tale is recreated every time it is told, and therefore *every* telling is correct in its own way. A great deal of variation is also acceptable in print versions, where literary style carries the same uniqueness as the teller's voice. Popular culture often adopts a recorded version of a folktale as a standard, such as the Grimm Brother's books, Perrault's versions, or Disney movies, but it is important to remember that these tales have previously been told in countless forms. Authors and illustrators may also add original twists, customize their stories for a chosen audience, or adapt a familiar tale to an unfamiliar setting, as oral storytellers do. There might be a problem, however, when a print version suggests by its title, or lack of an author's note, that it represents a tale derived directly from a previously printed source when it has greatly customized the story. Readers of a story identified as recorded and published by the Grimm brothers, for instance, have a right to find that the text has been published without major additions, omissions, or distortions.

One way to check how traditional a version of a tale might be is to see where your local library has it shelved. If the book can be found in the 398 section like Paul Galdone's version of *The Three Little Pigs,* then it is close to the most traditional tellings. In this case, Galdone has tightened up one of the earliest recorded versions but stayed mostly true to Joseph Jacob's text from 1890. On the other hand, David Wiesner's *The Three Pigs* is shelved in picturebooks under his last name because he takes artistic liberties with the tale, as the three pigs escape from the book. Many books will be found along a continuum from classic to innovative, but this chapter concentrates attention on the more traditional tales.

Types of Folktales

The folktales that have found their way into the hands and hearts of children come from many cultures. There will be features of these stories that are unique to each culture, but children will also find particular aspects of plot or characterization that occur across cultures. Recognizable literary patterns can be found in cumulative tales, pourquoi tales, beast tales, wonder tales, and realistic tales.

Cumulative Tales Very young children are fascinated by such cumulative stories as "The Old Woman and Her Pig" with its "Rat! rat! gnaw rope; rope won't hang butcher; butcher won't kill ox; ox won't drink water; water won't quench fire; fire won't burn stick; stick won't beat dog; dog won't bite pig; piggy won't get over the stile; and I shan't get home tonight." (See versions by Margaret Read MacDonald and Eric Kimmel.) In cumulative tales, the story itself is not as important as the increasing repetition of the details building up to a quick climax.

Hungry jackal repeats the tune from each previous episode as the story progresses in *Gobble You Up!* by Gita Wolf, a cumulative tale from northern India with traditional Mandna finger paintings by Sunita. Cover to *Gobble You Up!* by Gita Wolf and Sunita, ©Tara Books Pvt Ltd., Chennai, India https://tarabooks.com/

The story of the gingerbread boy who ran away from the old woman, defiantly crying "Catch me if you can!" as in Paul Galdone's *The Gingerbread Boy,* has been told in many different versions, including Beatrice Rodriguez's *The Gingerbread Man,* Jim Aylesworth's *The Gingerbread Man,* and Jan Brett's *Gingerbread Baby.* Dotti Enderle sets the traditional story in a library with a gingerbread man. Characters from different sections of the Dewey decimal system chase him through the stacks until an Arctic fox, from section 998, shows up and the librarian puts him safely back on his 398.2 shelf.

In another familiar cumulative tale, one day an acorn falls on Chicken Little (see Steven Kellogg's or Mara Alperin's *Chicken Little*). Thinking the sky is falling down, she persuades Henny Penny, Ducky Lucky, and Turkey-Lurkey to go along with her to tell the king. Children delight in the sound of the rhyming double names, which are repeated over and over. Young children, especially, enjoy extending and personalizing these cumulative tales through dramatic play. You will find repetitive stories in practically all folklore.

Pourquoi Tales Some folktales are "why," or *pourquoi,* stories that explain certain animal traits or characteristics or human customs. These tales often come from religious traditions. They appear in cultures around the globe including Greek mythology, the epic of Gilgamesh from Mesopotamia, and Aboriginal Australians. Beverley Naidoo includes several pourquoi tales in her collection, *Who Is King? Ten Magical Stories from Africa.* These stories from a variety of countries and peoples tell why monkeys live in trees (Ewe tale from Ghana), why hippos have no hair (Luo tale from Kenya), how elephant got his trunk (Venda tale from South Africa), and why the cockerel crows (Chichewa tale from Malawi). Fellow South African Piet Grobler illustrates the tales in vivid watercolors with light-hearted penwork in his trademark scratchy style. *The Beckoning Cat* by Koko Nishizuka chronicles the origin of the small cat statues, or maneki-neko, displayed near the entrances of shops for good luck, explaining a human custom.

Many Native American stories are "why" stories that explain animal features, the origin of certain natural features, or how humans and their customs came to be. These stories are some of the most popular pourquoi stories and are typically easy to find. *Pine and the Winter Sparrow* by Alexis York Lumbard shares a Cherokee story of why pine trees stay green. Paul Goble's collection of twenty-three traditional stories from five different nations, *The Man Who Dreamed of Elk Dogs & Other Stories from the Tipi,* tells such stories as how horses first appeared to the tribes of the American Plains. *The Girl Who Helped Thunder and Other Native American Folktales,* legends from Native peoples across North America that were gathered and retold by James and Joseph Bruchac, includes many pourquoi tales such as "The Sister and Her Seven Brothers" from the Cheyenne, which explains how certain stars came to be.

Beast Tales Probably the favorite folktales of young children are beast tales in which animals act and talk like human beings. The best known of these frequently appear in newly illustrated versions. In his version of *The Three Little Pigs,* Paul Galdone portrays the wolf as a ferocious doggy creature. James Marshall's red-capped wolf looks like a thug in his red-striped polo shirt. Steven Guarnaccia's version, *The Three Little Pigs: An Architectural Tale,* casts each pig as a different famous architect, dressing them in appropriate human clothing, and the details of their houses reflect their architectural style. Other beast tales found in several versions include *The Three Billy Goats Gruff* (versions by Jerry Pinkney and Paul Galdone), *The Little Red Hen* (Jerry Pinkney, Paul Galdone, and Leslie Kimmelman), and *Puss in Boots* (Jerry Pinkey, Joy Cowley, and Charles Perrault).

Many stories are "wise beast/foolish beast" tales of how one animal, such as a spider or rabbit, outwits a lion, hyena, leopard, or other foe. Tales of the trickster can be found in cultures all around the world. One of the most well-known tricksters is Anansi the Spider. Anansi tales, such as those told in *The First Adventures of Spider* by Joyce Cooper Arkhurst and *The Parade* by KP Kojo, spread from Ghana to West Africa, the Caribbean, and many other places where enslaved Africans were taken. These stories often include pourquoi tales such as "How Spider Got a Thin Waist." Gerald McDermott's retelling of the classic trickster tale, *Monkey: A Trickster Tale from India,* explains how Monkey outwits Crocodile. The trickster can take many forms in Native American folklore, from raccoon, to rabbit, to raven. Matt Dembicki compiled and edited *Trickster,* a graphic anthology of twenty-one Native American trickster tales. Native American storytellers wrote the stories, then collaborated with illustrators to adapt each trickster tale into comic form.

Many beast tales that traveled to the United States with enslaved Africans were collected by Joel Chandler Harris in the late 1800s. Although perhaps starting as tales about the spider Anansi, these tales focus on the trickster character of Brer Rabbit, who is often seen to represent the African Americans as they sought to outwit the white slave owners. Julius Lester was awarded a Coretta Scott King author honor award for *The Tales of Uncle Remus: The Adventures of Brer Rabbit.*

Talking animals appear in folktales of all cultures. Fish are often in English, Scandinavian, German, and South Seas stories. Tales of bears, wolves, and the firebird are found in Russian folklore. Spiders, rabbits, tortoises, crocodiles, monkeys, and lions are very much a part of African tales; rabbits, badgers, monkeys, and even bees are represented in Japanese stories. A study of just the animals in folklore would be fascinating.

Wonder Tales Children call wonder tales about magic and the supernatural "fairy tales." Very few tales have fairies or even a fairy godmother in them, but the name persists. Wicked witches, Baba Yaga in Russian folklore, demons such as the *oni* of Japanese tales, or monsters and dragons abound in these stories. Traditionally, we have thought of the fairy tale as involving romance and adventure. "Cinderella," "Snow White and the Seven Dwarfs," and "Beauty and the Beast" all have elements of both. The long quest tales—such as the Norwegian tale told in George Webbe Dasent's *East o' the Sun and West o' the Moon*—are complex wonder tales in which the hero or heroine triumphs against all odds to win the hand of a spouse and makes a fortune. Children expect that these tales will end with ". . . and they lived happily ever after." In fact, part of the appeal of the wonder tale is the secure knowledge that no matter what happens, love, kindness, and truth will prevail—and hate, wickedness, and evil will be punished. Wonder tales have always represented the glorious fulfillment of human desires.

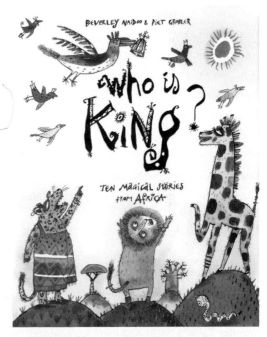

Realistic Tales Surprisingly, there are a few realistic tales included in folklore. The story in Marcia Brown's *Dick Whittington and His Cat* could have happened; in fact, there is evidence that a Richard Whittington did indeed live and was mayor of London. Like the American story in Reeve Lindbergh's *Johnny Appleseed,* the tale began with a real person but has become so embroidered through various tellings that it takes its place in the folklore of its culture.

Dianne Snyder's *The Boy of the Three-Year Nap* is a humorous realistic folktale involving trickery. A poor widow, tired of supporting her son Taro, who is "lazy as a rich man's cat," pesters him to go to work for a rich rice merchant. Declining to work, the boy tricks the merchant into betrothing him to his daughter. Taro's mother works her own ruse, however, and in the end Taro is caught in his own tricks.

Teaching Feature 4.1: A Cross-Cultural Study of Folktale Types is the first of two features in this

Beverley Naidoo's *Who is King?* retells tales of the native animals of Africa amid Piet Grobler's whimsical ink line drawings of flora and fauna cheerfully tinted with blots of watercolor. From *Who is King? And Other Tales from Africa* by Beverley Naidoo, illustrated by Piet Grabler, published by Frances Lincoln Ltd, copyright ©2015. Reproduced by permission of Frances Lincoln Ltd, an imprint of The Quarto Group.

A Cross-Cultural Study of Folktale Types

Tale (Author)	Culture or Country/Place of Origin
Cumulative Tales: An increasing repetition of the details builds up to a quick climax.	
The Bossy Gallito (Gonzalez)	Cuba
The Cazuela That the Farm Maiden Stirred (Vamos)	Spain
Chicken Little (Kellogg)	England
Farmer Falgu Goes on a Trip (Soundar)	India
One Fine Day (Hogrogian)	Armenia
This Is the House That Jack Built (Taback)	United States
What About Me? (Young)	Sufi (Middle East)
Pourquoi Tales: Folktales that explain why ("pourquoi" in French) certain animal traits or characteristics or human customs have developed.	
The Golden Flower (Jaffe)	Puerto Rico
How Chipmunk Got His Stripes (Bruchac and Bruchac)	Native American
Pine and the Winter Sparrow (Lumbard)	Cherokee
The Princess and the Warrior (Tonatiuh)	Mexico
Tiger and Turtle (Rumford)	India
Tuko and the Birds (Climo)	Philippines
Why the Sun and the Moon Live in the Sky (Dayrell)	Africa
Beast Tales: Tales in which animals act and talk like human beings.	
The Bremen Town Musicians (Orgel); The Musicians of Bremen (Puttapipat)	Germany
Chukfi Rabbit's Big, Bad Bellyache: A Trickster Tale (Rodgers)	Choctaw
Deep in the Woods (Corr)	Russia
Give Up, Gecko! (MacDonald)	Uganda
King Pom and the Fox (Souhami)	Japan
Mabela the Clever (MacDonald)	Africa
Wonder Tales: Longer and more complicated tales about magic and the supernatural, often called fairy tales.	
The Bearskinner (Schlitz)	Germany
Baba Yaga (Leysen)	Russia
Beauty and the Beast: A Retelling (Lee)	France/West Africa
The Crane Girl (Manley)	Japan
The Great Smelly, Slobbery, Small-Tooth Dog (MacDonald)	Great Britain

(continued)

teaching feature 4.1

Tale (Author)	Culture or Country/Place of Origin
Jack and the Beanstalk (Crews)	England/New York City
Realistic Tales: Stories from the oral tradition that involve no magic.	
The Boy of the Three-Year Nap (Snyder)	Japan
Dick Whittington and His Cat (Brown, in Cresswell's *A Treasury of Fairy Tales*)	England
The Empty Pot (Demi)	China
"Gelert the Hound" in *A Year Full of Stories* (McAllister)	Wales
My Grandfather's Coat (Aylesworth)	Yiddish/United States

chapter that group folktales from various countries in specific ways to help teachers more easily plan curricula. This box groups together titles that tell particular tale types.

Evaluating Folktales

Because folktales have been told and retold from generation to generation within a particular culture, we may ask how they reflect the place of their origin and its oral tradition. An authentic tale from the Ashanti people will include references to the flora and fauna of southern Ghana and to the people's food, huts, customs, foibles, and beliefs. It will sound like it is being *told,* making a good read aloud. Although folktales have many elements in common, it would be difficult to confuse a folktale from Japan with a folktale from the fjords of Norway. What are some of the things to look for when reading folktales? What are the characteristics common to all folktales? The box **Guidelines: Evaluating Traditional Literature** summarizes the criteria to consider when evaluating this genre for children.

Characteristics of Folktales

Plot Structures Of the folktales best known in children's literature, even the longer stories are usually simple and direct. A series of episodes maintains a quick flow of action. If it is a "wise beast/foolish beast" story, the characters are quickly delineated, the action shows the inevitable conflict and resolution, and the ending is usually brief. If the tale is a romance, the hero or heroine sets forth on a journey, often helps the poor on the way, frequently receives magical power, overcomes obstacles, and returns to safety. The plot that involves a weak or innocent child going forth to meet the monsters of the world is another form of the "journey-novel." In the Germanic *Hansel and Gretel,* the children go out into a dark world and meet the witch, but goodness and purity triumph.

Evaluating Traditional Literature

Go to Connect® to access study resources, practice quizzes, and additional materials.

Consider the following when evaluating folktales for children:

- Is there some mention or citation of the original source in appropriate cultural specificity?
- Is the plot simple and direct?
- Is the language lively and engaging and in keeping with the oral tradition?

- Does a theme emerge from the telling of the tale? If so, what is the story's message or moral?
- Do illustrations add to and extend the story? Are illustrations and details true to the culture represented?
- Does the story represent cultural norms, or is it rewritten to white Anglo-European conventions?

Almost all folktale plots are success stories of one kind or another (unlike many myths, in which characters meet a sad end through their own human failings).

Repetition is a basic element in many folktale plots, and "three" is often the magic number. There are three little pigs whose three houses face the puffing of the wolf. In longer versions of the story, the wolf gives three challenges to the pig in the brick house—to get turnips, to get apples, and to go to the fair. Each of the three tasks becomes increasingly more difficult, and the intensity of the wonders becomes progressively more marvelous. This repetition satisfies listeners or readers with its orderliness.

Time and place are established quickly in the folktale. Virginia Hamilton opens *The Girl Who Spun Gold* with "There be this tale told about a tiny fellow who could hide in a foot of shade amid old trees." Time is always past and frequently described by such conventions as "Once upon a time" or "In olden times when wishing still helped." The setting of the folktale is typically generic: in some faraway land, in a cottage in the woods, or in a beautiful palace.

The conclusion of the story follows the climax very quickly and includes few details. In the German bearskin tale, such as Laura Amy Schlitz's *The Bearskinner,* a poor soldier makes a pact with the devil. He must wear a hideous bearskin for seven years in return for all the money he wants. A gambler's middle daughter promises to wait for the loathsome Bearskinner in return for settling her father's debts. When the soldier returns, rid of his bearskin and looking young and handsome, the middle daughter recognizes him by his kind eyes. The story ends as follows:

> So the middle daughter married the Bearskinner. The love between them lasted a lifetime and so did the soldier's fortune. He always had more than enough and always shared with people who had nothing.
>
> And never again did he bargain with the devil. (unpaged)[1]

Even this is a long ending compared with the traditional line, "And so they were married and lived happily ever after."

The structure of the folktale, with its quick introduction, economy of incident, and logical and brief conclusion, maintains interest through suspense and repetition. Because the storyteller has to keep the attention of the audience, each episode must contribute directly to the theme of the story. Written versions, then, should follow the oral tradition, adding little description and avoiding lengthy asides or admonitions.

Characterization Characters in folktales are shown in flat dimensions, symbolic of the completely good or entirely evil. Character development is seldom depicted. The beautiful girl is usually virtuous, humble, patient, and loving. Stepmothers are ugly, cross, and mean. The hero is strong, virile, brave, kind, and sympathetic. The poor are often kind, generous, and long-suffering; the rich are imperious, hard-hearted, and often conniving, if not actually dishonest. Physical characteristics may be described briefly, but readers can rely on accompanying pictures or form their own as they read.

Qualities of character or special strengths or weaknesses of the characters are revealed quickly because this factor will be the cause of conflict or lead to resolution of the plot. The heroine in *Clever Beatrice* by Margaret Willey is established in a few phrases:

> "Sure, she was little but Beatrice loved riddles and tricks and she could think fast on her feet. Sharp as a tack," said her mother.[2]

Seeing folktale characters as symbols of good, evil, power, trickery, wisdom, and other traits, children begin to understand the basis of literature that distills and exemplifies the essences of human experience.

Style Folktales offer children many opportunities to hear rich qualitative language and a wide variety of language patterns. Story introductions may range from the familiar "Once upon a time" to the Persian "There was a time and there wasn't a time"; and then there are Ashanti tales that start "We do not mean, we do not really mean that what we are going to say is true."

The introductions and language of the folktale should maintain the feel of the culture of origin but still be understood by its present audience. Some folktales include proverbs of the country. Drawing on this convention of folklore, Jonathan Emmett closes his original story in *Prince Ribbit*, "just because it's in a book doesn't mean it's true!"

Frequently storytellers imitate the sounds of the story. In Verna Aardema's retelling of a West African tale in *Why Mosquitoes Buzz in People's Ears*, a python slithers into a rabbit's hole *wasawusu, wasawusu, wasawusu*, and the terrified rabbit scurries away *krik, krik, krik*. Chitra Soundar and Kanika Nair's *Farmer Falgu Goes on a Trip* brings the bothersome noises to life with the "tap-tap-tap," "phee-phee," "dum-dum," and "trot-trot" of the dancers, snake charmer, drums, and oxen. These onomatopoeic words help listeners hear the story and are wonderful embellishments for those who perform stories.

When the tales are written as though the storyteller is speaking directly to the reader, the oral tradition is more clearly communicated. Rachel Qitsualik draws readers into her frightening Inuit folktales in *The Shadows that Rush Past*:

> Imagine an old woman. Then, in your mind's eye, make her gigantic, maybe twice the size of a large grownup. Make her filthy too, with leathery skin and big, greedy, fishlike eyes. Later, I'll tell you what is under her parka, though I don't think you'll like it. (p. 4)

Dialect enhances a story, but it can be difficult to read. A reader will need to practice reading or telling a story with dialect, but it is worth the effort if it is done well. Julius Lester, in his retellings of the Uncle Remus stories collected by Joel Chandler Harris, tried to do what Harris had done: namely, to write tales "so that the reader (listener) would feel as if he or she were being called into a relationship of warmth and intimacy with another human body."[3] His contemporary storyteller communicates through asides, imagery, and allusions. For instance, in "Brer Rabbit Gets Even," in Julius Lester's *The Tales of Uncle Remus,* Brer Rabbit decides to visit with Miz Meadows and the girls:

> Don't come asking me who Miz Meadows and her girls were. I don't know, but then again, ain't no reason I got to know. Miz Meadows and the girls were in the tale when it was handed to me, and they gon' be in it when I hand it to you. And that's the way the rain falls on that one. . . . (p. 16)

The major criteria for style in the written folktale, then, are that it maintain the atmosphere of the country and culture from which it originated and that it sound like a tale *told* by a storyteller.

Themes The basic purpose of the folktale is to tell an entertaining story, yet these stories do include important themes. Some tales might be merely humorous accounts of foolish people who are so ridiculous that the listeners see their own foolish ways exaggerated in them. Many of the stories once provided an outlet for feelings against the kings and nobles who oppressed the poor. Cultural values are expressed in folklore. Humility, kindness, patience, sympathy, hard work, and courage are invariably rewarded. These rewards reflect the goals of people—long life, a good spouse, beautiful homes, fine clothing, plenty of food, and freedom from fear of the ogre or giant. Sometimes these themes are stated explicitly at the end of the book as in Ed Young's *What About Me?* In this story, a young boy approaches the Grand Master to ask for knowledge. He is sent out to get a small carpet for the Master's work. This, of course, is not as simple a task as it sounds. After many arduous trials, the boy finds that the knowledge he sought was already his. The Grand Master cautions, "Some of the most precious gifts that we receive are those we receive when we are giving," and "Often, knowledge comes to us when we least expect it." (p. 32). In Kim Jacob's *Princess Sophie and the Six Swans,* Sophie's stepmother turns her brothers into swans as a repayment for speaking ill of her to their father. To break the spell, the heroine must spin six shirts from thorny thistle without speaking a single word, discovering "what determination and love can do" and "the vast power of words" (p. 38).

Many folktales feature the small and powerless achieving good ends by perseverance and patience. In Gail Haley's African tale *A Story, A Story,* Anansi the spider man wins stories for his people by outsmarting a leopard, the hornets, and a fairy and presenting them all to the Sky God. Characters such

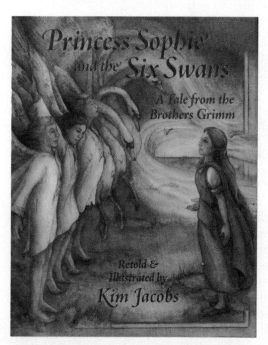

In *Princess Sophie and the Six Swans* retold by Kim Jacobs, a girl makes sacrifices to free her brothers from a curse. Jacobs, Kim, *Princess Sophie and the Six Swans: A Tale from the Brothers Grimm.* Bloomington, IN: Wisdom Tales Press, 2017, Cover. Copyright ©2017 by Wisdom Tales Press. All rights reserved. Used with permission.

as Blanche in Robert D. San Souci's *The Talking Eggs* and Manyana in John Steptoe's *Mufaro's Beautiful Daughters* have good luck when they are kind to objects and animals. In the case of the latter, the sister who takes time to stop and help people is the one who wins the prince's love. The theme of rewarding a generous and willing person and punishing a greedy and disobedient one seems to be universal.

Feminists have expressed concern that folktale themes most often favor courageous, independent boy adventurers and leave girl characters languishing at home. Though it is true that it is easier to find tales that feature plucky boys, there are folktales that portray resourceful, courageous, clever, and independent girls (even if still within a historical, sexist milieu). In the Grimm brothers' *Princess Furball,* the heroine doesn't need a fairy godmother; she wins a prince because of her own cleverness.

Parents, teachers, and some psychologists have expressed concern about themes of cruelty and horror in folktales. "Little Red Riding Hood," for example, has been rewritten so that the wolf eats neither the grandmother nor the heroine. Goals are not accomplished easily in folktales; they frequently require sacrifice. But usually harsh acts occur very quickly with no sense of pain and little description. In the Grimm brothers' *Snow White and the Seven Dwarfs,* illustrated by Nancy Ekholm Burkert, Snow White's stepmother dances to death in her iron shoes but we do not see this action, only the empty shoes at the top of a staircase. Children accept these stories as they are—symbolic interpretations of life in an imaginary land of another time.

Motifs Folklorists analyze folktales according to motifs or patterns, numbering each tale and labeling its episodes. *Motif* has been defined as the smallest part of a tale that can exist independently.[4] Motifs can be seen in the recurring parade of characters in folktales—the younger brother, the wicked stepmother, the abused child, the clever trickster—or in supernatural beings like the fairy godmother, the evil witch, and the terrifying giant. The use of magical objects (e.g., a slipper, a doll, a ring, a tablecloth) is another pattern found in many folktales. Stories of enchantment, long sleeps, or marvelous transformations are typical motifs. Some motifs have been repeated so frequently that they have been identified as a type of folk story. Thus, we have beast tales about talking animals and wonder tales about supernatural beings.

Even the story plots have recurring patterns—three tasks to be performed, three wishes that are granted, three trials to be endured. A simple tale will have several motifs; a complex one will have many. Recognizing some of the most common motifs in folklore will help a teacher to suggest points of comparison and contrast in a cross-cultural approach to folk literature.

Versions and Variants Editions of folktales can be considered as either versions or a variant of the traditional tale. When the text and plot of a folktale are close to the preserved records of the traditional oral telling but reinterpreted visually by an illustrator, we refer to it as a *version* of a folktale. These types of tales typically attribute the text to a specific historic collector. For example, *The Frog Prince* is attributed as "a story by the Brothers Grimm, retold by Joy Cowley." Rachel Isadora has illustrated several tales from the Brothers Grimm, including *Hansel and Gretel* and *Rapunzel*. In these tales, Isadora preserves much of the text as recorded by the Grimm Brothers in 1812 but adds a lively African locale in her striking patterned collages.

In contrast to folktale versions, folktale *variants* do not preserve the text and exact plot of a tale but share many characters, similarities, or motifs in common. These variations

Illustrator Rachel Isadora has reinterpreted the traditional Grimm brothers' story of *Rapunzel* with an African setting. Isadora, Rachel. *Rapunzel.* New York, NY: G.P. Putnam's Sons Books for Young Readers, 2008, Cover. Copyright ©2008 by G.P. Putnam's Sons Books for Young Readers. All rights reserved. Used with permission.

represent the differences through translation, modification, and personalization as a tale is told and retold. For example, Eric Kimmel and illustrator Martha Aviles set the Grimm brothers' story of "The Fisherman and His Wife" in the Aztec culture in *The Fisherman and the Turtle*. To adapt the tale to its new setting, Kimmel casts Opochtli, the god of the sea, as a turtle instead of a fish and the greedy wife finds her end as a stone statue among the portrayals of the Aztec gods.

As one of the most reinterpreted tales, the "Cinderella" story illustrates differences in theme and motif that can be found in cultures from around the world. Scholars have found variants of this story in ancient Egypt, in ninth-century China, and in tenth-century Iceland. Cinderella receives her magical gifts in many different ways. In the French and most familiar tale (see Charles Perrault's *Cinderella* illustrated by Marcia Brown), a fairy godmother gives them to her; in the Grimms' recording, a dove appears on the tree that grew from the tears she had shed on her mother's grave; in Ai-Ling Louie's Chinese variant titled *Yeh-Shen,* magical fish bones bestow gifts on her. Cinderella attends three balls in some stories, and her treatment of the stepsisters varies from blinding them to inviting them to live at the palace. Many of these variants have been creatively combined into the remarkable story *Glass Slipper, Gold Sandal* by Paul Fleischman.

Another way to consider folk literature is by comparing the origin of the tale to its depiction. Although some stories seem to have developed independently in different cultures, retellings of tales may set them in a separate culture. The origins of the tale recounted in *Beauty and the Beast: A Retelling* seem to primarily originate from France before proliferating across Europe. When H. Chuku Lee sets the tale in West Africa, the two cultures become blended together. Consequently, children have the opportunity to see people who aren't white given revered roles. Unfortunately, these most excellent tales may also perpetuate Eurocentrism when they draw predominantly on tales from Europe. Tales depicted in their native setting and tales adopted into other locales both have a place in the classroom. Teachers should look critically at the traditional literature they are introducing and attempt to present a selection that respects the wide varieties of peoples, cultures, and tales from across the world.

Studying Folktales in the Classroom Knowledge of the variants of a tale, common motifs, and common types of folktales enables teachers to help children see similar elements in folktales across cultures. Knowledge of the folklore of a particular country or cultural group aids in identifying the uniqueness and individuality of that group. Both approaches to a study of folklore seem meaningful.

Although realistic fiction is typically used more commonly today to learn about non-dominant cultures both near and far, folklore embodies the history of many peoples.

In-depth studies of the folktales of diverse places may provide insights into the traditional beliefs of these peoples, their values, their jokes, and their histories. Teachers should be aware that modern people cannot be fully represented by their traditional literature and should supplement the curriculum with other sources of information. At the same time, a cross-cultural study of folk literature by types, motifs, and variants can address some of the universal qualities of humankind. **Teaching Feature 4.2: A Cross-Cultural Study of Folktale Motifs and Variants** can help you organize tales by variants for classroom presentation.

teaching **feature 4.2**

A Cross-Cultural Study of Folktale Motifs and Variants

Theme (Author)	Culture or Country/Place of Origin
Cinderella	
Adelita (dePaola)	Mexico
Domítíla (Coburn)	Mexico
Cendrillon (San Souci)	Caribbean
Cinderella (Perrault)	France
The Egyptian Cinderella (Climo)	Egypt
Fair, Brown, & Trembling (Daly)	Ireland
The Gift of the Crocodile (Sierra)	Indonesia
The Golden Sandal (Hickox)	Middle East
The Korean Cinderella (Climo)	Korea
Little Gold Star (San Souci)	Spanish American
Princess Furball (Grimm brothers, Huck)	Germany
The Rough-Face Girl (Martin)	Native American
Yeh-Shen (Louie)	China
Magical Objects or Gifts	
Gabriel's Horn (Kimmel)	Jewish
"The Gifts of the North Wind" in *A Year Full of Stories* (McAllister)	Norway
The Magic Gourd (Diakité)	Mali
The Magic Porridge Pot (Galdone)	Germany
The Runaway Wok (Compestine)	China
"Sweet Porridge" in Fairy Tale Comics (Duffy)	Germany
Tunjur! Tunjur! Tunjur! (MacDonald)	Palestine

(continued)

teaching feature 4.2

Theme (Author)	Culture or Country/Place of Origin
Generous Person/Greedy Person	
"The Fairies" in *The World Treasury of Fairy Tales & Folklore* (Gray)	France
The Goat-Faced Girl (Sharpe)	Italy
"Mbango and the Whirlpool" in *Girls and Goddesses* (Don)	Cameroon
Mufaro's Beautiful Daughters (Steptoe)	Africa (Zimbabwe)
The Talking Eggs (San Souci)	African American
Toads and Diamonds (Huck, in Maccarone's *Princess Tales Around the World*)	France
The Wishing Foxes (MacDonald)	Appalachia
Helpful Companions	
Anansi the Spider (McDermott)	West Africa
The Fool of the World and the Flying Ship (Ransome)	Russia
"Kari Woodenskirt" in *D'Aulaires' Book of Norwegian Folktales*	Norway
The Monkey King (Seow)	China
"The Poor Miller's Boy and the Little Cat" in *Tales From the Brothers Grimm* (Zwerger)	Germany
The Shark King (Johnson)	Hawaii
Naming	
Ananse and the Lizard (Cummings)	West Africa
Duffy and the Devil (Zemach)	England
The Girl Who Spun Gold (Hamilton)	West Indies
Nelly May Has Her Say (DeFelice)	England
Rumpelstiltskin (Grimm brothers)	Germany

Fables

In Western culture, fables are most commonly associated with Aesop, a Greek slave who is supposed to have been born in Asia Minor about 600 B.C. Some scholars doubt his actual existence and believe that his works were the product of several storytellers. We know that some of the fables he is said to have told appeared in Greek literature two centuries before Aesop's birth and in India and Egypt before that.

Beyond Aesop, the best-known sources for fables have come from India, including the Jataka tales—animal stories that told of the previous births of the Buddha—and the

Panchatantra, a Hindi collection of interrelated animal tales written within the frame story of educating three ignorant princes. These stories, longer than Aesop's fables, have moralistic verses interspersed throughout. Fables also appear in the collections of oral tales recorded by Hsieh-yü in Chinese, Sulkhan-Saba Orbeliani in Georgian, Jean de La Fontaine in French, Ignacy Krasicki in Polish, and James Thurber in English as well as in *One Thousand and One Nights in Arabic.*

Characteristics of Fables

Fables are traditionally brief, didactic tales in which animals, or occasionally the elements, speak as human beings. Examples of these might be the well-known race between the tortoise and the hare (Pinkney) or the contest between the north wind and the sun (in *Fable Comics* by Duffy). Humans do appear in a few fables, such as *The Boy Who Cried Wolf* (Hennessy). The characters are impersonal, with no name other than "fox," "rabbit," or "cow." They do not have the lively personalities of Anansi the spider, Brer Rabbit, or Raven the trickster of folktale fame. The animals merely represent aspects of human nature—the lion stands for kingliness, the fox for cunning, the sheep for innocence and simplicity, and so on. Fables seldom have more than three characters, and the plots are usually based on a single incident. In comparison to beast tales, fables are shorter, simpler, have the most archetypal characters, and highlight obvious moral and didactic intent. Fables were primarily meant to instruct; therefore, all of them contain either an implicit or an explicit moral.

Although they extend beyond short animal tales, longer instructional tales may also be considered as fables. Cautionary tales, such as the yu-yen from China, have been told all around the world. Dating as far back as the third century BCE or more, Shiho Nunes retells nineteen short but keen tales in *Chinese Fables,* with traditional illustrations in hazy yellow tones by Lak-Khee Tay-Audouard. The parables of Jesus from the Christian Bible, such as the stories of the prodigal son, about a wayward child returning to his family, and the Good Samaritan, who is the only traveler to offer aid despite being a traditional enemy, are some of the best-known traditional tales. Collections of parables, such as those by Mary Hoffman and Tommie dePaola, are often thought-provoking, asking readers to consider different viewpoints in order to fully explore the lesson. Retelling a Jewish parable filled with humor, *The Rooster Prince of Breslov,* Ann Redisch Stampler's prince grows into a wise ruler when an old man cultivates his thoughtfulness.

Because of their brevity, fables appear to be simple. However, they convey an abstract idea in relatively few words, and for that very reason, they are highly complex. Younger children might appreciate some fables, but they are not usually able to extract a moral spontaneously until about second or third grade. There are many fine collections of fables to share with children.

Fables in Children's Literature

Aesop's fables are popular material for authors and illustrators. Jerry Pinkney applies his characteristic style to *Aesop's Fables* with grand results. His exquisite watercolor illustrations for sixty of Aesop's best tales make this an essential collection for classrooms and libraries. The book is meticulously designed, and Pinkney's multicultural interpretation of human and animal characters is highly original. Beverley Naidoo's story collection, *Aesop's Fables,* portrays the classic tales in an African setting. Piet Grober's vivid illustrations complement Naidoo's wise and witty retellings. In *Fox Tails: Four Fables from Aesop,* Amy Lowry weaves four fables about a tricky fox into a single story.

Beyond Aesop, many excellent collections portray tales of other origins. Mark McGinnis's treasury of Jataka Tales, *When the Buddha Was an Elephant,* features striking full-page illustrations with bold white outlines of the realistically rendered animals. *The Pandas and their Chopsticks* by Demi draws on Chinese and other Asian sources, including the Jataka tales for both story and calligraphy-inspired artwork. Focusing on fables from Islamic culture, Micha Archer brings the merry but shrewd character of Mulla Nasruddin to life with roughly shaped collages of lively patterned and painted papers in Shahrukh Husain's *The Wise Fool.* Marcia Williams sets fables from India into panels with comic asides in speech bubbles and exaggerated body language that at once feels native to storytelling traditions and freshly invigorating in *The Elephant's Friends.* With a little bit from everywhere, the *Lion Classic Wisdom Stories* by Mary Joslin collects twenty-eight insightful tales from around the world.

Other illustrators have chosen single tales for interpretation. Jerry Pinkney highlights the passage of time in Aesop's *The Grasshopper and the Ants* with shifting color palettes that float over his lyrical pencil sketches. The smoky speckles of John Burningham's mixed media illustration over dense, oily pastels showcase the bulk of the West African creatures in *Tug of War.* These tales are available from a wide variety of cultures. In this way, children become familiar with the spare language, the conventional characters, and the explicit or implied morals of fables.

Older children might enjoy comparing treatments of several of these fables, such as the two versions of *The Lion & the Mouse* in the vignette at the beginning of Chapter 3. Ed Young's classic version of *Seven Blind Mice* showcases vividly colored collages on a bold black background. In contrast, Jude Daly uses the soft warm browns of southern Africa and the smooth textures of acrylics to take a more gentle approach in *Six Blind Mice and an Elephant.* After such comparisons, discussions, and readings, children would then be well prepared to write their own fables and variations.

Epic and Legendary Heroes

An epic is a long narrative or a cycle of stories that cluster around the actions of a single hero. Epics often grew out of myths or along with them, as the gods play active roles in earlier epics like the *Iliad* and the *Odyssey.* Moreover, many heroes, such as Gilgamesh, Sun Wukong, and Quetzalcoatl, are gods or demigods. In some tales, the center of action shifts from the gods to human heroes. For examples, in "Robin Hood," the focus is completely on the daring adventures of one person.

The epic hero is a cultural or national hero embodying all the ideal characteristics of greatness in his or her time. King Arthur and Robin Hood appealed to the English love of justice and freedom: King Arthur and his knights represented the code of chivalry; Robin Hood was the champion of the commoner—the prototype of the "good outlaw." Many of these epics continue to shape literature today by providing archetypes of characters and plots[5] while the themes of the stories can be molded and remolded to fit the time of the retelling.

The Epic of Gilgamesh, composed more than four thousand years ago in Mesopotamia, is one of the oldest hero stories and perhaps the first great work of literature. It is a tale about the power and importance of human compassion, centering on an oppressive ruler. In order to balance his power, the gods create Enkidu, who is as wild and innocent as

Gilgamesh is cultured and cruel. Found on clay tablets dating to about 650 BCE, the epic poem known today assembles several earlier myths. Ludmila Zeman has retold and illustrated three episodes of the Gilgamesh epic in a highly readable trio of picturebooks beginning with *Gilgamesh the King*. In the third book, *The Last Quest of Gilgamesh*, Gilgamesh encounters a story of a great flood (similar to those found in many other cultures including the Genesis flood narrative) in his search for immortality after Enkidu's death. Zeman's majestic illustrations, done in mixed media and incorporating motifs from Mesopotamian art, have a wonderful sense of timelessness. Perfect for middle school, Geraldine McCaughrean's superb retelling of the epic in *Gilgamesh the Hero* provides more details while maintaining the themes of friendship and mortality.

The most popular hero of Western cultures must be the Greek hero Odysseus (known to the Romans as Ulysses). Surviving through wit rather than strength, Odysseus and his wife, Penelope, represent the Greek ideals of intelligence, persistence, and resourcefulness. Mary Pope Osborne's multipart set, *Tales from the Odyssey,* provides a good introduction for upper elementary school, while Rosemary Sutcliff's *The Wanderings of Odysseus,* with tender but historically inspired paintings by Alan Lee, addresses middle-grade readers. Although older, Padraic Colum's *The Children's Homer* is still considered to be one of the best at keeping the essence of the traditional poem and is available in a number of editions. Gareth Hinds paints Odysseus's world in gritty realism using lush watercolors and pastels in his somber graphic novel retelling, *The Odyssey*.

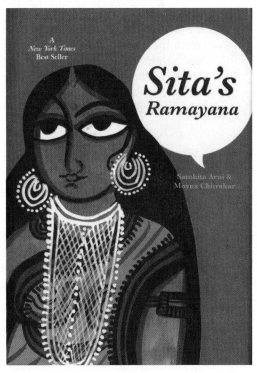

Also worthy of note, Neil Packer's rich paintings ornament Gillian Cross's vivid but accessible text in *The Odyssey*. As shown in all these fine editions, the wanderings of Odysseus are a mainstay of Western literature, even providing a template for many contemporary journey stories.

The Ramayana is the great epic tale of India that tells how the noble Rama, his devoted brother, and his beautiful, virtuous wife, Sita, manage to defeat the evil demon Ravana. Composed by the sage Valmiki during the fourth century BCE, the Ramayana represented some 24,000 couplets that were memorized and repeated. It constitutes part of the gospel of Hindu scripture, for Rama and his wife are held as the ideal man and woman. Rama also is believed to be an incarnation of the god Vishnu, who has come to the earth in human form. In *Sita's Ramayana,* Samhita Arni's version of the epic poem is told from Sita's perspective in a graphic novel format for older readers. *The Story of Divaali,* retold by Jatinder Verma, frames Rama and Sita's story for younger audiences in an informative, but lengthy, text.

Sun Wukong, also known as the Monkey King, is one of the main characters in the sixteenth-century Chinese epic, *Journey to the West*. A trickster with immense strength, speed, and energy, his tales will appeal to a wide range of ages. Younger readers will

Sita's Ramayana by Samhita Arni retells the classic Indian tale from Sita's point of view in a graphic novel format. Cover to *Sita's Ramayana* by Samhita Arni and Moyna Chitrakar, ©Tara Books Pvt Ltd., Chennai, India www.tarabooks.com.

enjoy *Monkey King* by Ed Young or even *The Monkey King* by David Seow. Written for middle schoolers, Wei Dong Chen's series of graphica begins with *Birth of the Stone Monkey*. Readers may also recognize Sun Wukong from Gene Yang's award-winning graphic novel *American Born Chinese* that weaves together legend and the struggles with racial stereotypes of contemporary realistic fiction.

Famed from an Anglo-Saxon poem, the hero Beowulf battles three terrible foes to save the Scandinavian Kingdom of Heorot in several notable editions for children. In *Beowulf: A Hero's Tale Retold,* James Rumford maintains a sense of authentic language, using only words that can be traced back to Old English. Rumford's exceptional illustrations frame the dark scratchy line drawings with shadowy tentacles that seem to advance as the grim story progresses. Nicky Raven's *Beowulf: A Tale of Blood, Heat, and Ashes* provides a lengthier version for older readers cloaked in literal darkness and looming landscapes by John Howe.

As already seen in the descriptions of the great heroes, the epic heroic tradition is almost exclusively masculine. Female characters, both god and mortal, like Athena and Penelope in the Odyssey, take active roles in many of these stories but never that of the main character. Heroines such as Amaterasu the Japanese Shinto Sun goddess, Penthesilea the Amazon Queen, the French saint Joan of Arc, and Hua Mulan from China feature in ancient epics in their own right but are rarely seen in children's literature today.

Epic hero stories from cultures across the world abound. *Ancient & Epic Tales: From Around the World* by Heather Forest collects a global overview of vignettes from a variety of multicultural epics appropriate for elementary school. Some of these lesser known epics including those featuring heroines may be better known locally, but their wonder and gentle lessons would soon make them beloved of children all around the globe. These epics can be considered to express the highest moral values of a society. Knowledge of an epic invites children into that particular culture; more importantly, it provides them with models of greatness through the ages.

Myths and Sacred Stories

Myth can be defined as a story that explains natural, historical, or social phenomenon, including how the world began, how nature works, and systems of values. These stories have been considered as having historically happened and typically involve supernatural beings who are worshiped as gods. These gods frequently took the forms of men, women, and animals, but they were immortal and possessed supernatural powers.

Myths deal with relationships, especially those among the gods, with other spiritual beings, and with humans. They also address how people accept or fulfill their destiny, and how people struggle with good and evil forces, both within and outside themselves. The myths are good stories, too, for they contain action, suspense, and basic conflicts. Usually, each story is short and can be enjoyed by itself, without deep knowledge of the general mythos in which it resides.

Although the word "myth" can also mean fictitious or false belief, it is important to remember that these stories are still believed in many cultures today. Our use of the term *mythology* to include many religious and spiritual tales follows academic practice and provides a useful framework for examining culturally significant literature.

All children should know the spiritual and religious beliefs that have shaped the world in which they live. This religious heritage is often conveyed in the form of stories. Many

Jonah's Whale by Eileen Spinelli is a retelling of Jonah and the whale, a story taken from the Old Testament. Illustration from *Jonah's Whale* written by Eileen Spinelli and illustrated by Giuliano Ferri. Used by permission of Wm. B. Eerdmans Publishing.

peoples around the world have creation stories, and there are numerous accounts of a great flood. Many Native American stories reflect the religious beliefs of their tellers. The Jataka and Panchatantra stories come from Buddhist traditions and the Ramayana from Hindu scriptures. Other sources of story such as the Muslim Qur'an, the Christian Bible, and the Jewish Tanakh also have an important and rightful place in any comprehensive discussion of traditional literature. These books are a written record of people's continuing search to understand themselves and their relationships with others and their creator. It makes little sense to tell children the stories of Jack the Giant Killer, Odysseus, or Utnapishtim and then deny them the stories about Adam and Eve, Abraham (Ibrahim), Muhammad, Moses (Musa), Mary (Maryam), Jesus (Isa), and Noah (Nuh).

The legal division between church and state seems to prohibit religious instruction in public schools and, indeed, we do not propose that teachers advocate for or instruct in the practice of religious customs. The 1963 Supreme Court decision in *Abington School District v. Schempp* asserted that "religious exercises" in public schools violated the First Amendment, but also encouraged study of the religious texts as literature. Recent research furthermore recommends including learning about religion in public education as an important part of cultural studies.

Creation Myths

Every culture may have its own story about how the world began, how people were made, and how the sun and the moon got into the sky. These are called creation myths, or origin myths; they give an explanation for the beginnings of things. Virginia Hamilton chose creation stories from around the world for her collection *In the Beginning*. Her introduction explains:

> These myths from around the world were created by people who sensed the wonder and glory of the universe. Lonely as they were, by themselves, early people looked inside themselves and expressed a longing to discover, to explain who they were, why they were, and from what and where they came. (p. xi)

Barry Moser's watercolor portraits and representations are mysterious and dramatic accompaniments to these tales. An Inuit story tells how Raven the Creator made a pea pod from which humans sprang. A Chinese story explains how Phan Ku burst from a cosmic egg to create the world. A Maidu legend from California, "Turtle Dives to the Bottom of the Sea," begins with a sea turtle that dives underwater to bring up enough earth to make dry land. *Creation* by Cynthia Rylant is a poetically simple rendition of the story from the Christian and Hebrew bibles set to sweeping brushstrokes of acrylic paint. Going a step further, Paul Fleischman's *First Light, First Life* weaves together elements of creation stories from around the world, celebrating both the variety and commonalities between different cultures.

Nature Myths

Nature myths include stories that explain seasonal changes, animal characteristics, earth formations, constellations, and the movements of the sun and earth. They can be found in books like *Ganesha: The Curse on the Moon* by Sourav Dutta and *Persephone* by Sally Pomme Clayton. In *Ganesha,* the phases of the moon are created when the Hindu god Ganesha takes away the Moon's light for making fun of him. Fortunately, Ganesha's father, Shiva, mitigated the punishment to a monthly cycle. In *Persephone,* Demeter, the Greek goddess of agriculture, curses the earth with the cold of winter when her daughter, Persephone, is carried off to the underworld as Hades's queen. Zeus allows Persephone to return to her mother for nine months of the year, after which Demeter's grief once again brings winter's cold. Many of these types of myths have been previously discussed in the section "Pourquoi Tales," as the two categories share many tales in common.

Greek Mythology

Stories from Greek mythology are often the easiest to find in Anglo-American children's literature. Sparked by the discoveries of ruins at Crete and Mycenae, the historical interest in this culture has inspired documentation and proliferation of the many stories of gods and goddesses, heroes, and monsters revered by the ancient Greeks (approximately 800 BCE to 500 CE). As their culture became more sophisticated and complex, so too did their stories of the gods. These personified gods could do anything that humans could do, but on a much mightier scale. The gods, although immortal, freely entered into the lives of mortals, helping or hindering them, depending on their particular moods. Many of the myths are concerned with the gods' conflicts and loves, often as they inadvertently caused troubles for humans.

Children will find that many of the same elements of folktales are present in the many excellent editions of Greek myths. With bold stone lithograph illustration, the classic *D'Aulaires' Book of Greek Myths* presents a well-woven selection of tales ranging from the birth of Cronus's children to the stories of the mortal descendants of Zeus. Caldecott Medal winner Mordicai Gerstein focuses on just one of the Greek gods in *I Am Pan!* with energetic pencil sketches roughly plastered with watercolor in a comic book style that matches Pan's wild antics. Professional folklorist Lise Lunge-Larsen's *Gifts from the Gods: Ancient Words and Wisdom from Greek and Roman Mythology* chronicles how many of the words we use today have their origin in characters from Greek and Roman myths, such as "Achilles' heel," with action-oriented watercolor and pencil illustrations by Gareth Hinds. Another unique collection, *Echo Echo* by Marilyn Singer, combines reverso poems (in which the second half of the poem reverses the first with different punctuation in order to change the meaning) of twelve tales, with the richly stylized acrylics of Josée Masse.

Greek mythology also features some glorious hero myths that do not attempt to explain anything at all. Similar in many ways to wonder tales, the hero is given certain tasks or, in the case of Heracles, labors to accomplish. These tales differ from heroic epics in that their stories are shorter and are typically limited to the quest at hand beyond some basic backstory. Hero myths can be found in *Strong Stuff: Herakles and His Labors* by John Harris, *Jason and the Argonauts* by Robert Byrd, and *The Fate of Achilles* by Bimba Landmann, a heavily illustrated novel for older readers.

Myths from Around the World

Beyond Greco-Roman mythology, Norse tales with their giants and dwarfs, eight-legged horses and vicious wolves, magic hammers, and rings are also quite popular in English language publications for children. Primarily these are bold, powerful stories of the relationships among the gods and their battles against the evil frost giants. Norse myths have particularly influenced European literary culture. Today, references can still be found in fantasy, superhero comics, role-playing games, webcomics, and manga. *D'Aulaires' Book of Norse Myths* remains the classic introduction to the body of Norse myths and heroes for children of all ages. Despite tastefully incorporating some of the coarser traditional details, Neil Gaiman's lilting (as well as amusing) *Norse Mythology* would also be appropriate for middle-grade readers.

Although myths from other cultures may be less accessible, their stories are just as rich as those from ancient Greece. *Stories from the Billabong* by James Vance Marshall, *Way Back When* by Neil Christopher, and *Whiskers, Tails & Wings* by Judy Goldman, respectively, collect sacred stories from the Yorta-Yorta people of Australia, the Inuits of the Canadian arctic, and a variety of indigenous peoples of Mexico. In addition to fine volumes on Greek and Norse mythology, Donna Jo Napoli and Christina Balit have produced a similarly opulent illustrated *Treasury of Egyptian Mythology: Classic Stories of Gods, Goddesses, Monsters, & Mortals*. One of pop-up-book master Robert Sabuda's collaborations with Matthew Reinhart, *Encyclopedia Mythologica: Gods & Heroes* presents a global assortment of stories in a novel format, adding in Hawaiian, Egyptian, Aztec, Asian, and Native American myths.

Sacred stories from today's major religions—Christianity, Islam, Buddhism, Hinduism, Taoism, Shinto, Judaism, and Earth Religions—also abound in children's literature. When treated with the same respect due all sacred stories, their role in contemporary religious practice as instructional tools should not preclude their use as cultural artifacts in the classroom. Collections such as *Sacred Stories: Wisdom from World Religions* by Marilyn McFarlane provide a good overview, in this case complete with a brief introduction to each religion before a sampling of its stories. *With a Mighty Hand,* Amy Ehrlich's adaptation of the Jewish Torah, condenses the familiar tales of the Abrahamic traditions (Judaism, Islam, and Christianity) into verse highlighted with Daniel Nevins' solemn but saturated oil paintings.

The many individual picturebooks based on a specific story can speedily introduce children to this literature. Linda Wolfgruber's dusky monoprints in *The Camel in the Sun* tenderly illuminates the growth of empathy in a Muslim tale of the Prophet Muhammad. The glorious birds of the Sufi tale, *The Conference of Birds,* wing delicately around the gilt frames of abundant white space in Demi's Asian-inspired illustrations. Noah's Ark remains a popular tale for children: Jerry Pinkey's majestic watercolors with pencil highlights a traditional version, while Holly Meade mixes watercolor and collage in Susan Campbell Bartoletti's soothing lullaby to the ark's passengers in *Naamah and the Ark at Night.* Even secular editions such as *The Animal's Ark* by Marianne Dubuc have been produced.

Myths and sacred stories, epic heroes, fables, and folktales represent the literary and preliterary traditions of people through the ages. This traditional literature is deeply rooted in basic human feelings. McFarlane considers:

> [A myth] may not be literal fact, but it tells a story deeper than fact because it holds an important truth about life. We put the truth into story form because humans use stories and pictures to understand what cannot be seen and touched. . . . Collectively, these stories are part of our global heritage, the wisdom passed down through generations. They are important to human identity as our music, art, laws, and other aspects of civilization. (p. xii)

Through this literature, children can form a link with the common bonds of humanity from the beginnings of recorded time, as well as form a foundation for much of their future reading.

Challenging Perspectives on Traditional Literature

An important point to consider when teaching traditional literature is that not all children will view fairy tales in predictable ways. Some children will opt not to participate in classroom activities that center on reading fairy tales, fables, or myths. Simply put, this would not be their genre of choice. Their perceptions about traditional literature present particular challenges for the classroom teacher. This can be especially challenging if fairy tales, well liked by the teacher, are used to teach across the curriculum. In that context, a student's lack of engagement and lack of response can eventually create a barrier to academic achievement.

Some educators assert that there are universals across all cultures and create spaces for more communal reading and responding to traditional literature. This is not always the case. Teachers' childhood experiences and those of their students, particularly those from diverse backgrounds, may find themselves at disparate crossroads. Therefore, the mediation of responses rooted in lived experiences may be especially challenging. There are some lived experiences that fuel responses to literature that are germane to a particular set of everyday life understandings.[6,7] For example, a study conducted by Tyson with African American male fifth-grade students reported the children were not engaged in the classroom when the story of Little Red Riding Hood was part of a unit to teach several literacy skills. This led her to explore the teaching and learning implications connected to the selection and use of traditional children's literature. In this study, she opened the door to extended responses to the literature and coupled it with the use of contemporary realistic fiction. She stated,

> As they responded to the texts, the boys began to discover and supplement the fictional information with factual information. They began to scrutinize and interrupt the information through cause and effect, hypothesizing ideas and predictions, inferring or deciphering character traits or identifying the author's purpose, as well as bringing personal insight and

their own experience to their literary interpretations . . . they did look for connections to their lives including, but not limited to, school, family, and community experiences.[8]

Tyson later concluded that their responses were often related to their own lives. The boys in the study began to respond to the issues raised in the texts in ways that increased their engagement and enhanced their success with literacy tasks.

So the questions arise: When looking at reader response and reading engagement, how do we recognize that culture, geography, language, and other influences impact reader response? How can a teacher meet the challenge of using traditional literature with children that may not connect and engage with the genre?

First, teachers and librarians can look outside the realm of what is the traditional. For example, *The Princess and the Packet of Frozen Peas* by Tony Wilson and illustrator Sue deGennao is a humorous twenty-first-century twist on the story of the Princess and the Pea. This princess looks like a "normal" girl and the prince's quest to find a non-whiny princess will offer an alternative connection for engagement with the traditional story.

Throughout this chapter, we have highlighted many texts that are considered the "classics" in traditional children's literature. Today's teachers should remember that children, even the youngest learners in our classrooms, are no longer exposed only to what is on the shelves of their neighborhood, classroom, and home libraries. They are no longer even confined to the "traditional" printed page.

Children today may have more options. They can download books and other multimedia from the Internet to their smartphones, tablets, and much more. Given the wealth of cross-over technological experiences that children can have in a multimodal literary world, the first responses to the traditional genre of literature may not be "traditional" at all. Smith[9] conducted a study where she explored body punctuation as a part of children's response to literature, adding depth of meaning to spoken responses that were absent to written ones. In her article, "Body Punctuation: Reader-Response in Motion," Smith focused on particular body language used by students as part of their response process, which she called "body punctuation." Smith defined the gestures and the exaggerated body movements as ways that students extended their understandings and responses to literature, suggesting procedures and clues for processes that might be used by all teachers.

Second, teachers can expand their understanding of what it means to respond to traditional literature.[10] If the only legitimate way to respond is to discuss the literature within its genre—plot structures, style, themes, motif and variants, and other strategies used to capture students' responses to literature—then we may lose the opportunity to use traditional literature to open up a whole world of imagination, cross-cultural understanding, and pure enjoyment. Children will come to the classroom with many varied lived experiences that will be the foundation of engagement and response to literature. What happens when a teacher wants to use a traditional folktale to teach all the objectives found in a reading standard and some of the children's responses indicate they are not engaged with the text? The teacher may decide to continue with the unit and hope those students will change their attitude or the teacher may want to develop teaching strategies that will facilitate creating classroom spaces for multiple ways of responding to literature. The Ten-Point Model sample found in Connect® provides suggestions for using traditional literature to respond to the perspectives some children bring to a reading of this genre.

curriculum connections

Using Traditional Literature to Address Standards

Traditional literature can provide windows into many people, places, and experiences. It brings to life the values and material surroundings of groups all over the world, demonstrating both our differences and our similarities. The variety of styles and stories that encompass the genre of traditional literature offer an opportunity for implementing curriculum standards in the classroom.

Suggested Children's Book: *Interrupting Chicken* by David Ezra Stein (Candlewick Press, 2010)

Chicken is ready for her bedtime story and Papa is ready to read, on one condition: Chicken must

not interrupt. Each time Papa begins one of her favorite folktales, Chicken listens quietly until the main character approaches the conflict in the story. At that point, Chicken cannot contain herself, and she interrupts to warn the character of the impending danger, ending the story abruptly. Whether it is *Hansel and Gretel, Little Red Riding Hood,* or *Chicken Little*, Chicken wants to edit the story, frustrating her father. In the end, it is Chicken who reads a bedtime story of her own making to her papa.

Subject	Standard	Classroom Ideas
Language Arts	**NCTE/ILA (Reading):** Students apply a wide range of strategies to comprehend, interpret, evaluate, and appreciate texts.	Compare Chicken's version to a traditional version of one of the three stories Chicken modifies: *Hansel and Gretel, Little Red Riding Hood,* or *Chicken Little*.
Art, Language Arts, and Technology	**NCTE/ILA (Writing):** Students employ a wide range of strategies as they write and use different writing process elements appropriately to communicate with different audiences for a variety of purposes.	In groups, rewrite other folktales that Chicken might interrupt to perform for the class. Create masks that characters wear during the production. Film each performance to share with families.
	NCCAS: Students realize artistic ideas and work through interpretation and presentation.	
	ISTE: Students create original works or responsibly repurpose or remix digital resources into new creations.	
Social Studies, Science, and Math	**NCSS:** Describe ways in which language, stories, folktales, music, and artistic creations serve as expressions of culture and influence behavior of people living in a particular culture.	Research, read, and reflect on traditional literature from a variety of cultures. Create a table that compares and contrasts the different versions of the traditional literature.

curriculum connections

Subject	Standard	Classroom Ideas
	NGSS: Obtain and combine information from books and other reliable media to explain phenomena.	
	NCTM: Represent data using tables and graphs.	
Textual Connections	**Traditional Literature:** *The Twelve Dancing Princesses* (Isadora); *Little Red Riding Hood* (Hyman); *Chicken Little* (Emberley and Emberley); *Seven Blind Mice* (Young)	
	Other Fractured Tales: *The True Story of the Three Pigs* (Scieszka); *Sleeping Ugly* (Yolen); *The Three Pigs* (Wiesner), *Prince Ribbit* (Emmett)	
Other Books by Stein	*Ice Boy; The Nice Book; Pouch!; Leaves; Cowboy Ned & Andy; Ol' Mama Squirrel*	
Author's Website	https://davidezrastein.com/	

Sources: International Society for Technology in Education (ITSE); National Coalition for Core Arts Standards (NCCAS); National Council of Teachers of English (NCTE)/International Literacy Association (ILA); National Council of Teachers of Mathematics (NCTM); National Council for the Social Studies (NCSS); Curriculum Standards; and Next Generation Science Standards (NGSS).

Notes

1. Laura Amy Schlitz, *The Bearskinner: A Tale of the Brothers Grimm,* illustrated by Max Grafe (Candlewick, 2007).
2. Margaret Willey, *Clever Beatrice,* illustrated by Heather Solomon (Atheneum, 2001).
3. Julius Lester, "The Storyteller's Voice: Reflections on the Rewriting of Uncle Remus," *New Advocate* 1.3 (summer, 1988): 144.
4. Stith Thompson, *Motif Index of Folk Literature,* 6 vols. (Bloomington, Ind.: Indiana University Press, 1955–1958).
5. See discussions of "The Hero's Journey" such as those in *The Hero with a Thousand Faces* by Joseph Campbell (Pantheon, 1949/2008).
6. R. Sims Bishop, "Mirrors, Windows, and Sliding Glass Doors," *Perspectives* 6 (1990): ix–xi.
7. V. Harris, *Teaching Multicultural Literature in Grades K–8* (Norwood, Mass.: Christopher-Gordon Publishers, 1992).
8. C. Tyson, "'Shut My Mouth Wide Open': Realistic Fiction and Social Action," *Theory into Practice* 38.3 (1999): 155–59.
9. E. B. Smith, "Body Punctuation: Reader-Response in Motion," in *Reader Response in Elementary Classrooms: Quest and Discovery,* ed. Nicholas J. Karolides (Mahwah, N.J.: Lawrence Erlbaum Associates, 1997).
10. L. Eckert, *How Does It Mean? Engaging Reluctant Readers through Literary Theory* (Portsmouth, N.H.: Heinemann, 2006).

Children's Literature

Go to **Connect**® to access study resources, practice quizzes, and additional materials.

Titles in blue = multicultural titles

Except where obvious from the title, the country or culture of origin follows each entry in parentheses. Dates in square brackets are original publication dates.

Folktales

Aardema, Verna. *Why Mosquitoes Buzz in People's Ears*. Illustrated by Leo Dillon and Diane Dillon. Dial, 1975. (West Africa)

Alperin, Mara. *Chicken Little*. Illustrated by Nick East. Tiger Tales, 2016. (Europe)

Arkhurst, Joyce Cooper. *The First Adventures of Spider*. Illustrated by Jerry Pinkey. Little Brown and company, 2012. (West Africa)

Aylesworth, Jim. *The Gingerbread Man*. Illustrated by Barbara McClintock. Scholastic, 1998. (England)

_____. *My Grandfather's Coat*. Illustrated by Barbara McClintok. Scholastic, 2014. (Yiddish)

Azizi, Sara. *The Knight, the Princess, and the Magic Rock: A Classic Persian Tale*. Wisdom Tales, 2012. (Persia)

Brett, Jan. *Gingerbread Baby*. Putnam, 1999. (England)

Brown, Marcia. *Dick Whittington and His Cat*. Scribner's, 1950. (England)

Bruchac, Joseph, and James Bruchac. *Raccoon's Last Race: A Traditional Abenaki Story*. Dial, 2004.

_____. *The Girl Who Helped Thunder and Other Native American Folktales (Folktales of the World)*. Illustrated by Stefano Vitale. Sterling, 2008.

_____. *How Chipmunk Got His Stripes: A Tale of Bragging and Teasing*. Illustrated by Jose Aruego and Ariane Dewey. Dial, 2001. (Native American)

Bryan, Ashley. *Beat the Story-Drum, Pum-Pum*. Atheneum, 1980. (Africa)

Climo, Shirley. *The Egyptian Cinderella*. Illustrated by Ruth Heller. Crowell/Harper, 1989.

_____. *The Korean Cinderella*. Illustrated by Ruth Heller. HarperCollins, 1993.

_____. *Tuko and the Birds: A Tale from the Philippines*. Illustrated by Francisco X. Mora. Holt, 2008.

Coburn, Jewell Reinhart. *Domitila: A Cinderella Tale from the Mexican Tradition*. Illustrated by Connie McLennan. Shens Books, 2000.

Compestine, Ying Chang. *The Runaway Wok: A Chinese New Year Tale*. Dutton Children's Books, 2011.

Corr, Christopher. *Deep in the Woods*. Frances Lincoln Children's Books, 2017. (Russia)

Cowley, Joy. *The Frog Prince*. Illustrated by Yeon-joo Kim. Learner, 2016. (Germany)

_____. *Puss in Boots*. Illustrated by Sam-Hyeon Kim. Lerner, 2015. (France)

Cresswell, Helen. *A Treasury of Fairy Tales*. Illustrated by Sian Bailey. HarperCollins, 2013. (various)

Crews, Nina. *Jack and the Beanstalk*. Henry Holt, 2011. (England/New York City)

Cummings, Pat. *Ananse and the Lizard. A West African Tale*. Holt, 2002.

Daly, Jude. *Fair, Brown and Trembling: An Irish Cinderella Story*. Farrar, 2001. (Ghana)

Daly, Niki. *Pretty Salma: A Red Riding Hood Story from Africa*. Clarion, 2007.

Dasent, George. *East o'the Sun and West o'the Moon*. Illustrated by Gillian Barlow. Philomel, 1988. (Norway)

D'Aulaire, Ingri and Edgar Parin. *D'Aulaires' Book of Norwegian Folktales*. University of Minnesota Press, 2016.

Davis, David. *Fandango Stew*. Sterling Pub., 2011. (Southwest United States)

DeFelice, Cynthia. *Nelly May Has Her Say*. Illustrated by Henry Cole. Farrar, 2013. (England)

Dembicki, Matt. *Trickster. Native American Tales: A Graphic Collection*. Fulcrum, 2010.

Demi. *The Empty Pot*. Holt, 1990. (China)

dePaola, Tomie. *Adelita: A Mexican Cinderella Story*. Putnam, 2002.

Diakité, Baba Wagué. *The Magic Gourd*. Scholastic, 2003. (Mali)

Divakaruni, Chitra Banerjee. *Grandma and the Great Gourd: A Bengali Folktale*. Illustrated by Susy Pilgrim Waters. Roaring Brook, 2013.

Don, Lari. *Girls and Goddesses (World of Stories)*. Darby Creek, 2016. (various)

Duffy, Chris (editor). *Fairy Tale Comics: Classic Tales Told by Extraordinary Cartoonists*. (various)

Emmett, Jonathan. *Prince Ribbit*. Illustrated by Poly Bernatene. Macmillan, 2016. (not traditional)

Enderle, Dotti. *The Library Gingerbread Man*. Upstart, 2010. (Europe)

Fleischman, Paul. *Glass Slipper, Gold Sandal: A Worldwide Cinderella*. Illustrated by Julie Paschkis. Holt, 2007.

Gagne, Terry. *Robin Hood*. Mitchell Lane Publishers, 2015. (England)

Galdone, Paul. *The Gingerbread Boy*. Clarion, 1984 [1968]. (England)

_____. *The Little Red Hen*. Clarion, 1979 [1974]. (England)

_____. *The Magic Porridge Pot*. Clarion, 1979 [1976]. (Germany)

_____. *The Three Billy Goats Gruff*. HMH, 2011. (Norway)

_____. *The Three Little Pigs*. Clarion, 1981 [1973]. (England)

Gilani, Fawzia. *Cinderella: An Islamic Tale*. Illustrated by Shireen Adams. Islamic Society, 2011.

Goble, Paul. *The Man Who Dreamed of Elk-Dogs & Other Stories from the Tipi (Wisdom Tales)*. Illustrated by Lauren Waukau-Villagomez. Wisdom Tales, 2012.

Gonzalez, Lucia M. *The Bossy Gallito*. Illustrated by Lulu Delacre. Lorito Books, 2009. (Cuba)

Gray, William. *The World Treasury of Fairy Tales and Folklore: A Family Heirloom of Stories to Inspire and Entertain*. Wellfleet Press, 2016. (various)

Grimm, Jacob, and Wilhelm Grimm. *Princess Furball*. Retold by Charlotte Huck. Illustrated by Anita Lobel. Greenwillow, 1989. (Germany)

_____. *Rumpelstiltskin*. Retold and illustrated by Paul O. Zelinsky. Dutton, 1986. (Germany)

_____. *Snow White and the Seven Dwarfs*. Translated by Randall Jarrell. Illustrated by Nancy Ekholm Burkert. Farrar, 1972. (Germany)

Guarnaccia, Steven. *The Three Little Pigs: An Architectural Tale*. Abrams Books for Young Readers, 2010. (England)

Haley, Gail E. *A Story, a Story*. Atheneum, 1970. (Africa)

Hamilton, Virginia. *The Girl Who Spun Gold*. Illustrated by Leo Dillon and Diane Dillon. Scholastic, 2000. (West Indies)

Han, Suzanne Crowder. *The Rabbit's Tail: A Tale from Korea*. Illustrated by Richard Wehrman. Holt, 1999.

Hickox, Rebecca. *The Golden Sandal: A Middle Eastern Cinderella*. Illustrated by Will Hillenbrand. Holiday, 1998.

Hogrogian, Nonny. *One Fine Day*. Macmillan, 1971. (Armenia)

Huck, Charlotte S. *Toads and Diamonds*. Illustrated by Anita Lobel. Greenwillow, 1996. (France)

Isadora, Rachel. *Hansel and Gretel*. Putnam Juvenile, 2009. (Germany)

_____. *Rapunzel*. Putnam, 2008. (Germany/Africa)

Jaffe, Nina. *The Golden Flower: A Taino Myth from Puerto Rico*. Illustrated by Eric O. Saná. Piñata, 2005.

Jacobs, Kim. *Princess Sophie and the Six Swans: A Tale from the Brothers Grimm*. Wisdom Tales, 2017. (Germany)

Javaherbin, Mina. *Elephant in the Dark*. Illustrated by Eugene Yelchin. Scholastic, 2015. (Persia)

Johnson, R. Kikuo. *The Shark King*. Toon Books, 2012. (Hawaii)

Kellogg, Steven. *Chicken Little*. Morrow, 1988. (United States)

Kimmel, Eric. *The Fisherman and the Turtle*. Illustrated by Martha Aviles. Cavendish, 2008. (Germany/Aztec)

_____. *The Old Woman and Her Pig*. Illustrated by Giora Carmi. Holiday, 1993. (England)

Kimmel, Eric A. *Gabriel's Horn*. Illustrated by Maria Surducan. Kar-Ben Publishing, 2016. (Judaism)

Kimmelman, Leslie. *The Little Red Hen and the Passover Matzah*. Illustrated by Paul Meisel. Holiday House, 2010. (Judaism)

Kojo, KP. *The Parade: A Stampede of Stories About Ananse, the Trickster Spider*. Illustrated by Karen Little. Frances Lincoln, 2010. (Ghana)

Lee, H. Chuku. *Beauty and the Beast: A Retelling*. Illustrated by Pat Cummings. Harper, 2014. (France/West Africa)

Lester, Julius. *Tales of Uncle Remus: The Adventures of Brer Rabbit*. Illustrated by Jerry Pinkney. Puffin, 2006. (United States)

Leysen, An. *Baba Yaga*. Clavis, 2015. (Russia)

Lindbergh, Reeve. *Johnny Appleseed*. Illustrated by Kathy Jakobsen. Little, 1990. (United States)

Louie, Ai-Ling. *Yeh-Shen: A Cinderella Story from China*. Illustrated by Ed Young. Philomel, 1982.

Lumbard, Alexis York. *Pine and Winter Sparrow*. Illustrated by Beatriz Vidal. Wisdom Tales, 2015. (Cherokee)

Maccarone, Grace. *Princess Tales Around the World: Once Upon a Time in Rhyme with Seek-and-Find Pictures*. Illustrated by Gail De Marcken. Feiwel and Friends, 2017. (various)

MacDonald, Margaret Read. *The Great Smelly, Slobbery, Small-Tooth Dog: A Folktale from Great Britain*. Julie Paschkis. August, 2007.

MacDonald, Margaret Read. *Give Up, Gecko! A Folktale from Uganda*. Illustrated by Deborah Melmon. Two Lions, 2013.

MacDonald, Margaret Read. *The Wishing Foxes*. Illustrated by Kitty Harvill. Plum Street, 2017. (Appalachia)

_____. *Mabela the Clever*. Illustrated by Tim Coffey. Whitman, 2001. (Limba/Africa)

_____. *The Old Woman and Her Pig: An Appalachian Folktale*. Illustrated by John Kanzler. HarperCollins, 2007.

_____. *Tunjur! Tunjur! Tunjur! A Palestinian Folktale*. Illustrated by Alik Arzoumanian. Cavendish, 2006.

Manley, Curtis. *The Crane Girl*. Illustrated by Lin Wang. Shen's Books, 2017. (Japan)

Marshall, James. *The Three Little Pigs*. Grosset & Dunlap, 2000. (England)

Martin, Rafe. *The Rough-Face Girl*. Illustrated by David Shannon. Putnam, 1992. (Native American)

McAllister, Angela. *A Year Full of Stories: 52 Folktales and Legends from Around the World*. Illustrated by Christopher Corr. Frances Lincoln, 2016. (various)

McDermott, Gerald. *Monkey: A Trickster Tale from India*. Harcourt Children's Books, 2011.

_____. *Anansi the Spider*. Holt, 1972. (Africa)

Naidoo, Beverley. *Who Is King? Ten Magical Stories from Africa*. Illustrated by Piet Grobler. Frances Lincoln, 2015.

Nishizuka, Koko. *The Beckoning Cat*. Illustrated by Rosanne Litzinger. Holiday House, 2009. (Japan)

Qitsualik, Rachel A. *The Shadows that Rush Past*. Iqaluit, 2011. (Inuit)

Orgel, Doris. *The Bremen Town Musicians and Other Animal Tales from Grimm*. Roaring Brook Press, 2004. (Germany)

Perrault, Charles. *Cinderella*. Illustrated by Marcia Brown. Scribner's, 1954. (France)

_____. *Puss in Boots*. Translated by Malcolm Arthur. Illustrated by Fred Marcellino. Farrar, 1993 [1990]. (France)

Pinkney, Jerry. *The Lion & the Mouse*. Little, Brown Books, 2009. (Greece)

_____. *The Little Red Hen*. Dial, 2006. (England)

_____. *Puss in Boots*. Dial Books for Young Readers, 2012. (France)

_____. *The Three Billy Goats Gruff*. Little, Brown and Company, 2017. (Norway)

Puttapipat, Niroot. *The Musicians of Bremen*. Candlewick, 2005. (Germany)

Ransome, Arthur. *The Fool of the World and the Flying Ship*. Illustrated by Uri Shulevitz. Farrar, 1968. (Russia)

Rodgers, Greg. *Chufki Rabbit's Big, Bad Bellyache: A Trickster Tale*. Illustrated by Leslie Stall Widener. Cinco Puntos, 2014. (Choctaw)

Rodriguez, Beatrice. *The Gingerbread Man*. North-South, 2012. (Europe)

Rumford, James. *Tiger and Turtle*. Roaring Brook Press, 2010. (India)

San Souci, Robert D. *Cendrillon, a Caribbean Cinderella*. Illustrated by Brian Pinkney. Simon, 1998.

_____. *The Little Gold Star. A Spanish American Cinderella Story*. Illustrated by Sergio Martinez. HarperCollins, 2000.

_____. *The Silver Charm: A Folktale from Japan*. Illustrated by Yoriko Ito. Doubleday, 2002.

_____. *The Talking Eggs*. Illustrated by Jerry Pinkney. Dial, 1989. (African American)

Schlitz, Laura Amy. *The Bearskinner: A Tale of the Brothers Grimm*. Illustrated by Max Grafe. Candlewick, 2007. (Germany)

Seow, David. *The Monkey King: A Classic Chinese Tale for Children*. Illustrated by L.K. Tay-Audouard. Tuttle Publishing, 2017.

Sharpe, Leah Marinsky. *The Goat-Faced Girl*. Illustrated by Jane Marinsky. David R Godine, 2009. (Italy)

Sierra, Judy. *The Gift of the Crocodile: A Cinderella Story*. Illustrated by Reynold Ruffins. Simon, 2000. (Indonesia)

Snyder, Dianne. *The Boy of the Three-Year Nap*. Illustrated by Allen Say. Houghton, 1988. (Japan)

Souhami, Jessica. *King Pom and the Fox*. Frances Lincoln, 2007. (Japan)

Soundar, Chitra. *Farmer Falgu Goes on a Trip*. Karadi Tales, 2016. (India)

Steptoe, John. *Mufaro's Beautiful Daughters: An African Tale*. Lothrop, 1987. (Zimbabwe)

Taback, Simms. *This Is the House That Jack Built*. Puffin, 2003. (England)

Vamos, Samantha R. *The Cazuela That the Farm Maiden Stirred*. Illustrated by Rafael López. Charlesbridge Publishing, 2011. (Latin America)

Willey, Margaret. *Clever Beatrice*. Illustrated by Heather Solomon. Atheneum, 2001. (Canada)

Young, Ed. *What About Me?* Philomel, 2002. (Sufi)

Wiesner, David. *The Three Pigs*. Clarion, 2001. (not traditional)

Zemach, Harve. *Duffy and the Devil*. Illustrated by Margot Zemach. Farrar, Straus and Giroux, 1973. (Cornwall, England)

Zwerger, Lisbeth. *Tales from the Brothers Grimm*. Michael Neugebauer Publishing, 2013. (Germany)

Fables

Burningham, John. *Tug of War* Candlewick, 2013. (Nigeria)

Daly, Jude. *Six Blind Mice and an Elephant*. Otter-Barry Books, 2017. (India/Southern Africa)

DePaola, Tomie. *The Parables of Jesus*. Holiday House, 1987. (Christianity)

Duffy, Chris (editor). *Fable Comics*. First Second, 2015. (various)

Hennessy, B. G. *The Boy Who Cried Wolf*. Illustrated by Boris Kulikov. Simon, 2006. (Greece)

Hoffman, Mary. *Parables: Stories Jesus Told*. Illustrated by Jackie Morris. Phyllis Fogelman, 2000. (Christianity)

Husain, Shahrukh. *The Wise Fool: Fables from the Islamic World*. Illustrated by Micha Archer. Barefoot Books, 2011.

Joslin, Mary. *The Lion Classic Wisdom Tales*. Lion Children's, 2013. (various)

Lowry, Amy. *Fox Tails: Four Fables from Aesop*. Holiday House, 2012. (Greece)

McGinnis, Mark W. *When Buddha Was an Elephant: 32 Animal Wisdom Tales from the Jataka*. Shambhala, 2015. (India)

Naidoo, Beverley. *Aesop's Fables*. Illustrated by Piet Grobler. Frances Lincoln Children's Books, 2011. (Greece/Africa)

Nunes, Shiho S. *Chinese Fables: "The Dragon Slayer" and Other Timeless Tales of Wisdom*. Tuttle Publishing, 2013.

Pinkney, Jerry. *Aesop's Fables*. North-South, 2000. (Greece)

———. *The Grasshopper and the Ants*. Little, Brown and Company, 2015. (Greek)

———. *The Tortoise and the Hare*. Little, Brown and Company, 2013. (Greek/Southwest United States)

Stampler, Ann Redisch. *The Rooster Prince of Breslov*. Clarion, 2010. (Judaism)

Williams, Marcia. *The Elephant's Friends and Other Tales from Ancient India*. Candlewick, 2012.

Young, Ed. *Seven Blind Mice*. Philomel, 1992. (India)

Epic and Legendary Heroes

Arni, Samhita. *Sita's Ramayana*. Illustrated by Moyna Chitrakar. (India)

Chen, Wei Dong. *Birth of the Stone Monkey (Monkey King #1)*. Illustrated by Chao Peng. JR*Comics, 2012. (China)

Colum, Padraic. *The Children's Homer: The Adventures of Odysseus and the Tale of Troy*. Illustrated by Willy Pogany. Macmillan, 1962. (Greece)

Cross, Gillian. *The Odyssey*. Illustrated by Neil Packer. Candlewick, 2012. (Greece)

Forest, Heather. *Ancient & Epic Tales: From Around the World*. August House, 2016. (various)

Hinds, Gareth. *The Odyssey*. Candlewick, 2010. (Greece)

McCaughrean, Geraldine. *Gilgamesh the Hero*. Illustrated by David Parkins. Eerdmans, 2004. (Mesopotamia)

Osborne, Mary Pope. *Tales from the Odyssey*. Hyperion Books for Children, 2010. (Greece)

Raven, Nicky. *Beowulf: A Tale of Blood, Heat, and Ashes*. Illustrated by John Howe. Candlewick, 2007. (Greece)

Rumford, James. *Beowulf: A Hero's Tale Retold*. Houghton, 2007. (Scandinavia)

Seow, David. *The Monkey King: A Classic Chinese Tale for Children*. Illustrated by L.K. Tay-Audouard. Tuttle Publishing, 2017.

Sutcliff, Rosemary. *The Wanderings of Odysseus: The Story of the Odyssey*. Illustrated by Alan Lee. Delacorte, 1996. (Greece)

Verma, Jatinder. *The Story of Divaali*. Illustrated by Nilesh Mistry. Barefoot, 2016. (India)

Yang, Gene. *American Born Chinese*. First Second, 2006. (not traditional)

Young, Ed. *Monkey King*. HarperCollins, 2001. (China)

Zeman, Ludmila. *Gilgamesh the King*. Tundra, 1992. (Mesopotamia)

———. *The Last Quest of Gilgamesh*. Tundra, 1995. (Mesopotamia)

Myths and Sacred Stories

Bartoletti, Susan Campbell. *Naamah and the Ark at Night*. Illustrated by Holly Meade. Candlewick, 2011. (Judaism)

Byrd, Robert. *Jason and the Argonauts*. Dial Books for Young Readers, 2016. (Greece)

Christopher, Neil. *Way Back Then*. Illustrated by Germaine Arnaktauyok. Inhabit Media, 2015. (Inuit)

Clayton, Sally Pomme. *Persephone*. Illustrated by Virginia Lee. Eerdmans Books, 2009. (Greece)

D'Aulaire, Ingri, and Edgar Parin D'Aulaire. *D'Aulaires' Book of Greek Myths*. Doubleday, 1962.

———. *D'Aulaires' Book of Norse Myths*. New York Review of Books, 2005 [1967]. (Scandinavia)

Dubuc, Marianne. *The Animal's Ark*. Kids Can Press, 2016. (Abrahamic tradition)

Dutta, Sourav. *Ganesha: The Curse on the Moon*. Illustrated by Rajesk Nagulakonda. Random House, 2015. (India)

Ehrlich, Amy. *With a Mighty Hand: The Story in the Torah*. Candlewick, 2013. (Judaism)

Fleischman, Paul. *First Light, First Life*. Illustrated by Julie Paschkis. (various)

Gaiman, Neil. *Norse Mythology*. W.W. Norton, 2017. (Scandinavia)

Gerstein, Mordicai. *I Am Pan!* Roaring Book Press, 2016. (Greece)

Goldman, Judy. *Whiskers, Tails & Wings: Animal Folktales from Mexico*. Illustrated by Fabricio Vanden Broeck. Charlesbridge, 2013.

Hamilton, Virginia. *In the Beginning: Creation Stories from around the World*. Illustrated by Barry Moser. Harcourt, 1988. (various)

Harris, John. *Strong Stuff: Herakles and His Labors*. Illustrated by Gary Baseman. J. Paul Getty Museum, 2005. (Greece)

Lunge-Larsen, Lise. *Gifts from the Gods: Ancient Words and Wisdom from Greek and Roman Mythology*. Illustrated by Gareth Hinds. Houghton Mifflin Books for Children, 2011.

Landmann, Bimba. *The Fate of Achilles*. J. Paul Getty Museum, 2011. (Greece)

Marshall, James Vance. *Stories from the Billabong*. Illustrated by Francis Firebrace Jones. Francis Lincoln, 2009. (Yorta-Yorta)

McFarlane, Marilyn. *Sacred Stories: Wisdom from World Religions*. Illustrated by Daniel Nevins. Aladdin, 2012. (various)

Napoli, Donna Jo. *Treasury of Egyptian Mythology: Classic Stories of Gods, Goddesses, Monsters, & Mortals*. Illustrated by Christina Balit. National Geographic Children's Books, 2013.

Ondaatje, Griffin. *The Camel in the Sun*. Illustrator Linda Wolfsgruber. Groundwood, 2013. (Islam)

Pinkney, Jerry. *Noah's Ark*. Chronicle Books, 2002. (Christianity)

Reinhart, Matthew. *Gods & Heroes (Encyclopedia Mythologica #2)*. Candlewick, 2010. (various)

Rylant, Cynthia. *Creation*. Beach Lane Books, 2016. (Christianity)

Singer, Marilyn. *Echo Echo: Reverso Poems About Greek Myths*. Illustrated by Josée Masse. Dial Books for Young Readers, 2016.

Spinelli, Eileen. *Jonah's Whale*. Illustrated by Giuliano Ferri. Eerdmans Books for Young Readers, 2012. (Abrahamic tradition)

Modern Fantasy

Chapter Outline

**Bree, a fifth grader, read Philip
Pullman's *The Golden Compass* and
found it "stupendous."** She passed
it on to her best friend Madeline who
also responded to it with passionate
enthusiasm. Soon the two were in
a continuing dialogue about Pullman's
daemons, pronunciations, and auroras.
They loved assigning daemons to each
other. Then, during sleepovers, they
began assigning each person they knew
their *true* type of daemon. *The Golden
Compass* became their measuring
stick for other fantasy. They asked each
other, "But is it as good as *The Golden
Compass*? Are the characters as realistic?
Is the setting as vivid? Is the plot as
compelling?" For these friends, fantasy
became a way of examining their own
worlds and evaluating the world
of literature.

After twenty-plus years, Bree reflects on the lasting impressions the book left on her. "In the early days of the internet, I remember googling 'Skraeling' to try to separate fact from fiction. A trip to Oxford as a young adult inspired me to re-read the series and I found it just as good as I remembered. I look forward to rediscovering the trilogy—and the upcoming additions to the series—with my newborn daughter, Eleanor, in the future." For now, William Steigs's *Brave Irene,* another book about a feisty heroine, will start Eleanor on her reading journey.

©Nell Bang-Jensen.

Fantasy for Today's Child

Some educators and parents question the value of fantasy for today's child. They argue that children want contemporary stories that are relevant and speak to the problems of daily living—"now" books about the real world, not fantasies about unreal worlds. Others object to any fantasy at all for children, afraid that reading fantasy stories that include goblins, trolls, and witches could lead children to practices of satanism or belief in the occult.

But the genre of fantasy is rich and varied with numerous types of stories. Good fantasy can support children's understanding of themselves and of the struggles they will face as human beings. Lloyd Alexander, master of the craft of writing fantasy, argues that fantasy is of the utmost value for children.

> We call our individual fantasies dreams, but when we dream as a society, or as a human race, it becomes the sum total of all our hopes. Fantasy touches our deepest feelings and in so doing, it speaks to the best and most hopeful parts of ourselves. It can help us learn the most fundamental skill of all—how to be human.[1]

The great fantasies frequently reveal new insights into the world of reality. Both E. B. White's *Charlotte's Web* and Kenneth Grahame's *The Wind in the Willows* detail the responsibilities and loyalties required of true friendship. The fundamental truth underlying Ursula Le Guin's story *A Wizard of Earthsea* is that each of us is responsible for the

Artist Jerry Pinkney visualizes Hans Christian Andersen's The *Nightingale* in a fabled kingdom in Morocco. Illustrations from THE NIGHTINGALE by Hans Christian Andersen, adapted and illustrated by Jerry Pinkney, Copyright ©2000 by Jerry Pinkney. Used with permission of Dial Books for Young Readers, a division of Penguin Young Readers Group, a division of Penguin Random House LLC. Used with permission of the Sheldon Fogelman Agency. All rights reserved.

wrong that we do and that we are free of it only when we face it directly. In a book of realism, such a theme might appear to be a thinly disguised ethics lesson; in fantasy, it becomes an exciting quest for identity and self-knowledge. Fantasy consistently asks the universal questions concerning the struggle of good versus evil, the humanity of humankind, and the meaning of life and death.

A modern realistic fiction novel can be out of date in five years, but well-written fantasy endures. Hans Christian Andersen's *The Nightingale* speaks directly to this century's adoration of mechanical gadgetry to the neglect of what is simple and real. Lois Lowry's *The Giver* asks how the freedom of an individual can be weighed against the needs of the group. Natalie Babbitt's *Tuck Everlasting* questions whether anything or anyone would wish to live forever.

More important, however, fantasy helps the child develop imagination. To be able to imagine, to conceive of alternative ways of life, to entertain new ideas, to create strange new worlds, to dream dreams—these are all skills vital to human survival.

These arguments aside, children themselves have shown that they continue to want books that satisfy this hunger. J. K. Rowling's Harry Potter books are undoubtedly the most popular children's books to be published in the past fifty years. E. B. White's *Charlotte's Web,* C. S. Lewis's Narnia series, and Madeleine L'Engle's *A Wrinkle in Time* are all fantasies that rank among children's favorite books. And many of the classics, books that have endured through generations—such as Lewis Carroll's *Alice in Wonderland,* A. A. Milne's *Winnie the Pooh,* Kenneth Grahame's *The Wind in the Willows,* and J. M. Barrie's *Peter Pan*—are also fantasies.

The modern literature of fantasy is diverse. We have contemporary fairy tales written by known authors; stories of magic, talking toys, and other wonders; quests for truth in lands that never were; and narratives that speculate on the future. Though these types of stories might seem very different, they do have something in common: they have roots in earlier sources—in folktales, legends, myths, and the oldest dreams of humankind. All literature borrows from itself, but the fantasy genre is particularly dependent. The motifs, plots, characters, settings, and themes of new fantasy books often seem familiar. And well they should, for we have met them before, in other, older stories.

Many authors borrow directly from the characters and motifs of folklore, which can vary between local and regional cultures. The African American folk heroes John de Conquer and John Henry Roustabout enliven the unusual fantasy *The Magical Adventures of Pretty Pearl* by Virginia Hamilton. Grace Lin's *When the Sea Turns to Silver* is one of three books she based on Chinese folklore. Ian Beck's Tom Trueheart series and Adam Gidwitz's *A Tale Dark and Grimm* and *In a Glass Grimmly* are peopled by characters from German and English folktales. Nancy Farmer (*The Islands of the Blessed,* book three of The Sea of Trolls trilogy), Neil Gaiman (*Odd and the Frost Giants*), Rick Riordan (Magnus Chase series), Maggie Stiefvater (*The Scorpio Races*), and Patrick Ness (*A Monster Calls*) all rely on places, motifs, and creatures from Celtic and Norse mythology to tell their thrilling stories. Greek mythology forms the basis for Gail Carson Levine's *Ever* and Riordan's *The Mark of Athena,* the final book in the popular The Heroes of Olympus series.

The ultimate taproot of all fantasy is the human psyche. Like the ancient tale-tellers and the medieval bards, modern fantasy writers speak to our deepest needs, our darkest fears, and our highest hopes. In fantasy for children, adults might find many of the collective images or shared symbols called archetypes by the great psychologist Carl Jung. Children will simply recognize that such a fantasy is "true." All our best fantasies, from the briefest modern fairy tale to the most complex novel of high adventure, share this quality of truth.

Types of Fantasy

Literary Fairy Tales

As discussed in Chapter 4, the traditional folklore or fairy tale had no identifiable author but was passed on by retellings by one generation to the next. Even though the names Grimm and Jacobs have become associated with some of these tales, they did not write the stories; they compiled and edited the folktales of Germany and England. The modern literary fairy tale, on the other hand, utilizes the form of the old but has an identifiable author.

Hans Christian Andersen is generally credited with being the first author of modern fairy tales, although some of his stories, such as *The Wild Swans,* are definite adaptations of the old folktales. Many of Andersen's stories bear his unmistakable stamp of gentleness, melancholy, and faith in God. Often even his retellings of old tales are embellished with deeper meanings, making them very much his creations.

Other well-known authors have been captivated by the possibilities of the literary fairy tale. Kenneth Grahame's *The Reluctant Dragon* is the droll tale of a peace-loving dragon who is forced to fight Saint George. James Thurber's *Many Moons* is the story of a petulant princess who desires the moon. *The Purloining of Prince Oleomargarine,* an unfinished story by Mark Twain, has been rewritten by Philip Stead. Erin Stead's ethereal illustrations complement the melancholy story. Evan Turk's vibrant *The Storyteller* is a more recent addition to the subgenre of literary fairy tale. Contemporary authors have brought a sense of playfulness to tales and characters that originated in the oral tradition. (See Modern Folktale Style in Chapter 3.)

Animal Fantasy

Children might first be introduced to fantasy through tales of talking animals, toys, and dolls. The young child frequently ascribes powers of thought and speech to pets or toys and might already be acquainted with some of the Beatrix Potter stories or the more sophisticated tales of William Steig.

One of the most beloved animal fantasies of our time is E. B. White's delightful tale *Charlotte's Web*. While much of our fantasy is of English origin, *Charlotte's Web* is as American as the Fourth of July and just as much a part of our children's heritage. Eight-year-old Fern can understand all of the animals in the barnyard—the geese who always speak in triplicate ("certainly-ertainlyertainly"); the wise old sheep; and Templeton, the crafty rat—yet she cannot communicate with them. The true heroine of the story is Charlotte A. Cavatica—a beautiful, large gray spider who befriends Wilbur, a humble little pig. When the kindly old sheep inadvertently drops the news that as soon as Wilbur is nice and fat he will be butchered, Charlotte promises to save the hysterical pig. By miraculously spinning words into her web that describe the pig as "radiant," "terrific," and "humble," she makes Wilbur famous. The pig is saved, but Charlotte dies alone at the fairgrounds. Wilbur manages to bring Charlotte's egg sac back to the farm so that the continuity of life in the barnyard is maintained. Wilbur never forgets his friend Charlotte, though he loves her children and grandchildren dearly. This story has humor, pathos, wisdom, and beauty. Its major themes speak of the web of true friendship and the cycle of life and death. All ages find meaning in this most popular fantasy.

The well-loved *The Wind in the Willows* by Kenneth Grahame endures even though it is slow-paced, idyllic, and more sentimental than a more modern animal fantasy. It is the story of four friends: kindly and gruff old Badger; practical and good-natured Ratty; gullible Mole; and boisterous, expansive, and easily misled Toad. Toad gets into one scrape after another, and the other three loyally rescue their errant friend and finally save his elegant mansion from a band of wicked weasels and stoats. The themes of friendship, the importance of a home place, and love of nature pervade this pastoral fantasy.

The villainous animals threatening Toad Hall in *The Wind in the Willows* are the same sorts who threaten Redwall Abbey in Brian Jacques's Redwall books. But this series is swiftly told, complexly plotted, and action-packed by comparison. Redwall tells of Matthias, a clumsy, young, and peace-loving mouse, who galvanizes himself to defeat the evil rat, Cluny the Scourge. Aided by Cornflower the Fieldmouse, Constance the Badger, and Brother Methuselah, Matthias's efforts to fortify the Abbey alternate with chapters of the terrible Cluny subduing woodland creatures to his will. The sinister names of Cluny's band (Fangborn, Cheesethief, Ragear, Mangefur) alert

Carmen Agra Deedy and Randall Wright's *The Cheshire Cheese Cat: A Dickens of a Tale* is a story of an alley cat who teams up with the mice population to save the nation during the time of Charles Dickens. First published in the United States under the title *The Cheshire Cheese Cat: A Dickens of a Tale* by Carmen Agra Deedy and Randall Wright, drawings by Barry Moser. Text Copyright ©2011 by Carmen Agra Deedy and Randall Wright. Illustrations Copyright ©2011 by Barry Moser. Published by arrangement with Peachtree Publishers.

young readers to the evil characters. In fact, one of the major appeals of the Redwall stories is that one never doubts that good will triumph. Fans of this popular series have ample opportunity to follow the Redwall saga; the series includes twenty-two books.

Gorilla characters have become a recent addition to animal fantasy. Katherine Applegate's *The One and Only Ivan* is a poignant novel in verse that exposes the mistreatment of animals in roadside attractions and circuses. Older readers will find a more complex story in Jakob Wegelius's *The Murderer's Ape*. A large cast of characters (illustrated in the first eight pages of the book) follow the long journey of Sally Jones—a gorilla—to clear her best human friend of murder. Sally can read and type but cannot speak, and so she encounters many perils and misunderstandings along the way.

Carmen Agra Deedy and Randall Wright's *The Cheshire Cheese Cat: A Dickens of a Tale* is an animal fantasy set in Victorian England. Skilley is an alley cat who becomes the mouser of Ye Olde Cheshire Cheese, an inn frequented by Charles Dickens and other writers from the time. But instead of killing the mice, the cat makes a deal to protect them in exchange for the inn's delectable Cheshire cheese. Skilley and the mice face many challenges throughout the book, from a tyrannical cook to an evil tomcat. Moser's black-and-white pencil drawings bring the talking characters to life.

The World of Toys and Dolls

As authors have endowed animals with human characteristics, so, too, have they personified toys and dolls. Young children enjoy stories that bring inanimate objects such as a tugboat or a steam shovel to life. Seven-, 8-, and 9-year-olds still like to imagine that their favorite playthings have a life of their own.

Probably no one has made toys seem quite so much like people as has A. A. Milne in his well-loved Pooh stories. Each chapter contains a separate adventure about the favorite stuffed toys of Milne's son, Christopher Robin. The good companions introduced in *Winnie the Pooh* include Winnie-the-Pooh, "a bear of little brain"; Eeyore, the doleful donkey; Piglet, the happy follower and devoted friend of Pooh; and Rabbit, Owl, Kanga, and little Roo. A bouncy new friend, Tigger, joins the group in Milne's second book, *The House at Pooh Corner*. They all live in the "100 Aker Wood" and spend most of their time getting into—and out of—exciting and amusing situations. The humor in these stories is not hilarious but quiet, whimsical, and subtle. If teachers and children know only the Disney version of these stories, they are in for a treat when they read the original Milne.

Emily Jenkins has created a memorable cast of toy characters in the Toys trilogy. The first book, *Toys Go Out: Being the Adventures of a Knowledgeable Stingray, a Toughy Little Buffalo, and Someone Called Plastic*, introduces readers to three toys: a stuffed stingray, a stuffed buffalo, and a plastic bouncy ball. The toys belong to the Little Girl who lives on the high bed with the fluffy pillows. The toys continue to have adventures in *Toy Dance Party: Being the Further Adventures of a Bossyboots Stingray, a Courageous Buffalo, & a Hopeful Round Someone Called Plastic*. The final book in the trilogy is *Toys Come Home: Being the Early Experiences of an Intelligent Stingray, a Brave Buffalo, and a Brand-New Someone Called Plastic*. Each book contains six interconnected chapters in which the toys compete for the affections of the Little Girl and have many adventures together. The stories, told from the toys' point of view, offer readers an entertaining glimpse into the secret lives of toys. The detailed black-and-white illustrations were done by Caldecott Award–winning Paul O. Zelinsky.

Annabelle Doll is 8 years old going on 108 in Ann M. Martin and Laura Godwin's trilogy about dolls who are alive. In *The Doll People*, readers are introduced to Annabelle and her family, who live in a lovely Victorian dollhouse from 1898. The dollhouse and the porcelain dolls have been handed down through succeeding generations of girls to their present owner, Kate Palmer. Although she is allowed to move around at night when Kate is sleeping, Annabelle becomes restless and bored, longing for an adventure. When she meets a plastic doll from a modern new dollhouse, the two girls become fast friends and go on an adventure together, searching for Annabelle's long-lost aunt. The two dolls have many more exciting encounters in *The Meanest Doll in the World, The Runaway Dolls,* and *The Doll People Set Sail.* The four books are charming stories and will resonate with every child who has wondered if her dolls might come to life at night after she has gone to sleep. Brian Selznick's pencil illustrations add detail and depth to the characters and their experiences. The action, suspense, and engaging dialogue make the books excellent read-alouds.

Eccentric Characters and Preposterous Situations

Many fantasies for children are based on eccentric characters or preposterous situations. Cars or people might fly, eggs might hatch into dinosaurs or dragons, ancient magical beings might come up against modern technology. Often these characters and situations occur in otherwise very normal settings—which allows readers to believe more readily.

Ian Fleming, author of the James Bond novels, only wrote one book for children, and it has become a classic: *Chitty Chitty Bang Bang: The Magical Car.* Fleming wrote this book about the spirited adventures of a wild British family for his son, Caspar. Recently, Frank Cottrell Boyce was asked by the Fleming family to write a sequel to the book that was originally published in 1964 and illustrated by John Birmingham. Boyce's *Chitty Chitty Bang Bang Flies Again* features the Tooting family on vacation in their 1966 VW camper van. Little do they know that the old engine they find and install in their van actually belonged to the original magical car. Chitty flies the family on an adventure around the world searching for all of her parts so she can restore her original self.

Pippi Longstocking, a notoriously funny character created by Astrid Lindgren, has delighted children for more than fifty years. Pippi is an orphan who lives alone with her monkey and her horse in a child's utopian world where she tells herself when to go to bed and when to get up! Although she is only 9 years old, Pippi can hold her own with anyone, for she is so strong that she can pick up a horse or a man and throw him into the air. Children love this amazing character who always has the integrity to say what she thinks, even if she shocks adults. Seven-, 8-, and 9-year-olds enjoy her madcap adventures in *Pippi Longstocking* and in the sequels *Pippi Goes on Board* and *Pippi in the South Seas.* Lauren Child, the award-winning creator of the Charlie and Lola books, illustrated Tiina Nunnally's 2007 translation of Astrid Lindgren's *Pippi Longstocking.*

Mr. Popper's Penguins by Richard Atwater and Florence Atwater has long been the favorite funny story of many primary-grade children. Mr. Popper is a mild little house painter whose major interest in life is the study of the Antarctic. When an explorer presents Mr. Popper with a penguin, he promptly names him Captain Cook, and he obtains Greta from the zoo to keep Captain Cook company. After the arrival of ten baby penguins, Mr. Popper puts a freezing plant in the basement of his house and moves his furnace upstairs to the living room. The Atwaters' serious account of a highly implausible situation adds to the humor of this truly funny story.

Roald Dahl's many books are populated with highly eccentric characters involved in highly preposterous adventures. One of the most popular fantasies for children is Dahl's tongue-in-cheek morality tale *Charlie and the Chocolate Factory*. Mr. Willie Wonka suddenly announces that the five children who find the gold seal hidden in their chocolate bar wrappers will be allowed to visit his fabulous factory. One by one the children disobey Willie and meet with horrible accidents in the chocolate factory, except of course for the virtuous and humble Charlie, who by the story's conclusion has brought his poor family to live in the chocolate factory and is learning the business from his benefactor. M. T. Anderson's Pals in Peril series follows the mad-cap adventures of Jasper Dash and his two crime-fighting friends. The series of five books offers readers a zany mishmash of mystery and fantasy, peppered with silly footnotes and asides from the narrator. Anderson, author of the popular YA dystopia *Feed,* has an extensive interactive website for the series at www.mt-anderson.com/delaware/.

Garth Nix and Ingrid Law have turned to folktales to find their eccentric characters. Nix's *Frogkisser* turns the Frog Prince on its head as a young princess sets out on a quest to return various amphibians to human form after her evil uncle casts a spell on them. In Law's *Savvy,* each of the members of the Beaumont family finds a special gift ("savvy") revealed on his or her thirteenth birthday. Brother Rocket puts out electrical charges, young Fish causes storms and hurricanes when he gets upset. Two days before her own thirteenth birthday, young Mibs eagerly awaits the revelation of her own savvy. The funny events that take place as she sets off on her journey to identity lighten the tone but don't hide the worthy theme that we all have our individual savvy, magical or not. *Scumble* continues the adventures of the unique Beaumont family.

Peter Brown combines science fiction and animal fantasy with his eccentric *The Wild Robot*. When a boat carrying a shipment of robots sinks, one of the crates ends up on an island inhabited by animals. Playful otters knock over the crate, accidentally activating a robot. The robot, a female, ends up as a nurturing member of the animal kingdom. Warm and touching, *The Wild Robot* is followed

The Wild Robot by Peter Brown features a mechanical creature who is shipwrecked on an island inhabited only by animals. From *The Wild Robot* by Peter Brown. Text and illustrations copyright ©2016 by Peter Brown. Used by permission of Little Brown Books for Young Readers. All rights reserved.

by *The Wild Robot Escapes*. H. M. Bowman's *A Crack in the Sea* also begins on an island. This watery land consists of Islanders and Raft Worlders, both expelled from another world. They have coexisted peacefully for all the years of their exile. However, when a crack opens to the other world, Kinchen and her strange brother Pip are called upon to mend the crack. Their story intertwines with two others. The second story involves a brother and sister who are captured and put on a slave ship in the other world in 1871. The third story takes place in a boat on a stormy sea as a brother and sister try to escape post-war Vietnam. The sea and a Kracken are the unifying element as these six children eventually come together in a complex and satisfying tale.

Incredible Worlds

When Alice followed the White Rabbit down his rabbit hole and entered a world that grew "curiouser and curiouser," she established a pattern for many modern books of fantasy. Often starting in the world of reality, they move quickly into a world where the everyday becomes extraordinary, yet still believable. The plausible impossibilities of Lewis Carroll's *Alice's Adventures in Wonderland* include potions and edibles that make poor Alice grow up and down like an elevator. Always the proper Victorian young lady, however, Alice maintains her own personality despite her bizarre surroundings, and her acceptance of this nonsense makes it all seem believable. She is the one link with reality in this amazingly fantastic world.

The British landscape where Alice's adventures began has formed the setting for many other fine works of fantasy. *Harry Potter and the Sorcerer's Stone*, the first book in J. K. Rowling's phenomenally popular series, begins in what seems to be a run-of-the-mill middle-class neighborhood as Mr. Dursley picks up his briefcase, bids his wife and son goodbye, and heads off to work. As he drives off, however, he fails to notice a cat sitting on the street reading a map. Mr. Dursley might be clueless, but readers know immediately that this is no ordinary work of realism. They are soon immersed in the magical world of Harry Potter, his awful Dursley relatives, and a host of magical and muggical characters. Rowling has adapted the familiar characters of school stories—a well-meaning and earnest hero and his likable friends, a school bully, an acerbic teacher, and a kindhearted one, and finally a wise if uneducated janitor to whom the kids go for advice and comfort. Her plots are fast moving and straightforward. The hero is confronted with serious problems that, in spite of many obstacles, are eventually solved. What makes these books so enjoyable are the good humor and obvious zest with which Rowling writes and the wonderful details of Harry's extraordinary world. Sage Blackwood has created an equally magical kingdom in *Miss Ellicott's School for the Magically Minded*. The school takes in orphan girls who are trained as sorceresses to guard the wall that protects a xenophobic city from the outside world. When the adult sorceresses go missing, it's up to two of the pupils, with help of a kitchen boy and a boy from outside the wall, to save the city.

Steampunk is a recent trend within fantasy that re-imagines or projects a world in which steam power rather than electronics has driven innovation, often drawing on the Victorian times in which this split took place. Scott Westerfeld's Leviathan trilogy portrays the Central Powers in World War I as "Clankers" dependent upon large, steam-powered machines, concluding in *Goliath*. In *The Boundless* is Kenneth Oppel's innovative machine, the "longest train ever," that barrels through the alternative Canadian world. Philip Reeve is another popular steampunk author for children with several series of books, most recently including *Traction City* and *Scrivener's Moon* in the Mortal Engines

Two sorceress apprentices, a kitchen boy, and a war refugee are the main characters in Sage Blackwood's delightful *Miss Ellicott's School for the Magically Minded.* Jacket art copyright ©2016 by Glenn Thomas. Used by permission of HarperCollins Publishers.

and Fever Crumb series, respectively, that propose a post-apocalyptic future where giant mechanical cities roam the earth, often attacking and consuming each other.

Miniature worlds have always fascinated children, and Mary Norton's Borrowers series tells a fascinating story about tiny people who try to coexist with normal-size humans. The Borrowers derive their names from their occupation, which is "borrowing" from human "beans," those "great slaves put there for them to use." "Borrowing" is a dangerous trade, for if one is seen by human beings, disastrous things may happen. Therefore, in *The Borrowers,* Pod and Homily Clock are understandably alarmed when they learn of their daughter Arrietty's desire to explore the world upstairs. In the end, the Borrowers are "discovered" and flee for their lives. This surprise ending leads directly to the sequel, *The Borrowers Afield.* Strong characterizations and apt descriptions of setting make the small-scale world of the Borrowers come alive. Other titles continue the series.

Once children have discovered the delights of series fantasy, they will want to be introduced to others. See **Teaching Feature 5.1: Chronicles, Sagas, and Trilogies: Recent Fantasy Series for Children** for descriptions of more popular series fantasies.

Magical Powers

The magical people, creatures, and objects that are found in traditional literature are just as prevalent in children's fantasy. The children in books of fantasy often possess a magical object, know a magical saying, or have magical powers themselves. In *Half Magic* by Edward Eager, the nickel that Jane finds turns out to be a magical charm, or at least half of a magical charm, for it provides half of all the children's wishes, so that half of them will come true.

In John Stephens's *The Emerald Atlas,* book one in The Books of Beginning series, three siblings have passed through a series of orphanages in the ten years since their parents disappeared in order to protect them. At the latest orphanage, they find an

Chronicles, Sagas, and Trilogies: Recent Fantasy Series for Children

Author	Series Title	Description	Grade Level
M. T. Anderson	Pals in Peril	Three close friends encounter humorous adventures in a parody of formula fiction.	5–8
Avi	Dimwood Forest	These charming animal fantasies feature Poppy the mouse and her friends and family.	3–6
T. A. Barron	The Great Tree of Avalon	These stories of the battle between good and evil take place in the legendary land of Avalon.	5 and up
T. A. Barron	The Lost Years of Merlin	These tales relate the childhood of Merlin and his rise to power.	5 and up
Ian Beck	Tom Trueheart	Tom, youngest of seven brothers all named Jack, enters the land of stories to seek happy endings.	3–6
Hilary Bell	The Goblin Wood Trilogy	Tobin and Makenna come from different sides of a war but must work together in the interests of both humans and goblins.	4–6
L. M. Boston	Green Knowe Chronicles	A thirteenth-century Anglo Saxon manor serves as the locus of past and present.	3–6
Michael Buckley	The Sisters Grimm	Two sisters move in with their grandmother to find that she lives in a town populated with characters from fairy tales.	3–6
Cathy Camper	*Lowriders to the Center of the Earth* (Lowriders series)	Three animal friends with distinctly Mexican characteristics take their lowrider car on fantastic journeys in graphic novel format.	5–8
Eoin Colfer	Artemis Fowl	A young criminal mastermind captures a LEPrecon to hold for ransom and finds himself involved in the fairy world.	5–8
Suzanne Collins	Underland Chronicles	Gregor and his baby sister fall into the Underland where they encounter an alliance of giant bats and humans and battle against the evil rats who have captured his father.	4–8
Suzanne Collins	The Hunger Games	Teens compete in survival games where the last one living wins.	6 and up
Barry Deutsch	Hereville	Mirka, an 11-year-old Orthodox Jewish girl, slowly works toward her dreams of fighting dragons and trolls in these fascinating graphic novels.	3–7

(continued)

teaching feature 5.1

Author	Series Title	Description	Grade Level
Tony DiTerlizzi and Holly Black	The Spiderwick Chronicles	Three children move into an old estate and experience new adventures with fairies and other magical creatures.	3–6
Chitra Banerjee Divakaruni	The Brotherhood of the Conch	Indian mythology and culture form the backdrop for this series about a poor boy from Kolkata who joins an ancient brotherhood to fight evil.	4–7
Jeanne Duprau	The City of Ember	Lina and Doon struggle to escape their existence in a devastated future world.	4–7
Nancy Farmer	Northern Saga	Jack, a young Saxon boy, enters into adventures with heroes from Celtic and Norse Mythology.	5 and up
Cornelia Funke	Inkheart	Meggie and her father can live in two worlds: their own and the world of the book.	4–7
Ben Hatke	*Mighty Jack*	A reimagining of Jack and the Beanstalk in graphic novel form.	4–7
Erin Hunter	Survivors	This Erin Hunter animal series features dogs trying to work together to survive in a post apocalyptic world without humans.	5–7
Brian Jacques	Redwall	A large cast of animal characters fight for right in the mythical medieval kingdom of Redwall.	4 and up
Catherine Jinks	Genius Squad	Thaddeus Roth is a young genius who is recruited into the Axis Institute for World Domination.	5 and up
Catherine Jinks	How to Catch a Bogle	Celtic characters appear in these exciting books and a young singer is at the center of the action.	4–6
Jeramey Kraatz	The Cloak Society	Superpowered Alex is a member of a secret society of villains but must make some difficult choices.	4–6
Brandon Mull	Fablehaven	Two children must help protect a nature preserve for creatures from myths and legends.	4 and up
Nnedi Okorafor	*Akata Witch; Akata Warrior*	An albino Nigerian girl battles serial killers, magic, and witches.	6 and up
Lauren Oliver and H. C. Chester	*Curiosity House: The Fearsome Firebird* (Curiosity series)	Four orphans who perform in a bizarre circus battle an evil villain and solve mysteries.	4–6
Kenneth Oppel	Silverwing	A young bat ventures out into the wide world to save his colony and find his identity.	3–6

(continued)

teaching feature 5.1

Author	Series Title	Description	Grade Level
Christopher Paolini	Inheritance	A boy bonds with a dragon to fight evil in his kingdom.	4–7
David Petersen	Mouse Guard	These graphic novels chronicle the brave mice who help protect those who wish to travel from the dangers of the road.	3–6
Tamora Pierce	Circle of Magic; The Circle Opens; The Circle Reforged	These series follow the adventures of four mages from their training to the major roles they play in their society.	4–7
Philip Reeve	The Hungry City Chronicles	In a future world, mechanized cities travel around the globe trying to destroy each other.	5 and up
Philip Reeve	Larklight	Mad adventure and wacky episodes follow Art and his sister Myrtle through a Victorian world set in outer space.	5 and up
Adam Rex	Fangbone! Third-Grade Barbarian	Fangbone recruits his new classmates to help keep a powerful weapon out of the hands of the vile Venomous Drool.	2–4
Rick Riordan	Percy Jackson & the Olympians	A boy with attention deficit hyperactivity disorder finds out he is the half human son of a Greek god. His quest is to restore order in the supernatural realm and discover his true identity.	5–9
Brian Sanderson	Alcatraz Versus the Evil Librarians	Alcatraz uses his talent for breaking things and magical glasses to fight against the evil librarians in this humorous series.	4–7
Eta Spalding	Fitzgerald-Trout series	The Fitzgerald-Trouts have madcap adventures on an island where only children can drive.	4–7
John Stephens	Books of Beginning	Three orphans must make a dangerous journey with a book that can take them back in time.	4–7
Jon Scieszka	The Time Warp Trio	A magic book provides adventures in time to three zany boys.	2 and up
Trenton Lee Stewart	The Benedict Society	Four uniquely talented youngsters are recruited to fight evil.	4–6
Jonathan Stroud	The Bartimaeus Trilogy	Bartimaeus, the djinni, an ambitious young magician, and a young resistance fighter struggle for power in an alternate Victorian universe.	5 and up

(continued)

teaching feature 5.1

Author	Series Title	Description	Grade Level
Lian Tanner	The Keepers Trilogy	Goldie, a natural thief, must help protect the Museum of Dent.	4–6
Kate Thompson	Tír na n'Óg	A family of Irish musicians travel back and forth between the present and the land of Faerie.	7 and up
Catherynne M. Valente	*The Girl Who Raced Fairyland All the Way Home* (Fairyland series)	A girl from Nebraska finds herself on multiple adventures in Fairyland.	5–8
Mark Walden	H.I.V.E.: Higher Institute of Villainous Education	A kid criminal genius goes to a top secret school where all may not be what it seems.	4–6
Django Wexler	*The Mad Apprentice; The Palace of Glass* (The Forbidden Library series)	When her father disappears, Alice is sent to live in the gloomy mansion of an uncle. When she takes a book from the forbidden library, she opens herself up to all kinds of dangers.	4–6
Patricia Wrede	Enchanted Forest Chronicles	The unconventional Princess Cimorene befriends dragons, battles wizards, and rescues princesses in this lighthearted series.	4–7
J. A. White	*The Last Spell* (The Thickety series)	A girl accused by her community of being a witch is mysteriously called into the dark woods where her magical powers are revealed.	4–6

enchanted atlas that transports them back in time, where they learn that they have special powers and are the key to an ancient prophecy. Embarking on a quest to save the world, their journey is filled with magic, dangerous enemies, and powerful allies. Their adventures continue in *The Fire Chronicle*.

Authors Sarah Prineas and Sid Fleischman set their fantasies in a much lighter vein. Prineas's protagonist in *The Magic Thief* is Conn, a wily young pickpocket. When he picks the pocket of the wizard Nevery Elinglas, Conn has met his match, and he finds himself apprenticed to a mage whose difficult task is to discover why magic is seeping out of the city of Wellmet. A lively battle of wits between Nevery and the villainous

Underlord ensues with Conn playing the role of a bumbling if ingenious helper. *The Girl Who Drank the Moon* by Kelly Barnhill is filled with the magic, magical characters, and magical creatures found in traditional folktales. However, the characters in the story do not fit our expectations of good and evil. The witch is a good witch who, each year, rescues the baby left as a sacrifice to keep the community safe from the perceived dangers. As the story begins, the annual sacrifice is made, despite the terrible anguish of the child's mother. Xan, the witch, takes the baby, intending to take it to a free city to give to a loving family. On the journey through the woods to the home, the witch mistakenly feeds the baby from the moon rather than the usual starlight. The baby drinks deeply and is imbued with a special magic. Xan cannot give baby Luna away. *The Girl Who Drank the Moon* is a powerful story that is reflective of xenophobic peoples who fear the "other" and judge people by outward appearances.

Readers with a tolerance for invented worlds and the ability to follow a large cast of characters will enjoy the many books by Diana Wynne Jones. *Howl's Moving Castle* features Sophie Hatter, an adolescent who is turned into an old woman by the Wicked Witch of the Waste. In *Charmed Life,* the magician Chrestomanci must help young Eric Chant (called "Cat" for short) to discover his own powers while he preserves his household against the evil that assails it from outside the castle walls. *The Lives of Christopher Chant* and *The Pinhoe Egg* round out the series. These imaginatively plotted stories reveal the author's wry humor, her love of language, and her ability to balance aspects of time and space in impossible but believable ways.

Suspense and the Supernatural

Interest in the occult and the supernatural, usually an adult preoccupation, also captures the imagination of children. They enjoy spooky, scary stories, just as they like being frightened by TV or theater horror stories. This may in part explain the popularity of authors like John Bellairs, whose mysteries, such as *The House with a Clock in Its Walls,* are full of spooky old houses, scary characters, fast-moving plots, and plenty of dialogue. Increasingly, publishers are issuing finely crafted suspense fantasies that are often superior to the usual ghost story or mystery tale. These well-written tales of suspense and the supernatural deserve attention. One such book is Patrick Ness's *A Monster Calls,* a novel from an original idea by Siobhan Dowd and winner of the 2012 Carnegie and Kate Greenaway Medals. An ancient monster is terrifying in its relentless mission to force Conor, a 13-year-old boy, to tell the truth about his deepest fear, that of losing his mother to cancer. The novel explores grief and loss in a brutally honest manner. Using a mixture of printmaking and markmaking, Jim Kay's black-and-white ink illustrations bring the horror of the monster to life. Ness's *The Nest* tells an equally chilling story, as does David Almond in *Skellig.* These books portray children left alone with their fears when a family member falls ill.

Several recent books don't pull any stops when it comes to horror. All involve resourceful heroines who are forced to act in the face of their terror when their parents disappear. Neil Gaiman's Newbery-winning *The Graveyard Book* is an inventive tale of Nobody Owens, an orphan whose family is brutally murdered. Known as Bod, the boy lives in a graveyard, where he is raised by ghosts and watched over by an otherworldly guardian. Gaiman's coming-of-age story follows Bod from babyhood to adolescence, exploring timeless themes of family, loyalty, and a child's desire for independence. *The Graveyard Book* is horror writing at its best, with intriguing characters, a well-constructed and eerie setting, and a thrilling and suspenseful plot. Dave McKean, who also illustrated Gaiman's *Coraline* and *The Wolves in the Walls,* adds his black-and-white illustrations to the macabre tale.

Joseph Bruchac's *The Dark Pond, Whisper in the Dark,* and *Skeleton Man,* although set in the present, are based on traditional Native American tales. In *Skeleton Man,* the heroine, Molly, relates this traditional Abenaki tale at the beginning of her own narrative story. As her story proceeds, Molly becomes involved with a mysterious great-uncle who turns up when her parents disappear. Locked in her room each night, Molly suspects that the uncle may be Skeleton Man, a legendary creature who devoured himself and then, still hungry, ate everyone around him. Molly realizes that, like the young girls in the original tale, she is the only one who can defeat him. These novels are flat-out terrifying through their final pages.

Mary Downing Hahn's ghost stories are not for the fainthearted. In *Wait Till Helen Comes,* a ghost child named Helen has perished in a fire and now waits by a pond to drag children to their deaths as play companions. When Molly and Michael's mother remarries, their new father's child joins the family, but Heather is a brat who forever whines about imagined injustices. Nobody believes Heather's stories of the ghostly Helen until Molly begins to develop some sympathy for her stepsister's point of view. In a chilling ending, Molly pieces together the mystery, saves Heather from a sure death, and forges a hopeful beginning of a loving family. *The Ghost of Crutchfield Hall* is a spine-tingling story of Florence, a 12-year-old orphan who goes to live with her great-aunt and uncle in a spooky old manor. The house is haunted by the ghost of her cousin, Sophia, who tries to enlist Florence's help in avenging her death. Florence feels powerless to resist Sophia's malicious plans in this chilling gothic mystery. Hahn's fast-paced stories consistently win young-readers' awards presented by various states, showing how much children appreciate a good, scary ghost story. Hahn's *One for Sorrow: A Ghost Story* is set in a girls' school during the flu epidemic of 1918. The new girl Annie is befriended by Elsie,

Florence finds her great-aunt and uncle's manor is haunted by the ghost of her cousin, Sophia, in *The Ghost of Crutchfield Hall* by Mary Downing Hahn.

who turns out to be quite nasty. Annie makes other friends to Elsie's dismay. When Elsie dies of the flu, she comes back to claim Annie as a friend for eternity.

In *Spirit Hunters* by Ellen Oh, Harper has always been sensitive to the spirit world; so sensitive that she once ended up in a mental institution. When her family moves into an old house in the Washington D. C. area, Harper is the only one who understands that her younger brother Michael is being possessed by the ghost of a malevolent child. Harper seeks to battle the spirit for her brother's life and protect her family. This terrifying story culminates in a battle between spirits. The book is best read with the lights on!

Sweet Whispers, Brother Rush by Virginia Hamilton is a haunting story of the supernatural in which 14-year-old Tree must take care of her older brother Dab while her mother, Viola, works in another city as a practical nurse. Tree painfully accepts her mother's absences and devotes her time to schoolwork and caring for her brother. As Dab's occasional bouts of sickness suddenly become more frequent, a spectral character named Brother Rush appears to Tree and enables her to understand what is happening. Making use of African American cadences and inflections, Hamilton has created complex characters whose steady or fumbling reachings for each other may linger with middle-school readers long past the end of this story.

Time-Shift Fantasy

Probably everyone at one time or another has wondered what it would be like to visit the past. Recognizing this, authors of books for children have written many fantasies that are based on characters who appear to shift easily from their particular moment in the present to a long-lost point in someone else's past. Usually, these time leaps are linked to a tangible object or place that is common to both periods. In *Tom's Midnight Garden* by Philippa Pearce, for example, the old grandfather clock that strikes thirteen hours serves as the fixed point of entry for the fantasy.

No one is more skillful in fusing the past with the present than L. M. Boston in her stories of Green Knowe, the mysterious old English house in which the author lived. Each story of Green Knowe blends a child of the present with characters and situations from previous centuries while creating for the reader a marvelous sense of place.

While the characters in most time fantasies slip in and out of the past, the problem in *Tuck Everlasting* is that the Tuck family is trapped forever in the present. Natalie

Babbitt's elegant prose leads the reader to expect a quiet Victorian fantasy, but the book holds many surprises—including a kidnapping, a murder, and a jailbreak. The simplicity of the Tucks and their story belies the depth of the theme of *Tuck Everlasting*. With its prologue and epilogue, the story is reminiscent of a play, a kind of *Our Town* for children.

In some books where characters are shifted from modern times into specific periods of history, the concern with social and political issues of the past is very strong. Margaret Peterson Haddix, author of the popular series The Shadow Children, has a highly suspenseful series that is part mystery, part science fiction, and part historical fiction. In *Found,* the main characters learn that they are actually famous missing children from history who were sent forward in time to save their lives. Throughout the series, they travel back in time to try and fix history so they can return to their present-day lives. In *Caught,* the fifth book in the series, the time-traveling children are charged with returning the daughter of Albert Einstein to history. Jane Yolen's devastating story of the Holocaust, *The Devil's Arithmetic,* begins in the present when Hannah, bored with all the remembering of the Passover Seder, opens the door to welcome symbolically the prophet Elijah and finds herself in the unfamiliar world of a Polish village in the 1940s.

Susan Cooper has created a richly detailed time-travel story in *King of Shadows*. Nat Field is a passionate actor and a member of a group of boys who have been chosen to perform William Shakespeare's *A Midsummer Night's Dream* at the recently opened replica of the Globe Theatre in London. Nat keeps himself busy with rehearsals and throws himself into his role as Puck, partly out of love for acting and partly to block out thoughts about his father's suicide. Soon after his arrival in London, Nat becomes ill and wakes from his fever to find himself in sixteenth-century London. There he is still called Nat Field and he is still an actor. But now he finds he is to play the part of Puck alongside Will Shakespeare on the boards of the original Globe. Readers captivated by the world of the Elizabethan theater in *King of Shadows* will also enjoy Jane Louise Curry's *The Black Canary*. In this time-shift fantasy, 13-year-old James, a biracial child, has rejected the musical world of his career-oriented parents. When he accompanies them to London, he finds a mysterious door in the cellar of their borrowed flat. Stepping through, James is plunged into Elizabethan times, where he is forced to join the Queen's performers. In addition to dealing with issues of race, Curry tells a gripping coming-of-age story in *The Black Canary*. Both *The Black Canary* and *King of Shadows* introduce themes of interest to early adolescents. In addition, they present readers with the historical background of a vivid age.

Brian Selznick's *The Marvels* takes place in two different time periods. In 1766, the family of the Marvels performs a play about a shipwreck. In 1900, a boy runs away from school to London and finds an uncle who lives in an old house. How the two time periods are connected is the subject of this complex tale, told equally in images and words.

Imaginary Realms

Many authors of fantasy create believability by setting their stories in an imaginary society where kings and queens rule feudal societies that resemble the Middle Ages. Often lighter in tone than high fantasy, these stories might nonetheless feature some of its attributes—such as a human character's search for identity, a quest, or the struggle against evil—and are good introductions to the more complex and more serious works of high fantasy. Children are often drawn to this kind of fantasy, as it seems so closely related in many ways to folktales and traditional literature.

Authors have long enjoyed playing with the characters and elements of traditional tales. Adam Gidwitz used Geoffrey Chaucer's *The Canterbury Tales* to frame *The*

Inquisitor's Tale: Or, The Three Magical Children and Their Holy Dog. Set in an imaginary kingdom in France, the story begins with a traveler arriving at an inn. He asks if anyone knows a story about three children. The various patrons of the inn then retell their own encounters with the children, leading to a surprising and satisfying ending. Gail Carson Levine, Diane Stanley, and Patricia Wrede are three writers who have relied on familiar fairy tales to create humorous, highly readable fantasies. In *Ella Enchanted,* Levine has taken the Cinderella story and provided a reasonable interpretation for Cinderella's subservience to her stepmother and stepsisters. A well-meaning fairy has given her the gift of obedience, but the gift turns into a curse when her stepfamily starts ordering her around. This wily heroine eventually breaks the wish through willing self-sacrifice and wins the Prince through her own devices. In *Bella at Midnight,* Diane Stanley serves up a delightful twist on the Cinderella story, with a bit of the Joan of Arc legend thrown in. Patricia Wrede's Enchanted Forest Chronicles feature the unconventional Princess Cimorene. In *Dealing with Dragons,* Cimorene runs off to be librarian and cook for the dragon Kazul rather than stay in the palace, sew, and wait for a suitor. This same audience will appreciate the many series of books by Tamora Pierce, which feature characters who will not stay put in the roles their societies have dictated for them. While all of Pierce's books like *Mastiff* feature feisty heroines, her classic series The Song of the Lioness and Protector of the Small focus on girls who want to enter the male world of knighthood. Alana in *Alana: The First Adventure* disguises herself as a boy and Keladry in *First Test* starts training unfairly as a page on probation. Gail Carson Levine's *A Tale of Two Castles* features another character who won't stick to traditional gender roles. Elodie is a spirited young heroine who sets out to become an actress and finds herself cast in the role of assistant to a dragon. Together they work to solve a series of mysteries involving an entertaining cast of characters who inhabit the castle.

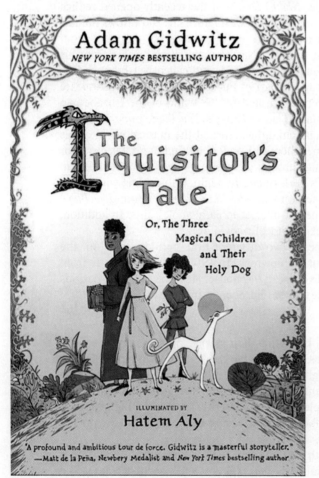

The Inquisitor's Tale: Or, The Three Magical Children and Their Holy Dog is inspired by Chaucer's The Canterbury Tales. Illuminated borders by Hatem Aly add veracity to the book's setting in an imaginary France.

Gerald Morris, Nancy Springer, and Kevin Crossley-Holland have placed their stories squarely within the tradition of Arthurian legend. We have chosen to discuss these books in the fantasy chapter because of some instances of magic and their focus on legendary characters such as Arthur and Morgan le Fay. However, these books are so well researched in the history of the Middle Ages that they could qualify as historical fiction. Morris's stories are clearly set in mythical Arthur's time period. *The Squire's Tale* and *The Squire, His Knight, and His Lady* are the somewhat lighthearted stories of 14-year-old Terence's apprenticeship to Sir Gawain and his adventures at King Arthur's court. Springer's *I Am Mordred* and *I Am Morgan le Fay* are more somber but ultimately uplifting stories of the traditional villains in King Arthur's tale. Crossley-Holland's series, which includes *The Seeing Stone, At the Crossing Place,* and *King of the Middle March,* takes place in the latter part of the twelfth century in England. This England is not a mythical place but a carefully researched historical setting. It is a time when the English face great danger as the villainous King John assumes the throne after King Richard's death. The Arthur of this period is given access to King Arthur's life through the magical seeing stone. *Crossing to Paradise* follows Arthur's childhood friend Gatti, a young field girl, who is asked to accompany Lady Gwyneth as a maidservant on a pilgrimage to the Holy Land. In return for her services on this dangerous journey, Gatti will be taught to read and write and to be trained in how to use her marvelous singing voice. The geographical journey is mirrored by Gatti's journey to self-understanding and self-confidence.

High Fantasy

Many readers who learn to enjoy popular stories of magic, ghosts, time travel, and the like go on to become fans of a more serious and demanding type of story called high fantasy. These complex narratives, which often extend into sequels, are characterized by certain recurring themes and motifs. For instance, the stories frequently take place in created worlds or imaginary realms. Characters might call on ancient and fundamental powers, for good or ill. The conflict between these opposing forces becomes the focus of many stories. Frequently the protagonists of high fantasy have a quest to fulfill. Finally, although there may be touches of humor, the overall tone of high fantasy is serious, because its purpose is serious. High fantasy concerns itself with cosmic questions and ultimate values: goodness, truth, courage, and wisdom.

The age-old conflicts between good and evil, light and darkness, life and death are recurring themes in modern fantasy as well as in traditional literature. The setting for the struggle might be the world as we know it, or an invented land like Narnia, which some children know as well as their own backyards or city blocks. C. S. Lewis, a well-known English scholar and theologian, created seven fantasies about the country of Narnia. The best of the series is the first one published, *The Lion, the Witch, and the Wardrobe,* although it was the second in the sequence according to the history of Narnia.

Susan Cooper has written a series of five books about the cosmic struggle between good and evil. The second book in the series, *The Dark Is Rising,* features Will Stanton who discovers that he is the last of the Old Ones, immortals dedicated throughout the ages to keeping the world safe from the forces of evil, the Dark. Will must find the six Signs of Life in order to complete his power and defeat, even temporarily, the rising of the Dark. While rich in symbolism and allegory, the story is grounded in reality so that both Will's "real" life and his quest in suspended time are distinct, yet interwoven. In the fourth book of the series, *The Grey King,* Will once again must prepare for the coming battle between the Dark and the Light. *Silver on the Tree* draws together characters from

In his Great Tree of Avalon series, T. A. Barron has created complex works of high fantasy based in ancient legends and myths. Barron, T.A.. *The Great Tree of Avalon: The Eternal Flame, Book III*. New York, NY: Philomel Books, a division of Penguin Young Readers Group, 2002, Cover. Copyright ©2002 by Philomel Books, a division of Penguin Young Readers Group. All rights reserved. Used with permission.

the previous four novels for a final assault on the Dark. Much that was hidden in the other tales is made explicit here, and knowledge of the major threads of the first four books is necessary to understand this exciting and fulfilling climax to the saga.

T. A. Barron has also drawn on myths surrounding King Arthur in his five-book The Lost Years of Merlin series. This saga begins with a young boy who finds himself lying on a rocky shore robbed of his memory and his identity. Over the course of the series, this child will uncover his past and his magical gifts. More important, however, as he faces increasingly difficult trials, he will learn to control his marvelous talents and to accept the responsibilities that come with power. Barron's Great Tree of Avalon series continues his exploration of Celtic lore and the myth of Merlin.

Philip Pullman, whose skillful writing has given us such fine books as the suspenseful *The Ruby in the Smoke,* the supernatural *Clockwork,* and the farcical *The Firework-Maker's Daughter* and *I Was a Rat,* has created high fantasy of matchless proportion in His Dark Materials series. The trilogy, which includes *The Golden Compass, The Subtle Knife,* and *The Amber Spyglass,* is a richly complex work of the imagination. Inspired by a phrase from Milton's *Paradise Lost,* Pullman wrestles with profound issues of innocence, individuality, and spirituality. *La Belle Sauvage Dust* is the first "Book of the Dust" in a long-awaited prequel series. These compelling books, with their connections to Judeo-Christian traditions, their underpinnings in literary classics, and their references to theories of quantum physics, demand much of readers, but those willing to accept the challenging puzzles will be rewarded with an exceptionally satisfying experience.

High fantasy is almost always the story of a search—for treasure, justice, identity, understanding—and of a hero figure who learns important lessons in the adventuring. Welsh legends and mythology are the inspiration for the intriguing chronicles of the imaginary land of Prydain as told by Lloyd Alexander. In *The Book of Three,* the reader is introduced to Taran, an assistant pigkeeper who dreams of becoming a hero. With a strange assortment of companions, he pursues Hen Wen, the oracular pig, and struggles to save Prydain from the forces of evil. The chronicles are continued in the most exciting of all the books, *The Black Cauldron.* Over the course of the chronicles Taran gradually learns what it means to become a man among men. He experiences treachery, tragedy, and triumph; yet a thread of humor runs throughout to lighten the tension. Good does prevail, and Taran has matured and is ready for his next adventure. *The High King,* the masterful conclusion to this cycle of stories about the kingdom of Prydain, received the Newbery Medal.

A superior tale against which other novels of high fantasy may be judged is *A Wizard of Earthsea* by Ursula K. Le Guin. Studying at the School for Wizards, Sparrow-hawk is taunted by a jealous classmate to use his powers before he is ready. Pride and arrogance drive him to call up a dreadful malignant shadow that threatens his life and all of Earth-sea. Thus, begins a chase and the hunt between the young wizard and the shadowbeast across the mountains and the waters of this world. Sparrow-hawk, or Ged, his true name known only by his most trusted friends, is a well-developed character who transforms from an intelligent, impatient adolescent into a wise and grateful mage, or wizard. A major theme of the story is the responsibility that each choice carries with it. The power of knowing the true name of someone or something, a common motif in traditional literature, is of central importance to this story. So, too, is the value of self-knowledge:

> Ged's "ultimate quest . . . had made him whole: a man who knowing his whole true self, cannot be used or possessed by another power other than by himself, and whose life therefore is lived for life's sake and never in the service of ruin, or pain, or hatred, or the dark." (p. 203)

The metaphors in all Le Guin's books speak clearly and profoundly to today's world.

Science Fiction

The line between fantasy and science fiction has always been difficult to draw, particularly in children's literature. Children are likely to use the label *science fiction* for any book that includes the paraphernalia of science, although critics make finer distinctions. It has been suggested that fantasy (even "science fantasy") presents a world that never was and never could be, whereas science fiction speculates on a world that, given what we now know of science, might just one day be possible.

Science fiction is relevant for today's rapidly changing world. Writers must speculate about future technology and how new discoveries will affect our daily lives and thoughts. To do this, they must construct a world in which scientific frontiers of genetic engineering, artificial intelligence, space exploration, or robotics have advanced beyond our present knowledge. As in modern fantasy, detailed descriptions of these "scientific principles" and the characters' acceptance of them make the story believable. In addition, authors who speak to today's reader about the future must consider the ethical or social implications inherent in the scientific issues they raise.

One of the most popular motifs in science fiction, especially for the youngest readers, is humorous tales of alien encounters. These books present imaginative nonhuman characters that could possibly be encountered in our vast universe but, due to the scientific likelihood of encountering extraterrestrial life, often seem more like fantasy. Visitors to earth can be found in popular picturebooks like *Aliens in Underpants Save the World* by Claire Freedman and Ben Cort, graphica like *Legends of Zita the Spacegirl* by Ben Hatky, and wacky novels like *The True Meaning of Smekday* by Adam Rex and Jon Scieszka's *Spaceheadz #4: Sphdz 4life!* As these books begin to cater to higher developmental needs, they can become more thought-provoking, such as *Enchantress from the Stars* by Sylvia Louise Engdahl.

Science fiction of the highest level presents the reader with complex hypotheses about the future of humankind. Many novels raise questions about the organization of society or the nature of the world following a massive ecological disaster. Writers such as

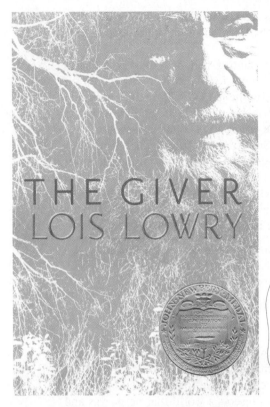

In her Newbery Medal–winning book *The Giver*, Lois Lowry raises fundamental questions about human nature and human society. Cover from *The Giver* by Lois Lowry. Cover copyright ©2012 by Houghton Mifflin Harcourt. Reprinted by permission of Houghton Mifflin Harcourt Publishing Company. All rights reserved.

Madeleine L'Engle imagine other life forms and their interactions with our world. In L'Engle's *A Swiftly Tilting Planet,* the past is altered to change the present and future. Throughout these novels of speculation runs the question of which human qualities and responsibilities will become—or remain—essential in time to come. *A Wrinkle in Time* suggests that love and individuality will continue to be important for the future. If there is a classic in the field of science fiction for children, it might be this Newbery Medal winner by Madeleine L'Engle, which celebrated its fiftieth anniversary with a special commemorative edition of the book. See **Teaching Feature 5.2: Exploring Possible Futures** for an overview of recent science fiction about future worlds.

One of the values of science fiction is its ability to develop children's imagination and intuition as well as exercise their speculative and improvisational abilities. Most literature offers a view of society as it is; science fiction assumes a vastly different society. Much science fiction that considers cosmic questions falls within the realm of young-adult novels. For instance, in *The Diary of Pelly D,* and the sequel *Cherry Heaven,* L. J. Adlington imagines a seemingly utopian world where growing prejudice about genetic ancestry leads society to a futuristic holocaust. In *Eva,* Peter Dickinson considers the consequences when the mind of a human girl is transferred from her ruined body to that of a healthy chimpanzee. *The Adoration of Jenna Fox* by Mary E. Pearson and Nancy Farmer's *The House of the Scorpion* deal with ethical issues and cloning.

Neal Shusterman's *Unwind* portrays a future where issues of abortion and organ donation are taken to the extreme of being able to retroactively abort children at the age of 13. M. T. Anderson's *Feed* contemplates a frightening future where at birth almost everyone is wired to the Internet through brain implants. These books demand maturity in their readers but raise important questions about the world these young adults will inherit.

For younger adolescents, Lois Lowry's *The Giver* imagines a future that at first seems benign and idyllic. Pollution is gone, family life is tranquil, and communities are orderly and peaceful. In this world, young Jonas approaches the Ceremony of Twelve with anticipation, for this is when he will be assigned to his life's work. He is stunned when his name is passed over during the ceremony, but then the Chief Elder announces that Jonas has been selected to be the next Receiver of Memory. This is the one person in the community who holds memories, not just of events, but of feelings. As he is instructed by the old Receiver, now the Giver, he comes to understand the fullness of human experience in all its color, joy, and pain. He also begins to see beneath the orderly surface of his existence and to understand the terrible price his people have paid for their serenity.

Exploring Possible Futures: Science Fiction for Today's Youth

Author	Title	Description	Grade Level
M. T. Anderson	*The Game of Sunken Places*	Brian and Gregory unknowingly play an intergalactic game on behalf of two alien peoples.	3–6
Julie Bertagna	*Exodus; Zenith; Aurora*	Greenhouse gases have finally destroyed most of the planet, and refugees from the last island try to find sanctuary.	7 and up
Lisa Bunker	*Felix Yz*	Told in diary format, Felix shares his experiences before he is to be separated from a fourth-dimensional creature in an LGBTQIA inclusive family.	5–9
Frank Cotrell Boyce	*Sputnick's Guide to Life on Earth*	A wacky human family meets space aliens in this humorous story.	4–6
Emma Clayton	*The Roar; The Whisper*	Mika must play a virtual reality game in order to rescue his twin sister who dared to investigate outside their city, protected from the plague in an environmental dystopian tale.	5–8
Eoin Colfer	*The Supernaturalist: The Graphic Novel;*	When a group of kids discover that they can see supernatural Parasites that are attacking Satellite City, they resolve to protect humanity.	5 and up
	Artemis Fowl: The Last Guardian	Twelve-year-old master criminal Artemis Fowl battles evil fairies with the help of two sidekicks.	
Tony DiTerlizzi	*The Search for WondLa*	Raised by a robot, Eva Nine must now search for other humans.	5–8
Michael Grant	*Gone; Hunger; Lies; Plague; Fear; Light*	Everyone over the age of 13 has disappeared, and the survivors end up fighting each other rather than getting along.	6–9
Margaret Peterson Haddix	*Among the Hidden* (Shadow Children sequence)	Third children are illegal in a future world and thus exist in great peril.	4–7
Alaya Dawn Johnson	*The Summer Prince*	In post-apocalyptic Brazil, a young man is chosen to live as a king for a year and then be sacrificed.	7 and up
Susan Beth Pfeffer	*Life as We Knew It; The Dead and the Gone; This World We Live In The Shade of the Moon* (Life As We Knew It series)	An asteroid hits earth and causes havoc for human society.	7 and up

(continued)

teaching **feature 5.2**

Author	Title	Description	Grade Level
Philip Reeve and Sarah Mcintyre	*Cakes in Space* (Not-So-Impossible Tales)	A wacky space opera series for children set on a space ship traveling to a new planet.	2–5
Beth Revis	*Across the Universe; A Million Suns; Shades of Earth* (Across the Universe series)	After coming out of biofreeze, Amy discovers that the other colonists are being killed.	7 and up
Adam Rex	*The True Meaning of Smekday*	Tip writes a humorous essay about her experiences in the alien invasion.	3–5
Laura Ruby	*York: The Shadow Cipher*	Alternate history set in the streets of New York City.	5–8
Greg Leitich Smith	*Chronal Engine*	Three kids must use a time machine to travel to the time of dinosaurs in order to save their kidnapped friend and sister.	5–8
Greg van Eekhout	*Boy at the End of the World*	Fisher is the only survivor from his bunker, so he goes in search of other humans with a robot friend.	4–6

Determined to change the course of the future, Jonas and the Giver plan for his escape. But at the last moment, a terrible threat to Gabriel, a foster child about whom Jonas cares deeply, forces a change of plan, and Jonas sets out on a journey that might lead to his end or might bring him full circle to his humanity. *The Giver* is a richly rewarding fantasy, full of subtle clues, connections, and ideas. Lowry has given each reader the wonderful gift that Jonas's community lacked, the gift of choice. This is a book to be read, enjoyed, and understood on an intensely personal level. Lowry concludes her Giver Quartet, including *Gathering Blue* and *Messenger,* with *Son,* which is told in three separate story lines that incorporate elements from the first three books.

Jill Paton Walsh's *The Green Book* follows the exodus of a group of refugees who leave a dying Earth and travel to a new planet, which is covered by a crystalline vegetation. Pattie and her family are among the last group to flee Earth. Each person is allowed to bring only one book on the journey; to the consternation of her family, Pattie chooses to bring a blank green book. Life on the new planet becomes jeapordized when the only food that the colonists can grow is wheat, and all the grains look like glass. Pattie and her sister discover that the glass-like substance can be crushed and eaten, a discovery that saves the community. The book ends with the revelation that *The Green Book* is actually Pattie's book, a personal record of her experiences in helping to settle a new world.

The ability to change lives is the power of such good writing. Fantasy for children needs no defense. Whether a modern fairy tale like *Many Moons* or *The Little Prince,* modern fantasy like *Charlotte's Web* or *The Dark Is Rising,* or the science fiction of *A Wrinkle in Time, The Giver,* or *The Green Book,* these lasting books can speak for our time and the times to come. They stretch children's imaginations, present our own world in a new perspective, and ask readers to consider how present actions might affect earth's ecological, political, and social future.

Evaluating Modern Fantasy

Well-written fantasy, like other fiction, has a well-constructed plot, convincing character-ization, a worthwhile theme, and an appropriate style. However, additional considerations must guide the evaluation of fantasy. The primary concern is the way the author makes the fantasy believable. A variety of techniques can be used to create belief in the unbe-lievable. Many authors firmly ground a story in reality before gradually moving into fantasy. Not until chapter 3 in *Charlotte's Web* does author E. B. White suggest that Fern can understand the farm animals as they talk. And even then, Fern never talks to the animals; she only listens to them. By the end of the story, Fern is growing up and really is more interested in listening to Henry Fussy than to the animals. White's description of the sounds and smells of the barnyard allows readers to experience the setting as well.

Creating belief by careful attention to the detail of the setting is a technique also used by Mary Norton in *The Borrowers*. Norton's graphic description of the Borrowers' home beneath the clock enables the reader to visualize this domestic background and to feel what it would be like to be as small as the Borrowers. J. K. Rowling has created such wonderfully detailed settings for her Harry Potter series that children have no trouble accepting the magical creatures and the fantastic events that occur at Hogwarts School of Witchcraft and Wizardry.

Having one of the characters mirror the disbelief of the reader is another device for creating convincing fantasy. In *When You Reach Me,* Rebecca Stead convinces the reader of the possibility of time travel as her skeptical protagonist, Miranda, finds clues that lead her to believe her mystery friend is from the future.

The use of appropriate language adds a kind of authenticity to fantasy. In *The Incorrigible Children of Ashton Place* books, a clever series full of wordplay and quaint sayings, Maryrose Wood introduces three siblings who are brought to Ashton Place after they are found running wild in the forest. There, a young governess works to nurture their growling attempts at communication. The children's language is rudimentary, as seen in this comment by Cassiopeia, the youngest of the wild children, in which she asks if their squirrel may accompany them to London: "Nutsawoo come, too? . . . To Londawoo?" On the other hand, the governess, Miss Penelope Lumley, is the proper model of Victorian upper class English.

The proof of real objects gives an added dimension of truth in books. How can we explain the origin of Greta's kitten or her father's penknife if not from Blue Cove in Julia Sauer's story *Fog Magic*? In *Tom's Midnight Garden* by Philippa Pearce, it is the discovery of a pair of ice skates that confirms the reader's belief in Tom's adventures. Another point to be considered when evaluating fantasy is the consistency of the story. Each fantasy should have a logical framework and an internal consistency in the world set forth by the author. For instance, characters should not become invisible whenever they face difficulty unless invisibility is a well-established part of their natures. The laws of fantasy may be strange indeed, but they must be obeyed.

Lloyd Alexander explains the importance of internal consistency within the well-written fantasy:

> Once committed to his imaginary kingdom, the writer is not a monarch but a subject. Characters must appear plausible in their own setting, and the writer must go along with the inner logic. Happenings should have logical implications. Details should be tested for consistency. Shall animals speak? If so, do *all* animals speak? If not, then which—and how? Above all, why? Is it essential to the story, or lamely cute? Are there enchantments? How powerful? If an enchanter can perform such-and-such, can he not also do so-and-so?[2]

Finally, while all plots should be original, the plots of fantasy must be ingenious and creative. A contrived or trite plot seems more obvious in a fanciful tale than in a realistic story.

Modern fantasy makes special demands on authors. The box **Guidelines: Evaluating Modern Fantasy** summarizes the criteria that need to be considered when evaluating this genre for children.

Guidelines

Evaluating Modern Fantasy

Go to Connect® to access study resources, practice quizzes, and additional materials.

Consider the following when evaluating modern fantasy:

- What are the fantasy elements of the story?
- How has the author made the story believable?
- Is the story logical and consistent within the framework established by the author?
- Is the plot original and ingenious?
- Is there a universal truth underlying the metaphor of the fantasy?
- How does the story compare with other books of the same kind or by the same author?

Challenging Perspectives on Modern Fantasy

Children have always loved fantasy. Whether it is Beatrix Potter's *Tales of Peter Rabbit*, Maurice Sendak's *Where the Wild Things Are,* or the lovable adventures of Don Freeman's *Corduroy,* children have read and reread and come back for more. In fantasies, people and animals live in a make-believe world. Some fantasies begin realistically or contain bits of reality so that they seem believable to the reader.

As children enter the world of make-believe through imagination and play, reading provides a conduit for expanding the terrain of reality to include the world of suspended belief. It is often with fantasy through nursery rhymes, fairy tales, and folk tales that younger children engage in dramatic play. Pretending that inanimate objects can come to life has always been popular for readers of all ages.

Some parents, caregivers, and teachers have become concerned when reading materials, either selected for or given to their children, include tales of fantasy that in their minds is an affront to religious and spiritual family values. However, the question of appropriateness is not a new one. In the early work of developmental psychologist Piaget, he determined that children move through several stages of development (see Chapter 2). Some teachers and parents often cite this research to support claims that children are not developmentally ready to traverse between the worlds of imagination and reality. However, researchers continue to find that children who are encouraged to engage in these imaginative ways make significant gains in readiness skills.[3,4]

The development and use of imagination is crucial to a child's intellectual and social development. The ability to suspend belief to expand their worlds through fantasy can develop school readiness for younger children and foster creativity.

The major challenge, however, is to respond to critiques that fantasy is dangerous literature for children. Parents and guardians of children have the expressed right to determine what their children read. It is not the teacher's role to determine if parents or caregivers should include or exclude fantasy from their child's "personal-at-home" library.

What does fall under the purview of teachers is to engage in language arts instruction that is not limited to grammar and vocabulary, or even to the development of language skills. They must encourage creative language and understand that the role of imagination in reading good children's literature can be facilitated with the genre of fantasy in ways that for some children can jump-start their imagination and increase the development of general skills and specific strategies of the reading process.

The challenge that remains, however, is how a teacher can deal with a parent's objection to a particular book. Should teachers, as professionals, be free to exercise their judgment in the selection of children's literature to be read in the classroom? The professional autonomy of teachers can be an important source of strength in an education system, and as such, should be valued by the broader society as well as by colleagues of the profession. Using children's literature is just one area where teachers are experiencing many limitations and challenges to their professional autonomy. For example, in some school districts, challenges to a teacher's academic freedom to present multiple perspectives of science content have arisen from both social and political communities. These challenges can be met in many cases when teachers work in partnership with parents, caregivers, communities, and school administrators to negotiate the best way to approach these controversial topics as they arise with challenged texts.

Some school districts have established policies on the rights of teachers to teach good literature, thereby supporting the selection of fantasy, science fiction, and other genres of children's literature. If a policy does not exist, it may be appropriate to first talk with an administrator in the building to discuss if the book has been used before or how challenges to the use of controversial texts have been dealt with in the past. It might also require a note home to parents letting them know before a book is used in the classroom, and that an alternative reading assignment may be given to their child if they so choose. It could also be helpful to check with other teachers in the building as well as district or local professional teacher organizations for advice. There are no predetermined rules to follow because every community context is different. It is best to gather as much information as you can and make your best professional decision. Surprisingly, the types of controversies that may arise, such as with J. K. Rowling's Harry Potter books, often actually generate even greater reader interest and enthusiasm in the books!

If the challenge to a book prohibits using it in the classroom, this could lead to what is called a "teachable moment." These unplanned moments create a wonderful classroom space to have discussions about books that are banned, censored, challenged, or feature controversial issues. Language arts teacher Shiela Siegfried wrote, "teachers must be ready at the drop of a hat to leap into curriculum development. The teachable moment is also the curriculum-design moment. The children are letting us know what sparks their interest all the time." She further stated, "Spur-of-the-moment curriculum development should be occurring regularly in our classrooms. Opportunities arise daily that lend themselves to further exploration" (p. 285).[5] Access Connect® for an example of how to use the Ten-Point Model for discussions with students about books that are banned or censored.

In his book, *Critical Incidents in Teaching: Developing Professional Judgment,* David Tripp states, ". . . we have to develop professional judgment, when we have to move beyond our everyday 'working' way of looking at things." He argues that teachers need a "professional consciousness" to meet the everyday challenges to teaching.[6] It is this professional consciousness that should permeate teachers' decisions in the selection and use of any genre of children's literature. The consciousness will help teachers respond to the pressure of contemporary concerns while simultaneously showing high degrees of skill and competence in their instruction of fantasy literature.

curriculum connections

Using Modern Fantasy to Address Standards

As a genre, fantasy opens up possibilities to explore alternative societies that emulate and expose the hopes, despairs, and possibilities of our own society. In fantasy, the characters are not only people like us, but also trolls, kings, fairies, and sorcerers who form coalitions to fight against darkness and evil. As described in this chapter, one type of fantasy is Animal Fantasy, in which the story is presented from the perspective of an animal. Fantasy provides a space for characters and readers alike to wrestle with the inadequacies of our human limits and imagine ways our world might be otherwise. The genre has strong connections to the language arts because of many titles' dependence on epic structures and more traditional extended narratives.

Suggested Children's Book: *The Girl Who Drank the Moon* by Kelly Barnhill (Algonquin, 2016).
Every year, a baby is left in a forest as a sacrifice to keep the people of Cattail from harm. Xan,

thought to be the evil witch who takes the babies, actually saves them, feeds them starlight, and finds them happy homes with families on the far side of the forest. But one baby is just too special to give away. Xan accidentally feeds her moonlight (powerful magic) instead of starlight. She names her Luna. By the time she is 5 years old, Luna's unique magical powers could put her in danger. Xan puts a protective spell on the child that suppresses her magic until she is 13 years old. Meanwhile, the baby's mother, heartbroken and furious with the town's people for taking her baby, is locked away in a tower and finds magical powers of her own. Kelly Barnhill's intricate tale explores the capacity of the human heart. In the event of seemingly unbearable sorrow, one has choices.

curriculum connections

Subject	Standard	Classroom Ideas
Language Arts and Social Studies Technology	**NCTE/ILA (Reading):** Students apply a wide range of strategies to comprehend, interpret, evaluate, and appreciate texts. They draw on their prior experience, their interactions with other readers and writers, their knowledge of word meaning and of other texts, their word identification strategies, and their understanding of textual features (e.g., sound-letter correspondence, sentence structure, context, and graphics). **NCSS:** Identify and describe ways that family, groups, and community influence the individual's daily life and personal choices.	Map the character development of Luna, Fyrian, and Glerk. Then compare the role that Glerk and Fyrian play in Luna's life. Compare and contrast the traditional views of witches, monsters, and dragons to the characters found in *The Girl Who Drank the Moon*.
Science, Math, and Art	**NGSS:** Construct an argument with evidence, data, and/or a model. **NCTM:** Identify and describe line and rotational symmetry in two- and three-dimensional shapes and designs. **NCTM:** Identify and build a three-dimensional object from two-dimensional representations of that object. **NCCAS:** Generate and conceptualize artistic ideas and work.	Create origami birds, exploring symmetry and angles. Predict which birds will fly the furthest and/or highest. Test your hypothesis.
Textual Connections	*Miss Ellicott's School for the Magically Minded* (Blackwood), *A Most Magical Girl* (Foxlee); *My Diary from the Edge of the World* (Anderson); *Castle Hangnail* (Vernon)	
Other Books by Barnhill	*The Witch's Boy*; *The Unlicensed Magician*; *The Mostly True Story of Jack*; *Iron Hearted Violet*	
Author's Website	https://kellybarnhill.wordpress.com	

Sources: International Society for Technology in Education (ITSE); National Coalition for Core Arts Standards (NCCAS); National Council of Teachers of English (NCTE)/International Literacy Association (ILA); National Council for Teachers of Mathematics (NCTM); National Council for Social Studies Curriculum Standards (NCSS); and Next Generation Science Standards (NGSS).

Notes

1. Lloyd Alexander, "Fantasy and the Human Condition," *New Advocate* 1.2 (spring, 1983): 83.
2. Lloyd Alexander, "The Flat-Heeled Muse," in *Children and Literature*, ed. Virginia Haviland, p. 243. From March/April 1965 issue of *The Horn Book Magazine*.
3. D. G. Singer and J. L. Singer, eds., *Handbook of Children and the Media* (Thousand Oaks, Cal.: Sage Publications, 2001).
4. D. G. Singer and J. L. Singer, *The House of Make-Believe* (Cambridge, Mass.: Harvard University Press, 1992).
5. S. Siegfried, "Carpe diem," *Language Arts* 69 (1992): 284–85.
6. D. Tripp, *Critical Incidents in Teaching: Developing Professional Judgment* (New York: Routledge, 1993).

Children's Literature

Go to Connect® to access study resources, practice quizzes, and additional materials.

Titles in blue = multicultural titles

Adlington, L. J. *The Diary of Pelly D.* Greenwillow, 2005.
_____. *Cherry Heaven.* Greenwillow, 2008.
Alexander, Lloyd. *The Black Cauldron.* Holt, 1965.
_____. *The Book of Three.* Holt, 1964.
_____. *The Castle of Llyr.* Holt, 1966.
_____. *The High King.* Holt, 1968.
_____. *Taran Wanderer.* Holt, 1967.
Almond, David. *Skellig.* Delacorte, 1999.
Andersen, Hans Christian. Only see this used on Amazon. Illustrated by Jerry Pinkney. Fogelman/Putnam, 2002.
Anderson, M. T. Only see this used on Amazon (The Norumbegan Quartet). Scholastic, 2010.
_____. *Feed.* Candlewick, 2002.
_____. *Zombie Mommy: Pals in Peril.* Beach Lane, 2011.
Antle, Bhagavan. *Suryia and Roscoe.* Holt, 2011.
Applegate, Katherine. *The One and Only Ivan.* HarperCollins Collins, 2012.
Atwater, Richard, and Florence Atwater. *Mr. Popper's Penguins.* Illustrated by Robert Lawson. Little, 1938.
Avi. *Poppy.* Illustrated by Brian Floca. Orchard, 1995.
Babbitt, Natalie. *Tuck Everlasting.* Farrar, 1975.
Barnhill, Kelly. *The Girl Who Drank the Moon.* Algonquin, 2016.
Barrie, J. M. *Peter and Wendy.* Hodder & Stoughton, 1911. (Peter Pan, CreateSpace, 2011)
Barron, T. A. *Atlantis Lost.* Philomel, 2016.
_____.*The Fires of Merlin.* Philomel, 1998.
_____. *The Great Tree of Avalon: Child of the Dark Prophecy.* Philomel, 2004.
_____. *The Great Tree of Avalon: The Eternal Flame.* Philomel, 2006.
_____. *The Great Tree of Avalon: Shadows on the Stars.* Philomel, 2005.
_____. *The Lost Years of Merlin.* Philomel, 1996.
Beck, Ian. Only see this used on Amazon. Harper-Collins, 2007.
_____. *Tom Trueheart and the Land of the Dark Stories.* HarperCollins, 2008.
Bellairs, John. *The House with a Clock in Its Walls.* Dial, 1973.
Bell, Hilari. Only see used on Amazon. HarperCollins, 2003.
Bertagna, Only see used on Amazon. Walker, 2008.
_____. Only see used on Amazon. Walker, 2009.
Blackwood, Sage. *Miss Ellicott's School for the Magically Minded.* Katherine Tegen Books, 2017.
Boston, L. M. *The Children of Green Knowe.* Illustrated by Peter Boston. Harcourt, 1955.
_____. *An Enemy at Green Knowe.* Illustrated by Peter Boston. Harcourt, 1964.
_____. *The River at Green Knowe.* Illustrated by Peter Boston. Harcourt, 1959.
_____. *The Treasure of Green Knowe.* Illustrated by Peter Boston. Harcourt, 1958.
Bouwman, H. M. *A Crack in the Sea.* Putnam, 2017.
Boyce, Frank Cottrell. *Chitty Chitty Bang Bang Flies Again.* Illustrated by Joe Berger. Candlewick, 2012.
_____. *Sputnick's Guide to Life on Earth.* Harper, 2017.
Brown, Peter. *The Wild Robot.* Little, 2016.
_____. *The Wild Robot Escapes,* Little, 2018.
Bruchac, Joseph. *The Dark Pond.* HarperCollins, 2004.
_____. *Skeleton Man.* HarperCollins, 2001.
_____. *Whisper in the Dark.* HarperCollins, 2005.

Buckley, Michael. *The Sisters Grimm: The Council of Mirrors*. Amulet, 2012.

Bunker, Lisa. *Felix Yz*. Viking, 2017.

Camper, Cathy. *Lowriders to the Center of the Earth*. Illustrated by Raul the Third. Chronicle, 2016.

Carroll, Emma. *In a Darkling Wood*. Delacorte, 2017.

Carroll, Lewis [Charles L. Dodgson]. *Alice's Adventures in Wonderland and Through the Looking Glass*. Illustrated by John Tenniel. Macmillan, 1963 [1865, 1872].

Clayton, Emma. *The Roar*. Scholastic, 2012.

_____. Only see used on Amazon. Scholastic, 2012.

Colfer, Eoin. *Artemis Fowl*. Hyperion, 2009.

_____. *The Supernaturalist*. Hyperion, 2005.

Collins, Suzanne. *Gergor the Overlander: Underland Chronicles*. Scholastic, 2007.

_____. *The Hunger Games*. Scholastic, 2008.

Cooper, Susan. *The Dark Is Rising*. Illustrated by Alan E. Cober. Atheneum, 1973.

_____. *The Grey King*. Atheneum, 1975.

_____. *King of Shadows*. McElderry, 1999.

_____. *Over Sea, Under Stone*. Illustrated by Marjorie Gill. Harcourt, 1966.

_____. *Silver on the Tree*. Atheneum, 1977.

Crossley-Holland, Kevin. *At the Crossing Place*. Scholastic, 2002.

Curry, Jane Louise. *The Black Canary*. Simon, 2005.

Dahl, Roald. *Charlie and the Chocolate Factory*. Illustrated by Joseph Schindelman. Knopf, 1972.

Deedy, Carmen Agra, and Randall Wright. *The Cheshire Cheese Cat: A Dickens of a Tale*. Illustrated by Barry Moser. Peachtree, 2011.

Delaney, Joseph. *The Last Apprentice: Lure of the Dead*. Illustrated by Patrick Arrasmith. Greenwillow, 2012.

Deutsch, Barry. *How Mirka Got Her Sword*. (Hereville) Amulet, 2010.

DiCamillo, Kate. *The Miraculous Journey of Edward Tulane*. Illustrated by Bagram Ibatoulline. Candlewick, 2006.

Dickinson, Peter. *Eva*. Laurel Leaf, 1990.

DiTerlizzi, Tony, and Holly Black. *The Field Guide: The Spider-wick Chronicles*. Simon, 2003.

_____. *The Nixie's Song*. Beyond the Spiderwick Chronicles. Simon, 2007.

DuPrau, Jeanne. *The City of Ember*. Random, 2003.

Eager, Edward. *Half Magic*. Illustrated by N. M. Bodecker. Harcourt, 1954.

Engdahl, Sylvia Louise. *Enchantress from the Stars*. Walker, 2001.

Farmer, Nancy. *The House of the Scorpion*. Atheneum, 2002.

_____. *The Land of the Silver Apples*. Atheneum, 2007.

_____. *The Lord of Opium*. Atheneum, 2014.

_____. *The Islands of the Blessed*. Atheneum, 2009.

Fleischman, Sid. *The Midnight Horse*. Illustrated by Peter Sis. Greenwillow, 1990.

Fleming, Ian. *Chitty Chitty Bang Bang: The Magical Car*. Random House, 1964.

Fleischman, Sid. *The Whipping Boy*. Illustrated by Peter Sis. Greenwillow, 1986.

Freedman, Claire. *Aliens in Underpants Save the World*. Illustrated by Ben Cort. Aladdin, 2012.

Freeman, Don. *Corduroy*. Viking, 1968.

Funke, Cornelia. *Inkdeath*. Scholastic, 2008.

_____. *Inkheart*. Scholastic, 2003.

_____. *Inkspell*. Scholastic, 2005.

Gaiman, Neil. *Coraline*. Illustrated by Dave McKean. Harper-Collins, 2002.

_____. *The Graveyard Book*. HarperCollins, 2008.

_____. *The Wolves in the Walls*. HarperCollins, 2003.

Gardner, Lyn. *Into the Woods*. Random, 2007.

_____. *Out of the Woods*. Random, 2010.

Gidwitz, Adam. *A Tale Dark and Grimm*. Dutton, 2011.

_____. *In a Glass Grimmly*, Dutton, 2012.

_____. *The Grimm Conclusion*. Dutton, 2014.

_____. *The Inquisitor's Tale: Or, The Three Magical Children and Their Holy Dog*. Illustrated by Hatem Aly. Dutton, 2016.

Grahame, Kenneth. *The Reluctant Dragon*. Illustrated by Ernest H. Shepard. Holiday, 1938.

_____. *The Wind in the Willows*. Illustrated by E. H. Shepard. Scribner's, 1940 [1908].

Grant, Michael. Fear. HarperCollins Children's/Tegen, 2012.

_____. *Gone*. HarperCollins Children's/Tegen, 2009.

_____. *Hunger*. HarperCollins Children's/Tegen, 2010.

_____. *Lies*. HarperCollins Children's/Tegen, 2011.

_____. *Light*. HarperCollins Children's/Tegen, 2013.

_____. *Plague*. HarperCollins Children's/Tegen, 2012.

Haddix, Margaret. *Among the Hidden*. Simon, 1999.

_____. *Caught*. Simon, 2012.

_____. *Found*. Simon, 2009.

Hahn, Mary Downing. *All the Lovely Bad Ones*. Clarion, 2008.

_____. *The Ghost of Crutchfield Hall*. Sandpiper, 2011.

_____. *One for Sorrow: A Ghost Story*. Clarion, 2017.

_____. *Wait Till Helen Comes: A Ghost Story*. Houghton, 1986.

Hamilton, Virginia. *Sweet Whispers, Brother Rush*. Philomel, 1982.

Hatke, Ben. *Legends of Zita the Spacegirl*. First Second, 2012.

_____. *Mighty Jack*. First Second, 2016.

_____. *Mighty Jack and the Goblin King*. First Second, 2017.

Hunter, Erin. *Into the Wild: Warriors*. HarperCollins, 2004.

_____. *The Empty City: Survivors*. HarperCollins, 2012.

Jacques, Brian. *Redwall*. Illustrated by Gary Chalk. Philomel, 1987.

Jenkins, Martin. *Can We Save the Tiger?* Illustrated by Vicky White. Candlewick, 2011.

Jinks, Catherine. *The Last Bogler*. Houghton, 2016.

Johnson, Alaya Dawn. *The Summer Prince*. Scholastic, 2014.

Jones, Diana Wynne. *House of Many Ways*. Greenwillow, 2008.

_____. *Howl's Moving Castle*. Harper, 2001.

_____. *The Lives of Christopher Chant*. Greenwillow, 1988.

_____. *The Pinhoe Egg*. Greenwillow, 2006.

Kibuishi, Kazu. *Explorer: The Mystery Boxes*. Amulet, 2012.

Kraatz, Jeramey. *The Cloak Society*. HarperCollins, 2012.

Law, Ingrid. *Savvy*. Dial, 2008.

_____. *Scumble*. Dial, 2010.

Le Guin, Ursula K. *The Farthest Shore*. Illustrated by Gail Garraty. Atheneum, 1972.

_____. *The Tombs of Atuan*. Illustrated by Gail Garraty. Atheneum, 1971.

_____. *A Wizard of Earthsea*. Illustrated by Ruth Robbins. Parnassus, 1968.

L'Engle, Madeleine. *A Swiftly Tilting Planet*. The Time Trilogy. Farrar, 1978.

_____. *A Wind in the Door*. The Time Trilogy. Farrar, 1973.

_____. *A Wrinkle in Time*. The Time Trilogy. Farrar, 1962.

Levine, Gail Carson. *A Tale of Two Castles*. HarperCollins Children's, 2012.

_____. *Ella Enchanted*. HarperCollins, 1997.

Lewis, C. S. *The Horse and His Boy*. Illustrated by Pauline Baynes Macmillan, 1962.

_____. *The Last Battle*. Illustrated by Pauline Baynes. Macmillan, 1964.

_____. *The Lion, the Witch, and the Wardrobe*. Illustrated by Pauline Baynes. Macmillan, 1961.

_____. *The Magician's Nephew*. Illustrated by Pauline Baynes. Macmillan, 1964.

_____. *Prince Caspian: The Return to Narnia*. Illustrated by Pauline Baynes. Macmillan, 1964.

_____. *The Silver Chair*. Illustrated by Pauline Baynes. Macmillan, 1962.

_____. *The Voyage of the "Dawn Treader."* Illustrated by Pauline Baynes. Macmillan, 1962.

Lindgren, Astrid. *Pippi Goes on Board*. Translated by Florence Lamborn. Illustrated by Louis S. Glanzman. Viking, 1957.

_____. *Pippi in the South Seas*. Translated by Florence Lamborn. Illustrated by Louis S. Glanzman. Viking, 1959.

_____. *Pippi Longstocking*. Illustrated by Louis S. Glanz-man. Viking, 1950.

_____. *Pippi Longstocking*. Illustrated by Lauren Child. Translated by Tina Nunnally. Viking, 2007.

Lin, Grace. *When the Sea Turns to Silver*. Little, 2016.

Lowry, Lois. *Gathering Blue*. Houghton, 2000.

_____. *The Giver*. Houghton, 1993.

_____. *Messenger*. Houghton, 2004.

_____. *Son*. Houghton, 2012.

Martin, Ann M., and Laura Godwin. *The Doll People*. Hyperion, 2000.

_____. *The Doll People Set Sail*. Disney, 2014.

_____. *The Meanest Doll in the World*. Hyperion, 2008.

_____. *The Runaway Dolls*. Hyperion, 2003.

McDougal, Sophia. *Mars Evacuees*. Harper, 2015.

Milne, A. A. *Winnie the Pooh*. Illustrated by Ernest H. Shepard. Dutton, 1926.

Morris, Gerald. *The Squire, His Knight and His Lady*. Houghton, 1999.

_____. *The Squire's Tale*. Houghton, 1998.

Mull, Brandon, and Brandon Dorman. *Fablehaven*. Aladdin, 2007.

Ness, Patrick. *A Monster Calls*. Illustrated by Jim Kay. Candlewick, 2011.

Nix, Garth. *Frogkisser!* Scholastic, 2017.

Norton, Mary. *The Borrowers*. Illustrated by Beth and Joe Krush. Harcourt, 1953.

_____. *The Borrowers Afield*. Illustrated by Beth and Joe Krush. Harcourt, 1955.

Oh, Ellen. *Spirit Hunters*. Harper, 2017.

Okorafor, Nnedi. *Akata Witch*. Viking, 2011.

_____. *Akata Warrior*. Viking, 2017.

Oliver, Lauren. *Liesl & Po*. Illustrated by Kei Acedera. HarperCollins Children's, 2011.

Oliver, Lauren, and H. C. Chester. *Curiosity House: The Fearsome Firebird*. Harper, 2017.

Oppel, Kenneth. *Silverwing*. Simon, 1997.

_____. *The Nest*. Illustrated by Jon Klassen. Simon, 2015.

172 Part 2 Exploring Genres in Children's Books

Paolini, Christopher. *Eragon*. Knopf, 2003.

Pearce, Jackson, and Maggie Stiefvatter. *Pip Bartlett's Guide to Magical Creatures*. Scholastic, 2015.

Pearce, Philippa. *Tom's Midnight Garden*. Illustrated by Susan Einzig. Lippincott, 1959.

Pearson, Mary E. *The Adoration of Jenna Fox*. Holt, 2008.

Petersen, David. *Mouse Guard*. Villard, 2008.

Pfeffer, Susan Beth. *The Dead and the Gone*. Harcourt, 2008.

Pierce, Tamora. *Boodhound: The Legend of Beka Cooper*. Random, 2009.

——. *Battle Magic*. Scholastic, 2015.

——. *Terrier: The Legend of Beka Cooper*. Random, 2006.

Potter, Alicia. *Mrs. Harkness and the Panda*. Illustrated by Melissa Sweet. Knof, 2012.

Prineas, Sarah. *The Magic Thief*. HarperCollins, 2008.

Pullman, Philip. *The Amber Spyglass*. His Dark Materials. Knopf, 2000.

——. *Clockwork: Or All Wound Up*. Scholastic, 1998.

——. *The Firework-Maker's Daughter*. Illustrated by S. Saelig Gallagher. Levine, 1999.

——. *The Golden Compass*. His Dark Materials. Knopf, 1996.

——. *I Was a Rat*. Knopf, 2000.

——. *La Belle Sauvage: The Book of Dust*. Random, 2017.

——. *The Ruby in the Smoke*. Knopf, 1994.

——. *The Subtle Knife*. His Dark Materials. Knopf, 1997.

Reeve, Philip. *Cakes in Space (A Not-So-Impossible Tale)*. Illustrated by Sarah McIntyre. Random House, 2015.

——. *Darkling Plain*. The Hungry Cities Chronicles. HarperCollins, 2007.

——. *Fever Crumb*. Scholastic, 2011.

——. *Infernal Devices*. The Hungry Cities Chronicles. HarperCollins, 2003.

——. *A Million Suns*. Penguin, 2012.

——. *Mortal Engines*. The Hungry City Chronicles. Harper-Collins, 2003.

——. *Oliver and the Sea Wigs (A Not-So-Impossible Tale)*. Random House, 2014.

——. *Predator's Gold*. The Hungry City Chronicles. Harper-Collins, 2003.

——. *Predator's Gold*. The Hungry Cities Chronicles. HarperCollins, 2004.

——. *Pugs of the Frozen North (A Not-So-Impossible Tale)*. Yearling, 2017.

——. *Scrivener's Moon: (Fever Crumb)*. Scholastic, 2012.

Revis, Beth. *Across the Universe*. Penguin, 2011.

Rex, Adam. *The True Meaning of Smekday*. Hyperion, 2007.

Rex, Michael. *Fangbone: Third Grade Barbarian*. Putnam, 2012.

Riordan, Rick. *The Lightning Thief*. Percy Jackson and the Olympians, Book 1. Hyperion, 2005.

——. *Magnus Chase and The Gods of Asgard: The Ship of the Dead*. Disney, 2017.

——. *Magnus Chase and The Gods of Asgard: The Sword of Summer*. Disney, 2017.

——. *The Mark of Athena*. Hyperion/Disney, 2012.

Rowling, J. K. *Harry Potter and the Sorcerer's Stone*. Scholastic, 1998.

Ruby, Laura. *York: The Shadow Cipher*. Harper, 2017.

Sachar, Louis. *Fuzzy Mud*. Random, 2015.

Saint-Exupéry, Antoine de. *The Little Prince*. Translated by Katherine Woods. Harcourt, 1943.

Sanderson, Brandon. *Alcatraz Versus the Evil Librarians*. Scholastic, 2007.

Sauer, Julia. *Fog Magic*. Illustrated by Lynd Ward. Viking, 1943.

Schlitz, Amy Laura. *Splendors and Glooms*. Candlewick, 2012.

Scieszka, Jon. *Da Wild, Da Crazy, Da Vinci*. Viking, 2004.

——. *The Frog Prince, Continued*. Illustrated by Steve Johnson. Puffin, 1994.

——. *Spaceheadz: Sphdz 4life!*. Simon and Schuster, 2013.

Selznick, Brian. *The Marvels*. Scholastic, 2015.

Sendak, Maurice. *Where the Wild Things Are*. Harper-Collins, 1963.

Sherman, Delia. *The Evil Wizard Smallbone*. Delacorte, 2016.

Shusterman, Neal. *Unwind*. Simon, 2009.

Smith, Greg Leitich. *Chronal Engine*. Clarion, 2012.

Spalding, Esta. *Knock About With the Fitzgerald-Trouts*. Illustrated by Sydney Smith. Little, 2017.

Springer, Nancy. *I Am Mordred: A Tale from Camelot*. Philomel, 1998.

——. *I Am Morgan le Fay*. Philomel, 2002.

Stanley, Diane. *Bella at Midnight: The Thimble, the Ring, and the Slippers of Glass*. Illustrated by Bagram Ibatoulline. Harper, 2006.

——. *The Giant and the Beanstalk*. HarperCollins, 2004.

Stead, Rebecca. *When You Reach Me*. Wendy Lamb, 2009.

Stephens, John. *The Emerald Atlas*. Knopf, 2011.

_____. *The Fire Chronicle*. Knopf, 2012.

Stewart, Trenton Lee. *The Extraordinary Education of Nicholas Benedict*. Little, 2012.

_____.*The Mysterious Benedict Society*. Illustrated by Carson Ellis. Little, 2007.

_____. *The Mysterious Benedict Society and the Perilous Journey*. Illustrated by Carson Ellis. Little, 2008.

_____. *The Secret Keepers*. Illustrated by Diana Sudyka. Little, Brown, 2016.

Stiefvater, Maggie. *The Scorpio Races*. Scholastic, 2011.

Tanner, Lian. *Museum of Thieves*. The Keepers Trilogy. Yearling, 2011.

Thompson, Kate. *The New Policeman*. Greenwillow, 2007.

Thurber, James. *Many Moons*. Illustrated by Marc Simont. Harcourt, 1990.

Tolkien, J. R. R. *The Fellowship of the Ring. The Two Towers. The Return of the King*. The Lord of the Rings trilogy. Houghton, 1965.

_____. *The Hobbit*. Houghton, 1938.

Turk, Evan. *The Storyteller*. Atheneum, 2016.

Twain, Mark, and Philip Stead. *The Purloining of Prince Oleomargarine*. Illustrated by Erin Stead. Doubleday, 2017.

Valente, Catherynne M. *The Girl Who Raced Fairyland All the Way Home*. Feiwel, 2016.

van Eekhout, Greg. *Boy at the End of the World*. Bloomsbury, 2011.

Walden, Mark. *H.I.V.E.: Higher Institute of Villainous Education*. Simon, 2011.

Walsh, Jill Paton. *The Green Book*. Square Fish, 2012.

Wegelius, Jakob. *The Magician's Ape*. Illustrated by Peter Graves. Delacorte, 2017.

Weisenberg, Marit. *Select*. Chronicle, 2017.

Westerfeld, Scott. *Behemoth: Leviathan Trilogy*. Simon, 2011.

_____. *Goliath: Leviathan Trilogy*. Simon, 2012.

_____. *Leviathan Trilogy*. Simon, 2009.

Wexler, Django. *The Mad Apprentice* (Forbidden Library Series). Penguin, 2015.

_____. Wexler, Django. *The Palace of Glass*. Penguin, 2016.

White, E. B. *Charlotte's Web*. Illustrated by Garth Williams. Harper, 1952.

White, J. A. *The Thickety: The Last Spell*. Harper, 2017.

Williams, Margery. *The Velveteen Rabbit*. Illustrated by William Nicholson. Doubleday, 1969 [1922].

Willems, Mo. *Goldilocks and the Three Dinosaurs*. HarperCollins, 2012.

Wood, Maryrose. *The Incorregible Children of Ashton Place: The Hidden Gallery*. Balzer & Bray, 2011.

_____. *The Incorregible Children of Ashton Place: The Interrupted Tale*. Balzer & Bray, 2013.

_____. *The Incorregible Children of Ashton Place: The Mysterious Howling*. Balzer & Bray, 2011.

_____. *The Incorregible Children of Ashton Place: The Unseen Guest*. Balzer & Bray, 2012.

Wrede, Patricia C. *Dealing with Dragons*. Harcourt, 1990.

Yolen, Jane. *The Devil's Arithmetic*. Viking Penguin, 1990.

Chapter Six

Poetry

Chapter Outline

A little boy and his mother board a crowded city bus and find two seats together toward the front. As the bus leaves the stop, the child begins to sing softly to himself; his legs dangling a few inches from the floor keeping pace with his song:

> *Going for a bus ride*
> *Going for a bus ride*
> *Going for a BUS ride*
> *Bus Bus Bus Bus Bus*
> *Going for a BUS ride*

©Cynthia Tyson.

Oblivious to the passing world, he continues these refrains through several more stops, altering the variations in pitch and beat to suit his happy mood. Like most young children, he has a ready affinity for the elements of poetry—the delightful musicality he finds in his language. And he has no hesitation in creating his own poems to accompany the rhythms of his life. His love of rhythm and rhyme will be nurtured as he encounters good books shared with him by those he loves.

Poetry for Children

There is an elusiveness about poetry that makes it defy precise definition. It is not so much what it is that is important, as how it makes us feel. In her *Poems for Children*, Eleanor Farjeon tells us that poetry is "not a rose, but the scent of the rose. . . . Not the sea, but the sound of the sea."[1] Fine poetry is this distillation of experience that captures the essence of an object, a feeling, or a thought. Such intensification requires a more highly structured patterning of words than prose does. Each word must be chosen with care for both sound and meaning, because poetry is language in its most connotative and concentrated form. Laurence Perrine defines poetry as "a kind of language that says more and says it more intensely than ordinary language."[2]

Poetry for children differs little from poetry for adults, except that it comments on life in dimensions that are meaningful for children. Its language should be poetic and its content should appeal directly to children. For example, in "Firefly July," poet J. Patrick Lewis captures the magic of a summer night from a child's point of view.

Firefly July
When I was ten, one summer night,
The baby stars that leapt
Among the trees like dimes of light,
I cupped, and capped, and kept.

–J. PATRICK LEWIS. ©2008 by J. Patrick Lewis. Reprinted by permission of Curtis Brown, Ltd.

The emotional appeal of children's poetry should reflect the real emotions of childhood. Poetry that is coy, nostalgic, or sentimental might be *about* children, but it is not *for* them. Whittier's "The Barefoot Boy," for example, looks back on childhood in a nostalgic fashion characteristic of adults, not children.

Sentimentality is another adult emotion that is seldom felt by children. Joan W. Anglund's poetry is as cute and sentimental as her pictures of "sweet little boys and girls." The poem "Which Loved Best," frequently quoted before Mother's Day, drips with sentiment and morality. Poems that are about childhood or aim to instruct are usually disliked by children.

Yet children do feel deep emotions; they can be hurt, fearful, bewildered, sad, happy, expectant, and satisfied. The best poetry for children succeeds in capturing the real feelings of children, and the best poets have found many ways of speaking to the needs and interests of children.

Where Poetry Begins

For many children, finger plays, nursery rhymes, and songs are their first introduction to the world of literature. These folk rhymes are passed down from generation to generation and are found across many cultures. What is the attraction of nursery rhymes that makes them so appealing to these young children? What accounts for their survival through these many years? Much of the language in these rhymes is obscure; for example, modern-day children have no idea what "curds" and "whey" are, yet they delight in "Little Miss Muffet." Nothing in current literature has replaced the venerable traditional finger plays and rhymes for the nursery-school age.

Nursery Rhymes and Games Finger rhymes are a traditional way to provide for young children's participation as they play "Five Little Pigs" or sing "Where Is Thumbkin?" and the ever popular "Eensy, Weensy Spider." Finger plays date back to the time of Friedrich Froebel, the so-called father of the Kindergarten Movement, who collected the finger plays and games that the peasant mothers in the German countryside were using with their children. In *Let's Clap, Jump, Sing, & Shout; Dance, Spin, & Turn It Out!: Games, Songs, & Stories from an African American Childhood*, Newbery Honor winner Patricia McKissack draws on her own experiences growing up in the American South to collect her favorite poems, songs, games, and stories for children. Brian Pinkney, winner of two Caldecott Honors, uses his signature ink and watercolor art to illustrate the playful collection. As teachers recognize, this folklore of childhood continues beyond the preschool set and onto the grade-school playground. *Steppin' Out: Jaunty Rhymes for Playful Times* by Lin Oliver, *Nursery Rhyme Comics* edited by Chris Duffy, and *Over the Hills and Far Away: A Treasury of Nursery Rhymes* by Elizabeth Hammill are wonderful collections to keep in the classroom library.

collected by PATRICIA C. McKISSACK
illustrated by BRIAN PINKNEY

LET'S CLAP, JUMP, SING & SHOUT; DANCE, SPIN & TURN IT OUT!

Games, Songs & Stories from an African American Childhood

Patricia McKissack has collected many favorite songs and games in *Let's Clap, Jump, Sing, & Shout; Dance, Spin, & Turn It Out!: Games, Songs, & Stories From an African American Childhood*, illustrated by Brian Pinkney. McKissack, Patricia C., *Let's Clap, Jump, Sing, & Shout; Dance, Spin, & Turn It Out!: Games, Songs, & Stories From an African American Childhood*. New York, NY: Schwartz & Wade, 2017, Cover. Copyright ©2017 by Schwartz & Wade. All rights reserved. Used with permission.

Mother Goose The terms *nursery rhymes* and *Mother Goose rhymes* are interchangeable. The character of Mother Goose has come to represent the type of speech play we have discussed but the reason for the association of these traditional rhymes with a character called Mother Goose is unclear. The oldest surviving nursery rhyme book was published by Mary Cooper in 1744 in two or perhaps three little volumes under the title *Tommy Thumb's Pretty Song Book*; a single copy of volume 2 is a treasured possession of the British Museum.

Today's children are fortunate in being able to choose among many beautifully illustrated

Mother Goose editions. There is no *one* best Mother Goose book, for this is a matter for individual preference. The children in every family deserve at least one of the better editions, however. Preschool and primary teachers will also want to have one that can be shared with small groups of children who might not have been fortunate enough ever to have seen a really beautiful Mother Goose. Some of the most delightful collections are *Tomie dePaola's Mother Goose*, Iona Opie and Rosemary Wells's *My Very First Mother Goose* and *Here Comes Mother Goose*, David McPhail's *Mother Goose: A Collection of Favorite Rhymes, Songs, and Concepts*, Susan Middleton Elya's *La Madre Goose: Nursery Rhymes for Los Niños*, and Petra Mathers's *The McElderry Book of Mother Goose*.

The Elements of Poetry

As children become more sophisticated through their exposure to films and television, the dividing line between what is poetry for adults and what is poetry for children becomes fainter. It is, however, possible to identify those poems that contain the elements of fine poetry that still speak to children.

Rhythm The young child is naturally rhythmical. She beats on the tray of her high chair, kicks her foot against the table, and chants her vocabulary of one or two words in a singsong fashion. She delights in the sound of "Pat-a-cake, pat-a-cake, baker's man" or "Ride a cock-horse to Banbury Cross" before she understands the meaning of the words. This response to a measured beat is as old as humans themselves. Primitive people had chants, hunting and working songs, dances, and crude musical instruments. Rhythm is a part of the daily beat of our lives—the steady pulse rate, regular breathing, and pattern of growth.

Poetry satisfies the child's natural response to rhythm. In poetry, it is the stresses and pauses in language that set up the rhythm. The term *meter* refers to this pattern of stresses that fall in each line. The rhythm helps create a kind of music of its own, and the child responds to it. The very young child enjoys the rocking rhythm of Mother Goose and expects it in all other poems. In the following poem from *The Llama Who Had No Pajama*, Mary Ann Hoberman explores various rhythms in the child's life as she links weather and seasonal patterns to the rhythm of a child's swinging.

Collections such as Mary Ann Hoberman's *The Llama Who Had No Pajama* introduce children to the delights of poetry. Cover from *The Llama Who Had No Pajama: 100 Favorite Poems* by Mary Ann Hoberman. Jacket illustrations copyright ©1998 by Betty Fraser. Reprinted by permission of Harcourt Children's Books, an imprint of Houghton Mifflin Harcourt Publishing Company. All rights reserved.

Hello and Good-bye

Hello and good-bye
When I'm in a swing
Swinging low and then high,
Good-bye to the ground
Hello to the sky.
Hello to the rain
Good-bye to the sun,
Then hello again sun
When the rain is all done.
In blows the winter,
Away the birds fly.
Good-bye and hello
Hello and good-bye.

—MARY ANN HOBERMAN. "Hello and Good-bye," from *The Llama Who Had No Pajama: 100 Favorite Poems*. Copyright ©1959 and renewed 1987 by Mary Ann Hoberman. Reprinted with permission of Houghton Mifflin Harcourt Publishing Company.

Amy Ludwig VanDerwater's poems in *Read! Read! Read!* celebrate the joy of reading. *READ! READ! READ!* Illustrations copyright ©2017 by Ryan O'Rourke. First published by WordSong, an imprint of Highlights for Children. Used with permission.

In some poems, both the rhythm and the pattern of the lines are suggestive of the movement or mood of the poem. The arrangement of these poems forces the reader to emphasize a particular rhythm. For example, in Eleanor Farjeon's "Mrs. Peck-Pigeon," "Mrs. Peck-Pigeon is picking for bread, Bob-bob-bob goes her little round head"—the repetition of the hard sounds of *b* and *p* helps to create the bobbing rhythm of the pigeon herself.

Rhyme and Sound In addition to the rhythm of a poem, children respond to its rhyme—for rhyme helps to create the musical qualities of a poem, and children enjoy the "singingness of words." The Russian poet Kornei Chukovsky maintains that in the beginning of childhood, we are all "versifiers," and that it is only later in life that we begin to speak in prose.[3] Chukovsky is referring to the young child's tendency to double all syllables, so that *mother* is first "mama" and *water* is "wa-wa." This, plus the regular patterning of such words as *daddy*, *mommy*, and *granny* makes for a natural production of rhyme. The young child's enjoyment of Mother Goose is due almost entirely to the rhyme and rhythm of these verses.

Rhyme is only one aspect of sound; *alliteration*, or the repetition of initial consonant sounds, is another; *assonance*, or the repetition of particular vowel sounds, is still another. Jack Prelutsky frequently uses alliteration to create the humor in his poetry collections such as *I've Lost My Hippopotamus* and *My Dog May Be a Genius*. The quiet *s* sound and the repetition of the double *o* in *moon* and *shoon* suggest the mysterious beauty of the moon in Walter de la Mare's poem "Silver" (in Helen Ferris's *Favorite Poems Old and New*). The term *onomatopoeia* refers to the use of words that make a sound like the action represented by the word, such as *crack*, *hiss*, and *sputter*. Occasionally, a poet will create an entire poem that resembles a particular sound. Tony Mitton has successfully imitated the sound of a railroad train in "Rickety Train Ride."

Rickety Train Ride

I'm taking the train to Ricketywick
Clickety clickety clack.
I'm sat in my seat
With a sandwich to eat
As I travel the trickety track.

It's ever so rickety trickety train,
And I honestly thickety think.
That before it arrive
At the end of the line
I will tip up my drippety drink.

—Tony Mitton. "Rickety Train Ride," in Jane Yolen and Andrew Fusek Peters *Here's a Little Poem*, 2007; originally published in *Pip*, Scholastic Inc., NY. Used with permission from David Higham Agency.

Repetition is another way the poet creates particular sound effects in a poem. Robert Frost frequently used repetition of particular lines or phrases to emphasize meaning in his poems. The repetition of the last line "miles to go before I sleep" in his famous "Stopping by Woods on a Snowy Evening" (in de Regniers et al., *Sing a Song of Popcorn*) adds to the mysterious element in that poem.

Children are intrigued with the sound of language and enjoy unusual and ridiculous combinations of words. The light-hearted nonsense of Laura Richards's "Eletelephony" is as much in the sound of the ridiculous words as in the plight of the poor elephant who tried to use the "telephant." Children love to trip off the name "James James Morrison Morrison Weatherby George Dupree" in A. A. Milne's "Disobedience." Poets use rhyme, rhythm, and the various devices of alliteration, assonance, repetition, and coined words to create the melody and sound of poetry loved by children.

Imagery Poetry draws on many kinds of language magic. The imagery of a poem involves direct sensory images of sight, sound, touch, smell, or taste. This aspect of poetry has particular appeal for children, as it reflects one of the major ways they explore their world. The very young child grasps an object and immediately puts it in her mouth. Children love to squeeze warm, soft puppies, and they squeal with delight as a pet mouse scampers up their arms. Taste and smell are also highly developed in the young child.

Poetry can never be a substitute for actual sensory experience. A child can't develop a concept of texture by hearing a poem or seeing pictures of the rough bark of a tree;

he must first touch the bark and compare the feel of a deeply furrowed oak with the smooth-surfaced trunk of a beech tree. Then the poet can call up these experiences and extend them or invite the child to see them in a new way.

Because children are visually minded, they respond readily to the picture-making quality of poetry. In Tennyson's "The Eagle," the description of the eagle is rich in the use of visual imagery. In the first verse, the reader can see the eagle perched on the crest of a steep mountain, poised and ready for his swift descent whenever he sights his quarry. But in the second verse, the poet "enters into" the eagle's world and describes it from the bird's point of view. Looking down from his lofty height, the might of the waves is reduced to wrinkles and the sea seems to crawl:

> He clasps the crag with crooked hands;
> Close to the sun in lonely lands,
> Ringed with the azure world, he stands.
>
> The wrinkled sea beneath him crawls;
> He watches from his mountain wall,
> And like a thunderbolt he falls.
>
> —ALFRED, LORD TENNYSON. "The Eagle," in *Piping Down the Valleys Wild*, ed. Nancy Larrick.

The lonely, peaceful scene is shattered by the natural metaphor of the final line: "And like a thunderbolt he falls." In your mind's eye, you can see, almost feel, the wind on your wings as you plunge down the face of the cliff.

Most poetry depends on visual and auditory imagery to evoke a mood or response, but imagery of touch, taste, and smell is also used. Psychologists tell us that some of children's earliest memories are sensory, recalling particularly the way things smell and taste. Most children have a delicate sense of taste that responds to the texture and smell of a particular food. Rose Rauter captures both the feel of a fresh-picked peach and its delicious taste in "Peach":

> Touch it to your cheek and it's soft
> as a velvet newborn mouse
> who has to strive to be alive.
> Bite in. Runny
> honey blooms on your tongue—
> as if you've bitten open
> a whole hive.
>
> —ROSE RAUTER. "Peach," from *Knock at a Star: A Child's Introduction to Poetry* by Dorothy
> M. Kennedy, X. J. Kennedy, Karen L. Baker. Text copyright ©1999 by X. J. Kennedy
> and Dorothy M. Kennedy. Illustrations copyright ©1999 by Karen Lee Baker. Used by
> permission of Little, Brown Books for Young Readers. All rights reserved.

Figurative Language: Comparison and Contrast Because the language of poetry is so compressed, every word must be made to convey the meaning of the poem. Poets do this by comparing two objects or ideas with each other in such a way that the connotation of one word gives added meaning to another. In "Peach," Rose Rauter compared the soft fuzzy feel of a peach to a velvety newborn mouse; its sweet taste made her think of a whole hive of honey. In "A Cold-Air Balloon," Chris Harris compares the burrowing action to that of gophers and sinking like that of a stone.

I'M JUST NO GOOD AT RHYMING

AND OTHER NONSENSE FOR MISCHIEVOUS KIDS AND IMMATURE GROWN-UPS

WRITTEN BY Chris Harris
(without William Shakespeare)

ILLUSTRATED BY Lane Smith

A Cold-Air Balloon

Let's grind through the earth in our
cold-air balloon!
On down through the ground in our
magic cocoon,
We'll burrow like gophers! We'll sink
like a stone!
We'll gaze at the world up above us,
and moan!
We'll sob in the darkness, we'll cry in
the cold
At the slugs and the bugs and the
slime and the mold.
As worms wiggle by us in worlds
anaerobic
We'll weep and we'll whimper! We'll feel claustrophobic!

And just when we're at our most frightened and nervous,
Right then we'll ascend to the heavenly surface.
We'll soak in the sunlight! We'll breathe in the air!
We'll jump up and down and around without care!
And thanks to our flight in that horrid balloon,
For the rest of our lives, we'll feel high as the moon.

When writers compare one thing with another, using such connecting words as *like* or *as*, they are using a *simile*. In a *metaphor*, the poet speaks of an object or idea as if it *were* another object. In recent years, we have paid little attention to the difference between these two techniques, referring to both as examples of metaphorical or figurative language.

It is not important that children know the difference between a simile and a metaphor. It is important that they know what is being compared and that the comparison is fresh and new and helps them view the idea or object in a different and unusual way. Two well-known poems containing metaphors that help children see their world afresh are Carl Sandburg's "Fog" and Vachel Lindsay's "The Moon's the North Wind's Cookie" (both in

Jack Prelutsky's *The Random House Book of Poetry for Children*). Perhaps the reason these poems have endured is that they also reveal a true understanding of a child's point of view.

Personification is a way of speaking about inanimate objects and animals as though they were persons. Human beings have always personified inanimate objects. Young children personify their toys; adolescents and adults name their computers, their cars, and boats. Poetry simply extends this process to a wider range of objects. In *Dirty Laundry Pile: Poems in Different Voices*, Paul Janeczko has collected twenty-seven poems written in the voices of animals such as mosquitoes, cats, and turtles and objects like washing machines, scarecrows, and kites. In *Button Up!: Wrinkled Rhymes*, Alice Schertle's poems personify various articles of clothing with distinct and humorous voices.

Shape The first thing children notice about reading a poem is that it looks different from prose. And usually it does. Most poems begin with capital letters for each line and have one or more stanzas. Increasingly, however, poets are using the shape of their poems to reinforce the image of the idea. Eve Merriam's "Windshield Wiper" (in Bernice Cullinan and Deborah Wooten's *Another Jar of Tiny Stars*, Wordsong, 2009) places the reader inside a car looking out as a rainstorm begins and ends.

Windshield Wiper

fog smog	fog smog
tissue paper	tissue paper
clear the blear	clear the smear
fog more	fog more
splat splat	downpour
rubber scraper	rubber scraper
overshoes	macintosh
bumbershoot	muddle on
slosh through	slosh through
drying up	drying up
sky lighter	sky lighter
nearly clear	nearly clear

    clearing, clearing, veer
    clear here, clear

—EVE MERRIAM. From *OUT LOUD* by Eve Merriam. Copyright ©1973 Eve Merriam. All rights renewed and reserved. Used by permission of Marian Reiner.

Children enjoy mounting their own poems on a piece of paper shaped in the image of their poem, such as a verse about a jack-o'-lantern on a pumpkin shape or a poem about a plane mounted on the silhouette of an airplane. Later, the words themselves may form the shape of the content, as in concrete poetry.

The Overall Impact of Poetry

We have seen how sound, language, and the shape of a poem can all work together to create the total impact of the poem. Considered individually, the rhyme scheme, imagery, figurative language, and appearance of the poem are of little importance unless all of these interrelate to create an emotional response in the reader. The craft of the poem is not the poem.

In the following poem, Naomi Shihab Nye entreats the reader to empathize with refugees from the Mediterranean Sea:

Mediterranean Blue

If you are the child of a refugee, you do not
sleep easily when they are crossing the sea
on small rafts and you know they can't swim.
My father couldn't swim either. He swam through
sorrow, though, and made it to the other side
on a ship, pitching his old clothes overboard
at landing, then tried to be happy, make a new life.
But something inside him was always paddling home,
clinging to anything that floated – a story, a food or face.
They are the bravest people on earth right now,
don't dare look down on them. Each mind a universe
swirling as many details as yours, as much love for
a humble place. Now the shirt is torn,
the sea too wide for comfort, and nowhere
to receive a letter for a very long time.

And if we can reach out a hand, we better.

"Mediterranean Blue" by Naomi Shihab Nye, from *Traveling the Blue Road: Poems of the Sea.*
Copyright 2017. Used by permission of Naomi Shihab Nye.

All elements of this poem work together to communicate the emotional and physical challenges of a child's refugee experience. A teacher could destroy the total impact of this poem for children by having them count the number of metaphors in it, looking at their increasing force and power. Children should have a chance to hear the poem, comment on it if they wish, or compare it with other similar poems.

Good poetry has the power to make readers moan in despair, catch their breath in fear, gasp in awe, smile with delight, or sit back in wonder. Poetry heightens emotions and increases one's sensitivity to an idea or mood.

Evaluating Poetry

A child responds to the total impact of a poem and should not be required to analyze it. However, teachers need to understand the language of poetry if they are to select the best to share with children. How, for example, can you differentiate between real poetry and mere verse? Mother Goose, jump-rope rhymes, tongue twisters, and the lyrics of some songs are not poetry, but they *can* serve as a springboard for diving into more formal poetry. Elizabeth Coatsworth, who has written much fine poetry and verse for children, refers to rhyme as "poetry in petticoats."[4] Such rhymes might have the sound of poetry, but they do not contain the quality of imagination or the depth of emotion that characterizes real poetry.

In looking for real poetry for children, teachers should examine the content and form of the poetry. However, it is important to note that modern poets are breaking traditional molds in both content and form. Frequently, the words are spattered across pages in a random fashion, or they become poem-pictures, as in concrete poetry. Many authors are revisiting story in one of its earliest forms, the epic narrative poem. Writers for older children and young adults are using poetry to redefine the form of the novel, such as Thanhha Lai's

Newbery Honor-winning *Inside Out & Back Again*. Other poet novelists examine historical events, such as the story of the Tuskegee Airmen, told by Marilyn Nelson in *American Ace* and Carole Boston Weatherford in *You Can Fly: The Tuskegee Airmen*. Poet novelists use the verse novel form to build a bridge between the world of poetry and the world of prose, merging the elements of poetry with the narrative structure of prose. In *Applesauce Weather*, Helen Frost explores loss and hope in a gentle tale set against the backdrop of a family's applesauce-making tradition. In *Catching a Storyfish*, Janice N. Harrington explores the power of story to help a young girl find her voice within the isolation of her new home.

Teachers need to be able to identify the characteristics of good poetry and be aware of new trends in contemporary poetry in order to make wise selections to share with children. They need to know the various kinds of poetry and the range of content available in poetry for children. Then they can select poems that will gradually develop children's appreciation of poetry and its form. The questions listed in the feature **Guidelines: Evaluating Poetry for Children** would not be appropriate to use for every poem. However, they can serve as a starting point for exploring the world of poetry with children.

Forms of Poetry for Children

Children are more interested in the "idea" of a poem than in knowing about the various forms of poetry. However, teachers will want to expose children to various forms of poetry and note their reactions. Do these children like only narrative poems? Do they think all poetry must

Guidelines

Evaluating Poetry for Children

Go to Connect® to access study resources, practice quizzes, and additional materials.

Consider the following when evaluating poetry:

- How does the rhythm of the poem reinforce and create the meaning of the poem?
- If the poem rhymes, does it sound natural or contrived?
- How does the sound of the poem add to its meaning?
- Does the poem use alliteration? Onomatopoeia? Repetition?
- Does the poem create sensory images of sight, touch, smell, or taste?
- Are these images related to children's delight in their particular senses?
- What is the quality of imagination in the poem? Does the poem invite the child to see something in a fresh, new way, or does it rely on tired clichés?

- Is the figurative language appropriate to children's lives? Are the similes and metaphors ones that a child would appreciate and understand?
- What is the tone of the poem? Does it patronize childhood by talking down to it? Is it didactic and preachy? Does it see childhood in a sentimental or nostalgic way?
- Is the poem appropriate for children? Will it appeal to them, and will they like it?
- How has the poet created the emotional intensity of the poem? Does every word work to heighten the feelings conveyed?
- Does the shape of the poem contribute to the poem's meaning?
- What is the purpose of the poem? To amuse? To describe in a fresh way? To comment on humanity? To draw parallels to our lives? How well has the poet achieved this purpose?

A Kick in the Head: An Everyday Guide to Poetic Forms, selected by Paul B. Janeczko and illustrated by Chris Raschka, introduces budding poets to twenty-nine different poetic forms. A KICK IN THE HEAD. This Collection copyright ©2005 by Paul B. Janeczko. Illustrations copyright ©2005 by Chris Raschka. Reproduced by permission of Candlewick Press, Somerville, MA.

rhyme, or will they listen to some free verse? Are they ready for the seemingly simple, yet highly complex, form of haiku? Understanding of and appreciation for a wide variety of poetry grow gradually as children are exposed to different forms and types of poems. Paul Janeczko's *A Kick in the Head: An Everyday Guide to Poetic Forms* is a lively introduction to forms of poetry that will appeal to children. Each form is accompanied by poems of example and a brief explanation of poetic structure. Janeczko's choice of poems and Chris Raschka's illustrations liven up what might otherwise be just a tedious list of definitions. Although we do not have the space in this chapter to cover the many forms found in *A Kick in the Head*, we have singled out a few that are worth sharing with children in **Teaching Feature 6.1: Forms of Poetry for Children.**

teaching feature 6.1

Forms of Poetry for Children

Forms	Title/Author	Grade Level
Narrative The narrative poem relates a particular event or episode or tells a long tale. It may be a lyric, a sonnet, or free verse; its one requirement is that it must tell a story.	*Our Farm: By the Animals of Farm Sanctuary* (Gottfried)	PreK–2
	Knock Knock: My Dad's Dream for Me (Beaty)	PreK–3
	The Night Before Christmas (Moore) (multiple books)	K–3
	The Tale of Custard the Dragon (Nash)	K–3
	Once Upon a Poem: Favorite Poems That Tell Stories (Crossley-Holland)	K–3
	Wynken, Blynken, & Nod (Field) (multiple books)	K–3
	Tony (Galing)	K–3
	A Song About Myself (Keats)	K–3
	Before Morning (Sidman)	

(continued)

teaching feature 6.1

Forms	Title/Author	Grade Level
Lyrical The term *lyrical* derives from the word *lyric* and means poetry that sings its way into the minds and memories of its listeners. It is usually personal or descriptive poetry, with no prescribed length or structure other than its melody.	*Wake Up!* (Frost) "The Swing" and "The Wind," both in *A Child's Garden of Verses* (Stevenson) "Lone Dog" (McLeod) in *Favorite Poems Old and New* (Ferris) "Sea Fever" (Masefield) in *Favorite Poems Old and New* (Ferris)	K–3 K–3 3–6 3–6
Limerick This is a five-line verse in which the first and second lines rhyme, the third and fourth rhyme, and the fifth line rhymes with lines 1 and 2 and usually is a surprise or humorous statement. Freak spellings, oddities, and humorous twists characterize this form of poetry.	"Limericks" in *Knock at a Star* (Kennedy and Kennedy) *Poetry for Young People: Edward Lear* (Mendelson) *Grimericks* (Pearson) *Something Sure Smells Around Here: Limericks* (Cleary)	3–6 3–6 3–6 3–6
Free Verse Free verse does not have to rhyme but depends on rhythm or cadence for its poetic form. It may use some rhyme, alliteration, and pattern. Though it frequently looks different on the printed page, it sounds very much like other poetry when read aloud.	*Fresh-Picked Poetry: A Day at the Farmers' Market* (Schaub) *A Child's Garden of Verses* (Stevenson) *The Pet Project: Cute and Cuddly Vicious Verses* (Wheeler) *Read! Read! Read!* (VanDerwater) *Poetry for Kids: Emily Dickinson* (Snively) *Night Guard* (Lea)	K–3 K–3 K–3 K–6 3–6 6 and up
Haiku Haiku is an ancient Japanese verse form that can be traced back to the thirteenth century. There are only seventeen syllables in the haiku; the first and third lines contain five syllables, the second line seven. Almost every haiku can be divided into two parts: first, a simple picture-making description that usually includes some reference, direct or indirect, to the season; and second, a statement of mood or feeling. A relationship between these two parts is implied—either a similarity or a telling difference.	*The Hound Dog's Haiku and Other Poems for Dog Lovers* (Rosen) *Wabi Sabi* (Reibstein) *The Cuckoo's Haiku and Other Birding Poems* (Rosen) *Yum! ¡MmMm! ¡Qué Rico!* (Mora) *If Not for the Cat* (Prelutsky) *Today and Today* (Issa)	K–3 K–3 4–6 6–8 6–10 6–10

(continued)

Forms	Title/Author	Grade Level
Invented Forms	*A Meal of the Stars* (Jensen)	PreK–2
Many poets are breaking new ground with their invented poetic forms. From poetry word puzzles, to poems that can be read up or down, to the Reverso, these unique collections will entice children to try writing their own invented forms of poetry.	*Lemonade: and Other Poems Squeezed from a Single Word* (Raczka)	3–6
	Mirror Mirror: A Book of Reverso Poems (Singer)	3–6
	Follow Follow: A Book of Reverso Poems (Singer)	3–6
	Echo Echo: Reverso Poems about Greek Myths (Singer)	3–6
Concrete	*A Poke in the I* (Janeczko)	K–3
Concrete poems are picture poems that invite the reader see what they are saying. The message of the poem is presented not only in the words (sometimes just letters or punctuation marks) but also in the arrangement of the words. Meaning is reinforced, or even carried, by the shape of the poem.	*Flicker Flash* (Graham)	K–3
	Wet Cement: A Mix of Concrete Poems (Raczka)	3–6
	Blue Lipstick: Concrete Poems (Grandits)	6 and up
Classic	*The Watcher* (Grimes)	8–12
Many modern poets write poetry in classic forms, such as the sonnet or the cento.		

Selecting Poetry for Children

Before they enter school, children seem to have a natural enthusiasm for the sounds and rhythms of language. Schoolteachers and librarians will want to select poems and poets that will build upon these inclinations and that appeal to children's interests. They will also want to find ways to extend and deepen children's initial preferences into a lifelong love of poetry.

Children's Poetry Preferences

Starting in the early 1920s, children's interest in poetry has been the subject of many research studies. The interesting fact about all these studies is the similarity of the findings and the stability of children's poetry preferences over the years. According to Ann Terry, these studies suggest the following:

1. Children are the best judges of their preferences.
2. Reading texts and courses of study often do not include the children's favorite poems.

In *The Watcher*, Nikki Grimes uses the poetic form of the golden shovel, invented by Terrance Hayes, whereby the poet takes a line (or lines) from a poem and uses each word in the line (or lines) as the end word in each line of a new poem.

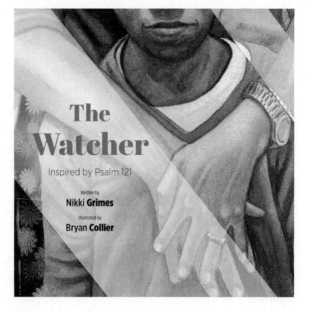

3. Children's poetry choices are influenced by (1) the poetry form, (2) certain poetic elements, and (3) the content, with humor and familiar experience being particularly popular.
4. A poem enjoyed at one grade level may be enjoyed across several grade levels.
5. Children do not enjoy poems they do not understand.
6. Thoughtful, meditative poems are disliked by children.
7. Some poems appeal to one sex more than the other; girls enjoy poetry more than boys do.
8. New poems are preferred over older, more traditional ones.
9. Literary merit is not necessarily an indication that a poem will be liked.[5]

Terry also reported that in her study of children in grades 4 through 6, narrative poems, such as John Ciardi's "Mummy Slept Late and Daddy Fixed Breakfast" (in *A Jar of Tiny Stars*, ed. Bernice E. Cullinan) and Giselle Potter's illustrated picturebook of Eugene W. Field's "Wynken, Blynken, and Nod," and limericks, including both modern and traditional, were the children's favorite forms of poetry. Haiku was consistently disliked by all grade levels. Elements of rhyme, rhythm, and sound increased children's enjoyment of the poems, as evidenced by their preference for David McCord's "The Pickety Fence" (in *A Jar of Tiny Stars*, ed. Bernice E. Cullinan) and "Lone Dog" (in *Favorite Poems Old and New*, ed. Helen Ferris). Poems that contained much figurative language or imagery were disliked. Children's favorite poems at all three grade levels contained humor or were about familiar experiences or animals. All children preferred contemporary poems containing modern content and today's language to the older, more traditional poems. Research by Carol Fisher and Margaret Natarella[6] found similar preferences among first, second, and third graders, as did Karen Kutiper[7] among seventh, eighth, and ninth graders.

How then can we most effectively select poetry for children? Certainly a teacher will want to consider children's needs and interests, their previous experience with poetry, and the types of poetry that appeal to them. A sound principle to follow is to begin where the children are. Teachers can share poems that have elements of rhyme, rhythm, and sound, such as Tony Mitton's "Rickety Train Ride" in Jane Yolen and Andrew Fusek Peters's *Here's a Little Poem* or Nicola Davies's "Dragonfly Babies" and "Fireflies" in her collection of animal poems in *Song of the Wild*. They can read many narrative verses and limericks and look for humorous poems and poems about familiar experiences and animals. They should share only those poems that they really like themselves; enthusiasm for poetry is contagious. However, teachers will not want to limit their sharing only to poems that they know children will like, for taste needs to be developed, too. Children should go beyond their delight in humorous and narrative poetry to develop an appreciation for variety in both form and content. We want children to respond to more poetry and to find more to respond to in poetry.

Poetry Books for Children

Today poetry anthologies do not stay in print as long as they used to due to time limits placed on permissions to use certain poems. This has meant the publication of fewer large anthologies and the proliferation of many specialized collections containing fewer than twenty poems. Teachers will want to have a good classroom library of both anthologies and specialized collections, including some for their personal use and some for the children's use. These can be enhanced by selecting volumes from the school library for special studies that link poetry to all the many areas of the curriculum.

Poetry Anthologies Every family with children will want to own at least one excellent anthology of poetry for children. Many parents and teachers will be attracted to the large *Random House Book of Poetry for Children*, with its 572 poems selected by Jack Prelutsky and profusely illustrated with Arnold Lobel's lively pictures. Though much of the book is dominated by humorous verse (including some thirty-eight poems by Prelutsky himself), fine poems by Robert Frost, Eve Merriam, Eleanor Farjeon, Emily Dickinson, Myra Cohn Livingston, Dylan Thomas, and others are interspersed with them. Arnold Lobel's humorous full-color illustrations also draw children to this anthology. Another worthwhile collection is Jack Prelutsky's *The 20th Century Children's Poetry Treasury*, containing a selection of 211 poems by 137 different poets. Meilo So's watercolor illustrations are saturated in bright colors. Editors Bill Martin Jr. and Michael Sampson chose almost 200 traditional and contemporary children's poems for *The Bill Martin Jr. Big Book of Poetry*. The poems are illustrated by a wide range of award-winning artists, including Ashley Bryan, Lois Ehlert, Steven Kellogg, Chris Raschka, Nancy Tafuri, and Dan Yaccarino.

Knock at a Star: A Child's Introduction to Poetry, compiled by the well-known adult poet and anthologist X. J. Kennedy and his wife, Dorothy, is a memorable collection of poetry for children 8 years old and up. The poets represented range widely, from adult poets like James Stephens, Emily Dickinson, Robert Frost, and William Stafford to children's poets such as Aileen Fisher, David McCord, and Lillian Morrison. Many familiar poems are here, but most are new and fresh to children's collections. The three section headings in this book also are addressed to children and provide an understanding of how poetry does what it does: (1) "What Do Poems Do?" (make you laugh, tell stories, send messages, share feelings, start you wondering); (2) "What's Inside a Poem?" (images, word music, beats that repeat, likenesses); and (3) "Special Kinds of Poems." Teachers, librarians, and parents as well as children can learn from this wise book, which teaches at the same time as it develops enthusiasm for poetry.

Two anthologists have collected poems particularly well suited for children to memorize and speak aloud: *Forget-Me-Nots: Poems to Learn by Heart* by former Children's Poet Laureate, Mary Ann Hoberman (illustrated by Michael Emberley), and *Poems to Learn by Heart*, by

Caroline Kennedy (with paintings by Jon J. Muth). Donald Hall's *The Oxford Illustrated Book of American Children's Poems* is a wonderful collection that includes poems from contemporary poets and classic favorites. Twelve award-winning picturebook artists have come together in *Goodnight Songs* to illustrate a charming collection of lullabies by beloved author Margaret Wise Brown. A CD of the songs, composed and performed by Tom Proutt and Emily Gray, accompanies the book. In 1994, Valerie Worth's series of books featuring small poems was published in a collection (*All the Small Poems and Fourteen More*) and illustrated by Natalie Babbitt. Recently, the form of the small poem has experienced a resurgence in children's poetry. In *Firefly July: A Year of Very Short Poems*, illustrated by Melissa Sweet, Paul B. Janeczko has selected delightfully short poems for the seasons. Kenn Nesbitt selected "60-Second Poems to Send You Off to Sleep" in his anthology, *One Minute till Bedtime*, with art by Christoph Niemann. Polly Dunbar provides exuberant illustrations to accompany Jane Yolen and Andrew Fusek Peters's collection for younger children titled *Here's a Little Poem: A Very First Book of Poetry*. Lin Oliver's *Little Poems for Tiny Ears*, illustrated by Tomie dePaola, offers short and playful poems for reading aloud to babies and toddlers.

Three specialized collections make excellent additions to classroom and home libraries. Editor Elise Paschen's *Poetry Speaks to Children*, an anthology of classic and contemporary poetry, comes with a CD on which fifty poems are read or performed, many by the poets themselves. The poems are paired with colorful illustrations by Judy Love, Wendy Rasmussen, and Paula Zinngrabe Wendland. J. Patrick Lewis, the U.S. Children's Poet Laureate from 2011 to 2013, is the editor of *National Geographic Book of Animal Poetry: 200 Poems with Photographs That Squeak, Soar, and Roar!* as well as the *National Geographic Book of Nature Poetry: More than 200 Poems with Photographs that Float, Zoom, and Bloom!* The animal and nature poems are paired with spectacular wildlife photographs.

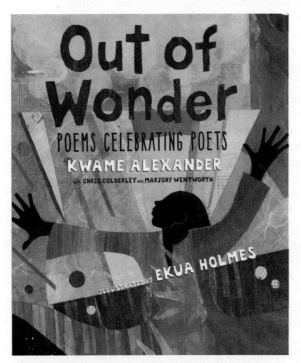

In the collection, *Out of Wonder: Poems Celebrating Poets*, Kwame Alexander, Chris Colderley, and Marjory Wentworth have penned homage poems honoring famous poets. OUT OF WONDER. Text copyright ©2017 by Kwame Alexander. Illustrations copyright ©2017 by Ekua Holmes. Reproduced by permission of the publisher, Candlewick Press, Somerville, MA.

In *Out of Wonder: Poems Celebrating Poets*, Newbery Medal-winning author and poet Kwame Alexander and fellow poets Chris Colderley and Marjory Wentworth honor twenty famous poets "out of gratitude for the joys of poetry." Homage is paid in the form of poetry to some of the world's most beloved poets: from Maya Angelou to Naomi Shihab Nye and from Langston Hughes to Pablo Neruda. Extensive biographical notes are included at the end of the book about the poets chosen to be celebrated. Caldecott Honor-winning Ekua Holmes created the vibrant and colorful collage on paper illustrations.

One of the most enduring anthologies is *Reflections on a Gift of Watermelon Pickle and Other Modern Verses*, edited by Stephen Dunning and others. Illustrated with superb black-and-white photographs surrounded by much white space, this anthology appeals to the eye as well as the ear of older students in middle school. They will take delight in "Sonic Boom" by John Updike, "Ancient History" by Arthur Guiterman, "Dreams" by Langston Hughes, and "How to Eat a Poem" by Eve Merriam. They will appreciate the honesty and realistic viewpoint of "Husbands and Wives," in which Miriam Hershenson tells of couples who ride the train from station to station without ever speaking to each other. In *Death of the Hat: A Brief History of Poetry in 50 Objects*, award-winning anthologist Paul Janeczko provides a tour of poetry through the ages, beginning with the early Middle Ages and ending with the present day. Chris Raschka's watercolor and ink illustrations illuminate the common theme of objects that threads among all the poems.

Several volumes of multicultural poetry for older children deserve to be considered among the "must-haves" in any home or classroom. Catherine Clinton has edited a fine anthology of poetry called *I, Too, Sing America: Three Centuries of African American Poetry*. Illustrated in muted tones by Stephen Alcorn, the book provides a chronological history of African American poetry by including poets from the 1700s to today. Poet and anthologist Naomi Shihab Nye has edited an international collection with universal connections: *This Same Sky: A Collection of Poems from Around the World*. Inspired by a collection of slave-related documents, Ashley Bryan tells the stories of eleven slaves listed for sale on the Fairchilds Appraisement of the Estate document in *Freedom Over Me: Eleven Slaves, Their Lives and Dreams Brought to Life by Ashley Bryan*. Bryan painted their portraits and gave voice to their dreams through the poetic form, endeavoring to "bring these slaves to life and have them tell their stories."

Specialized Collections As mentioned earlier, as poetry permissions have become more expensive and more difficult to obtain for long lengths of time, anthologists have turned to making small, specialized collections. Most of these are organized for a particular age level or around certain subjects, such as dogs or seasons. Some are related to the ethnic origin of the poems, such as portraying the lives of famous Latinos found in Margarita Engle's *Bravo! Poems about Amazing Hispanics*. Rafael López's mixed media art brings the biographical poems to life. Two esteemed books that celebrate the experiences of African Americans were named the 2012 Coretta Scott King Author Honor Books. Eloise Greenfield's *The Great Migration: Journey to the North*, illustrated by Jan Spivey Gilchrist, is a collection of poems about African Americans who left their homes in the South in the early 1900s to make their way up North to a better life. Patricia C. McKissack's *Never Forgotten*, illustrated by Leo and Diane Dillon, is a story-in-verse set in West Africa that explores the pain and grief of family members who

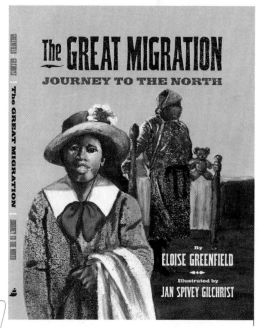

Writer Eloise Greenfield and illustrator Jan Spivey Gilchrist's *The Great Migration: Journey to the North* depicts the experiences of families like their own who courageously journeyed North to new lives. Cover from *The Great Migration* by Eloise Greenfield. Used by permission of HarperCollins Publishers.

Supplement?

are left behind when a young black boy is kidnapped and sold into slavery. In *Somos como las nubes/We Are Like the Clouds*, Salvadoran poet Jorge Argueta portrays the journeys of young refugee children from Mexico and countries in Central America. Based on his personal experiences working with immigrant children in El Salvador and the United States, these bilingual poems chronicle the emotional lives of displaced children. Alfonso Ruano's acrylic illustrations sensitively bring the young people's experiences to life. An increasing number of specialized collections contain stunning illustrations. Some of the best of these are listed in **Teaching Feature 6.2: Specialized Collections of Poetry**. Children will find imaginative connections to themes such as time or animals and to subjects as varied as American history, music, and science through many of these books.

teaching **feature 6.2**

Specialized Collections of Poetry

Author or Compiler	Title	Grade Level	Description
Children's Everyday Experiences			
Kristine O'Connell George	*Emma Dilemma: Big Sister Poems*	K–3	George perfectly captures the highs and lows of being a big sister.
Eloise Greenfield	*Brothers & Sisters: Family Poems*	K–3	This collection of poems for and about African American families explores and celebrates sibling experiences.
Gail Carson Levine	*Forgive Me, I Meant to Do It: False Apology Poems*	3–6	Inspired by William Carlos Williams's poem "This Is Just to Say," this collection of light verse imagines how tricksters feel about their mischief.
Jorge Elias Luján	*Con el sol en los ojos/ With the Sun in My Eyes*	K–3	A little boy and girl describe their everyday experiences in these bilingual poems written in Spanish and English.
Patricia McKissack	*Stitchin' and Pullin': A Gee's Bend Quilt*	K–3	Using free verse, McKissack follows the experiences of a young African American girl in rural Alabama when she is finally invited to join the intergenerational quilting circle.

(continued)

teaching feature 6.2

Author or Compiler	Title	Grade Level	Description
Pat Mora	*Love to Mama: A Tribute to Mothers*	K–3	Poems honor mothers, grandmothers, and caregiving women.
Naomi Shihab Nye	*A Maze Me: Poems for Girls*	6 and up	Nye's poems reflect the inner life and concerns of adolescent girls.
Poetry of Nature and Seasons			
Nicola Davies	*Outside Your Window: A First Book of Nature*	PreK–2	A unique blend of poetry and science, these poems about a child's interactions with nature are divided up by the seasons.
Douglas Florian	*Poetrees*	K–3	Lovely watercolors and mixed media illustrate these poems about trees.
Julie Fogliano	*When Green Becomes Tomatoes: Poems for All Seasons*	K–3	Journal entries in poetic form celebrate the seasons.
Mary Ann Hoberman and Linda Winston	*The Tree That Time Built: A Celebration of Nature, Science, and Imagination*	3–6	An anthology of more than 100 poems celebrates the natural world with an accompanying CD.
Joyce Sidman	*Red Sings from Treetops: A Year in Colors*	K–3	This 2010 Caldecott Honor–winning book of seasonal color poems is stunningly illustrated by Pamela Zagarenski using mixed-media paintings on wood along with computer art.
Joyce Sidman	*Ubiquitous: Celebrating Nature's Survivors*	K–3	Combining poems, scientific facts, and hand-colored linocuts, this collection explores the life forms that have survived long enough to become "ubiquitous."
Marilyn Singer	*A Stick Is an Excellent Thing: Poems Celebrating Outdoor Play*	K–3	Eighteen poems capture the timeless outdoor activities that children delight in.
Sallie Wolf	*The Robin Makes a Laughing Sound: A Birder's Observations*	3–6	Arranged by season, Wolf's journal is full of poems, field notes, and sketches that record her bird-watching experiences over the course of a year.

(continued)

teaching feature 6.2

Author or Compiler	Title	Grade Level	Description
Jane Yolen	*The Alligator's Smile and Other Poems*	K–3	Yolen and her photographer son, Jason Stemple, collaborate on several volumes about the natural world that pair poetry with scientific facts.
Charlotte Zolotow	*Changes: A Child's First Poetry Collection*	PreK–2	Published on the occasion of her one hundredth birthday, Zolotow's poems offer young children a celebration of the seasons.

Animal Poems

Author or Compiler	Title	Grade Level	Description
Douglas Florian	*UnBEElievables: Honeybee Poems and Paintings*	K–3	Humorous and rhythmic verse explores the world of bees.
Amy Gibson	*Around the World on Eighty Legs*	K–3	More than fifty poems about a variety of animals are arranged geographically by regions from around the world.
Avis Harley	*African Acrostics: A Word in Edgeways*	3–6	This collection of acrostic poems about African animals is illustrated with vibrant color photographs by Deborah Noyes.
Katherine Hauth	*What's for Dinner?: Quirky, Squirmy Poems from the Animal World*	K–3	Clever poems explore what animals eat along the food chain; many include gory eating habits.
Lee Bennett Hopkins	*Nasty Bugs*	K–3	Sixteen poems about creatures that bite in the night.
J. Patrick Lewis	*National Geographic Book of Animal Poetry: 200 Poems with Photographs That Squeak, Soar, and Roar!*	PreK–6	Two hundred animal poems paired with spectacular wildlife photographs.
Carol Murray	*Cricket in the Thicket: Poems About Bugs*	K–3	Playful poems about insects are paired with facts.
Marilyn Singer	*A Strange Place to Call Home: The World's Most Dangerous Habitats & the Animals That Call Them Home*	K–3	A fascinating look at fourteen animals that defy the odds to survive in their inhospitable habitats.

(continued)

teaching feature 6.2

Author or Compiler	Title	Grade Level	Description
Marilyn Singer	*Every Day's a Dog's Day: A Year in Poems*	PreK–2	This collection of short poems follows the antics of dogs through the seasons and holidays.
Lee Wardlaw	*Won Ton: A Cat Tale Told in Haiku*	K–3	Using a series of senryu (similar to haiku) poems, a shelter cat chronicles his experiences of being adopted by a family.
Amy Ludwig VanDerwater	*Every Day Birds*	K–3	Poems to help children learn about and identify common North American birds.
Humorous Poetry			
Allan Ahlberg	*Everybody Was a Baby Once: And Other Poems*	2–4	A creative cast of characters, from babies to witches, inhabits these fun poems.
Angela Dominguez	*Maria Had a Little Llama/María Tenía Una Llamita*	PreK–2	A bilingual English/Spanish retelling of the classic rhyme.
Douglas Florian	*Shiver Me Timbers: Pirate Poems & Paintings*	K–3	Set sail with a band of pirates in Florian's wildly entertaining pirate poetry.
John Keats	*A Song About Myself*	K–3	Keat's letter poem to his sister is brought to life by Chris Raschka.
J. Patrick Lewis	*Keep a Pocket in Your Poem: Classic Poems and Playful Parodies*	K–6	Patrick painlessly introduces children to classic poems through humorous parodies.
J. Patrick Lewis and Jane Yolen	*Last Laughs: Animal Epitaphs*	3–6	This darkly funny collection of epitaph poems will leave children laughing.
Multicultural Poetry Collections			
Arnold Adoff	*Roots and Blues: A Celebration*	4 and up	Using his signature "shaped speech" poetic style, Adoff traces the history and culture of blues music.
Jorge Argueta	*Talking with Mother Earth: Poems/Hablando con Madre Tierra: Poemas*	3–6	Bilingual poems describe the childhood experiences of a Pipil Nahua Indian boy.

(continued)

teaching feature 6.2

Author or Compiler	Title	Grade Level	Description
Gwendolyn Brooks	*Bronzeville Boys and Girls*	3–6	Faith Ringgold has illustrated a new edition of Brooks's classic collection.
Lorie Marie Carlson	*Cool Salsa: Bilingual Poems on Growing Up Latino in the United States; Red Hot Salsa: Bilingual Poems on Being Young and Latino in the United States*	6 and up	Two collections of bilingual poems describe growing up Latino.
Margarita Engle	*Bravo! Poems About Amazing Hispanics*	3–6	Engle writes poems to celebrate Hispanics from all countries.
Cynthia Grady	*I Lay My Stitches Down: Poems of American Slavery*	3–6	Using a quilt block poetic structure of ten lines with ten syllables each, these poems give voice to the experiences of American slaves. Historical notes and Michele Wood's quilt paintings accompany each poem.
Eloise Greenfield	*The Great Migration: Journey to the North*	3–6	A collection of poems about African Americans who left their homes in the South to make their way up North to a better life in the early 1900s.
Nikki Grimes	*When Daddy Prays*	3–6	Poems from a young African American child's perspective as he ponders his father's relationship with God.
Nikki Grimes	*One Last Word: Wisdom from the Harlem Renaissance*	6 and up	Grimes' "shovel" poems are paired with original poems from the Harlem Renaissance.
Lee Bennett Hopkins	*Amazing Faces*	K–3	A collection of poems that celebrates the many faces of multicultural America with contributions from Joseph Bruchac, Nikki Grimes, and Jane Yolen.

(continued)

teaching feature 6.2

Author or Compiler	Title	Grade Level	Description
Langston Hughes	*Sail Away*	PreK–2	A collection of poems about the oceans, including mermaids.
Langston Hughes	*The Dream Keeper and Other Poems*	2 and up	This is a must-have collection of poems from a great American poet.
Walter Dean Myers	*Here in Harlem: Poems in Many Voices*	6 and up	The people of Harlem are seen through many different poetic forms.
Naomi Shihab Nye	*19 Varieties of Gazelle: Poems of the Middle East*	4 and up	Nye holds up a magnifying glass to capture the smallest nuances of Middle Eastern culture.

Creating a Climate for Enjoyment

There have always been teachers who love poetry and who share their enthusiasm for poetry with students. There are teachers who make poetry a natural part of the daily program of living and learning. They realize that poetry should not be presented under the pressure of a tight time schedule, but should be enjoyed every day. Children should be able to relax and relish the humor and beauty that the sharing of poetry affords.

Hmm → I used to do that.....

Finding Time for Poetry

Teachers who hope to develop children's delight in poetry will find time to share poetry with them sometime each day and find ways to connect poetry to the experiences in children's lives. They know that anytime is a good time to read a poem to children, but they will especially want to capitalize on exciting experiences like the first snow, a birth-day party, or the arrival of a classmate's new baby brother. Perhaps there has been a fight on the playground and someone is still grumbling and complaining—that might be a good time to share poetry about feelings. The teacher could read Karla Kuskin's "I Woke Up This Morning" (in *A Jar of Tiny Stars*), and then everyone could laugh the bad feelings away. Poetry can also be thought of as a delicious snack to nibble on during transition times between going out to recess or the last few minutes of the day. Anytime is a good time for a poetry snack! Sylvia Vardell and Janet Wong's *Poetry Friday Anthologies* provide excellent resources for teachers who wish to share poetry with their students. The newest titles in the series are *The Poetry Friday Anthology for Celebrations* and *The Poetry Anthology for Science*. Teachers will also find support in the authors' Poetry Friday

Power series *Here We Go* and *You Just Wait*, which are filled with activities for both readers and writers of poetry.

One way to be sure to share poetry every day is to relate children's favorite prose stories to poetry. One teacher who keeps a card file of poems always slips one or two cards into the book that is to be read aloud that day. For example, after sharing *Whistle for Willie* by Ezra Jack Keats, Jack Prelutsky's "Whistling" (in *Read-Aloud Rhymes for the Very Young*) could be read. A fifth-grade teacher paired Gail Carson Levine's *Ella Enchanted* with Laura Whipple's *If the Shoe Fits: Voices from Cinderella*. Students then went on to read other novelizations of fairy tales and to write poems in the voices of the characters. Librarians and teachers will want to make their own poetry/prose connections.

Teachers have also found that a good way to integrate poetry into the entire day is to link poems to content areas. A science unit could be built around Jane Yolen and Jason Stemple's extensive series of books that combines poems, facts, and photographs of nature, such as their latest book in the series *The Alligator's Smile and Other Poems*, or Joyce Sidman's many books about ecosystems, including *Dark Emperor and Other Poems of the Night*, *Song of the Water Boatman*, *Ubiquitous: Celebrating Nature's Survivors*, *Swirl by Swirl: Spirals in Nature*, and *Winter Bees & Other Poems of the Cold*. A math lesson might be introduced with one of the poems from J. Patrick Lewis's collection *Edgar Allan Poe's Pie: Math Puzzlers in Classic Poems* or Joyce Sidman's *Round*, in which a young child takes the reader on a tour of all that is round in the natural world, exploring both the concept and the shape. Jane Yolen and Jason Stemple collaborate on two math-related poetry/photography collections: *Count Me a Rhyme: Animal Poems by the Numbers* (counting animals from 1 to 10) and *Shape Me a Rhyme: Nature's Forms in Poetry* (shapes in nature).

Many poems can enhance social studies. Geography need not be neglected when we have a collection such as *Amazing Places*, in which anthologist Lee Bennett Hopkins has gathered poems that celebrate famous places in the United States. American history is also well represented by collections such as Ntozake Shange's *Freedom's a-Callin Me*. Carole Boston Weatherford's *Freedom in Congo Square*, winner of the Charlotte Zolotow Award, brings to life the history of Congo Square in New Orleans, where both enslaved and free people of African heritage came together to celebrate the break from work allowed on Sunday afternoon. Illustrator R. Gregory Christie won a Caldecott Honor and a Coretta Scott King Illustrator Honor for his vibrant art. In *Jazz Day: The Making of a Famous Photograph*, Roxanne Orgill's poems chronicle the history of Art Kane's famous photograph that was taken for *Esquire* magazine's issue on American jazz. Francis Vallejo's acrylic and pastel paintings capture the musicians and the vibrant atmosphere of Harlem in 1958. Father–son team Walter Dean Myers and Christopher Myers explore what it means to be an American in *We Are America: A Tribute from the Heart*. Caldecott Honor–winning artist Bryan Collier interprets Langston Hughes's beloved poem in *I, Too, Am America*.

Several volumes pair poetry and art in unique ways. Jan Greenberg, with Sandra Jordan, has written many books about twentieth-century art, inviting poets to choose a work of twentieth-century art and write a poem about it. The results, *Heart to Heart* and *Side by Side*, are a delight and a revelation. Belinda Rochelle's *Words with Wings: A Treasury of African-American Poetry and Art* pairs twenty poems by renowned African American poets with twenty works of art by celebrated African American artists. In Ashley Bryan's *Puppets*, the Coretta Scott King Award winner pairs his puppets made with

Dark Emperor

Perched   missile,
  almost invisible, you
    preen silent feathers,
  swivel your sleek satellite
dish of head. What fills the
cool moons of your mesmerizing
eyes? What waves of sound
funnel toward those waiting
ears? What symphonies of
squeaks and skitters, darts
and rustles, swell the vast,
breathing darkness of your
  realm? O Dark Emperor
    of hooked face and
      hungry eye: turn that
        awful beak away
          from me;
        disregard

the tiny hiccup
of my heart
as I flee.

Nocturnal animals have specially adapted senses for hunting. Whereas raccoons use extrasensitive paws to feel for prey, great horned **owls** have huge eyes and extraordinary hearing; their wide, flat faces channel sound toward two large ear cavities on the sides of their head. They can also swivel their head more than halfway in either direction, although not all the way around. As night falls, the great horned owl moves from its deep-woods roost to a high perch near the forest's edge. With eyes and ears a hundred times more sensitive than a human's, it scouts for anything from salamanders to mice to rabbits. Like other owls', its feathers are soft-edged, so it can fly silently and pounce without warning on unsuspecting prey.

Poems from books such as *Dark Emperor and Other Poems of the Night* or *Winter Bees & Other Poems of the Cold* by Joyce Sidman can serve as models for writing or springboards for curriculum studies. Illustration from *Dark Emperor and Other Poems of the Night* by Joyce Sidman, illustrated by Rick Allen. Illustrations copyright ©2010 by Rick Allen. Reprinted by permission of Houghton Mifflin Harcourt Publishing Company. All rights reserved.

treasures washed ashore on the beach with personified poems that breathe life into the original puppets.

Children will also be delighted with excellent poetry books on sports, such as Jack Prelutsky's *Good Sports*, Douglas Florian's *Poem Runs: Baseball Poems*, illustrated by the poet, and Ayana Lowe's *Come and Play: Children of Our World Having Fun*, with photographs by Julie Collins. There are poems on every subject, from dinosaurs to quasars and from black holes to whales.

Reading Poetry to Children

Poetry should be read in a natural voice with a tone that fits the meaning of the poem. Generally, the appropriate pace for reading poetry is slower than for reading prose. It is usually recommended that a poem be read aloud a second time, perhaps to refresh children's memories, to clarify a point, or to savor a particular image. Most poetry, especially good poetry, is so concentrated and compact that few people can grasp its meaning in one exposure. Following the reading of a poem, discussion should be allowed to flow naturally. In certain instances, discussion is unnecessary or superfluous. Spontaneous chuckles might follow the reading of Kaye Starbird's "Eat-It-All Elaine" (in *The Random House Book of Poetry for Children*, ed. Jack Prelutsky), while a thoughtful silence might be the response to Robert P. Tristram Coffin's "Forgive My Guilt" (in *Reflections on a Gift of Watermelon Pickle*, ed. Stephen Dunning et al.). It is not necessary to discuss or do something with each poem read, other than to enjoy it. The most important thing you as a teacher or librarian can do when you are reading poetry is share your enthusiasm for the poem.

A former United States poet laureate provides four simple but useful tips for reading poetry aloud. These tips are elaborated on the Library of Congress Poetry 180 project website. They are, in brief:

1. Read the poem slowly. A good way for a reader to set an easy pace is to pause for a few seconds between the title and the poem's first line.
2. Read in a normal, relaxed tone of voice. Let the words of the poem do the work.
3. Poems come in lines but pausing at the end of every line will create a choppy effect and interrupt the flow of meaning. Readers should pause only where there is punctuation, just as you would when reading prose.
4. Use a dictionary to look up unfamiliar words. In some cases, a reader might want to write a poem phonetically as a reminder of how it should sound.[8]

Choral Reading

The reading and sharing of poetry through choral speaking is another way to foster interest in poetry. Choral speaking or reading is the interpretation of poetry by several voices speaking as one. At first, young children *speak* it as they join in the refrains. Middle-grade children might prefer to *read* their poems. They are not always read in unison; in fact, this is one of the most difficult ways to present a poem.

Several types of choral speaking are particularly suited for use in the elementary school. In the "refrain" type, one person (teacher or child) reads the narrative and the rest of the class joins in on the refrain. The teacher might use the well-known folk poem that begins "In a dark, dark wood there was a dark, dark path" and let children join in on the "dark dark" phrases. Eve Merriam's "Windshield Wiper" (in *Knock at a Star*, ed. X. J. Kennedy and D. M. Kennedy) and Sara Holbrook's "Copycat" (in *Wham! It's a Poetry Jam*) are good echo poems to try.

Another way to do a group reading, called antiphonal, is to divide the class into two groups and let the groups take turns reading each verse. An effective approach with young children is the "line-a-child" arrangement, where different children say, or read, individual lines, with the class joining in unison at the beginning or end of the poem. "One, Two, Buckle My Shoe" is a good rhyme to introduce this type of choral reading.

Several books come ready-made for multiple-voice readings. Younger children can get started on this technique with Mary Ann Hoberman's series of books beginning with *You Read to Me, I'll Read to You: Very Short Stories to Read Together* or Betsy Franco's *Messing Around on the Monkey Bars: And Other School Poems for Two Voices*. Older children particularly enjoy practicing reading Paul Fleischman's poems for multiple voices found in his Newbery Medal book *Joyful Noise* and in his *I Am Phoenix*. In *Big Talk*, Fleischman challenges older readers by presenting poems for four voices.

If children are to develop appreciation for the deep satisfactions that poetry brings, they should have many opportunities to share poetry in interesting and meaningful situations. Appreciation for poetry develops slowly. It is the result of long and loving experiences with poetry over a period of years. Children who are fortunate enough to have developed a love of poetry will always be the richer for it.

Challenging Perspectives on Poetry

During playground duty, Ms. Berlyn walked toward two little girls playing what looked like a game of very sophisticated patty-cake. The rhythm and rhyme of the game was almost hypnotic. The girls were singing and reciting the words of a popular rhyme, "Apple on the stick, you make me sick, you make my heart go 2-40-6, not because you dirty, not because you clean, not because you kiss the boy behind the magazine! Come on girls let's have some fun, here comes Jenny with the short skirt on." The rhyme went on and then Ms. Berlyn realized that the rhyme went "down hill" as the girls' language became inappropriate.

"Let's find another game to play," Ms. Berlyn interrupted.

Startled, one little girl asked why. Ms. Berlyn responded, "The language is not school language and you should not be talking about some of those things—you are too young."

"It's just like poetry," Crystal protested. "It rhymes and everything!"

Ms. Berlyn did not know what to say. "Well, that's not poetry, find something else to do." The girls walked away discussing in hushed tones their feelings about Ms. Berlyn's request.

Poetry can be extremely engaging and fun word play for children, but today certain uses present challenges for teachers. Its value begins in the early grades, when poetry can be used to jump-start language development and as a support for a wide range of literacy skills, including phonemic awareness, repetition, and predictability, and to enhance reading fluency and emergent writing, especially for children with limited vocabulary.

Poetry today is not "your mother's poetry." When a first grader was asked to define poetry, he responded, "Poetry is rhyming words, but not all the time, and can be like hip-hop and rap too." For many young people, the most popular form of poetry is called *spoken word*. Spoken word is the presentation of poetry in which the formal elements of poetry are dramatic performances and recitation. Often imitating song lyrics found in hip-hop and rap music, the verses are spoken rather than sung.

Spoken word is often performed competitively. Poetry slams—a competitive event in which poets perform their work and are judged based on content and performance—are organized locally, nationally, and internationally. These events invite poets to participate in either the individual or group categories for awards, prize money, and possibly television or Internet exposure. In *performance poetry*, the poet either reads previously published poems or reads poems specifically written to be performed aloud. Another kind of spoken word poetry gaining popularity recently is political and social commentary, which is more artistic than a typical speech.

Outside of the classical poetry taught in schools, the poetry of today, in "slams" for example, are full of social and political commentary and are often mixed with great energy, enthusiasm, and strong language. This context provides an exciting segue for teachers to discuss the wonderful world of poetry with their students in the classroom. The challenge for many teachers will be how to use contemporary forms of expression in poetry and negotiate use of controversial language and content. Nikki Giovanni's *Hip Hop Speaks to Children: A Celebration of Poetry with a Beat* highlights the use of rhythm and vernacular in hip-hop, rap, and African American poetry. Giovanni explains in her informative introduction that jazz and blues rhythms and language from the historic fields of enslavement and the everyday life of the city streets are represented in this contemporary approach to poetry. This collection comes with a CD, allowing readers to hear

more than thirty of the spoken word pieces or poetry as they are performed by many of the artists themselves.

Social and political commentary in poetic forms can take one down a slippery slope. Some language is deeply political and loaded with the historical and contemporary baggage of racism, sexism, homophobia, and other systemic oppressions. The polarization caused by a single word can be seen in the use of the racial slur "nigger." This word was used as a derogatory way to impose a view of inferiority upon a race of people. Books written for children and young adults have grappled with the use of language that captures the milieu of historical or contemporary times. One publisher responded to this dilemma by removing from Mark Twain's classic *Huck Finn* the 219 instances where the racial epitaph appears and is replacing it with the word "slave." There are two schools of thought represented in this decision. Some feel it is "censorship" and "political correctness." Others feel this is a transgression of epic proportions, altering the words of a literary icon. Still others feel the word is offensive and has no place in school.

While many teachers report they hear "worse" language in the hallways of their schools than they will ever read in any children's book, decisions about the inclusion or exclusion of books with historical or contemporary language that may be offensive has and will continue to be a challenge.

Additional challenges can arise when language dialects are heard as deficits. Issues of identity and validation of a child's home language can present challenges to the teaching and learning process. If we want children to adopt the language of schooling, teachers should not view language variation as deficits. In her book *The Skin That We Speak*, Lisa Delpit provides a variety of positive ways to view the language variations that students bring to school. "Since language is one of the most intimate expressions of identity, indeed, 'the skin that we speak,' then to reject a person's language can only feel as if we are rejecting him" (p. 47).[9]

This is not suggesting that the use of offensive or what is now deemed "strong language" is appropriate for school. When students use language in poetry or other forms of creative writing, there is a way to simultaneously affirm a student's peer culture and home language and provide a segue to teaching and learning standard, edited English. Most often the discussion of affirming a student's home language is in part helping English Language Learners (ELL) to speak, read, write, and communicate in English. In *Rethinking Schools*, author Linda Christensen uses the poem "Raised by Women" by Kelly

Norman Ellis. This poem connects home and heritage in a celebration of the women in the poet's life. Christensen stated she uses poetry to "build community and teach poetic traits . . . to build relationships with students and between students." She further says, "I love Ellis' celebration of the women in her life, her use of home language, and the wit and wisdom of her rhythmic lines."[10] Christensen uses poetry to help honor the use of students' home language rather than standard English, and, like the poet, encouraged students to experiment with language in their poems. The students felt validated while they learned about metaphor, meter, rhyme, simile, and tone. Arnold Adoff's *Roots and Blues* is another example of using poetry to inform and affirm. Using short poems and prose vignettes, Adoff uses language variation and unique stylistic presentation to tell the the story of the uniquely American musical art form—the Blues.

Teachers can engage students in conversations of the debates around language and literary works. Using this approach, we start by affirming a student's home language, culture, attitudes, beliefs, and values. We can begin with the "funds of knowledge" the students bring to every teaching and learning event.[11] By changing our vantage point and increasing *our* "cultural competence" in our classrooms, we come to understand, affirm, and draw upon students' home and school linguistic experiences for their own learning and development.[12]

Using the many new and familiar voices found in poetry written for children, teachers can engage students in reading, writing, and performing poetry in ways that can serve as a bridge to reading and understanding other forms of classical work. The ultimate goal is to get students to read, and write, and then read and write again and again—increasing student engagement and participation with poetry. (Go to Connect® to use the Ten-Point Model to engage students in conversations of the debates surrounding language and literary works in contemporary times.)

curriculum connections

Using Poetry to Address Standards

The topic of poetry often gets groans from students and teachers alike who relate the genre more to ancient verse than to the new, imaginative, and engaging titles for children that have come out more recently. Poetry can be a tool for exploring language, emotion, and the world around us, while also implementing curriculum standards.

Suggested Children's Book: *Echo Echo: Reverso Poems About Greek Myths* by Marilyn Singer, illustrated by Josée Masse (Dial Books, 2015)
Singer pens a poem for a Greek myth, like *Narcissus* or *Icarus,* and then reverses it so the poem can be read from top to bottom or bottom to top. For each myth, she cleverly weaves poetic language with well-known stories to provide two different perspectives. At the bottom of each double-page spread, Singer provides a concise summary of each original myth for those who may not be familiar with the story.

(continued)

(continued)

Subject	Standard	Classroom Ideas
Science, Math, and Art	**NGSS:** Ask questions based on observations to find more information. **NCTM:** Describe, extend, and make generalizations about patterns. **NCCAS:** Interpret intent and meaning in artistic work.	What do you notice about these poems by just looking at them? Identify characteristics and patterns found in one of the pages. Compare their descriptions of the patterns found in this form of poetry to other forms they have read and/or studied. What do you notice in the art on this page? Identify characteristics and patterns found in the art. How do the patterns in the poems connect with the art?
Art, Language Arts, Math, Social Studies, and Technology	**NCTE/ILA (Reading):** Students read a wide range of print to build an understanding of texts, of themselves, and of the cultures of the United States and the world. **NCTE/ILA (Reading):** Students apply a wide range of strategies to comprehend, interpret, evaluate, and appreciate texts. **NCTE/ILA (Writing):** Students apply knowledge of language structure, language conventions, media techniques, figurative language, and genre to create, critique, and discuss print and non-print texts. **NCSS:** Describe ways in which language, stories, folktales, music, and artistic creations serve as expressions of culture and influence behavior of people living in a particular culture. **NCCAS:** Synthesize and relate knowledge and personal experiences to make art. **ISTE:** Students publish or present content that customizes the message and medium for their intended audiences.	Research myths from around the world, charting similarities and differences. Create reverso poems based on myths they have researched from other countries. Students use digital media to create symmetrical designs to depict their reverso poems.

(continued)

curriculum connections

(continued)

Subject	Standard	Classroom Ideas
Textual Connections	*Norse Mythology* (Gaiman); *Treasury of Greek Mythology: Classic Stories of Gods, Goddesses, Heroes, & Monsters* (Napoli); *Treasury of Egyptian Mythology: Classic Stories of Gods, Goddesses, Monsters, & Mortals* (Napoli); *Treasury of Norse Mythology: Stories of Intrigue, Trickery, Love, and Revenge* (Napoli); *Jason and the Argonauts: The First Great Quest in Greek Mythology* (Byrd); *I Am Pan!* (Gerstein); *Norse Myths: Tales of Odin, Thor, and Loki* (Crossley-Holland)	
Other Books by Singer	*Mirror Mirror; Follow Follow; A Stick Is an Excellent Thing; A Full Moon Is Rising; Twosomes: Love Poems from the Animal Kingdom; Central Heating: Poems About Fire and Warmth*	
Author's Website	http://marilynsinger.net	

Sources: International Society for Technology in Education (ITSE); National Coalition for Core Arts Standards (NCCAS); National Council of Teachers of English (NCTE)/International Literacy Association (ILA); National Council of Teachers of Mathematics (NCTM); National Council for the Social Studies Curriculum Standards (NCSS); and Next Generation Science Standards (NGSS).

Notes

1. *Poetry* originally appeared in *Sing for Your Supper*. Copyright ©1938 by Eleanor Farjeon; renewed 1966 by Gervase Farjeon. Used by permission of HarperCollins Publishers, New York, NY.

2. Laurence Perrine, *Sound and Sense: An Introduction to Poetry*, 10th ed. (New York: Harcourt Brace Jovanovich, 2000), p. 3.

3. Kornei Chukovsky, *From Two to Five*, trans. and ed. Miriam Morton (Berkeley: University of California Press, 1963), p. 64.

4. Elizabeth Coatsworth, *The Sparrow Bush*, ill. Stefan Martin (New York: Norton, 1966), p. 8.

5. Ann Terry, "Children's Poetry Preferences: A National Survey of the Upper Elementary Grades," *NCTE Research Report* 16 (Urbana, Ill.: National Council of Teachers of English, 1974), p. 10.

6. Carol J. Fisher and Margaret A. Natarella, "Young Children's Preferences in Poetry: A National Survey of First, Second and Third Graders," *Research in the Teaching of English* 16 (December 1982): 339–53.

7. Karen Sue Kutiper, *A Survey of the Adolescent Poetry Preferences of Seventh, Eighth and Ninth Graders* (Ed.D. dissertation, University of Houston, 1985).

8. Poetry 180, October 2008 <www.loc.gov.poetry/180/p180-howtoread.html>. Used by permission of Billy Collins.

9. L. Delpit and J. Dowdy, eds. *The Skin That We Speak: Thoughts on Language and Culture in the Classroom* (New York: New Press, 2002).

10. L. Christensen, "Raised by Women: Building Relationships Through Poetry," *Rethinking Schools* 21.3. (2007). Also online at <www.rethinking-schools.org/archive/21_03/21_03.shtml>.

11. G. J. Ladson-Billings, *The Dreamkeepers: Successful Teachers of African-American Children* (San Francisco, CA: Jossey-Bass, 1997).

12. L. C. Moll et al., "Funds of Knowledge for Teaching: Using a Qualitative Approach to Connect Homes and Classrooms," *Theory into Practice* 31(2),1992: 132–41.

Children's Literature

Go to **Connect**® to access study resources, practice quizzes, and additional materials.

Titles in blue = multicultural titles

Ada, Alma Flor, and E. Isabel Campoy, selectors. *¡Muu, Moo!: Rimas de Animales/Animal Nursery Rhymes.* Illustrated by Vivi Escrivá. English version by Rosalina Zubizarreta. HarperCollins, 2010.

Adoff, Arnold. *Roots and Blues.* Illustrated by R. Gregory Christie. Clarion, 2011.

Ahlberg, Allan. *Everybody Was a Baby Once: And Other Poems.* Illustrated by Bruce Ingman. Candlewick, 2010.

Alexander, Kwame (with Chris Colderley and Marjory Wentworth). *Out of Wonder: Poems Celebrating Poets.* Illustrated by Ekua Holmes. Candlewick, 2017.

Alexander, Kwame, Mary Rand Hess and Deanna Nikaido. *Animal Ark: Celebrating Our Wild World in Poetry and Picture.* Photographs by Joel Sartore. National Geographic Children's Books, 2017.

Argueta, Jorge. *Somos como las nubes/We are Like the Clouds.* Illustrated by Alfonso Ruano. Groundwood, 2016.

_____. *Talking with Mother Earth/Hablando con Madre Tierra: Poems/Poemas.* Illustrated by Lucia Angela Pérez. Groundwood, 2006.

Beaty, Daniel. *Knock Knock: My Dad's Dream for Me.* Illustrated by Bryan Collier. Little, Brown, 2013.

Brooks, Gwendolyn. *Bronzeville Boys and Girls.* Illustrated by Faith Ringgold. HarperCollins, 2007.

Brown, Margaret Wise. *Goodnight Songs.* Illustrated by a variety of artists. Sterling, 2014.

Bryan, Ashley. *Ashley Bryan's Puppet.* Atheneum, 2014.

_____. *Freedom Over Me: Eleven Slaves, Their Lives and Dreams Brought to Life by Ashley Bryan.* Atheneum, 2016.

Carlson, Lori M., ed. *Cool Salsa: Bilingual Poems on Growing Up Latino in the United States.* Holt, 1994.

_____. *Red Hot Salsa: Bilingual Poems on Being Young and Latino in the United States.* Holt, 2005.

Caswell, Deanna. *Guess Who, Haiku.* Illustrated by Bob Shea. Harry N. Abrams, 2016.

Cleary, Brian P. *Something Sure Smells Around Here: Limericks.* Illustrated by Andy Rowland. Millbrook, 2015.

Clinton, Catherine. *I, Too, Sing America: Three Centuries of African American Poetry.* Illustrated by Stephen Alcorn. Houghton, 1998.

Crossley-Holland, Kevin. *Once Upon a Poem: Favorite Poems That Tell Stories.* Chicken House, 2004.

Cullinan, Bernice E., and Deborah Wooten, eds. *Another Jar of Tiny Stars.* Boyds Mills, 2009.

Davies, Nicola. *Outside Your Window: A First Book of Nature.* Illustrated by Mark Hearld. Candlewick, 2012.

_____. *Song of the Wild: A First Book of Animals.* Illustrated by Petr Horáček. Candlewick, 2016.

dePaola, Tomie. *Tomie dePaola's Mother Goose.* Putnam, 1988.

De Regniers, et al. *Sing a Song of Popcorn: Every Child's Book of Poems.* Scholastic Press, 1988.

Dominguez, Angela. *Maria Had a Little Llama/María Tenía Una Llamita.* Henry Holt, 2013.

Duffy, Chris (Ed.). *Nursery Rhyme Comics.* First Second, 2011.

Dunning, Stephen, Edward Lueders, and Hugh Smith. *Reflections on a Gift of Watermelon Pickle and Other Modern Verse.* Lothrop, 1966.

Elya, Susan Middleton. *La Madre Goose: Nursery Rhymes for Los Niños.* Illustrated by Juana Martinez-Neal. G. P. Putnam's Sons, 2016.

Engle, Margarita. *Bravo! Poems About Amazing Hispanics.* Illustrated by Rafael López. Henry Holt, 2017.

Farjeon, Eleanor. *Poems for Children.* Lippincott, 1951.

Ferris, Helen, ed. *Favorite Poems Old and New.* Illustrated by Leonard Weisgard. Doubleday, 1957.

Field, Eugene. *Wynken, Blynken, and Nod.* Illustrated by Giselle Potter. Schwartz & Wade, 2008.

Fleischman, Paul. *Big Talk: Poems for Four Voices.* Illustrated by Beppe Giacobbe. Candlewick, 2000.

_____. *I Am Phoenix: Poems for Two Voices.* Illustrated by Ken Nutt. Harper, 1985.

_____. *Joyful Noise: Poems for Two Voices.* Illustrated by Eric Beddows. Harper, 1988.

Florian, Douglas. *Poem Runs: Baseball Poems.* Harcourt, 2012.

_____. *Poetrees.* Beach Lane, 2010.

_____. *Shiver Me Timbers! Pirate Poems & Paintings.* Illustrated by Robert Neubecker. Beach Lane, 2012.

_____. *UnBEElievables: Honeybee Poems and Paintings*. Beach Lane, 2012.

Fogliano, Julie. *When Green Becomes Tomatoes: Poems for All Seasons*. Illustrated by Julie Morstad. Roaring Brook, 2016.

Foreman, Michael. *Michael Foreman's Playtime Rhymes*. Candlewick, 2002.

Franco, Betsy. *Messing Around on the Monkey Bars: And Other School Poems for Two Voices*. Candlewick, 2009.

Frost, Helen. *Applesauce Weather*. Illustrated by Amy June Bates. Candlewick, 2016.

_____. *Wake Up!* Photographs by Rick Lieder. Candlewick, 2017.

Galing, Ed. *Tony*. Illustrated by Erin E. Stead. Roaring Brook, 2017.

George, Kristine O'Connell. *Emma Dilemma: Big Sister Poems*. Illustrated by Nancy Carpenter. Clarion, 2011.

Giovanni, Nikki, ed. *Hip Hop Speaks to Children: A Celebration of Poetry with a Beat*. Illustrated by Kristen Balouch, Michele Noiset, Jeremy Tugeau, Alicia Vergel de Dios, and Damian Ward. Sourcebooks, 2008.

Gottfried, Maya. *Our Farm: By the Animals of Farm Sanctuary*. Illustrated by Robert Rahway Zakanitch. Knopf, 2010.

Grady, Cynthia. *I Lay My Stitches Down: Poems of American Slavery*. Illustrated by Michele Wood. Eerdmans, 2011.

Graham, Joan Bransfield. *Flicker Flash*. Illustrated by Nancy Davis. Houghton Mifflin, 1999.

_____. *Splish, Splash*. Illustrated by Steve Scott. Ticknor & Fields, 1994.

Grandits, John. *Blue Lipstick: Concrete Poems*. Clarion, 2007.

Greenberg, Jan, ed. *Heart to Heart: New Poems Inspired by Twentieth-Century American Art*. Abrams, 2001.

_____. *Side by Side: New Poems Inspired by Art from around the World*. Abrams, 2008.

Greenfield, Eloise. *Brothers & Sisters: Family Poems*. Illustrated by Jan Spivey Gilchrist. Amistad, 2008.

_____. *The Great Migration: Journey to the North*. Illustrated by Jan Spivey Gilchrist. Amistad, 2010.

Grimes, Nikki. *Planet Middle School*. Bloomsbury, 2011.

_____. *One Last Word: Wisdom from the Harlem Renaissance*. Illustrated by Cozbi Cabrera. Bloomsbury, 2017.

_____. *When Daddy Prays*. Illustrated by Tim Ladwig. Eerdmans, 2002.

Hall, Donald, ed. *The Oxford Illustrated Book of American Children's Poems*. Oxford University Press, 1999.

Hammill, Elizabeth. *Over the Hills and Far Away: A Treasury of Nursery Rhymes*. Candlewick, 2015.

Harley, Avis. *African Acrostics: A Word in Edgeways*. Photographs by Deborah Noyes. Candlewick, 2009.

Harrington, Janice N. *Catching a Storyfish*. WordSong, 2016.

Hauth, Katherine B. *What's for Dinner?: Squirmy Poems from the Animal World*. Illustrated by David Clark. Charlesbridge, 2011.

_____. *The Tree That Time Built: A Celebration of Nature, Science, and Imagination*. Sourcebooks, 2009.

Hoberman, Mary Ann. *Forget-Me-Nots: Poems to Learn by Heart*. Little, Brown, 2012.

_____. *The Llama Who Had No Pajama*. Illustrated by Betty Fraser. Harcourt, 1998.

_____. *You Read to Me, I'll Read to You: Very Short Stories to Read Together*. Illustrated by Michael Emberley. Little, 2001.

Hoberman, Mary Ann and Linda Winston. *The Tree That Time Built: A Celebration of Nature, Science, and Imagination*. Illustrated by Barbara Fortin. Sourcebooks, 2009.

Holbrook, Sara. *Wham! It's a Poetry Jam*. Wordsong, 2002.

Hopkins, Lee Bennett, selector. *Amazing Faces*. Illustrated by Chris Soentpiet. Lee & Low, 2010.

_____. *Amazing Places*. Illustrated by Chris Soentpiet and Christy Hale. Lee & Low, 2015.

_____. *Nasty Bugs*. Illustrated by Will Terry. Dial, 2012.

Hughes, Langston. *The Dream Keeper and Other Poems*. Illustrated by Brian Pinkney. Knopf, 2007 (1932).

Issa, Kobayashi. *I, Too, Am America*. Illustrated by Bryan Collier. Simon & Schuster, 2012.

_____. *Sail Away*. Illustrated by Ashley Bryan. Atheneum, 2015.

_____. selector. *Dirty Laundry Pile: Poems in Different Voices*. Illustrated by Melissa Sweet. HarperCollins, 2001.

Janeczko, Paul B. (Ed.). *Death of the Hat: A Brief History of Poetry in 50 Objects*. Illustrated by Chris Raschka. Candlewick, 2015.

_____. *Firefly July: A Year of Very Short Poems*. Illustrated by Melissa Sweet. Candlewick, 2014.

_____. *A Kick in the Head*. Illustrated by Chris Raschka. Candlewick, 2009.

_____, compiler. *A Kick in the Head: An Everyday Guide to Poetic Forms*. Illustrated by Chris Raschka. Candlewick, 2005.

_____, selector. *A Poke in the I: A Collection of Concrete Poems*. Illustrated by Chris Raschka. Candlewick, 2001.

Jensen, Dana. *A Meal of the Stars: Poems Up and Down*. Illustrated by Tricia Tusa. Houghton Mifflin, 2012.

Keats, Ezra Jack. *Whistle for Willie*. Viking, 1964.

Keats, John. *A Song About Myself.* Illustrated by Chris Raschka. Candlewick, 2017.

Kennedy, Caroline. *Poems to Learn by Heart*. Illustrated by Jon J. Muth. Disney Hyperion, 2013.

Kennedy, X. J., and Dorothy M. Kennedy, comp. *Knock at a Star: A Child's Introduction to Poetry*. Illustrated by Karen Ann Weinhaus. Little, 1999 [1982].

Kuskin, Karla. *Moon, Have You Met My Mother?* Illustrated by Sergio Ruzzier. Harper, 2003.

Lai, Thanhha. *Inside Out & Back Again*. HarperCollins, 2011.

Larrick, Nancy, ed. *Piping Down the Valleys Wild*. Illustrated by Ellen Raskin. Delacorte, 1985 [1968].

Lea, Synne. *Night Guard*. Illustrated by Stian Hole. Eerdmans, 2016.

Levine, Gail Carson. *Ella Enchanted*. HarperCollins, 1997.

_____. *Forgive Me, I Meant to Do It: False Apology Poems*. Illustrated by Matthew Cordell. HarperCollins, 2012.

Lewis, J. Patrick. *Doodle Dandies*. Illustrated by Lisa Desimini. Atheneum, 1998.

_____. *Edgar Allan Poe's Pie: Math Puzzlers in Classic Poems*. Illustrated by Michael Slack. Harcourt, 2012.

_____. *Keep a Poem in Your Pocket: Classic Poems and Playful Parodies*. Illustrated by Johanna Wright. WordSong, 2017.

_____. *National Geographic Book of Animal Poetry: 200 Poems with Photographs That Squeak, Soar, and Roar!* National Geographic, 2012.

_____. *National Geographic Book of Nature Poetry: More than 200 Poems with Photographs That Float, Zoom, and Bloom!* National Geographic Children's Books, 2015.

Lewis, J. Patrick, and Jane Yolen. *Last Laughs: Animal Epitaphs*. Illustrated by Jeffrey Stewart Timmins. Charlesbridge, 2012.

_____. *Take Two!: A Celebration of Twins*. Illustrated by Sophie Blackall. Candlewick, 2012.

Lowe, Ayana, ed. *Come and Play: Children of Our World Having Fun*. Photographs by Julie Collins. Bloomsbury, 2008.

Luján, Jorge Elias. *Con el sol en los ojos/With the Sun in My Eyes*. Illustrated by Morteza Zahedi. Groundwood, 2012.

Martin Jr., Bill, and Michael Sampson, eds. *The Bill Martin Jr. Big Book of Poetry*. Simon & Schuster, 2008.

Mathers, Petra, compiler. *The McElderry Book of Mother Goose*. Illustrated by Petra Mathers. Margaret K. McElderry Books, 2012.

McKissack, Patricia. *Let's Clap, Jump, Sing, & Shout; Dance, Spin, & Turn It Out! Games, Songs, & Stories from an African American Childhood*. Illustrated by Brian Pinkney. Schwartz & Wade, 2017.

_____. *Never Forgotten*. Illustrated by Leo and Diane Dillon. Schwartz & Wade, 2011.

_____. *Stitchin' and Pullin': A Gee's Bend Quilt*. Illustrated by Cozbi A. Cabrera. Random House, 2008.

McPhail, David. *Mother Goose: A Collection of Favorite Rhymes, Songs, and Concepts*. Roaring Brook, 2013.

Mendelson, Edward. *Poetry for Young People: Edward Lear*. Illustrated by Laura Huliska-Beith. Sterling, 2001.

Moore, Clement. *The Night Before Christmas*. Illustrated by Jan Brett. Putnam, 1998.

Mora, Pat. *Love to Mama: A Tribute to Mothers*. Illustrated by Paula S. Barragán. Lee, 2001.

Murray, Carol. *Cricket in the Thicket: Poems About Bugs*. Illustrated by Melissa Sweet. Henry Holt, 2017.

Muth, Jon J. *Hi, Koo! A Year of Seasons*. Scholastic, 2014.

Myers, Walter Dean. *Here in Harlem: Poems in Many Voices*. Holiday House, 2008.

_____. *We Are America: A Tribute from the Heart*. Illustrated by Christopher Myers. Collins, 2011.

Nash, Ogden. *The Tale of Custard the Dragon*. Illustrated by Lynn Munsinger. Little, 1995.

Nelson, Marilyn. *American Ace*. Dial, 2016.

_____, (Ed.). *Mrs. Nelson's Class*. World Enough Writers, 2017.

Nesbitt, Kenn. *One Minute till Bedtime: 60-Second Poems to Send You Off to Sleep*. Illustrated by Christoph Niemann. Little, Brown, 2016.

Nye, Naomi Shihab. *19 Varieties of Gazelle: Poems of the Middle East*. Greenwillow, 2002.

_____. *A Maze Me: Poems for Girls*. Greenwillow, 2005.

_____. *This Same Sky: A Collection of Poems from Around the World*. Four Winds, 1992.

Oliver, Lin. *Little Poems for Tiny Ears*. Illustrated by Tomie dePaola. Nancy Paulsen, 2017.

_____. *Steppin' Out: Jaunty Rhymes for Playful Times*. Illustrated by Tomie dePaola. Penguin/Nancy Paulsen, 2017.

Opie, Iona, ed. *Here Comes Mother Goose*. Illustrated by Rosemary Wells. Candlewick, 1999.

_____, ed. *My Very First Mother Goose*. Illustrated by Rosemary Wells. Candlewick, 1996.

Orgill, Roxanne. *Jazz Day: The Making of a Famous Photograph*. Illustrated by Francis Vallejo. Candlewick, 2016.

Paschen, Elise, ed. *Poetry Speaks to Children*. Illustrated by Judy Love, Wendy Rasmussen, and Paula Zinngrabe Wendland. Sourcebooks, 2005.

_____, selector. *The 20th Century Children's Poetry Treasury*. Illustrated by Meilo So. Knopf, 1999.

Paschkis, Julie. *Flutter and Hum/Aleteo y Zumbido: Animal Poems/Poemas de Animales*. Henry Holt, 2015.

Pearson, Susan. *Grimericks*. Illustrated by Gris Grimly. Cavendish, 2005.

Prelutsky, Jack. *Good Sports: Rhymes About Running, Jumping, Throwing and More*. Illustrated by Chris Raschka. Knopf, 2007.

_____. *In Aunt Giraffe's Green Garden*. Illustrated by Petra Mathers. Greenwillow, 2007.

_____. *My Dog May Be a Genius*. Illustrated by James Stevenson. Greenwillow, 2008.

_____, ed. *The Random House Book of Poetry for Children*. Illustrated by Arnold Lobel. Random, 1983.

_____. *Read-Aloud Rhymes for the Very Young*. Illustrated by Marc Brown. Knopf, 1986.

Raczka, Bob. *GUYKU: A Year of Haiku for Boys*. Illustrated by Peter H. Reynolds. Houghton Mifflin Harcourt, 2010.

_____. *Lemonade: And Other Poems Squeezed from a Single Word*. Illustrated by Nancy Doniger. Roaring Brook, 2011.

_____. *Wet Cement: A Mix of Concrete Poems*. Roaring Brook, 2016.

Reibstein, Mark. *Wabi Sabi*. Illustrated by Ed Young. Little, Brown, 2008.

Rochelle, Belinda, selector. *Words with Wings: A Treasury of African-American Poetry and Art*. Amistad, 2000.

Rosen, Michael J. *The Cuckoo's Haiku: And Other Birding Poems*. Illustrated by Stan Fellows. Candlewick, 2009.

Schaub, Michelle. *Fresh-Picked Poetry: A Day at the Farmers' Market*. Illustrated by Amy Huntington. Charlesbridge, 2017.

Schertle, Alice. *Button Up!: Wrinkled Rhymes*. Illustrated by Petra Mathers. Harcourt, 2009.

Shange, Ntozake. *Freedom's a-Callin Me*. Illustrated by Rod Brown. Amistad, 2012.

Sidman, Joyce. *Before Morning*. Illustrated by Beth Krommes. Houghton Mifflin Harcourt, 2016.

_____. *Dark Emperor & Other Poems of the Night*. Illustrated by Rick Allen. Houghton Mifflin, 2011.

_____. *Red Sings from Treetops*. Illustrated by Pamela Zagarenski. Houghton Mifflin, 2009.

_____. *Round*. Illustrated by Taeeum Yoo. Houghton Mifflin Harcourt, 2017.

_____. *Song of the Water Boatman & Other Pond Poems*. Illustrated by Beckie Prange. Houghton Mifflin, 2005.

_____. *Swirl by Swirl: Spirals in Nature*. Illustrated by Beth Krommes. Houghton Mifflin, 2011.

_____. *This Is Just to Say*. Illustrated by Pamela Zagarenski. Houghton, 2007.

_____. *Ubiquitous: Celebrating Nature's Survivors*. Illustrated by Beckie Prange. Houghton Mifflin, 2010.

_____. *Winter Bees & Other Poems of the Cold*. Illustrated by Rick Allen. Houghton Mifflin Harcourt, 2014.

Singer, Marilyn. *Echo Echo: Reverso Poems About Greek Myths*. Illustrated by Josée Masse. Dial, 2016.

_____. *Every Day's a Dog's Day: A Year in Poems*. Illustrated by Miki Sakamoto. Dial, 2012.

_____. *Feel the Beat: Dance Poems That Zing from Salsa to Swing*. Illustrated by Kristi Valiant. Dial, 2017.

_____. *Follow, Follow: A Book of Reverso Poems*. Illustrated by Josée Masse. Dial, 2013.

_____. *Footprints on the Roof: Poems About the Earth*. Illustrated by Meilo So. Knopf, 2002.

_____. *Mirror, Mirror: A Book of Reversible Verse*. Illustrated by Josée Masse. Dutton, 2010.

_____. *A Stick is an Excellent Thing: Poems Celebrating Outdoor Play*. Illustrated by LeUyen Pham. Clarion, 2012.

_____. *A Strange Place to Call Home: The World's Most Dangerous Habitats & the Animals that Call them Home*. Illustrated by Ed Young. Chronicle, 2012.

Smith, Hope Anita. *My Daddy Rules the World: Poems About Dads*. Henry Holt, 2017.

Snively, Susan (Ed.). *Poetry for Kids: Emily Dickinson*. Illustrated by Christine Davenier. Moon Dance, 2016.

Soto, Gary. *Worlds Apart: Traveling with Fernie and Me*. Putnam, 2005.

Stevenson, Robert Louis. *A Child's Garden of Verses*. Illustrated by Alice Provensen and Martin Provensen. Golden Books, 2017.

VanDerwater, Amy Ludwig. *Every Day Birds*. Illustrated by Dylan Metrano. Orchard, 2016.

_____. *Read! Read! Read!* Illustrated by Ryan O'Rourke. WordSong, 2017.

Vardell, Sylvia and Janet Wong. *Here We Go: A Poetry Friday Power Book*. Pomelo, 2017.

_____. *The Poetry Friday Anthology for Celebrations: Holiday Poems for the Whole Year in English and Spanish*. Pomelo, 2015.

_____. *The Poetry Friday Anthology for Science: Poems for the School Year Integrating Science, Reading, and Language Arts*. Pomelo, 2014.

_____. *You Just Wait: A Poetry Friday Power Book*. Pomelo, 2016.

Wardlaw, Lee. *Won Ton* and Chopstick: A Cat and Dog Tale Told in Haiku. Illustrated by Eugene Yelchin. Henry Holt, 2015.

Weatherford, Carole Boston. *Freedom in Congo Square*. Illustrated by R. Gregory Christie. Little Bee, 2016.

_____. *You Can Fly: The Tuskegee Airmen*. Illustrated by Jeffery Boston Weatherford. Atheneum, 2016.

Wheeler, Lisa. *The Pet Project: Cute and Cuddly Vicious Verses*. Illustrated by Zachariah OHora. Atheneum, 2013.

Whipple, Laura. *If the Shoe Fits: Voices from Cinderella*. Illustrated by Laura Beingessner. McElderry, 2002.

Wolf, Sallie. *The Robin Makes a Laughing Sound: A Birder's Journal*. Designed by Micah Bornstein. Charlesbridge, 2010.

Worth, Valerie. *All the Small Poems and Fourteen More*. Illustrated by Natalie Babbitt. Farrar, 1994.

Yolen, Jane. *The Alligator's Smile and Other Poems*. Photographs by Jason Stemple. Millbrook, 2016.

_____. *Count Me a Rhyme: Animal Poems by the Numbers*. Photographs by Jason Stemple. WordSong, 2014.

_____. *Shape Me a Rhyme: Nature's Forms in Poetry*. Photographs by Jason Stemple. WordSong, 2015.

_____. *Thunder Underground*. Illustrated by Josée Masse. WordSong, 2017.

Yolen, Jane, and Andrew Fusek Peters. *Here's a Little Poem: A Very First Book of Poetry*. Illustrated by Polly Dunbar. Candlewick, 2007.

Yolen, Jane and Rebecca Kai Dotlich. *Grumbles from the Town: Mother-Goose Voices with a Twist*. Illustrated by Angela Matteson. WordSong, 2016.

Zolotow, Charlotte. *Changes: A Child's First Poetry Collection*. Illustrated by Tiphanie Beeke. Sourcebooks, 2015.

Chapter Seven

Contemporary Realistic Fiction

Chapter Outline

It was Thursday—library day at school. Jayla loved library day. She was always excited to get a new book to read. As she stood in line waiting for her class to walk down the hall, she asked Jake if he was excited about library day. "No," he replied. "Why not?" Jayla asked. "Library day is fun and . . ." Before Jayla could finish her sentence, Jake interrupted, "All the library books are dumb and I hate to read!" Overhearing the conversation, Mr. Hussain asked, "Jake why do you hate to read?" With his head down, he quietly shrugged his shoulders. "Tell me," he continued, "what do you like to watch on television?" "I like real stories and

©Bettie Parsons Barger.

the Discovery Channel." Mr. Hussain quickly realized that contemporary realistic fiction just might be of interest to Jake. "How about this, Jake. If I make a suggestion for a book, will you at least try it out?" "Okay," he answered. Mr. Hussain went to the shelves of the school library and quickly found a book. Later that day, when the students were given free time before recess, Mr. Hussain noticed that Jake was reading the book. Mr. Hussain smiled to himself thinking "Yes! Got him!" But quickly he began to ask himself, "Now how can I keep him reading?"

Realism in Contemporary Children's Literature

Realistic fiction may be defined as imaginative writing that accurately reflects life in the past or as it could be lived today. Everything in such a story can conceivably happen to real people living in our natural physical world, in contrast to fantasy, where impossible happenings are made to appear quite plausible even though they are not possible. Historical fiction (see Chapter 8) portrays life as it may have been lived in the past; contemporary realism focuses on the problems and issues of living today. In considering where to draw the line between historical and contemporary fiction, we classified books firmly contextualized in specific historical events as historical fiction. A recent example would be Anne Nesbet's *Cloud and Wallfish* set in 1989 in communist East Germany. On the other hand, there are many books in which the time period is relatively unimportant but that address contemporary issues of today's children. For example, in considering the effects of recent wars such as the Afghanistan or Iraq conflicts, Gary Schmidt's *The Wednesday Wars* and *Okay for Now* still reflect the experiences of contemporary children despite the vague setting during the Vietnam War.

Though other genres in children's literature, such as fantasy, are very popular, many children connect best to realistic fiction. The books discussed in this chapter can be categorized as contemporary realistic fiction for children. Many are stories about growing up today and finding a place in the family, among peers, and in modern society. In addition, aspects of coping with the problems of the human condition may be found in contemporary literature for children. Books that are humorous or reflect special interests—such as animal or sports stories and mysteries—can also be classified as realistic literature and so are addressed in this chapter.

Realistic fiction serves children who are in the process of understanding and coming to terms with themselves. Books that honestly portray the realities of life help children gain a fuller understanding of human problems and human relationships and, thus, a fuller understanding of themselves and their own potential.

This is not a function unique to contemporary realism. Other types of books can show children a slice of the world. Some fantasy is nearer to truth than realism; biography and autobiography frequently provide readers with models of human beings who offer "hope and courage for the journey." The ability to maintain one's humanity and courage in the midst of deprivation is highlighted in *Number the Stars,* Lois Lowry's historical fiction

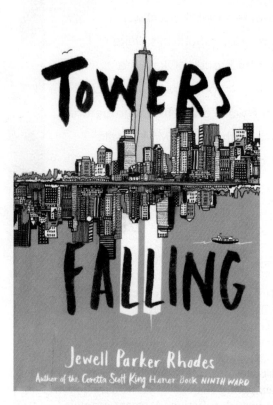

about Danish efforts to save Jewish citizens in World War II. Personal bravery and responsible behavior under dire circumstances is also one of the themes of the high fantasy *A Wizard of Earthsea* by Ursula Le Guin. However, most children appear to identify more readily with characters in books of contemporary realism than with those of historical fiction or fantasy.

Realistic fiction helps children enlarge their frames of reference while seeing the world from another perspective. For example, *Towers Falling* by the Coretta Scott King author honor award winner Jewell Parker Rhodes reviews the attacks of 9/11 from the perspective of today. Learning about the events in her fifth grade class, Dèja comes to better know her community, her country, and even her father. Children who have had little contact with the problems of the elderly might come to understand the older adults as real people through Sharon Creech's *Moo* or Naomi Shihab Nye's *The Turtle of Oman*. Stories like these help young people develop compassion for and an understanding of human experiences.

Realistic fiction also reassures young people that they are not the first in the world to have faced problems. In Kwame Alexander's *Booked*, Ali Benjamin's *The Thing About Jellyfish*, and Emma Shevah's *Dream On, Amber*, they read of other children whose parents have separated or divorced. In Nikki Grimes's *Planet Middle School*, Tim Federle's *Five, Six, Seven, Nate!*, and Raina Telgemeier's *Drama*, they read about characters who are beginning to be concerned about romantic relationships. They gain some solace from recognizing the problems a low-income background poses for Jackson in Katherine Applegate's *Crenshaw*, Star in Robin Herrera's *Hope Is a Ferris Wheel*, and Bart in Arne Svingen's *The Ballad of a Broken Nose*. This knowledge that they are not alone brings a kind of comfort to child readers.

Realistic fiction can also illuminate experiences that children have not had. A child with loving parents whose only chore consists of making a bed may have a deeper need to read Nicole Helget's *The End of the Wild*, Tara Sullivan's *The Bitter Side of Sweet*, or Erin Entrada Kelly's *Land of Forgotten Girls* than a child of poverty whose life is more nearly reflected in the story. A child who takes school for granted might gain much from Andrea Davis Pinkney's novel in verse, *The Red Pencil*, about a girl fleeing conflict in Sudan who finds joy in the promise of education. Realistic fiction can be a way of experiencing a world we do not know.

Some books also serve as a kind of preparation for living. Far better to have read Katherine Paterson's *Bridge to Terabithia* or Alan Silberberg's *Milo: Sticky Notes and Brain Freeze* than to experience firsthand at age 10 or 12 the death of your best friend or the suicide of your mother. For many years, death was a taboo subject in children's literature. Yet, as children face the honest realities of life in books, they are developing a kind of courage for facing problems in their own lives. Madeleine L'Engle, whose *Meet the Austins* was among the first works of modern children's literature to treat the subject of death, maintained that "to pretend there is no darkness is another way of extinguishing light."[1]

Realistic fiction for children does provide many possible models, both good and bad, for coping with problems of the human condition. As children experience these stories, they may begin to filter out some meaning for their own lives. This allows children to organize and shape their own thinking about life as they follow, through stories, the lives of others.

More controversy surrounds the writing of contemporary realistic fiction for children than perhaps any other kind of literature. Everyone is a critic of realism, for everyone feels he or she is an expert on what is real in today's world. But realities clash, and the fact that "what is real for one might not be real for another" is a true and lively issue. Some of the issues that seem uniquely related to contemporary realism in writing for children raise some questions.

What Is Real?

The question of what is "real" or "true to life" is a significant one. C. S. Lewis, the British author of the well-known Narnia stories, described three types of realistic content:

> But when we say, "The sort of thing that happens," do we mean the sort of thing that usually or often happens, the sort of thing that is typical of the human lot? Or do we mean "The sort of thing that might conceivably happen or that, by a thousandth chance, may have happened once?"[2]

Middle graders reading the Narnia series know that these stories are fantasy and couldn't happen in reality. However, middle graders might read stories like Gary Paulsen's *Hatchet,* or Alexandra Diaz's *The Only Road* and believe that children can survive any hardship or crisis if only they possess determination. These well-written books cast believable characters in realistic settings facing real problems. Teachers might ask readers to compare these books to Graham Salisbury's *Night of the Howling Dogs,* which is based on Salisbury's cousin's experience surviving a tsunami. Book discussions can help readers ask whether this sort of thing "by a thousandth chance, may have happened once."

Night of the Howling Dogs is a thrilling survival story based on real events that were experienced by author Graham Salisbury's cousin. Salisbury, Graham. *Night of the Howling Dogs.* New York, NY: Wendy Lamb Boos, an imprint of Random House Children's Books, a division of Random House, Inc., 2007, Cover. Copyright ©2007 by Random House Children's Books. All rights reserved. Used with permission.

Adding to the question of what is real is the recent trend in literature for children in which fantastical or unexplained phenomena occur in a realistic story. The definition of what is "real" or "fantastical" can vary from culture to culture. Consequently, it could help readers to remember that their own worldviews and ideas may differ significantly from the perspectives and beliefs of the characters in a story. For example, in reading the Hurricane Katrina story *Ninth Ward* by Jewell Parker Rhodes, some readers might need to keep in mind that Lanesha's ability to see the spirit of her deceased mother is a culturally accepted gift of second sight. This magical realism is often associated with Latin American culture in which these events may be considered to be real and/or spiritual.

As with the question of whether a book belongs with contemporary realism or historical fiction, contemporary realistic fiction can include books with minor elements of magic that speak predominantly to contemporary real-life concerns. For example, Michael encounters an unexplainable phenomenon in his new garage as he copes with his newborn sister's serious illness in *Skellig* by David Almond. If the story focused more on the magic and explanations of its mechanics rather than simply accepting it, we would be more likely to identify it as fantasy. We suspect that as the twenty-first century moves forward, the lines between traditional genres will continue to blur.

How Real May a Children's Book Be?

Much controversy centers on how much graphic detail may be included in a book for children. How much violence is too much? How explicit may an author be in describing bodily functions or sexual relations? These are questions that few would have asked until the 1960s. But there are new freedoms today. Childhood is not the innocent time we like to think it is (and it probably never was). In addition, authors of young adult literature (defined by the American Library Association's Printz Award as ages 12–18) have been more willing to tackle issues for adolescents as frankly as they would in a book for adults. In this book, we focus on children ages 6 to 14. It is therefore often difficult to make decisions about what literature is appropriate for those adolescents in middle school. Basically, we have worked under the assumption that although these youth might not need protection, they do still need the perspective that literature can give. A well-written book makes the reader aware of the human suffering resulting from inhumane acts by others.

News coverage of local killings or the body count in the latest "peacekeeping" effort seldom shows the pain and anguish that each death causes. The rebuilding of human lives is too slow and tedious to portray in a five-minute newscast. Even many video games are based on violence. The winner of the game is the one who can eliminate or destroy the "enemy." Reasons or motivations are never given, and the aftereffects of violence are not a part of the game.

By way of contrast to the daily news, a well-written story provides perspective on the pain and suffering of humankind. In a literary story, the author has time to develop the characters into fully rounded human beings. The reader knows the motives and pressures of each individual and can understand and empathize with the characters. If the author's tone is one of compassion for the characters, if others in the story show concern or horror for a brutal act, the reader gains perspective.

A story that makes violence understandable without condoning it is Suzanne Fisher Staples's *Shabanu: Daughter of the Wind*. In the Pakistani desert culture in which 12-year-old Shabanu lives, obedience to rules has enabled many tribes to live in peace in an environment that offers little material comfort. When Shabanu runs away to avoid an arranged marriage to a middle-aged man, she discovers her favorite camel has broken its leg. In choosing to remain with the camel, Shabanu tacitly agrees to the rules of her clan. Her father catches up with her and beats her severely. But she is soaked with his tears as he does what he must, and the reader realizes both are trapped in roles their society has defined for them.

James Giblin, a former children's book editor, suggests that a book can be realistic without being overly graphic:

> For instance, if the young detective in a mystery story was attacked by a gang of bullies, I wouldn't encourage an author to have them burn his arms with a cigarette to get him to talk (although that might conceivably happen in an adult mystery). However, I would accept a scene in which the gang *threatened* to do so: that would convey the reality and danger of the situation without indulging in all the gory details.[3]

Giblin maintains that very few subjects are inappropriate in themselves; it is all in how the author treats them. The facts of a situation, ugly as they might be, can be presented with feeling and depth of emotion, which carry the reader beyond the particular subject.

The same criteria are appropriate for evaluating explicitness about sex and bodily functions in books for children. Highlighted in the classic and often challenged book *Are You There God, It's Me Margaret* by Judy Blume, the physical aspects of puberty can be useful tools if they portray changes accurately. More recent books such as *Spurt* by Charles Miles are likely to present more positive views of sexuality.

Some books that directly address censorship issues for middle-grade audiences include *Ban This Book* by Adam Gratz, *Mr. Lemoncello's Library Olympics* by Chris Grabenstein, and *How to Get Suspended and Influence People* by Adam Selzer. Somewhat heavy handed but composed with more sensitivity and skill than most, Chris Crutcher's *The Sledding Hill* presents a situation regarding censorship. Here, a controversy is sparked by the reading of a young adult novel that includes a gay character. Although the book is about friendship and healing as well as sexual orientation, it will prompt interesting discussions.

Bias and Stereotyping

Children's books have always reflected the general social and human values of a society, so it is not surprising that they are also scrutinized for implied attitudes or biases of that society. Contemporary realistic fiction is examined for racism, cultural inaccuracies, sexism, ageism, and treatment of people with physical or mental impairments. Because consciousness generally has been raised in the world of children's book publishing, there are now more books that present diverse populations positively and fairly.

Thanhhà Lai's beautifully written *Listen, Slowly* captures the discontent of a 12-year-old girl exiled from California to Vietnam as her grandmother tries to find information about her grandfather who has been missing since the war. Cover art copyright ©2016 by Zdenko Basic. Used by permission of HarperCollins Publishers.

Historically, the political and social activism of the 1960s contributed to an awareness of racism in children's books. Since the beginning of the twenty-first century, children have been readily able to find fully realized characters from diverse cultures in books such as Thanhhà Lai's *Listen, Slowly,* Linda Sue Park's *A Long Walk to Water,* Julia Alvarez's Tia Lola series, and Jacqueline Woodson's *Peace, Locomotion.* Still, adults need to be alert to reissues of books from an earlier era—such as the 1945 Newbery Honor Book *The Silver Pencil,*[4] which contains many racist descriptions of people in Trinidad. Books like this help us recognize the gains of recent decades.

Because scholars have made us more aware of the subtle ways in which literature has perpetuated stereotypes, contemporary realistic fiction now does a much better job of portraying the complexity of gender expectations and roles. Girls can find caring female role models outside of the family; intelligent, independent, and strong girls and women; and romance as a consequence of strong friendship in the realistic fiction of today. They can also find characters like Wadjda in *The Green Bicycle* by Haifaa Al Mansour, Obayda in *One Half from the East* by Nadia Hashimi, or Joe in James Howe's *Totally Joe,* who challenge traditional roles and expectations.

Boys, too, can get beyond such beliefs as "men don't cry." Modern realistic fiction shows that there are different ways of being a man, as exemplified in the variety of male role models in Richard Peck's light-hearted novel, *The Best Man.* The issue of presenting multiple role models in books for boys has led to a campaign by popular author Jon Scieszka. Scieszka's website, called Guys Read <www.guysread.com>, has suggestions for books and activities that will appeal to boys. Scieszka has also selected various authors to contribute humorous short stories to the Guys Read series.

People with mental or physical disabilities have in the past been depicted as "handicapped." Books such as Sharon Draper's *Out of My Mind* or R. J. Palacio's *Wonder* provide more enlightened views that suggest that the person is more important than the condition; one can be differently abled without necessarily being "disabled." Older people (and other adults) in children's literature have often been dismissed as irrelevant in a young person's life, as ineffectual in contrast to the vibrancy of young spirits, or as unable to do certain things because of their age. High-quality contemporary realistic fiction stories depict adults and older people in many ways—as mentors to young people, for instance, and as having their own romances, problems, and triumphs.

Children's books have made great gains in the depiction of our changing society. However, today's books need to continue to reflect the wide ranges of

In R. J. Palacio's masterfully written *Wonder,* August's story of starting school for the first time ever in fifth grade with mandibulofacial dysostosis is told from several points of view. Palacio, R.J. *Wonder.* New York, NY: Alfred A. Knopf, an imprint of Random House Children's Books, 2012, Cover. Copyright ©2012 by Alfred A. Knopf, an imprint of Random House Children's Books All rights reserved. Used with permission.

occupations, education, speech patterns, lifestyles, and futures that are possible for all, regardless of race, gender, age, ability, or belief.

The Author's Background

The subject of an author's racial background has become another source of controversy in children's contemporary realistic fiction. Must an author be black to write about African Americans, or Native American to write about Native Americans? As Virginia Hamilton states:

> It happens that I know Black people better than any other people because I am one of them and I grew up knowing what it is we are about. . . . The writer uses the most comfortable milieu in which to tell a story, which is why my characters are Black. Often being Black is significant to the story; other times, it is not. The writer will always attempt to tell stories no one else can tell.[5]

It has been generally accepted that an author should write about what he or she knows about his or her own culture. But Ann Cameron, a white Anglo-American author who has lived in Guatemala for many years, is the author of many books about children from diverse places and cultures, including *The Stories Julian Tells, Gloria Rising, The Most Beautiful Place in the World,* and *Colibrí.* Cameron maintains a different point of view:

> It seems to me that the people who advise "write about what you know" drastically underestimate the human capacity for imagining what lies beyond our immediate knowledge and for understanding what is new to us. Equally, they overestimate the extent to which we know ourselves. A culture, like a person, has blind spots. . . . Often the writer who is an outsider—an African writing about the United States, an American writing about China—sees in a way that enriches him as an observer, the culture he observes, and the culture he comes from.[6]

Moreover, although it may be true that Cameron and other writers who have spent years living and working in other countries (Elizabeth Laird, Jane Kurtz, and Nancy Farmer, for example) may not be able to give an entirely culturally authentic picture of the characters they write about, they do Western children a great service by pointing out issues of social justice and human rights. As world cultures become more and more interdependent in the twenty-first century, offering such service is surely a worthwhile goal. We agree with children's author and scholar Alma Flor Ada who suggests, "The merit of a book is determined not by the heritage of the author or illustrator, but by their intention, knowledge, sensitivity, responsibility, and artistry" (pp. 36–37).

Evaluating Contemporary Fiction

The hallmark of fine writing is the quality of imagining it calls forth from us. Imagination is not the exclusive trait of any race or gender but is a universal quality of all fine writers. No authors or artists want to be limited to writing about or portraying only the experiences of persons of a single gender, race, or other aspect of cultural background, nor should they be. We need to focus on two aspects of every book: (1) what is its literary merit? and (2) will children enjoy it? For additional criteria to keep in mind, see **Guidelines: Evaluating Contemporary Realistic Fiction.**

Evaluating Contemporary Realistic Fiction

Guidelines

Go to Connect® to access study resources, practice quizzes, and additional materials.

Consider the following when evaluating realistic fiction:

- Does the book honestly portray the realities of life for today's children?
- Does the book illuminate problems and issues of growing up in today's world?
- Does the story transcend the contemporary setting and have universal implications?
- Are the characters convincing and credible to today's child?

- Are controversial topics such as sexuality dealt with in an open and forthright way?
- If violence or other negative behavior is part of the story, does the author provide motivations and show aftereffects?
- Does the author avoid stereotyping?
- Does the book truly represent the experience of the culture depicted?
- Does the book help children enlarge their personal points of view and develop appreciation for our ever-changing pluralistic society?

Categorizing Literature

Reviewers, educators, and curriculum makers often categorize books according to their content. Categorizing serves textbook authors by allowing them to talk about several books as a group. It serves educators who hope to group books around a particular theme for classroom study. While one person might place Katherine Paterson's *Bridge to Terabithia* in a group of books about "making friends," it could just as easily be placed in other groups, such as books about "growing up" or "learning to accept death," or "well-written books." It is a disservice to both book and reader if, in labeling a book, we imply that this is all the book is about. Readers with their own purposes and backgrounds will see many different aspects and strengths in a piece of literature. It is helpful to remember that our experiences with art occur at many different, unique, and personal levels. Even though teachers might wish to lead children to talk about a particular aspect of a book, they will not want to suggest that this is the only aspect worth pursuing. Author Jean Little argues that teachers need to trust children to find their own messages in books:

> Individual readers come to each story at a slightly different point in their life's journey. If nobody comes between them and the book, they may discover within it some insight they require, a rest they long for, a point of view that challenges their own, a friend they may cherish for life. If we, in the guise of mentor, have all the good messages listed or discussed in small groups . . . the individual and vitally important meeting of child and story may never happen.[7]

A second issue in the categorizing of literature is age-appropriateness. Realistic fiction is often categorized as being for upper elementary or middle-grade and junior high or young-adult readers. Yet anyone who has spent time with 9- to 14-year-old readers has surely noticed the wide ranges of reading interests, abilities, and perceptions present. Judy Blume's *Are You There, God? It's Me, Margaret* and Matthew Quick's *Boy21* have challenged and entertained readers from fourth grade through high school. To suggest that these titles are only "for 10- to 12-year-old readers" would ignore the ages of half the readership of these popular authors.

The story of every man and every woman is the story of growing up, of becoming a person, of struggling to become one's own person. The kind of person you become has its roots in your childhood experiences—how much you were loved, how little you were loved; the people who were significant to you, the ones who were not; the places you've been, and those you did not go to; the things you had, and the things you did not get. Yet a person is always more than the totality of these experiences; the way a person organizes, understands, and relates to those experiences makes for individuality. Childhood is not a waiting room for adulthood but the place where adulthood is shaped by one's family, peers, society, and, most important, the person one is becoming. The passage from childhood to adulthood is a significant journey for each person. It is no wonder that children's literature is filled with stories about growing up in our society today.

In **Teaching Feature 7.1: A Sampling of Contemporary Realism for Children,** books are arranged according to categories based on theme and content merely for convenience of presentation.

teaching feature 7.1

A Sampling of Contemporary Realism for Children

Author	Title	Grade Level	Description
Families			
Leslie Connor	*All Rise for the Honorable Perry T. Cook*	4–7	After growing up in prison with his incarcerated mother, Perry is forced to join the new district attorney's family until she makes parole.
Jason Reynolds	*As Brave as You*	4–8	A summer with their grandparents in rural Virginia teaches Genie and Ernie more about their family, including their grandfather's blindness.
Caela Carter	*Forever, or a Long, Long Time*	4–7	Flora and Julian can't remember their past in years of foster care before they were adopted by their mom, Emily.

(continued)

teaching feature 7.1

Author	Title	Grade Level	Description
Margarita Engle	*Forest World*	4–6	After the reestablishment of diplomatic relations between the United States and Cuba, Edver is surprised when he meets the sister he never knew about on his way to be reunited with his father and grandfather in the jungles of Cuba in this novel in verse.
Thanhhà Lai	*Listen, Slowly*	5–8	A Vietnamese American girl visits Vietnam with her grandmother to reconnect with family.
Emma Donoghue	*The Lotterys Plus One*	4–7	When an estranged grumpy grandfather arrives, the two pairs of parents and seven diverse children are thrown into a tizzy.
Jane Kurtz	*Planet Jupiter*	4–6	Jupiter's cousin Edom, who was adopted from Ethiopia, comes to stay with them in Portland for the summer.
Beverly Cleary	*Ramona's World*	2–4	As with previous titles about this family, Ramona continues to be her irrepressible dramatic self.

Friends

Author	Title	Grade Level	Description
Beth Vrabel	*Caleb and Kit*	4–7	Caleb's cystic fibrosis may make him feel over-protected but when he makes a new friend, he must question the risks she encourages him to take.
Esther Ehrlich	*Nest*	4–6	When Chirp's mother is diagnosed with multiple sclerosis, she finds solace in a new friend.
John David Anderson	*Posted*	6–9	Four boys grow apart with the introduction of a new girl and a flurry of post-its swarming around their school.
Victoria Jamieson	*Roller Girl*	4–8	In this graphic novel, Astrid discovers roller derby as she grows apart from her best friend.
E.L. Konigsburg	*The View from Saturday*	4–8	Four sixth graders form strong bonds as they compete in a middle-school academic bowl.
Jerry Spinelli	*Wringer*	4–6	Spinelli examines the serious consequences of peer pressure as 9-year-old Palmer is pushed to be "one of the boys" by enduring physically painful rituals.

(continued)

teaching feature 7.1

Author	Title	Grade Level	Description
Growing Toward Maturity			
Alex Gino	*George*	4–6	George wants to take a female role in the class play but must confront gender identity barriers first.
Coe Booth	*Kinda Like Brothers*	4–6	Eleven-year-old Jarrett needs to work things out with a new foster brother his age.
Lisa Graff	*Lost in the Sun*	4–6	Middle school is a fresh start for Trevor, hopefully helping him move past a traumatic event in fifth grade.
Shelley Pearsall	*The Seventh Most Important Thing*	4–7	Arthur doesn't know that James Hampton (a.k.a. the Junk Man) is collecting junk for an art piece when he throws a brick at his head.
Kevin Henkes	*The Year of Billy Miller*	1–3	Second grade seems to start off on the wrong foot, complete with a lump on his head, but moves through funny and touching situations throughout the year.
Mariko Tamaki	*This One Summer*	6–12	Summer at a lakeside beach brings changes as Rose comes to new understandings of the trials besetting of her mother as well as some local teens in this graphic novel.
Survival in the Wilderness			
Nancy Farmer	*A Girl Named Disaster*	5–8	A young African girl runs away from her village and travels by river from Mozambique to Zimbabwe to find her father.
Eliot Schrefer	*Endangered*	7 and up	When civil war breaks out in Congo, an African American girl tries to rescue a young bonobo.
Gary Paulsen	*Hatchet*	4 and up	On his way to meet his father, the pilot of the aircraft suffers a heart attack, and Brian manages to land the plane in a lake in the Canadian wilderness.
Dan Gemeinhart	*The Honest Truth*	4–8	After his cancer recurs, Mark runs away with his dog to attempt to climb Mount Rainier while his best friend wonders what is the right thing to do.

(continued)

teaching feature 7.1

Author	Title	Grade Level	Description
Jean Craighead George	*Julie of the Wolves*	5–8	A Native Alaskan girl finds herself alone on the Alaskan tundra and must depend on a pack of wolves to survive.
Will Hobbs	*Never Say Die*	5–10	A half Inuit boy and his white brother navigate the Firth River in the Canadian Arctic while documenting climate change.
Terry Lynn Johnson	Survivor Diaries series; *Avalanche!*	4–8	On a ski trip, Ashley and Ryan are swept away by an avalanche.
Understanding Cognitive/Developmental Conditions			
Holly Goldberg Sloan	*Counting by 7s*	5–8	A gifted girl with social difficulties tries to connect with people after her parents are killed in a car accident.
Lynda Mullaly Hunt	*Fish in a Tree*	4–6	A teacher finally recognizes Ally's dyslexia and helps her discover how smart she really is.
Ellie Terry	*Forget Me Not*	5–8	A girl with Tourette syndrome makes friends with a popular boy at her new middle school.
Kathryn Erskine	*Mockingbird*	5–7	Caitlin, an 11-year-old girl with Asperger's Syndrome, has a hard time coping with the death of her brother.
Sharon Draper	*Out of My Mind*	4–6	Melody refuses to let her diagnosis of cerebral palsy define her. Instead, she is determined to let everyone know just how smart she is, even though she can neither walk nor talk.
Ann M. Martin	*Rain Reign*	4–6	Rose uses rules and homophones to deal with the challenges of Asperger's Syndrome when her dog goes missing.
Sally J. Pla	*The Someday Birds*	4–7	A cross-country road trip for his dad's brain surgery mitigates the difficulties of Charlie's autism and obsessive compulsive disorder with a list of birds to find.
Communities Around the Country			
Shelley Pearsall	*All of the Above*	5–8	Writing in the voices of four inter-city students, Pearsall tells the story of a math teacher who challenges his students in Cleveland, Ohio, to build the world's largest tetrahedron.

(continued)

Author	Title	Grade Level	Description
Daphne Benedis-Grab	*Army Brats*	3–6	Three military kids, one of whom is dyslexic and another adopted from China, explore a new army base.
Dana Alison Levy	*The Family Fletcher Takes Rock Island*	3–7	While on summer vacation, four adopted boys and their dads stumble into some humorous mishaps as well as a slightly more serious encounter with racism.
Erin Entrada Kelly	*Hello Universe*	3–7	Four friends draw on their unique Filipino, Japanese American, and deaf perspectives to deal with a bully.
Joseph Marshall	*In the Footsteps of Crazy Horse*	4–8	Jimmy's Lakota Indian grandfather takes him away from the reservation on a trip to learn about Lakota history.
Judith Robbins Rose	*Look Both Ways in the Barrio Blanco*	4–7	Jacinta's new mentor introduces her to the white upper-middle-class world while Jacinta's mother is in Mexico to care for her grandmother and hiding that her father is undocumented.
Virginia Hamilton	*M.C. Higgins, the Great*	6–8	M. C. daydreams of moving his family away from the slow-moving slag heap that threatens to engulf their southern Ohio home.
Gary D. Schmidt	*Orbiting Jupiter*	6–10	Jack's new foster brother brings some new issues to the family, including a baby that he fathered at age thirteen.

Glimpses of a Few Children's Experiences Across the Globe

Author	Title	Grade Level	Description
Maria Parr	*Adventures with Waffles*	3–5	A light-hearted tale of friendship between a girl and a boy translated from Norwegian.
Tara Sullivan	*The Bitter Side of Sweet*	6–10	Trapped in slavery that still exists, three children escape from a cacao plantation in the Ivory Coast.
Elizabeth Laird	*The Fastest Boy in the World*	3–6	An Ethiopian boy who loves to run has high hopes for a trip to Addis Abba with his grandfather.
Berlie Doherty	*The Girl Who Saw Lions*	7 and up	Two girls with Tanzanian roots grow up in widely different circumstances.

(continued)

teaching feature 7.1

Author	Title	Grade Level	Description
Marjorie Agosin	*I Lived on Butterfly Hill*	5–8	A girl flees Chile for America after a military coup.
Juana Medina	*Juana & Lucas*	K–3	A delightfully opinionated girl from Bogota, Colombia is rewarded with a special trip for learning English.
Nadia Hashimi	*One Half from the East*	5–8	A young Afghani girl lives as a boy in the tradition of bacha posh.
A.L. Sonnichsen	*Red Butterfly*	4–7	A Chinese orphan is separated from her American mother and sent to a home for disabled children since her hand is malformed.
Daniella Carmi	*Samir and Yonatan*	4–6	Samir, a Palestinian boy, must spend several months in an Israeli hospital on a ward with Jewish children who have also been damaged by the Israeli/ Palestinian conflict.
Rukhsana Khan	*Wanting Mor*	5–7	Jameela's father sells her to a cruel family because of her cleft lip, and she eventually ends up in an orphanage in Afghanistan. Through hard work, determination, and faith in Islam, Jameela tries to create a happy life for herself.

Popular Types of Realistic Fiction

Certain categories of realistic fiction are so popular that children ask for them by name. They want a good animal story, usually about a dog or horse; a sports book; a "funny" book; or a good mystery. Each decade seems to have a popular series, as well, that lingers on the bookshelves. From Gertrude Chandler Warner's Boxcar Children to Tom Angleberger's Origami Yoda series, from Nancy Drew and the Hardy Boys to Lincoln Peirce's Big Nate and Rachel Renee Russell's Dork Diaries series, children read one volume of a series and demand the next. Although many of these books are not typically considered high-quality literature, they do serve the useful function of getting children hooked on books so that they can enjoy better literature later.[8] Children also develop fluency and reading speed as they quickly read through popular books or a series.

Happily, the categories of popular fiction include many well-written, award-winning books, and children who love the easier series books have found their way to excellent

continued on page 232

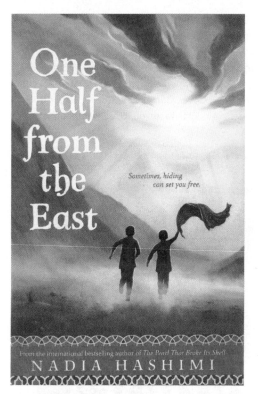

Obayda, the youngest of four Afghani sisters, dresses as a boy, or bacha posh, in order to bring their family luck in *One Half from the East* by Nadia Hashimi. Cover art copyright ©2016 by Jen Bricking. Used by permission of HarperCollins Publishers.

Twelve-year-old Nick struggles with family issues, bullying, and romance set against the backdrop of books, sports, and friends in *Booked*, a novel in verse by Kwame Alexander. Alexander, Kwame, *Booked*. New York, NY: HMH Books for Young Readers, 2016, Cover. Copyright ©2016 by HMH Books for Young Readers. All rights reserved. Used with permission.

A journey helps fill in memory gaps of 11-year-old Flora and her younger brother, two adopted fosters kids in Caela Carter's *Forever, or a Long, Long Time*. Cover art copyright ©2017 by Kenard Park. Used by permission of HarperCollins Publishers.

In *Unusual Chickens for the Exceptional Poultry Farmer* by Kelly Jones, a 12-year-old Latina girl is drawn into a humorous mystery when strange chickens start showing up at her uncle's farm. Jones, Kelly. *Unusual Chickens for the Exceptional Poultry Farmer*. New York, NY: Knopf Books for Young Readers, 2015, Cover. Copyright ©2015 by Knopf Books for Young Readers. All rights reserved. Used with permission.

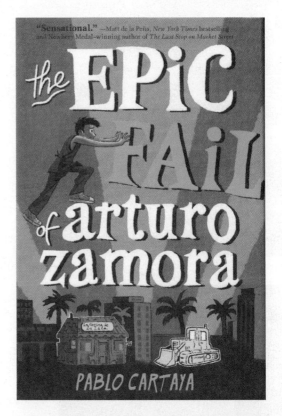

In *The Epic Fail of Arturo Zamora*, a 13-year-old learns about his Cuban roots and the power of resistance when his family's restaurant is threatened. Cartaya, Pablo, *The Epic Fail of Arturo Zamora*. New York, NY: Viking Books for Young Readers, 2017, Cover. Copyright ©2017 by Viking Books for Young Readers. All rights reserved. Used with permission.

Eleven-year-old Impy bravely takes on the challenge of public school for the first time so that she can work at the Renaissance Faire with her parents in Victoria Jamieson's new graphic novel, *All's Faire in Middle School.* Jamieson, Victoria, *All's Faire in Middle School*. New York, NY: Dial Books, Cover. 2017 Copyright ©2017 by Dial books. All rights reserved. Used with permission.

Third-grader Aref struggles to say goodbye to his grandfather when his family makes plans to move from Oman to the United States in Naomi Shihab Nye's *The Turtle of Oman*. Cover copyright ©2014 by Betsy Peterschmidt. Used by permission of HarperCollins Publishers.

In Ann M. Martin's *Rain Reign*, a girl with Asperger's Syndrome must search for her lost dog. Photo: ©Trevillion Images

In Silvey's thriller, *Jasper Jones,* a teenage boy and an outcast hide a body and investigate a murder in Australia in the 1960s. Silvey, Craig. *Jasper Jones*. New York, NY: Alfred A. Knopf, an imprint of Random House Children's Books, 2009, Cover. Copyright ©2009 by Alfred A. Knopf, an imprint of Random House Children's Books. All rights reserved. Used with permission.

titles such as Louis Sachar's *Holes,* Jerry Spinelli's *Maniac Magee,* and Kwame Alexander's *The Crossover.* Each of these books fits under the categories of "popular" literature but have transcended the formulaic nature of many popular books to win the John Newbery Medal. Newer, well-written works that middle-grade and middle-school readers will enjoy include Louis Sachar's *Fuzzy Mud* and Dana Alison Levy's *The Family Fletcher Takes Rock Island,* the sequel to *The Misadventures of the Family Fletcher.* Knowing and honoring the books children like increases an adult adviser's credibility, while also allowing him or her to recommend other titles that can broaden children's reading choices. In **Teaching Feature 7.2: Popular Fiction for Today's Readers,** we have selected some of the best fiction in categories that are especially appealing to children.

teaching feature 7.2

Popular Fiction for Today's Readers

Author	Title	Grade Level	Description
Humorous Stories			
Lenore Look	Alvin Ho series: *Allergic to the Great Wall, the Forbidden Palace, and Other Tourist Attractions*	1–4	Afraid of everything, Alvin is drawn into adventures on a family trip to China.
Jeff Kinney	Diary of a Wimpy Kid series: *Double Down*	3–6	Greg suffers the indignities and pains of adolescence in this funny illustrated novel.
James Patterson	I Funny series: *School of Laughs*	3–7	A wheelchair-bound aspiring comic tries to save the school library by teaching a comedy class.

(continued)

teaching feature 7.2

Author	Title	Grade Level	Description
Firoozeh Dumas	*It Ain't So Awful, Falafel*	5–7	Anti-immigrant sentiments make fitting in after a move hard for Iranian Zomorod (a.k.a. Cindy) despite a humorous outlook.
Tom Angleberger	Origami Yoda series: *Emperor Pickletine Rides the Bus*	3–6	Tommy and his friends set out on a field trip to Washington, DC, with a new "fruitgami" Yoda.
Jennifer L. Holm & Matthew Holm	*Sunny Side Up*	4–9	Comedy peppers the story of a girl spending a summer in Florida with her grandfather against the backdrop of some family issues with drug abuse.
Kelly Jones	*Unusual Chickens for the Exceptional Poultry Farmer*	4–7	Farm life gets interesting for a half-white, half-Latina 12-year-old when some peculiarly talented chickens start showing up.
Animal Stories			
Carl Hiaasen	*Chomp*	5–9	Wahoo and Tuna try to track down a missing reality TV survivalist in the Florida Everglades.
Ann M. Martin	*Rain Reign*	4–6	Rose uses rules and homophones to deal with the challenges of Asperger's Syndrome when her dog goes missing.
Nancy Bo Flood	*Soldier Sister, Fly Home*	5–8	When Tess's sister Gaby is deployed to Iraq, she asks Tess to take care of her horse on the Navajo reservation while she is away.
Jeanne Birdsall	*The Penderwicks in Spring*	4–7	Batty starts a dog-walking business as the family grieves the recent death of a dog.
Eric Dinerstein	*What Elephants Know*	4–7	Nandu must work to change the elephant stable in Nepal into a breeding center.
Phyllis Reynolds Naylor	*Shiloh*	4–6	Marty decides to hide an abused dog in the woods of his West Virginia mountain hollow. He deceives his family until a crisis forces him to fight for his principles and confront the owner of the dog.
Sheila Burnford	*The Incredible Journey*	4–6	Three runaway pets—a young Labrador retriever, an old bull terrier, and a Siamese cat—undertake an odyssey trying to reach their home more than 250 miles away.

(continued)

(continued)

teaching feature 7.2

Author	Title	Grade Level	Description
Sports Stories			
Deborah Wiles	*The Aurora County All-Stars*	4–6	Twelve-year-old star pitcher House Jackson has been out of commission due to a broken elbow. When he can finally pitch for the all-star game, he finds it is scheduled at the same time as the Aurora County Pageant.
Kwame Alexander	*Booked*	6–10	This novel in verse features family, love, and friendship on and around the soccer field.
Xavier Garza	Max's Lucha Libre Adventures series: *Maximilian & the Lucha Libre Club*	4–6	In this continuation of the bilingual series, Max is asked to join the Lucha Libre Club for the relations of Mexican wrestling royalty.
Jason Reynolds	*Patina*	5–9	New to the elite middle-school track team, Patina runs to escape her family issues.
Dirk McLean	*Team Fugee*	4–7	Soccer teams of Nigerian and Syrian refugee kids in Canada must unite to challenge the division champions.
School Stories			
Walter Dean Myers	*The Cruisers*	5–7	Zander and his friends start a school newspaper, *The Cruiser*, and find themselves reporting on a mock Civil War.
Nikki Grimes	*Garvey's Choice*	4–8	Written in verse, an overweight boy's choice of chorus over sports opens him up to new experiences and relationships.
Rebecca Stead	*Goodbye Stranger*	6–9	Seventh grade in Manhattan isn't easy for Bridge and her friends.
Megan Jean Soven	*The Meaning of Maggie*	4–7	Maggie starts middle school while her family rearranges work duties when her father becomes wheelchair-bound due to his Multiple Sclerosis.
John David Anderson	*Mrs. Bixby's Last Day*	4–6	When their teacher is diagnosed with cancer, three friends plan to make her last day the best ever.
Ruth Freeman	*One Good Thing About America*	3–7	A Congolese immigrant adjusts to school in Maine over the course of a year.

(continued)

teaching feature 7.2

Author	Title	Grade Level	Description
Mystery			
Andrew Clements	Benjamin Pratt & The Keepers of the School series: *We Hold These Truths*	4–6	Three sixth-graders' attempt to save their school leads them down a trail of secret passageways and into both treasure and trouble.
Jennifer Chambliss Bertman	Book Scavenger series: *The Unbreakable Code*	4–8	Emily and her friend James follow a trail of clues in books by Mark Twain set in San Francisco.
Jackson, Varian	Great Greene Heist series: *To Catch a Cheat*	5–8	Blackmail draws the group of multicultural middle schoolers back into another heist.
Bill Nye and Gregory Mone	*Jack and the Geniuses*	3–7	Jack and his foster siblings Ava and Matt explore science-based mysteries.
Amanda Hosch	*Mabel Opal Pear and the Rules for Spying*	4–7	When Mabel's parents don't return soon from their latest spy mission, things start to look fishy.
Sara St. Antoine	*Three Bird Summer*	5–8	An island summer friendship is catalyzed with mysterious notes from Adam's grandmother that suggest a hidden treasure.
Sheila Turnage	Tupelo Landing series: *The Odds of Getting Even*	4–7	Mo and Dale take on an intern to help solve a handful of cases in small town North Carolina when Dale's daddy breaks out of jail.
Laura Marx Fitzgerald	*Under the Egg*	4–7	Theodora uncovers an art mystery after her grandfather's death.
Ellen Raskin	*The Westing Game*	4–6	At the reading of a millionaire's will, sixteen characters are presented with a directive to discover the identity of his murderer and other clues cleverly hidden within the will.

Challenging Perspectives on Realistic Fiction

The genre of contemporary realistic fiction includes books that are fictionalized narratives with plots, characters, and settings that might be found in real life. These stories reflect contemporary life, take place in familiar settings, and present situations with which the reader can identify. These stories are also often based on socially significant events. The classification of realistic fiction is given to stories that are convincingly true to life and that help children see their own lives, empathize with other people, and see the complexity of human interaction. For example, the *New York Times* best-seller for older readers, *The Hate U Give* by Angie Thomas, is the fictionalized journey of a 16-year-old African American protagonist as she traverses the world after her unarmed friend is killed by the police during a traffic stop. The story is full of "in-your-face" language and was reviewed as stunning, powerful, gut wrenching, and tragically timely. Another great example is the book *Ninth Ward,* a fictional account of a tight-knit community in New Orleans' Ninth Ward before Hurricane Katrina. A Coretta Scott King Author Honor Book, *Ninth Ward* is a deeply emotional story about transformation and a celebration of resilience, friendship, and family—in the face of a catastrophic natural disaster.

The question of whether to use contemporary realistic fiction in the classroom and how to use it continues to create challenges for teachers today. Some people have questioned the relevance of the topics in this type of fiction to the lives of children. Should we offer to children realistic depictions of social issues in literature? Claudia Mills, in *The Ethics of Representation: Realism and Idealism in Children's Fiction,* states:

> . . . in defense of realism, is the argument for the value of truth, for "telling it like it is," for an honest witness to the world as we actually find it. Children, this argument goes, have a right to be told the truth, as best as we can tell it. Besides, if we don't tell them the truth, they'll find it out anyway, eventually, and then distrust us for having withheld it from them.[9]

In recent times, what some deem inappropriate topics for books written for children and young adults, others have featured in this genre of contemporary realistic fiction. The topics that have been identified most often as unsuitable for certain age groups are inappropriate language, acts of racism, sexism or homophobia, implied sexual conduct, and violence. The appropriate or inappropriateness of these topics poses a challenge for the classroom teacher when using a genre of literature that features them. Teachers should always give attention to developmentally appropriate content and practices for children. Suggested guidelines for appropriate content were first introduced in 1987 by the National Association for the Education of Young Children[10] in order to enhance the quality of educational experiences for early childhood programs serving children from birth through age 8. Although the guidelines reflected a consensus definition of developmentally appropriate practices involving the input from thousands of early childhood professionals, a number of controversies, confusions, and myths surrounded their arrival in the field.

The appropriateness of content continues to be fodder for many lively debates in education circles and, as a result, the titles of many contemporary realistic children's literature books are relegated to the shelves of teachers' personal collections and are rarely a part of the curriculum development for teaching in content areas. This debate cannot be resolved in the few paragraphs of this chapter. However, we know that many children from all walks of life experience the difficulties of our world that are described in these books. This is not to suggest children living with violence, homelessness, poverty, or other injustices should only read or be read stories about protagonists dealing with the tough issues of life. It does suggest that children "need to have the book as a mirror—to mirror their physical self, their lives, and family experiences . . . they also need the window—the book that takes them into other worlds, that expands their horizons."[11] Using the genre of contemporary realistic fiction, we can help children to develop what we hold as a worthwhile, life-long learning goal: to develop empathy and respect the multiple ways of "seeing," "knowing," and "creating meaning in the world." The teacher can be the one who can guide, observe, facilitate, pose problems, extend discussions and activities, and, in Lev Vygotsky's words, "create a natural moment" in the child's environment.[12]

Finally, when using children's literature that has a focus on contemporary issues and problems, a teacher's choices should always reflect both the age and individual needs of the child and the goal of creating learning experiences that are meaningful. This should not discourage the use of literature that will focus on controversial issues, but rather should encourage its use to increase a child's ability to critique and ultimately participate in solving many of the problems in our world. (Access Connect® to address contemporary realistic fiction with the Ten-Point Model for Teaching Controversial Issues.)

curriculum connections

Using Realistic Fiction to Address Standards

Realistic fiction provides opportunities for students to engage in discussions about contemporary topics. Characters their age often struggle with familiar issues but prevail in the end. With the diversity of settings, characters, and conflicts, these books provide many opportunities for integration across the curriculum.

Suggested Children's Book: *Forever, or a Long, Long Time* by Caela Carter (Harper, 2017)

Forever is a long, long time—a sentiment that is hard to believe in after you've moved from foster home to foster home for seven of your eleven years. But Flora (age 11) and Julian's (age 9) adopted mom, Emily, has promised them that they will be a family forever. After living with Emily for two years, they are finally settling in and starting to believe that this will be their forever home. However, when Emily tells them that she is pregnant, their world spirals out of control. In order to move forward, they will have to dig into their past to answer tough questions. This incredibly well-written novel details the emotional, social, and academic struggles of both Flora and Julian. Carter deftly shares the important role one's past has on shaping the future.

(continued)

curriculum connections

(continued)

Subject	Standard	Classroom Ideas
Art, Language Arts, Social Studies, and Technology	**NCTE/ILA:** Students use spoken, written, and visual language to accomplish their own purposes (e.g., for learning, enjoyment, persuasion, and the exchange of information). **NCSS:** Identify and describe ways family, groups, and community influence the individual's daily life and personal choices. **NCSS:** Explore factors that contribute to one's personal identity such as interests, capabilities, and perceptions. **NCCAS:** Synthesize and relate knowledge and personal experiences to make art. **ISTE:** Students know and use a deliberate design process for creating innovative artifacts.	Using an online service, like Shutterfly or Mixbook, create a digital memory book with photographs and accompanying narratives. Use a variety of layouts to design an effective memory book. Write about family members and how they influence who you are, what you are interested in, and your capabilities.
Science and Math	**NGSS:** Generate and compare multiple solutions to a problem based on how well they meet the criteria and constraints of the design problem. **NCTM:** Apply and adapt a variety of appropriate strategies to solve problems.	Flora and Julian create a number of stories to explain how they came into the world, as they are both convinced they were not born. Think about, record, and evaluate other creative explanations of this "problem."
Textual Connections	*The Misadventures of the Family Fletcher* (Levy); *The Door by the Staircase* (Marsh); *All Rise for the Honorable Perry T. Cook* (Connor)	
Other Books by Carter	For middle-grade readers: *My Life with the Liar* For young adult readers: *Tumbling; My Best Friend, Maybe; Me, Him, Them, and It*	
Author's Website	http://caelacarter.com	

Sources: International Society for Technology in Education (ITSE); National Coalition for Core Arts Standards (NCCAS); National Council of Teachers of English (NCTE)/International Literacy Association (ILA); National Council for Teachers of Mathematics (NCTM); National Council for Social Studies Curriculum Standards (NCSS); and Next Generation Science Standards (NGSS).

Notes

1. Madeleine L'Engle, in a speech before the Florida Library Association, May 1965, Miami.
2. C. S. Lewis, *An Experiment in Criticism* (Cambridge: Cambridge University Press, 1961), p. 57.
3. James Cross Giblin, *Writing Books for Young People* (Boston: Writer, 1990), p. 73.
4. Alice Dalgliesh, *The Silver Pencil* (New York: Puffin, 1991 [1944]).
5. Virginia Hamilton, "Writing the Source: In Other Words," *Horn Book Magazine* (December 1978): 618.
6. Ann Cameron, "Write What You Care About," *School Library Journal* 35.10 (June 1989): 50.
7. Jean Little, "A Writer's Social Responsibility," *New Advocate* 3 (spring, 1990): 83.
8. See Margaret Mackey's "Filling the Gaps: 'The Baby-Sitters Club,' the Series Book, and the Learning Reader," *Language Arts* 67.5 (September 1990): 484–89; and "Bad Books, Good Reading," special issue of *Bookbird* 33.3/4 (fall/winter, 1995–1996).
9. Claudia Mills, "The Ethics of Representation: Realism and Idealism in Children's Fiction," report from the Institute for Philosophy and Public Policy, vol. 19, no. 1 (winter, 1999): 13–18.
10. S. Bredekamp and C. Copple, eds., *Developmentally Appropriate Practice in Early Childhood Programs,* rev. ed. (Washington, DC: NAEYC, 1997).
11. R. Sims Bishop, "Mirrors, Windows, and Sliding Glass Doors," *Perspectives* 6 (1990): ix–xi.
12. L. S. Vygotsky, "Interaction Between Learning and Development," in *Minds in Society,* ed. M. Cole, V. John-Steiner, S. Scribner, and E. Souberman (Cambridge, Mass.: Harvard University Press, 1978).

Children's Literature

Go to Connect® to access study resources, practice quizzes, and additional materials.

Titles in blue = multicultural titles

Agosin, Marjorie. *I Lived on Butterfly Hill.* Atheneum Books for Young Readers, 2014.

Al Mansour, Haifaa. *The Green Bicycle.* Penguin/Dial, 2015.

Alexander, Kwame. *Booked.* Houghton Mifflin Harcourt, 2016.

——. *The Crossover.* Houghton Mifflin Harcourt, 2014.

Almond, David. *Skellig.* Delacorte Books for Young Readers, 2009.

Alvarez, Julia. *How Tia Lola Ended Up Starting Over* (The Tia Lola Stories). Yearling, 2011.

Anderson, John David. *Mrs. Bixby's Last Day.* HarperCollins/Walden Pond, 2016.

——. *Posted.* HarperCollins/Walden Pond, 2017.

Angleberger, Tom. *Emperor Pickletine Rides the Bus (Origami Yoda #6).* Amulet Books, 2014.

Applegate, Katherine. *Crenshaw.* Feiwel and Friends, 2015.

Benedis-Grab, Daphne. *Army Brats.* Scholastic, 2017.

Benjamin, Ali. *The Thing About Jellyfish.* Little, Brown Books for Young Readers, 2015.

Bertman, Jennifer Chambliss. *The Unbreakable Code.* Christy Ottaviano Books, 2017.

Birdsall, Jeanne. *The Penderwicks in Spring.* Knopf Books for Young Readers, 2015.

Blume, Judy. *Are You There God? It's Me, Margaret.* Bradbury, 1970.

Booth, Coe. *Kinda Like Brothers.* Scholastic, 2015.

Burnford, Sheila. *The Incredible Journey.* Illustrated by Carl Burger. Little, 1961.

Cameron, Ann. *Colibrí.* Farrar, 2003.

——. *Gloria Rising.* Illustrated by Lis Toth. Farrar, 2002.

——. *The Most Beautiful Place in the World.* Illustrated by Thomas B. Allen. Knopf, 1988.

——. *The Stories Julian Tells.* Illustrated by Ann Strugnell. Knopf, 1981.

Carmi, Daniella. *Samir and Yonatan.* Levine/Scholastic, 2000.

Carter, Caela. *Forever, or a Long, Long Time.* Harper, 2017.

Cleary, Beverly. *Ramona's World.* Illustrated by Alan Tiegreen. Morrow, 1999.

Clements, Andrew. *We Hold These Truths (Benjamin Pratt & The Keepers of the School #5).* Illustrated by Adam Stower. Atheneum, 2013.

Connor, Leslie. *All Rise for the Honorable Perry T. Cook.* Katherine Tegen, 2016.

Creech, Sharon. *Moo.* HarperCollins, 2016.

Crutcher, Chris. *The Sledding Hill.* Greenwillow, 2005.

Dalgliesh, Alice. *The Silver Pencil.* Scribners, 1944.

Diaz, Alexandra. *The Only Road.* Simon & Schuster/ Paula Wiseman, 2016.

Dinerstein, Eric. *What Elephants Know.* Disney/ Hyperion, 2016.

Doherty, Berlie. *The Girl Who Saw Lions.* Roaring Brook Press, 2008.

Donoghue, Emma. *The Lotterys Plus One.* Arthur A. Levine Books, 2017.

Draper, Sharon M. *Out of My Mind.* S & S/Atheneum, 2010.

Dumas, Firoozeh. *It Ain't So Awful Falafel.* Clarion, 2016.

Ehrlich, Esther. *Nest.* Random House/Wendy Lamb, 2014.

Engle, Margarita. *Forrest World.* Atheneum, 2017.

Erskine, Kathryn. *Mockingbird.* Philomel, 2010.

Farmer, Nancy. *A Girl Named Disaster.* Orchard, 1996.

Federle, Tim. *Five, Six, Seven, Nate!* Simon & Schuster, 2014.

Fitzgerald, Laura Marx. *Under the Egg.* Penguin/Dial, 2014.

Flood, Nancy Bo. *Soldier Sister, Fly Home.* Charlesbridge, 2016.

Freeman, Ruth. *One Good Thing About America.* Holiday House, 2017.

Garza, Xavier. *Maxmillian & the Lucha Libre Club: A Bilingual Lucha Libre Thriller (Max's Lucha Libre Adventures #3).* Cinto Puntos Press, 2016.

Gemeinhart, Dan. *The Honest Truth.* Scholastic, 2015.

George, Jean Craighead. *Julie of the Wolves.* Illustrated by John Schoenherr. Harper, 1972.

Gino, Alex. *George.* Scholastic, 2015.

Grabenstein, Chris. *Mr. Lemoncello's Library Olympics.* Random House, 2016.

Graff, Lisa. *Lost in the Sun.* Penguin/Philomel, 2015.

Gratz, Alan. *Ban This Book.* Starscape, 2017.

Grimes, Nikki. *Garvey's Choice.* Boyds Mills/Wordsong, 2016.

Hamilton, Virginia. *Cousins.* Thorndike Press, 2001.

_____. *M. C. Higgins, the Great.* Macmillan, 1974.

Hashimi, Nadia. *One Half from the East.* HarperCollins, 2016.

Hiaasen, Carl. *Chomp.* Knopf, 2012.

Helget, Nicole. *The End of the Wild.* Little, Brown and Company, 2017.

Henkes, Kevin. *The Year of Billy Miller.* Greenwillow, 2014.

Herrera, Robin. *Hope Is a Ferris Wheel.* Abrams/ Amulet, 2014.

Hobbs, Will. *Never Say Die.* HarperCollins Children's Books, 2013.

Holm, Jennifer L. & Matthew Holm. *Sunny Side Up.* Graphix, 2015.

Hosch, Amanda. *Mabel Opal Pear and the Rules for Spying.* Capstone Young Readers, 2017.

Howe, James. *Totally Joe.* Atheneum Books for Young Readers, 2007.

Hunt, Lynda Mullaly. *Fish in a Tree.* Penguin/Nancy Paulsen, 2015.

Johnson, Terry Lynn. *Avalanche (Survivor Diaries #2).* Illustrated by Jani Orban. HMH, 2018.

Johnson, Varian. *To Catch a Cheat.* Scholastic/ Arthur A. Levine, 2016.

Jamieson, Victoria. *Roller Girl.* Dial Books for Young Readers, 2015.

Jones, Kelly. *Unusual Chickens for the Exceptional Poultry Farmer.* Knopf Books for Young Readers, 2015.

Kelly, Erin Entrada. *Hello Universe.* HarperCollins/ Greenwillow, 2017.

_____. *Land of Forgotten Gils.* HarperCollins/ Greenwillow, 2016.

Khan, Rukhsana. *Wanting Mor.* Groundwood Books, 2009.

Kinney, Jeff. *Double Down (Diary of a Wimpy Kid #11).* Amulet Books, 2016.

Konigsburg, E. L. *The View from Saturday.* Atheneum, 1996.

Kurtz, Jane. *Planet Jupiter.* Greenwillow Books, 2017.

Lai, Thanhhà. *Listen, Slowly.* HarperCollins, 2015.

Laird, Elizabeth. *The Fastest Boy in the World.* Macmillan Children's Books, 2014.

L'Engle, Madeleine. *Meet the Austins.* Dell, 1981 [1960].

Le Guin, Ursula K. *A Wizard of Earthsea.* Illustrated by Ruth Robbins. Houghton, 1968.

Levy, Dana Alison. *The Family Fletcher Takes Rock Island (The Misadventures of the Family Fletcher #2).* Delacourt, 2016.

_____. *The Misadventures of the Family Fletcher (Book #1).* Delacourt, 2014.

Look, Lenore. *Alvin Ho: Allergic to the Great Wall, the Forbidden Palace, and Other Tourist Attractions.* Schwartz & Wade, 2014.

Lowry, Lois. *Number the Stars.* Houghton, 1989.

Martin, Ann M. *Rain Reign.* Feiwel and Friends/ Macmillan, 2014.

Marsh, Katherine. *The Door by the Staircase.* Illustrated by Kelly Murphy. Disney-Hyperion, 2016.

Marshall, Joseph. *In the Footsteps of Crazy Horse.* Amulet Books, 2015.

McLean, Dirk. *Team Fugee.* Lorimer, 2017.

Medina, Juana. *Juana & Lucas.* Candlewick, 2016.

Miles, Charles. *Spurt*. Simon & Schuster, 2017.

Myers, Walter Dean. *The Cruisers*. Scholastic Press, 2011.

Naylor, Phyllis Reynolds. *Shiloh*. Atheneum, 1991.

Nesbet, Anne. *Cloud and Wallfish*. Candlewick, 2017.

Nye, Bill. *Jack and the Geniuses: At the Bottom of the World (Jack and the Geniuses #1)*. Abrams, 2017.

Nye, Naomi Shihab. *The Turtle of Oman*. HarperCollins/Greenwillow, 2014.

Palacio, R. J. *Wonder*. Knopf Books for Young Readers, 2012.

Park, Linda Sue. *A Long Walk to Water: Based on a True Story*. Clarion, 2011.

Parr, Maria. *Adventures with Waffles*. Candlewick, 2015.

Paterson, Katherine. *Bridge to Terabithia*. Illustrated by Donna Diamond. Crowell, 1977.

Patterson, James. *School Story*. Little, Brown and Company, 2017.

Paulsen, Gary. *Hatchet*. Bradbury, 1987.

Pearsall, Shelley. *All of the Above*. Little, Brown Books for Young Readers, 2008.

_____. *The Seventh Most Important Thing*. Knopf, 2015.

Peck, Richard. *The Best Man*. Dial, 2016.

Pinkney, Andrea Davis. *The Red Pencil*. Little, Brown Books for Young Readers, 2014.

Pla, Sally J. *The Someday Birds*. HarperCollins Publishers, 2017.

Quick, Mathew. *Boy21*. Little, Brown Books for Young Readers, 2012.

Raskin, Ellen. *The Westing Game*. Dutton, 1978.

Rhodes, Jewell Parker. *Ninth Ward*. Little Brown Books for Young Readers, 2010.

_____. *Towers Falling*. Little, Brown Books for Young Readers, 2016.

Reynolds, Jason. *As Brave as You*. Atheneum/Caitlyn Dlouhy, 2016.

Reynolds, Jason. *Patina*. Atheneum/Caitlyn Dlouhy, 2017.

Robbins Rose, Judith. *Look Both Ways in the Barrio Blanco*. Candlewick, 2015.

Sachar, Louis. *Fuzzy Mud*. Random/Delacorte, 2015.

_____. *Holes*. Illustrated by Vladimir Radunsky and Bagram Ibatoulline. Dell Yearling, 2000.

Salisbury, Graham. *Night of the Howling Dogs*. Random, 2007.

Schmidt, Gary D. *Okay for Now*. Clarion, 2011.

_____. *Orbiting Jupiter*. Clarion, 2015.

_____. *The Wednesday Wars*. Clarion, 2007.

Schrefer, Eliot. *Endangered*. Scholastic, 2012.

Scieszka, Jon. *Heroes & Villians* (Guys Read series). Walden Pond Press, 2016.

Selzer, Adam. *How to Get Suspended and Influence People*. Delacorte, 2007.

Shevah, Emma. *Dream On, Amber*. Chicken House, 2015.

Silberberg, Alan. *Milo: Sticky Notes and Brain Freeze*. Aladdin, 2011.

Sloan, Holly Goldberg. *Counting by 7s*. Dial Books for Young Readers, 2013.

Sonnichsen, A.L. *Red Butterfly*. Simon & Schuster, 2015.

Soven, Megan Jean. *The Meaning of Maggie*. Chronicle, 2014.

Spinelli, Jerry. *Maniac Magee*. Little, Brown Books for Young Readers, 1999.

_____. *Wringer*. HarperCollins, 1997.

St. Antoine, Sara. *Three Bird Summer*. Candlewick, 2014.

Staples, Suzanne Fisher. *Shabanu: Daughter of the Wind*. Knopf, 1989.

Stead, Rebecca. *Goodbye Stranger*. Wendy Lamb Books, 2015.

Sullivan, Tara. *The Bitter Side of Sweet*. Putnam, 2016.

Svingen, Arne. *The Ballad of a Broken Nose*. Margaret K. McElderry, 2016.

Tamaki, Mariko. *This One Summer*. Illustrated by Jillian Tamaki. First Second, 2014.

Telgemeier, Raina. *Drama*. Graphix, 2012.

Terry, Ellie. *Forget Me Not*. Feiwel and Friends, 2017.

Thomas, Angie. *The Hate U Give*. Harper Collins, 2016.

Turnage, Sheila. *The Odds of Getting Even*. Kathy Dawson Books, 2015.

Vrabel, Beth. *Cabel and Kit*. Running Press Kids, 2017.

Wiles, Deborah. *The Aurora County All-Stars*. Harcourt, 2007.

Woodson, Jacqueline. *Peace, Locomotion*. Puffin, 2010.

Historical Fiction

Chapter Outline

Dinha loves to escape with a good book. Today, she is in her getaway—a nice, cool tree house. This time she's reading *Town Is by the Sea*, written by Joanne Schwartz and illustrated by Sydney Smith. Dinha is imagining what her life would be like if her father was a coal miner in 1950s Canada or if her grandfather was a coal miner before that. She puts herself in the shoes of the young narrator, trying to understand something she herself has never and will never experience.

When reflecting on her love for historical fiction, Dinha is quick to say, "I love books that take me to

Photo by Sara Dashner Photography, Gahanna, Ohio.

make-believe places in real history." For her, well-written historical fiction breaks the boundaries of time and place, allowing her to feel part of the culture, the climate, and the history. She connects better with the history because she feels a connection with the fictional characters that "lived" it.

Historical Fiction for Today's Child

Historical fiction must draw on two sources, fact and imagination—the author's information about the past and her or his power to speculate about how it was to live in that time. By personalizing the past and making it live in the mind of the reader, such books can help children understand both the public events that we usually label "history" and the private struggles that have characterized the human condition across the centuries.

Historical fiction is not as popular with readers today as it was a generation or two ago. Today's children generally select realistic fiction, the so-called "I" stories with modern-day characters and settings. Even so, children have more historical fiction available now than in any other decade. Publishers have capitalized on children's interest in series books by developing collectible sets of historical fiction titles. The American Girl books offer many different series, each chronicling the adventures of a girl in a particular time. These books, along with the expensive dolls and period costumes that go with them, have been phenomenally successful. Other publishers have also targeted the 7-to-11 age range. In 1996, Scholastic introduced the Dear America series of fictional journals by young girls, which provide "eyewitness" accounts of events in American history. All the books are written by well-known authors, though with mixed results. Joyce Hansen's *I Thought My Soul Would Rise and Fly* received a Coretta Scott King Honor Book Award in 1998; other titles have been severely criticized.[1] Perhaps most disturbing is the series' attempt to look like authentic diaries rather than like fiction. No author's name is given on the cover or spine. Following the diary entries is an epilogue describing what happened to the character following the accounts in the diary. An historical note and archival photographs follow. Buried at the back of the book is a brief "About the Author" section, and the dedication, acknowledgments, and CIP information are given on the final page. It is no wonder that many children and teachers believe these stories are real accounts. The popularity of the series has spawned three others that use a similar format. The My America series is for a younger audience and has a continuing series of books narrated by the same fictional character. The My Name Is America series features fictional boys' reports of significant happenings in American history, and the Royal Diaries series provides fictional chronicles of famous young women such as Elizabeth I and Cleopatra. Teachers who want to share these books with children will want to select titles carefully and ensure that children read them with a critical eye.[2]

Historical fiction continues to provide ideas to authors and illustrators of picture storybooks that portray the life of a particular period. For example, children can experience both the grueling reality and the hopeful dreams of eleven slaves, based on an

Kadir Nelson's illustrations for *Henry's Freedom Box* by Ellen Levine represent the dramatic true story of a slave's escape from Virginia to Philadelphia. From *Henry's Freedom Box* by Ellen Levine, illustrated by Kadir Nelson, Scholastic, Inc. / Scholastic Press. Illustration copyright ©2007 by Kadir Nelson, Inc. Reprinted by permission.

1828 document, as Ashley Bryan does in his award-winning *Freedom Over Me: Eleven Slaves, Their Lives and Dreams Brought to Life*. They can cheer for the extraordinary bravery of Henry Brown as he escapes from slavery by shipping himself from Richmond to Philadelphia in *Henry's Freedom Box* by Ellen Levine and Kadir Nelson. In Eve Bunting's *Dandelions*, readers can travel across the prairie, or they can greet the arrival of Lewis and Clark from a Native American perspective in Virginia Driving Hawk Sneve's *Bad River Boys*. They can experience the detention of a young Chinese immigrant newly arrived in San Francisco in Katrina Saltonstall Currier's *Kai's Journey to Gold Mountain*. They can walk among the tenements of an immigrant community in New York City in Elisa Bartone's *Peppe the Lamplighter* or experience the horrors of World War II and the Holocaust in books such as *The Cats in Krasinski Square* by Karen Hesse, *Rose Blanche* by Roberto Innocenti and Christophe Gallaz, or *Stone Angel* by Jane Yolen. They can experience the desperation for rain during the Dust Bowl in *The Storm in the Barn* by Matt Phelan. In Joanne Schwartz's *Town Is by the Sea*, illustrated by the award-winning Sydney Smith, readers can venture deep underground with miners and bask in the sun by the sea.

The Value of Historical Fiction

Historical novels for children help a child to experience the past—to enter into the conflicts, the suffering, the joy, and the despair of those who lived before us. There is no way children can feel the jolt of a covered wagon, the tediousness of the daily trek in the broiling sun, or the constant threat of danger unless they take an imaginative journey in books like Jean Van Leeuwen's *Bound for Oregon* or Gary Paulsen's *Mr. Tucket* and *Call Me Francis Tucket*. Well-written historical fiction offers young people the vicarious experience of participating in the life of the past.

Historical fiction encourages children to think as well as feel. Every book set in the past invites a comparison with the present. In addition, opportunities for critical thinking and judgment are built into the many novels that provide conflicting views on an issue and force characters to make hard choices. Readers of *Chains* by Laurie Halse Anderson can weigh the decision of Isabel, a teenage slave, to become a spy during the American Revolution in an attempt to gain her freedom. In *Forge* and *Ashes*, Anderson continues her portrayal of the fight for freedom, both by individuals and by a nation. Readers will

[handwritten margin note: vicarious experience]

experience the horrors of the Civil War in Rodman Philbrick's Newbery Honor–winning *The Mostly True Adventures of Homer P. Figg*. Homer uses witty tall tales to tell the story of how he runs away from home to search for his brother who has been sold as a soldier to the Union Army.

An historical perspective also helps children see and judge the mistakes of the past more clearly. They can read such books as *Day of Tears* by Julius Lester, *Nory Ryan's Song* by Patricia Reilly Giff, *Salt to the Sea* by Ruta Sepetys, or *Under the Blood-Red Sun* by Graham Salisbury and realize the cruelty people are capable of inflicting on each other, whether by slavery, persecution, or the internment of Japanese Americans in "relocation centers." Such books will quicken children's sensibilities and bring them to a fuller understanding of human problems and human relationships. We hope that children will learn not to repeat the injustices of the past. Many years ago George Santayana cautioned: "Those who cannot remember the past are condemned to repeat it."

Stories of the past help children see that times change, nations rise and fall, but universal human needs have remained relatively unchanged. All people need and want respect, belonging, love, freedom, and security, regardless of whether they lived during the period of the Vikings or the pioneers or are alive today. The pain of moving from home to home and place to place is present in many books such as Louise Erdrich's *The Birchbark House*, *The Game of Silence*, *The Porcupine Year*, *Chickadee*, and *Makoons*. But the solace drawn from loving families is what gives all the characters hope. Children today living in tenements, trailers, or suburban homes seek the same feeling of warmth and family solidarity that Erdrich portrays so effectively in her books.

Historical fiction also enables children to see human interdependence. We are all interconnected and interrelated. We need others as much as the boys did when they were left to survive in the woods during World War II in Aharon Appelfeld's *Adam and Thomas*. Ellen Rosen needed Annemarie Johansen's family in order to escape the Nazis in Lois Lowry's award-winning book *Number the Stars*. Michael remembers the kindness of strangers from Czechoslovakia that restored his faith in people and provided hope when he had none in 1939 in *It Rained Warm Bread*, written by Michael's daughter, Gloria Moskowitz-Sweet, and illustrated by Hope Anita Smith. Such books also dramatize the courage and integrity of the thousands of people who willingly take a stand for what they believe. History does not record their names, but their stories are frequently the source of inspiration for books of historical fiction.

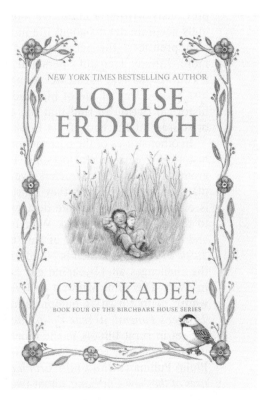

NEW YORK TIMES BESTSELLING AUTHOR

LOUISE ERDRICH

CHICKADEE

BOOK FOUR OF THE BIRCHBARK HOUSE SERIES

Louise Erdrich's *Chickadee* continues the adventures of the Ojibwa community with the next generation in the mid-nineteenth century. Cover art copyright ©2012 by Aza Erdrich Dorris. Used by permission of HarperCollins Publishers.

Children's perceptions of chronology are inexact and develop slowly. Even so, stories about the past can develop a feeling for the continuity of life and help children to see themselves and their present place in time as part of a larger picture. Books such as Bonnie Pryor's *The House on Maple Street* provide this sense for younger elementary students. In Pryor's book, lost objects from early times are unearthed in a contemporary child's yard. Paintings by Beth Peck link past and present, showing changes that came to that specific setting over the intervening centuries. In *The House*, written for older readers, a stone house narrates its transformation over time through J. Patrick Lewis's quatrains and Roberto Innocenti's artwork. Reading historical fiction is one way children can develop this sense of history and begin to understand their place in the sweep of human destiny.

Types of Historical Fiction

The genre of historical fiction can be used to designate all realistic stories that are set in the past. Even though children tend to see these in one undifferentiated category (because all the action happened "in the olden days" before they were born), readers will want to keep in mind that various distinctions can be made on the basis of the author's purpose and the nature of the research and writing tasks required. Teachers and librarians should help children differentiate between the fictionalized aspects and the factual aspects in all types of historical fiction.

In the most obvious type of historical fiction, an author weaves a fictional story around actual events and people of the past. *Johnny Tremain* by Esther Forbes, the story of a fictional apprentice to Paul Revere, is a novel of this sort. The author had previously written a definitive adult biography of Revere and had collected painstakingly accurate details about life in Boston just before the Revolutionary War: the duties of apprentices, the activities of the Committee for Public Safety, and much, much more. Johnny Tremain's personal story, his development from an embittered boy into a courageous and idealistic young man, is inextricably connected with the political history and way of life of his place and time. It is not uncommon in recent books of historical fiction to find that the author has added an author's note and bibliography of sources at the end of the book.

In other stories of the past, fictional lives are lived with little or no reference to recorded historical events or real persons. However, the facts of social history dictate the background for how the characters live and make their living; what they wear, eat, study, or play; and what conflicts they must resolve. Kimberly Willis Holt's *Dear Hank Williams* is of this type. Quirky Tate decides to write her year-long school pen-pal project letters to the famous singer Hank Williams, providing insights into the social history of 1948 and 1949. Another book of this type is Jennifer L. Holm's Newbery Honor–winning *Turtle in Paradise*, which is based on the author's great-grandmother's stories and follows the challenges an 11-year-old girl faces when she is sent to live with relatives in Florida in 1935. The rural Midwest and western America provide the setting for several books whose main thrust is humor rather than historical detail. Richard Peck's books *The Teacher's Funeral*, *A Year Down Yonder*, *A Long Way from Chicago*, and *A Season of Gifts* are set in rural Illinois in the nineteenth and mid-twentieth centuries. Their main focus is on wonderfully eccentric characters and amusing plot lines. These same qualities make Philip Pullman's *Two Crafty Criminals!: And How They Were Captured by the Daring Detectives of the New Cut Gang*, about two boys who lead a neighborhood gang of crime solvers in Victorian London, so appealing.

In 1894, the "New Cut Gang" of children uncovers several mysteries by cleverly outsmarting the elders of the town. Pullman, Philip. *Two Crafty Criminals!: And How They Were Captured By The Daring Detectives Of The New Cut Gang*. New York, NY: Alfred A. Knopf, an imprint of Random House Children's Book, 2012, Cover. Copyright ©2012 by Alfred A. Knopf, an imprint of Random House Children's Books. All rights reserved. Used with permission.

Often in this type of historical fiction the historical setting simply provides the background for ripping good adventure stories that rely on the structures of Robert Louis Stevenson's *Treasure Island* or Johann David Wyss's *The Swiss Family Robinson*. Christopher, in Kevin Sands' *The Blackthorn Key*, uses his wit and all of the apothecary training he learned when his mentor, Master Blackthorn, is killed. Sands' adventure thriller, set in the 1600s, has secrets, intrigue, and danger.

Some historical fiction turns traditional female roles upside down. Nancy Springer has chosen an historical London setting for her likable mystery series. Springer's heroine Enola Holmes is the very rebellious younger sister to Mycroft and Sherlock Holmes and determined to solve her own mysteries in books such as *The Case of the Missing Marquess* and *The Case of the Gypsy Good-bye*. In Jacqueline Kelly's Newbery-honor winner, *The Evolution of Calpurnia Tate*, Callie prefers to study botanical science in the woodshed with her grandfather, as she is determined to become a scientist like Charles Darwin. She is the only girl with six brothers, and her mother expects her to learn how to cook and sew and to be an accomplished lady, as all girls should be in 1899. However, Callie prefers to be out in nature, observing and making discoveries. In Kelly's sequel, *The Curious World of Calpurnia Tate*, we find Calpurnia's thirst for knowledge and understanding still strong, as she finds a way to work with a local vet, learning more about the science of medicine, much to her mother's dismay.

In a third type of historical fiction, authors recreate, largely from memory, their own personal experiences of a time that is "history" to their child audience. The Little House books, for example, are all based on actual childhood experiences in the life of their author, Laura Ingalls Wilder, or her husband. Such books require searching one's memory for details and then sorting and imaginatively retelling significant events, but extensive research is seldom done and books written in the past often reflect the prejudices of the past. This is one reason to make sure to offer children many books about a time period. Louise Erdrich's The Birchbark House series takes place during the same time period as Wilder's Little House books but presents historical events from the point of view of a Native American community.

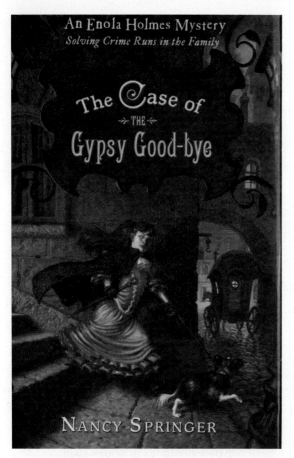

In other instances, a purely contemporary story about a significant event might endure until it acquires historical significance. *Snow Treasure* by Marie McSwigan is the exciting story of Norwegian children who heroically strapped gold bullion under their sleds and slid downhill to the port past the watchful Nazi commandant. Written as realism in 1942, this book is read by children today as historical fiction. We must also realize that Katherine Paterson's *Park's Quest*, Gary Schmidt's *Trouble*, and other books about the Vietnam War might be read as historical fiction by today's child, despite the fact that, for some of us, these events were lived firsthand.

Some historical stories defy commonly accepted classifications. Walter Mosley's graphically moving *47* vividly portrays the experiences of slavery in 1832 Georgia. The story's narrator is named only Number Forty-Seven, following the practice of dehumanization that was common to slave owners in the South. However, Forty-Seven is looking back on his life from the ripe old age of 180. Furthermore, the other major character in the story is a runaway slave named Tall John, whom many on the plantation suspect of being the legendary African hero High John the Conqueror. Instead of being this mythical African, however, Tall John is actually an alien from another planet. Clearly, Mosley has broken the format of traditional historical fiction for children. But the book presents such an accurate and brutal picture of slavery that it will provide important historical insights to mature readers.

A few authors tell stories of the past in the guise of another genre to draw the hesitant reader in more quickly. Jane Yolen's devastating story of the Holocaust, *The Devil's Arithmetic*, begins in the present when Hannah, bored with all the remembering of the Passover Seder, opens the door to welcome symbolically the prophet Elijah and finds herself in the unfamiliar world of a Polish village in the 1940s. Margaret Peterson Haddix's The Missing series draws readers into history via the storytelling construct of time travel. Throughout these suspenseful books, the main characters, who are famous missing children from history, go back in time to right historical wrongs. Brian Selznick does a masterful job of using illustrations to draw readers into the story. In the Caldecott-winning *The Invention of Hugo Cabret*, Selznick tells about Georges Méliès through the eyes of the fictional character Hugo. Selznick continues to use illustrations to tell the story in *Wonderstruck* and *The Marvels*.

Historical fiction has also been shaped in the form of theatrical scripts. *Day of Tears* by Julius Lester, *Good Masters! Sweet Ladies!* by Laura Amy Schlitz, and *Colonial Voices* by Kay Winters all contain multiple voices witnessing historical events and provide children with wonderful opportunities for dramatic presentation. *The Watch That Ends the Night* by Allan Wolf is a verse novel that tells the historic event of the sinking of the Titanic from the perspective of twenty-five different voices, including the iceberg. Categorizing books like these is far less important than bringing them to the attention of children, for they all tell good stories and make their subjects memorable.

No type of historical story is intrinsically better than another. However, the type of story might influence a teacher's selection process when choosing books for specific classroom purposes. However, when evaluating historical fiction, for which the criteria are described in the following section, standards of authenticity must be applied most rigorously to stories that give a prominent place to real people and real events and are used as part of the social studies curriculum.

Evaluating Historical Fiction

Books of historical fiction must, first of all, tell a story that is interesting in its own right. The second, and unique, requirement is balancing fact with fiction. Margery Fisher maintains that a good story should not be overwhelmed by facts:

> For the more fact he [the author] has to deal with, the more imagination he will need to carry it off. It is not enough to be a scholar, essential though this is. Without imagination and enthusiasm, the most learned and well-documented story will leave the young reader cold, where it should set him on fire.[3]

Historical fiction *does* have to be accurate and authentic. However, the research should be thoroughly digested, making details appear as an essential part of the story, not tacked on for effect. Mollie Hunter, a well-known Scottish writer of fine historical fiction for children, maintains that an author should be so steeped in the historical period of the book that "you could walk undetected in the past. You'd wake up in the morning and know the kind of bed you'd be sleeping in, ... even the change you'd have in your pocket!"[4] The purpose of research, she said, is

> to be able to think and feel in terms of a period so that the people within it are real and three-dimensional, close enough to hear the sound of their voices, to feel their body-warmth, to see the expression in their eyes.[5]

This obligation applies not only to the details of person, place, and time but also to the values and norms of the culture or cultures depicted. To provide a faithful representation of a culture, an author needs to grasp the language, emotions, thoughts, concerns, and experiences of her character rather than shape that character to fit a mainstream point of view. Louise Erdrich's depiction of Ojibwa families in *The Porcupine Year*, *The Birchbark House*, *The Game of Silence*, *Chickadee*, and *Makoons* reveals the importance of accurate depiction of culture in historical fiction for children. Erdrich's books make for a valuable comparison of the way Native peoples are depicted in Laura Ingalls Wilder's Little House books set in the same location about the same time. To fail in this regard is, at the very least, insensitive to children who are members of that culture. Such a failure also does a disservice to children from outside that culture whose worldview and understanding could be enriched by exposure to the attitudes, values, and goals of another group.

Although fictional characters and invented turns of plot are accepted in historical novels, nothing should be included that contradicts the actual record of history. If President Lincoln was busy reviewing Union troops in Virginia on a given day in 1863, an author must not "borrow" him for a scene played in New York City, no matter how great the potential dramatic impact. It breaks the unwritten contract between author and child reader to offer misinformation in any form.

Stories must accurately reflect the spirit and values of the time, as well as the events. Historical fiction cannot be made to conform to today's more enlightened point of view concerning medical knowledge, women's rights, or civil rights. George Washington can't be saved with a shot of penicillin. Although in Carol Ryrie Brink's *Caddie Woodlawn*, Caddie's father allows her to be a tomboy while she is growing up in the Wisconsin backwoods, it is highly unlikely that girls raised in the Victorian era could refuse to assume the persona of a "proper lady" in adulthood. Many African Americans may have suffered the indignity of racism in silence as the family in William Armstrong's *Sounder* did. But there were also people of many cultures in our history who fought against the roles that society dictated for them. Authors of historical fiction can inspire us with their stories in books based on real characters such as *Tucky Jo and Little Heart* by Patricia Polacco, *The Wren and the Sparrow* by J. Patrick Lewis, Christopher Paul Curtis's *Elijah of Buxton*, and Margi Preus's *Heart of a Samurai*.

The historian Christopher Collier, who has collaborated with his brother James Lincoln Collier on several novels set during the era of the American Revolution, maintains that authors should pay careful attention to historiography, "that is, the way that professional historians have approached and interpreted the central episode of the story."[6] Collier believes that authors should weigh opposing views on the causes or meaning of a conflict and decide which should be predominant in the story, but also find a way to include the other significant interpretations. One way is to have different characters espouse different points of view. In *Bull Run*, Paul Fleischman deals with this reality by telling the story of this early battle of the Civil War through the voices of sixteen different characters—northerner and southerner, male and female, civilian and military, slave and free.

However, fiction that draws the reader into the thoughts and feelings of a central character cannot be truly impartial. In the middle of a massacre scene, a bleeding settler who cries "But the Indians are only fighting for what is theirs!" will sacrifice the story's credibility. Many fine books, like Michael Morpurgo's *An Elephant in the Garden* and Gene Yang's *Boxers & Saints*, let the reader feel more than one side of an issue. But for a more inclusive viewpoint, teachers and librarians will want to provide a variety of books, each with its own point of view and approach to the topic.

The authenticity of language in historical fiction should be given careful attention. We have no recordings of the speech of people from much earlier times, but the spoken word in a book with an historical background should give the flavor of the period. However, too many *prithee*s and *thou*s will seem artificial and might discourage children's further reading. Some archaic words can be used if they are explained in the content. For example, the book *The Cabin Faced West* notes that George Washington "bated" at the Hamiltons. The author, Jean Fritz, makes it very clear by the action in the story that "bated" means "stopped by for dinner."

Some words commonly used in earlier times are offensive by today's standards. Authors must consider whether it would be misleading to omit such terms entirely and how necessary such language is for establishing a character. In Graham Salisbury's *Under the Blood-Red Sun*, "haoles," or white Hawaiians, refer to the Japanese as "Japs." The word "nigger" is used by African American authors Julius Lester in *Day of Tears* and Walter Mosley in *47*. It would have defeated the purpose and softened the brutality of the times of these stories to have these characters use more acceptable language. Walter Mosley explains 47's use of the phrase "a nigger like me" in a footnote: "That was before I met Tall John and he taught me about the word 'nigger' and how wrong it was for me to use such a term" (p. 7). Authors' notes about the reasons for choices they have made regarding language are useful to both students and teachers. Explaining the dilemma she faced in *Crooked River*, a story about the clash of Anglo and Native Americans in Ohio in 1812, Shelley Pearsall remarks:

> Sadly, the language of the past also reflected the prejudices and hatreds of the past. Some of the characters in *Crooked River* use words such as *savages, half-breeds,* and *beasts* to describe the Native American people. It was with a heavy heart that I put those words into the story. They were used on the frontier and found in the historical documents I read. Appallingly, even the governor of Ohio used this language in an 1812 address to the Ohio Legislature where he called the Indians "hordes of barbarians." As a historical writer I could not ignore the language of the past, but I hope that it causes readers to reflect upon the destructive power that words of hate can wield. (p. 239)

Pearsall counteracts the sting of such language by her sensitive shaping of the character of John Mic, an Ojibwa man accused of the murder of a white man. In the chapters narrated by John, Pearsall chose to use story poems, which she felt best expressed "the powerful, descriptive language" of the Ojibwa.

As discussed in the chapter on poetry, some language is deeply political and loaded with the historical and contemporary baggage of racism, sexism, homophobia, and other systemic oppressions. The polarization caused by a single word can be seen in the use of the word "nigger" or "injun" (Huck Finn). Debates range from thinking we must use the word, because it is a part of our lexicon, to thinking of it as a racial epitaph that should be erased from even the "classic" literary texts. We will not settle that debate here. Our objective should be to expose children and young adults to the best literature, helping readers suspend belief long enough to maybe get through life's tough situations, to rise above their own challenges, to consider multiple perspectives, to respect diversity, and to become more self-reflective.

Well-written historical fiction also makes use of figurative language that is appropriate for the times and characters in the story. For example, in Katherine Paterson's powerful story *Lyddie*, about a farm girl who goes to work in the fabric mills of Lowell, Massachusetts, in the 1840s, all allusions and metaphors are those of an uneducated rural girl. In the very beginning of the story, a bear gets into their farm cabin and Lyddie stares him down while the other children climb the ladder to the loft. Finally, she herself backs up to the ladder, climbs it, and pulls it up behind her. Throughout the book Lyddie alludes to "staring down the bears." She thinks of the huge machines as "roaring clattering beasts ... great clumsy bears" (p. 97). And when she throws a water bucket at the overseer to get him to let go of a young girl, she laughs as she imagines she hears the sound of an angry bear crashing the oatmeal bucket in the cabin. Everything about this book works together to capture Lyddie's view of the world. At the same time, the long thirteen hours a day of factory work, life in the dormitories, the frequency of tuberculosis, and the treatment of women all reflect the spirit and the values of the times. More important than the authenticity of the writing is the fast-paced story and Lyddie's grit, determination, and personal growth.

A book of historical fiction should do even more than relate a good story of the past authentically and imaginatively. It should illuminate today's problems by examining those of other times. The themes of many historical books are basic ones about the meaning of freedom, loyalty and treachery, love and hate, acceptance of new ways, closed minds versus questioning ones, and, always, the age-old struggle between good and evil. Many tales of the past echo recent experience. Books like *Revolution* by Deborah Wiles, *Stella by Starlight* by Sharon Draper, *Esperanza Rising* by Pam Muñoz Ryan, and *Firefly Letters: A Suffragette's Journey to Cuba* by Margarita Engle could well be used in a discussion of the history of women's roles. All these books can shed light and understanding on today's problems.

To summarize, historical fiction must first meet the requirements of good writing, but it demands special criteria beyond that. In evaluating historical fiction, the reader will want to consider whether the story meets these specialized needs. Historical fiction can dramatize and humanize facts of history that can seem sterile in so many textbooks. It can give children a sense of participation in the past and an appreciation for their historical heritage. It should enable the child to see that today's way of life is a result of what people did in the past and that the present will influence the way people live in the future. For some of the most important criteria to keep in mind, see **Guidelines: Evaluating Historical Fiction.**

Esperanza Rising, **by Pam Muñoz Ryan, is a moving story of a family transitioning from a life of privilege in Mexico to living as migrant workers in California during the Great Depression. The character of Esperanza is based on Ryan's grandmother.** Illustration ©2000 by Joe Cepeda from ESPERANZA RISING by Pam Muñoz Ryan. Scholastic Inc. Scholastic Press. Used by permission.

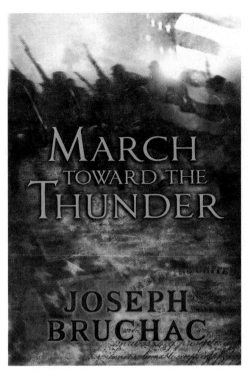

Joseph Bruchac's *March Toward the Thunder* is based on the story of Bruchac's Abenaki great-grandfather's service in the Irish Brigade in 1864. Bruchac, Joseph. *March Toward the Thunder*. New York, NY: Dial Books for Young Readers, A Division of Penguin Young Readers Group, 2008, Cover. Copyright ©2008 by Dial Books for Young Readers, A Division of Penguin Young Readers Group. All rights reserved. Used with permission.

Evaluating Historical Fiction

Guidelines

Go to Connect® to access study resources, practice quizzes, and additional materials.

Consider the following when evaluating historical fiction for children:

- Does the book tell a good story? Is fact blended with fiction in such a way that the background is subordinate to the story?
- Is the story as accurate and authentic as possible?
- Does the author provide background information in an afterword, or author's note, that will help readers distinguish between what is fact and what has been fictionalized?
- Does the story accurately reflect the values and norms of the culture depicted?

- Does the author avoid any contradiction or distortion of the known events of history?
- Are background details authentic, in keeping with accurate information about the period?
- Does the story accurately reflect the values and spirit of the time?
- Are different points of view on the issues of the time presented or acknowledged?
- Does the dialogue convey a feeling of the period without seeming artificial? Does it reflect character as well as setting?
- Is the language of the narrative appropriate to the time, drawing figures of speech from the setting?
- Does the theme provide insight and under-standing for today's problems as well as those of the past?

Classroom Approaches to Historical Fiction

One way to approach historical fiction is to look at common topics or themes as they are presented in different settings across the centuries and to group titles by such themes. Such a thematic approach helps emphasize the universality of human experiences over time and place.

Another approach is to plan to read books chronologically, according to the periods and settings they represent. **Teaching Feature 8.1: Historical Fiction and the Social Studies Sequence by Grade Level** includes historical fiction titles that correspond with the National Council for the Social Studies curriculum standards, broken down by grade level.

teaching feature 8.1

Historical Fiction and the Social Studies Sequence by Grade Level

Title (Author, Illustrator)	Place/Time (if specified)	Grade Level
KINDERGARTEN: Understanding Then and Now		
Ox-Cart Man (Hall, Cooney)	New England, 1800s	K–3
The House on Maple Street (Pryor, Peck)	1700s	K–3
Good Times Travel Agency series (Bailey, Slavin)	Variety of times	K–3
A Medieval Feast (Aliki)	Medieval	K–3
GRADE 1: Schools/Transportation Methods of the Past		
Hornbooks and Inkwells (Kay, Schindler)	1700s	K–3
Mailing May (Tunnell, Rand)	Idaho, 1914	K–3
The Bicycle Man (Say)	Japan, 1940s	K–3
Virgie Goes to School with Us Boys (Howard, Lewis)	Tennessee, 1870s	K–3
The Secret Subway (Corey, Red Nose Studio)	New York City, 1860s	K–3
Wagons Ho! (Hallowell and Holub, Avril)	Missouri and Oregon, 1846 and 2011	1–3
GRADE 2: Family Histories		
Three Names (MacLachlan, Pertzoff)	Prairie, recent past	K–3
Uncle Jed's Barbershop (Mitchell, Ransome)	South, Great Depression	K–3
Town Is by the Sea (Schwartz, Smith)	Canada, 1950s	K–3
Show Way (Woodson, Talbott)	United States, Eight generations	K–3
GRADE 3: Voting, Rules and Laws		
I Could Do That! Esther Morris Gets Women the Vote (White, Carpenter)	Wyoming, 1869	K–3
The Day Gogo Went to Vote (Sisulu, Wilson)	South Africa, 1994	K–3

Title (Author, Illustrator)	Place/Time (if specified)	Grade Level
George Washington's Birthday: A Mostly True Tale (McNamara, Blitt)	Virginia, 1700s	K–3
Granddaddy's Turn: A Journey to the Ballot Box (Bandy and Stein, Ransome)	South, 1960s	K–3
John, Paul, George & Ben (Smith)	New England, 1700s	K–4
The Ballot Box Battle (McCully)	New York, 1880	3–5
GRADE 4: State History: The Impact of the Great Depression and the Dust Bowl on States' Histories		
The Truth about Sparrows (Hale)	Texas, 1933	4–6
Out of the Dust (Hesse)	Oklahoma, 1934	4–6
Esperanza Rising (Ryan)	California, 1930s	4–6
Moon over Manifest (Vanderpool)	Manifest, Kansas, 1936	4–6
The Mighty Miss Malone (Curtis)	Indiana and Michigan	4–6
GRADES 4 to 8: US History: World War II		
Hidden (Dauvillier, Lizano and Salsedo)	France	3–5
The Whispering Town (Elvgren, Santomauro)	Denmark	3–5
Stone Angel (Yolen, Green)	England and France	4–6
Soldier Bear (Tak, Hopman)	Poland and Iran	4–6
The War that Saved My Life (Bradley)	England	4–6
GRADES 4 to 8: US History: Civil Rights Era		
Stella by Starlight (Draper)	North Carolina, 1932	4–6
Revolution (Wiles)	Mississippi, 1964	4–6
Night on Fire (Kidd)	Alabama, 1964	4–6
Goin' Someplace Special (McKissack, Pinkney)	Tennessee, 1960s	4
The Port Chicago 50: Disaster, Mutiny, and the Fight for Civil Rights (Sheinkin)	Chicago, 1940s	7 and up
GRADES 5 to 8: U.S. History: Revolutionary Era		
Gingerbread for Liberty!: How a German Baker Helped Win the American Revolution (Rockliff, Kirsch)	Baker for George Washington's Troops	1–4
Seeds of America series: *Chains*; *Forge*; *Ashes* (Anderson)	African American sisters in Revolutionary War, New York City	4–6

(continued)

teaching **feature** 8.1

Title (Author, Illustrator)	Place/Time (if specified)	Grade Level
Liberty or Death (Blair)	Runaway slaves side with the British during the American Revolution	4–6
Johnny Tremain (Forbes)	Prior to and during the Revolutionary War	4–6
Early Thunder (Fritz)	Loyalist in Massachusetts	4–6
The Winter People (Bruchac)	Abenaki Village in Canada	4–6
Colonial Voices: Hear Them Speak (Winters, Day)	Multiple voices describing events leading to the Revolution	4–6
The Arrow Over the Door (Bruchac, Watling)	American Revolution	4–6
The Fighting Ground (Avi)	Battle near Trenton, New Jersey	5–7
My Brother Sam Is Dead (Collier and Collier)	Two brothers on opposing sides during the Revolution	5 and up
Jump Ship to Freedom (Arabus Family Saga series) (Collier and Collier)	African Americans' experiences during the Revolution	5 and up
GRADES 5 to 8: State/U.S. History: Resistance to Slavery		
Henry's Freedom Box (Levine, Nelson)	Henry Brown, a slave, ships himself to freedom	2–5
Elijah of Buxton; *The Madman of Piney Woods* (Curtis)	Free settlement of former slaves; Canada early 1860s	4–6
Jefferson's Sons: A Founding Father's Secret Children (Bradley)	Jefferson and Heming's children's experiences	4–6
Nightjohn (Paulsen)	Life of slaves on a southern plantation, c. 1850	4–6
The Underground Abductor (Nathan Hale's Hazardous Tales series) (Hale)	Delaware, early nineteenth century	4–6
Copper Sun (Draper)	Parallel stories of an African girl and a white indentured servant who find themselves subject to a brutal slave owner	6 and up
Day of Tears: A Novel in Dialogue (Lester)	Slave auction, 1859 Georgia	7 and up
Letters from a Slave Boy (Lyons)	Based on the life of Joseph Jacobs	7 and up
Letters from a Slave Girl (Lyons)	Based on the life of Harriet Jacobs	7 and up

Title (Author, Illustrator)	Place/Time (if specified)	Grade Level
GRADES 4 to 8: State/U.S. History: The Civil War		
Thunder at Gettysburg (Gauch)	Girl caught in middle of battle of Gettysburg	1–4
Pink and Say (Polacco)	Georgia	2–5
The Mostly True Adventures of Homer P. Figg (Philbrick)	U.S. South	3–5
How I Found the Strong (McMullan)	Southern boy left to care for his family	4–6
The Storm Before Atlanta (Schwabach)	Georgia	4–6
With Every Drop of Blood (Collier and Collier)	Southern boy and African American Union soldier	4–6
March Toward the Thunder (Bruchac)	Abenaki Indian youth in Irish Brigade, 1864	7 and up
Red Moon at Sharpsburg (Wells)	Virginia, beginning in 1862	7 and up
GRADES 5 to 8: U.S. History: The Age of Industrial Revolution		
Fire at the Triangle Factory (Littlefield, Young)	New York, 1911	2–5
Billy Creekmore (Porter)	Coal mines, 1900	4–6
Bread and Roses, Too (Paterson)	Massachusetts Mill Strike, 1912	4–6
Counting on Grace (Winthrop)	Vermont Mill Town, 1910	4–6
Fair Weather (Peck)	Chicago World's Fair, 1893	4–6
Lyddie (Paterson)	Massachusetts Mills, 1843	4 and up
Searching for Sarah Rector: The Richest Black Girl in America (Bolden)	Oklahoma, 1920s	6 and up
Ashes of Roses (Auch)	Triangle Shirt Factory, 1911	7 and up
GRADE 6: Ancient Civilizations: Ancient Times		
The Golden Goblet (McGraw)	Egypt, 1450 BC	5 and up
The Roman Britain Trilogy series (Sutcliff): *The Eagle of the Ninth*; *The Silver Branch*; *The Lantern Bearers*	Roman Britain, fifth-century England	5 and up
The Roman Mysteries series (Lawrence): *The Thieves of Ostia*; *The Gladiators from Capua*	Roman Empire, first century C.E.	6 and up
Mara, Daughter of the Nile (McGraw)	Egypt, 1450 BC	6 and up

(continued)

Title (Author, Illustrator)	Place/Time (if specified)	Grade Level
GRADE 7: World History: The Middle Ages		
Adam of the Road (Gray, Lawson)	England, thirteenth century	3–5
Blood Red Horse (Grant)	The Crusades	4–6
Crispin: The Cross of Lead (Avi)	England, fourteenth century	4–6
Good Masters! Sweet Ladies! Voices from a Medieval Village (Schlitz Byrd)	English village, 1255	4–6
The Midwife's Apprentice (Cushman)	England	4–6
A Single Shard (Park)	Korea, twelfth century	4–6
The Door in the Wall (de Angeli)	England, fourteenth century	5 and up
Catherine, Called Birdy (Cushman)	England, 1290	6 and up
The King's Shadow (Alder)	England, 1053	7 and up
The Kite Rider (McCaughrean)	China, thirteenth century in the time of Genghis Kahn	7 and up

Source: National Council for the Social Studies Curriculum Standards.

Challenging Perspectives on Historical Fiction

When children are asked to name their least favorite school subject, the answer is often social studies. Anything to do with history, ancient or modern, seems to turn off young readers. The question for educators then becomes, "How can I pique the interest of my students in historical events? And especially those events that link the past experiences of people near and far to the lived experiences of contemporary times?"

Researchers and observant teachers have concluded that students' interest in social studies (history, political science, economics, religious studies, geography, psychology, anthropology, and civics) and their ability to learn, retain, and think critically about social studies content increases considerably when their instruction included literature.[7,8]

One efficient way to accomplish this is by integrating social studies education into the language arts curriculum using historical fiction. Students can integrate literacy skills with social studies content as they read historical fiction and informational texts.

Originally written in German, *My Family for the War* by Anne C. Voorhoeve presents a challenge to typical perspectives. When Ziska is taken out of Berlin in 1939 on a kindertransport, she must deal with the fact that while her family's heritage is Jewish, her family's practice of Protestantism doesn't protect them from abuse. In England, Ziska learns about Judaism as practiced by two very different Jewish families, enlightening readers with these new perspectives in addition to the conditions of World War II in both Berlin and London.

Another book to consider is *Fish for Jimmy* (2013), a story of two Japanese-American brothers after Japan bombed Pearl Harbor and the United States entered the war. The family is forced to leave their home and go to an internment camp. Jimmy loses his appetite, becomes weak, and is getting ill. His older brother sneaks out of the camp and catches fresh fish for Jimmy to help make him strong again.

Today, many students are interested in book series. The You Choose Books series presents multiple yet challenging perspectives in an "interactive history adventure." Books like *World War I* by Gwenyth Swain present three different stories to follow—a Belgian resistance fighter, a British soldier, and an American Field Service volunteer—in a fact-saturated, choose-your-own-adventure that explores these multiple angles.

In kindergarten and first grades, students learn to distinguish among past, present, and future and learn about significant American holidays and people. A selection for younger readers could include *All Different Now: Juneteenth, the First Day of Freedom* by Angela Johnson and illustrator E.B. Lewis. Through the eyes of one little girl, they chronicle the story of Juneteenth, also known as Juneteenth Independence Day or Freedom Day—a holiday that commemorates the June 19, 1865, announcement of the abolition of slavery in Texas, and more generally the emancipation of African American slaves throughout the Confederate South. In *The House Baba Built* by Caldecott winner Ed Young, the author describes in detail how the home built by his father became a refuge for friends and relatives during Japan's invasion. An afterword, author's note, and timeline provide rich historical information for curricular connections.

The use of historical fiction raises a challenge for some who believe there is a "truth," and factual evidence of an event should not be distorted by fictional accounts. For example, some teachers did not want to use Faith Ringgold's book, *Aunt Harriet's Underground Railroad in the Sky*. In the book, Cassie returns to the skies, flying way up, so far up that the mountains look like rock candy and the oceans like tiny cups of tea. Cassie and her brother, BeBe, encounter a fantastic train—the Underground Railroad train—and a tiny woman in a conductor's uniform. The woman is Harriet Tubman, who takes Cassie and BeBe on an imaginary journey to the terrifying world of a slave plantation and on a desperate, but ultimately triumphant, escape to freedom.

Drawing on historical accounts of the Underground Railroad, the facts of Harriet Tubman's life, and on the rich resources of her own imagination, Ringgold created a book that both recounts the chilling realities of slavery and joyfully celebrates freedom. How can this award-winning book be a problem? One teacher reported, "After spending so much time on the Underground Railroad—teaching the children it was not a REAL railroad but a metaphor for the escape route of enslaved Africans—the last thing I needed was a book that said it was in the sky!" While the accuracy of historical events have a place in the curriculum, when using a work of historical fiction, the focus should be placed on expanding the reader's perspective of a given time. Instructional strategies should also be developed to encourage critical thinking, research to understand the historical context of book, and the development of their historical thinking.

Yet another concern is how history is fraught with controversy. When discussing historical fiction and controversial issues, the most common objection raised is, "Why should we impose contemporary values and ideals upon the past?" As mentioned in earlier chapters, discussing controversial issues with children helps to foster their critical thinking and problem-solving ability. Using historical fiction creates an open forum for debating the historical issues juxtaposed with contemporary concerns. As children recognize a literary selection as a reflection of its social, cultural, and historical context, they should read considering the issues raised in light of situations, conflicts, and themes common to the human experiences of the time. Contemporary values should only be juxtaposed for the purpose of critique, comparison, or debate.

With careful selection, one can find examples of historical fiction through which two or more strands of the social studies can be taught, and engaging discussions of historical and contemporary controversial issues will promote increased literacy skills. This can happen while the children suspend belief and are enthralled with the story. Combining historical fiction and informational texts with social studies standards with engaging and interactive literacy activities will facilitate students' reading comprehension and understanding of social studies content. As mentioned earlier in this chapter, historical fiction can be used to designate all realistic stories that are set in the past. It is also the hope that reading, analyzing, and interpreting this genre can facilitate the development of an increased understanding of human dignity, basic rights, and responsibilities of citizens in a democracy—and open-minded respect for individual and cultural differences. (Go to Connect® to use the Ten-Point Model to facilitate classroom discussion of historical fiction.)

curriculum connections

Using Historical Fiction to Address Standards

Historical fiction provides children with a lens to the past. By reading and engaging in discussions about fictionalized historical events, students have the opportunity to experience a range of emotions and gain knowledge about what life was like during different time periods.

Suggested Children's Book: *The War that Saved My Life* by Kimberly Brubaker Bradley (Dial Books, 2015)
Ada lives with her brother, Jamie, in a tiny apartment over a pub. Her abusive mother, ashamed of Ada's twisted foot, confines Ada to a solitary life indoors while Jamie is allowed to run and play. Ada discovers that children are being evacuated to the countryside to escape the bombings, *and* that her mother is planning to only send Jamie. Ada takes her future into her own hands to stay with her brother and escape her reality. Bradley's novel blends this wonderful story with historical facts about what life was like for children evacuated to the English countryside during World War II.

curriculum connections

Subject	Standards	Classroom Ideas
Language Arts and Social Studies	**NCSS:** Describe personal changes over time, such as those related to physical development and personal interests. **NCSS:** Describe personal connections to place. **NCTE/ILA:** Students apply a wide range of strategies to comprehend, interpret, evaluate, and appreciate texts.	Analyze the development of Ada throughout the story, using textual evidence to describe her changes throughout the story. Analyze characters' connections to place, as Ada learns to live at Susan's house.
Science and Mathematics	**NGSS:** Define a simple design problem reflecting a need or a want that includes specified criteria for success and constraints on materials, time, or cost. **NCTM:** Develop fluency in adding, subtracting, multiplying, and dividing whole numbers.	Design a housing solution, using a budget, for citizens who become homeless due to the bombing. Build a model.
Art, Social Studies, Technology, and Language Arts	**NCAS:** Generate and conceptualize artistic ideas and work. **NCSS:** Identify and use various sources for reconstructing the past, such as documents, letters, diaries, maps, textbooks, photos, and others. **ISTE:** Students plan and employ effective research strategies to locate information and other resources for their intellectual or creative pursuits. **NCTE/ILA:** Students employ a wide range of strategies as they write and use different writing process elements appropriately to communicate with different audiences for a variety of purposes.	After researching famous posters from both the United States and United Kingdom, students write and design propaganda multimedia posters used during World War II.
Textual Connections	*The Boy in the Striped Pajamas* (Boyne); *Rose Blanche* (Gallaz, Innocenti); *Number the Stars* (Lowry); *The Butterfly* (Polacco); *The Lion, the Witch, and the Wardrobe* (Lewis); *The Tree in the Courtyard* (Gottesfeld)	
Other Books by Bradley	*The War I Finally Won*; *Jefferson's Sons: A Founding Father's Secret Children*; and *For Freedom: The Story of a French Spy*	
Author's website	http://www.kimberlybrubakerbradley.com	

Sources: International Society for Technology in Education (ITSE); National Coalition for Core Arts Standards (NCCAS); National Council of Teachers of English (NCTE)/International Literacy Association (ILA); National Council for Teachers of Mathematics (NCTM); National Council for Social Studies Curriculum Standards (NCSS); and Next Generation Science Standards (NGSS).

Notes

1. See Marlene Atleo, et al., "A Critical Review of Ann Rinaldi's *My Heart Is on the Ground*," and Beverly Slapin's "A Critical Review of Ann Turner's *The Girl Who Chased Away Sorrow*," available at <www.oyate.org>.
2. See Daniel Hade, "Storyselling: Are Publishers Changing the Way Children Read?" *Horn Book Magazine* 78.5 (2002): 509.
3. Margery Fisher, *Intent Upon Reading: A Critical Appraisal of Modern Fiction for Children* (New York: Watts, 1962), p. 225.
4. Mollie Hunter in a lecture at Ohio State University, Columbus, Ohio, November 1968.
5. Mollie Hunter, "Shoulder the Sky," in *Talent Is Not Enough* (New York: Harper, 1976), pp. 43–44.
6. Christopher Collier, "Criteria for Historical Fiction," *School Library Journal* 28 (August 1982): 32.
7. M. Cai, "Variables and Values in Historical Fiction for Children," *The New Advocate* 5.4 (1992): 279–91.
8. E. Freeman and L. Levstick, "Recreating the Past: Historical Fiction in the Social Studies Curriculum," *Elementary School Journal* 88.4 (1988): 329–37.

Children's Literature

*Go to **Connect**® to access study resources, practice quizzes, and extending materials.*

Titles in blue = multicultural titles

Alder, Elizabeth. *The King's Shadow*. Farrar, 1995.

Aliki. *A Medieval Feast*. HarperCollins, 1986.

Anderson, Laurie Halse. *Ashes*. Atheneum/Caitlyn Dlouhy Books, 2016.

———. *Chains*. Simon, 2008.

———. *Forge*. Atheneum Books for Young Readers, 2012.

Appelfeld, Aharon. *Adam and Thomas*. Triangle Square, 2015.

Armstrong, Alan. *Raleigh's Page*. Random, 2007.

Armstrong, William H. *Sounder*. Illustrated by James Barkley. Harper, 1969.

Auch, M. J. *Ashes of Roses*. Holt, 2002.

Avi [Avi Wortis]. *Crispin: The Cross of Lead*. Hyperion, 2002.

———. *The Fighting Ground*. Lippincott, 1984.

———. *Prairie School*. Illustrated by Bill Fransworth. HarperCollins, 2010.

Bailey, Linda. *Adventures in Ancient Greece (Good Times Travel Agency)*. Illustrated by Bill Slavin. Kids Can Press, 2002.

Bandy, Michael S. and Eric Stein. *Granddaddy's Turn: A Journey to the Ballot Box*. Illustrated by James Ransome. Candlewick, 2015.

Bartone, Elisa. *Peppe the Lamplighter*. Illustrated by Ted Lewin. Lothrop, 1993.

Blaire, Margaret Whitman. *Liberty or Death: The Surprising Story of Runaway Slaves Who Sided with the British during the American Revolution*. National Geographic Children's Books, 2010.

Bolden, Tonya. *How to Build a Museum*. Viking, 2016.

———. *Searching for Sarah Rector: The Richest Black Girl in America*. Harry N. Abrams, 2014.

Borden, Louise. *Sleds on Boston Common: A Story from the American Revolution*. Illustrated by Robert Andrew Parker. McElderry, 2000.

Boyne, John. *The Boy in the Striped Pajamas*. Random House, 2006.

Bradley, Kimberly Brubaker. *For Freedom: The Story of a French Spy*. Delacourte Press, 2003.

———. *Jefferson's Sons: A Founding Father's Secret Children*. Dial, 2015.

———. *The War I Finally Won*. Dial Books, 2017.

———. *The War that Saved My Life*. Dial Books, 2015.

Brink, Carol Ryrie. *Caddie Woodlawn*. Illustrated by Trina Schart Hyman. Macmillan, 1973.

Bruchac, Joseph. *The Arrow Over the Door*. Dial, 1998.

———. *March Toward the Thunder*. Dial, 2008.

———. *The Winter People*. Dial, 2002.

Bryan, Ashley. *Freedom over Me: Eleven Slaves, Their Lives and Dreams Brought to Life*. Atheneum/Caitlyn Dlouhy Books, 2016.

Bunting, Eve. *Dandelions*. Illustrated by Greg Shed. Harcourt, 1995.

Carbonne, Elisa. *Blood on the River: James Town 1607*. Viking Juvenile, 2006.

Collier, James Lincoln, and Christopher Collier. *Jump Ship to Freedom*. Delacorte, 1981.

_____. *My Brother Sam Is Dead*. Four Winds, 1974.

_____. *With Every Drop of Blood*. Delacorte, 1994.

Corey, Shana. *The Secret Subway*. Schwartz & Wade, 2016.

Curtis, Christopher Paul.

_____. *Elijah of Buxton*. Scholastic, 2007.

_____. *Madman of Piney Woods*. Scholastic Press, 2014.

_____. *The Mighty Miss Malone*. Wendy Lamb Books, 2012.

Cushman, Karen. *Catherine, Called Birdy*. Clarion, 1994.

_____. *The Midwife's Apprentice*. Clarion, 1995.

Dauviller, Loic, and Greg Salsedo. *Hidden*. Illustrated by Marc Lizano. First Second, 2014.

de Angeli, Marguerite. *The Door in the Wall*. Doubleday, 1949.

Draper, Sharon. *Copper Sun*. Atheneum, 2006.

_____. *Stella by Starlight*. Atheneum Books for Young Readers, 2015.

Elvgren, Jennifer. *The Whispering Town*. Illustrated by Fabio Santomauro. Kar-Ben Publishing, 2014.

Engle, Margarita. *Firefly Letters: A Suffragette's Journey to Cuba*. Henry Holt and Co., 2010.

Erdrich, Louise. *The Birchbark House*. Hyperion, 1999.

_____. *The Game of Silence*. HarperCollins, 2005.

_____. *Makoons*. HarperCollins. 2016.

_____. *The Porcupine Year*. HarperCollins, 2008.

_____. *Chickadee*. HarperCollins, 2012.

Fleischman, Paul. *Bull Run*. HarperCollins, 1993.

Forbes, Esther. *Johnny Tremain*. Illustrated by Lynd Ward. Houghton, 1946.

Fritz, Jean. *The Cabin Faced West*. Illustrated by Feodor Rojankovsky. Coward-McCann, 1958.

_____. *Early Thunder*. Illustrated by Lynd Ward. Coward-McCann, 1967.

Gallaz, Christophe, and Roberton Innocenti. *Rose Blanche*. Creative Editions, 1985.

Garfield, Henry. *The Lost Voyage of John Cabot*. Atheneum, 2004.

Gauch, Patricia Lee. *Thunder at Gettysburg*. Illustrated by Stephen Gammell. Putnam, 1990 [1975].

Giff, Patricia Reilly. *Nory Ryan's Song*. Delacorte, 2000.

Gottesfeld, Jeff. *The Tree in the Courtyard*. Illustrated by Peter McCarthy. Knopf Books for Young Readers, 2016.

Grant, K. M. *Blood Red Horse*. de Granville Trilogy. Walker, 2005.

Gray, Elizabeth Janet. *Adam of the Road*. Illustrated by Robert Lawson. Viking, 1942.

Haddix, Margaret Peterson. *Found (The Missing: Book 1)*. Simon & Schuster, 2008.

Hale, Marian. *The Truth About Sparrows*. Holt, 2004.

Hale, Nathan. *The Underground Abductor: An Abolitionist Tale about Harriet Tubman*. Harry N. Abrams, 2015.

Hall, Donald. *OxCart Man*. Illustrated by Barbara Cooney. Puffin, 1983.

Hallowell, George, and Joan Holub. *Wagons Ho!* Illustrated by Lynne Avril. Albert Whitman & Company, 2011.

Hansen, Joyce. *I Thought My Soul Would Rise and Fly: The Diary of Patsy, a Freed Girl*. Scholastic, 1997.

Hesse, Karen. *The Cats in Krasinski Square*. Illustrated by Wendy Watson. Scholastic, 2004.

_____. *Out of the Dust*. Scholastic, 1997.

_____. *Stowaway*. McElderry, 2000.

Holm, Jennifer L. *The Trouble with May Amelia*. Illustrated by Adam Gustavson. Atheneum Books for Young Readers, 2011.

_____. *Turtle in Paradise*. Yearling, 2010.

Holt, Kimberly Willis. *Dear Hank Williams*. Henry Holt and Co., 2015.

Howard, Elizabeth Fitzgerald. *Virgie Goes to School with Us Boys*. Illustrated by E. B. Lewis. Simon & Schuster, 2011.

Innocenti, Roberto, and Christophe Gallaz. *Rose Blanche*. Illustrated by Roberto Innocenti. Creative Education, 1985.

Johnson, Angela. *All Different Now: Juneteenth, the First Day of Freedom*. Illustrated by E.B. Lewis. Simon & Schuster Books for Young Readers, 2014.

Jones, Elizabeth McDavid. *Mystery on Skull Island*. Pleasant, 2002.

Kay, Verla. *Hornbooks and Inkwells*. Illustrated S. D. Schindler. Putnam Juvenile, 2011.

Kelly, Jacqueline. *The Curious World of Calpurnia Tate*. Henry Holt and Co., 2011.

_____. *The Evolution of Calpurnia Tate*. Henry Holt and Co., 2009.

Kidd, Ronald. *Night on Fire*. Albert Whitman & Company, 2015.

Lawrence, Caroline. *The Gladiators from Capua*. Roaring Brook Press, 2005.

_____. *The Thieves of Ostia*. Roaring Brook Press, 2002.

Lester, Julius. *Day of Tears: A Novel in Dialogue*. Hyperion, 2005.

_____. *Pharaoh's Daughter: A Novel of Ancient Egypt*. Harcourt, 2000.

Levine, Ellen. *Henry's Freedom Box: A True Story from the Underground Railroad*. Illustrated by Kadir Nelson. Scholastic, 2010.

Lewis, C. S. *The Lion, the Witch, and the Wardrobe*. HarperCollins, 1950.

Lewis, J. Patrick. *The House*. Illustrated by Roberto Innocenti. Creative Editions, 2009.

———. *The Wren and the Sparrow*. Kar-Ben Publishing, 2015.

Littlefield, Holly. *Fire at the Triangle Factory*. Illustrated by Mary O'Keefe Young. Carolrhoda Books, 1996.

Lowry, Lois. *Number the Stars*. HMH Books for Young Readers, 2014.

Lyons, Mary E. *Letters from a Slave Boy: The Story of Joseph Jacobs*. Atheneum, 2007.

———. *Letters from a Slave Girl: The Story of Harriet Jacobs*. Scribner's, 1992.

MacLachlan, Patricia. *Three Names*. Illustrated by Alexander Pertzoff. Perfection Learning, 1994.

McCaughrean, Geraldine. *The Kite Rider*. HarperCollins, 2002.

McCully, Emily Arnold. *The Ballot Box Battle*. Knopf, 1996.

McGraw, Eloise Jarvis. *The Golden Goblet*. Viking Penguin, 1986 [1961].

———. *Mara, Daughter of the Nile*. Viking Penguin, 1985 [1953].

McKissack, Patricia C. *Goin' Someplace Special*. Illustrated by Jerry Pinkney. Atheneum Books for Young Readers, 2001.

McMullan, Margaret. *How I Found the Strong*. Houghton, 2005.

McNamara, Margaret. *George Washington's Birthday: A Mostly True Tale*. Illustrated by Barry Blight. Schwartz & Wade, 2012.

Mitchell, Margaree King. *Uncle Jed's Barbershop*. Illustrated by James E. Ransome. Simon & Schuster, 1993.

Morpurgo, Michael. *An Elephant in the Garden*. Feiwel & Friends, 2011.

Moses, Sheila. *The Legend of Buddy Bush*. McElderry, 2004.

Moskowitz-Sweet, Gloria. *It Rained Warm Bread*. Illustrated by Home Anita Smith. Henry Holt & Company, 2018.

Park, Linda Sue. *A Single Shard*. Clarion, 2001.

Paterson, Katherine. *Bread and Roses, Too*. Clarion, 2006.

———. *Lyddie*. Lodestar, 1988.

———. *Park's Quest*. Dutton, 1988.

Paulsen, Gary. *Nightjohn*. Delacorte, 1993.

———. *Call Me Francis Tucket*. Yearling, 1995.

———. *Mr. Tuckett*. Yearling, 1994.

Pearsall, Shelley. *Crooked River*. Knopf, 2005.

Peck, Richard. *Fair Weather*. Dial, 2001.

———. *A Long Way from Chicago*. Dial, 1999.

———. *A Season of Gifts*. Dial, 2009.

———. *The Teacher's Funeral: A Comedy in Three Parts*. Dial, 2004.

———. *A Year Down Yonder*. Dial, 2000.

Phelan, Matt. *The Storm in the Barn*. Candlewick, 2009.

Philbrick, Rodman. *The Mostly True Adventures of Homer P. Figg*. The Blue Sky Press, 2009.

Polacco, Patricia. *The Butterfly*. Philomel Books, 2000.

———. *Pink and Say*. Philomel, 1994.

———. *Tucky Jo and Little Heart*. Simon & Schuster, 2015.

Porter, Tracey. *Billy Creekmore: A Novel*. HarperCollins, 2007.

Pryor, Bonnie. *The House on Maple Street*. Illustrated by Beth Peck. Morrow, 1987.

Raum, Elizabeth. *Orphan Trains: An Interactive History Adventure*. You Choose Books, 2011.

Reeder, Carolyn. *Shades of Gray*. Macmillan, 1989.

Ringgold, Faith. *Aunt Harriet's Underground Railroad in the Sky*. Perfection Learning, 1995.

Rockliff, Mara. *Gingerbread for Liberty!: How a German Baker Helped Win the American Revolution*. Illustrated by Vincent X. Kirsch. HMH Books for Young Readers, 2015.

Ryan, Pam Muñoz. *Esperanza Rising*. Scholastic, 2000.

Salisbury, Graham. *Under the Blood-Red Sun*. Delacorte, 1994.

Sands, Kevin. *The Blackthorn Key*. Alladin, 2015.

Say, Allen. *The Bicycle Man*. Sandpiper, 1989.

Schlitz, Laura Amy. *Good Masters! Sweet Ladies! Voices from a Medieval Village*. Illustrated by Robert Byrd. Candlewick, 2008.

Schmidt, Gary. *Trouble*. HMH Books for Young Readers, 2010.

Sepetys, Ruta. *Salt to the Sea*. Philomel Books, 2016.

Sheinkin, Steve. *The Port Chicago 50: Disaster, Mutiny, and the Fight for Civil Rights*, Roaring Brook Press, 2014.

Schwabach, Karen. *The Storm Before Atlanta*. Random House, 2010.

Schwartz, Joanne. *Town Is by the Sea*. Illustrated by Sydney Smith. Groundwood Books, 2017.

Selznick, Brian. *The Invention of Hugo Cabert*. Scholastic, 2007.

_____. *The Marvels*. Scholastic, 2015.

_____. *Wonderstruck*. Scholastic, 2011.

Sisulu, Elinor Batezat. *The Day Gogo Went to Vote*. Illustrated by Sharon Wilson. Little, Brown & Co, 1996.

Smith, Lane. *John, Paul, George & Ben*. Hyperion Books for Children, 2012.

Sneve, Virginia Driving Hawk. *Bad River Boys: A Meeting of the Lakota Sioux with Lewis and Clark*. Illustrated by Bill Farnsworth. Holiday, 2005.

Speare, Elizabeth George. *The Sign of the Beaver*. Houghton, 1983.

_____. *The Witch of Blackbird Pond*. Houghton, 1958.

Springer, Nancy. *The Case of the Gypsy Good-bye*. Philomel, 2011.

_____. *The Case of the Missing Marquess: An Enola Holmes Mystery*. Philomel, 2006.

Stevenson, Robert Louis. *Treasure Island*. Illustrated by John Lawrence. Candlewick, 2009.

Sutcliff, Rosemary. *The Eagle of the Ninth*. Oxford University Place, 1954.

_____. *The Lantern Bearers*. Oxford University Place, 1959.

_____. *The Silver Branch*. Oxford University Place, 1957.

Swain, Gwenyth. *World War I: An Interactive History Adventure* (You Choose Books). Capstone Press, 2012.

Tak, Bibi Dumon. *Soldier Bear*. Illustrated by Philip Hopman. Translated by Laura Watkinson. Eerdmans Books for Young Readers, 2011.

Tak, Bibi Dumon. *Soldier Bear*. Illustrated by Philip Hopman. Eerdmans Books for Young Readers, 2011.

Tunnell, Michael O. *Mailing May*. Illustrated by Ted Rand. Greenwillow Books, 2000.

Vanderpool, Clare. *Moon Over Manifest*. Delacourt, 2010.

Voorhoeve, Anne C. *My Family for the War*. Dial, 2012.

Wells, Rosemary. *Red Moon at Sharpsburg*. Viking, 2007.

White, Linda Arms. *I Could Do That! Esther Morris Gets Women the Vote*. Illustrated by Nancy Carpenter. Farrar, Straus and Giroux, 2005.

Wilder, Laura Ingalls. *Little House on the Prairie*. Illustrated by Garth Williams. Harper, 1953 [1935].

_____. *Little Town on the Prairie*. Illustrated by Garth Williams. Harper, 1953 [1932].

Wiles, Deborah. *Revolution*. Scholastic Press, 2014.

Winters, Kay. *Colonial Voices: Hear Them Speak*. Illustrated by Larry Day. Dutton, 2008.

Winthrop, Elizabeth. *Counting on Grace*. Random, 2006.

Wolf, Allan. *The Watch That Ends the Night: Voices from the Titanic*. Candlewick, 2011.

Woodson, Jaqueline. *Show Way*. Illustrated by Hudson Talbott. G.P. Putnam's Sons Books for Young Readers, 2005.

Wyss, Johann David. *The Swiss Family Robinson*. Sharon, 1981 [1814].

Yamasaki, Katie. *Fish for Jimmy*. Holiday House, 2013.

Yang, Gene. *Boxers and Saint*. First Second, 2013.

Yolen, Jane. *Stone Angel*. Illustrated by Katie May Green. Philomel Books, 2015.

Young, Ed. *The House Baba Built: An Artist's Childhood in China*. Little, Brown & Co., 2011.

Chapter Nine

Nonfiction

Chapter Outline

Tati is a lively 6-year-old who loves to go to the school library because there she can choose any book she wants. At story time she listens eagerly to picture storybooks and other fiction, but the books she chooses to check out, to

©Bettie Parsons Barger.

keep for a time and to pore over at home, are nonfiction. Her favorites are about animals, insects, and the natural world. She often chooses books far above her level of understanding. Part of her fun is looking at the illustrations over and over again, but she also wants an adult to "read" these difficult books to her. In this case, she means reading the picture captions and talking through main ideas or intriguing details in response to her many questions. She joins in the reading by looking for words she knows or can figure out in the boldface headings or diagram labels.

Nonfiction for Today's Child

The audience for nonfiction books is broad, including young children as well as older students, girls as well as boys. Adult ideas about what is appropriate for a given age level are often less important than a child's desire to know about a particular topic. When reading nonfiction, young readers often read selected parts, like the captions, or choose their own order for exploring the pages. In this type of reading, visual materials play a vital part by focusing interest and clarifying or extending information. Most of all, our example of Tati shows how nonfiction literature can provide a powerful motivation to read and to enjoy experiences with books. Children are curious about the world and how it works, and they develop passionate attachments to the right books at the right time. They deserve teachers and librarians who can help them discover this particular kind of satisfaction in reading.

What Is Nonfiction?

Children's literature scholars use the term *nonfiction* books to designate literature for children that is based in the actual rather than the imagined. This includes a wide range of books written for children, such as biographies, history, true adventures, science, sports, photographic essays, and memoirs. Author Penny Colman argues that nonfiction "can be just as compelling, engaging, and beautifully written as good fiction."[1] In this chapter, we will address the wide variety of nonfiction available for children. Biographies will be addressed in Chapter 10.

New worlds and new interests await children between the covers of nonfiction books. The intrigue of the moonlight hunt of a mother coyote, the fascinating world of entomologists, or the search for the elusive snow leopards of Mongolia have all been revealed in attractive and inviting formats. For proof, have a look at Maria Gianferrari's *Coyote Moon*, Caitlin O'Connell and Donna M. Jackson's *The Elephant Scientist*, or Sy Montgomery's *Saving the Ghosts of the Mountain: An Expedition Among Snow Leopards of Mongolia*. Nonfiction books also offer children new perspectives on familiar topics, as can be found in David Macaulay's *Toilets: How It Works*. Some nonfiction books, like Sneed B. Collard's *Insects: The Most Fun Bug Book Ever* or Stephen Kramer's *Hidden Worlds: Looking Through a Scientist's Microscope*, have tremendous eye appeal and invite browsing. Others are

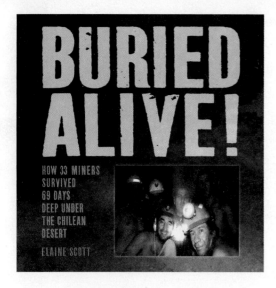

designed to reward sustained attention, like Russell Freedman's *Vietnam: A History of the War* or Elaine Scott's *Buried Alive!: How 33 Miners Survived 69 Days Deep Under the Chilean Desert*. Nonfiction books for children are more numerous, more varied, and more appealing than ever.

Awards for Nonfiction

For many years, nonfiction books were overlooked in awards given to children's literature. In 1981, author Betty Bacon pointed out that nonfiction books had won the Newbery Medal only six times in fifty-eight years, and those winners were from history or biography, in which the chronological narrative form is very much like fiction.[2] This is quite a contrast to literature for adults, where authors like John McPhee and Mary Roach regularly win critical acclaim for their work, and nonfiction frequently dominates the best-sellers lists. As a result of this imbalance, in 1990 the National Council of Teachers of English established the Orbis Pictus Award for Outstanding Nonfiction for Children. Its name commemorates what is considered to be the first book of facts produced for children, dating back to the seventeenth century. Recent winners include Jason Chin's *Grand Canyon*, Don Brown's *Drowned City: Hurricane Katrina & New Orleans*, and Candace Fleming's *The Family Romanov: Murder, Rebellion & the Fall of Imperial Russia*.

In 2000, the Association for Library Service to Children established the Robert F. Sibert Informational Book Medal to honor an author whose work of nonfiction has made a significant contribution to the field of children's literature in a given year. Candace Fleming's *Giant Squid* and Duncan Tonatiuh's *Funny Bones: Posada and His Day of the Dead*

Calaveras are among those titles named as Sibert Award winners or honor books. The Boston Globe-Horn Book Awards have included a nonfiction category since 1976. Some of the books recently recognized in this category have been Steve Jenkin's *The Animal Book: A Collection of the Fastest, Fiercest, Toughest, Cleverest, Shyest—and Most Surprising—Animals on Earth*, Christy Hale's *Dreaming Up: A Celebration of Building*, and Caitlin O'Connell and Donna M. Jackson's *The Elephant Scientist*. With the number of prestigious awards, there are now many more opportunities for all kinds of nonfiction books for children to receive the acclaim they deserve.

Evaluating Nonfiction Books

Critic Jo Carr has suggested that teachers and librarians who want to choose the very best books available should be guided by her view that a nonfiction writer is first a teacher, then an artist, and should be concerned with feeling as well as thinking and passion as well as clarity.[3] Specific criteria can be used to help identify this level of achievement. Being familiar with these criteria and with the types of books in which information is presented will make it easier to choose the best books at the right time. The individual reviewer must judge the relative value of the various criteria in terms of particular books. Sometimes a book's strengths in one or two categories may far outweigh its weakness in others. See **Guidelines: Evaluating Nonfiction Books** for an overview of these criteria.

Accuracy and Authenticity

Accuracy is of primary importance in nonfiction books for children. Inaccurate information, no matter how well it is presented, is problematic because young readers are likely to believe what is printed in a book is truth. The author's qualifications, the way in which the author presents facts and generalizations, the correctness of the illustrations, and many other factors need to be considered in evaluating a book's accuracy and authenticity.

The Author's Qualifications Nonfiction books are written by people who are authorities in their fields, such as astronaut Sally Ride, or they are written by writers who study a subject, interview specialists, and compile the data. A few, like naturalist Jean Craighead George, are both specialists and writers. It is always a good idea to check the book's jacket copy, title page, introduction, or "About the Author" page for information about the author's special qualifications, often expressed in terms of professional title or affiliation. Expertise in one field does not necessarily indicate competency in another, however, so we expect a high degree of authenticity only if the author has limited the book to what appears to be his or her specialty.

   If a book is written by a "writer," not by an expert in the field, facts can be checked by authorities and the authorities cited. For example, Donna M. Jackson is an insect enthusiast but is not a trained scientist. In *The Bug Scientists*, however, she acknowledges and names a long list of experts she interviewed and consulted, and photo credits show that the illustrations were furnished by individuals and universities with an established expertise. The record of sources and research provided here gives assurance that the book is accurate. A number of authors have earned the reputation of writing dependably good nonfiction books. When in doubt, teachers and librarians are likely to turn first to writers who have

Evaluating Nonfiction Books

Go to Connect® to access study resources, practice quizzes, and additional materials.

Consider the following when evaluating nonfiction books for children:

Accuracy and Authenticity
- Is the author qualified to write about this topic?
- Has the manuscript been checked by authorities in the field?
- Are the facts accurate according to other sources?
- Is the information up-to-date?
- Are all the significant facts included?
- Do text and illustrations reveal diversity and avoid stereotypes?
- Are generalizations supported by facts?
- Is there a clear distinction between fact and theory?
- Are the text and illustrations free of anthropomorphism or philosophical explanations?

Content and Perspective
- For what purpose was the book designed?
- Is the book within the comprehension and interest range of its intended audience?
- Is the subject adequately covered?
- Are different viewpoints presented?
- Does the book lead to an understanding of the scientific method?

- Does it foster the spirit of inquiry?
- Does the book show interrelationships?
- If it is a science book, does it indicate related social issues?

Style
- Is information presented clearly and directly?
- Is the text appropriate for the intended audience?
- Does the style create the feeling of reader involvement?
- Is the language vivid and interesting?

Organization
- Is the information structured clearly, with appropriate subheadings?
- Does the book have reference aids that are clear and easy to use, such as a table of contents, index, bibliography, glossary, and appendix?

Illustrations and Format
- Do illustrations clarify and extend the text or speak plainly for themselves?
- Are size relationships made clear?
- Are media suitable to the purposes for which they are used?
- Are illustrations explained by captions or labels where needed?
- Does the total format contribute to the clarity and attractiveness of the book?

proven their integrity with facts—Penny Colman, Candace Fleming, Marc Aronson, Philip Hoose, Laurence Pringle, and Seymour Simon, among others. But authorship, while it may be a valuable rule of thumb, is a dangerous final criterion. Each book must be evaluated on its own merits.

Factual Accuracy Fortunately, many of the errors of fact in children's nonfiction books are often minor. Children who have access to a variety of books on one topic should be encouraged to notice discrepancies and pursue the correct answer, a valuable exercise in critical reading.

Errors that teachers and children recognize are less distressing than those that pass for fact because the topic is unfamiliar or highly specialized; then the reader must depend on a competent reviewer to identify inaccuracies. Ideally, a book with technical information should be reviewed by someone with expertise in that field. *Appraisal: Science Books for Young People* is a periodical that offers paired reviews (a science professional and a teacher or librarian). *Science Books and Films* includes reviews by specialists in the field. *Horn Book Magazine* singles out natural science books for special reviewing efforts, although other nonfiction is included. The *School Library Journal* often provides helpful criticism. *Social Education* and *Science and Children* magazines also give some attention to appropriate books, and both publish a list of outstanding books in their respective fields each year. Both of these lists can be accessed through the Children's Book Council website at <www.cbcbooks.org>. Generally speaking, although natural science books may be easier for experts to challenge, representation issues in nonfiction about history and other topics in the humanities have been more frequently investigated.

Up-to-Dateness Some books that are free of errors at the time of writing become inaccurate with the passage of time, as new discoveries are made in the sciences or as changes occur in world politics. Books that focus on the past are less likely to be rapidly outdated, although new discoveries in archaeology or new theories in history and anthropology call for a reevaluation of these materials. Kathleen Weidner Zoehfeld's *Dinosaur Parents, Dinosaur Young* details the mistakes that, for many years, led scientists to believe that dinosaur parents did not care for their young. She describes how scientists Michael Novacek and Mark Norell were able to deduce that the oviraptor actually sat on its nest and incubated its eggs. This type of information helps children to understand how what we know about an extinct species changes as scientists continue to ask questions. Books that focus on subjects in which vigorous research and experimentation are being done, such as viruses and disease or space technology, are even more quickly outdated. It is worth noting that the latest trade books are almost always more up-to-date than the latest textbooks or print encyclopedias.

It is also difficult, but important, to provide children with current information about other countries where national governments are emerging or where future political developments are uncertain. Current events that generate an interest in books about a particular country also call attention to the fact that those books might be out-of-date. Internet sites provide an excellent way to keep track of current events, although these too require critical evaluation. The American Library Association lists more than seven hundred great sites for children. (Go to <www.ala.org> and search "Great Websites for Kids.") Teachers will want to make note of other sites vetted by professional organizations, such as the website for the National Council for the Social Studies <www.ncss.org> and the website for the National Science Teachers Association <www.nsta.org>. Books about diverse cultures also need to include material on contemporary experience, as well as heritage. Deborah Heiligman's *Holidays Around the World: Celebrate Ramadan and Eid al-Fitr with Praying, Fasting, and Charity* explains the reason for the Muslim holy month and provides a look at various ways its end is celebrated around the world. Sharing such books is a good way of combating stereotypes.

Inclusion of All the Significant Facts Although the material presented in a book might be current and technically correct, the book cannot be totally accurate if it omits significant facts. Forty years ago, biology books that dealt with animal reproduction frequently glossed over the specifics of mating or birth. Robert McClung's *Possum*, published in 1963, explains the process like this: "All night long the two of them wandered through the woods together. But at dawn each went his own way again. Possum's babies were born just twelve days later."[4] Fortunately, the changing social mores that struck down taboos in children's fiction in the 1990s have also encouraged a new frankness in nonfiction books. For instance, close-up photographs and forthright text in *How You Were Born* by Joanna Cole mark this as a straightforward book about human reproduction and birth. Gail Saltz's *Amazing You!* is a frank and engaging look at male and female sexual organs.

Human reproduction and sexuality have so often been distorted by omissions that books with accurate terminology and explicit information are particularly welcome. Robie H. Harris's *It's Not the Stork! A Book About Girls, Boys, Babies, Bodies, Families, and Friends* and *Who Has What?: All About Girls' Bodies and Boys' Bodies* are aimed at children in grades kindergarten to third. Older children and adolescents will find that Harris's *It's So Amazing: A Book About Eggs, Sperm, Birth, Babies, and Families* or *It's Perfectly Normal: A Book About Changing Bodies, Growing Up, Sex, and Sexual Health* are thorough and frank guides to adolescent and adult sexuality. In each of these books Michael Emberley's detailed illustrations add a wonderful touch of humor to what is often a touchy subject for this age group. *Sex Is a Funny Word: A Book About Bodies, Feelings, and YOU*, by Cory Silverberg, encourages upper-elementary and middle-grade readers to set boundaries, think for themselves, and ask questions about topics related to sexuality. Overall, in this inclusive book, Silverberg covers a variety of relationships, highlights gender diversity, and emphasizes the importance of trust, respect, and joy.

The honest presentation of all information necessary for understanding a topic is just as important in historical or cultural accounts as in the natural sciences. This may be difficult to achieve because social issues are complex, and writing for a young audience requires that the author be brief. Judging whether a book includes all the significant facts can also be difficult, for deciding what really counts is a matter of interpretation, often dependent on the book's intended audience. For many years, myths surrounding the first Thanksgiving went unchallenged. In *1621: A New Look at Thanksgiving*, Catherine O'Neill Grace and Margaret M. Bruchac, in cooperation with the staff of Plimoth Plantation, show how those myths evolved and present new information. They state:

> In 1947, the founders of Plimoth Plantation created a museum to honor the 17th-century English colonists who would come to be known to the world as the Pilgrims. In doing so, the founders left out the perspective of the Wampanoag people who had lived on the land for thousands of years. At Plimoth Plantation today, we ask questions about what really happened in the past. We draw from the new research of scholars who study documents, artifacts, home sites, culture, and formerly untapped sources such as the Wampanoag people themselves. (p. 7)

This fascinating account includes photographs taken at the museum site and shows children what the harvest festival was probably like. The book also provides an important lesson about historical research and the need to include many sources and many points of view when interpreting historical events. More recent books such as *Sarah Gives Thanks* by Mike Allegra have further contextualized this traditional holiday by examining the construction of the holiday.

Careful research by Catherine O'Neill Grace and Margaret M. Bruchac for *1621: A New Look at Thanksgiving* helps undo many of the stereotypes about the first "Thanksgiving" feast.
©S. Brimberg & C. Coulson/National Geographic Stock.

Avoidance of Stereotypes A book that omits significant facts tells only part of the truth; a book that presents stereotypes pretends, wrongly, to have told the truth. One very common sort of stereotyping is by omission. If we never see women or diverse races in science books, for instance, we are left with the incorrect impression that all scientists must be white males. In recent years, fortunately, more authors, illustrators, and publishers have made conscious efforts to represent the great variety of roles that women and underrepresented groups play in science and the world of work. Susan Kuklin's *Families*, which includes photographs and voices of children describing their families, surveys the many groupings of loving adults and children who make up today's families. This type of no-fanfare approach helps combat stereotypes because it encourages children to understand the contributions of people as a matter of course.

Another way authors try to avoid stereotyping is by relating the story of one individual within a community. Diane Hoyt-Goldsmith's books about Native Americans each focus on one Sovereign Nation and then on a particular child's family, school, and community experiences. Readers associate the facts in these books with specific persons and places. Consequently, they should be less likely to assume that this particular description of Native American life represents the way *all* people of Native American heritage live.

Use of Facts to Support Generalizations To be distinguished from stereotype or simple opinion, a proper generalization needs facts for support. Phillip Hoose provides such support throughout *The Race to Save the Lord God Bird*. Hoose is careful to make sure his readers understand that scientists are not sure if the ivory-billed woodpecker (nicknamed the Lord God Bird for its magnificent plumage) is extinct or not. Instead, Hoose takes readers through the tantalizing mystery of the bird's existence with facts about the sightings and search for the elusive bird. He also provides extensive notes of his sources in an afterword. Seymour Simon works with the Smithsonian Institute to give readers an introduction to climate change in *Global Warming*, using full-page color photographs and an exploration of the complex factors related to global warming. Critical readers need to be aware of generalizations and judge for themselves whether adequate facts are provided to support them.

Distinction Between Fact and Theory In their introduction to *The World Made New: Why the Age of Exploration Happened & How It Changed the World*, Marc Aronson and John W. Glenn state:

> In this book you will often notice us saying "we are not sure" ... That is not because we were lazy and forgot to check. Rather it is that, recently, historians have been re-examining evidence on these issues and making exciting new discoveries. (p. 5)

Careful writers like these make distinctions between fact and theory; but even so, children need guidance in learning to recognize the difference. Often the distinction depends on key words or phrases—such as *scientists believe*, *so far as we know*, or *perhaps*. Consider the importance of the simple phrase *may have* in this description of a prehistoric reptile: "Pterodactyls lived near the shores of prehistoric seas and may have slept hanging from trees." Books about the disappearance of the dinosaurs make good material for helping children sort out the difference between fact and theory, because the problem is dramatic and the evidence provides for legitimate disagreement among scientists. Franklyn Branley's *What Happened to the Dinosaurs?* does a particularly good job of helping primary-age children understand what a theory is. James Deem's *Faces from the Past: Forgotten People of North America* does a fine job (for older children) of examining the processes used by anthropologists and archaeologists that help artists to reconstruct the features of the people from the past.

"...gripping and informative."
—JARED DIAMOND, author of the best-selling Pulitzer-Prize-winner *Guns, Germs, and Steel*

NATIONAL GEOGRAPHIC

The World Made New

WHY THE AGE OF EXPLORATION
HAPPENED & HOW IT
CHANGED THE WORLD

Marc Aronson & John W. Glenn

Marc Aronson and John W. Glenn explain that what we know about history is constantly being updated by new research in *The World Made New: Why the Age of Exploration Happened & How It Changed the World*. ©Ngs Books/National Geographic Stock.

James Deem explains the process scientists use and the information they can glean when studying the skulls and skeletons found in archaeological digs in *Faces from the Past: Forgotten People of North America*.
Cover from *Faces from the Past: Forgotten People of North America* by James M. Deem. Copyright ©2012 by James M. Deem. Reprinted by permission of Houghton Mifflin Harcourt Publishing Company. All rights reserved.

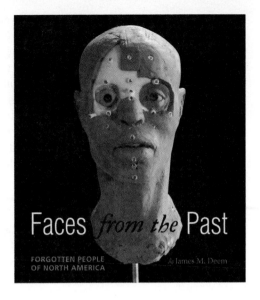

Although it is important to distinguish between fact and theory in all of the sciences, including the social sciences, the matter receives most attention in books dealing with evolution and human origins. This can be a very sensitive topic, but children have the right to access scientific knowledge, which would encompass well-supported theories regarding our origins. Laurence Pringle and Steve Jenkins have provided scientifically valid explanations. Their *Billions of Years, Amazing Changes: The Story of Evolution* is an excellent and visually appealing introduction for younger readers. Catherine Thimmesh's *Lucy Long Ago: Uncovering the Mystery of Where We Came From*, aimed at older children and adolescents, concentrates on the scientific process that built our present-day understanding. It is reassuring to note that balanced coverage of this important topic is available in nonfiction books at a time when many school districts are reluctant to include the topic in their curricula.

Avoidance of Anthropomorphism In poetry and fiction, the assignment of human feelings and behavior to animals, plants, or inanimate objects is called *personification*—an accepted literary device that can be used with great effect. In nonfiction, however, this device is unacceptable and is known as *anthropomorphism*. According to clinical psychologist Jean Piaget, the "magical beliefs of the child are integrally connected with the belief in animism, where the child regards as living and conscious a large number of inanimate objects."[5] Science writer Millicent Selsam addressed the problem of interpreting what animals do in one of her early books on animal behavior:

> It is hard to keep remembering that animals live in a different kind of world from our own. They see, hear, smell, and taste things differently. And they do not have human intelligence or emotions, so we must avoid interpreting their behavior in terms of our own feelings and thoughts. For example, it looks to us as though parent birds are devoted to their young in the same way that human parents are devoted to theirs. But only experimental work can show whether this interpretation is true.[6]

Many books with these anthropomorphic touches are still being published. Lorrie Mack's *Animal Families*, aimed at a preschool to primary-grade audience, looks at first glance as if it has all the qualities we ask for in nonfiction. There is a table of contents, a simple glossary and an index, appealing photographs, and attractive layout. The style of writing seems typically expository: "There are all kinds of animal families with different ways of life" (p. 8). Look more closely, however, and you will see that in addition to captions and labels on photographs there are speech bubbles where the animal "talks" to the audience. "'My brothers and sisters and I are all VERY hungry,' states a grizzly bear cub" (p. 13). Then in one double-page spread, a baby duck actually narrates the entire text. In *Antarctica*, an otherwise lovely book about the animal life on this great continent, Helen Cowcher tries to convey the negative impact of human intrusion on the animal life. She states, "Out at sea anxious songs ring out from the depths. Weddell seals call to their friends under the ice."[7] The words *anxious* and *friends* attribute human emotions and human relationships to the seals and may lead children to the types of interpretation that Selsam cautions against. Sandra Markle's *A Mother's Journey* is an emotionally gripping book about the Antarctic and its emperor penguins, but Markle and illustrator Alan Marks achieve that response through good writing and fine illustration.

Content and Perspective

Consideration of the purpose of a book, its intended audience, and the objectivity of its author can help readers evaluate a nonfiction book's content and perspective. A good nonfiction book should also foster reflective inquiry in children and enable them to see relationships across disciplines.

Purpose It is futile to try to pass judgment on the content of a nonfiction book without first determining the purpose for which the book was designed. Identifying the scope of the book lets us know what we can reasonably expect. A quick look at Steve Jenkin's *Animals by the Numbers: A Book of Animal Infographics* reveals a fascinating collection of facts for browsing, whereas both the title and the appearance of Nicola Davies's *Many: The Diversity of Life on Earth* indicate a comprehensive treatment of the topic. Titles can be misleading, particularly those that promise to tell "all about" a subject but offer limited coverage instead. At best, titles indicate the scope of the book's content and pique the reader's curiosity, as do titles such as Bridget Heos's *Stronger Than Steel: Spider Silk DNA and the Quest for Better Bulletproof Vests, Sutures, and Parachute Rope* and *Hidden Worlds: Looking Through a Scientist's Microscope* by Stephen Kramer. More about the scope and purpose of nonfiction books can be found in **Teaching Feature 9.1: Types of Nonfiction**.

teaching feature 9.1

Types of Nonfiction

Type	Description	Example Title	Author	Grade Level
Concept Books	Explore the characteristics of a class of objects or of an abstract idea.	*Snakes*	Nic Bishop	PreK–2
		Fabulous Frogs	Martin Jenkins	PreK–2
		Egg: Nature's Perfect Package	Steve Jenkins and Robin Page	PreK–2
		Round	Joyce Sidman	PreK–2
		Just a Second	Steve Jenkins	K–3
		Seeing Symmetry	Loreen Leedy	K–3

Type	Description	Example Title	Author	Grade Level
Craft and How-To Books	Give directions for making and doing.	*Super Simple Backyard Critter Crafts: Fun and Easy Animal Crafts*	Sammy Bosch	K–3
		Three-Dimensional Art Adventures: 36 Creative, Artist-Inspired Projects in Sculpture, Ceramics, Textiles, and More	Maja Pitamic and Jill Laidlaw	3–5
		Inkblot: Drip, Splat, and Squish Your Way to Creativity	Margaret Peot	4–6
Documents and Journals	Based on sketchbooks, journals, and original documents.	*Puffling Patrol*	Ted Lewin and Betsy Lewin	2–5
		America Is Under Attack: September 11, 2001: The Day the Towers Fell	Don Brown	2–5
		Ancient Earth Journal: The Late Jurassic: Notes, Drawing, and Observations from Prehistory	Juan Carlos Alonso and Gregory S. Paul	4–6
		A Dream of Freedom: The Civil Rights Movement from 1954 to 1968	Diane McWhorter	4 and up
		Far From Shore	Sophie Webb	4 and up
Experiment and Activity Books	Present activities or experiments to clarify concepts.	*Rosie Revere's Big Project Book for Bold Engineers*	Andrea Beaty	2–6
		Citizen Scientists: Be a Part of Scientific Discovery from Your Own Backyard	Loree Griffin Burns	3–6
		Catch the Wind, Harness the Sun: 22 Super-Charged Science Projects for Kids	Michael J. Caduto	4–6
Identification Books	Generally naming books, usually with simple drawings or photographs with appropriate labels.	*Transportation!*	Gail Gibbons	PreK–2
		Cars, Trains, Ships & Planes: A Visual Encyclopedia of Every Vehicle	Clive Gifford	2–5
		The Story of Buildings: From the Pyramids to the Sydney Opera House and Beyond	Patrick Dillon	4–6

(continued)

teaching feature 9.1

Type	Description	Example Title	Author	Grade Level
Life-Cycle Books	Cover all or some part of the life cycle of animals or plants.	*Owls*	Gail Gibbons	K–3
		Good Trick, Walking Stick!	Sheri Mabry Bestor	K–3
		The Hidden Life of a Toad	Doug Wechsler	K–3
Nonfiction Picturebooks	Convey information in well-designed picturebook format.	*A Beetle Is Shy*	Dianna Hutts Aston	PreK–3
		Underground	Shane W. Evans	K–3
		Bird Talk: What Birds Are Saying and Why	Lita Judge	K–3
		Coyote Moon	Maria Gianferrari	K–3
		Best in Snow	April Pulley Sayre	K–3
Photographic Essays	Photographs are used to particularize general information, to document emotion, and to assure the reader of truth in an essentially journalistic fashion.	*Leopard & Silkie: One Boy's Quest to Save the Seal Pups*	Brenda Peterson	PreK–3
		Face to Face with Wolves	Jim Brandenburg	2–5
		The School the Aztec Eagles Built: A Tribute to Mexico's World War II Air Fighters	Dorinda Makanaōnalani Nicholson	3–5
		¡Ole! Flamenco	George Ancona	3–5
		We Will Not Be Silent: The White Rose Student Resistance Movement That Defied Adolf Hitler	Russell Freedman	4–6
Specialized Books	Designed to give specific information about a relatively limited topic.	*Celebritrees: Historic & Famous Trees of the World*	Margi Preus	K–3
		Glow: Animals with Their Own Night-Lights	W. H. Beck	K–3
		Giant Squid	Candace Fleming	K–3
		The Great White Shark Scientist	Sy Montgomery	4 and up
		Animals by the Numbers: A Book of Animal Infographics	Steve Jenkins	K–3
Survey Books	Give an overall view of a substantial topic and furnish a representative sampling of facts, principles, or issues.	*Heart and Soul: The Story of Americans and African Americans*	Kadir Nelson	4–6
		Grover Cleveland, Again! A Treasury of American Presidents	Ken Burns	4–6
		Those Amazing Musical Instruments!	Genevieve Helsby	4 and up
		Venom	Marilyn Singer	4 and up

Intended Audience Before evaluating content, we have to know not just for what purpose the book was intended, but for whom. Book jackets and book reviews often indicate an age range according to reading level or interest. It is difficult to know whether one or both of these factors are reflected in the age recommendation. Generally, a book's reading level is not as important as its content in relation to the reader's actual interest in a subject. Older students and adults might turn to children's nonfiction books for introductory material on an unfamiliar topic. In using nonfiction books, children will read "beyond their abilities" when reading for particular facts. Children will frequently turn to difficult books if they contain interesting pictures or useful diagrams. At the same time, vocabulary, sentence length, size of type, and the book's organization are factors to be considered. Children might reject a book that contains useful information if they see crowded pages, relatively small type, and few pictures.

The choice of topic, then, is an important factor in determining whether a book will be suitable for its intended audience. Books for young children most often reflect their basic egocentric concerns and their curiosity about themselves and other living things; it is a mistake to assume that they will not be interested in other subjects, however. Many early primary children enjoy browsing through the widely diverse titles of the Eyewitness series, such as Laurence Mound's *Insect* or Colin McCarthy's *Reptiles*, even though these books are published for an older audience.

Adequacy of Coverage Recognizing the purpose of a book and its intended level, the reader has a basis for deciding if the author has said too much about the topic or too little. Jim Murphy's many fine books, such as *Breakthrough!: How Three People Saved "Blue Babies" and Changed Medicine Forever* and *Truce: The Day the Soldiers Stopped Fighting*, are more than one hundred pages. The focus of the topic is limited, but the treatment is detailed. Broader topics, like the history or culture of a nation, might require many pages in order to give even brief attention to all the significant material. History textbooks have earned particularly harsh criticism for faulty coverage,[8] and good trade books help fill in perspectives that the textbooks omit. A generation ago, Gerald Johnson expressed the need for careful writing in the introduction to his book *America Is Born*:

> Part of the story is very fine, and other parts are very bad, but they all belong to it, and if you leave out the bad parts you never understand it all. (pp. viii–ix)[9]

Authors who fail to acknowledge more than one viewpoint or theory fail to help children learn to critically examine issues. Even young children should know that authorities do not always agree, though the context might be simple. It is far more common, though, and certainly more necessary, for books about complex issues to deal with varying points of view.

Demonstration of Scientific Inquiry Because we are concerned about *how* as well as *what* children learn, it is important to note what kind of thinking a book encourages, as well as the body of facts it presents. Nonfiction books should illustrate the process of scientific inquiry, the excitement of discovery. Sandra Markle's *The Great Leopard Rescue: Saving the Amur Leopards* and Sy Montgomery's *The Great White Shark Scientist* give readers a good idea of the problems scientists try to solve and the kind of day-to-day work that is involved.

While these are fine accounts of the scientific method at work, the reader's involvement is still vicarious. Some books are designed to give children more direct experience with the skills of inquiry. Millicent Selsam's *How to Be a Nature Detective* encourages children to ask "What happened, who was here, and where did he go?" in order to learn how to read animal tracks. At each step of the process, Marlene Donnelly's illustrations help children follow this sequence as if they were actually outdoors, tracking various animals. Many of Jim Arnosky's books, such as *Hidden Wildlife: How Animals Hide in Plain Sight* and *Frozen Wild: How Animals Survive in the Coldest Places on Earth*, direct attention to important features in the outdoor environment and give background information that helps children interpret what they see.

Methods of scientific inquiry apply to the social sciences, too. In *Ain't Nothing But a Man: My Quest to Find the Real John Henry*, Scott Reynolds Nelson reveals the story of his own historical research as he attempts to find the story behind the legend of John Henry. The search leads him into many dead ends, but he eventually lays out a case for what he believes is the truth. The book is a fascinating tale of a real person who might have been behind the legend, and Nelson includes details about the building of a railroad in the story. *Ain't Nothing But a Man* is also a guide to conducting historical research with an afterword by Marc Aronson that encourages students to do their own research. Penny Colman's *Thanksgiving: The True Story* is also told in the first person and begins with the results of an informal survey she sent out asking adults and teens several questions about their understanding of the Thanksgiving story. One hundred percent of the teens and a majority of adults surveyed had learned that the first Thanksgiving was celebrated by Pilgrims and Indians in Plymouth, Massachusetts, in 1621. Colman went on to conduct further research and found at least twelve competing claims for holding the holiday first, from Texas in 1541 to Boston in 1631. In subsequent chapters, Colman elucidates on the competing claims, some of the oldest traditions of the holiday, Sarah Josepha Hale's campaign to have a national day of Thanksgiving, and the "Pilgrim and Indian" story. The book's second section surveys the types of gatherings, the food, and the activities that usually take place on Thanksgiving. The methodology and the organization of the book could easily be replicated by students who want to conduct their own research.

Interrelationships and Implications A list of facts is fine for an almanac, but nonfiction books should be expected to put facts into some sort of perspective. After all, linking facts in one way or another transforms information into knowledge. In *The Tragic Tale of the Great Auk*, Jan Thornhill provides an in-depth look at the multiple factors, from human predators to evolutionary changes, that led to the extinction of the Great Auk. Thornhill ends by highlighting the now-thriving ecosystems because the Great Auk no longer hunts there.

Interrelationships of a different sort are pointed out in Tonya Bolden's *How to Build a Museum*. This book helps readers see the cultural context of the building of the National Museum of African American History and Culture. The author uses photographs and artwork to tell the story of how it took a hundred years, and hundreds of people, to make the dream a reality. The vivid presentations of museum artifacts are especially good for prompting discussion about the relationship of one culture to another.

Intertwining science and technology with culture has become crucial, and many recent nonfiction books have taken this issue as a focus. In *Voyager's Greatest Hits*, Alexandra Siy details the journey of Voyager 1 and Voyager 2, launched in 1977. Each chapter describes a historical scientific discovery that connected with images sent back to Earth from the Voyagers in space over the past 40 years, using culture to ground the narrative. Even books not specifically designed to call attention to the related social problems of science and technology ought to acknowledge that such problems exist. Where the uses

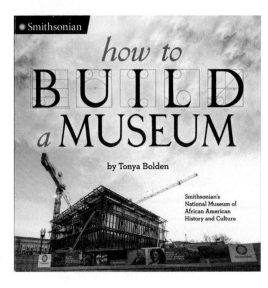

of science have serious implications for society, the relationships should be made clear.

Style

The style of a nonfiction book can be crucial in attracting children to the book and in helping them understand the concepts presented. The clarity of presentation and the appropriateness of the language for its intended audience are important matters to consider in evaluating a book's style. In addition, the writing should involve readers in the topic and provide them with an absorbing and vivid learning experience. Author Penny Colman suggests that in evaluating nonfiction writing, we should ask how authors effect transitions, craft the ending, "establish a point of view, create a sense of time, use adjectives, adverbs, metaphors, or varied sentence lengths."[10] These qualities of style are just as important in nonfiction as they are in fiction.

Clarity and Directness It is difficult to list all of the criteria that influence clarity. The use of precise language and specific detail is one important factor. Nothing is vague in Candace Fleming's *Giant Squid*. She explains that the size of a giant squid's eye is large "so it can spy pinpoints of light in its pitch-black world and that "some have even grown as large as 10 inches in diameter—the size of human head." The language is simple and direct, giving the reader a clear picture.

Many writers and publishers of nonfiction for children seem to believe that information needs to be presented in the guise of fiction. Some of the most popular nonfiction picturebooks of recent years are the Magic School Bus stories by Joanna Cole and Bruce Degen. *The Magic School Bus Inside the Earth* was followed by other titles. Although the story element in books like these might help children understand facts, they could also confuse children who are still sorting out real and make believe. In addition, when a picturebook is only loosely based in fact, as in *George Washington's Birthday: A Mostly True Tale* by Margaret McNamara or *Ice Boy* by David Ezra Stein, we cannot call it nonfiction (perhaps *informational fiction*[11] would be a good term), and we need to make sure children understand the difference. Across grade levels, teachers will need to help children develop their own criteria for evaluating nonfiction that includes ever finer distinctions between what is made up and what is not made up.

Level of Difficulty Although the vocabulary does have to be within the child's range, books for primary-grade children need not be restricted to a narrow list of words. New terms can be explained in context. In *Follow the Water from Brook to Ocean*, Arthur Dorros provides a two-paragraph description of the effects of moving water before introducing the word *erosion*. He also gives helpful context through examples and illustrations for the words *meanders* and *reservoir*. Context does not serve to explain everything, however; a writer aware of the background of the intended audience takes pains to make new words clear. Words that look unpronounceable are another stumbling block for most children. A glossary is helpful, but youngsters who are intent on a book's content might not take time to look in the back. In some cases, authors provide pronunciation guides in parentheses for daunting words. Such is the case in Caroline Arnold's *Global Warming and the Dinosaurs: Fossil Discoveries at the Poles* and Sara Gillingham's *Alpha, Bravo, Charlie: The Complete Book of Nautical Codes*.

Reader Involvement Authors use many different techniques to engage their readers' attention and help them stay involved with a book's subject matter. Alexandra Siy begins *Mosquito Bite* with black-and-white photographs of a girl and a boy playing a backyard game of hide-and-seek. As the boy peeks from behind a tree, the tantalizing text reads like the introduction to a horror film:

> He listens. He hears the girl's footsteps near the garden, or the driveway, now by the flowers along the walk. She's getting closer. Suddenly there's another sound. A droning buzz. The boy's hand flutters across his face and brushes the back of his neck. Something else is looking for the boy. (p. 5)

Siy and photographer Dennis Kunkel then go on to describe the life cycle of the *Culex pipiens* mosquito using stunning colorized electron micrographs.

Nonfiction authors also use direct address sentences that speak to the reader as "you," as in Giles Laroche's *If You Lived Here, Houses of the World*. Sometimes an author asks direct questions to claim a bond of communication with the reader. Robin Page hooks the primary-grade audience with intriguing questions in *A Chicken Followed Me Home! Questions and Answers about a Familiar Fowl*.

One technique that lends itself to nonfiction for children is called "creative nonfiction." Such writers of adult nonfiction as Annie Dillard and Frank Conroy have long used this approach to invigorate their topics.[12] Author Penny Colman explains that in writing creative nonfiction, "I adhere to the basic tenets of nonfiction writing as well as use stylistic and narrative strategies traditionally found in fiction."[13] Colman begins *Corpses, Coffins, and Crypts: A History of Burial* with her own reflection about spending the day with her uncle's dead body. In subsequent chapters, she relays the real-life experiences of many others to cover subjects such as autopsies, embalming and cremation, and burial customs. These real-life experiences and personal reflections add zest to her explanations, yet her meticulous research and attention to detail are evident not only in her writing but also in her extensive use of archival material and site visits. The results are highly engaging books.

Vividness of Language The writer of nonfiction books uses the same techniques as the writer of fiction to bring a book to life, although the words must be accurate as well as attractive. Imagery is used to appeal to the senses, as in Juan Carlos Alonso and Gregory S. Paul's *The Late Jurassic: Notes, Drawings, and Observations from Prehistory*:

> Standing in lush green surroundings, you take a deep breath and notice how thick the air is with humidity. The unique smell of wet and decomposing plant matter overwhelms you as the sound of insects rings endlessly in your ears. The air is stifling hot, making it exhausting to get around. The Late Jurassic does not welcome visitors. (p. 6)

Phillip Hoose's *Moonbird: A Year on the Wind with the Great Survivor B95* begins with this soaring image:

> B95 can feel it: stirring in his bones and feathers. It's time. Today is the day he will once again cast himself into the air, spiral upwards into the clouds and bank into the wind, working his newly molted flight feathers for real. (p. 3)

Children probably will not be able to describe an author's style, but they certainly will respond to it. They know that a well-written nonfiction book somehow does not sound the same as an encyclopedia essay, and they enjoy the difference.

Organization

Even if a book is vividly written, accurate, and in command of its topic, children will not find it very useful unless it also furnishes a clear arrangement of information. The way a book's content is structured and the reference aids it includes should help readers find and understand key concepts and facts.

Structure Every author must choose a structure, or organizing principle, as a basis for presenting facts. Sometimes an author uses a very obvious principle, such as organizing a collection of facts alphabetically. This format allows Lulu Delacre to introduce readers to interesting details about the Ecuadoran Andes in the bilingual book *¡Olinguito, de la A a la Z!: Descubriendo el Bosque Nublado/ Olinguito, from A to Z! : Unveiling the Cloud Forest.* In this book, as in others, the alphabet device makes a good format for browsing and is easily understood by children, although it pays less attention to the relationships among facts.

The question-and-answer approach has become more widely used in recent years. For very young children, questions and pictured answers can change a concept book into an engaging guessing game. Steve Jenkins and Robin Page's *What Do You Do With a Tail Like This?* repeats the question in the book's title with changes to the animal's body part each time and supplies multiple answers when readers turn the page and discover what indeed the various animals do with the body part. Etta Kaner's Have You Ever Seen? series includes hard-to-resist titles such as *Have You Ever Seen a Duck in a Raincoat?, Have You Ever Seen a Stork Build a Log Cabin?*, and *Have You Ever Seen a Hippo with Sunscreen?* These books, meant for children in the primary grades, follow a question-and-answer pattern such as: "Have you ever seen a polar bear build an igloo? That's silly. People build igloos. How could a polar bear build an igloo?" followed by a page of information about how female polar bears do indeed "build dens in hard-packed snow." National Geographic Kids has a board book series, called Look and Learn, for younger readers to enjoy. Titles, like *Birds, In My Garden*, and *Big Cats*, provide vivid images, introductory information, and engaging questions.

A common and sensible arrangement for many books, especially about history or biological processes, is based on chronology. Kate Waters's *Samuel Eaton's Day* and *Sarah Morton's Day* allow modern-day children to compare their own morning-to-nighttime activities to those of children who lived almost four hundred years ago.

Regardless of its topic, a general survey type of book should have a system of headings that helps the reader get an overview of the content, unless the book is very brief and has pictures that serve as graphic guides for skimming. The longer the book and the more complex its topic, the greater the need for manageable division. Subheadings are helpful as indicators of structure, especially for less-practiced readers.

Reference Aids With the exception of certain simple and special types, factual books should offer help at both front and back for the reader who needs to locate information quickly. It is important for children to develop reference skills early, so a table of contents and an index should be included in any book whose structure warrants it. Ann Morris's concept books for younger children, including *Shoes, Shoes, Shoes,* provide visual indexes with additional information about each of the countries that she has visited in photographs in the books. A map identifies each of the countries shown in the pictures. This is a good way to introduce younger readers to indexes and other reference aids. For older children, an index will be truly useful only if it is complete and has necessary cross-references. It is difficult to think of all the possible words children might use to look up a topic or to answer a question, yet writers should consider as many possibilities as seem reasonable.

Other helpful additions to a book are glossaries, bibliographies, pronunciation guides, suggestions for further reading, and nonfiction appendixes. Picture glossaries are on the increase with the growing number of nonfiction picturebooks. Anne Schreiber includes a picture glossary of photographs in her National Geographic Readers series of books such as *Sharks, Penguins,* and *Monkeys.* These books would be good for demonstrating to children the use of reference aids, because they have touches of humor that add appeal as well as a full range of devices for locating and extending information.

If children are to understand methods of inquiry, they need to learn that a writer uses many sources of information. Penny Colman's *Corpses, Coffins, and Crypts* has five pages of references. In an author's note Colman provides information about the people whose experiences she related, and she lists the sources that were particularly helpful to her. Photo credits that include many of her own photographs show how thorough and wide-ranging her research was.

Appendixes are used to extend information in lists, charts, or tabulations of data that would seem cumbersome in the text itself. *Commodore Perry in the Land of the Shogun,* Rhoda Blumberg's award-winning account of the opening of Japanese harbors to American ships, seems all the more credible because of the documents and lists presented in the appendixes. Having read that lavish gifts were exchanged during the negotiations, children can discover in an appendix that the emperor was offered more than thirty items, including two telegraph sets, a copper lifeboat, champagne, tea, muskets, swords, and two mail-bags with padlocks.

Illustrations and Format

In our visually oriented culture, readers of all ages demand that a book's illustrations make it more interesting and attractive. In a nonfiction book, the illustrations and design must do that, and much more. Researchers who have traditionally focused on the grammar or structures of written text have turned to the construction of visual text and have demonstrated how important these visual elements are to understanding of meaning and concepts, especially in nonfiction. Even young children readily learn to "read" the information in pictures and format.

Clarification and Extension of Text One of the basic functions of the visual material in nonfiction books is to clarify and extend the text. The visual material consists of illustrations and photographs but can also include such devices as labels, cutaways, cross-sections, diagrams, and graphs. Books by Gail Gibbons such as *Ladybugs* and *The Fruits We Eat* provide younger readers with a first look at these visual devices.

The more abstract the topic, the more important it is that pictures help children "see" explanations. Latitude, longitude, and other mapping concepts, for instance, are often hard for children to grasp, so it is especially important that they be illustrated clearly, as they are in Heather Alexander's *Child's Introduction to the World: Geography, Cultures, and People.* These big, bright pictures use color to focus attention on the equator, contour lines, and other specific aspects of simplified maps.

Illustrations are especially important in clarifying size relationships. The photographs for Teruyuki Komiya's oversized books—*Life-Size Zoo*, *Life-Size Farm*, and *Life-Size Aquarium*—show the actual size of familiar animals. Illustrator Steve Jenkins has delighted younger children with his *Actual Size*, which makes use of an extra-large trim size, double-page spreads, and foldouts to give children a sense of their own size in relation to different animals. For example, only the teeth of the great white shark are shown on a twelve-inch by twenty-inch double-page spread. Not many topics lend themselves to life-size portrayals, of course, and that makes it important for artists to find other ways to be clear. Photographs and drawings often show magnified parts or wholes, and often some information about actual size is needed.

In nonfiction books such as *Ladybugs* by Gail Gibbons, children learn to recognize visual materials such as cross-sections, labels, and diagrams. ©2012 by Gail Gibbons.

In many books, the visual materials add detail and extend the information of the text; in others, the illustrations themselves provide the bulk of the information, or become the subject of the text. In Walter Wick's *A Drop of Water*, the amazing photographs invite the reader to ask questions about such things as how a straight pin can indent the surface of water in a glass or how a huge bubble can rest on a metal frame. The text functions here to clarify and extend the pictures rather than the other way around. When illustrations are this important to a book, they need to have substantive content, high-quality reproduction, and a logical presentation or layout. For other good examples of effective presentation, look at Seymour Simon's books about rocks and minerals or Ted Lewin and Betsy Lewin's *How to Babysit a Leopard*.

In some picturebooks, the aesthetic quality of the illustrations and book format further enhance the book's information. *Circle* by Jeannie Baker is a stunningly beautiful description of the migration of Godwits birds whose 7,000-mile journey is one of the longest migratory routes of the animal world. Baker uses collage and changes points of view and the depiction of space to leave the reader in awe of these amazing bird feats. The book format for Jean Fritz's *Leonardo's Horse* has a rounded dome added to the traditional rectangular cover. This, along with the gold foil endpapers and Hudson Talbot's lovely illustrations, pays visual tribute to Leonard's artistic genius.

Suitability of Media Both illustrations and photographs can be clear and accurate, but one medium might be more suitable than another for a given purpose. We have talked with some young children who believe that a book is nonfiction because it has photographs and fiction because it has illustrations. It is important for teachers to help students think about why a particular medium has been chosen for a particular subject.

Paul Carrick and Bruce Shillinglaw's paintings in *Dinosaur Parents, Dinosaur Young: Uncovering the Mystery of Dinosaur Families* by Kathleen Weidner Zoehfeld are important in allowing the reader to visualize the circumstances that may have led to the creation of the oviraptor fossils. Illustrators can also create cutaways, diagrams, and other visuals that would not be possible with photographs. On the other hand, paintings would not create the sense of wonder that photographs do in *Hidden Worlds: Looking through a Scientist's Microscope* by Stephen Kramer. It is important for teachers to help children consider the reasons for the choices of media for nonfiction books. Diagrams and drawings have an impact of their own and also have many uses especially appropriate to science books. Diagrams can reduce technological processes to their essentials or show astronomical relationships that represent distances too great to be photographed.

Sometimes the perception of a graphic artist is vital to the purpose of a book. David Macaulay's *The Way Things Work*, *The Way Things Work Now*, and *The Way We Work* explain how mechanical devices and human bodies work, and though all books have an engaging, almost lighthearted approach, they represent years of research from this talented author. His *Cathedral*, *City*, *Castle*, *Pyramid*, and *Mosque* lead us step-by-step through the building of these amazing constructions and also demonstrate the ways in which humans have been involved in their conception and their use. Macaulay certainly set the standard for excellence, attention to detail, and touches of humor in his illustrated nonfiction.

In spite of the range of media available for nonfiction books, the medium of choice is now photography. Photographs help establish credibility for real-life stories like Diane Hoyt-Goldsmith's *Las Posadas: An Hispanic Christmas Celebration* and add to the fascination of such topics as bog people in James M. Deem's *Bodies from the Ash*. Photographs reveal the natural world in its astonishing variety, recording minute detail in an instant. The photos by Nic Bishop for Joy Cowley's *Chameleon, Chameleon* and *Red-Eyed Tree Frog* and for his book *Lizards* reveal marvels of skin textures, colors, and patterns that would be difficult to reproduce with complete accuracy in a painting.

Photographs in nonfiction books furnish more than technical accuracy, however. Photographers

Eye-catching photographs and an appealing title will invite children to pick up *Hidden Worlds: Looking Through a Scientist's Microscope* **by Stephen Kramer.**

can be artists as well as recorders of information. Sometimes artistry results not from a single photographer's work but from the careful choice of pictures to accompany a nonfiction text. The photographs that illustrate Seymour Simon's many books come from a variety of sources, but their effect is breathtaking in such books as *Butterflies, Insects, Horses, Water,* and *Crocodiles and Alligators.*

Captions Children need to be able to look at an illustration and know what they are seeing, and that requires a wise use of captions and labels. Many writers use the text itself, if it is brief, to explain the pictures, eliminating the need for additional captions. The short paragraphs in much of Seymour Simon's *Extreme Earth Records* and Peter Lourie's *The Polar Bear Scientists* are clearly situated next to their photographs. The arrangement of the text on the page and clear references to details in each picture help readers get maximum information about the biologists' study of the threatened species and their conservation efforts.

Sometimes it is helpful to have labels or other text printed within the illustration itself. In *Far from Shore: Chronicles of an Open Ocean Voyage* by naturalist Sophie Webb, the birder uses a journal to record her observations on a research cruise. Webb's field guide-like documentation includes paintings, detailed notes, and a variety of drawings with labels and captions. However an author chooses to use captions, they should be clear.

Format The total look of a book is its *format,* involving type size, leading (space between the lines), margins, placement of text and pictures, and arrangement of front and back matter—these include title and copyright pages in the front and indexes, bibliographies, and other aids at the back. *Mummies Made in Egypt* by Aliki incorporates hieroglyphic writing on the dedication and half-title pages, and many of the illustrations are arranged like the friezes that decorated the tombs of antiquity. This author frequently arranges sequences of pictures on the page in a comic strip or storyboard variation.

There are no absolute rules for format; the look of a book should be responsive to its purpose and its content. The broad coverage of topic intended in the Eyewitness series published by DK makes the busy layout of its pages seem rich rather than crowded. On the other hand, Steve Jenkins's nonfiction books for younger children including *Actual Size* and *Down, Down, Down: A Journey to the Bottom of the Sea,* as well as his book with Robin Page, *My First Day,* feature a less complicated page layout with bright full-color collage illustrations. Even a book that is sparingly illustrated can be notable for its overall design. Spacious margins and tastefully ornamented headings can make a long text seem less forbidding. The format of a nonfiction book is an asset if it contributes to clarity or if it makes the book more appealing to its audience.

Challenging Perspectives on Nonfiction

Children are naturally curious about the world around them. For some children, however, reading nonfiction may be difficult as it requires a different repertoire of skills, or a mastery of a different set of reading strategies, than those needed to read fiction. As teachers help students learn to read in the content areas (e.g., math, science, and social studies), the understanding of the structure and specialized vocabulary of nonfiction produce particular challenges for both teaching and learning.

When reading fiction, we start at the beginning of the book, we read all the words, on all the pages, until we get to the end of the text. This strategy is fine for reading most traditional fiction, but some readers have difficulty transferring this skill set to reading nonfiction. For instance, students would not read a cookbook from beginning to end if they want to find out how to cook french toast or two pasta dishes. They would go to the table of contents, find the recipe, turn to that page, and follow those directions. Similarly, students reading *Atlas of Adventures* may enjoy skimming through the pages, finding a map of a particular continent and reading about what makes the continent unique before moving to another place in the book. For example, if they want to look up information about the continent of Africa, they would use the index and map and globe skills learned from social studies to find and read about the location.

Gathering of information and learning about new things may require developing instructional strategies focused on the study of illustrations, diagrams, charts, and graphs, and less time with print awareness, phonemic awareness, phonics, or fluency. To increase comprehension, readers will have to stop and think about what they are reading and make sure they understand how to synthesize the content before they can can continue reading and taking in new information. It may require students to look in other books for more information and to learn unfamiliar vocabulary and concepts.

For elementary classroom teachers, the controversies with this genre are usually reduced to how much "reality" children can handle. *Gay & Lesbian History for Kids: The Century-Long Struggle for LGBT Rights* is a book of powerful stories chronicling the historical and contemporary struggles and contributions of LGBTQIA people in America. Some teachers believe the nature of some of the content is not developmentally appropriate for young readers, even though the book received the 2016 National Council for the Social Studies Notable Book List. The point is that books that are reviewed and receive awards or teaching recommendation may still not be used by teachers due to what they believe is inappropriate content.

As with contemporary realistic fiction, some parents, caregivers, administrators, and community members feel that some nonfiction materials are excessively violent or too scary for children. Cynthia Levinson, author of *We Got A Job*, a book that follows four young children who took part in the volatile 1963 civil rights protests in Birmingham, Alabama, received starred reviews from multiple children's book reviewers. However, Levinson said that although she didn't want to write "revisionist" history, she, her editor, and publisher did debate whether the vicious dog attacks described in the text and the photographs would be "too scary" for young children. They mulled over what age recommendation to set. The book is recommended for children aged 10 and older, though Levinson points out that Audrey, one of the children she writes about is, was only 9 years old when she lived through the marches and arrests.

Concerns range from texts with mature themes (e.g., human sexuality or graphic language) to disturbing illustrations some feel are unsuitable for children. Examples of children's books that have received both school and public library request for removal include the following:

- *And Tango Makes Three* by Peter Parnell and Justin Richardson (true story/homosexuality, religious views, developmentally inappropriate).

- *It's Perfectly Normal: Changing Bodies, Growing Up, Sex, and Sexual Health* by Robie H. Harris and Michael Emberley (nudity, sex education).

- *I am Jazz*, by Jazz Jennings and Shelaugh McNichols (transgender child, language, sex education, offensive viewpoints).

There is no recipe or formula that a teacher can use to know whether a book will be appropriate or not. Teachers must know their children in order to make selections that are appropriate to the development of their students. The nonfiction collections found in classrooms and school libraries are intended to serve a wide variety of interests and a very diversified student population. When an issue of current interest seems controversial or unresolved, the classroom teacher should gather from the genre, nonfiction in this case, materials showing a variety of viewpoints and differing opinions on that issue. Today's children have an immense capacity to analyze, critique, and challenge the realities of their daily lives. Using nonfiction can be just one tool to help facilitate increasing the knowledge base as children continue to make sense of the world.

There are a number of important reasons that support using nonfiction with children:[14]

- **Nonfiction provides the key to success in later schooling.** As readers advance in grade, they more frequently face content-area textbooks as well as informational passages on tests. Including more nonfiction texts in early schooling puts them in a better position to handle reading and writing demands in later grades.

- **Nonfiction prepares students to handle real-life reading.** Studies show that adults read a great deal of nonfiction both at home and on the job.[15,16] Also, there is a growing reliance upon web-based material and the need for information competency, including how to interpret and evaluate information. Thus, students must be able to read and write informational text.

- **Nonfiction appeals to readers' preferences.** As Ron Jobe and Mary Dayton-Sakari describe in *Info-Kids: How to Use Nonfiction to Turn Reluctant Readers into Enthusiastic Learners*, some students simply prefer information text. Using these resources in your classroom may improve attitudes toward reading and even serve as a catalyst for overall literacy development.[17]

- **Nonfiction addresses students' questions and interests.** Many studies have illustrated that regardless of readers' text preferences, when the text *topic* interests them, their reading is likely to improve. Not surprisingly then, approaches emphasizing reading for the purpose of addressing students' real questions tend to lead to higher achievement and motivation.[18]

- **Nonfiction builds knowledge of the natural and social world.** Students who are reading and listening to nonfiction will develop a greater knowledge of the world,[19,20] acquiring background knowledge that will help them comprehend subsequent texts.[21] Overall, the more background knowledge readers have, the stronger their comprehension skills are likely to be.

- **Nonfiction boosts vocabulary and other kinds of literacy knowledge.** According to researchers, parents and teachers focus more on vocabulary and literacy concepts when reading nonfiction texts aloud versus when they read narrative text.[22,23] This extra attention from parents and teachers may make nonfiction well suited for building a student's word knowledge.[24,25] Learning to read diagrams, tables, and other graphical devices that are often part of informational text may develop visual literacy.

Go to Connect® for a sample of how to use the Ten-Point Model to incorporate nonfiction into the classroom.

Using Nonfiction to Address Standards

Nonfiction books have been written on many topics, but even books on a single topic can be used to support content standards from a range of subjects. For example, books about animals could teach about social studies, language arts, and even math concepts in addition to science. Animals and their effects on people, whether from the distant past like dinosaurs or the present, can come to life for students through books.

Suggested Children's Book: *Animals by the Numbers: A Book of Animal Infographics* by Steve Jenkins (Houghton Mifflin Harcourt, 2016).

Steve Jenkins's fresh approach to fascinating information about animals is visually depicted in charts, graphs, and numbers. His colorful art, combined with the incredible infographics, will grab the attention of readers of all ages. Which animal jumps the farthest? What animal is considered the most deadly? How far can animals jump? All of these questions and more are explored.

Subject	Standards	Classroom Ideas
Language Arts, Math, Science, and Social Studies	**NCTM:** Recognize the differences in representing categorical and numerical data. Evaluate how well each representation shows important aspects of the data. **NCTE/ILA (reading):** Students read a wide range of print and nonprint texts to acquire new information. **NCSS:** Demonstrate the ability to correctly use vocabulary associated with time, such as past, present, future, and long ago; read and construct simple timelines. **NGSS:** For any particular environment, some kinds of organisms survive well, some survive less well, and some cannot survive at all.	Pick a topic, like horns or temperature, and study that double-page spread. Reflect on what the visual infographics tell you about each topic. Reflect on how the visuals tell you the information.
Art, Language Arts, and Technology	**NCCAS:** Convey meaning through the presentation of artistic work. **NCTE/ILA:** Students participate as knowledgeable, reflective, creative, and critical members of a variety of literacy communities.	Research another topic that is not in *Animals by the Numbers* in a small group. Determine your facts and create a multimodal infographic to display your information.

Subject	Standards	Classroom Ideas
	ISTE: Students know and use a deliberate design process for creating innovative artifacts.	
	NCTE/ILA (writing): Students apply knowledge of language structure, language conventions (e.g., spelling and punctuation), media techniques, figurative language, and genre to create, critique, and discuss print and nonprint texts.	
Textual Connections	*The Animal Book* (Jenkins); *Can an Aardvark Bark*? (Stewart); *The Big Book of Animals of the World* (Könnecke); *National Geographic Book of Animal Poetry: 200 Poems with Photographs That Squeak, Soar, and Roar!* (Lewis)	
Other Books by Jenkins	Written by Jenkins: *Apex Hunters: The World's Deadliest Hunters, Past and Present*; *Down, Down, Down: A Journey to the Bottom of the Sea*; and *Actual Size*	
	Written by Jenkins and Robin Page: *What Do You Do With a Tail Like This?*; *How to Swallow a Pig*; *Creature Features*; *Egg*; and *Sleep*.	
	Illustrated by Jenkins: *Eat Like a Bear* (Sayre); *Hello Baby!* (Fox); and *Animal Poems* (Worth)	
Author's Website	http://www.stevejenkinsbooks.com	

Sources: International Society for Technology in Education (ITSE); National Coalition for Core Arts Standards (NCCAS); National Council of Teachers of English (NCTE)/International Literacy Association (ILA); National Council of Teachers of Mathematics (NCTM); National Council for the Social Studies (NCSS) Curriculum Standards; and Next Generation Science Standards (NGSS).

Notes

1. Penny Colman, "Nonfiction Is Literature Too," *New Advocate* 12.3 (summer, 1999): 217.
2. Betty Bacon, "The Art of Nonfiction," *Children's Literature in Education* 12 (spring, 1981): 3.
3. Jo Carr, "Writing the Literature of Fact," in *Beyond Fact: Nonfiction for Children and Young People* (Chicago: American Library Association, 1982), pp. 3–12.
4. Robert McClung, *Possum* (New York: Morrow, 1963), p. 41.
5. Andre F. Favat, "Child and Tale : The Origins of Interest." National Council of Teachers of English Research Committee. Research Report No. 19. National Council of Teachers of English, 1977.
6. Millicent Selsam, *Animals as Parents*, illustrated by John Kaufmann (New York: 1965), p. 16.
7. Helen Cowcher, *Antarctica* (New York: Farrar, Strauss & Giroux, 1990), unpaged.
8. See Frances FitzGerald, *America Revised* (Boston: Atlantic/Little, Brown, 1979).

9. Gerald White Johnson, *America Is Born*, illustrated by Leonard Everett Fisher (New York: William Morrow, 1959).

10. Colman, "Nonfiction Is Literature Too," p. 220.

11. See Carol Avery, "Nonfiction Books: Naturals for the Primary Level," in *Making Facts Come Alive: Choosing Quality Nonfiction for Children*, ed. Rosemary Banford and Janice Kristo (Norwood, Mass.: Christopher Gordon, 1998).

12. Lee Gutkind, "From the Editor: The 5R's of Creative Nonfiction," *Creative Nonfiction* 6 (1996): 1–16.

13. Colman, "Nonfiction Is Literature Too," p. 219.

14. N. K. Duke, V. S. Bennett-Armistead, and E. M. Roberts, "Bridging the Gap Between Learning to Read and Reading to Learn," in *Literacy and Young Children: Research-Based Practice*, ed. D. M. Barone and L. M. Morrow (New York: Guilford Press, 2003), pp. 226–42.

15. R. L. Venezky, "The Origins of the Present-Day Chasm Between Adult Literacy Needs and School Literacy Instruction," *Visible Language* 16 (1982): 112–27.

16. M. C. Smith, "The Real-World Reading Practices of Adults," *Journal of Literacy Research* 32 (2000): 25–32.

17. Ron Jobe and Mary Dayton-Sakiri, *Info-Kids: How to Use Nonfiction to Turn Reluctant Readers into Enthusiastic Learners* (Portland, Maine: Stenhouse Publishers, 2002).

18. J. T. Guthrie, P. Van Meter, A. D. McCann, A. Wigfield, L. Bennett, et al. "Growth in Literacy Engagement: Changes in Motivations and Strategies During Concept-Oriented Reading Instruction," *Reading Research Quarterly* 31 (1996): 306–32.

19. E. Anderson and J. T. Guthrie, *Motivating Children to Gain Conceptual Knowledge from Text: The Combination of Science Observation and Interesting Texts*, paper presented to the annual meeting of the American Educational Research Association, Montreal, Canada, April 1999.

20. N. K. Duke and J. Kays, "Can I Say Once Upon a Time? Kindergarten Children Developing Knowledge of Information Book Language," *Early Childhood Research Quarterly* 13 (1998): 295–318.

21. P. T. Wilson and R. C. Anderson, "What They Don't Know Will Hurt Them: The Role of Prior Knowledge in Comprehension," in *Reading Comprehension from Research to Practice*, ed. J. Oransano (Hillside, N.J.: Erlbaum, 1986).

22. J. M. Mason, C. L. Peterman, B. M. Powell, and B. M. Kerr, "Reading and Writing Attempts by Kindergarteners After Book Reading by Teachers," in *Reading and Writing Connections*, ed. J. M. Mason (Boston: Allyn & Bacon, 1989), pp. 105–120.

23. A. D. Pelligrini, J. C. Perlmutter, L. Galda, and G. H. Brody, "Joint Reading Between Head Start Children and Their Mothers," *Child Development* 61 (1990): 443–53.

24. M. J. Dreher, "Fostering Reading for Learning," in *Engaging Young Readers: Promoting Achievement and Motivation*, ed. L. Baker, M. J. Dreher, and J. Guthrie (New York: Guilford, 2000), pp. 94–118.

25. N. K. Duke, V. S. Bennett-Armistead, and E. M. Roberts, "Incorporating Information Text in the Primary Grades," in *Comprehensive Reading Instruction Across Grade Levels*, ed. C. Roller (Newark, Del.: International Reading Association, 2002).

Children's Literature

*Go to **Connect**® to access study resources, practice quizzes, and additional materials.*

Titles in blue = multicultural titles

Aliki (Aliki Brandenberg). *Mummies Made in Egypt.* Crowell, 1979.

Allegra, Mike. *Sarah Gives Thanks: How Thanksgiving Became a National Holiday.* Illustrated by David Gardner. Albert Whitman, 2012

Alexander, Heather. *Child's Introduction to the World: Geography, Cultures, and People.* Illustrated by Meredith Hamilton. Black Dog & Leventhal, 2010.

Alonso, Juan Carlos and Gregory S. Paul. *Ancient Earth Journal: The Late Jurassic: Notes, Drawing, and Observations from Prehistory.* Illustrated by Juan Carols Alonso. Walter Foster Junior, 2016.

Ancona, George. *¡Ole! Flamenco.* Lee & Low, 2010.

Arnold, Caroline. *Global Warming and the Dinosaurs: Fossil Discoveries at the Poles.* Illustrated by Laurie Caple. Clarion, 2009.

Arnosky, Jim. *Frozen Wild: How Animals Survive in the Coldest Places on Earth.* Sterling Children's Books, 2015.

_____. *Hidden Wildlife: How Animals Hide in Plain Sight*. Sterling Children's Books, 2017.

Aronson, Marc, and John W. Glenn. *The World Made New: Why the Age of Exploration Happened & How It Changed the World*. Illustrated by Gil Davies. National Geographic, 2007.

Aston, Diana Hutt. *A Beetle Is Shy*. Illustrated by Sylvia Long. Chronicle, 2016.

Baker, Jeannie. *Circle*. Candlewick, 2016.

Beaty, Andrea. *Rosie Revere's Big Project Book for Bold Engineers*. Illustrated by David Roberts. Abrams Books for Young Readers, 2017.

Beck, W. H. *Glow: Animals with Their own Night-Lights*. HMH Books for Young Readers, 2015.

Bestor, Sheri M. *Good Trick, Walking Stick!* Illustrated by Johnny Lambert. Sleeping Bear Press, 2016.

Bishop, Nic. *Lizards*. Scholastic, 2010.

_____. *Snakes*. Scholastic, 2012.

Bolton, Tonya. *How to Build a Museum: Smithsonian's National Museum of African American History and Culture*. Viking, 2016.

Bosch, Sammy. *Super Simple Backyard Critter Crafts: Fun and Easy Animal Crafts*. Super Sandcastle, 2016.

Brandenburg, Jim. *Face to Face with Wolves*. National Geographic Children's Books, 2008.

Branley, Franklyn M. *What Happened to the Dinosaurs?* Illustrated by Marc Simont. Crowell, 1989.

Brenner, Barbara. *If You Were There in 1492*. Bradbury, 1991.

Brown, Don. *America Is Under Attack: September 11, 2001: The Day the Towers Fell*. Flash Point, 2011.

Brown, Don. *Drowned City: Hurricane Katrina & New Orleans*. HMH Books for Young Readers, 2015.

Burns, Ken. *Grover Cleveland, Again! A Treasury of American Presidents*. Illustrated by Gerald Kelley. Knopf Books for Young Readers, 2016.

Burns, Loree Griffin. *Citizen Scientists: Be a Part of Scientific Discovery from Your Own Backyard*. Photographs by Ellen Harasimowicz. Henry Holt, 2012.

Caduto, Michael J. *Catch the Wind, Harness the Sun: 22 Super-Charged Science Projects for Kids*. Storey, 2011.

Chin, Jason. *Grand Canyon*. Roaring Brook Press, 2017.

Cole, Joanna. *How You Were Born*. Photographs by Margaret Miller. HarperCollins, 1994.

_____. *The Magic School Bus Inside the Earth*. Illustrated by Bruce Degen. Perfection Learning, 1989.

Collard III, Sneed B. *Insects: The Most Fun Bug Book Ever*. Charlesbridge, 2017.

Colman, Penny. *Corpses, Coffins, and Crypts: A History of Burial*. Holt, 1997.

_____. *Thanksgiving: The True Story*. Holt, 2008.

Cowcher, Helen. *Antarctica*. Farrar, 1990.

Cowley, Joy. *Chameleon, Chameleon*. Photographs by Nic Bishop. Scholastic, 2005.

_____. *Red-Eyed Tree Frog*. Photographs by Nic Bishop. Scholastic, 1999.

Davies, Nicola. *Many: The Diversity of Life on Earth*. Illustrated by Emily Sutton. Candlewick, 2017.

Deem, James M. *Bodies from the Ash: Life and Death in Ancient Pompeii*. Houghton Mifflin, 2005.

_____. *Faces from the Past: Forgotten People of North America*. Houghton Mifflin, 2012.

Delacre, Lulu. *¡Olinguito, de la A a la Z!: Descubriendo el Bosque Nublado / Olinguito, from A to Z!: Unveiling the Cloud Forest*. Children's Book Press, 2016.

Dillon, Patrick. *The Story of Buildings: From the Pyramids to the Sydney Opera House and Beyond*. Illustrated by Stephen Biesty. Candlewick, 2014.

Dorros, Arthur. *Follow the Water from Brook to Ocean*. HarperCollins, 1991.

Evans, Shane W. *Underground*. Roaring Brook Press, 2011.

Hale, Christy. *Dreaming Up: A Celebration of Building*. Lee & Low Books, 2012.

Fleming, Candace. *The Family Romanov: Murder, Rebellion, and the Fall of Imperial Russia*. Schwartz & Wade Books, 2014.

_____. *Giant Squid*. Illustrated by Eric Rohmann. Roaring Brook Press, 2016.

Fox, Mem. *Hello Baby!* Illustrated by Steve Jenkins. Little Simon, 2008.

Freedman, Russell. *Vietnam: A History of the War*. Holiday House, 2016.

Freedman, Russell. *We Will Not Be Silent: The White Rose Student Resistance Movement That Defied Adolf Hitler*. Clarion Books, 2016.

Fritz, Jean. *Leonardo's Horse*. Illustrated by Hudson Talbot. Putnam, 2001.

Gianferrari, Maria. *Coyote Moon*. Illustrated by Bagram Ibatoulline. Roaring Brook Press, 2016.

Gibbons, Gail. *The Fruits We Eat*. Holiday House, 2015.

_____. *Ladybugs*. Holiday House, 2012.

_____. *Owls*. Holiday, 2005.

_____. *Transportation*. Holiday House, 2017.

Gillingham, Sara. *Alpha, Bravo, Charlie: The Complete Book of Nautical Codes*. Phaidon Press, 2016.

Glifford, Clive. *Cars, Trains, Ships & Planes: A Visual Encyclopedia of Every Vehicle*. DK Children, 2015.

Grace, Catherine O'Neill, and Margaret M. Bruchac. *1621: A New Look at Thanksgiving*. Photographs by Sisse Brimberg and Cotton Coulson. National Geographic, 2001.

Guiberson, Brenda. *Cactus Hotel*. Illustrated by Megan Lloyd. Henry Holt, 1991.

Harris, Robie H. *It's Not the Stork! A Book About Girls, Boys, Babies, Bodies, Families, and Friends*. Illustrated by Michael Emberley. Candlewick, 2006.

——. *It's Perfectly Normal: A Book About Changing Bodies, Growing Up, Sex, and Sexual Health*. Illustrated by Michael Emberley. Candlewick, 1994.

——. *It's So Amazing: A Book About Eggs, Sperm, Birth, Babies, and Families*. Illustrated by Michael Emberley. Candlewick, 1999.

——. *Who Has What?: All About Girls' Bodies and Boys' Bodies*. Illustrated by Nadine Bernard Wescott. Candlewick, 2011.

Heiligman, Deborah. *Holidays Around the World: Celebrating Ramadan and Eid Al-Fitr: With Praying, Fasting, and Charity*. National Geographic, 2006.

Helsby, Genevieve. *Those Amazing Musical Instruments!* Sourcebooks, 2007.

Heos, Bridget. *Stronger Than Steel: Spider Silk DNA and the Quest for Better Bulletproof Vests, Sutures, and Parachute Rope*. Illustrated by Andy Comins. Houghton Mifflin, 2013.

Herthel, Jessica and Jazz Jennings. *I am Jazz*. Illustrated by Shelaugh McNichols. Dial Books, 2014.

Hoose, Phillip. *The Race to Save the Lord God Bird*. Farrar, 2004.

Hoyt-Goldsmith, Diane. *Celebrating Ramadan*. Photographs by Lawrence Migdale. Holiday, 2001.

Jackson, Donna M. *The Bug Scientists*. Houghton, 2002.

Jenkins, Martin. *Fabulous Frogs*. Illustrated by Tim Hopgood. Candlewick, 2016.

Jenkins, Steve. *Actual Size*. Houghton, 2004.

——. *The Animal Book*. HMH Books for Young Readers, 2015.

——. *Animals by the Numbers: A Book of Animal Infographics*. HMH Books for Young Readers, 2016.

——. *Apex Hunters: The World's Deadliest Hunters, Past and Present*. HMH Books for Young Readers, 2017.

——. *Down, Down, Down: A Journey to the Bottom of the Sea*. HMH Books for Young Readers, 2009.

——. *Just a Second: A Different Way to Look at Time*. Houghton Mifflin, 2011.

Jenkins, Steve, and Robin Page. *Creature Features: Twenty-Five Animals Explain Why They Look the Way They Do*. Illustrated by Steve Jenkins. HMH Books for Young Readers, 2014.

——. *How to Swallow a Pig*. Illustrated by Steve Jenkins. HMH Books for Young Readers, 2015.

——. *My First Day*. Illustrated by Steve Jenkins. Houghton Mifflin, 2013.

——. *Time to Sleep*. Illustrated by Steve Jenkins. HMH Books for Young Readers, 2011.

——. *What Do You Do With a Tail Like This?* Illustrated by Steve Jenkins. Houghton Mifflin, 2003.

Judge, Lita. *Bird Talk: What Birds Say and Why*. Flash Point, 2012.

Kaner, Etta. *Have You Ever Seen a Duck in a Raincoat?* Illustrated by Jeff Szuc. Kids Can Press, 2009.

——. *Have You Ever Seen a Hippo with Sunscreen?* Illustrated by Jeff Szuc. Kids Can Press, 2010.

——. *Have You Ever Seen a Stork Build a Log Cabin?* Illustrated by Jeff Szuc. Kids Can Press, 2010.

Komiya, Teruyuki. *Life-Size Aquarium*. Seven Footer Press, 2009.

——. *Life-Size Farm*. Seven Footer Press, 2012.

——. *Life-Size Zoo: From Tiny Rodents to Gigantic Elephants, An Actual Size Animal Encyclopedia*. Seven Footer Press, 2009.

Könnecke, Ole. *The Big Book of Animals of the World*. Gecko Press, 2015.

Kramer, Stephen. *Hidden Worlds: Looking Through a Scientist's Microscope*. Photographs by Dennis Kunkel. Houghton, 2001.

Kuklin, Susan. *Families*. Hyperion, 2006.

Laroche, Giles. *If You Lived Here: Houses of the World*. Houghton Mifflin, 2011.

Leedy, Loreen. *Seeing Symmetry*. Holiday House, 2012.

Levinson, Cynthia. *We Got a Job: The 1963 Birmingham Children's March*. Peachtree, 2012.

Lewin, Ted. *Puffling Patrol*. Illustrated by Betsy Lewin. Lee & Low Books, 2014.

Lewin, Ted, and Betsy Lewin. *How to Babysit a Leopard: And Other True Stories from our Travels*

Across Six Continents. Roaring Brook Press, 2015.

Lewis, J. Patrick, ed. *National Geographic Book of Animal Poetry: 200 Poems with Photographs That Squeak, Soar, and Roar!* National Geographic Children's Books, 2012.

Lourie, Peter. *The Polar Bear Scientists*. Houghton Mifflin, 2012.

Macaulay, David. *Castle*. Houghton, 1977.

_____. *Cathedral: The Story of Its Construction*. Houghton, 1973.

_____. *City: The Story of Roman Planning and Construction*. Houghton, 1974.

_____. *Mosque*. Houghton, 2003.

_____. *Pyramid*. Houghton, 1975.

_____. *The Way Things Work*. Houghton, 1988.

_____. *The Way We Work*. Houghton, 2008.

_____. *The Way Things Work Now*. HMH Books for Young Readers, 2016.

_____. *Toilets: How It Works*. Macmillan Children's Publishing Group, 2013.

Mack, Lorrie. *Animal Families*. DK, 2008.

Markle, Sandra. *A Mother's Journey*. Illustrated by Alan Marks. Charlesbridge, 2005.

_____. *The Great Leopard Rescue: Saving the Amur Leopards*. Millbrook Press, 2017.

McCarthy, Colin. *DK Eyewitness Books: Reptiles*. DK Children, 2012.

McClung, Robert. *Possum*. Morrow, 1963.

McNamara, Margaret. *George Washington's Birthday: A Mostly True Tale*. Illustrated by Barry Blitt. Schwarts & Wade, 2012.

McWhorter, Diane. *A Dream of Freedom: The Civil Rights Movement from 1954 to 1968*. Scholastic, 2004.

Montgomery, Sy. *Quest for the Tree Kangaroo: An Expedition to the Cloud Forest of New Guinea*. Photographs by Nic Bishop. Houghton, 2006.

_____. *The Great White Shark Scientist*. Photographs by Keith Ellenbogen. HMH Books for Young Readers, 2016.

Morris, Ann. *Shoes, Shoes, Shoes*. Lothrop, 1995.

Murphy, Jim. *Breakthrough!: How Three People Saved "Blue Babies" and Changed Medicine Forever*. Clarion Books, 2015.

_____. *Truce: The Day the Soldiers Stopped Fighting*. Scholastic, 2009.

National Geographic Kids. *Look and Learn: Big Cats*. National Geographic Children's Books, 2017.

_____. *Look and Learn: Birds*. National Geographic Children's Books, 2017.

_____. *Look and Learn: In My Garden*. National Geographic Children's Books, 2017.

Nelson, Kadir. *Heart and Soul: The Story of America and African Americans*. Balzer and Bray, 2011.

Nelson, Scott Reynolds, with Marc Aronson. *Ain't Nothing But a Man: My Quest to Find the Real John Henry*. National Geographic, 2008.

Nicholson, Dorinda Makanaōnalani. *The School the Aztec Eagles Built: A Tribute to Mexico's World War II Air Fighters*. Lee & Low Books Inc., 2016.

O'Connell, Caitlin, and Donna M. Jackson. *The Elephant Scientist*. Illustrated by Timothy Rodwell. Houghton Mifflin, 2011.

Page, Robin, *A Chicken Followed Me Home! Questions and Answers about a Familiar Fowl*. Beach Lane Books, 2015.

Page, Robin, and Steve Jenkins. *Egg: Nature's Perfect Package*. Illustrated by Steve Jenkins. HMH Books for Young Readers, 2015.

Parnell, Peter, and Justin Richardson. *And Tango Makes Three*. Illustrated by Henry Cole. Simon & Schuster, 2005.

Peot, Margaret. *Inkblot: Drip, Splat, and Squish Your Way to Creativity*. Boyds Mill Press, 2011.

Peterson, Brenda. *Leopard & Silkie: One Boy's Quest to Save the Seal Pups*. Photographs by Robin Lindsey. Henry Holt, 2012.

Pholen, Jerome. *Gay & Lesbian History for Kids: The Century-Long Struggle for LGBT Rights*. Chicago Review Press, 2015.

Pitmac, Maja. *Three-dimensional Art Adventures: 36 Creative, Artist-Inspired Projects in Sculpture, Ceramics, Textiles, and More*. Chicago Review Press, 2016.

Preus, Margi. *Celebritrees: Historic and Famous Trees of the World*. Illustrated by Rebecca Gibbon. Henry Holt, 2011.

Pringle, Laurence. *Billions of Years, Amazing Changes: The Story of Evolution*. Illustrated by Steve Jenkins. Boyds Mill Press, 2001.

Mound, Laurence. *DK Eyewitness Books: Insect*. DK Children, 2017.

Saltz, Gail. *Amazing You: Getting Smart about Your Private Parts*. Illustrated by Lynne Cravath Dutton, 2005

Sayre, April Pulley. *Best in Snow*. Beach Lane Books, 2016.

_____. *Eat Like a Bear*. Illustrated by Steve Jenkins. Henry Holt and Co., 2013.

Schreiber, Anne. *National Geographic Readers: Monkeys*. National Geographic Children's Books, 2013.

____. *Pandas*. National Geographic Children's Books, 2010.

____. *Penguins*. National Geographic Children's Books, 2009.

____. *Sharks!* National Geographic Children's Books, 2008.

Scott, Elaine. *Buried Alive!: How 33 Miners Survived 69 Days Deep Under the Chilean Desert*. Clarion, 2012.

Selsam, Millicent. *How to Be a Nature Detective*. Illustrated by Marlene Hill Donnelly. HarperCollins, 1995.

Sidman, Joyce. *Round*. Illustrated by Taeeun Yoo. HMH Books for Young Readers, 2017.

Silverberg, Cory. *Sex Is a Funny Word: A Book About Bodies, Feelings, and YOU*. Illustrated by Fiona Smyth. Seven Stories Press, 2015.

Simon, Seymour. *Butterflies*. Collins, 2011.

____. *Crocodiles and Alligators*. HarperCollins, 1999.

____. *Extreme Earth Records*. Chronicle, 2012.

____. *Global Warming*. Collins, 2010.

____. *Horses*. HarperCollins, 2006.

____. *Insects*. HarperCollins, 2016.

____. *Water*. HarperCollins, 2017.

Singer, Marilyn. *Venom*. Darby Creek, 2007.

Siy, Alexandra. *Voyager's Greatest Hits: The Epic Trek to Interstellar Space*. Charlesbridge, 2017.

Siy, Alexandra, and Dennis Kunkel. *Mosquito Bite*. Charlesbridge, 2005.

Stewart, Melissa. *Can an Aardvark Bark?* Illustrated by Steve Jenkins. Beach Lane Books, 2017.

Thimmesh, Catherine. *Lucy Long Ago: Uncovering the Mystery of Where We Came From*. Houghton Mifflin, 2009.

Thornhill, Jan. *The Tragic Tale of the Great Auk*. House of Anansi Press, 2016.

Tonatiuh, Duncan. *Funny Bones: Posada and His Day of the Dead Calaveras*. Abrams Books for Young Readers, 2015.

Waters, Kate. *Samuel Eaton's Day: A Day in the Life of a Pilgrim Boy*. Illustrated by Russ Kendall. Scholastic, 1996.

____. *Sarah Morton's Day: A Day in the Life of a Pilgrim Girl*. Illustrated by Russ Kendall. Scholastic, 1993.

Webb, Sophie. *Far from Shore: Chronicles of an Open Ocean Voyage*. Houghton Mifflin, 2011.

Wechsler, Doug. *The **H**idden **L**ife of a Toad*. Charlesbridge, 2017.

Wick, Walter. *A Drop of Water*. Scholastic, 1997.

Williams, Rachel. *Atlas of Adventures: A Collection of Natural Wonders, Exciting Experiences, and Fun Festivities from the Four Corners of the Globe*. Illustrated by Lucy Letherland. Wide Eyed Editions, 2015.

Worth, Valerie. *Animal Poems*. Illustrated by Steve Jenkins. Farrar, Straus and Giroux, 2007.

Zoehfeld, Kathleen Weidner. *Dinosaur Parents, Dinosaur Young: Uncovering the Mystery of Dinosaur Families*. Illustrated by Paul Carrick and Bruce Shillinglaw. Clarion, 2001.

Biography

Chapter Outline

Following a classroom study of biographies, a fourth-grade teacher asked her students to reflect on their experiences in their response journals. Gabriel, age 10, wrote:

> Reading about the lives of other people could be very interesting. Each person has his unique life experiences. You can learn

©Sara Dashner Photography, Gahanna, Ohio.

about when and where he was born, how he was raised, what kind of family he came from. You can also learn about where he went to school and what kind of student he was when he went to school. Most of all, you can learn about his dreams and how he fulfilled his dreams. For example if I happened to be reading a book about Michael Jordan, I would be very interested to know how he trained himself to be a great basketball star. Also why did he all of a sudden switch his career as a basketball player to become a baseball player? I would want to know who was his role model when he was young like me. How did he become interested in basketball games? What kind of advice would he give to young people who have the same kind of dream to become a basketball star?

Elementary and middle-school students are in the process of becoming themselves, and reading about real people can provide glimpses of the kinds of lives they might choose to live. Biographies can answer questions that are important to young readers like Gabriel and raise questions about how their futures might unfold.

Biography for Today's Child

In children's literature, biography often bridges the gap between realistic fiction and nonfiction books. A life story might read like fiction, but, like other types of nonfiction, it will center on facts and events that can be documented. In the past, writers of biography for children have been allowed more freedom in the use of fictional techniques than have those who write for adults. As a result, children's biographies over the years have shown a wide range of factual orientations, from strict authenticity to liberal fictionalization.

Authentic biography follows many of the same rules as serious scholarly works written for adults. A book of this type is a well-documented, carefully researched account of a person's life. Typically, only statements that are known to have been made by the subject are included as dialogue. Jean Fritz was one of the first authors to demonstrate that biographies for children could be authentic as well as lively and readable. Her writing helped set a new standard. Her books about famous figures of the American Revolution, including *And Then What Happened, Paul Revere?* and *Can't You Make Them Behave, King George?*, are based on detailed research. Candace Fleming's *Amelia Lost: The Life and Disappearance of Amelia Earhart*, as well as Steve Sheinkin's *The Notorious Benedict Arnold: A True Story of Adventure, Heroism & Treachery* and *Undefeated: Jim Thorpe and the Carlisle Indian School Football Team* are among many other excellent examples of authentic biography.

Fictionalized biography is grounded in thorough research, but the author dramatizes certain events and personalizes the subject. In contrast to those who write authentic biography, authors of fictionalized biography may invent dialogue and even ascribe

Candace Fleming brilliantly elaborates on the life of Amelia Earhart, alternating between her childhood and the mystery of her disappearance and the search for her plane. Fleming, Candace. *Amelia Lost: The Life and Disappearance of Amelia Earhart*. New York, NY: Schwartz and Wade Books, an imprint of Random House Children's Books, 2011, Cover. Copyright ©2011 by Random House Children's Books. All rights reserved. Used with permission.

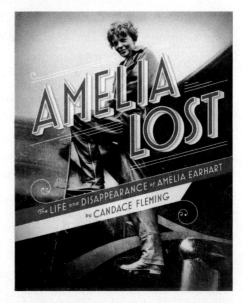

unspoken thoughts to the subject. These conversations might be based on facts taken from diaries, journals, or other period sources, but it is important for teachers to help children understand the spectrum between fictionalized and authentic biographies in addition to picturebooks and novels that fit into the category of historical fiction. Several picturebook biographies, such as *Bambino and Mr. Twain* by P. I. Maltbie and *The Adventures of Mark Twain by Huckleberry Finn* (written and illustrated by Robert Burleigh and Barry Blitt) relate events in the life of Mark Twain. Barbara Kerley's *The Extraordinary Mark Twain (According to Susy)* presents a fictional narrative about Twain's daughter, Susy, along with actual quotes from a biography Susy wrote about her father. These are fictionalized biographies, however; the factual details are essentially true, but their presentation is imagined.

Not everyone agrees where to draw the line between fictionalized biography or memoirs and historical fiction. When Jean Fritz wrote about her childhood in China and her much-longed-for trip to the United States in *Homesick: My Own Story*, she found that her "memory came out in lumps," and she finally chose not to worry about exact sequence. She telescoped events of all her childhood into a two-year span. The library cataloging information in the front of this book designates it as fiction, but many readers will think of it as the autobiography of Jean Fritz. The inclusion of a section of family photographs from their days in China strengthens the book's claim to authenticity. Fritz's humor, her depth of feeling, and her vivid portrayal of the turmoil in China during the 1920s make *Homesick* worth reading, regardless of the label that is put on it.

Publishers of biography for children have been quick to capitalize on trends in the social studies curriculum as well as shifts in children's interests. In the mid-1970s, many biographies about leaders in the American Revolution appeared in connection with the bicentennial. Likewise, dozens of new books about Lewis and Clark came out in time for the bicentennial that began in 2003. Several recent biographies reflect a new emphasis on encouraging girls in science, technology, engineering, and math fields. One pioneering role model can be found in two biographies about Eugenie Clark: Heather Lang's *Swimming with Sharks: The Daring Discoveries of Eugenie Clark* and Jess Keating's *Shark Lady: The True Story of How Eugenie Clark Became the Ocean's Most Fearless Scientist*. Such attention is also paid to Ada Lovelace in Fiona Robinson's *Ada's Ideas: The Story of Ada Lovelace, the World's First Computer Programmer* and Diane Stanley's *Ada Lovelace, Poet*

Jess Keating's *Shark Lady: The True Story of How Eugenie Clark Became the Ocean's Most Fearless Scientist* (2017) introduces readers to the pioneering zoologist who changed how the world viewed sharks. Keating, Jess, *Shark Lady: The True Story of How Eugenie Clark Became the Ocean's Most Fearless Scientist*. Naperville, IL: Sourcebooks, 2017, Cover. Copyright ©2017 by Sourcebooks. All rights reserved. Used with permission.

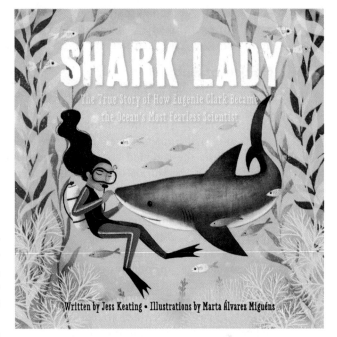

of Science: The First Computer Programmer. As attention to multicultural education has grown, stories about women, African Americans, and other underrepresented groups continue to be reflected in publishing trends.

Biographies of popular-culture celebrities and other contemporary figures continue to feed children's tremendous interest in sports and entertainment personalities. Although such books tend to be objective and almost journalistic in their approach, many are superficial in scholarship and poorly written. A great number of these and other biographies are published as parts of series, and the result is often life stories that are tailored to fit certain format specifications rather than explored in all their uniqueness.

An interest in the lives of historical figures, the appearance of many autobiographies by children's authors, the use of photographs and other primary source materials, and the picturebook format itself have all had significant impact on the genre of biography. Mediocre biographies continue to be published, but the number of available high-quality books grows season by season. Biographies have received many prestigious awards in the past several decades. In 2009, Melissa Sweet received a Caldecott honor for *A River of Words: The Story of William Carlos Williams*, written by Jen Bryant. In 2014, Jen Bryant received an NCTE Orbis Pictus honor and a Robert F. Sibert honor, as well as the Schneider Family Book Award, for *A Splash of Red: The Life and Art of Horace Pippin*. Bryant went on to win both the Orbis Pictus Award and the Robert F. Sibert Medal for *The Right Word: Roget and His Thesaurus* in 2015, and Melissa Sweet received another Caldecott honor for her illustrations in the book.

Criteria for Juvenile Biography

The criteria for evaluating biographies for children differ somewhat from those established for other juvenile nonfiction. They also diverge somewhat from generally accepted patterns for adult biography. Readers may enjoy biography as they read fiction—for the story, or *plot*. Children often demand a fast-moving narrative. In biography, events and actions become even more exciting because "they really happened." Thus, children may like biography written as a story with continuity rather than just a collection of facts and dates. An encyclopedia gives them facts in a well-organized fashion. Biography, to do more than this, can help readers *know* the person as a living human being.

Choice of Subject

Formerly, most biographies for children were about familiar figures of the past in the United States, particularly those whose lives offered the readiest action material, such as Daniel Boone or Abraham Lincoln. Now the range of subjects is much broader, including artists and intellectuals as well as soldiers and presidents, plus world figures whose presence suggests the widened concerns of our pluralistic society. Biographies of contemporary figures in the worlds of sports and entertainment continue to reflect the influence of the mass media.

For many years, biography for children was limited to subjects whose lives were considered worthy of emulation. This is no longer true. There are books about people remembered for their misdeeds, like *The Notorious Benedict Arnold* by Steve Sheinkin, and controversial persons like Adolf Hitler. Fidel Castro, Ho Chi Minh, and Lenin have all been subjects of juvenile biographies. As long as the biographies attempt to take an objective stance and recognize the various points of view concerning the subjects, these books can serve a useful purpose in presenting a worldview to readers.

Biographies of lesser-well-known figures or subjects whose accomplishments are highly specialized also have value for children. Rhoda Blumberg tells a fascinating survival story in *Shipwrecked!: The True Adventures of a Japanese Boy.* Shipwrecked on an island off the coast of isolationist Japan in 1841, young Manjiro had no hope of returning home. Rigid Japanese laws mandated death to anyone who left the country. Rescued by the crew of an American whaleboat, Manjiro traveled to America, the first Japanese citizen to do so. He lived an amazing life, eventually returning home to Japan despite the risk of execution. The story of another little-known immigrant to America is told in *Adrift at Sea: A Vietnamese Boy's Story of Survival,* Tuan Ho's autobiographical account of his family's experience escaping Vietnam following the fall of Saigon. His survival, as told to Marsha Forchuk Skrypuch, depends on a small fishing boat overloaded with refugees. Children should be encouraged to read biographies about a wide range of subjects—famous persons, great human beings who were not famous, and even antiheroes. In *Shackleton: Antarctic Odyssey,* Nick Bertozzi explores the ambitious expedition of Ernest Shackleton from 1914 to 1915 in a graphic novel format for older readers. For younger readers, William Grill's *Shackleton's Journey* provides a visual narrative of the explorer's adventures in Antarctica.

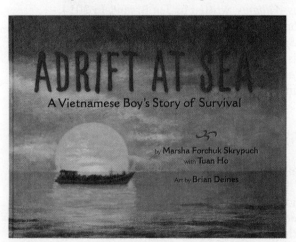

Brian Deines's illustrations add drama and emotional impact to Tuan Ho's moving account of his family's escape from Vietnam told with Marsha Forchuk Skrypuch in *Adrift at Sea: A Vietnamese Boy's Story of Survival.* Skrypuch, Marsha Forchuk. *Adrift at Sea: A Vietnamese Boy's Story of Survival.* Illustrated by Brian Deines. Contributions by Tuan Ho. Toronto, Canada. Copyright ©2016 by Pajama Press. All rights reserved. Used with permission.

Accuracy and Authenticity

Accuracy is the hallmark of good biographical writing, whether it is for adults or for children. More and more, writers of juvenile biography are acknowledging primary sources for their materials in either an introductory note or an appended bibliography. Conscientious authors of well-written children's biographies frequently travel to the locale of the story in order to get a personal sense of the place. They visit museums to study actual objects that were used by their subjects; they spend hours poring over original letters and documents. Much of this research might not be used in the actual biography, but its effect will be evident in the author's insight into the character of the subject and in the accuracy of the historical detail.

The same kind of careful research should be reflected in the accuracy of the illustrations that convey the time, place, and setting. The dress of the period, the interiors of the houses, and the very utensils that are used must be authentic representations. Many books, such as Harold Holzer's *Father Abraham: Lincoln and His Sons*, Dorothy Hinshaw Patent's *Charles Darwin: The Life of a Revolutionary Thinker*, and Candace Fleming's *Ben Franklin's Almanac: Being a True Account of the Good Gentleman's Life*, make use of reproductions of maps, letters, and artwork of the period to authenticate the subject matter.

But most difficult of all, perhaps, is the actual portrayal of the subject. There are many drawings and paintings of most historical figures, but an accurate likeness is problematic, particularly for subjects who lived before the advent of photography. In their book *Christopher Columbus: The Great Adventure and How We Know About It*, Delno West and Jean West point out:

> There are hundreds of paintings, engravings, woodcuts, and statues of Christopher Columbus, but they were all made after he died by people who never saw him. (p. 13)

Several of these competing portraits are reproduced in their book. They also quote Columbus's son, Ferdinand, who described his father's long face, light eyes, big nose, and red hair, so that readers have a basis for reacting to the illustrations.

Photographs provide authentic illustrations for many biographical accounts, such as Russell Freedman's highly acclaimed photobiographies, Elizabeth Partridge's *Restless Spirit: The Life and Work of Dorothea Lange*, Kathi Appelt and Jeanne Schmitzer's *Down Cut Shin Creek: The Pack Horse Librarians of Kentucky*,

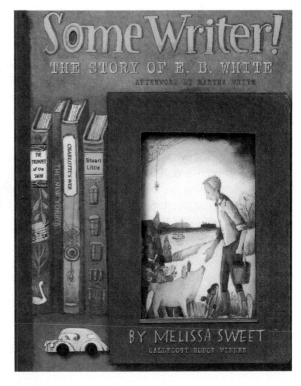

Melissa Sweet used her signature watercolor and mixed-media collage artwork, along with archival materials shared by E.B. White's granddaughter, to create *Some Writer!: The Story of E. B. White*. Sweet, Melissa. *Some Writer!: The Story of E. B. White*. New York, NY: HMH Books for Young Readers, 2016, Cover. Copyright ©2016 by HMH Books for Young Readers. All rights reserved. Used with permission.

Jim Murphy's *The Giant and How He Humbugged America*, and Candace Fleming's *The Family Romanov: Murder, Rebellion, and the Fall of Imperial Russia*.

An authentic biography should be true in every detail. A fictionalized biography must also be true to the factual record, and any invented dialogue or background detail must be plausible and true to the times. Yet the truth of what is included in a biography does not quite answer the entire question of its accuracy. Sometimes, what is left out is just as important as what is put in.

Formerly, authors of biographies for children avoided writing about certain aspects of the lives of their subjects. Serious criticism has been leveled at biographies of Washington and Jefferson that did not include the fact that they owned many slaves. More-recent biographies, even those for younger children, do include this information. In *Thomas Jefferson: A Picture Book Biography*, James Cross Giblin approaches his subject with the same meticulous research he applies to his many nonfiction books and writes of Jefferson's ambivalence about slavery. In her biography for older readers, *This Land Was Made for You and Me: The Life and Songs of Woody Guthrie*, Elizabeth Partridge writes honestly about Guthrie's irresponsible and often reckless behavior, as well as his passionate regard for the plight of the working classes.

When writing for younger children, certain biographers might present only a portion of a person's life. In planning their picturebook *Abraham Lincoln*, Ingri d'Aulaire and Edgar Parin d'Aulaire deliberately omitted his assassination and closed the book with the end of the Civil War. The authors' purpose was to present the greatness of the man as he lived, for too frequently, they believed, children remember only the manner of Lincoln's death. There is a danger, however, that omissions might oversimplify and thereby distort the truth about a person's life. Although the critic Jo Carr has argued that it is better not to offer biography to young children at all than to present them with unbalanced portraits distorted by flagrant omissions,[1] books with a comprehensive approach can be used in combination with those selectively focused for particular effect.

Style

The author's language is especially important to biography because it bears the burden of making the subject seem alive and sound real. Documented quotes should be woven smoothly into the narrative. When dialogue is invented, it should have the natural rhythms of speech, regardless of the period it represents, because stilted writing makes characters seem wooden.

In today's authentic biography, the author's way with words makes all the difference between a dull and a lively book. In *Cloth Lullaby: The Woven Life of Louise Bourgeois*, Amy Novesky uses lyrical language to describe Louise's childhood spent helping her family repair tapestries:

> At the family 's workshop, Louise's mother, like her mother before her, repaired fabric grown threadbare with time.
>> She loved to work in the warm sun, her needle rising and falling beside the lilting river, perfect, delicate spiderwebs glinting with caught drops of water above her. (p. 11)

The narrator's tone always pervades the presentation, but a dispassionate point of view is usually reserved for authentic biography. Whatever the form or viewpoint, the background materials should be integrated into the narrative with smoothness and proportion. The judicious use of quotes from letters or journals may support the authenticity of the biography, but it should not detract from the absorbing account of the life of the subject.

Children enjoy a style that is clear and vigorous. The research must be there, but it should be a natural part of the presentation.

The choice of narrator, or point of view, is also an important consideration in the style of a biography. Writers of biography most often use the third person, but some authors take a more intimate point of view. Carole Boston Weatherford chose to tell the story of Fannie Lou Hamer from a first-person point of view. In her author's note for the Caldecott honor and Sibert honor-winning *Voice of Freedom: Fannie Lou Hamer: Spirit of the Civil Rights Movement*, Weatherford shares that Hamer "was known as the spirit, or the voice, of the civil rights movement." Telling her story in first person highlights Hamer's courageous "Voice of Freedom."

Hearing Hamer's story in her own, passionate voice lends the book immediacy and impact.

Characterization

The characterization of the subject of a biography must be true to life, neither adulatory nor demeaning in tone. The reader should have the opportunity to know the person as a real human being with both shortcomings and virtues. To emphasize the worthiness of their subjects, juvenile biographers sometimes portray them as too good to be true.

Jean Fritz is one author who manages to create vivid portraits of great figures without according them pseudo-sainthood. She has presented Paul Revere as a busy and sometimes forgetful human being in her humorous yet authentic picturebook biography *And Then What Happened, Paul Revere?* He didn't always meet his deadlines, once producing a hymnbook some eighteen months after he had promised it! A dreamer, he even left one page in his "Day Book" simply for doodling. The author does not discredit her character; she simply makes him come alive by admitting his foibles, as well as describing his accomplishments.

Comparing two or more biographies of the same subject is one way of understanding the importance of characterization. Barb Rosenstock's *Dorothea's Eyes: Dorothea Lange Photographs the Truth* and Carole Boston Weatherford's *Dorothea Lange: The Photographer Who Found the Faces of the Depression* are similar in length and coverage. Both are generally suitable for grades 3 through 5. Although both books emphasize Dorothea's ability to see what others fail to see, they provide somewhat different views of the deep emotional intelligence that informed Dorothea's ability to see what others looked past. While each book discusses how ostracized Dorothea felt due to her lingering limp

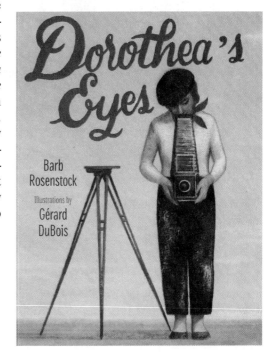

Barb Rosenstock writes that "Dorothea's eyes help us see with our hearts," and she uses Lange's documentary photographs to help the reader do just that. (p. 30). Rosenstock, Barb. *Dorothea's Eyes: Dorothea Lange Photographs the Truth.* Honesdale, PA: Calkins Creek, 2016, Cover. Copyright ©2016 by Calkins Creek. All rights reserved. Used with permission.

after being stricken with polio, each focuses on a different outcome: Rosenstock emphasizes Dorothea's ability to become invisible as a result of learning to hide her limp, while Weatherford highlights the empathy for others that Dorothea developed. *Jim Thorpe's Bright Path* by Joseph Bruchac and *Undefeated: Jim Thorpe and the Carlisle Indian School Football Team* by Steve Sheinkin would provide a similar comparison for older readers.

Biography must not degenerate into mere eulogy; reexamining should not become denigrating. The background of subjects' lives, their conversations, their thoughts, and their actions should be presented as faithfully to the facts as possible. The subject should also be seen in relation to her or his times, for no person can be "read" in isolation. For example, in *A Poem for Peter: The Story of Ezra Jack Keats and the Creation of The Snowy Day*, Andrea Davis Pinkey's tribute "bio-poem" situates *The Snowy Day* against the backdrop of an American publishing industry blatantly missing portrayals of African American characters in literature for children.

Theme

Underlying the characterization in all biography is the author's interpretation of the subject. No matter how impartial an author might attempt to be, composing a cohesive life story requires some interpretation. An author's selection of facts can limit the dimensions of the portraiture or highlight certain features. In this context, every author walks a thin line between theme and bias. Time usually lends perspective and objectivity, but contemporary biography might tend more toward bias. Teachers and librarians need to help children realize that all biographies have a point of view determined by their authors. Again, a comparison of several biographies of the same person written in different time periods would help children discover this fact.

Frequently, in juvenile biography, the author's take will be identified in the title, as in Andrea Davis Pinkney's *A Poem for Peter: The Story of Ezra Jack Keats and the Creation of The Snowy Day*, as well as Vaunda

The picturebook biography *Sequoyah* by James Rumford evokes important cultural themes and information through both pictures and words. Illustration from *Sequoyah: The Cherokee Man Who Gave His People Writing* by James Rumford. Copyright ©2004 by James Rumford. Reprinted by permission of Houghton Mifflin Harcourt Publishing Company. All rights reserved.

Micheaux Nelson's *Bad News for Outlaws: The Remarkable Life of Bass Reeves, Deputy U. S. Marshal*. These titles name their subjects and point out the theme of the books.

In picturebook biographies, illustrations also reveal the theme. James Rumford's illustrations for *Sequoyah: The Cherokee Man Who Gave His People Writing* pay homage to the woodblock prints of such Japanese artists of the nineteenth century as Hokusai and Hiroshige. They evoke the contrast between Eastern and Western art styles and subtly emphasize the two cultures Sequoyah represented and brought together through his invention of a Cherokee alphabet. Demi pays reverent attention to customs of Islam in her biography of *Muhammad*, never representing his human form but showing only a silhouette of Muhammad in gold leaf. The style of her illustrations, resembling the miniatures of ancient Persia, also conveys the wonder and piety of the life of this holy prophet.

There is a danger in oversimplifying and forcing all facts to fit a single mold. An author must not re-create and interpret a life history in terms of one fixed picture, particularly in a biography that covers the full scope of a subject's life. Ordinary people have several facets to their personalities; the great are likely to be multidimensional. The perceptive biographer concentrates on those events from a full life that helped mold and form that personality. It is this selection and focus that create the theme of the biography. The **Guidelines: Evaluating Juvenile Biography** summarizes the criteria we have discussed in this section.

Guidelines

Evaluating Juvenile Biography

Go to Connect® to access study resources, practice quizzes, and additional materials.

Choice of Subject
- Does the subject's life offer interest and meaning for today's child?
- Will knowing this historical or contemporary figure help children understand the past or the present?
- Can the subject's experiences widen children's views on the possibilities for their own lives?

Accuracy and Authenticity
- Do the text and illustrations reflect careful research and consistency in presentation?
- Does the author provide notes about original source material, a bibliography, or other evidence of documentation?
- Are there discrepancies of fact in comparison with other books?

- Are there significant omissions that result in a distorted picture of the subject's life?

Style
- Are quotations or dialogue used in a way that brings the subject to life?
- For a fictionalized biography, does the choice of narrator's point of view add to the story?
- Is the author's style clear and readable, with background material included naturally?

Characterization
- Is the subject presented as a believable, multidimensional character, with both strengths and weaknesses?
- Does the author avoid both eulogizing and debunking?

Theme
- Does the author's interpretation of the subject represent a fair and balanced approach?
- Does the author avoid oversimplifying or manipulating the facts to fit the chosen theme?

Types of Presentation and Coverage

Writers of adult biography are by definition bound to try to re-create the subject's life as fully as possible, with complete detail and careful documentation. Writers of children's biography, however, may use one of several approaches. The resulting types of biography need individual consideration, for each offers to children a different perspective and a different appeal. **Teaching Feature 10.1: Types of Biography** provides an overview of the scope of coverage for children. Keep in mind, however, that a single book might fit into more than one of the following categories.

Biographies of all types give children a glimpse into other lives, other places, and other times. The best of them combine accurate information and fine writing in a context that children enjoy—the story that really happened. Children may know about historical events or contemporary figures from textbooks, but literature that depicts this content will introduce a different way of knowing that is more intimate and more memorable. These biographies put facts into the frame of human feeling. All children deserve to have such books as part of their experience.

teaching feature 10.1

Types of Biography

Note: Most subjects of the biographies listed below are named in the book's title. When this is not the case, the subject is noted after the author's name.

Type	Title and Author	Grade Level
Picturebook Biographies: A biography in a picturebook form. The pictures carry a substantial part of the interpretation.	**Activists for Human Rights**	
	A Picture Book of Sojourner Truth (Adler)	K–3
	César (Bernier-Grand) [César Chavez]	K–3
	Rosa (Giovanni) [Rosa Parks]	K and up
	The Youngest Marcher: The Story of Audrey Faye Hendricks, a Young Civil Rights Activist (Levinson)	K and up
	The House That Jane Built: A Story About Jane Addams (Stone)	1 and up
	Artists	
	Maya Lin: Artist-Architect of Light and Lines (Harvey)	K–3
	Dave the Potter: Artist, Poet, Slave (Hill)	K–3
	The Iridescence of Birds: A Book About Henri Matisse (MacLachlan)	K–3
	Balloons over Broadway: The True Story of the Puppeteer of Macy's Parade (Sweet) [Tony Sarg]	K–3
	The Pot That Juan Built (Andrews-Goebel) [Juan Quezada]	1 and up

teaching feature 10.1

Type	Title and Author	Grade Level
	Frida (Winter) [Frida Kahlo]	1 and up
	Draw What You See: The Life and Art of Benny Andrews (Benson)	2 and up
	Fancy Party Gowns: The Story of Fashion Designer Ann Cole Lowe (Blumenthal)	2 and up
	A Splash of Red: The Life and Art of Horace Pippin (Bryant)	2 and up
	Cloth Lullaby: The Woven Life of Louise Bourgeois (Novesky)	2 and up
	Dorothea's Eyes: Dorothea Lange Photographs the Truth (Rosenstock)	2 and up
	Leonardo da Vinci (Stanley)	2 and up
	Radiant Child: The Story of Young Artist Jean-Michel Basquiat (Steptoe)	2 and up
	It Jes' Happened: When Bill Traylor Started to Draw (Tate)	2 and up
	Dorothea Lange: The Photographer Who Found the Faces of the Depression (Weatherford)	2 and up
Dancers, Musicians, Singers, and Performers		
	Trombone Shorty (Andrews) [Troy Andrews]	1 and up
	Firebird: Ballerina Misty Copeland Shows a Young	1 and up
	Girl How to Dance Like the Firebird (Copeland)	1 and up
	Ella Fitzgerald: The Tale of a Vocal Virtuosa (Pinkney)	1 and up
	Josephine: The Dazzling Life of Josephine Baker (Powell)	2 and up
	Little Melba and Her Big Trombone (Russell-Brown) [Melba Liston]	2 and up
	When Marian Sang (Ryan) [Marian Anderson]	2 and up
	Monsieur Marceau (Schubert)	2 and up
	Swan: The Life and Dance of Anna Pavlova (Snyder)	2 and up
Overcoming Challenges		
	Fifty Cents and a Dream: Young Booker T. Washington (Asim)	2 and up
	Malala: Activist for Girls' Education (Frier) [Malala Yousafzai]	2 and up
	The Boy Who Harnessed the Wind (Kamkwamba)	2 and up
	Frederick Douglass: The Lion Who Wrote History (Myers)	2 and up
	Emmanuel's Dream: The True Story of Emmanuel Ofosu Yeboah (Thompson)	2 and up

(continued)

teaching feature 10.1

Type	Title and Author	Grade Level
Poets and Writers		
	Pablo Neruda: Poet of the People (Brown)	K–3
	A Boy, a Mouse, and a Spider: The Story of E.B. White (Herkert)	K–3
	The Right Word: Roget and His Thesaurus (Bryant)	2 and up
	A River of Words: The Story of William Carlos Williams (Bryant)	2 and up
	Enormous Smallness: A Story of E. E. Cummings (Burgess)	2 and up
	A Poem for Peter: The Story of Ezra Jack Keats and the Creation of The Snowy Day (Pinkney)	3 and up
	Some Writer!: The Story of E. B. White (Sweet)	3 and up
	Poet: The Remarkable Story of George Moses Horton (Tate)	3 and up
Scientists		
	Me . . . Jane (McDonnell) [Jane Goodall]	K–3
	Odd Boy Out: Young Albert Einstein (Brown)	K–3
	On a Beam of Light: A Story of Albert Einstein (Berne)	K–4
	Shark Lady: The True Story of How Eugenie Clark Became the Ocean's Most Fearless Scientist (Keating)	K–4
	Swimming with Sharks: The Daring Discoveries of Eugenie Clark (Lang)	K–4
	Life in the Ocean: The Story of Oceanographer Sylvia Earle (Nivola)	K–4
	Ada's Ideas: The Story of Ada Lovelace, the World's First Computer Programmer (Robinson)	K–4
	Star Stuff: Carl Sagan and the Mysteries of the Cosmos (Sisson)	K–4
	Ada Lovelace, Poet of Science: The First Computer Programmer (Stanley)	K–4
Sports		
	Martina & Chrissie: The Greatest Rivalry in the History of Sports (Bildner)	2 and up
	Miss Mary Reporting: The True Story of Sportswriter Mary Garber (Macy)	2 and up
	Trudy's Big Swim: How Gertrude Ederle Swam the English Channel and Took the World by Storm (Macy)	2 and up

Type	Title and Author	Grade Level
	Touch the Sky: Alice Coachman, Olympic High Jumper (Malaspina)	2 and up
	Something to Prove: The Great Satchel Paige vs. Rookie Joe DiMaggio (Skead)	2 and up
	The Kid from Diamond Street: The Extraordinary Story of Baseball Legend Edith Houghton (Vernick)	2 and up
	Wangari Maathai Biography Text Set	
	Seeds of Change: Wangari's Gift to the World (Johnson)	2 and up
	Mama Miti: Wangari Maathai and the Trees of Kenya (Napoli)	2 and up
	Planting the Trees of Kenya: The Story of Wangari Maathai (Nivola)	2 and up
	Wangari Maathai: The Woman Who Planted Millions of Trees (Prévot)	2 and up
	Wangari's Trees of Peace: A True Story from Africa (Winter)	2 and up
	Doreen Rappaport Biography Series	
	Abe's Honest Words: The Life of Abraham Lincoln (Rappaport)	2 and up
	Eleanor, Quiet No More (Rappaport) [Eleanor Roosevelt]	2 and up
	Frederick's Journey: The Life of Frederick Douglass (Rappaport)	2 and up
	Helen's Big World: The Life of Helen Keller (Rappaport)	2 and up
	Jack's Path of Courage: The Life of John F. Kennedy (Rappaport)	2 and up
	John's Secret Dreams: The Life of John Lennon (Rappaport)	2 and up
	Martin's Big Words (Rappaport) [Martin Luther King, Jr.]	2 and up
	To Dare Mighty Things: The Life of Theodore Roosevelt (Rappaport)	2 and up
Graphic: Biography in graphic novel format.	*X: A Biography of Malcolm X* (Gunderson)	4 and up
	Anne Frank: The Anne Frank House Authorized Graphic Biography (Jacobson)	4 and up
	Annie Sullivan and the Trials of Helen Keller (Lambert)	4 and up
	Boys of Steel: The Creators of Superman (Nobleman) [Jerry Siegel and Joe Shuster]	4 and up
	Primates: The Fearless Science of Jane Goodall, Dian Fossey, and Biruté Galdikas (Ottaviani)	4 and up

(continued)

teaching feature 10.1

Type	Title and Author	Grade Level
	Feynman (Ottaviani) [Richard Feynman]	4 and up
	Lily Renée, Escape Artist: From Holocaust Survivor to Comic Book Pioneer (Robbins)	5 and up
	Bessie Stringfield: Tales of the Talented Tenth (Gill)	5 and up
	Shackleton: Antarctic Odyssey (Bertozzi) [Ernest Shackleton]	6 and up
	Sammy Sosa: Home-Run Hero (Driscoll)	6 and up
Simplified Biographies: Various kinds of biographies for less fluent readers, usually short with many illustrations.	*Ben Franklin: His Wit and Wisdom from A–Z* (Schroeder)	K–3
	Thomas Jefferson (Harness)	1–3
	Sacajawea: Her True Story (Milton)	1 and up
	Mary McLeod Bethune (Greenfield)	4–6
	Who Was Charles Darwin? (Hopkinson)	4–6
	Maritcha: A Nineteenth-Century American Girl (Bolden) [Maritcha Lyons]	4–6
Partial Biographies: Biographies about only part of the subject's life.	*We Are One: The Story of Bayard Rustin* (Brimner)	K–3
	Abigail Adams: Witness to a Revolution (Bober)	K–3
	The Young Hans Christian Andersen (Hesse)	4–6
	Frederick Douglass: The Last Days of Slavery (Miller)	4–6
	Jack: The Early Years of John F. Kennedy (Cooper)	5 and up
Complete Biographies: Complete biography spans the subject's lifetime in a view that has some depth, some balance, and some sense of perspective.	*Franklin Delano Roosevelt* (Freedman)	4–6
	Christo and Jeanne-Claude: Through the Gates and Beyond (Greenberg and Jordan)	4–6
	Vincent and Theo: The Van Gogh Brothers (Heiligman)	4 and up
	Amelia Lost: The Life and Disappearance of Amelia Earhart (Fleming)	6 and up
	The World at Her Fingertips: The Story of Helen Keller (Dash)	6 and up
	The Great Little Madison (Fritz) [James Madison]	6 and up
	Claudette Colvin: Twice Toward Justice (Hoose)	6 and up
	Restless Spirit: The Life and Work of Dorothea Lange (Partridge)	6 and up
	The Brontë Sisters: The Brief Lives of Charlotte, Emily, and Anne (Reef)	6 and up
	Samurai Rising: The Epic Life of Minamoto Yoshitsune (Turner)	6 and up
	Adventurous Women: Eight True Stories About Women Who Made a Difference (Colman)	6 and up

Type	Title and Author	Grade Level
Collective Biographies: Biographical information about specific people or endeavors.	*Chuck Close: Face Book* (Close)	3–5
	Bad Girls: Sirens, Jezebels, Murderesses, Thieves & Other Female Villains (Yolen and Stemple)	3–6
	Lives of the Artists: Masterpieces, Messes (and What the Neighbors Thought) (Krull)	4–6
	Motor Girls: How Women Took the Wheel and Drove Boldly Into the Twentieth Century (Macy)	4–6
	Kids of Kabul: Living Bravely Through a Never-Ending War (Ellis)	4–8
	Let It Shine: Stories of Black Women Freedom Fighters (Pinkney)	5 and up
	Good Night Stories for Rebel Girls (Favilli)	6 and up
Autobiography and Memoir: Life stories recalled and written down by the subjects themselves and drawn from personal memory.	*Drawing from Memory* (Say)	K–3
	I Will Plant You a Lilac Tree: A Memoir of a Schindler's List Survivor (Hillman)	K–3
	A Boy and a Jaguar (Rabinowitz)	2–4
	Brown Girl Dreaming (Woodson)	3–5
	The Abracadabra Kid: A Writer's Life (Fleischman)	4 and up
	Red Scarf Girl: A Memoir of the Cultural Revolution (Jiang)	6 and up
	The Upside Down Boy/El niño de cabeza (Herrera)	7 and up
	To the Mountaintop: My Journey Through the Civil Rights Movement (Hunter-Gault)	7 and up
	The Way West: Journal of a Pioneer Woman (Knight)	7 and up
	The House Baba Built: An Artist's Childhood in China (Young)	7 and up

Challenging Perspectives on Biography

Rachael sits quietly at her desk with her book closed. Noticing this, her teacher, Mrs. Craig, walks over to her desk and asks, "Rachael, it's D.E.A.R. [Drop Everything And Read] time and you are not reading. Is there a problem?" Rachael doesn't look up at her teacher. Mrs. Craig repeats her question. Rachael slowly raises her head, "I don't want to read a book that has something in it about Hitler. He was a very bad man."

Earlier in this chapter, we discussed that biographies written for children are no longer limited to people whose lives are worthy of emulation. Chronicling the lives of those who may be guilty of "high crimes and misdemeanors" in biographies has become part of the canon. This may lead some teachers to question whether they should provide biographies about men and women who have participated in atrocities such as genocide or treason.

For some, the answer is easy—no. Others may deliberate and find this a very difficult decision. Why? Many teachers may believe inclusion of such material expands the world-view of young readers. This view is supported with content objectives and curricular benchmarks, especially in the social studies. However, having such objectives and benchmarks does not remove the challenge of how to navigate reading and responding to biographies that are written about people and cultural contexts that are full of historical or contemporary controversy.

While many of us would like to expose children and young adults to books that would provide positive role models (leaders, political thinkers, inventors, scientists, artists, writers, actors, sportspersons), we may find ourselves sharing biographies written about people who both negatively and positively changed and influenced the world. This provides a very important space for teachers to engage students in responses that reflect various and multiple points of view. These books can serve a useful purpose in presenting an expanded worldview to readers.

As a teacher plans to read or assign a potentially "controversial" biography, a few points to remember are:

1. **Openly discuss the reality of both positive and negative life stories.** Don't pretend the lives of some people (historical and contemporary) are not controversial. Along with their positive contributions, openly discuss the poor choices that had negative consequences in their life or the lives of others. Annette Gordon-Reed's *The Hemingses of Monticello: An American Family* can create an opportunity to discuss Thomas Jefferson, who was not only the author of the Declaration of Independence, the President of the United States, and a founder of the University of Virginia, but also a slave owner.

2. **Emphasize the human capacity to grow and change.** Some life stories begin with people in very difficult circumstances. *X: A Biography of Malcolm X* by Jessica Gunderson, illustrated by Seitu Hayden, presents opportunities for discussions of compassion and empathy as well as deliberation around how choices can have a constructive or destructive impact on a single person or society.

3. **Cultivate democratic ideals.** Reading a children's book with less than "perfect" people provides an excellent opportunity to reiterate the importance of a democratic and legal system of checks and balances to ensure liberty and justice for all. For instance, a teacher could use Susan Goldman Rubin's *Irena Sendler and the Children of the Warsaw Ghetto*, illustrated by Bill Farnsworth, which is an account of a Catholic social worker's courage and ingenuity in rescuing, documenting, and relocating hundreds of Jewish children during the terror of Nazi-occupied Poland.

The challenge—and opportunity—is to provide children with biographies that will spark new ideas and discoveries on their own through the stories and experiences of others. It may come from reading about those "of whom the world was not worthy" or from those guilty of everything from corruption to homicide. (Go to Connect® for a sample of how to use the Ten-Point Model to address biography in the classroom.)

Using Biography to Address Standards

Reading biography presents children with challenges that are similar to reading nonfiction. To become critical readers of biography, they must ask questions of the text. Children should be encouraged to think about what is really factual in a book and what is made up and to ask questions. Comparing biographies of the same person can be a useful exercise in critical reading. Such an activity can also help children focus on the style of each writer (and illustrator) and how the writing and illustrations affect their own understanding and enjoyment of the biography.

Suggested Children's Book: *Some Writer!: The Story of E. B. White* by Melissa Sweet (Houghton Mifflin Harcourt, 2016)

Melissa Sweet's unique storytelling format that blends collage, illustrations, and text enthralls readers interested in learning more about the life of E. B. White. Excerpts from letters and family photographs provide a more intimate knowledge of White's passions, work, and sense of humor. Readers will finish this book with a deep appreciate for the thought and care White put into his writings for children and indeed think he was "some writer."

Subject	Standards	Classroom Ideas
Language Arts, Social Studies, and Technology	**NCSS:** Use appropriate resources, data sources, and geographic tools such as atlases, databases, grid systems, charts, graphs, and maps to generate, manipulate, and interpret information.	Research saltwater farms, like the one the Whites purchased on Allen Cove in Maine.
	ISTE: Students plan and employ effective research strategies to locate information and other resources for their intellectual or creative pursuits.	Draw connections between what life was like on a farm in Maine in Sweet's biography to facts learned from your research. Extend these connections to characters in White's novels.
	NCTE/ILA: Students conduct research on issues and interests by generating ideas and questions, and by posing problems. They gather, evaluate, and synthesize data from a variety of sources (e.g., print and nonprint texts, artifacts, people) to communicate their discoveries in ways that suit their purpose and audience.	
Science and Math	**NGSS:** Plan and conduct an investigation to determine whether plants need sunlight and (salt) water to grow.	Investigate plant growth in saltwater versus freshwater.
	NCTM: Design investigations to address a question. Collect data using observations and experiments. Represent data using tables and graphs such as line plots, bar graphs, and line graphs.	Collect, analyze, and represent data about how much of each type of water and the amount of sunlight impacts plant growth each day.

(continued)

curriculum connections

Subject	Standards	Classroom Ideas
Language Arts and Art	**NCTE/ILA:** Students adjust their use of spoken, written, and visual language to communicate effectively with a variety of audiences and for different purposes. **NCCAS:** Convey meaning through the presentation of artistic work.	Study a character from one of White's novels, like Templeton, to explore character motivation and interest. Create a "chapter" collage with sketches, dialogue from the book, and your writing.
Textual Connections	*Charlotte's Web* (White), *The Trumpet of the Swan* (White), and *Stuart Little* (White); *A Boy, a Mouse, and a Spider: The Story of E.B. White* (Herkert)	
Other books by Sweet	Written by Sweet: *Balloons over Broadway: The True Story of the Puppeteer of Macy's Parade*; *Tupelo Rides the Rails* Illustrated by Sweet: *Listen to Our World* (Martin); *Little Red Writing* (Holub); *The Right Word: Roget and His Thesaurus* (Bryant); *A River of Words: The Story of William Carlos Williams* (Bryant); *A Splash of Red: The Life and Art of Horace Pippin* (Bryant)	
Author's Website	http://melissasweet.net	

Sources: International Society for Technology in Education (ITSE); National Coalition for Core Arts Standards (NCCAS); National Council of Teachers of English (NCTE)/International Literacy Association (ILA); National Council of Teachers of Mathematics (NCTM); National Council for the Social Studies Curriculum Standards (NCSS); and Next Generation Science Standards (NGSS).

Notes

1. Jo Carr, "What Do We Do about Bad Biographies?" in *Beyond Fact: Nonfiction for Children and Young People* (Chicago: American Library Association, 1982), pp. 119–29.

Children's Literature

*Go to **Connect**® to access study resources, practice quizzes, and additional materials.*

Titles in blue = multicultural titles

Adler, David A. *A Picture Book of Sojourner Truth*. Illustrated by Gershom Griffith. Holiday, 1994.

Andrews, Troy. *Trombone Shorty*. Illustrated by Bryan Collier. Harry N. Abrams, 2015.

Andrews-Goebel, Nancy. *The Pot That Juan Built*. Illustrated by David Diaz. Lee, 2002.

Appelt, Kathi, and Jeanne Cannella Schmitzer. *Down Cut Shin Creek: The Pack Horse Librarians of Kentucky*. HarperCollins, 2001.

Asim, Jabari. *Fifty Cents and a Dream: Young Booker T. Washington*. Illustrated by Bryan Collier. Little, Brown, 2012.

Benson, Kathleen. *Draw What You See: The Life and Art of Benny Andrews*. Illustrated with paintings by Benny Andrews. Clarion, 2015.

Berne, Jennifer. *On a Beam of Light: A Story of Albert Einstein*. Illustrated by Vladimir Radunsky. Chronicle, 2013.

Bernier-Grand, Carmen T. *César: ¡Si, Se Puede! Yes, We Can!* Illustrated by David Diaz. Cavendish, 2005.

Bertozzi, Nick. *Shackleton: Antarctic Odyssey*. First Second, 2014.

Bildner, Phil. *Martina & Chrissie: The Greatest Rivalry in the History of Sports*. Illustrated by Brett Helquist. Candlewick, 2017.

Blumenthal, Deborah. *Fancy Party Gowns: The Story of Fashion Designer Ann Cole Lowe*. Illustrated by Laura Freeman. Little Bee, 2017.

Blumberg, Rhoda. *Shipwrecked!: The True Adventures of a Japanese Boy*. HarperCollins, 2001.

Bober, Natalie S. *Abigail Adams: Witness to a Revolution*. Atheneum, 1995.

Bolden, Tonya. *Maritcha: A Nineteenth-Century American Girl*. Abrams, 2005.

Brimner, Larry Dane. *We Are One: The Story of Bayard Rustin*. Calkins Creek, 2007.

Brown, Don. *Odd Boy Out: Young Albert Einstein*. Houghton, 2004.

Brown, Monica. *Pablo Neruda: Poet of the People*. Illustrated by Julie Paschkis. Holt, 2011.

Bruchac, Joseph. *Jim Thorpe's Bright Path*. Illustrated by S. D. Nelson. Lee & Low, 2004.

Bryant, Jen. *The Right Word: Roget and His Thesaurus*. Illustrated by Melissa Sweet. Eerdmans Books for Young Readers, 2014.

_____. *A River of Words: The Story of William Carlos Williams*. Illustrated by Melissa Sweet. Eerdmans Books for Young Readers, 2008.

_____. *A Splash of Red: The Life and Art of Horace Pippin*. Illustrated by Melissa Sweet. Knopf Books for Young Readers, 2013.

Burgess, Matthew. *Enormous Smallness: A Story of E. E. Cummings*. Illustrated by Kris Di Giacomo. Enchanted Lion, 2015.

Burleigh, Robert, and Barry Blitt. *The Adventures of Mark Twain by Huckleberry Finn*. Atheneum, 2011.

Close, Chuck. *Chuck Close: Face Book*. Abrams, 2012.

Colman, Penny. *Adventurous Women: Eight True Stories About Women Who Made a Difference*. Holt, 2006.

Cooper, Ilene. *Jack: The Early Years of John F. Kennedy*. Dutton, 2003.

Copeland, Misty. *Firebird: Ballerina Misty Copeland Shows a Young Girl How to Dance Like the Firebird*. Illustrated by Christopher Myers. G.P Putnam's Sons Books for Young Readers, 2014.

d'Aulaire, Ingri, and Edgar Parin d'Aulaire. *Abraham Lincoln*. Rev. ed. Doubleday, 1957.

Dash, Joan. *The World at Her Fingertips: The Story of Helen Keller*. Scholastic, 2001.

Driscoll, Laura. *Sammy Sosa: Home-Run Hero*. Illustrated by Ken Call. Grosset, 1999.

Ellis, Deborah. *Kids of Kabul: Living Bravely through a Never-Ending War*. Groundwood, 2012.

Faber, Doris. *Eleanor Roosevelt, First Lady of the World*. Illustrated by Donna Ruff. Viking, 1985.

Favilli, Elena. *Good Night Stories for Rebel Girls*. Illustrated by Francesca Cavallo. Timbuktu Labs, 2016.

Fleischman, Sid. *The Abracadabra Kid: A Writer's Life*. Greenwillow, 1996.

Fleming, Candace. *Amelia Lost: The Life and Disappearance of Amelia Earhart*. Schwartz & Wade. 2011.

_____. *Ben Franklin's Almanac: Being a True Account of the Good Gentleman's Life*. Simon, 2003.

_____. *The Family Romanov: Murder, Rebellion, and the Fall of Imperial Russia*. Schwartz & Wade, 2014.

Freedman, Russell. *Franklin Delano Roosevelt*. Clarion, 1990.

Frier, Raphaële. *Malala: Activist for Girls' Education*. Illustrated by Aurélia Fronty. Translated by Julie Cormier. Charlesbridge, 2017.

Fritz, Jean. *The Great Little Madison*. Putnam, 1989.

_____. *And Then What Happened, Paul Revere?* Illustrated by Margot Tomes. Coward, 1973.

_____. *Can't You Make Them Behave, King George?* Illustrated by Tomie dePaola. Coward, 1982.

_____. *Homesick: My Own Story*. Illustrated by Margot Tomes. Putnam, 1982.

Giblin, James Cross. *Thomas Jefferson*. Illustrated by Michael Dooling. Scholastic, 1994.

Gill, Joel Christian. *Bessie Stringfield (Tales of the Talented Tenth #2)*. Fulcrum, 2016.

Giovanni, Nikki. *Rosa*. Illustrated by Bryan Collier. Holt, 2005.

Goodall, John. *The Story of a Farm*. McElderry, 1989.

Greenberg, Jan, and Sandra Jordan. *Christo and Jeanne-Claude: Through the Gates and Beyond*. Roaring Brook Press, 2008.

Greenfield, Eloise. *Mary McLeod Bethune*. Illustrated by Jerry Pinkney. Crowell, 1993 [1977].

Grill, William. *Shackleton's Journey*. Flying Eye, 2014.

Gunderson, Jessica Sarah. *X: A Biography of Malcom X*. Illustrated by Seitu Hayden. Capstone, 2011.

Harness, Cheryl. *Thomas Jefferson*. National Geographic, 2007.

Harvey, Jeanne Walker. *Maya Lin: Artist-Architect of Light and Lines*. Illustrated by Dow Phumiruk. Holt, 2017.

Heiligman, Deborah. *Vincent and Theo: The Van Gogh Brothers*. Holt, 2017.

Herkert, Barbara. *A Boy, a Mouse, and a Spider: The Story of E.B. White*. Illustrated by Lauren Castillo. Henry Holt and Co., 2017.

Herrera, Juan Felipe. *The Upside Down Boy/El niño de cabeza*. Illustrated by Elizabeth Gómez. Children's, 2000.

Hesse, Karen. *The Young Hans Christian Andersen*. Illustrated by Erik Blegvad. Scholastic, 2005.

Hill, Laban Carrick. *Dave the Potter: Artist, Poet, Slave*. Illustrated by Bryan Collier. Little Brown, 2010.

Hillman, Laura. *I Will Plant You a Lilac Tree: A Memoir of a Schindler's List Survivor*. Atheneum, 2005.

Holub, Joan. *Little Red Writing*. Illustrated by Melissa Sweet. Chronicle Books, 2013.

Holzer, Harold. *Father Abraham: Lincoln and His Sons*. Boyds Mills, 2011.

Hoose, Phillip. *Claudette Colvin: Twice Toward Justice*. Farrar, 2009.

____. *Who Was Charles Darwin?* Illustrated by Nancy Harrison. Grosset, 2005.

Hunter-Gault, Charlene. *To the Mountaintop: My Journey Through the Civil Rights Movement*. Roaring Brook Press, 2012.

Jacobsen, Sid. *Anne Frank: The Anne Frank House Authorized Graphic Biography*. Illustrated by Ernesto Colón. Hill and Wang, 2011.

Johnson, Jen Cullerton. *Seeds of Change: Wangari's Gift to the World*. Illustrated by Sonia Lynn Sadler. Lee & Low, 2010.

Jiang, Ji-li. *Red Scarf Girl: A Memoir of the Cultural Revolution*. HarperCollins, 1997.

Kamkwamba, William and Bryan Mealer. *The Boy Who Harnessed the Wind*. Illustrated by Elizabeth Zunon. Puffin, 2012.

Keating, Jess. *Shark Lady: The True Story of How Eugenie Clark Became the Ocean's Most Fearless Scientist*. Illustrated by Marta Alvarez Miguens. Sourcebooks Jabberwocky, 2017.

Kerley, Barbara. *The Extraordinary Mark Twain (According to Susy)*. Illustrated by Edwin Fotheringham. Scholastic, 2010.

Knight, Amelia. *The Way West: Journal of a Pioneer Woman*. Adapted by Lillian Schisse. Illustrated by Michael McCurdy. Simon, 1993.

Krull, Kathleen. *Lives of the Artists: Masterpieces, Messes (and What the Neighbors Thought)*. Illustrated by Kathryn Hewitt. Harcourt, 1995.

Lang, Heather. *Swimming with Sharks: The Daring Discoveries of Eugenie Clark*. Illustrated by Jordi Solano. Albert Whitman, 2016.

Levinson, Cynthia. *The Youngest Marcher: The Story of Audrey Faye Hendricks, a Young Civil Rights Activist*. Illustrated by Vanessa Brantley-Newton. Atheneum, 2017.

Macy, Sue. *Miss Mary Reporting: The True Story of Sportswriter Mary Garber*. Illustrated by C.F. Payne. Simon & Schuster, 2016.

____. *Motor Girls: How Women Took the Wheel and Drove Boldly Into the Twentieth Century*. National Geographic, 2017.

____. *Trudy's Big Swim: How Gertrude Ederle Swam the English Channel and Took the World by Storm*. Illustrated by Matt Collins. Holiday House, 2017.

MacLachlan, Patricia. *The Iridescence of Birds: A Book About Henri Matisse*. Roaring Brook, 2014.

Malaspina, Ann. *Touch the Sky: Alice Coachman, Olympic High Jumper*. Illustrated by Eric Velasquez. Albert Whitman, 2012.

Maltbie, P. I. *Bambino and Mr. Twain*. Illustrated by Daniel Miyares. Charlesbridge, 2011.

McDonnell, Patrick. *Me . . . Jane*. Little Brown, 2011.

Miller, William. *Frederick Douglass: The Last Days of Slavery*. Illustrated by Cedric Lucas. Lee, 1995.

Milton, Joyce. *Sacajawea: Her True Story*. Illustrated by Shelley Hehenberger. Putnam, 2001.

Murphy, Jim. *The Giant and How He Humbugged America*. Scholastic, 2012.

Myers, Walter Dean. *Frederick Douglass: The Lion Who Wrote History*. Illustrated by Floyd Cooper. HarperCollins, 2017.

Napoli, Donna Jo. *Mama Miti: Wangari Maathai and the Trees of Kenya*. Illustrated by Kadir Nelson. Simon & Schuster, 2010.

Nelson, Vaunda Micheaux. *Bad News for Outlaws: The Remarkable Life of Bass Reeves, Deputy U. S. Marshal*. Illustrated by R. Gregory Christie. Carolrhoda, 2009.

Nivola, Claire A. *Life in the Ocean: The Story of Oceanographer Sylvia Earle*. Farrar, 2012.

———. *Orani: My Father's Village.* Farrar/Frances Foster, 2011.

———. *Planting the Trees of Kenya: The Story of Wangari Maathai.* Farrar, Straus and Giroux, 2008.

Nobleman, Marc Tyler. *Boys of Steel: The Creators of Superman.* Knopf, 2008.

Novesky, Amy. *Cloth Lullaby: The Woven Life of Louise Bourgeois.* Illustrated by Isabelle Arsenault. Harry N. Abrams, 2016.

Ottaviano, Jim. *Primates: The Fearless Science of Jane Goodall, Dian Fossey, and Biruté Galdikas.* Illustrated by Maris Wicks. First Second, 2013.

Partridge, Elizabeth. *Restless Spirit: The Life and Work of Dorothea Lange.* Viking, 1998.

Patent, Dorothy Hinshaw. *Charles Darwin: The Life of a Revolutionary Thinker.* Holiday, 2001.

Pinkney, Andrea Davis. *Ella Fitzgerald: The Tale of a Vocal Virtuosa.* Illustrated by Brian Pinkney. Hyperion, 2002.

———. *Let It Shine: Stories of Black Women Freedom Fighters.* Illustrated by Stephen Alcorn. Harcourt/Gulliver, 2000.

———. *A Poem for Peter: The Story of Ezra Jack Keats and the Creation of The Snowy Day.* Illustrated by Steve Johnson and Lou Fancher. Viking, 2016.

———. *Sojourner Truth's Step-Stomp Stride.* Illustrated by Brian Pinkney. Jump at the Sun, 2009.

Powell, Patricia Hruby. *Josephine: The Dazzling Life of Josephine Baker.* Illustrated by Christian Robinson. Chronicle, 2014.

Prévot, Franck. *Wangari Maathai: The Woman Who Planted Millions of Trees.* Illustrated by Aurélia Fronty. Charlesbridge, 2015.

Rabinowitz, Alan. *A Boy and a Jaguar.* Illustrated by Catia Chien. HMH Books for Young Readers, 2014.

Rappaport, Doreen. *Martin's Big Words.* Illustrated by Bryan Collier. Hyperion/Jump at the Sun, 2001.

———. *Abe's Honest Words: The Life of Abraham Lincoln.* Illustrated by Kadir Nelson. Disney-Hyperion, 2008.

———. *Eleanor, Quiet No More.* Illustrated by Gary Kelley. Disney-Hyperion, 2009.

———. *Frederick's Journey: The Life of Frederick Douglass.* Illustrated by London Ladd. Jump at the Sun, 2015.

———. *Helen's Big World: The Life of Helen Keller.* Illustrated by Matt Tavares. Disney-Hyperion, 2012.

———. *Jack's Path of Courage: The Life of John F. Kennedy.* Illustrated by Matthew Todd Borgens. Disney-Hyperion, 2010.

———. *John's Secret Dreams: The Life of John Lennon.* Illustrated by Bryan Collier. Disney-Hyperion, 2004.

———. *To Dare Mighty Things: The Life of Theodore Roosevelt.* Illustrated by C.F. Payne. Disney-Hyperion, 2013.

Reed, Annette Gordon. *The Hemingses of Monticello: An American Family.* Norton, 2008.

Reef, Catherine. *The Brontë Sisters: The Brief Lives of Charlotte, Emily, and Anne.* Clarion, 2012.

Robbins, Trina. *Lily Renée: Escape Artist.* Lerner, 2011.

Robinson, Fiona. *Ada's Ideas: The Story of Ada Lovelace, the World's First Computer Programmer.* Harry N. Abrams, 2016.

Rosenstock, Barb. *Dorothea's Eyes: Dorothea Lange Photographs the Truth.* Illustrated by Gerard DuBois. Calkin's Creek, 2016.

Rubin, Susan Goldman. *Irena Sendler and the Children of the Warsaw Ghetto.* Illustrated by Bill Farnsworth. Holiday, 2012.

Rumford, James. *Sequoyah: The Cherokee Man Who Gave His People Writing.* Translated into Cherokee by Anna Sixkiller Huckaby. Houghton, 2004.

Russell-Brown, Katheryn. *Little Melba and Her Big Trombone.* Illustrated by Frank Morrison. Lee & Low, 2014.

Ryan, Pam Muñoz. *When Marian Sang: The True Recital of Marian Anderson: The Voice of a Century.* Illustrated by Brian Selznick. Scholastic, 2002.

Say, Allen. *Drawing from Memory.* Scholastic, 2011.

Schroeder, Alan. *Ben Franklin: His Wit and Wisdom.* Illustrated by John O'Brien. Holiday, 2012.

Schubert, Leda. *Monsieur Marceau.* Illustrated by Gérard Dubois. Roaring Brook, 2012.

Sheinkin, Steven. *The Notorious Benedict Arnold: A True Story of Adventure, Heroism, & Treachery.* Flash Point, 2011.

———. *Undefeated: Jim Thorpe and the Carlisle Indian School Football Team.* Roaring Brook, 2017.

Sisson, Stephanie Roth. *Star Stuff: Carl Sagan and the Mysteries of the Cosmos.* Roaring Brook, 2014.

Skead, Rob. *Something to Prove: The Great Satchel Paige vs. Rookie Joe DiMaggio.* Illustrated by Floyd Cooper. Lerner, 2013.

Skrypuch, Marsha Forchuk. *Adrift at Sea: A Vietnamese Boy's Story of Survival*. Illustrated by Brian Deines. Contributions by Tuan Ho. Pajama Press, 2016.

Snyder, Laurel. *Swan: The Life and Dance of Anna Pavlova*. Illustrated by Julie Morstad. Chronicle, 2015.

Stanley, Diane. *Ada Lovelace, Poet of Science: The First Computer Programmer*. Illustrated by Jessie Hartland. Simon & Schuster, 2016.

_____. *Leonardo da Vinci*. Morrow, 1996.

Steptoe, Javaka. *Radiant Child: The Story of Young Artist Jean-Michel Basquiat*. Little, Brown, 2016.

Stone, Tanya Lee. *The House That Jane Built: A Story About Jane Addams*. Illustrated by Kathryn Brown. Henry Holt, 2015.

Sweet, Melissa. *Balloons Over Broadway: The True Story of the Puppeteer of Macy's Parade*. Houghton Harcourt, 2011.

_____. *Some Writer!: The Story of E. B. White*. HMH Books for Young Readers, 2016.

_____. *Tupelo Rides the Rails*. HMH Books for Young Readers, 2008.

Tate, Don. *It Jes' Happened: When Bill Traylor Started to Draw*. Illustrated by Gregory Christie. Lee & Low, 2012.

Thompson, Laurie Ann. *Emmanuel's Dream: The True Story of Emmanuel Ofosu Yeboah*. Illustrated by "https://www.goodreads.com/author/show/2771307.Sean_Qualls" Sean Qualls. Schwartz & Wade, 2015.

Turner, Pamela S. *Samurai Rising: The Epic Life of Minamoto Yoshitsune*. Illustrated by Gareth Hinds. Charlesbridge, 2016.

Vernick, Audrey. *The Kid from Diamond Street: The Extraordinary Story of Baseball Legend Edith Houghton*. Illustrated by Steven Salerno. Clarion, 2016

Weatherford, Carole Boston. *Dorothea Lange: The Photographer Who Found the Faces of the Depression*. Illustrated by Sarah Green. Albert Whitman, 2017.

_____. *Voice of Freedom: Fannie Lou Hamer: Spirit of the Civil Rights Movement*. Illustrated by Ekua Holmes. Candlewick, 2015.

West, Delno, and Jean West. *Christopher Columbus: The Great Adventure and How We Know About It*. Atheneum, 1991.

White, E. B. *Charlotte's Web*. HarperCollins, 1952.

_____. *Stuart Little*. HarperCollins, 1945.

_____. *The Trumpet of the Swan*. HarperCollins, 1970.

Winter, Jeanette. *Wangari's Trees of Peace: A True Story from Africa*. Harcourt, 2008.

Winter, Jonah. *Frida*. Illustrated by Ana Juan. Scholastic, 2002.

Woodson, Jacqueline. *Brown Girl Dreaming*. Puffin, 2014.

Yolen, Jane, and Heidi V. Y. Stemple. *Bad Girls: Sirens, Jezebels, Murderesses, Thieves & Other Female Villains*. Illustrated by Rebecca Guy. Charlesbridge, 2013.

Young, Ed. *The House Baba Built: An Artist's Childhood in China*. Little, Brown, 2011.

Part Three

The Literature Program Across the Curriculum

Chapter Eleven

Planning the Literature Program

Chapter Outline

One October morning, a group of first graders were gathered in a circle on the rug. They had been studying monarch butterflies, observing their metamorphosis from tiny caterpillar to adult caterpillar, chrysalis, and butterfly. In addition to learning about their life cycle, students also learned about their defense mechanisms, migration patterns, and their dependence on the milkweed plant.

The teacher read them Helen Frost's picturebook, *Monarch and Milkweed*, to highlight the structure and function of the milkweed pod and seed dispersal. Frost parallels the life cycle of the milkweed plant with that of the monarch, describing how the monarch drinks nectar from the milkweed's fragrant purple flowers and how the "flowers fall away; green pods push out. Inside these bumpy fists, new seeds are forming." As the weather turns cooler and the leaves of the milkweed plant begin to yellow and fall away, and the monarch readies to fly south for the winter, the milkweed pods turn brown and dry. Finally, as the monarch takes flight, Mexico bound, the milkweed's pods split open, sending the silky tendrils of white fluff into the air, brown seeds dangling below, ready to drop to the ground and start the life cycle of the milkweed plant again.

©Brian MacDonald.

After one initial read through of the book in its entirety, the teacher returned to the page that shows the milkweed pods releasing the seeds into the air. "Milkweed's pods split open. Brown seeds lay close together on a soft, white bed. October wind catches a silky tendril, opens it, and lifts a seed into the air, carrying it out and away, across a river, to an old white house." She and the children reviewed what they'd learned about how some seeds travel via animal, wind, water, or fling, and students quickly decided that the milkweed's seeds travel by air.

The teacher then revealed the milkweed pod she had been concealing in her pocket. It had already begun to crack open, so students could see the brown seeds nestled neatly inside, the white fluffy tendrils still straight and flat.

"What do you think happens when the pod dries out and splits all the way open?" she asked. Eager hands raised, and students predicted that the white silk would fluff up, catch a breeze, and carry the seed to its new destination. "Let's find out!"

The teacher handed each eager child a bumpy, dry milkweed pod. Some examined them carefully before prying them open, while others couldn't wait and dove right in. Before they knew it, the classroom was full of white fluff, children blowing the milkweed seeds in all directions. They observed how some fell to the ground quickly, while others stayed airborne longer. Some landed in friends' hair or on clothing, eventually finding their way to the floor. Many ended up in pockets and joyful hands, determined to plant them at home.

After a rowdy and rather comical effort to retrieve all the stray fluff and seeds, the group gathered again on the carpet. "So what did you discover about the milkweed pods and seeds?" Students excitedly recounted their experiences, concluding that the fluff was a very effective structure to transport the milkweed seeds to different locations near and far.

"What would happen if there wasn't any fluff?" In addition to being way less fun to open up in their classroom, the children decided that the seeds would end up right underneath the old plant. They were able to articulate the concept of how structure dictates function in their reflections. "The fluff helps the seeds go somewhere new, so new plants can grow," said one student.

"Yeah, like in the book how one floated over the river to get to someone's yard," said another. "It's kind of like the seeds wanted to fly away and not just drop down right there."

"Well then the monarchs have more milkweed plants for when they come back!"

In this vignette, we see how children's literature was central to the first-grade curriculum. The teacher knew that if children had the opportunity to listen, read, and explore good books through a variety of activities, they would grow to appreciate and understand fine books and big ideas. The class read-aloud sessions took place several times a day, giving children and teacher the opportunity to explore many concepts, in this case the concept of structure and function from the Next Generation Science Standards (NGSS). The episode is also typical of how an inquiring community of learners can be built around and beyond quality books. The teacher had been working with a literature-based curriculum over a period of years, not only to help students learn, but also to develop their love of reading. At the same time, she also found many ways to integrate curricular standards through the exploration of literature.

Purposes of the Literature-Based Curriculum

A literature-based curriculum includes relevant children's books in the study of multiple subject areas. Each school will want to develop its own curriculum in terms of the background and abilities of the children it serves. Teachers and librarians need to know both their children and the potential of their material and have an understanding of the structure of literature; then they will be free to make the right match between child and book.

This chapter can suggest guidelines and give examples, but it cannot prescribe the literature-based curriculum that will work with all children.

One of the major purposes of any literature-based curriculum is to provide children with the opportunity to experience literature, to enter into and become involved in a book. The goal of all literature-based curricula should be not only to meet the content-area standards but also to help them learn to love reading, to discover joy in reading. Their every activity, every assignment, should pass this test: "Will this increase children's desire to read? Will it make them want to continue reading?" A literature-based curriculum must get children excited about reading, turned on to books, and tuned in to literature.

A second goal of a literature-based curriculum is to build critical knowledge and understanding (currently represented by content-area standards) through integrated experiences with genres and disciplines. This type of integration builds on current theories of how individual children develop and learn.[2] It gives children opportunities for critical inquiry in areas that have relevance to their lives and futures. A literature-based curriculum also allows teachers to provide opportunities for learning for children of widely differing abilities and interests.[3] **Teaching Feature 11.1: Fact and Fiction: Books to Use Together** provides examples of how to link various genres of books with themes of study at different grade levels.

A school literature program should also help children develop literary awareness and appreciation. We want children to develop an understanding of literary genres and to recognize the unique qualities and criteria of many types of literature. We want to introduce children to literary classics and contemporary works highlighting the authors and illustrators who create the books that they love. We expect that over time children will become familiar with the many components of fiction and nonfiction literature. However, their knowledge about literature should be secondary to experiencing the joy of reading good literature. Too frequently, we have substituted the study of literary criticism for the experience of becoming fully engaged with the literature itself. Attention to content, rather than literary criticism of the form, should be the first concern.

A story map of "The Story of the Three Little Pigs" helped first-grade children to retell the story. Columbus Public Schools, Columbus, Ohio. Connie Compton, teacher.

Fact and Fiction: Books to Use Together

Poultry and Eggs (Grades K–2)

Big Fat Hen (Baker)	Counting Book
The Talking Eggs (San Souci)	Traditional
The Sky Is Falling! (Teague)	Traditional
A Chicken Followed Me Home!: Questions and Answers About a Familiar Fowl (Page)	Nonfiction
A Nest Full of Eggs (Jenkins)	Nonfiction
Guess What Is Growing Inside This Egg (Posada)	Nonfiction
Where Do Chicks Come From? (Sklansky)	Nonfiction
An Egg Is Quiet (Aston)	Nonfiction
Hatch! (Munro)	Nonfiction
The Perfect Nest (Friend)	Nonfiction
Daniel's Mystery Egg (Ada)	Easy Picturebook
Nana's Big Surprise / Nana, ¡que sorprésa! (Peréz)	Picturebook
An Extraordinary Egg (Lionni)	Picturebook
Egg Drop (Grey)	Picturebook
P. Zonka Lays an Egg (Paschkis)	Picturebook
Just Plain Fancy (Polacco)	Picturebook
The Odd Egg (Gravett)	Picturebook
Cook-a-Doodle-Doo! (Stevens)	Picturebook
Chicken Man (Edwards)	Picturebook

Insects and Invertebrates (Grades 2–3)

The Beetle Book (Jenkins)	Nonfiction
Butterflies (Simon)	Nonfiction
Bugs (Wright)	Nonfiction
Monarch and Milkweed (Frost)	Nonfiction
Monarch Butterfly (Gibbons)	Nonfiction
Spiders (Bishop)	Nonfiction
Flip the Flaps: Creepy Crawlies (Wallace)	Nonfiction
Bugs Are Insects (Rockwell)	Nonfiction
Honey in a Hive (Rockwell)	Nonfiction
Face to Face with Caterpillars (Murawski)	Nonfiction
The Tarantula Scientist (Montgomery)	Nonfiction
I, Fly: The Buzz About Flies and How Awesome They Are (Heos)	Nonfiction
Insects: The Most Fun Bug Book Ever (Collard)	Nonfiction
My Awesome Summer by P. Mantis (Meisel)	Picturebook
Worm Loves Worm (Austrian)	Picturebook
Du Iz Tak? (Ellis)	Picturebook
A Butterfly Is Patient (Aston)	Picturebook
Diary of a Spider (Cronin)	Picturebook
Diary of a Fly (Cronin)	Picturebook
James and the Giant Peach (Dahl)	Fantasy

(continued)

teaching feature 11.1

Insects and Invertebrates (Grades 2–3) (continued)

Bug Off!: Creepy, Crawly Poems (Yolen)	Poetry
Nasty Bugs (Hopkins)	Poetry
Bugs: Poems About Creeping Things (Harrison)	Poetry
Joyful Noise (Fleischman)	Poetry
The Grasshopper & the Ants (Pinkney)	Traditional

Wet Weather (Grades 1–3)

Weather (Cosgrove)	Nonfiction
Wild Science Projects About Earth's Weather (Gardner)	Nonfiction
Down Comes the Rain (Branley)	Nonfiction
Flash, Crash, Rumble, and Roll (Branley)	Nonfiction
Boy, Were We Wrong About the Weather! (Kudlinski)	Nonfiction
Storms (Simon)	Nonfiction
Weather! Watch How Weather Works (Rupp)	Nonfiction
Ready, Set . . . WAIT!: What Animals Do Before a Hurricane (Zelch)	Nonfiction
Flood Warning (Kenah)	Nonfiction
The Storm (Miyakoshi)	Picturebook
Storm in the Barn (Phelan)	Picturebook
Terrible Storm (Hurst)	Picturebook
Hurricane! (London)	Picturebook
The First Tortilla: A Bilingual Story (Anaya)	Picturebook
Rainstorm (Lehman)	Picturebook
Twister (Beard)	Picturebook
In the Rain with Baby Duck (Hest)	Picturebook
Ling & Ting: Together in All Weather (Lin)	Picturebook
Float (Miyares)	Picturebook
The Storm Makers (Smith)	Fantasy
When the Rain Comes (Fullerton)	Fantasy

Celebrating the Life of Dr. Martin Luther King Jr. and Understanding the Context of his Work (Grades 3–5)

Marching for Freedom: Walk Together, Children, and Don't You Grow Weary (Partridge)	Nonfiction
My Brother Martin: A Sister Remembers Growing Up with the Rev. Dr. Martin Luther King Jr. (Farris)	Nonfiction
Freedom Walkers: The Story of the Montgomery Bus Boycott (Freedman)	Nonfiction
Voice of Freedom: Fannie Lou Hamer: Spirit of the Civil Rights Movement (Weatherford)	Nonfiction
Blood Brother: Jonathan Daniels and His Sacrifice for Civil Rights (Wallace)	Nonfiction
Love Will See You Through (Watkins)	Nonfiction
The Assassination of Martin Luther King Jr. (Bodden)	Nonfiction

Celebrating the Life of Dr. Martin Luther King Jr. and Understanding the Context of his Work (Grades 3–5) *(continued)*

The Assassination of John F. Kennedy (Bodden)	Nonfiction
The Youngest Marcher: The Story of Audrey Faye Hendricks, a Civil Rights Activist (Levinson)	Biography
March On!: The Day My Brother Martin Changed the World (Farris)	Biography
Martin's Big Words: The Life of Dr. Martin Luther King, Jr. (Rappaport)	Biography
Coretta Scott (Shange)	Biography
Through My Eyes (Bridges)	Memoir
White Socks Only (Coleman)	Picturebook
We March (Evans)	Picturebook
Belle, The Last Mule at Gee's Bend (Ramsey)	Picturebook
Sit-In: How Four Friends Stood Up by Sitting Down (Pinkney)	Picturebook
Freedom Summer (Wiles)	Picturebook
The Other Side (Woodson)	Picturebook
If a Bus Could Talk: The Story of Rosa Parks (Ringgold)	Picturebook
Goin' Someplace Special (McKissack)	Picturebook
A Sweet Smell of Roses (Johnson)	Picturebook
Freedom on the Menu: The Greensboro Sit-Ins (Weatherford)	Picturebook
Abby Takes a Stand (Scraps of Time series) (McKissack)	Fiction
The Watsons Go to Birmingham (Curtis)	Fiction
One Crazy Summer (Williams-Garcia)	Fiction
March (March Trilogy series) (Lewis)	Graphic Novel

Displaced Children and Families (Grades 5–8)

These texts raise awareness about displaced people who have been forced to flee their homes under threat of persecution, conflict, and violence. The United Nations has established June 20 as World Refugee Day to honor the courage, strength, and determination of women, men, and children who are refugees.

Adrift at Sea: A Vietnamese Boy's Story of Survival (Skrypuch) (Cambodia)	Nonfiction
Escape from Saigon: How a Vietnamese War Orphan Became an American Boy (Warren) (Vietnam)	Nonfiction
Frederick's Journey: The Life of Frederick Douglass (Rappaport) (nineteenth-century America)	Nonfiction
Polish Orphans of Tengeru: The Dramatic Story of Their Long Journey to Canada 1941–49 (Taylor) (post-WWII)	Nonfiction
Red Bird Sings: The Story of Zitkala-Sa, Native American Author, Musician, and Activist (Capaldi) (late nineteenth-century America)	Nonfiction
Rescue: The Story of How Gentiles Saved Jews in the Holocaust (Meltzer) (WWII)	Nonfiction

(continued)

teaching **feature** 11.1

Displaced Children and Families (Grades 5–8) *(continued)*

Stormy Seas: Stories of Young Boat Refugees (Leatherdale) (5 stories)	Nonfiction
The Hidden Children (Greenfeld) (WWII)	Nonfiction
Far Apart, Close in Heart: Being A Loved One When a Family Member Is Incarcerated (Birtha) (U.S. prison system)	Picturebook
My Beautiful Birds (Del Rizzo) (Syria)	Picturebook
Stepping Stones: A Refugee Family's Journey (Ruurs) (Syria)	Picturebook
Pancho Rabbit and the Coyote (Tonatiuh) (Mexico)	Picturebook
Two White Rabbits (Buitrago) (Mexico)	Picturebook
The Journey (Sanna) (various stories)	Picturebook
The Whispering Cloth (Shea) (Hmong refugee camp in Thailand)	Picturebook
Walk with Me (Buitrago) (Latin America)	Picturebook
A Different Pond (Phi) (Vietnam)	Fiction
A Long Walk to Water (Park) (Sudan)	Fiction
Adam and Thomas (Appelfeld) (France, WWII)	Fiction
Between Shades of Grey (Sepetys) (Lithuania, WWII)	Fiction
Bronze and Sunflower (Wenxuan) (China 1960–70s)	Fiction
Cloud and Wallfish (Nesbet) (Cold War Europe)	Fiction
Emil and Karl (Glatshteyn) (Pre-WWII Austria)	Fiction
How I Became a Ghost: A Choctaw Trail of Tears Story (Tingle)	Fiction
How Many Days to America? (Bunting) (Caribbean)	Fiction
Kiss the Dust (Laird) (Kurdish refugee camp)	Fiction
La Línea (Jaramillo) (Central America)	Fiction
My Brigadista Year (Paterson) (Cuba 1961)	Fiction
Never Full Down (McCormick) (Cambodia)	Fiction
My Freedom Trip: A Child's Escape from North Korea (Park) (Korean War)	Fiction
Number the Stars (Lowry) (WWII)	Fiction
Paper Wishes (Sepahban) (Japanese Internment)	Fiction
Secrets in the Fire (Mankell) (Mozambique)	Fiction
Soldier Boy (Hutton) (Uganda)	Fiction
The Bitter Side of Sweet (Sullivan) (Ivory Coast)	Fiction
The Clay Marble and Related Readings (Ho) (Cambodia)	Fiction
The Elephant in the Garden (Morpurgo) (Germany WWII)	Fiction
The Endless Steppe (Hautzig) (Siberia WWII)	Fiction
The War That Saved My Life (Bradley) (WWII)	Fiction
The Only Road (Diaz) (Guatemala to the United States)	Fiction
Under the Persimmon Tree (Staples) (Afghan War refugee)	Fiction
Home of the Brave (Applegate) (Sudanese refugee in the United States)	Novel in Verse
Inside Out and Back Again (Lai) (Vietnam Was refugee in the United States)	Novel in Verse
The Red Pencil (Pinkney) (Somalia)	Novel in Verse

teaching **feature 11.1**

Displaced Children and Families (Grades 5–8) *(continued)*

I Never Saw Another Butterfly: Children's Drawings and Poems from the Terezin Concentration Camp, 1942-1944 (Volavková) (Czechoslovakia WWII)	Poetry
Somos como los nubes: We Are Like the Clouds (Argueta) (Central America)	Poetry

Landscapes (Grades 5–8)

These texts encompass a broad concept of landscape or "place," exploring geological, archeological, mathematical, and biological concepts, as well as strongly-built settings in realistic and fantasy fiction.

Brooklyn Bridge (Curlee)	Nonfiction
Built to Last (Macaulay)	Nonfiction
From Mud Huts to Skyscrapers (Paxmann)	Nonfiction
Home (Ellis)	Nonfiction
How To Make A Planet: A Step-By-Step Guide To Building The Earth (Forbes)	Nonfiction
If You Lived Here: Houses of the World (Laroche)	Nonfiction
Maya Lin: Artist-Architect of Light and Lines (Harvey)	Nonfiction
Nature Anatomy: The Curious Parts and Pieces of the Natural World (Rothman)	Nonfiction
Our Patchwork Planet (Sattler)	Nonfiction
Round Buildings, Square Buildings, & Buildings That Wiggle Like a Fish (Issacson)	Nonfiction
Seismology: Our Violent Earth (Baxter)	Nonfiction
Skywalkers: Mohawk Ironworkers Build the City (Weitzman)	Nonfiction
The Channel Tunnel (Donovan)	Nonfiction
The Lithosphere: Earth's Crust (Vogt)	Nonfiction
The Secret Subway (Corey)	Nonfiction
The Story of Buildings (Dillon)	Nonfiction
Uncovering Earth's Crust (Storad)	Nonfiction
Underground (Macaulay)	Nonfiction
Walk This World (Broom)	Nonfiction
Sam & Dave Dig a Hole (Barnett)	Picturebook
The Curious Garden (Brown)	Picturebook
Earth Verse: Haiku from the Ground Up (Walker)	Poetry
Amazing Places (Hopkins)	Poetry
Here in Harlem: Poems in Many Voices (Myers)	Poetry
Sugar Hill: Harlem's Historic Neighborhood (Weatherford)	Poetry
Thunder Underground (Yolen)	Poetry
Lost in NYC: A Subway Adventure (Spiegelman)	Graphica
Blue Mountain Trouble (Mordecai)	Fiction

(continued)

Landscapes (Grades 5–8) *(continued)*

Clayton Byrd Goes Underground (Williams-Garcia)	Fiction
Each Little Bird That Sings (Wiles)	Fiction
Gentle's Holler (Madden)	Fiction
Lost in the Labyrinth (Kindl)	Fiction
Saint Louis Armstrong Beach (Woods)	Fiction
The Architect's Apprentice (Shafak)	Fiction
The Killer's Tears (Bondoux)	Fiction
When Zachary Beaver Came to Town (Holt)	Fiction
York (Ruby)	Fiction
The Night Gardener (Fan)	Fiction
Tokyo Digs a Garden (Lappano)	Fiction
Out of the Dust (Hesse)	Historical Fiction
Maybe Something Beautiful: How Art Transformed a Neighborhood (Campoy)	Historical Fiction
Cartwheeling in Thunderstorms (Rundell)	Realistic Fiction
Harry Potter and the Sorcerer's Stone (Rowling)	Fantasy
Miss Ellicott's School for the Magically Minded (Blackwood)	Fantasy
City of Glass (Clare)	Fantasy
City of Halves (Inglis)	Fantasy
The Underneath (Appelt)	Fantasy

In this colorful picturebook, James Ransome depicts a model teacher and the wonderful experiences she provides in an urban classroom. Illustrations from MY TEACHER by James Ransome, copyright ©2012 by James Ransome. Used by permission of Dial Books for Young Readers, an imprint of Penguin Young Readers Group, a division of Penguin Random House LLC. All rights reserved.

Components of a Literature Program

The day-to-day routines in classrooms centered around children's literature may vary greatly according to the age of the students, the needs of the community, and the common core standards of local and state curricula. But children in all literature-based classrooms need to be surrounded by enthusiastic, book-loving adults and many, many good books.

One important aspect of any classroom is what has been called the "climate." Each classroom teacher creates the climate of the classroom by setting up and arranging the teaching and learning environment. The climate in the classroom is of course more than the physical classroom space. It is a process that sets the tone for all activity that happens in the classroom. If the teacher is a reader and loves books, shares them with children, and provides time and space for children to read, the students are likely to become enthusiastic readers. Additionally, a teacher who reads to the children every day, talks about books and characters in books as if they were good friends, and knows poems and stories is serving the class as an adult model—someone who reads and enjoys books. Children will find any teacher who is an avid reader and excited about books to be the best inspiration to spark a love for reading. In James Ransome's *My Teacher*, the young protagonist narrates a story about an urban classroom teacher who did many wonderful things with her students, one of which focused on helping them take charge of building their own class library.

One teacher regularly used to read a new children's book while her class was reading. She would keep the book in an old beat-up briefcase that she delighted in carrying. A kind of game she played with her 7- and 8-year-old students was to keep the book hidden from them. Their delight was to find out what book she was reading, so they could read the same one. Of course they always found out, which was what she had in mind in the first place. Enthusiasm for books is contagious; if the teacher has it, so will the children.

If we want children to become readers, we will want to surround them with books of all kinds. We know that wide reading is directly related to accessibility; the more books available and the more time for reading, the more children will read and the better readers they will become.

Books should be a natural part of the classroom environment. There should be no argument about whether to have a classroom collection of books or a library media center; both are necessary. Children should have immediate access to books whenever they need them. The books in the classroom collection will vary from those in the library media center. Many classrooms have an extensive paperback collection (400 to 500 titles). Frequently, there are five or six copies of the same title, so several children can read the same book and have an in-depth discussion of it.

The classroom teacher will also want to provide for a changing collection of books depending on the themes or units the children are studying. The librarian might provide a rolling cart of materials that will enhance children's study of insects or folktales or the Civil War or explorers. It is important that teachers be thoroughly acquainted with the content of these books so they can help their students use them. If the library media center does not have particular books that the children or the teacher needs, they might be obtained from local public libraries or from a bookmobile. Many public libraries offer special services to teachers, putting together collections of books with limited advance notice. Some state libraries will send boxes of books to teachers in communities that are not serviced by public libraries. An increasing number of teachers are demanding and receiving their share of monies allocated for instructional materials. Teachers using children's literature as the heart of their curriculum should receive the same amount of money as those using basal readers, workbooks, social studies, science, and other textbooks. We admire the number of teachers who spend their own money to buy trade books for their classrooms, but at the same time we question the practice. Children's literature is an essential component in the making of a fluent reader and should be an unquestioned item of every school budget.

Sharing Literature with Children

Because literature serves many educational purposes in addition to entertainment and enjoyment, teachers should place a high priority on sharing literature with children. Boys and girls of all ages should have the opportunity to hear and read good literature every day.

One of the best ways to interest children in books is to read to them frequently from the time they are first able to listen. Preschoolers and kindergartners should have an opportunity to listen to stories three or four times a day. Parents, caregivers, or grandparents, high school and college students, and community members—all can be encouraged to come to the classroom and read to individuals or to small groups of children throughout the day. Children should have a chance to hear their favorite stories repeated over and over again either in the classroom or at a listening/multimedia center. A child from a book-loving family might have heard more than a thousand stories before she ever comes to kindergarten; some children might never have heard one.

Teachers accept the idea of reading at least twice a day to the primary-grade child. The daily read-aloud time is supported by reading research and advocated by almost all authorities in reading. The research reported in Chapter 1 emphasizes the importance of reading aloud to all children, not only for enjoyment, but also for the development of their reading skills and strategies. Reading to children improves children's reading and writing. Rereading favorite books is as important as the initial reading.

Unfortunately, daily story times are not as common in the upper elementary and middle-school grades as in the primary grades, yet we know that they are just as essential for those age groups. Older children, like many adults, like to be read to, as evidenced by the many books available in electronic formats. Reading comprehension is improved as students listen to and discuss events, characters, and motivation. They learn to predict what will happen in exciting Newbery Award–winning tales like Kate DiCamillo's *The Tale of Despereaux* or Louis Sachar's *Holes*. Their vocabulary increases as they hear fine texts such as Sy Montgomery's *Amazon Adventure: How Tiny Fish Are Saving the World's Largest Rainforest* or Katrina Goldsaito's *The Sound of Silence*. Older students can discuss homelessness and prejudice as they hear Deborah Ellis's *No Ordinary Day*, Avi's *City of Orphans*, or Alexandra Diaz's *The Only Road*. They can add to their knowledge of Abraham Lincoln's presidency by reading Russell Freedman's remarkable photobiography *Lincoln*. Teachers can take advantage of this time to introduce various genres, such as fantasy, biography, or poetry, that students might not be reading on their own.

Primarily, however, the read-aloud time will cause children to want to read. For older children it models the cadence and fluency of good oral reading. Once children have heard a good book read aloud, they can hardly wait to savor it again. Reading aloud thus generates further interest in books, language, and literary events. Good oral reading should develop a taste for fine literature.

Selecting Books to Read Aloud

Teachers and librarians will want to select read-aloud books in terms of the children's interests and background in literature and the quality of writing. Usually teachers will not select books that children in the group are reading avidly on their own or books that may appear to be controversial. This is the time to stretch their imaginations, to extend interests, and to develop appreciation of fine writing and alternative perspectives. If children have not had much experience in listening to stories, begin where they are.

Appreciation for literature appears to be developmental and sequential. Children aged 6 and 7 years who have had little exposure to literature still need to hear many traditional fairy tales, including "Hansel and Gretel" and "Sleeping Beauty." Rachel Isadora and Jerry Pinkney are excellent read-aloud resources; both have many illustrated picturebooks of popular fairy tales. Young children delight in such favorite picture storybooks as David Ezra Stein's *Interrupting Chicken*.

Other young children who have had much exposure to literature might demand longer chapter books like *James and the Giant Peach* or *The BFG* by Roald Dahl. Older children with a strong foundation and wide exposure to literature might enjoy series chapter books by authors such as Rick Riordan, Mildred Taylor, J. K. Rowling, Tom Angleberger, and Sharon Draper.

Picturebooks are no longer just for "little kids." There is a real place for sharing beautiful picturebooks with older children as well as younger ones. Frances O'Roark Dowell's *Sam the Man & the Rutabaga Plan* and Uri Shulevitz's *Dawn* create the same feeling visually as one of Emily Dickinson's clear, rarefied poems. It is a literary experience for all ages, but particularly for anyone who has felt a deep connection with the world before the sunrise. Older students particularly enjoy Jon Scieszka's *Battle Bunny*, Shaun Tan's *Lost & Found,* and Chris Van Allsburg's *The Mysteries of Harris Burdick.*

The teacher should strive for balance in what is read aloud to children. Like children, teachers tend to enjoy what they know best. Expanding the repertoire of what is read aloud may require researching multiple book lists for reviews, asking for recommendations from other teachers, and looking up professional organizations whose focus is children's literature.

Many teachers have thought of read-aloud time as a time to read fiction to children. However, there is a wealth of excellent nonfiction that is every bit as compelling as a good fictional story. For example, Russell Freedman's book *Freedom Walkers: The Story of the Montgomery Bus Boycott* gives the historical account of the events that led to the civil rights movement, but its prose style also captivates readers as a narrative, using the actual recorded words of the people whose experiences tell the story.

Poetry is another genre that can be read aloud, even in the brief minutes of transition between subjects or before lunch or recess breaks. Word play and spoken word can engage the reluctant reader as well as the better reader. Reading poems for two or more voices can help children enhance fluency in reading aloud. They will find it irresistible fun to work together dramatically reading aloud poetry. *Forget-Me-Nots: Poems to Learn by Heart,* selected by Children's Poet Laureate Mary Ann Hoberman, is an exceptional resource.

Primary-grade teachers should read many books to their children. Middle-grade teachers might present parts of many books to their students during book talks or as teasers to interest children in reading the books. But how many entire books will a teacher read in the course of one school year? An educated guess might be that starting with 8-year-olds—when teachers begin to read longer, continuous stories to boys and girls—an average of some six to ten books are read aloud during the year. This means that for the next four years, when children are reaching the peak of their interest in reading, they might hear no more than forty or so books read by their teachers!

Today when there are thousands of children's books in print, read-aloud choices must be selected with care in terms of their relevance for students and the quality of their writing. Only a teacher who knows the children, their interests, and their background of experience can truly select appropriate books for a particular class. The teacher will want to consider children's backgrounds in literature, or lack of background, as he or she selects appropriate books to capture their attention. A read-aloud program should be planned. What books are too good to miss? These should be included in the overall plan.

Teachers should keep a record of the books that they have shared with the children they teach and a brief notation of the class's reaction to each title. This enables teachers to see what kind of balance is being achieved and what the particular favorites of the class are. Such a record provides the children's future teachers with information on the likes and dislikes of the class and their exposure to literature. It also might prevent the situation that was discovered by a survey of one school in which every teacher in the school, with the exception of the kindergarten and the second-grade teachers, had read E. B. White's *Charlotte's Web* aloud to the class! *Charlotte's Web* is a great book, but not for every class several years in a row. Perhaps teachers in a school need to agree on what is the most appropriate time for reading particular favorites. Teachers and librarians should be encouraged to try reading new books to children, instead of always reading the same ones. But some self-indulgence should be allowed for every teacher who truly loves a particular book because that enthusiasm can't help but rub off on children.

Effective oral reading is an important factor in capturing children's interest. Some teachers can make almost any story sound exciting; others plod dully through. The storyteller's voice, timing, and intonation patterns should communicate the meanings and mood of the story. To read effectively, the teacher should be familiar with the story and communicate his or her enthusiasm for the book. **Teaching Feature 11.2: Effective Practices for Reading Aloud** might prove useful. Check the list before selecting and reading a story to a whole class.

Storytelling

A 5-year-old said to his teacher: "Tell the story from your face." His preference for the story told by the teacher or librarian instead of the story read directly from the book is echoed by boys and girls everywhere. The art of storytelling is frequently neglected in the elementary school today. There are so many beautiful books to share with children, we rationalize, and our harried life allows little time for learning stories. Yet children should not be denied the opportunity to hear well-told stories. Through storytelling, the teacher helps transmit the literary heritage. In addition, oral stories told in many cultures throughout the world have not been retold in written form. What better way to celebrate these stories than to invite members of the children's families and communities to come to school for storytelling time?

Storytelling provides for intimate contact and rapport with the children. No book separates the teacher from the audience. The story may be modified to fit group needs. A difficult word or a phrase can be explained in context. Stories can be personalized for very young children by substituting their names for those of the characters. Such a phrase as "and, David, if you had been there you would have seen the biggest Billy Goat Gruff . . ." will redirect the child whose interest has wandered. The pace of the story can be adapted to the children's interests and age levels.

Folktales like "The Three Billy Goats Gruff," "The Little Red Hen," and "Cinderella" are particular favorites of younger children. The repetitive pattern of these tales makes them easy to tell. Originally passed down from generation to generation by word of mouth, these tales were polished and embellished with each retelling; 6-, 7-, and 8-year-olds enjoy hearing longer folktales such as Ashley Bryan's *Beautiful Blackbird*, a folktale from Zambia. They also enjoy some of the tall tales about American folk heroes such as Paul Bunyan, Pecos Bill, and John Henry. Incidents from biographies and chapters from longer books may be told as a way of interesting children in reading them.

Effective Practices
for Reading Aloud

1. Select a book appropriate to the developmental age of the children and their previous exposure to literature.
2. Determine whether you will share the book with the whole class, a small group, or an individual child.
3. Select books that will stretch children's imaginations, extend their interests, and expose them to fine art and writing.
4. Read a variety of types of books to capture the interests of all.
5. Remember that favorite books should be reread at the primary level.
6. Plan to read aloud several times a day.
7. Select a book that you like so that you can communicate your enthusiasm.
8. Choose a book or section that can be read in one session.
9. Read the book first so that you are familiar with the content.
10. Seat the children close to you so that all can see the pictures.
11. Hold the book so that children can see the pictures at their eye level.
12. Communicate the mood and meaning of the story and characters with your voice.
13. Introduce books in various ways:
    - Through a display
    - Through a brief discussion about the author or illustrator
    - By asking children to predict what the story will be about through looking at the cover and interpreting the title
    - By linking the theme, author, or illustrator to other books children know
14. Encourage older children to discuss the progress of the story or predict the outcome at the end of the chapter.
15. Help children to link the story with their own experiences or other literature.
16. Keep a list of the books read aloud to the whole class that can be passed on to their next teachers.

For more on effective practices for reading aloud, see Judy Freeman and Caroline Feller Bauer's *The Handbook for Storytellers* (Chicago: American Library Association, 1995) or Mem Fox's *Reading Magic: Why Reading Aloud to Our Children Will Change Their Lives Forever* (Boston: Mariner Books, 2008).

Book Talks

Librarians and teachers frequently use a book talk to introduce books to children. The primary purpose of a book talk is to interest children in reading the book themselves. Rather than reveal the whole story, the book talk tells just enough about the book to entice others to read it. A book talk may be about one title; it may be about several unrelated books that would have wide appeal; or it may revolve around several books with a similar theme, such as "getting along in the family" or "courage" or "survival stories." The book talk should begin with the recounting of an amusing episode or exciting moment in the book. The narrator might want to assume the role of a character in

Love this — *thematic groupings*

a book, such as Julie in *Julie of the Wolves* by Jean Craighead George, and tell of her experience of being lost without food or a compass on the North Slope of Alaska. The speaker should stop before the crisis is over or the mystery is solved. Details should be specific. It is better to let the story stand on its own than to characterize it as a "terribly funny" story or the "most exciting" book you've ever read. The speaker's enthusiasm for the book will convey itself. This is one reason why book talks should be given only about stories the speaker genuinely likes. Children will then come to trust this evaluation. It is best if the book is on hand as it is discussed, so that the children can check it out as soon as the book talk is finished.

Providing Time to Read Books

One of the primary purposes of giving book talks, telling stories, and reading aloud to children is to motivate them to read. A major goal of every school should be to develop children who *can* read but also *do* read—who love reading and will become lifetime readers. To become fluent readers, children need to practice reading from real books that capture their interest and imagination. No one could become a competent swimmer or tennis player by practicing four minutes a day. Teachers have limited influence on the out-of-school life of their students, but they do control the curriculum in school. If we want children to become readers, we must reorder our priorities and provide time for children to read books of their own choosing every day.

Recognizing this need, many teachers have initiated a sustained silent reading (SSR) time. Teachers have used other names, such as "recreational reading," "free reading," or even the acronym DEAR (Drop Everything and Read) used by the teacher in *Ramona Quimby, Age 8* by Beverly Cleary. Whatever the name, however, this is a time when everyone in the class (in some instances, the entire school, including the teachers, principals, clerical, and janitorial staff) reads. SSR times have been successfully established in kindergarten through middle schools. Usually, the reading period is lengthened gradually from ten minutes a day to twenty, thirty, or, in some upper-grade classes, forty-five minutes per day. Recognizing the importance of social interaction among readers, teachers often allow children to read in pairs. In classrooms that use real books for teaching reading and studying themes that cut across the curriculum, children are reading and writing throughout the day. Teachers still have a special time each day for children to read the books they have chosen to read for pleasure.

Providing Time to Talk About Books

Equally important as time for wide reading is time to talk about the books children are reading. When adults discuss books, we have good conversations about the ones we like, but we seldom quiz each other about character development, themes, or setting of the story. As teachers, we want to show this same respect for children as they share their thoughts about books. A good time for informal talk about books is after children have had time to read by themselves. In pairs, small groups, or as a class, children may be invited to tell something about a book, show a picture and tell what is happening, read an interesting or powerful paragraph, and so forth. In such discussions, teachers can learn much about what children are reading and how they talk about books.[4]

Maryann Eeds and Deborah Wells showed how well fifth and sixth graders explored the meaning of novels they were reading through nondirective response groups.[5] The literature discussion groups met two days a week, thirty minutes a day, for four to five weeks. The leaders were undergraduate education students who were instructed to let meaning emerge from the group rather than solicit it. The results of this study showed that the groups collaborated and built meaning that was deeper and richer than what they attained in their solitary reading. The authors concluded, "Talk helps to confirm, extend, and modify individual interpretations and creates a better understanding of the text."

As teachers listen carefully to children's responses in book discussion groups, they can identify teaching possibilities, plan future conversations, or make use of a teachable moment to make a point. When the teacher is an active participant rather than the director of a group, children more readily collaborate to fill their own gaps in understanding and make meaning together. More structured discussion may occur with the books a teacher chooses to read aloud or to read with small groups. The teacher can play an important role in engendering fruitful discussions by demonstrating the types of responses she hopes children will make. When the teacher introduces the story, she might invite children to recognize the author or illustrator, to notice the dedication, or to speculate on the book's content as they look at the cover. As she gives children time to look at the illustrations in picturebooks, she asks, "How do these pictures make you feel?" "What are you thinking about as you look at these illustrations?" "Do these illustrations remind you of anything in your home or community?" As she reads a chapter book, she asks what might happen next or why a character acts as he does. She might introduce Christopher Paul Curtis's *The Mighty Miss Malone* by reading Margaret King Mitchell's *When Grandmama Sings* and discussing segregation with the class. She might pause at a chapter's end and ask children how Curtis makes the reader feel that something dreadful is about to happen. She might ask what clues suggest that Jimmie would run off so that he could sing in clubs, just like Belle's grandmama. She might introduce the term *foreshadowing* and ask the children to listen for other examples as she reads. At first the teacher calls attention to aspects such as a well-written passage, an apt chapter heading, or a key moment when a character faces a choice. Later, children will begin noticing the kinds of things the teacher has brought out in these discussions. In this way, a teacher models reader behaviors that mature readers practice.

A third- and fourth-grade group heard Byrd Baylor's story *I'm in Charge of Celebrations* **and wrote about special days they wanted to remember.** Mangere Bridge School, Auckland, New Zealand. Colleen Fleming, teacher.

Providing Time for the In-Depth Study of Books

As the chapter opening scenario illustrates, if children are to have an opportunity to read and discuss widely, this activity should be balanced with a time for studying books deeply. When children work with books in ways that are meaningful to them—through talk, art making, writing, drama, mulltimodal activities, and music—many things happen. Children have greater satisfaction with, and clarify personal meanings about, what they have read. These activities allow many books to be visible in the classroom.

One child's work with a book can dramatically influence another child's willingness to read it. Children working on projects use various skills, exercise more choices, develop planning abilities, and experiment with a variety of learning experiences. In addition, these activities can allow children the opportunity to think more deeply about books and to return to them to explore responses in ways that deepen their understandings.

Teachers who know the children in their classes well recognize the diversity of learning styles this sort of active learning accommodates. They plan diverse activities that enhance children's delight in books, make them want to continue reading more and better books, and cause them to think both more widely and more specifically about what they have read. They know that many options should be open to children and do not expect all children to choose the same book or have the same type of response to a book. They consult with children about possibilities for projects and do not assign all children to do the same project; neither do they expect children to do an activity for every book that they read. The activities suggested here are planned to increase children's enjoyment and understanding of books.

Extending Literature Through Technology

The first decade of the twenty-first century saw the blossoming of transmedia (multi-platform) books for children. Transmedia books allow readers access to a virtual world to become part of the book's action through games, character interactions, and forums. Scholastic's The 39 Clues series, written by various authors, led publishers to enlist individual authors for such series as Tombquest (Northrop), Spaceheadz (Scieszka), and The Magnificent 12 (Grant). The Pottermore website (www.pottermore.com) created by J. K. Rowling offers readers a variety of experiences connected to her Harry Potter books.

Fan Response or Fandom (fan fiction, fan art, cosplay, fan casting, etc.) consists of sites that allow readers to share and extend their responses to books through multiple platforms. Such experiences connect readers beyond their local communities. The first modern "fandom" may be attributed to fans of Sherlock Holmes in the late 1800s, many who gathered to mourn his death. In the digital age, fandom has spawned a range of subcultures, many of which center around children's books. These include sites such as FanFiction.net, Archive of Our Own (Ao3), and Tumblr. Readers enthused about a series, such as *The Hunger Games*, will find abundant possibilities for continuing to live in the worlds of their favorite books alongside like-minded peers.

Technological connections to text can move beyond virtual spaces. Makerspaces are "places where people gather to make things."[6] Participants in the Makerspace culture are people who love to build things and share ideas. Makerspaces can be found in many school and public libraries and can range from high-budget centers funded by grants that include devices such as 3D printers, milling presses, and MakerBot replicators. A low-budget center can simply add materials such as circuitry kits, tools, and old or broken materials to a classroom art center full of more traditional art materials. Nonfiction titles such as David Adler's *Simple Machines* or the Chicago Review Press's "For Kids" series (such as *Leonardo da Vinci for Kids*) are a logical choice to include in makerspaces, but there are also many fiction books that inspire creativity. Ashley Spires's *The Most Magnificent Thing*, Kobi Yamada's *What Do You Do with an Idea?*, and Giselle Potter's *This Is My Doll House* are books that will inspire children to do some making of their own.

Children's Writing and Children's Books

Children's written work should grow out of their own rich experiences, whether with people, places, and things; research and observation; or literature. Children's writing about books can take many forms. Children should have many opportunities to write about the books they are reading. They should also be encouraged to use books as models for their own writing.

Real possibilities for writing are all around us in the classroom; however, it is literature that gives children a sense of how the written word sounds and looks. Literature has made a tremendous impact on reading programs, and so too has the writing process approach. Few teachers would consider teaching reading without including writing, because learning in one area means learning in the other. Literature informs both processes. As children become authors, they look at professional authors to see how a book works and sounds. They borrow and improvise on the language, patterns, and format of published books.[7] Writing and reading go on all day in a classroom where language arts and reading are intertwined and literature is at the heart of the curriculum.

Helping Children Write About Books In most schools, children are no longer required to write book reports, a particularly inert kind of writing. However, many teachers ask children to write about their reading in other ways. This writing resembles talk, in that a child shares ideas and someone responds to those ideas. Teachers find this is a time-saving idea and can set aside a weekly or biweekly time to react in writing to children's written responses. Some teachers demonstrate supportive responses and let pairs of children react to each other's written work as well. There are various ways a teacher can help children write about their reading.

A *reading log* is a simple record of the title and author of each book a child has read. Needless to say, this is a burden for young children, but it is a source of pride for second graders and older children who like to recall their reading and measure their progress. Teachers might give children six-by-eight-inch cards and let them fill in one side. Then the teacher and child can use these records for generalizing as they talk together about a child's reading. If a child takes her most recent card to the library, librarians might better help her find a book by seeing what she has enjoyed so far.

In a *response journal* children record their comments as they read a novel. Children respond freely as they think about their reading and write about the things that concern or interest them. A *double-entry draft* is a two-sided journal entry in which the reader copies or paraphrases a quote from the book on the left half of the paper. On the right, the reader comments on the quote. Teachers react to both of these journals and engage in a written dialogue with the reader (thereby creating a *dialogue journal*). Whatever we call them, children's written responses to the books they read provide teachers with another window into understanding how readers teach themselves to read.

Writing about books in the same way every day becomes tedious. Teachers may want to vary the way children can respond. They might invite children to keep a sketchbook/journal, where visual art serves as a preface to writing.[8] A single dialogue journal might be kept by a group reading the same book and children can take turns responding. Children might ask their own questions and consider which ones are more interesting to write about. They might keep journal entries in the form of a blog or post commentary or reviews on book websites.

What teachers need to avoid, however, is overusing written response or using a journal as a place in which children answer numbers of questions posed by the teacher. The primary power of journals is that the child owns the ideas, not the teacher. The child is director of the reading, and the child reflects on matters of interest to herself. When children write about their reading, they follow certain patterns, such as retelling, questioning particular words, clarifying meanings, reacting with like or dislike to a particular part of the story, relating a part of the story to their own lives, or otherwise reflecting.

Books That Support Children's Writing When children have a chance to become writers themselves, they begin to notice how other authors work. Literature suggests the many forms that stories, information, or poetry can take; as children experiment with the model, they begin to develop a sensitivity to the conventions of the form. This awareness in turn allows them to bring a wider frame of reference to the reading and writing that follow. Children in elementary classrooms should have an opportunity to experience a variety of well-written fiction, poetry, and nonfiction. At the same time, they can be encouraged to develop an appreciation of language and form through writing. In this way, children develop a sensitivity to language, an increasing control over the power of words, and a diverse writing repertoire.

Ideas for writing can come from the child's own life and from the classroom curriculum. They can also be inspired by books. Teachers can read aloud and then display individual books that serve as springboards or provocative formats for children's writing. Joyce Sidman's *This Is Just to Say: Poems of Apology and Forgiveness*, Gail Carson Levine's *Forgive Me, I Meant to Do It: False Apology Poems*, Margaret Wise Brown's *The Important Book*, or Vera B. Williams's *Three Days on a River in a Red Canoe* could serve as possible models for children to use. Many reading and writing connections have been explored in previous chapters. **Teaching Feature 11.3: Books That Serve as Writing Models** suggests stories that teachers might share as examples and incentives for children's own writing.

Exploring Literature Through the Visual Arts

Young children communicate through visual symbols as easily as they communicate through language, yet by the middle grades many children feel very insecure about making art. Children of all ages who have the opportunity to transform their responses to books through visual means are learning to be confident creators. In addition, their familiarity with art can increase their visual literacy and their aesthetic understanding.

Too often children are given a box of crayons and a small space at the top of some lined newsprint paper and told to "make a picture" of the story. How much better it is to work with children who are "filled to over-flowing" with knowledge about a book or theme. Children might produce higher-quality artwork if the teacher provided a variety of mediums from which to choose instead of the usual crayons and thin newsprint. Chalk, paints, markers, colored tissue papers, yarn, steel wool, cotton, material scraps, wires—anything that might be useful in depicting characters and scenes should be readily

Books That Serve as Writing Models

Title	Author	Grade Level	Type of Writing
Extra! Extra! Fairy-Tale News from Hidden Forest	Ada	2 and up	Newspaper
With Love, Little Red Hen	Ada	K–3	Letters
When Fish Got Feet, Sharks Got Teeth, and Bugs Began to Swarm: A Cartoon Prehistory of Life Long Before Dinosaurs	Bonner	4–6	Comics
Air Is All Around You	Branley	K and up	Expository nonfiction
Rufus the Writer	Bram	1–3	Narrative writing
Bad Kitty: Drawn to Trouble	Bruel	2–5	Writing and illustrating process
Tulip and Rex Write a Story	Capucilli	2–5	Narrative writing
Love That Dog; Hate That Cat; Moo	Creech	4–6	Poetry and journal entries
Diary of a Worm (Diary of a Worm series)	Cronin	K–3	Diary
Dead End in Norvelt	Gantos	4–6	Obituaries
Spiders	Gibbons	K and up	Expository nonfiction
I Spy with My Little Eye	Gibbs	PreK–2	Writing pattern
Meerkat Mail	Gravett	K–3	Postcards
Full Moon and Star	Hopkins	K–3	Poetry
Dear Mr. Blueberry	James	K–3	Letters
The Extraordinary Mark Twain (According to Susy)	Kerley	4–6	Personal journal
Dying to Meet You: 43 Old Cemetery Road	Klise	4–6	Letters
Forgive Me, I Meant to Do It: False Apology Poems	Levine	K–3	Poetry and journal entries
Hey World, Here I Am!	Little	4–7	Poetry and journal entries
Gooney Bird Greene series	Lowry	1–3	Story pattern
The Totally Made-Up Civil War Diary of Amanda MacLeish	Mills	4–6	Diary
Amelia's Notebook series	Moss	4 and up	Notebook
Autobiography of My Dead Brother	Myers	6 and up	Comics
Ways to Live Forever	Nicholls	4–6	Personal journal
I Wanna New Room	Orloff	K–3	Persuasive letters
The Perfect Pet	Palatini	PreK-2	Nonfiction persuasive

(continued)

teaching feature 11.3

Title	Author	Grade Level	Type of Writing
Now	Portis	1–3	Writing pattern
A Leaf Can Be . . .	Salas	K–3	Writing pattern
Do You Know Which Ones Will Grow?	Shea	PreK–2	Writing pattern
Red Sings from Treetops: A Year in Colors	Sidman	K–3	Poetry
This Is Just to Say: Poems of Apology and Forgiveness	Sidman	3–6	Poetry
Milo: Sticky Notes & Brain Freeze	Silberberg	4–6	Comics
Can an Aardvark Bark?	Stewart	PreK–3	Nonfiction expository
LaRue Across America: Postcards from the Vacation	Teague	K–3	Postcards
As Fast as Words Could Fly	Tuck	4–8	Persuasive letters
Hound Dog True	Urban	4–6	Notebook
Far From Shore: Chronicles of an Open Ocean Voyage	Webb	4–6	Personal journal
Each Little Bird That Sings	Wiles	4–6	Obituaries
Stringbeans' Trip to the Shining Sea and *Three Days on a River in a Red Canoe*	Williams	K–3	Postcards
Adam Canfield of the Slash	Winerip	5–8	School newspaper
The Robin Makes a Laughing Sound: A Birder's Observations	Wolf	4–6	Personal journal
Feathers	Woodson	4–6	Letters
Locomotion	Woodson	4–7	Poetry

accessible. Teachers might provide more interesting paper such as wallpaper samples, construction paper, hand-painted papers, and remainders from printers. Then when children are asked to make pictures of their favorite part of a story, of a character doing something in the book they have read, or illustrations for their own stories, the results are more exciting.

Paintings, murals, sculptures, crafts, constructions, assemblages, collages, mobiles and stabiles, stitchery, and multimedia creations are among the possibilities for visual expression in the classroom. Children's work should mirror the same range of artistic expression found in the world of visual art outside the classroom. The teacher's role is to design a

After reading Kathy Jakobsen's *My New York,* fourth graders created a map of the city that showed their own favorite places in the city. PS124, New York, New York. Mary S. Gallivan, teacher.

rich environment for creativity by providing materials, challenging children's thinking, and honoring children's work.

Displays of children's responses can be assembled and mounted carefully. They can be placed alongside a book or books that inspired the work or arranged as a summary of a thematic study. Often a study of a book or genre is extensive enough to warrant a museum exhibit. Explanations written by children help clarify for parents and other classroom observers how the work was created.

A teacher can also make use of a child's desire to replicate an illustrator's way of working by encouraging children to explore various media. Kindergarten children save their finger-painting pictures, cut them up, and use them to create their own story illustrated in the collage style of Eric Carle's stories such as *The Very Hungry Caterpillar.* Older children use dampened rice paper, ink, and watercolor to try to capture the look of traditional Japanese

Illustrator Eric Carle's bright collages inspire a kindergartner to experiment with forms.
Martin Luther King, Jr., Laboratory School, Evanston Public Schools, Evanston, Illinois. Barbara Friedberg, teacher.

A fourth grader carefully examined Suekichi Akaba's illustrations for *The Crane Wife* by Sumiko Yagawa before trying out his own watercolor response.
Barrington Elementary School, Upper Arlington, Ohio. Marlene Harbert, teacher.

artwork used by Meilo So in Leonore Look's *Brush of the Gods*. These children are answering for themselves the question "How did the illustrator make the pictures?"

Techniques that easily translate to the elementary classroom include collage, scratchboard, marbleized paper, many varieties of painting and printing, and stencil prints. By making these materials and processes readily available for children, teachers can extend the ways in which they visualize their world as well as their appreciation for illustrators' works. **Teaching Feature 3.2: The Artist's Media Choices** provides an overview of illustrators who work in some of these media and a list of materials that will allow children to explore these techniques.

Music and Movement in the Classroom

Children often enjoy singing to picturebook versions of well-known songs. They can also interpret literature by composing music or creating a dance. These activities help them think more carefully about the mood of a story or poem and consider their emotional responses to books more thoroughly. In recent years, there have been numerous fine picturebook interpretations of well-known songs, including Woody Guthrie's *This Land Is Your Land* by Kathy Jakobsen, Cecil Frances Alexander's *All Things Bright and Beautiful*, and Ashley Bryan's *Let It Shine: Three Favorite Spirituals*. To children who already know the song, the text of these books presents easy and enjoyable reading.

Many familiar folk songs have been researched and presented in authentic historic detail by such authors as Peter Spier and Woody Guthrie. Spier presents *The Star-Spangled Banner* with historical background so that the songs almost become an informational book, too. These various editions are a good way to make American history come alive as children are introduced to many folk songs that are a part of the American folk tradition.

In addition to the classroom extensions suggested, children might enjoy making their own book versions of other traditional songs like "Home on the Range," "Where Have All the Flowers Gone?," or "Old Dan Tucker." Some of these long and often funny stories would inspire fifth and sixth graders' imaginations.

Matching Music and Literature The process of identifying appropriate music to accompany prose and poetry selections helps children appreciate mood and tone in both literature and music. Second graders discussed the kind of music that could accompany the action of Maurice Sendak's *Where the Wild Things Are*. They recognized and created music with increasing tempo and volume, followed by a quiet conclusion of the story. Older children might enjoy reading one of Jack Prelutsky's *Nightmares* poems to music of their own choosing. Alternatively, a teacher might let children listen to Edvard Grieg's

"In the Hall of the Mountain King" or Richard Wagner's "Valkyries' Ride" and ask children which of Prelutsky's poems best suit these pieces. Many themes of subjects featured in literature have counterparts in music. For instance, the quiet awakening of the day in *Dawn* by Uri Shulevitz might be compared to the "Sunrise" movement from the *Grand Canyon Suite* by Ferde Grofé or to Cat Stevens's rendition of Eleanor Farjeon's poem "Morning Has Broken." Teachers can encourage older students to develop their sensitivity to recurring themes in art by juxtaposing literature and music.

Composing Music Poetry can be set to music as children create melody and identify the rhythmical elements. One group of talented 7-year-olds composed music to accompany their own sad tale of a princess who was captured during a battle and taken from her palace. Her knight-in-arms wandered the lonely countryside in search of her, while the poor princess grieved for him in her prison tower. The children made up a musical theme for each of the main characters, which they repeated during the various movements of their composition. The story was first told to their classmates, and then the song was played on the autoharp and glockenspiel. Older students composed a three-movement rhythmical symphony for Ged in Ursula K. Le Guin's *A Wizard of Earthsea*. A recorder repeated Ged's theme in appropriate places in this percussion piece. When literature provides the inspiration for children's musical compositions, children's appreciation for both literature and music will be enriched. Computer programs such as Apple's GarageBand not only make the creation of musical compositions to interpret literature and accompany projects possible but also motivate children to undertake such activities.

Movement and Literature Increasing attention has been given to children's control of their own body movements. The relationship between thought and movement has received much attention, particularly in England. Basic rhythmical movements might be introduced through Mother Goose rhymes. For example, children could walk to "Tommy Snooks and Bessie Brooks," gallop to "Ride a Cock Horse," jump to "Jack Be Nimble," and run to "Wee Willie Winkie." Nursery rhymes could also motivate dramatic action with such verses as "Hickory Dickory Dock," "Three Blind Mice," and "Jack and Jill." A favorite poem for young children to move to is "Holding Hands" by Lenore M. Link, which describes the ponderous way in which elephants walk. By way of contrast, Evelyn Beyer's poem "Jump or Jiggle" details the walk of frogs, caterpillars, worms, bugs, rabbits, and horses. It provides a wonderful opportunity for children to develop diverse movements. Both poems can be found in Jack Prelutsky's *Read-Aloud Rhymes for the Very Young*. In Marilyn Singer's poetry collection *A Stick Is an Excellent Thing: Poems Celebrating Outdoor Play*, LeUyen Pham's digitally colored pencil-and-ink illustrations portray young children engaged in imaginative play and activities, such as balancing on ledges in the poem "Edges."

As children learn basic movements, they can use them in different areas of space, at different levels, and at different tempos. Swinging, bending, stretching, twisting, bouncing, and shaking are the kinds of body movements that can be made by standing tall, at a middle position, or by stooping low. Other poetry that suggests movement includes "Stop, Go" by Dorothy Baruch, "The African Dance" by Langston Hughes, and "The Potatoes' Dance" by Vachel Lindsay. All of these poems can be found in *Favorite Poems Old and New*, compiled by Helen Ferris.

Extending Literature Through Drama

Books become more real to children as they identify with the characters through creative drama. Young children begin this identification with others through *dramatic play*. A 5-year-old engaged in impromptu play might become an airplane zooming to an airport built of blocks; another assumes the role of mother in the playhouse. Sometimes children of this age will play a very familiar story without adult direction. For example, "The Three Billy Goats Gruff" and "The Three Bears" are often favorites. Dramatic play represents this free response of children as they interpret experience. In schools, this type of natural response can find an outlet in activities that are part of a creative drama program. Creative drama is structured and cooperatively planned playmaking, an approach to learning that focuses on processes rather than production. While occasionally a play developed creatively will be shared with others, the value of creative drama lies in the process of playing and does not require an audience. Creative drama activities exist on a continuum from interpretation to improvisation and can include pantomime, story dramatization, readers' theater, and puppetry. All of these activities provide important ways for children to reenter the world of a book, to consider the characters, events, problems, and themes that are central in good literature. Such engagement brings children joy and zest in learning and living while broadening their understandings of both literature and life.

Dramatizing Stories Very young children aged 3 through 5 will become involved in dramatic play, but they usually do not have the sustained attention to act out a complete story. They might play a part of a favorite folktale (e.g., crossing the bridge as in "The Three Billy Goats Gruff"), but they seldom will complete a whole story. And no one should expect them to. Primary-grade children enjoy playing simple stories such as Aesop's fables, retold and illustrated by Eric Carle in *The Rabbit and the Turtle*, or those found in Paul Galdone's Folk Tale Classics series. Folktales are also a rich source of dramatization. They are usually short and have plenty of action, a quick plot, and interesting characters.

Stories from myths, such as "Pandora's Box" or "King Midas' Touch," are fine material for 9- to 11-year-olds to dramatize. Middle-grade children also enjoy presenting parts of books to each other in the form of debates, interviews, discussions, or television talk shows. A group of students played the roles of various characters in Natalie Babbitt's *Tuck Everlasting* and were interviewed by another student who took the role of a television talk-show host. They told about their own roles in the events that had taken place and voiced advantages and disadvantages of Winnie's living forever if she chose to drink water from a magic spring. Children then got into small groups to plan "tableau" of favorite scenes from the book. This time they had to use their bodies—facial expressions, poses, and gestures—rather than voices to convey their ideas. Activities such as these help children focus on important and complex issues that characters face in literature by providing these opportunities to explore ideas. This exploration is often a precursor of children's developing the ability to discover themes in literature or factors that influence characters to change.

Readers' Theater Teachers who are hesitant to try drama in their classroom might well begin with *readers' theater*, which involves a group of children in reading a play, a story, or a poem. Children are assigned to read particular parts. After reading through their parts silently, children read the text orally. Children thoroughly enjoy participating in

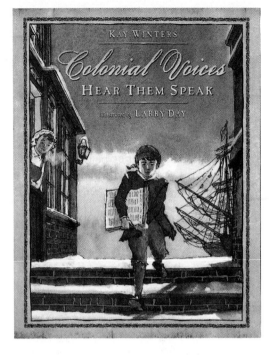

readers' theater. Even though they do not create the dialogue, as they do in improvisation or drama, they do interpret the character's personalities and the mood of the story. They also interact with each other in a kind of play form. The story provides the script, which makes it easy to try in the classroom.

In adapting a story for readers' theater, teachers or students must edit the text to omit phrases like *he said* and *she replied*. A child narrator needs to read the connecting prose between dialogue. Older children can write their own introductions and decide whether to leave out long descriptive passages or summarize them. Many teachers have found it useful to duplicate the parts of the story that children will read. This way, children can highlight their own parts and cross out unnecessary words. The most effective readers' theater selections contain a lot of dialogue. Folktales are easily adapted for primary children. Some good choices would be Steven Kellogg's *Chicken Little* or Paul Galdone's *The Little Red Hen*. At first, the teacher might read the narrator's part and let children take the different roles. When children become more capable readers and have had practice with readers' theater, they can take over the role of narrator. A variant of readers' theater best suited to younger children is a form of pantomime called *story theater*. Here a narrator reads a story aloud while children take the role of characters and act out the unfolding tale. Books that have a lot of action or emotional reaction make the best candidates for story theater. The teacher or librarian might read aloud Aleksei Tolstoy's *The Gigantic Turnip* while six children pantomime being the old man, the old woman, the little granddaughter, the dog, the calico cat, and the mouse. As the children gain confidence with this kind of drama, the teacher can stop at appropriate points when the old man calls to his wife and invite the designated child to create the dialogue. Moving from pantomime to extemporaneous dialogue is an easy transition to more complex forms of story reenactment.

Puppetry Many children will lose themselves in the characterization of a puppet while hidden behind a puppet stage even though they might hesitate to express ideas and feelings in front of the class. Through puppetry, children learn to project their voices and develop facility in varying their voice quality to portray different characters. For example, a rather quiet, shy child might use a booming voice as he becomes the giant in "Jack and the Beanstalk." Puppetry also facilitates the development of skills in arts and crafts.

Problems of stage construction, backdrops for scenery, and the modeling of characters provide opportunities for the development of creative thinking. A well-played puppet show extends children's appreciation and interpretation of stories and makes literature a more memorable experience for them. Beginning in kindergarten with the construction of paper-bag or simple stick figures, children can gain pleasure from their involvement with puppetry. Materials and types of puppets will range from the simple to the complex, depending on age and the child.

The teaching techniques used in creative drama should be followed, as puppet plays are created cooperatively by children and teachers. It is highly recommended that children "play out" stories before using their puppets. Written scripts are not necessary and can prove very limiting. Playing the story creatively allows the child to identify with the characters before becoming involved with the creation and mechanical manipulation of the puppet.

Connecting Literature and Life

Children sometimes have difficulty picturing life in other times or places or understanding historical time. They can experience books more completely through making maps and time lines and by compiling special collections. Children who thus ask questions about the details and events in literature are also introduced to methods of inquiry and research.

Creating Graphic Organizers

A graphic organizer is a visual representation of an idea. Semantic maps, attribute webs, or word webs often are used to help children group similar ideas into categories following a brainstorming session and display them to others. In these graphic organizers, a word or idea is placed at the center of a chart with spokes radiating toward related words, attributes, or other examples. One group listed "Outsiders in Literature" at the center of a semantic map and drew lines out to the various characters from novels who seem different from their peers. At the chart's center were clustered words describing insiders.

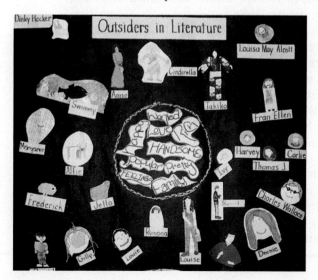

Word webs or semantic maps are also useful synthesizing aids for children who are organizing material from a variety of books and sources prior to writing a report.

Venn diagrams and comparison charts have been used as tools for organizing talk and thought, too. One teacher asked a group of children who had read many

Fifth and sixth graders made a type of sociogram to identify the "outsiders" in various stories. Personality traits that would make you an "insider" were written in the inner circle. Ridgemont Elementary School, Mt. Victory, Ohio. Sheryl Reed and Peggy Harrison, teachers.

novels by Betsy Byars to discuss how they are similar. Midway through the conversation children had raised such points as "The parents are never around," "The main character is usually about our age," and "Some big problem is always there." The teacher then helped children generate a chart with the titles of Byars's books, such as *Cracker Jackson* and *The Pinballs*, placed top-to-bottom on the left side of a large sheet of paper. Across the top of the chart, the children generated categories, such as "Where the Parents Are," "About the Main Character," "Big Problems," and "Who Helps and How." Now that the conversation was well under way, the graphic organizer helped children focus and continue the discussion while they filled in the grid they had created on the chart. Later, other Byars books were added, such as *The Summer of the Swans* and *Tornado*, which children also read to see how they fit the pattern. Children created artwork that represented some of the categories and wrote about how the books were alike and different. These were matted and hung next to the comparison chart. This activity helped the children analyze particular stories, synthesize several stories, and evaluate later readings. From the chart, they were able to generalize about books by one author, a sophisticated skill for 10- and 11-year-olds.

Nonfiction books are full of different types of graphic organizers that children learn to identify at a very young age. Kindergarteners may notice labeled drawings and cross-sections in books such as Gail Gibbons's *The Honey Makers* or *Tell Me Tree*, and first and second graders who have experience with nonfiction books readily incorporate such graphic organizers in their own nonfiction writing. Author Steve Moline argues that graphics such as flowcharts, tables, picture glossaries, cut-aways, and cross-sections aide children in deepening concepts and ideas from their all content-area learning.[9]

Artifacts and Collections

Items or artifacts mentioned in books often seem strange to children, even if explained in context. A child who reads that Ma Ingalls cooked prairie dinners in a spider would be puzzled until she could see this three-legged pan in a reference such as *Colonial Life* by Bobbie Kalman. Hefting a modern-day cast-iron replica would give a child a sense of the endurance of these utensils. This object, although a small part of the story, nonetheless connects reader experience with a part of the real world. A class collection could involve children in assembling book-related artifacts on a large scale. Second graders studying pioneers, for example, could make and collect items that pioneers might have taken west with them: such as a wooden spoon, a cornhusk doll, a flour sack, and a wagon wheel. As the teacher reads aloud *Bound for Oregon* by Jean Van Leeuwen, children add to the display their facsimiles of the route the family followed on their 2,000-mile journey from Arkansas to Oregon in 1852, a bouquet of wildflowers gathered by those who walked beside the moving wagons, and a "letter" from Mary Ellen Todd detailing her experiences with the wagon train. Labels can be made for each article as it is added to the display.

Maps, Primary Sources, and Time Lines

Often authors of books include a geographical map to help the reader locate the story setting. Other stories make sufficient reference to actual places so that children can infer a story location by carefully comparing the story and a contemporary map. One group of fourth graders found on a road map the probable route Ann Hamilton took in the 1780s when she walked across Pennsylvania in Jean Fritz's *The Cabin Faced West*. The movement of the Wilder family in the Little House books by Laura Ingalls Wilder can be followed on a map. Many fictional and biographical accounts of immigrants can be traced on world maps. As with many of the previous activities or projects in this chapter, maps, too, can help children look across a genre. The sources of folktales might be identified on a world map. The domains of tall-tale heroes and monsters might be located on a U.S. map. African folktales, fiction, and nonfiction might be located on a map of Africa as a way of differentiating features and regions of that continent—helping understand that Africa is not a country. Children need many encounters with maps and their working parts (key, symbols, scale, direction) before they become skilled users of all that a map can reveal.

Older children often enjoy making detailed maps of imaginary "countries of the mind," such as that in Lloyd Alexander's *The Remarkable Journey of Prince Jen* or his Prydain in *The Book of Three*, Ursula K. Le Guin's archipelagos in *A Wizard of Earthsea*, or Brian Jacques's Mossflower Woods surrounding *Redwall*. While fantasy provides ample opportunities for children to design their own maps imaginatively, other genres of books can be mapped as well.

The concept of time is difficult for children to grasp until sometime near the end of the concrete operational stage of thinking or the beginning of formal operations (ages 11 to 12). Prior to this period, time lines may help students organize events in a person's life as represented in a book. Time lines also allow children to represent a synthesis of events in several books. A time line from Jean Fritz's *And Then What Happened, Paul Revere?* might include the date of Paul Revere's birth, the date he took over his father's business, the summer he spent in the army, his famous ride, and his death in 1818. Events in the lives of Revere's contemporaries, such as Benjamin Franklin or George Washington, might be more easily compared if they were placed on a time line of the same scale as Revere's.

Placing book events in the world's time challenges even sophisticated readers to select relevant events in both the book and human history. A three-strand time line allows children to separate groups or types of events from others. While *Friedrich*, Hans Peter Richter's story of a Jewish boy caught in pre–World War II Germany, contains a "chronology" of dates in a reference at the back of the book, students might represent selected governmental decrees on one stratum of a time line. A second stratum might represent the number of Jews living in the Third Reich according to yearly censuses. A third stratum might list important events in Friedrich's life. In this way, children could see more clearly the political events against which Friedrich's tragic life was played out.

In making time lines, children need to agree on a scale so that events can be clearly shown—by year or by decade, for instance. Time lines can be made of string from which markers for events and years are hung. If children make time lines on a long roll of paper, entries can be written on cards or Post-it notes and placed temporarily along the line. In this way, corrections or realignments can be made easily.

Jackdaws

The term *jackdaw* comes from the British name for a relative of the crow that picks up brightly colored objects and carries them off to its nest. Commercially prepared jackdaw collections are sometimes available from museums and historical sites. These collections, based on an historical event or period, often include facsimile copies of diaries, letters, newspaper articles, advertisements, and other evidence from the time.

Teachers of elementary school children have modified this concept to suit activities and discussion with younger children. These teacher-made collections assemble resource materials that the teacher and children can handle in discussion, in display, or in actual construction and use. A jackdaw for Yoshiko Uchida's *Journey to Topaz*, for example, might include maps of the western United States on which children could locate the camps in which this Japanese American family was imprisoned in World War II. The jackdaw might also include photocopies of newspaper headlines of the time, relevant articles from that period from magazines such as *Time* and *Colliers*, a facsimile copy of one of the exclusion orders families were handed, and information about the author. Articles and documents that could accompany Laurence Yep's *Dragonwings* include reproductions of photographs of turn-of-the-century San Francisco's Chinatown, photographs of contemporary newspaper accounts of Chinese-built airplanes, a kite like the one Moon Shadow flew, and some green tea. Often sources for the factual material on which an historical fiction title is based are given in an author's note. Some jackdaws can then include copies of these actual source materials, or

This jackdaw was assembled to help children understand the many themes and historical events in Graham Salisbury's *Under the Blood-Red Sun.* ©Barbara Kiefer.

"facsimiles" can be created by the children. All materials can be placed in an appropriately decorated portfolio or box. **Figure 11.1** suggests some of the items that might be included in a jackdaw. Individual book titles will suggest other artifacts that children could include.

(figure **11.1**) Making a Jackdaw

Each book will suggest its own specific items or references to collect. Here is a general list of things that might be included.

- Recipes from the book's time (a typical dinner, a menu for a celebration)
- Price lists of commonly purchased goods then and now (milk, shoes, a dozen eggs, a car)
- A time line of the book's events
- A time line of the period surrounding the book's events
- A map, actual or imagined, of the setting
- A letter, diary, log, or news article that could have been written by or about a book character
- A photocopy of a book-related news article or document
- Artwork from the period (painting, architecture, sculpture)
- Songs, music, or dances from the book's setting (sheet music or lyrics, recordings)
- Clothes of characters of the period (paper dolls, catalog format, collage)
- Something about the author of the book

Helping children make connections between literature and their own experiences is an important teacher role. However, teachers need to recognize when enough is enough. After a six-week study of Laura Ingalls Wilder's *Farmer Boy*, one fifth grader said, "I hate this book." If teachers' first priority is to foster children's love of reading, they will be less likely to overburden children with factual inquiry. Teachers who appreciate the child's desire to know as a prior condition of learning can appreciate Louise Rosenblatt's criterion for the usefulness of background information: "It will have value only when the student feels the need of it and when it is assimilated into the student's experience of particular literary works."[10]

The School and the Community

To be successful, a classroom literature program needs an enthusiastic teacher, a good book collection, and students who are eager to read. However, to create a true community of readers, each teacher must also involve other teachers, students, administrators, librarians, and parents in discovering the delights of good books.

The Whole-School Program

Children learn what they live. Increasingly, educators are concerned that the quality of living in a school be equal to the quality of learning in that school. The physical environment of the school provides the context of that learning, but it is only one aspect of it. What teachers really believe in and want for their students will usually be taught. All teachers and librarians must have a strong commitment to literature. Few children discover books by themselves; in most instances, a parent, teacher, or librarian has served as the catalyst for bringing books and children together. As children grow up seeing significant adults as readers, they become readers. Find a teacher who is enthusiastic about children's books, and you will find a class of children who enjoy reading. Invariably, the teacher who reads, who knows books, and who shares this enthusiasm with students will inspire a love of reading. Many schools have made the development of readers their top priority. As a total school faculty they have met and planned certain activities to promote children's interest in reading.

Involving Administrators

No literature program can be successful without the support of the principal. More and more principals and curriculum coordinators are taking time to read aloud to children. One curriculum coordinator makes it a point to read aloud in one of the classrooms in his school district every day.[11] Children look forward to his coming, and he anticipates their response to his choice of books. Another principal has developed a two-tiered reading program called The Principal's Reading Club. Children from kindergarten through second grade make appointments to read with the principal for fifteen minutes from a book of their choice. Students in grades 3 to 6 select a book from a provided list and after three weeks return to discuss it with the principal. The participants receive a reading certificate, button, and pencil that has "I Read to the Principal" on it. More important, children see the principal as someone interested in them and their reading, and it's a wonderful way for the principal to get to know children and their reading abilities and preferences.

The School Library Media Center

Every school needs a trained librarian and a school library media center. Unfortunately, some schools do not have libraries or media centers. While the name has changed over the years to reflect the inclusion of nonprint materials such as films, videos, computers, and software as well as books, the purpose of the center is to provide the best services and materials to facilitate learning for children. The library media center should be open all day, every day, to serve students in its unique way. Flexible scheduling of story hours or lessons on library research may be directed by the librarian in a special area, leaving the rest of the resources free for others to use. Children can learn without the constant presence of a teacher or librarian. A trained aide can help children find relevant books, videos, and electronic and online materials. Parents have served most effectively as volunteers in the school media center. Children increase in their ability to do independent study by using a variety of sources. An abundance of materials should be readily and freely available.

Increasingly, new school library media centers have become the focal point of many schools, with classrooms radiating out from them. The space should be as flexible and fluid as possible to allow for growth and change. The environment should encourage free access to materials at all times. Children flow in and out, doing projects, finding resources, making their own books, producing films. As the library media center becomes more closely identified with the total instructional program, it becomes more integrated into the total school environment. The American Library Association lists the common characteristics of effective school libraries on their website (www.ala.org/research/librariesmatter/node/314).

The Library Media Specialist

The library media specialist plays a very important role in the quality of learning and living that takes place in the library media center, the school, and the community. Serving as a full-time contributing faculty member, the librarian works with children, teachers, parents, and volunteer and professional aides. Specialized training provides background knowledge of children's books and all media for instruction, library media procedures, knowledge of children's development and behavior, understanding of various teaching methods, and knowledge of school curriculum needs and organization. Increasingly, the library media specialist is called on to give leadership, not only in providing the materials for instruction, but also in shaping the curriculum itself. The library media program should be an integral part of the total school program. Working with teachers, the media specialist needs to be responsive to the curricular and instructional needs of the school. What units of study are the teachers planning this year? Books, films, and recordings on these subjects should be gathered together for the teachers' and children's use. Bibliographies of print and nonprint materials based on units of work should be developed cooperatively with teachers. Book lists and curriculum resources should be shared. The function of the school library media center is to provide an information-rich environment where teachers and students become effective users of print and nonprint materials.

Teachers and library media specialists become partners as they work together to help students learn to use information, to be critical of what they read and see, to make judgments about what is authentic and accurate, and to discover meaning. As students share their findings, they learn to question, compare, and combine information. Only such educated students can become contributing citizens to a democratic society.

Selecting Materials

With the increase of both numbers of books published and objections to the selection of certain books, it is essential that schools develop a selection policy. All professional library groups, and other professional organizations like the International Reading Association and the National Council of Teachers of English, strongly recommend that each school district develop a written statement that governs its selection of material. This policy statement should be approved by the school board and subsequently supported by its members if challenged. Factors to be considered in such a policy would include the following: who selects the materials, the quality of materials, appropriate content, needs and interests of special children, school curriculum needs, providing for balance in the collection, and procedures to follow for censorship and challenged material.

Because the subject matter of contemporary children's books is changing, the need for written criteria of selection has increased. Realism in children's books and young-adult novels reflects the same range of topics that can be seen on TV and the Internet, at the movies, and in current bestsellers. It makes no sense to "protect" children from well-written or well-presented materials on such controversial subjects as abortion, narcotics, or sexual orientation when they see stories elsewhere. Increased sensitivity to sexism, racism, and bias in books and nonbook materials is another area of recent concern that points to the need for a clear statement on selection policies. Here are some general guidelines to consider when developing policies for book selection:

1. **Who Selects the Materials?** Teachers, students, and parents might recommend particular titles, but the final selection of materials for the school library should be determined by professionally trained personnel. Reliable reviews of children's books play an important part in the selection of books. Four well-known review journals are *Booklist*, the *Bulletin of the Center for Children's Books*, *Horn Book Magazine*, and the *School Library Journal*. Other sources for reviews are listed in Appendix B.

2. **Quality of Materials.** Criteria for evaluation and selection of all types of instructional materials should be established and should be available in written form. Books for the collection should meet the criteria of good literature described in preceding chapters. There may need to be a balance between popular demand and quality literature, but this is a decision that must be made by individual librarians, based on their knowledge of the reading abilities and interests of the children they serve and their own basic philosophy of book selection. A written policy statement of the criteria to be used when purchasing books will help solve this dilemma.

3. **Appropriate Content.** The content of the materials to be selected should be evaluated in terms of the quality of the writing or presentation. Almost any subject can be written about for children, depending on the honesty and sensitivity of its treatment by the author. We should not deliberately shock or frighten children before they have developed the maturity and inner strength to face the tragedies of life. However, literature is one way to experience life, if only vicariously. In the process, a reader can be fortified and educated.

4. **Children's Needs and Interests.** Materials should be purchased with the children who will be using them in mind. This includes materials for children with special needs and books that represent a wide diversity of multicultural experiences. Children from a particular culture should have opportunities to see themselves reflected in books. In a pluralistic society, however, all children should have an

opportunity to read about children of different racial, religious, and ethnic backgrounds. Regardless of a child's background, a good selection policy should give children books that provide insight into their own lives but also take them out of those lives to help them see the world in its many dimensions.

5. **School Curriculum Needs.** Librarians should consider the particular needs of the school curriculum when ordering materials. Particular units in social studies or intensive study of the local region will require additional copies of books about the particular state, industries, and people of the region. The function of the school library media center is to provide a wide range of materials specially chosen to meet the demands of the school curriculum.

6. **Balance in the Collection.** Every school library needs to maintain a balanced collection. Keeping in mind the total needs of the school, the librarian should consider the following balances: book and nonbook material (including CDs, DVDs, and other materials), hardback and paperback books, reference books, and trade books, fiction and nonfiction, poetry and prose, classics (both old and "new"), realistic and fanciful stories, books for younger and older children, books for poor and superior readers at each grade level, books for teachers to read to students and use for enrichment purposes, and professional books for teachers and parents.

Selection Versus Censorship There is a fine line between careful selection of books for children and censorship. The goal of selection is to *include* a book on the basis of its quality of writing and total impact; the goal of censorship is to *exclude* a book in which the content (or even one part) is considered objectionable. Selection policies recommend a balanced collection representative of the various beliefs held by a pluralistic society; censors would impose their privately held beliefs on all. The American Library Association's "Library Bill of Rights" contains six policies relating to censorship of books and the right of free access to the library for all individuals or groups. (Go to <www.ala.org> and search "Library Bill of Rights.") This statement has been endorsed by the American Association of School Librarians and provides a firm foundation for schools to develop their own policies. Also see *Information Power: Building Partnerships for Learning* (Chicago: American Library Association, 1998).

Dealing with Censorship If there is a demand for censorship, how should it be handled? The first rule is to recognize that anyone has the right to question specific selections. The second rule is to be prepared—have an accepted response process. A written selection policy statement should contain a standardized procedure to follow when materials are challenged and should be part of district policy. The National Council of Teachers of English provides one in its booklet *The Students' Right to Know*.[12] The American Library Association suggests two items to include the following: (1) "What brought this title to your attention?" (2) "Please comment on the resource as a whole, as well as being specific about those matters that concern you."[13] The major consideration, then, is to have a form available when you need it and to make it specific to the book itself and simple enough to fill out.

Generally, if parents or other citizens feel their voices have been heard and that they have been dealt with fairly, they will abide by the decision of the book selection committee. If, however, they represent a group that is determined to impose its values on the schools, they will continue their pressure. This is why it is essential that every library have a selection policy supported by the board and administration. Librarians and teachers also need to be aware of the support they can obtain from organizations like the Office for Intellectual Freedom of the American Library Association, the Freedom to Read Foundation of ALA, the National Council of Teachers of English, the International Reading Association, the American Civil Liberties Union, and People for the American Way.

Working with Parents and the Community

Many schools have found that by informing and involving parents in school programs and plans, problems such as censorship are headed off or resolved before they can develop into serious discord. Even more important, parent volunteers can be a particularly rich resource for teachers and librarians. Sometimes these volunteers can be parents of students, sometimes they might be volunteers from a senior citizen center. One first-grade teacher has "grandmothers" from a senior citizen center who come once a week for the whole morning. They read stories to small groups of children, even individuals. They help make big books that the teacher uses. Whatever is needed, there is an extra pair of hands to do it. Parents can also serve as resource persons, depending upon their background of experience. One parent who is an Egyptologist became a tremendous resource for third-grade children who were studying mummies. In preparation for this parent's visit, the teacher read aloud *Mummies Made in Egypt* by Aliki, and the children prepared questions to ask him. He brought Egyptian artifacts and pictures to share with them. Another group of first-graders were studying about families. They wanted to interview the oldest member of their family about his or her childhood. One grandfather was invited to the class, and children learned how to conduct an interview. Wherever possible, teachers should draw on the expertise of parents, caregivers, and the community.

To help their students become part of a community of readers, teachers will want to plan time to communicate with them regularly about their reading. Parents and caregivers, too, are an integral part of this community, and they will appreciate being informed about the literacy program and their child's progress. Parents and the wider community can and should partner with both school and public libraries. The American Library Association "Libraries Matter" website (www.ala.org/research/librariesmatter) has a list of research studies showing the impact of libraries on early literacy, literacy and education, community development, and local economies.

Students can also reciprocate by contributing to the community themselves. Junior high school students in the Bronx so loved Katherine Paterson's *Bridge to Terabithia* that they wanted to share it with others. A literature group went out to the local senior citizens' residence and read it aloud to these new friends. Those seniors were invited to keep reading logs and join in the book discussions.

In one school, the parents and children created the Book Nook, a tiny paperback bookstore literally made from a broom closet. They decorated it with Maurice Sendak posters and a charming hanging lamp and even turned the old sink into a "trading pot" where children could place a "used" paperback and exchange it for another. The whole school takes justifiable pride in this paperback bookstore. In another school, the parents made a large wooden case on wheels that can be opened to create a bookstore anywhere in the building. Closed, it can be pushed flat against a wall. Parents will need help in getting such bookstores started and assuming responsibility for their operation. The librarian, a teacher who knows books, parents, and one or two children could serve as the selection committee to order new books. If teachers and parents support the store in the beginning, it will sustain itself once children know its regular hours and can find the books they want to buy and read.

With good planning, the community can be a wonderful resource for schools. The more a community participates, the more the people in that community will begin to take ownership and pride in their schools.

Evaluating the Literature Program

It is as easy to identify a school in which literature is an integral part of the curriculum as it is to recognize a home where books are loved and valued. Because we have not recommended any body of content that all children must learn, but rather have suggested that each school should plan its own literature program to include certain categories of experiences with literature, the **Guidelines: Evaluating a Literature Program** below could serve in two ways. First, they suggest to schools in the planning stages of a literature program what experiences ought to be offered to children. Second, they suggest measures for assessing a literature program already in place in an elementary or middle school. The first goal of all literature programs should be to develop lifetime readers. Because we know children are reading less and less in their free time at home, the school becomes their last best hope, not only for learning how to read, but also for *becoming readers.* Everything we do with books in schools should be measured against these criteria: Will this help children enjoy books? Will this help children become lifetime readers?

We know that children's reading for pleasure drops off when they are faced with the added homework and demands of middle school and high school. But if children have learned to love reading before that time, they will continue to read and increase their reading once they leave college. If they have not discovered the joys of reading before high school, it will be more difficult to cultivate that joy in adulthood—and it is possible they never will.

Guidelines

Evaluating a Literature Program

Go to *Connect®* to access study resources, practice quizzes, and additional materials.

Consider the following when evaluating a literature program:

Availability of Books and Other Media
- Is there a school library media center in each elementary school building?
- Does it meet American Library Association standards for books and other media?
- Is there a professionally trained librarian and adequate support staff in each building?
- Does every classroom contain several hundred paperbacks and a changing collection of hardbacks?
- Are reference books easily accessible to each classroom?
- May children purchase books in a school-run paperback bookstore?
- Do teachers encourage children to order books through various school book clubs?
- May children take books home without severe penalties for losing a book?
- Are children made aware of the programs of the public library? Do they have public library cards?

Time for Literature
- Do all children have time to read books of their own choosing every day?

(continued)

Guidelines

- Do all teachers read to the children once or twice a day?
- Do children have time to discuss their books with an interested adult or with other children every day?
- Are children allowed time to interpret books through art, drama, music, or writing?
- Do children seem attentive and involved as they listen to stories?
- Do they ask to have favorites reread?
- Is literature a part of all areas, across the curriculum?

Motivating Interest
- Do teachers show their enthusiasm for books by sharing new ones with children, reading parts of their favorite children's books, discussing them, and so on?
- Do classroom and library displays call attention to particular books?
- Are children encouraged to set up book displays in the media center, the halls, and their classrooms?
- Does the media specialist plan special events—such as story hours, book talks, sharing films, and working with book clubs?
- Do teachers and librarians work with parents to stimulate children's reading?
- Are special bibliographies prepared by the librarians or groups of children on topics of special interest—mysteries, animal stories, science fiction, fantasy, and so on?
- Are opportunities planned for contacts with authors and illustrators to kindle interest and enthusiasm for reading?

Balance in the Curriculum
- Do teachers and librarians try to introduce children to a wide variety of genres and to different authors when reading aloud?
- Do teachers share poetry as frequently as prose? Nonfiction as well as fiction?

- Do children read both fiction and nonfiction?
- Are children exposed to new books and contemporary poems as frequently as some of the old favorites of both prose and poetry?
- Do children have a balance of wide reading experiences with small-group, in-depth discussion of books?

Evaluating Children's Growth as Readers
- Do children keep reading logs or records of their free reading?
- Do older students (grade 3 and up) keep a response journal of their reading?
- Do teachers record examples of children's growth and understanding of literature as revealed in their play, talk, art, or writing?
- Do students and teachers together create an assessment portfolio with samples of children's best work?
- Are children allowed to respond to books in a variety of ways (art, drama, writing), rather than by required book reports?
- Is depth of understanding emphasized, rather than the number of books read?
- Are children responding to a greater range and complexity of work?
- What percentage of the children can be described as active readers? Has this percentage increased?
- Are some children beginning to see literature as a source of lifelong pleasure?

Evaluating Teachers' Professional Growth
- Are teachers increasing their knowledge of children's literature?
- What percentage of the staff have taken a course in children's literature in the past five years?
- Are some staff meetings devoted to ways of improving the use of literature in the curriculum?

- Do teachers attend professional meetings that feature programs on children's literature?
- Are in-service programs in literature made available on a regular basis?
- Are in-service programs, such as administering the running record or the Miscue Analysis, given regularly?
- Are such professional journals as *Horn Book Magazine*, *Book Links*, and *School*

Library Journal available to teachers and librarians?
- Are professional books on children's literature available?
- Have the teachers and librarians had a share in planning their literature programs?
- Do teachers feel responsible not only for teaching children to read but also for helping children find joy in reading?

Notes

1. Based on children's comments recorded by Susan Hepler in *Patterns of Response to Literature: A One-Year Study of a Fifth and Sixth Grade Classroom*, Ph.D. dissertation, Ohio State University, 1982.
2. See Christine C. Pappas, Barbara Z. Kiefer, and Linda L. S. Levstik, *An Integrated Language Perspective in the Elementary Classroom*, 4th ed. (Boston: Pearson Education, 2006).
3. Lesley M. Morrow, "The Impact of a Literature-Based Program on Literacy Achievement, Use of Literature, and Attitudes of Children from Minority Backgrounds," *Reading Research Quarterly* 27 (1992): 251–75.
4. See Taffy E. Raphael and Susan I. McMahon, "Book Club: An Alternative Framework for Reading Instruction," *Reading Teacher* 48.22 (1994): 102–116.
5. Maryann Eeds and Deborah Wells, "Grand Conversations: An Exploration of Meaning Construction in Literature Study Groups," *Research in the Teaching of English* 23.1 (1989): 4–29.
6. Ellyssa Kroski (editor), *The Makerspace Librarian's Sourcebook* (ALA Editions, 2017).
7. See Frederick R. Burton, "Writing What They Read: Reflections on Literature and Child Writers," in *Stories to Grow On*, ed. Julie M. Jensen (Portsmouth, N.H.: Heinemann, 1989), pp. 97–105.
8. See Karen Ernst, *Picturing Learning* (Portsmouth, N.H.: Heinemann, 1994).
9. Steve Moline, *I See What You Mean: Children at Work with Visual Information* (York, Me.: Stenhouse, 1995).
10. Louise Rosenblatt, *Literature as Exploration* (New York: Noble & Noble, 1976), p. 123.
11. James Mitchell, "Sound Bytes, Hamburgers and Billy Joel: Celebrating the Year of the Lifetime Reader," *Reading Today* 9 (August/September 1991): 29.
12. *The Students' Right to Know* (Urbana, Ill.: National Council of Teachers of English, 1982).
13. "Statement of Concern About Library/Media Center Resources," in *Intellectual Freedom Manual*, rev. ed. (Chicago: American Library Association, 1996), p. 167.

Children's Literature

*Go to **Connect**® to access study resources, practice quizzes, and additional materials.*

Titles in blue = multicultural titles

Ada, Alma Flor. *Extra Extra! Fairy-Tale News from Hidden Forest*. Illustrated by Leslie Tryon. Atheneum, 2007.

Adler, David A. *Simple Machines: Wheels, Levers, and Pulleys*. Illustrated by Ann Raff. Holiday, 2016.

———. *With Love, Little Red Hen*. Illustrated by Leslie Tryon. Atheneum Books for Young Readers, 2004.

Agosin, Marjorie. *I Lived on Butterfly Hill*. Illustrated by Lee White. Simon, 2015.

Alexander, Cecil Frances. *All Things Bright and Beautiful*. Illustrated by Bruce Whatley. Harper, 2001.

Alexander, Lloyd. *The Book of Three*. Holt, 1964.

———. *The Remarkable Journey of Prince Jen*. Dutton, 1991.

Aliki [Aliki Brandenberg]. *Mummies Made in Egypt*. Harper Collins, 1985 [1979].

Anaya, Rudolfo. *The First Tortilla: A Bilingual Story*. Illustrated by Amy Córdova. University of New Mexico Press, 2007.

Appelfeld, Aharon. *Adam and Thomas*. Illustrated by Philippe Dumas. Seven Stories/Triangle Square, 2015.

Appelt, Kathi. *The Underneath*. Simon, 2008.

Applegate, Katherine. *Home of the Brave*. Square Fish, 2008.

Argueta, Jorge. *Somos como las nubes/We Are Like the clouds*. Illustrated by Alfonso Ruano Groundwood, 2016.

Aston, Dianna Hutts. *A Butterfly Is Patient*. Illustrated by Sylvia Long. Chronicle, 2011.

———. *An Egg Is Quiet*. Illustrated by Sylvia Long. Chronicle, 2006.

Avi. *City of Orphans*. Illustrated by Greg Ruth. Atheneum, 2011.

Babbitt, Natalie. *Tuck Everlasting*. Farrar, 1975.

Baker, Keith. *Big Fat Hen*. Sandpiper, 1999.

Barnett, Mac. *Sam and Dave Dig a Hole*. Illustrated by Jon Klassen. Candlewick, 2014.

Bat-Ami, Miriam. *Two Suns in the Sky*. Puffin, 2001.

Bausum, Ann. *Unraveling Freedom: The Battle for Democracy on the Home Front During World War I*. National Geographic Children's Books, 2010.

Baxter, Roberta. *Seismology: Our Violent Earth*. Essential Library, 2015.

Beard, Darleen Bailey. *Twister*. Illustrated by Nancy Carpenter. Farrar, 1999.

Bertozzi, Nick. *Shackleton: Antarctic Odyssey*. First Second, 2014.

Birtha, Becky. *Far Apart, Close to the Heart: Being a Loved One When a Family Member Is Incarcerated*. Illustrated by Maja Kastelic. Whitman, 2017.

Bishop, Nic. *Spiders*. Scholastic Nonfiction, 2007.

Blackwood, Sage. *Miss Ellicott's School for the Magically Minded*. Harper, 2017.

Blos, Joan. *A Gathering of Days: A New England Girl's Journal, 1830–1832*. Scribner's, 1979.

Bodden, Valerie. *The Assassination of Martin Luther King Jr*. Creative Education, 2016.

Bonner, Hannah. *When Fish Got Feet, Sharks Got Teeth, and Bugs Began to Swarm: A Cartoon Prehistory of Life Long Before Dinosaurs*. National Geographic Children's Books, 2009.

Borden, Louise. *The Journey That Saved Curious George: The True Wartime Escape of Margaret and H. A. Ray*. Illustrated by Allan Drummond. Houghton, 2005.

Bouwman, H. M. *A Crack in the Sea*. Putnam, 2017.

Boyce, Frank Cottrell. *Sputnik's Guide to Life on Earth*. Walden Pond Press, 2017.

Bradley, Kimberly Brubaker. *The War That Saved My Life*. Penguin, 2015.

Bram, Elizabeth. *Rufus the Writer*. Illustrated by Chuck Groenink. Random, 2015.

Branley, Franklyn M. *Air Is All Around You*. Illustrated by Holly Keller. HarperCollins, 1986.

———. *Down Comes the Rain*. Illustrated by James Graham Hale. HarperCollins, 1997.

———. *Flash, Crash, Rumble, and Roll*. Illustrated by Barbara and Ed Emberley. Rev. ed. Crowell, 1985.

———. *The International Space Station*. Illustrated by True Kelley. Harper, 2000.

———. *Mission to Mars*. Illustrated by True Kelley. Harper, 2000.

Bridges, Ruby. *Through My Eyes*. Scholastic Press, 1999.

Broom, Jenny. *Walk This World*. Illustrated by Lotta Nieminen. Big Picture Press, 2013.

Brown, Margaret Wise. *The Important Book*. Illustrated by Leonard Weisgard. Harper, 1949.

Brown, Peter. *The Curious Garden*. Little, 2009.

Bruchac, Joseph. *Crazy Horse's Vision*. Illustrated by S. D. Nelson. Live Oak Media, 2007.

———. *Geronimo*. Scholastic Inc., 2006.

Bruel, Nick. *Bad Kitty: Drawn to Trouble*. Square Fish, 2015.

Bryan, Ashley. *Let It Shine: Three Favorite Spirituals*. Atheneum, 2007.

———. *Beautiful Blackbird*. Atheneum, 2003.

Buitrago, Jairo. *Two White Rabbits*. Illustrated by Rafael Yockteng. Translated by Elisa Amado. Groundwood, 2015.

———. *Walk with Me*. Illustrated by Rafael Yockteng. Translated by Elisa Amado. Groundwood, 2017.

Bunting, Eve. *How Many Days to America? A Thanksgiving Story*. Illustrated by Beth Peck. Houghton, 1988.

_____. *One Green Apple*. Illustrated by Ted Lewin. Clarion Books, 2006.

Burg, Ann E. *Unbound A Novel in Verse*. Scholastic, 2016.

Butler, Dori Hillestad. *King & Kayla and the Case of the Secret Code*. Nancy Meyers. Chronicle, 2017.

Byars, Betsy. *Cracker Jackson*. Puffin, 1986 [1985].

_____. *Goodbye, Chicken Little*. Harper, 1979.

_____. *The House of Wings*. Viking, 1972.

_____. *The Pinballs*. Harper, 1977.

_____. *The Summer of the Swans*. Viking, 1970.

_____. *Tornado*. Harper, 2004.

Campoy, F. Isabel and Theresa Howell. *Maybe Something Beautiful: How Art Transformed a Neighborhood*. Illustrated by Rafael López. Houghton, 2016.

Capaldi, Gian. *Red Bird Sings: The Story of Zitkala-Sa, Native American Author, Musician, and Activist*. Millerbrook Pr Trade, 2011.

Capucilli, Alyssa Satin. *Tulip and Rex Write a Story*. Illustrated by Sarah Massini. Harper, 2015.

Carbone, Elisa. *Night Running: How James Escaped with the Help of His Faithful Dog*. Illustrated by E. B. Lewis. Knopf, 2008.

_____. *Stealing Freedom*. Knopf, 1999.

Carle, Eric. *The Rabbit and the Turtle*. Orchard, 2008.

_____. *The Very Hungry Caterpillar*. Putnam, 1989 [1969].

Cheaney, J. B. *My Friend the Enemy*. Knopf, 2005.

Chotjewitz, David. *Daniel Half Human and the Good Nazi*. Translated by Doris Orgel. Atheneum, 2004.

Clare, Cassandra. *City of Glass*. McElderry, 2015.

Cleary, Beverly. *Ramona Quimby, Age 8*. Illustrated by Alan Tiegreen. Morrow, 1981.

Coleman, Evelyn. *To Be a Drum*. Illustrated by Aminah Brenda Lynn Robinson. Albert Whitman & Company, 1998.

_____. *White Socks Only*. Illustrated by Tyrone Geter. Albert Whitman & Company, 1996.

Collard, Sneed B. III. *Insects: The Most Fun Bug Book Ever*. Charlesbridge, 2017.

Cordell, Ryan and Evie Cordell. *Two Girls Want a Puppy*. Illustrated by Maple Lam. Harper, 2015.

Cory, Shana. *The Secret Subway*. Simon, 2016.

Cosgrove, Brian. *Weather*. DK Children, 2007.

Cousteau, Philippe, and Deborah Hopkinson. *Follow the Moon Home: A Tale of One Idea, Twenty Kids, and a Hundred Sea Turtles*. Illustrated by Meilo So. Chronicle, 2016.

Creech, Sharon. *Hate That Cat*. HarperCollins, 2010.

_____. *Love That Dog*. Perfection Learning, 2003.

Crews, Donald. *Sail Away*. Greenwillow, 1995.

Cronin, Doreen. *Diary of a Fly*. Illustrated by Harry Bliss. Live Oak Media, 2008.

_____. *Diary of a Spider*. Illustrated by Harry Bliss. HarperCollins, 2005.

_____. *Diary of a Worm*. Illustrated by Harry Bliss. HarperCollins, 2003.

Cummings, Pat. *Ananse and the Lizard: A West African Tale*. Holt, 2002.

Curlee, Lynn. *Brooklyn Bridge*. Atheneum, 2001.

Curtis, Christopher Paul. *The Watsons Go to Birmingham*. Laurel Leaf, 2000.

_____. *The Mighty Miss Malone*. Wendy Lamb Books, 2012.

Dahl, Roald. *James and the Giant Peach*. Illustrated by Lane Smith. Puffin, 1996 [1961].

_____. *James and the Giant Peach*. Illustrated by Nancy Ekholm Burkert. Knopf, 1961.

Decker, Timothy. *The Letter Home*. Front Street Press, 2005.

Del Rizzo, Suzanne. *My Beautiful Birds*. Pajama Press, 2017.

Diaz, Alexandra. *The Only Road*. Simon, 2016.

DiCamillo, Kate. *The Tale of Despereaux: Being the Story of a Mouse, a Princess, Some Soup, and a Spool of Thread*. Candlewick, 2004.

Dillon, Patrick. *The Story of Buildings: From the Pyramids to the Sydney Opera House*. Illustrated by Stephen Biesty. Candlewick, 2014.

Donovan, Sandy. *The Channel Tunnel*. Lerner, 2003.

Dowell, Frances O'Roark. *Sam the Man and the Rutabaga Plan*. Illustrated by Amy June Bates. Atheneum, 2017.

Edwards, Michelle. *Chicken Man*. Lothrop, 1991.

Ellis, Carson. *Du Iz Tak?* Candlewick, 2016.

_____. *Home*. Candlewick, 2015.

Ellis, Deborah. *No Ordinary Day*. Groundwood, 2011.

_____. *Kids of Kabul: Living Bravely Through a Never-Ending War*. Groundwood Books, 2012.

Erdrich, Louise. *The Birchbark House*. Hyperion, 1999.

_____. *The Game of Silence*. HarperCollins, 2005.

_____. *The Porcupine Year*. HarperCollins, 2008.

Evans, Shane W. *Underground: Finding the Light to Freedom*. Square Fish, 2015.

_____. *We March*. Roaring Brook Press, 2012.

Facklam, Margery. *The Big Bug Book*. Illustrated by Paul Facklam. Little, 1994.

Fan, Terry, and Eric Fan. *The Night Gardener*. Simon, 2016.

Farris, Christine King. *March On! The Day My Brother Martin Changed the World*. Illustrated by London Ladd. Scholastic Press, 2008.

_____. *My Brother Martin: A Sister Remembers Growing Up with the Rev. Dr. Martin Luther King, Jr.* Illustrated by Chris Soentpiet. Aladdin, 2005.

Ferris, Helen, comp. *Favorite Poems Old and New*. Illustrated by Leonard Weisgard. Doubleday, 1957.

Fisher, Leonard Everett. *The Architects: Colonial Craftsmen*. Cavendish, 1999.

Fleischman, Paul. *Joyful Noise: Poems for Two Voices*. Illustrated by Eric Beddows. Harper, 1988.

Forbes, Scott. *How to Make a Planet: A Step-by-Step Guide to Building the Earth*. Kids Can, 2014.

Freedman, Russell. *Freedom Walkers: The Story of the Montgomery Bus Boycott*. Holiday House, 2009.

Freeman, Judy, and Caroline Feller Bauer. *The Handbook for Story Tellers*. ALA, 2015.

French, Vivian. *Yucky Worms*. Illustrated by Jessica Ahlberg. Candlewick, 2012.

Friend, Catherine. *The Perfect Nest*. Illustrated by John Manders. Candlewick, 2007.

Fritz, Jean.

_____. *The Cabin Faced West*. Putnam, 1958.

_____. *And Then What Happened, Paul Revere?* Illustrated by Margo Tomes. Coward-McCann, 1973.

Frost, Helen. *Crossing Stones*. Farrar, Straus and Grioux, 2009.

_____. *Monarch and Milkweed*. Illustrated by Leonid Gore. Atheneum, 2008.

Fullerton, Alma. *When the Rain Comes*. Illustrated by Kim la Fave. Pajama Press, 2017.

Galdone, Paul. *The Little Red Hen*. Houghton, 1979 [1973].

Gantos, Jack. *Dead End in Norvelt*. Farrar, 2011.

Gardner, Robert. *Wild Science Projects About Earth's Weather*. Illustrated by Tom Labaff. Enslow, 2007.

George, Jean Craighead. *Julie of the Wolves*. Harper, 1972.

_____. *My Side of the Mountain*. Dutton, 1988 [1959].

Gibbons, Gail. *From Seed to Plant*. Holiday, 1991.

_____. *The Honey Makers*. HarperCollins, 2000 [1997].

_____. *Monarch Butterfly*. Holiday, 1989.

_____. *Spiders*. Holiday House, 1993.

_____. *Tell Me, Tree: All About Trees for Kids*. Little, 2002.

Gibbs, Edward. *I Spy With My Little Eye*. Templar, 2011.

Giff, Patricia Reilly. *Lily's Crossing*. Bantam Doubleday Dell, 1999.

Glatshteyn, Yankev. *Emil and Karl*. Translated by Jeffrey Shandler. Roaring Brook Press, 2006.

Goldsaito, Katrina. *The Sound of Silence*. Illustrated by Julia Kuo. Little, 2016.

Gravett, Emily. *Meerkat Mail*. Simon & Schuster Books for Young Readers, 2007.

_____. *The Odd Egg*. Simon & Schuster Books for Young Readers, 2009.

Greenfeld, Howard. *The Hidden Children*. Ticknor, 1993.

Grey, Mini. *Egg Drop*. Knopf Books for Young Readers, 2009.

Guthrie, Woody. *This Land Is Your Land*. Illustrated by Kathy Jakobsen. Little, 2002.

Hale, Shannon. *Real Friends*. Illustrated by Le Uyen Pham. First Second, 2017.

Hamilton, Virginia. *Anthony Burns: The Defeat and Triumph of a Fugitive Slave*. Laurel Leaf, 1993.

_____. *The House of Dies Drear*. Illustrated by Eros Keith. Macmillan, 1968.

Harris, Robie H. *It's So Amazing! A Book about Eggs, Sperm, Birth, Babies, and Families*. Candlewick, 2014.

Harrison, David L. *Bugs: Poems About Creeping Things*. Boyds, 2007.

Harrold, A. F. *The Song from Somewhere Else*. Illustrated by Levi Pinfold. Bloomsbury, 2017.

Harvey, Jeanne Walker. *Maya Lin: Artist-Architect of Light and Lines*. Illustrated by Dow Phumiruk. Holt, 2017.

Hautzig, Esther. *The Endless Steppe: Growing Up in Siberia*. Crowell, 1968.

Heos, Bridget. *I, Fly: The Buzz About Flies and How Awesome They Are*. Holt, 2015.

Herbert, Janis. *Leonardo for Kids: His Life and Ideas, 21 Activities*. Chicago Review Press, 1998.

Hesse, Karen. *Out of the Dust*. Scholastic, 1997.

Hest, Amy. *In the Rain with Baby Duck*. Illustrated by Jill Barton. Candlewick, 1995.

Ho, Minfong. *The Clay Marble: And Related Readings*. Houghton Mifflin Harcourt, 1997.

Hoberman, Mary Ann. *Forget-Me-Nots: Poems to Learn by Heart*. Illustrated by Michael Emberley. Little, 2012.

Holt, Kimberly Willis. *When Zachary Beaver Came to Town*. Holt, 2011.

Hopkins, Lee Bennett. *Amazing Places*. Illustrated by Chris Soentpiet. Lee & Low, 2015.

_____. *Full Moon and Stars*. Illustrated by Marcellus Hale. Abrams, 2011.

____. *Nasty Bugs*. Illustrated by Will Terry. Dial, 2012.

Hurst, Carol Otis. *Terrible Storm*. Illustrated by S. D. Schindler. Greenwillow Books, 2007.

Hutton, Keely. *Soldier Boy*. Farrar, 2017.

Inglis, Lucy. *City of Halves*. Scholastic, 2015.

Innocenti, Roberto, and Christophe Gallaz. *Rose Blanche*. Illustrated by Roberto Innocenti. Creative, 1985.

Isaacson, Philip. *Round Buildings, Square Buildings, Buildings That Wiggle Like a Fish*. Ember, 2016.

Jacques, Brian. *Redwall*. Philomel, 1986.

James, Simon. *Dear Mr. Blueberry*. Aladdin, 1996.

Jaramillo, Ann. *La Linea: A Novel*. Square Fish, 2008.

Jenkins, Martin. *Fabulous Frogs*. Candlewick, 2016.

Jenkins, Priscilla Belz. *A Nestful of Eggs*. Illustrated by Lizzy Rockwell. HarperCollins, 1995.

Jenkins, Steve. *The Beetle Book*. Houghton Harcourt, 2012.

Johnson, Angela. *A Sweet Smell of Roses*. Illustrated by Eric Velasquez. Simon & Schuster Books for Young Readers, 2007.

Jordan, Anne Devereaux, and Virginia Schomp. *Slavery and Resistance (The Drama of African-American History)*. Benchmark Books, 2006.

Judge, Lita. *One Thousand Tracings: Healing the Wounds of World War II*. Hyperion Book, 2007.

Kalman, Bobbie. *Colonial Life*. Crabtree, 1992.

Kaplan, William, and Shelley Tanaka. *One More Border: The True Story of One Family's Escape from War-Torn Europe*. Illustrated by Stephen Taylor. Groundwood Books, 1998.

Kellogg, Steven. *A-Hunting We Will Go*. Morrow, 1998.

____. *Chicken Little*. Morrow, 1985.

Kelly, Irene. *It's a Butterfly's Life*. Holiday, 2007.

Kenah, Katharine. *Flood Warning*. Illustrated by Amy Schimler-Safford. Harper, 2016.

Kerley, Barbara. *The Extraordinary Mark Twain (According to Susy)*. Illustrated by Edwin Fotheringham. Scholastic, 2010.

Kimmel, Elizabeth Cody. *Lily B. on the Brink of Love*. HarperCollins, 2005.

Kindl, Patrice. *Lost in the Labyrinth*. Houghton, 2002.

Klise, Kate. *Dying to Meet You (43 Old Cemetery Road)*. Illustrated by M. Sarah Klise. Sandpiper, 2010.

Krinitz, Esther Nisenthal, and Bernice Steinhardt. *Memories of Survival*. Hyperion, 2005.

Kudlinski, Kathleen V. *Boy, Were We Wrong About the Weather*. Illustrated by Sebastia Serra. Dial, 2015.

Kuntz, Doug. *Lost and Found Cat: The True Story of Kunkush's Incredible Journey*. Illustrated by Amy Stokes. Crown, 2017.

Lai, Thanhha. *Inside Out and Back Again*. HarperCollins, 2011.

Laird, Elizabeth. *Kiss the Dust*. Dutton, 1992.

Lappano, Jon-Erik. *Tokyo Digs a Garden* Illustrated by Kellen Hatanaka. Groundwood, 2016.

LaRoche, Giles. *If You Lived Here: Houses of the World*. Houghton, 2011.

Leatherdale, Mary Beth, and Eleanor Shakespeare. *Stormy Seas: Stories of Young Boat Refugees*. Annick, 2017.

Le Guin, Ursula K. *A Wizard of Earthsea*. Illustrated by Ruth Robbins. Parnassus, 1968.

Lehman, Barbara. *Rainstorm*. Houghton, 2007.

Levine, Gail Carson. *Forgive Me, I Meant to Do It: False Apology Poems*. Illustrated by Mathew Cordell. HarperCollins, 2012.

Levinson, Cynthia. *The Youngest Marcher: The Story of Audrey Faye Hendricks, a Civil Rights Activist*. Illustrated by Vanessa Brantley Newton. Atheneum, 2017.

Lewis, John, and Andrew Aydin. *March (Book One, Two, and Three)*. Illustrated by Nate Rowell. Top Shelf, 2016.

Lin, Grace. *Ling & Ting: Together in All Weather*. Little, 2015.

Lionni, Leo. *An Extraordinary Egg*. Knopf, 1994.

London, Jonathan. *Hurricane!* Illustrated by Henri Sorensen. HarperCollins, 1998.

Look, Lenore. *Brush of the Gods*. Illustrated by Meilo So. Schwartz and Wade, 2013.

Lowry, Lois. *Gooney Bird Greene*. Yearling, 2004.

____. *Number the Stars*. Houghton, 1989.

Lynne, Taylor. *Polish Orphans of Tengeru: The Dramatic Story of Their Long Journey to Canada 1941–49*. Dundurn, 2009.

Macaulay, David. *Built to Last*. Houghton, 2010.

____. *Underground*. Houghton, 1983.

MacLachlan, Patricia. *Sarah, Plain and Tall*. HarperCollins, 1985.

____. *Three Names*. Illustrated by Alexander Pertzoff. HarperCollins, 1991.

Madden, Kerry. *Gentle's Holler*. Puffin, 2007.

Mankell, Henning. *Secrets in the Fire*. Annick, 2003.

Marin, Albert. *Uprooted: The Japanese American Experience During WWII*. Knopf, 2016.

McClafferty, Carla Killough. *In Defiance of Hitler: The Secret Mission of Varian Fry*. Farrar, Straus and Giroux, 2008.

McCormick, Patricia. *Never Fall Down*. Harper, 2012.

McKissack, Patricia C. *Goin' Someplace Special*. Illustrated by Jerry Pinkney. Aladdin, 2008.

_____. *Scraps of Time 1960: Abby Takes a Stand*. Illustrated by Gordon James. Puffin, 2006.

Meisel, Paul. *My Awesome Summer* by P. Mantis. Holiday, 2017.

Meltzer, Milton. *Rescue: The Story of How Gentiles Saved Jews in the Holocaust*. HarperCollins, 1988.

Mills, Claudia. *The Totally Made-up Civil War Diary of Amanda MacLeish*. Farrar, Straus and Giroux, 2008.

Mitchell, Margaret King. *When Grandmama Sings*. Illustrated by James E. Ransome. HarperCollins, 2012.

Miyakoshi, Akiko. *The Storm*. Kids Can., 2016.

Miyares, Daniel, *Float*. Simon, 2015.

Montgomery, Sy. *Amazon Adventures: How Tiny Fish Are Saving the World's Largest Rainforest*. Photographs by Keith Ellenbogen. Houghton, 2017.

_____. *The Tarantula Scientist*. Photography by Nic Bishop. Houghton, 2004.

Mordecai, Martin. *Blue Mountain Trouble*. Scholastic, 2009.

Morpurgo, Michael. *The Elephant in the Garden*. Square Fish, 2013.

Moss, Marissa. *Amelia's Notebook*. Simon & Schuster/Paula Wiseman Books, 2006.

Munro, Roxie. *Hatch!* Amazon Children's Publishing, 2011.

Murawski, Darlyne. *Face to Face with Caterpillars*. National Geographic Children's Books, 2009.

Murphy, Jim. *Truce: The Day the Soldiers Stopped Fighting*. Scholastic, 2009.

Myers, Walter Dean. *Autobiography of My Dead Brother*. Illustrated by Christopher Meyers. HarperCollins, 2005.

_____. *Here in Harlem: Poems in Many Voices*. Holiday, 2004.

Naidoo, Beverley. *Making It Home: Real-Life Stories from Children Forced to Flee*. Puffin, 2005.

Nelson, Kadir. *Heart and Soul: The Story of America and African Americans*. HarperCollins, 2011.

Nelson, S. D. *Red Cloud: A Lakota Story of War and Surrender*. Abrams, 2017.

Nesbet, Anne. *Cloud and Wallfish*. Candlewick 2016.

Nicholls, Sally. *Ways to Live Forever*. Scholastic Paperbacks, 2011.

Nilsson, Ulf. *Detective Gordon: A Case in Any Case*. Illustrated by Gitte Spee. Translated by Julia Marshall. Gecko, 2017.

Northrop, Michael. *Book of the Dead (TombQuest 1)*. Scholastic, 2015.

O'Malley, Kevin. *Captain Raptor and the Moon Mystery*. Illustrated by Patrick O'Brien. Walker, 2005.

Oppenheim, Shulamith Levy. *The Lily Cupboard: A Story of the Holocaust*. Illustrated by Ronald Himler. HarperCollins, 1992.

Orloff, Karen Kaufman. *I Wanna Iguana*. Illustrated by David Catrow. Putnam, 2004.

_____. *I Wanna New Room*. Illustrated by David Catrow. Putnam, 2010.

Page, Robin. *A Chicken Followed Me Home: Questions and Answers about a Familiar Fowl*. Simon, 2015.

Palatini, Marge. *The Perfect Pet*. Illustrated by Bruce Whatley. Harper, 2009.

Park, Frances, and Ginger Park. *My Freedom Trip*. Illustrated by Debra Reid Jenkins. Boyds, 1998.

Park, Linda Sue. *A Long Walk to Water: Based on a True Story*. Clarion, 2011.

Partridge, Elizabeth. *Marching for Freedom: Walk Together Children and Don't You Grow Weary*. Viking Juvenile, 2009.

Paschkis, Julie. *P. Zonka Lays an Egg*. Peachtree, 2015.

Paterson, Katherine. *Bridge to Terabithia*. Illustrated by Donna Diamond. Crowell, 1977.

_____. *My Brigadista Year*. Candlewick, 2017.

Paxmann, Christine. *From Mud Huts to Skyscrapers*. Illustrated by Anne Ibelings. Prestel, 2012.

Peréz, Amada Irma. *Nana's Big Surprise / Nana, ¡Que sorprésa!*. Children's, 2007.

Phelan, Matt. *The Storm in the Barn*. Candlewick, 2011.

Phi, Bao. *A Different Pond*. Illustrated by Thi Bui. Capstone, 2017.

Pinkney, Andrea Davis. *The Red Pencil*. Little Brown, 2015.

_____. *Sit-In: How Four Friends Stood Up by Sitting Down*. Illustrated by Brian Pinkney. Little, Brown, 2010.

Pinkney, Jerry. *The Grasshopper and the Ants*. Little, 2015.

Polacco, Patricia. *Just Plain Fancy*. Bantam/Doubleday, 1990.

Pomeroy, Diana. *One Potato: A Counting Book of Potato Prints*. Sandpiper, 2000.

_____. *Wildflower ABC: An Alphabet of Potato Prints.* Sandpiper, 2001.

Portis, Annette. *Now.* Roaring Brook, 2017.

Posada, Mia. *Guess What Is Growing Inside This Egg?* Millbrook, 2007.

Potter, Giselle. *This Is My Doll House.* Random, 2016.

Prelutsky, Jack. *Nightmares: Poems to Trouble Your Sleep.* Illustrated by Arnold Lobel. Greenwillow, 1976.

_____, ed. *Read-Aloud Rhymes for the Very Young.* Illustrated by Marc Brown. Knopf, 1986.

Preston, Diana. *Remember the Lusitania!* Walker & Company, 2003.

Ramsey, Calvin Alexander, and Bettye Stroud. *Belle, The Last Mule at Gee's Bend: A Civil Rights Story.* Illustrated by John Holyfield. Candlewick, 2011.

Ransome, James. *My Teacher.* Dial, 2012.

Rappaport, Doreen. *Escape from Slavery: Five Journeys to Freedom.* Illustrated by Charles Lilly. HarperCollins, 1991.

_____. *Frederick's Journey: The Life of Frederick Douglas.* Jump At The Sun, 2015.

_____. *Freedom Ship.* Illustrated by Curtis James. Jump At The Sun, 2006.

_____. *Martin's Big Words: The Life of Dr. Martin Luther King, Jr.* Illustrated by Bryan Collier. Hyperion Book CH, 2001.

Richter, Hans Peter. *Friedrich.* Translated by Edite Kroll. Puffin, 1987 [1961].

Ringgold, Faith. *If a Bus Could Talk: The Story of Rosa Parks.* Aladdin, 2003.

Riordan, Rick. *39 Clues Series.* Scholastic Press, 2009.

Rockwell, Anne. *Bugs Are Insects.* Illustrated by Steve Jenkins. HarperCollins, 2001.

_____. *Honey in a Hive.* Illustrated by S. D. Schindler. HarperCollins, 2005.

Rodanas, Kristina. *Follow the Stars.* Cavendish, 1998.

Rosenthal, Amy Krouse. *This Plus That: Life's Little Equations.* Illustrated by Jen Corace. HarperCollins, 2011.

Rothman, Julia. *Nature Anatomy: The Curious Parts and Pieces of the Natural World.* Story, 2015.

Rowling, J. K. *Harry Potter and the Sorcerer's Stone.* Scholastic, 1998.

Ruby, Laura. *York: The Shadow Cipher.* Illustrated by Dave Stevenson. Walden Pond, 2017.

Rupp, Rebecca. *Weather! Watch How Weather Works.* Storey Publishing, 2003.

Ruurs, Margriet. *Stepping Stones: A Refugee Family's Journey.* Illustrated by Nizar Ali Badr. Orca, 2016.

Sachar, Louis. *Holes.* Farrar, 1998.

Salas, Laura Purdie. *A Leaf Can Be. . . .* Illustrated by Violeta Dabija. Millbrook Press, 2012.

Sanna. Francesca. *The Journey.* Flying Eye, 2016.

San Souci, Robert D. *The Talking Eggs.* Illustrated by Jerry Pinkney. Houghton Mifflin, 1992.

Sattler, Helen Roney. *Our Patchwork Planet.* Illustrated by Giulio Maestro. Harper, 1995.

Schulman, Janet. *Pale Male: Citizen Hawk of New York City.* Illustrated by Meilo So. Knopf, 2008.

Schwartz, Joanne. *Town Is by the Sea.* Illustrated by Sydney Smith. Groundwood, 2017.

Scieszka, Jon. *Battle Bunny.* Illustrated by Mac Barnett. Simon, 2013.

_____. *Spaceheadz.* Illustrated by Shane Prigmore. Simon, 2011.

Sendak, Maurice. *Where the Wild Things Are.* HarperCollins, 1963.

Sepahban, Lois. *Paper Wishes.* Farrar, 2016.

Sepetys, Ruta. *Between Shades of Gray.* Philomel, 2011.

Shafak, Elif. *The Architect's Apprentice.* Penguin, 2016.

Shange, Ntozake. *Coretta Scott.* Illustrated by Kadir Nelson. Katherine Tegen Books, 2009.

Shea, Pegi. *The Whispering Cloth. A Refugee's Story.* Illustrated by Anita Riggio. Boyds Mills Press, 1996.

Shea, Susan A. *Do You Know Which One Will Grow?* Illustrated by Tom Slaughter. Blue Apple, 2011.

Shingu, Susumu. *Traveling Butterflies.* Owlkids, 2015.

Shulevitz, Uri. *Dawn.* Farrar, 1974.

Sidman, Joyce. *Red Sings from Treetops: A Year in Colors.* Illustrated by Pamela Zagarenski. Houghton Mifflin Books for Children, 2009.

_____. *This Is Just to Say: Poems of Apology and Forgiveness.* Illustrated by Pamela Zagarenski. Houghton Mifflin, 2014.

Siegelson, Kim L. *Honey Bea.* Six Hens Press, 2010.

Silberberg, Alan. *Milo: Sticky Notes and Brain Freeze.* Aladdin, 2011.

Simon, Seymour. *Big Bugs.* Chronicle, 2005.

_____. *Butterflies.* Collins, 2011.

_____. *Storms.* Morrow, 1989.

Singer, Marilyn. *A Stick Is an Excellent Thing: Poems Celebrating Outdoor Play.* Illustrated by LeUyen Pham. Clarion, 2012.

Sklansky, Amy E. *Where Do Chicks Come From?* Illustrated by Pam Paparone. HarperCollins, 2005.

Skrypuch, Marsha Forchuk. *Adrift at Sea: A Vietnamese Boy's Story of Survival*. Pajama Press, 2016.

Smith, Jennifer E. *The Storm Makers*. Illustrated by Brett Helquist. Little Brown Books for Young Readers, 2012.

Sneve, Virginia Driving Hawk. *The Christmas Coat: Memories of My Sioux Childhood*. Illustrated by Ellen Beier. Holiday House, 2011.

Spier, Peter. *The Star-Spangled Banner*. Doubleday, 1973.

Spinelli, Jerry. *Milkweed*. Knopf, 2003.

Spires, Ashley. *The Most Magnificent Thing*. Kids Can, 2014.

Storad, Conrad J. *Uncovering the Earth's Crust*. Lerner, 2013.

Staples, Suzanne Fisher. *Under the Persimmon Tree*. Farrar, 2005.

Stein, David Ezra. *Interrupting Chicken*. Candlewick, 2010.

Stevens, Janet, and Susan Crummel Stevens. *Cook-a-Doodle-Doo!* Harcourt, 1999.

Stewart, Sarah. *The Gardener*. Illustrated by David Small. Square Fish, 2007.

Sullivan, Tara. *The Bitter Side of Sweet*. Putnam, 2016.

Swanson, Jennifer. *Everything Robotics*. National Geographic, 2016.

Sweet, Melissa. *Can an Aardvark Bark*? Illustrated by Steve Jenkins. Houghton, 2017.

Tan, Susan. *Cilla-lee Jenkins: Future Author Extraordinaire*. Illustrated by Dana Wulfekotte. Roaring Brook, 2017.

Tan, Shaun. *Lost & Found: Three by Shaun Tan*. Arthur A. Levine, 2011.

Taylor, Lynne. *Polish Orphans of Tengeru: The Dramatic Story of Their Long Journey to Canada 1941-1949*. Dundurn, 2009.

Taylor, Peter Lane, and Christos Nicola. *The Secret of Priest's Grotto: A Holocaust Survival Story*. Kar-Ben, 2007.

Teague, Mark. *LaRue Across America: Postcards from the Vacation*. Blue Sky Press, 2011.

____. *The Sky Is Falling!* Scholastic, 2015.

Tingle, Tim. *How I Became a Ghost: A Trail of Tears Story*. Roadrunner Press, 2013.

Tolstoy, Aleksei. *The Gigantic Turnip*. Illustrated by Niamh Sharkey. Barefoot, 2005.

Tonatiuh, Duncan. *Pancho Rabbit and the Coyote: A Migrant's Tale*. Abrams, 2014.

Tuck, Pamela M. *As Fast as Words Could Fly*. Illustrated by Eric Velasquez. Lee & Low, 2013.

Uchida, Yoshiko. *The Bracelet*. Illustrated by Joanna Yardley. Philomel, 1993.

____. *Journey to Topaz*. Illustrated by Donald Carrick. Creative Arts, 1985 [1971].

Urban, Linda. *Hound Dog True*. Harcourt Children's Books, 2011.

Van Allsburg, Chris. *The Mysteries of Harris Burdick*. Houghton, 1984.

____. *Queen of the Falls*. Houghton, 2011.

Van Laan, Nancy. *The Magic Bean Tree*. Illustrated by Beatriz Vidal. Houghton, 1998.

____. *Shingebiss: An Ojibwe Legend*. Illustrated by Betsy Bowen. Houghton, 1997.

Van Leeuwen, Jean. *Bound for Oregon*. Puffin, 1996 [1994].

Vogt, Gregory. *The Lithosphere: Earth's Crust*. Twenty-First Century, 2007.

Volavkova, Hana (ed). *I Never Saw Another Butterfly: Children's Drawings and Poems from the Terezin Concentration Camp, 1942–1944*. Schocken, 1994.

Walgren, Judy. *The Lost Boys of Natinga: A School for Sudan's Young Refugees*. Houghton, 1998.

Walker, Sally M. *Blizzard of Glass*. Holt, 2011.

____. *Earth Verse: Poetry from the Ground Up*. Illustrated by William Grill. Candlewick, 2017.

Wallace, Karen. *Creepy-Crawlies*. Illustrated by Tudor Humphries. Kingfisher, 2012.

Wallace, Rich, and Sandra Neil Wallace. *Blood Brother: Jonathan Daniels and His Sacrifice for Civil Rights*. Boyds Mills, 2016.

Warren, Andrea. *Escape from Saigon: How a Vietnam War Orphan Became an American*. Farrar, 2004.

Watkins, Angela Farris. *Love Will See You Through: Martin Luther King Jr.'s Six Guiding Beliefs (As Told by His Niece)*. Illustrated by Sally Wern Comport. Simon, 2015.

Watkins, Yoko Kawashima. *So Far from the Bamboo Grove*. Lothrop, 1986.

Weatherford, Carole Boston. *Freedom on the Menu: The Greensboro Sit-Ins*. Illustrated by Jerome Lagarrigue. Puffin, 2007.

____. *Sugar Hill: Harlem's Historic Neighborhood*. Illustrated by R. Gregory Christie. Whitman, 2014.

Webb, Sophie. *Far from Shore: Chronicles of an Open Ocean Voyage*. Houghton Mifflin Books for Children, 2011

Weitzman, David. *Skywalkers: Mohawk Ironworkers Build the City*. Roaring Brook, 2010.

Wenxuan, Cao. *Bronze and Sunflower*. Translated by Helen Wang. Illustrated by Meilo So. Candlewick, 2017.

Whelan, Gloria. *Goodbye Vietnam*. Knopf, 1992.

White, E. B. *Charlotte's Web*. Harper, 1952.

Wilder, Laura Ingalls. *Farmer Boy*. Illustrated by Garth Williams. Harper, 1953.

Wiles, Deborah. *Each Little Bird That Sings*. HMH Books for Young Readers, 2006.

———. *Freedom Summer*. Illustrated by Jerome Lagarrigue. Aladdin, 2005.

Williams-Garcia, Rita. *Clayton Byrd Goes Underground*. Harper, 2017.

———. *One Crazy Summer*. Amistad, 2010.

Williams, Mary. *Brothers in Hope: The Story of the Lost Boys of Sudan*. Illustrated by Gregory Christie. Lee & Low Books, 2005.

Williams, Vera B. *Three Days on a River in a Red Canoe*. Greenwillow, 1981.

Winerip, Michael. *Adam Canfeld of the Slash*. Candlewick, 2007.

Winters, Kay. *Voices from the Oregon Trail*. Illustrated by Larry Day. Dutton, 2014.

Wolf, Sallie. *The Robin Makes a Laughing Sound: A Birder's Observations*. Charlesbridge Publishing, 2010.

Woods, Brenda. *Saint Louis Armstrong Beach*. Penguin, 2001.

Woodson, Jacqueline. *Feathers*. Speak, 2010.

———. *Locomotion*. Speak, 2010.

———. *The Other Side*. Illustrated by E. B. Lewis. Putnam Juvenile, 2001.

———. *Visiting Day*. Illustrated by James Ransome. Puffin, 2015.

Wright, Joan Richards. *Bugs* (Reading Rainbow Books). Illustrated by Nancy Winslow Parker. Greenwillow Books, 1988.

Yamada, Kobi. *What Do You Do With an Idea*? Illustrated by Mae Besom. Compendium, 2014. Yolen, Jane. *Thunder Underground*. Illustrated by Josée Masse. WordSong, 2017.

Yep, Laurence. *Dragonwings*. HarperCollins, 1975.

Yolen, Jane. *Bug Off! Creepy, Crawly Poems*. Wordsong, 2012.

Zelch, Patti R. *Ready, Set . . . Wait!: What Animals Do Before a Hurricane*. Illustrated by Connie McLennan. Sylvan Dell Publishing, 2010.

Appendix A

Following are descriptions of some of the major awards in children's literature. We have included winners beginning with 1990. For a complete list of award winners, search the award's name online.

John Newbery Medal

The John Newbery Medal is named in honor of John Newbery, a British publisher and bookseller of the eighteenth century. He has frequently been called the father of children's literature because he was the first to conceive of the idea of publishing books expressly for children.

The award is presented each year to "the author of the most distinguished contribution to American literature for children." Only books published in the preceding year are eligible, and the author must be an American citizen or a permanent resident of the United States. The selection of the winner is made by a committee of the Association for Library Service to Children (ALSC) of the American Library Association. There are now fifteen members on this committee. The winning author is presented with a bronze medal designed by René Paul Chambellan and donated by Frederick G. Melcher. The announcement is made in January or early February. Later, at the summer conference of the American Library Association, a banquet is given in honor of the award winners.

In the following list, for each year the Medal winner is listed first (in boldface italic type), followed by the Honor Books for that year. The date is the year in which the award was conferred. All books were published the preceding year.

1990 *Number the Stars* by Lois Lowry. Houghton.
Afternoon of the Elves by Janet Taylor Lisle. Jackson/Orchard.
Shabanu: Daughter of the Wind by Suzanne Fisher Staples. Knopf.
The Winter Room by Gary Paulsen. Jackson/Orchard.

1991 *Maniac Magee* by Jerry Spinelli. Little.
The True Confessions of Charlotte Doyle by Avi. Jackson/Orchard.

1992 *Shiloh* by Phyllis Reynolds Naylor. Atheneum.
Nothing but the Truth by Avi. Jackson/Orchard.
The Wright Brothers by Russell Freedman. Holiday.

1993 *Missing May* by Cynthia Rylant. Jackson/Orchard.
The Dark-Thirty: Southern Tales of the Supernatural by Patricia C. McKissack. Knopf.
Somewhere in the Darkness by Walter Dean Myers. Scholastic.
What Hearts by Bruce Brooks. HarperCollins.

1994 *The Giver* by Lois Lowry. Houghton.
Crazy Lady by Jane Leslie Conly. HarperCollins.
Dragon's Gate by Laurence Yep. HarperCollins.
Eleanor Roosevelt: A Life of Discovery by Russell Freedman. Clarion.

1995 *Walk Two Moons* by Sharon Creech. HarperCollins.
Catherine, Called Birdy by Karen Cushman. Clarion.
The Ear, the Eye, and the Arm by Nancy Farmer. Jackson/Orchard.

1996 *The Midwife's Apprentice* by Karen Cushman. Clarion.
What Jamie Saw by Carolyn Coman. Front Street.
The Watsons Go to Birmingham: 1963 by Christopher Paul Curtis. Delacorte.
Yolonda's Genius by Carol Fenner. McElderry.
The Great Fire by Jim Murphy. Scholastic.

1997 *The View from Saturday* by E. L. Konigsburg. Atheneum.
A Girl Named Disaster by Nancy Farmer. Jackson/Orchard.
The Moorchild by Eloise McGraw. Simon.
The Thief by Megan Whalen Turner. Greenwillow.
Belle Prater's Boy by Ruth White. Farrar.

1998 *Out of the Dust* by Karen Hesse. Scholastic.
Ella Enchanted by Gail Carson Levine. HarperCollins.
Lily's Crossing by Patricia Reilly Giff. Delacorte.
Wringer by Jerry Spinelli. HarperCollins.

1999 *Holes* by Louis Sachar. Foster.
A Long Way from Chicago by Richard Peck. Dial.

2000 *Bud, Not Buddy* by Christopher Paul Curtis. Delacorte.
Getting Near to Baby by Audrey Couloumbis. Putnam.
Our Only May Amelia by Jennifer L. Holm. HarperCollins.
26 Fairmount Avenue by Tomie dePaola. Putnam.

2001 *A Year Down Yonder* by Richard Peck. Dial.
Because of Winn-Dixie by Kate DiCamillo. Candlewick.
Hope Was Here by Joan Bauer. Putnam.
Joey Pigza Loses Control by Jack Gantos. Farrar.
The Wanderer by Sharon Creech. HarperCollins.

2002   *A Single Shard* by Linda Sue Park. Clarion/Houghton.

Everything on a Waffle by Polly Horvath. Farrar.

Carver: A Life in Poems by Marilyn Nelson. Front Street.

2003   *Crispin: The Cross of Lead* by Avi. Hyperion.

The House of the Scorpion by Nancy Farmer. Atheneum.

Pictures of Hollis Woods by Patricia Reilly Giff. Random.

Hoot by Carl Hiaasen. Knopf.

A Corner of the Universe by Ann M. Martin. Scholastic.

Surviving the Applewhites by Stephanie S. Tolan. HarperCollins.

2004   *The Tale of Despereaux: Being the Story of a Mouse, a Princess, Some Soup, and a Spool of Thread* by Kate DiCamillo. Illustrated by Timothy Basil Ering. Candlewick.

Olive's Ocean by Kevin Henkes. Greenwillow.

An American Plague: The True and Terrifying Story of the Yellow Fever Epidemic of 1793 by Jim Murphy. Clarion.

2005   *Kira-Kira* by Cynthia Kadohata. Atheneum/Simon.

Al Capone Does My Shirts by Gennifer Choldenko. Putnam.

The Voice That Challenged a Nation: Marian Anderson and the Struggle for Equal Rights by Russell Freedman. Clarion/Houghton.

Lizzie Bright and the Buckminster Boy by Gary D. Schmidt. Clarion/Houghton.

2006   *Criss Cross* by Lynne Rae Perkins. Greenwillow.

Whittington by Alan Armstrong. Illustrated by S. D. Schindler. Random.

Hitler Youth: Growing Up in Hitler's Shadow by Susan Campbell Bartoletti. Scholastic.

Princess Academy by Shannon Hale. Bloomsbury.

Show Way by Jacqueline Woodson. Illustrated by Hudson Talbott. Putnam.

2007   *The Higher Power of Lucky* by Susan Patron. Illustrated by Matt Phelan. Simon.

Penny from Heaven by Jennifer L. Holm. Random.

Hattie Big Sky by Kirby Larson. Delacorte Press.

Rules by Cynthia Lord. Scholastic.

2008   *Good Masters! Sweet Ladies! Voices from a Medieval Village* by Laura Amy Schlitz. Candlewick.

Elijah of Buxton by Christopher Paul Curtis. Scholastic.

The Wednesday Wars by Gary D. Schmidt. Clarion.

Feathers by Jacqueline Woodson. Putnam.

2009   *The Graveyard Book* by Neil Gaiman. Illustrated by Dave McKean. HarperCollins.

The Underneath by Kathi Appelt. Illustrated by David Small. Atheneum Books for Young Readers/Simon & Schuster.

The Surrender Tree: Poems of Cuba's Struggle for Freedom by Margarita Engle. Henry Holt.

Savvy by Ingrid Law. Dial Books for Young Readers/Penguin Young Readers Group in partnership with Walden Media.

After Tupac & D Foster by Jacqueline Woodson. G.P. Putnam's Sons/Penguin Books for Young Readers.

2010   *When You Reach Me* by Rebecca Stead. Wendy Lamb Books/Random House Children's Books.

Claudette Colvin: Twice Toward Justice by Phillip Hoose. Melanie Kroupa Books/Farrar, Straus & Giroux.

The Evolution of Calpurnia Tate by Jacqueline Kelly. Henry Holt.

Where the Mountain Meets the Moon by Grace Lin. Little, Brown and Company Books for Young Readers.

The Mostly True Adventures of Homer P. Figg by Rodman Philbrick. The Blue Sky Press/Scholastic, Inc.

2011   *Moon Over Manifest* by Clare Vanderpool. Delacorte Press/Random House Children's Books.

Turtle in Paradise by Jennifer L. Holm. Random House Children's Books.

Heart of a Samurai by Margi Preus. Amulet Books/Abrams.

Dark Emperor and Other Poems of the Night by Joyce Sidman. Illustrated by Rick Allen. Houghton Mifflin Books for Children.

One Crazy Summer by Rita Williams-Garcia. Amistad/HarperCollins.

2012   *Dead End in Norvelt* by Jack Gantos. Farrar, Straus & Giroux.

Inside Out & Back Again by Thanhha Lai. HarperCollins Children's Books.

Breaking Stalin's Nose by Eugene Yelchin. Henry Holt and Company, LLC.

2013   *The One and Only Ivan* by Katherine Applegate. HarperCollins Children's Books.

Splendors & Glooms by Laura Amy Schlitz. Candlewick Press.

Bomb: The Race to Build—and Steal—the World's Most Dangerous Weapon by Steve Sheinkin. Flash Point/Roaring Brook Press.

Three Times Lucky by Sheila Turnage. Dial/Penguin Young Readers Group.

2014   *Flora & Ulysses: The Illuminated Adventures* by Kate DiCamillo. Candlewick Press.

Doll Bones by Holly Black. Margaret K. McElderry Books, an imprint of Simon & Schuster Children's Publishing.

The Year of Billy Miller by Kevin Henkes. Greenwillow Books, an imprint of HarperCollins Publishers.

One Came Home by Amy Timberlake. Alfred A. Knopf, an imprint of Random House Children's Books.

Paperboy by Vince Vawter. Delacorte Press, an imprint of Random House Children's Books.

2015 *The Crossover* by Kwame Alexander. Houghton Mifflin Harcourt.

El Deafo by Cece Bell. Amulet Press, an imprint of Abrams.

Brown Girl Dreaming by Jacqueline Woodson. Nancy Paulsen Books, an imprint of Penguin Group LLC.

2016 *Last Stop on Market Street* by Matt de la Peña. G.P. Putnam's Sons/Penguin.

The War That Saved My Life by Kimberly Brubaker Bradley. Dial Books for Young Readers/Penguin.

Roller Girl by Victoria Jamieson. Dial Books for Young Readers/Penguin.

Echo by Pam Muñoz Ryan. Scholastic Press/Scholastic Inc.

2017 *The Girl Who Drank the Moon* by Kelly Barnhill. Algonquin Young Readers, an imprint of Algonquin Books of Chapel Hill, a division of Workman Publishing.

Freedom Over Me: Eleven Slaves, Their Lives and Dreams Brought to Life by Ashley Bryan. Illustrated by Ashley Brown. Atheneum Books for Young Readers, an imprint of Simon & Schuster Children's Publishing Division.

The Inquisitor's Tale: Or, The Three Magical Children and Their Holy Dog by Adam Gidwitz. Illustrated by Hatem Aly. Dutton Children's Books, Penguin Young Readers Group, an imprint of Penguin Random House LLC.

Wolf Hollow by Lauren Wolk. Dutton Children's Books, Penguin Young Readers Group, an imprint of Penguin Random House LLC.

2018 *Hello, Universe* by Erin Entrada Kelly. Greenwillow Books, an imprint of HarperCollins Publishers.

Crown: An Ode to the Fresh Cut by Derrick Barnes. Illustrated by Gordon C. James. Bolden, an Agate Imprint, a Denene Millner Book.

Long Way Down by Jason Reynolds. Atheneum, an imprint of Simon & Schuster Children's Publishing Division, a Caitlyn Dlouhy Book.

Piecing Me Together by Renée Watson. Bloomsbury Children's Books.

Caldecott Medal

The Caldecott Medal is named in honor of Randolph Caldecott, a prominent English illustrator of children's books during the nineteenth century. This award, presented each year by an awards committee of the Association for Library Service to Children (ALSC) of the American Library Association, is given to "the artist of the most distinguished American picture book for children." In the following list, for each year the Medal winner is listed first (in boldface italic type), followed by the Honor Books for that year. If an illustrator's name is not cited, the author illustrated the book.

1990 *Lon Po Po: A Red-Riding Hood Story from China.* Adapted and illustrated by Ed Young. Philomel.

Bill Peet: An Autobiography by Bill Peet. Houghton.

Color Zoo by Lois Ehlert. Lippincott.

Herschel and the Hanukkah Goblins by Eric Kimmel. Illustrated by Trina Schart Hyman. Holiday.

The Talking Eggs by Robert D. San Souci. Illustrated by Jerry Pinkney. Dial.

1991 *Black and White* by David Macaulay. Houghton.

Puss in Boots by Charles Perrault. Translated by Malcolm Arthur. Illustrated by Fred Marcelino. di Capua/Farrar.

"More More More," Said the Baby by Vera B. Williams. Greenwillow.

1992 *Tuesday* by David Wiesner. Clarion.

Tar Beach by Faith Ringgold. Crown.

1993 *Mirette on the High Wire* by Emily Arnold McCully. Putnam.

Seven Blind Mice by Ed Young. Philomel.

The Stinky Cheese Man and Other Fairly Stupid Tales by Jon Scieszka. Illustrated by Lane Smith. Viking.

Working Cotton by Sherley Anne Williams. Illustrated by Carole Byard. Harcourt.

1994 *Grandfather's Journey* by Allen Say. Houghton.

Peppe the Lamplighter by Elisa Bartone. Illustrated by Ted Lewin. Lothrop.

In the Small, Small Pond by Denise Fleming. Holt.

Owen by Kevin Henkes. Greenwillow.

Raven: A Trickster Tale from the Pacific Northwest by Gerald McDermott. Harcourt.

Yo! Yes? by Chris Raschka. Jackson/Orchard.

1995 *Smoky Night* by Eve Bunting. Illustrated by David Diaz. Harcourt.

Swamp Angel by Paul O. Zelinsky. Dutton.

John Henry by Julius Lester. Illustrated by Jerry Pinkney. Dial.

Time Flies by Eric Rohmann. Crown.

1996 *Officer Buckle and Gloria* by Peggy Rathman. Putnam.

Alphabet City by Stephen T. Johnson. Viking.

Zin! Zin! Zin! a Violin by Lloyd Moss. Illustrated by Marjorie Priceman. Simon.

The Faithful Friend by Robert D. San Souci. Illustrated by Brian Pinkney. Simon.

Tops and Bottoms by Janet Stephens. Harcourt.

1997 *Golem* by David Wisniewski. Clarion.

Hush! A Thai Lullaby by Minfong Ho. Illustrated by Holly Meade. Kroupa/Orchard.

The Graphic Alphabet by David Pelletier. Orchard.

The Paperboy by Dav Pilkey. Orchard.

Starry Messenger by Peter Sis. Foster/Farrar.

1998 *Rapunzel* by Paul O. Zelinsky. Dutton.

The Gardener by Sarah Stewart. Illustrated by David Small. Farrar.

Harlem by Walter Dean Myers. Illustrated by Christopher Myers. Scholastic.

There Was an Old Lady Who Swallowed a Fly by Simms Taback. Viking.

1999 ***Snowflake Bentley*** by Jacqueline Briggs Martin. Illustrated by Mary Azarian. Houghton.

Duke Ellington: The Piano Prince and His Orchestra by Andrea Pinkney. Illustrated by Brian Pinkney. Hyperion.

No, David! by David Shannon. Scholastic.

Snow by Uri Shulevitz. Farrar.

Tibet Through the Red Box by Peter Sis. Foster.

2000 ***Joseph Had a Little Overcoat*** by Simms Taback. Viking.

A Child's Calendar by John Updike. Illustrated by Trina Schart Hyman. Holiday.

Sector 7 by David Wiesner. Clarion.

The Ugly Duckling by Hans Christian Andersen. Illustrated by Jerry Pinkney. Morrow.

When Sophie Gets Angry—Really, Really Angry. . . . by Molly Bang. Scholastic.

2001 ***So You Want to Be President?*** by Judith St. George. Illustrated by David Small. Philomel.

Casey at the Bat by Earnest Lawrence Thayer. Illustrated by Christopher Bing. Handprint.

Click, Clack, Moo: Cows That Type by Doreen Cronin. Illustrated by Betsy Lewin. Simon.

Olivia by Ian Falconer. Atheneum.

2002 ***The Three Pigs*** by David Wiesner. Clarion.

The Dinosaurs of Waterhouse Hawkins by Barbara Kerley. Illustrated by Brian Selznick. Scholastic.

Martin's Big Words by Doreen Rappaport. Illustrated by Brian Collier. Hyperion.

The Stray Dog by Marc Simont. HarperCollins.

2003 ***My Friend Rabbit*** by Eric Rohman. Roaring Brook Press.

The Spider and the Fly by Mary Howitt. Illustrated by Tony DiTerlizzi. Simon.

Hondo and Fabian by Peter McCarty. Holt.

Noah's Ark by Jerry Pinkney. Sea Star.

2004 ***The Man Who Walked Between the Towers*** by Mordicai Gerstein. Roaring Brook Press.

Ella Sarah Gets Dressed by Margaret Chodos-Irvine. Harcourt.

What Do You Do with a Tail Like This? by Steve Jenkins and Robin Page. Houghton.

Don't Let the Pigeon Drive the Bus by Mo Willems. Hyperion.

2005 ***Kitten's First Full Moon*** by Kevin Henkes. Greenwillow.

The Red Book by Barbara Lehman. Houghton.

Coming on Home Soon by Jacqueline Woodson. Illustrated by E. B. Lewis. Putnam.

Knuffle Bunny: A Cautionary Tale by Mo Willems. Hyperion.

2006 ***The Hello, Goodbye Window*** by Norton Juster. Illustrated by Chris Raschka. di Capua/ Hyperion.

Rosa by Nikki Giovanni. Illustrated by Bryan Collier. Holt.

Zen Shorts by Jon J. Muth. Scholastic.

Hot Air: The (Mostly) True Story of the First Hot-Air Balloon Ride by Marjorie Priceman. Schwartz/ Atheneum/Simon.

Song of the Water Boatman and Other Pond Poems by Joyce Sidman. Illustrated by Beckie Prange. Houghton.

2007 ***Flotsam*** by David Wiesner. Clarion.

Gone Wild: An Endangered Animal Alphabet by David McLimans. Walker.

Moses: When Harriet Tubman Led Her People to Freedom by Carole Boston Weatherford. Illustrated by Kadir Nelson. Hyperion.

2008 ***The Invention of Hugo Cabret*** by Brian Selnick. Scholastic.

Henry's Freedom Box: A True Story from the Underground Railroad by Ellen Levine. Illustrated by Kadir Nelson. Scholastic.

First the Egg by Laura Vaccaro Seeger. Brook/ Porter.

The Wall: Growing Up Behind the Iron Curtain by Peter Sis. Farrar/Foster.

Knuffle Bunny Too: A Case of Mistaken Identity by Mo Willems. Hyperion.

2009 ***The House in the Night*** by Susan Marie Swanson. Illustrated by Beth Krommes. Houghton Mifflin Company.

A Couple of Boys Have the Best Week Ever by Marla Frazee. Harcourt, Inc.

How I Learned Geography by Uri Shulevitz. Farrar, Straus & Giroux.

A River of Words: The Story of William Carlos Williams by Jen Bryant. Illustrated by Melissa Sweet. Wm. B. Eerdmans Publishing Co.

2010 ***The Lion & the Mouse*** by Jerry Pinkney. Little, Brown & Company.

All the World by Liz Garton Scanlon. Illustrated by Marla Frazee. Beach Lane Books.

Red Sings from Treetops: A Year in Colors by Joyce Sidman. Illustrated by Pamela Zagarenski. Children/Houghton Mifflin Harcourt.

2011 ***A Sick Day for Amos McGee*** by Philip C. Stead. Illustrated by Erin E. Stead. Holtzbrinck Publishing.

Dave the Potter: Artist, Poet, Slave by Laban Carrick Hill. Illustrated by Bryan Collier. Hachette Book Group, Inc.

Interrupting Chicken by David Ezra Stein. Candlewick Press.

2012 ***A Ball for Daisy*** by Chris Raschka. Random House, Inc.

Blackout by John Rocco. Disney Book Group.

Grandpa Green by Lane Smith. Holtzbrinck Publishing Holdings Limited Partnership.

Me...Jane by Patrick McDonnell. Hachette Book Group, Inc.

2013 *This Is Not My Hat* by Jon Klassen. Candlewick Press.

Creepy Carrots! by Aaron Reynolds. Illustrated by Peter Brown. Simon & Schuster Books for Young Readers, an imprint of Simon & Schuster Children's Publishing Division.

Extra Yarn by Mac Barnett. Illustrated by Jon Klassen. Balzer + Bray, an imprint of HarperCollins Publishers.

Green by Laura Vaccaro Seeger. Neal Porter Books, an imprint of Roaring Brook Press.

One Cool Friend by Toni Buzzeo. Illustrated by David Small. Dial Books for Young Readers, a division of Penguin Young Reader Group.

Sleep Like a Tiger by Mary Logue. Illustrated by Pamela Zagarenski. Houghton Mifflin Books for Children, an imprint of Houghton Mifflin Harcourt Publishing Company.

2014 *Locomotive* by Brian Floca. Atheneum Books for Young Readers, an imprint of Simon & Schuster Children's Publishing.

Journey by Aaron Becker. Candlewick Press.

Flora and the Flamingo by Molly Idle. Chronicle Books.

Mr. Wuffles! by David Wiesner. Clarion Books, an imprint of Houghton Mifflin Harcourt Publishing.

2015 *The Adventures of Beekle: The Unimaginary Friend* by Dan Santat. Little, Brown and Company, a division of Hachette Book Group, Inc.

Nana in the City by Lauren Castillo. Clarion Books, an imprint of Houghton Mifflin Harcourt.

The Noisy Paint Box: The Colors and Sounds of Kandinsky's Art by Barb Rosenstock. Illustrated by Mary GrandPré. Alfred A. Knopf, an imprint of Random House Children's Books.

Sam & Dave Dig a Hole by Mac Barnett. Illustrated by Jon Klassen. Candlewick Press.

Viva Frida by Yuyi Morales. Roaring Brook Press, a Neal Porter Book.

The Right Word: Roget and His Thesaurus by Jen Bryant. Illustrated by Melissa Sweet. Eerdmans Books for Young Readers.

This One Summer by Mariko Tamaki. Illustrated by Jillian Tamaki. First Second.

2016 *Finding Winnie: The True Story of the World's Most Famous Bear* by Lindsay Mattick. Illustrated by Sophie Blackall. Little, Brown and Company, a division of Hachette Book Group.

Trombone Shorty by Troy Andrews. Illustrated by Bryan Collier. Abrams Books for Young Readers, an imprint of Abrams.

Waiting by Kevin Henkes. Greenwillow Books/HarperCollins.

Voice of Freedom: Fannie Lou Hamer, Spirit of the Civil Rights Movement by Carole Boston Weatherford. Illustrated by Ekua Holmes. Candlewick Press.

Last Stop on Market Street by Matt de la Peña. Illustrated by Christian Robinson. G.P. Putnam's Sons/Penguin.

2017 *Radiant Child: The Story of Young Artist Jean-Michel Basquiat* by Javaka Steptoe. Little, Brown and Company, a division of Hachette Book Group.

Leave Me Alone! by Vera Brosgol. Roaring Brook Press, a division of Holtzbrinck Publishing Holdings Limited Partnership.

Freedom in Congo Square by Carole Boston Weatherford. Illustrated by R. Gregory Christie. Little Bee Books, an imprint of Bonnier Publishing Group.

Du Iz Tak? By Carson Ellis. Candlewick Press.

They All Saw a Cat by Brendan Wenzel. Chronicle Books, LLC.

2018 *Wolf in the Snow* by Matthew Cordell. Feiwel and Friends, an imprint of Macmillan.

Big Cat, Little Cat by Elisha Cooper. Roaring Brook Press, a division of Holtzbrinck Publishing Holdings Limited Partnership.

Crown: An Ode to the Fresh Cut by Derrick Barnes. Illustrated by Gordon C. James. Bolden, an Agate Imprint, a Denene Millner Book.

A Different Pond by Bao Phi. Illustrated by Thi Bui. Capstone Young Readers, a Capstone imprint.

Grand Canyon by Jason Chin. A Neal Porter Book, Roaring Brook Press, a division of Holtzbrinck Publishing Holdings Limited Partnership.

Batchelder Award

The Batchelder Award, established in 1966, is given by the Association of Library Service to Children (ALSC) of the American Library Association to the publisher of the most outstanding book of the year that is a translation, published in the United States, of a book that was first published in another country. In 1990, Honor Books were added to this award. The original country of publication is given in parentheses.

1990 *Buster's World* by Bjarne Reuter, translated by Anthea Bell. Dutton. (Denmark)

1991 *A Hand Full of Stars* by Rafik Schami, translated by Rika Lesser. Dutton. (Germany)

1992 *The Man from the Other Side* by Uri Orlev, translated by Hillel Halkin. Houghton. (Israel)

1993 No award

1994 *The Apprentice* by Molina Llorente, translated by Robin Longshaw. Farrar. (Spain)

1995 *The Boys from St. Petri* by Bjarne Reuter, translated by Anthea Bell. Dutton. (Denmark)

1996 *The Lady with the Hat* by Uri Orlev, translated by Hillel Halkin. Houghton. (Israel)

1997	*The Friends* by Kazumi Yumoto, translated by Cathy Hirano. Farrar. (Japan)
1998	*The Robber and Me* by Josef Holub, translated by Elizabeth C. Crawford. Holt. (Germany)
1999	*Thanks to My Mother* by Schoschana Rabinovici, translated by James Skofield. Dial. (Germany)
2000	*The Baboon King* by Anton Quintana, translated by John Nieuwenhuizen. Walker. (Netherlands)
2001	*Samir and Yonatan* by Daniella Carmi, translated by Yael Lotan. Scholastic. (Israel)
2002	*How I Became an American* by Karin Gündisch, translated by James Skofield. Cricket. (Germany)
2003	*The Thief Lord* by Cornelia Funke, translated by Oliver Latsch. Scholastic. (Germany)
2004	*Run, Boy, Run* by Uri Orlev, translated by Hillel Halkin. Lorraine. (Israel)
2005	*The Shadows of Ghadames* by Joëlle Stolz, translated by Catherine Temerson. Delacorte/Random. (France)
2006	*An Innocent Soldier* by Josef Holub, translated by Michael Hofmann. Levine/Scholastic. (Germany)
2007	*The Pull of the Ocean* by Jean-Claude Mourlevat, translated by Y. Maudet. Delacorte Press. (France)
2008	*Brave Story* by Miyuki Miyabe, translated by Alexander O. Smith. VIZ Media. (Japan)
2009	*Moribito: Guardian of the Spirit* by Nahoko Uehashi, translated by Cathy Hirano. Scholastic. (Japan)
2010	*A Faraway Island* by Annika Thor, translated by Linda Schenck. Random House. (Sweden)
2011	*A Time of Miracles* by Anne-Laure Bondoux, translated by Y. Maudet. Random House. (France)
2012	*Soldier Bear* by Bibi Dumon Tak, illustrated by Philip Hopman, translated by Laura Watkinson. Wm. B. Eerdmans Publishing Co. (Netherlands)
2013	*My Family for the War* by Anne C. Voorhoeve. Translated by Tammi Reichel. Dial. (Germany)
2014	*Mister Orange* by Truus Matti. Translated by Laura Watkinson. Enchanted Lion Books. (Netherlands)
2015	*Mikis and the Donkey* by Bibi Dumon Tak. Illustrated by Philip Hopman. Translated by Laura Watkinson. Eerdmans Books for Young Readers. (Netherlands)
2016	*The Wonderful Fluffy Little Squishy* by Beatrice Alemagna. Translated by Claudia Zoe Bedrick. Enchanted Lion Books. (France)
2017	*Cry, Heart, But Never Break* by Glenn Ringtved. Illustrated by Charlotte Pardi. Translated by Robert Moulthrop. Enchanted Lion Press. (Denmark)
2018	*The Murderer's Ape* by Jakob Wegelius. Translated by Peter Graves. Delacorte Press, an imprint of Random House Children's Books, a division of Penguin Random House LLC. (Sweden)

Children's Literature Legacy Award

Previously known as the Laura Ingalls Wilder Award, this award is given to an author or illustrator whose books (published in the United States) have made a substantial and lasting contribution to literature for children. Established in 1954, this award was given every five years through 1980. As of 1983, it is given every three years by the Association of Library Service to Children (ALSC) of the American Library Association. The following are the award winners since 1990.

1992	Marcia Brown
1995	Virginia Hamilton
1998	Russell Freedman
2001	Milton Meltzer
2003	Eric Carle
2005	Laurence Yep
2007	James Marshall
2009	Ashley Bryan
2011	Tomie dePaola
2013	Katherine Paterson
2015	Donald Crews
2016	Jerry Pinkney
2017	Nikki Grimes
2018	Jacqueline Woodson

Hans Christian Andersen Prize

The Hans Christian Andersen Prize, the first international children's book award, was established in 1956 by the International Board on Books for Young People. Given every two years, the award was expanded in 1966 to honor an illustrator as well as an author. A committee composed of members from different countries judges the selections recommended by the board or library associations in each country. The following have won the Hans Christian Andersen Prize since 1990.

1990	Tormod Haugen (author). Norway. Lisbeth Zwerger (illustrator). Austria.
1992	Virginia Hamilton (author). United States. Kveta Pacovská (illustrator). Czechoslovakia.
1994	Michio Mado (author). Japan. Jörg Müller (illustrator). Switzerland.
1996	Uri Orlev (author). Israel. Klaus Ensikat (illustrator). Germany.
1998	Katherine Paterson (author). United States. Tomi Ungerer (illustrator). France.
2000	Anna Maria Machado (author). Brazil. Anthony Browne (illustrator). United Kingdom.
2002	Aidan Chambers (author). United Kingdom. Quentin Blake (illustrator). United Kingdom.
2004	Martin Waddell (author). Ireland. Max Velthuijs (illustrator). Netherlands.

2006	Margaret Mahy (author). New Zealand.
	Wolf Erbruch (illustrator). Germany.
2008	Jürg Schubiger (author). Switzerland.
	Roberto Innocenti (illustrator). Italy.
2010	David Almond (author). United Kingdom.
	Jutta Bauer (illustrator). Germany.
2012	Maria Teresa Andruetto (author). Argentina.
	Peter Sis (illustrator). Czech Republic.
2014	Nauhoko Uehaski (author). Japan.
	Roger Mello (illustrator). Brazil.
2016	Cao Wenxuan (author). China.
	Rotraut Suzanne Berner (illustrator). Germany.
2018	Eiko Kadono (author). Japan.
	Igor Oleynikov (illustrator). Russia.

General Awards

Boston Globe–Horn Book Awards *Horn Book Magazine,* 56 Roland St., Suite 200, Boston, MA 02129. Currently given for outstanding fiction or poetry, outstanding nonfiction, and outstanding illustration. <www.hbook.com/magazine>.

Golden Kite Award Society of Children's Book Writers and Illustrators, 4727 Wilshire Blvd., Suite 301, Los Angeles, CA 90010. Presented annually by the Society of Children's Book Writers and Illustrators to members whose books of fiction, nonfiction, and picture illustration best exhibit excellence and genuinely appeal to interests and concerns of children. <www. scbwi.org>.

International Literacy Association Children's Book Award International Literacy Association, 258 Chapman Road, Suite 203 Newark, DE 19702. An annual award for a first or second book to an author from any country who shows unusual promise in the children's book field. Since 1987, the award has been presented to both a picturebook and a novel. <www.reading.org>.

New York Times Choice of Best Illustrated Children's Books of the Year New York Times, 229 W. 43rd St., New York, NY 10036. Books are selected for excellence in illustration by a panel of judges.

Awards Based on Special Content

Jane Addams Book Award Jane Addams Peace Association, 777 United Nations Plaza, 6th Floor, New York, NY 10017. For a book with literary merit stressing themes of dignity, equality, peace, and social justice. <www.janeaddamspeace.org>.

Association of Jewish Libraries Awards Association of Jewish Libraries, P.O. Box 1118, Teaneck, NJ 07666. Given to one or two titles that have made the most outstanding contribution to the field of Jewish literature for children and young people. The Sydney Taylor Body of Work Award, established in 1981, is given for an author's body of work. <https://jewishlibraries. org/>.

Catholic Book Awards Catholic Press Association of the United States and Canada, 205 W. Monroe St., Suite 470, Chicago, IL 60606. Honors selected in five categories and awarded to books with sound Christian and psychological values. <www.catholicpress.org>.

Charlotte Huck Award National Council of Teachers of English (NCTE), 1111 W. Kenyon Road, Urbana, IL 61801. Given annually for fiction that has the power to transform children's lives. <www.ncte.org>.

Child Study Children's Book Committee at Bank Street College Award Bank Street College of Education, 610 W. 112th St., New York, NY 10025. For a distinguished book for children or young people that deals honestly and courageously with problems in the world. <www.bnkst.edu>.

Christopher Awards The Christophers, 5 Hanover Square, 11th Floor, New York, NY 10004. Given to works of artistic excellence affirming the highest values of the human spirit. <www.christophers.org>.

Dolly Gray Award. Council for Exceptional Children. 2900 Crystal Dr. Suite 100. Arlington, VA 22202. Recognizes authors, illustrators, and publishers of high-quality fictional and biographical children, intermediate, and young adult books that appropriately portray individuals with developmental disabilities. http://www.daddcec.org/Awards/DollyGrayAwards. aspx

Jefferson Cup Award Children's and Young Adult Roundtable of the Virginia Library Association, P.O. Box 56312, Virginia Beach, VA 23456. Presented for a distinguished book in American history, historical fiction, or biography. <www.vla. org>.

Ezra Jack Keats Awards Given biennially to a promising new artist and a promising writer. The recipients receive a monetary award and a medallion from the Ezra Jack Keats Foundation, 450 14th Street, Brooklyn, NY 11215-5702. <www.ezra-jack-keats.org>.

Coretta Scott King Awards Social Responsibilities Round Table of the American Library Association, 50 E. Huron St., Chicago, IL 60611. Given to an African American author and an African American illustrator for outstanding inspirational and educational contributions to literature for children. <www. ala.org>.

National Council of Teachers of English Award for Excellence in Poetry for Children National Council of Teachers of English, 1111 Kenyon Rd., Urbana, IL 61801. Given formerly annually and presently every three years to a living American poet for total body of work for children ages 3 to 13. <www. ncte.org>.

National Jewish Book Awards Jewish Book Council, 520 8th Avenue, 4th Floor, New York, NY 10018. Various awards are given for work or body of work that makes a contribution to Jewish juvenile literature. <www.jewishbookcouncil.org>.

New York Academy of Sciences Children's Science Books Awards The New York Academy of Sciences, 7 World Trade Center, 250 Greenwich St., 40th Floor, New York, NY 10007. For books of high quality in the field of science for children, three awards are given: Younger Children, Older Children, and the Montroll Award for a book that provides unusual historical data or background on a scientific subject. <www.nyas.org>.

Scott O'Dell Award for Historical Fiction Honors a distinguished work of historical fiction set in the New World. <www. scottodell.com>.

Orbis Pictus Award for Outstanding Nonfiction for Children National Council of Teachers of English (NCTE), 1111 W. Kenyon Rd., Urbana, IL 61801. Presented annually by the

National Council of Teachers of English to the outstanding nonfiction book of the previous year. <www.ncte.org>.

Phoenix Award Children's Literature Association, 1301 W. 22nd Street, Suite 202, Oak Brook, IL 60523. Given to the author of a book published for children twenty years before that has not received a major children's book award. <https://chla.memberclicks.net/phoenix-award>.

Edgar Allan Poe Awards Mystery Writers of America, 1140 Broadway, Suite 1507, New York, NY 10001. For best juvenile mystery. <www.mysterywriters.org>.

Michael J. Printz Award American Library Association, 50 E. Huron St., Chicago, IL 60611. Given to a book that exemplifies literary excellence in young-adult literature. Sponsored by the Young Adult Library Services Association of the American Library Association. <www.ala.org>.

Robert F. Sibert Informational Book Award American Library Association, 50 E. Huron St., Chicago, IL 60611. Honors the author whose work of nonfiction has made a significant contribution to the field of children's literature in a given year. Sponsored by the Association of Library Services to Children. <www.ala.org>.

Washington Post/Children's Book Guild Nonfiction Award Washington Post, 1150 15th St. NW, Washington, DC 20071. Given to an author or an illustrator for a body of work in juvenile informational books.

Western Writers of America Spur Award Western Writers of America, Inc., 508 Senter Pl., Selah, WA 98942. For the best Western juvenile work in two categories, fiction and nonfiction. <www.westernwriters.org>.

Carter G. Woodson Book Award National Council for the Social Studies, 8555 16th Street, Suite 500, Silver Spring, Maryland 20910. Presented to outstanding social science books for young readers that treat sensitively and accurately topics related to ethnic minorities. <www.ncss.org>.

Awards for Lasting Contributions or Service to Children's Literature

Arbuthnot Award International Literacy Association, P.O. Box 8139, Newark, DE 19714. Named after May Hill Arbuthnot, an authority on literature for children, this award is given annually to an outstanding teacher of children's literature. <www.reading.org>.

Arbuthnot Honor Lecture The Association for Library Service to Children (ALSC) of the American Library Association, 50 E. Huron St., Chicago, IL 60611. This free public lecture is presented annually by a distinguished author, critic, librarian, historian, or teacher of children's literature. Both the lecturer and the site for the lecture are chosen by an ALSC committee. <www.ala.org>.

Grolier Foundation Award American Library Association Awards Committee, 50 E. Huron St., Chicago, IL 60611. Given to a community librarian or a school librarian who has made an unusual contribution to the stimulation and guidance of reading by children and young people. <www.ala.org>.

Lucile Micheels Pannell Award Women's National Book Association, National, PO Box 237, FDR Station, New York, NY 10150. Awards in the "general store" category and in the "children's specialty bookstore" category are presented annually by the Women's National Book Association to the owners of two bookstores whose innovative programs encourage children's reading. <http://www.wnba-books.org/pannell-award/>.

Regina Medal Catholic Library Association, 205 W Monroe Street, Suite 314, Chicago, IL 60606. For "continued distinguished contribution to children's literature." <www.cathla.org>.

University of Southern Mississippi Children's Collection Medallion University of Southern Mississippi Book Festival, USM Library, Hattiesburg, MS 39401. For a writer or an illustrator who has made an "outstanding contribution to the field of children's literature." <www.usm.edu>.

Appendix B

Book Selection Aids

Note: Publishers' addresses may change. For complete and up-to-date information, see the current edition of *Literary Market Place* or *Children's Books in Print*.

Comprehensive Lists and Directories

Children's Books in Print. **R.R. Bowker. Grey House Publishing. Annual.** A comprehensive listing of children's books currently in print. Includes titles for grades K–12. Titles are arranged alphabetically by author, title, and illustrator. A list of publisher addresses is provided. Also includes children's book awards for the previous ten years.

Guide to Reference Materials for School Media Centers, **6th ed. Barbara Ripp Safford. Libraries Unlimited, 2010.** Includes annotations and evaluations for useful reference tools for school media centers. Materials are arranged in order by subject. Also includes a list of sources and selection aids for print and non-print materials.

The Newbery and Caldecott Awards: A Guide to the Medal and Honor Books 2018 Edition. Association for Library Service to Children. This provides a comprehensive survey of the award processes and winners.

Subject Guide to Children's Books in Print. **R.R. Bowker. Grey House Publishing.** A companion volume to *Children's Books in Print*. Arranges all children's titles currently in print using more than 6,000 subject headings. Particularly useful for finding and ordering titles on specific subjects; however, titles are not annotated.

General Selection Aids

The Horn Book Guide to Children's and Young Adult Books. **Horn Book, Inc. Semiannual.** Provides short reviews of children's and young-adult books published in the United States during the prior publishing season with references to longer reviews in *Horn Book Magazine*. Books are given a numerical evaluation from 1 to 6. Published in a digital pdf format with an accompanying searchable database available by subscription. <https://www.hbook.com/horn-book-guide/>

Curriculum Areas and Genres of Literature

Anatomy of Wonder: A Critical Guide to Science Fiction. **Neil Barron 5th ed. Libraries Unlimited, 2004.** Includes a chapter that annotates titles for children and young adults, as well as 3,000 additional titles that would appeal to readers of the genre. Includes discussion of sci-fi poetry, film connections, and a chapter on classroom aids.

Sharing Books, Talking Science: Exploring Scientific Concepts with Children's Literature. Valerie Bang-Jensen and Mark Lubkowitz. *Sharing Books, Talking Science: Exploring Scientific Concepts with Children's Literature*. **Heinemann, 2017.**

This resource explores ways in which children's literature is a natural avenue for exploring Next Generation Science Standards.

Teaching with Text Sets. **Mary Ann Cappiello and Erika Thulin Dawes. Shell Education, 2012.** A resource for literature-based teaching across content areas and in line with National Standards.

Information About Authors and Illustrators

The Essential Guide to Children's Books and Their Creators. **Anita Silvey, ed. Houghton Mifflin, 2002.** This handsomely designed book includes biographical descriptions of and first-person reflections by important twentieth-century authors and illustrators and critical essays on a range of topics central to the study of children's literature.

Meet the Authors and Illustrators: 60 Creators of Favorite Children's Books Talk About Their Work. **Deborah Kovacs and James Preller. Scholastic Inc., 730 Broadway, New York, NY 10003. 1999. 142 pp.** Two children's book authors have collected information on favorite authors and illustrators from around the world. Each two-page highlight includes information about the author or illustrator, selected titles, pictures, and a "do-it-yourself" activity suggested for children.

Something About the Author. **Gale Research.** There are more than 200 volumes in print, added to periodically. Clear and sizable essays on contemporary authors and illustrators. Updating allows more-recent authors to be included. Contains photographs as well as reproductions from works of the illustrators. Suitable for middle-grade children to use for gathering biographical information.

Periodicals

Bookbird: A Journal of International Children's Literature. **IBBY, International Board on Books for Young People. Quarterly.** This excellent journal reflects the international character of children's literature through articles and profiles of authors and illustrators from member countries. Themed issues have included "Children's Poetry," "Southeast Asia," "Girls and Women," and "Philosophy for Children."

Book Links. **American Library Association. Four times/year.** This publication connects books, libraries, and classrooms. Special features include "book strategies" or guides for teaching a particular book, interviews with authors and illustrators to discover their personal story behind the book, book themes, poetry, and "just for fun," books for children to read and enjoy.

Booklist/BookListOnline.com. **American Library Association. Twice/month.** Reviews both adult and children's titles, including both print and nonprint materials. Reviews are annotated and graded by age levels and grades. Includes reviews of new selection tools. Often contains subject lists of good books in particular fields. Lists prize-winning books annually.

Book Review Digest. **H. W. Wilson Co. Annual.** Evaluates about 5,000 adult and children's books per year. For those books included, provides citations from several reviews that have appeared in other review periodicals.

The Bulletin of the Center for Children's Books. **Johns Hopkins University Press. 11 issues/year.** Reviews about 75 current children's books in each issue with negative as well as favorable reviews. Each entry is graded. Annotations stress curricular use, values, and literary merit.

CBC Newsletter. **Children's Book Council.** <www.cbcbooks.org/>. A website about children's books, including information about special events, free and inexpensive materials from publishers, and lists of prize-winners, as well as discussion of new books.

Childhood Education: Innovations. **Association for Childhood Education International.** Includes a column on children's books that contains annotated reviews on about 25 books.

Children and Libraries. **Association for Library Services to Children and Young Adult Services Division, American Library Association. Quarterly.** Provides articles on issues in children's literature and children's librarianship, international news, texts of speeches, and lists of upcoming events of interest in the field. Articles are often annotated bibliographies on subjects of current interest.

Children's Literature in Education. **Springer. Quarterly.** Publishes longer articles on English and American children's literature, including criticism, history, and biographical essays.

Cricket Magazines. **Cricket Media.** Various magazines for children of elementary school age.

The Dragon Lode. **Children's Literature and Reading Special Interest Group of the International Literacy Association.** <https://www.clrsig.org/dragonlode.html>. **Two issues/year.** The journal comes with membership in the International Literacy Association and features articles, book reviews, and classroom ideas that focus on children's literature.

Horn Book Magazine. **Horn Book, Inc. Bimonthly.** <https://www.hbook.com/horn-book-magazine-2/>. Includes detailed reviews of children's books judged by the editorial staff to be the best in children's literature. Contains articles about the literature, interviews with authors, and text of important speeches in the field of literature (Newbery and Caldecott acceptance speeches are published in the August issue each year). October issue lists the outstanding books of the previous year.

Journal of Children's Literature. **Children's Literature Assembly of the National Council of Teachers of English.** <http://www.childrensliteratureassembly.org/journal.html>. **Two issues/year.** The journal comes with membership in the Children's Literature Assembly and features articles, book reviews, and classroom ideas that focus on children's literature.

Knowledge Quest (formerly *School Library Media Quarterly*). **American Association of School Librarians, American Library Association. Quarterly.** Official journal of the AASL. Includes articles on book evaluations, censorship, library services, standards of service, and so on.

Language Arts. **National Council of Teachers of English. Six issues/year.** "Books for Children" section features regular reviews of new books. Several issues focus on literature and reading, containing articles on authors, using literature in the classroom, and so on.

The Lion and the Unicorn. **Johns Hopkins University Press. Three issues/year.** Literary criticism, book reviews, and interviews with authors of children's literature. Each issue presents a particular theme or genre around which articles are centered.

The New York Times Book Review. **New York Times Co.** Includes an online column devoted to Children's Books.

Publishers Weekly. Twice a year, in spring and fall, a "Children's Book Number" is published that includes new titles from all major publishers, as well as reviews. Negative reviews are included. Occasionally includes feature articles on children's books and publishing for children.

School Library Journal. **Monthly.** Reviews most children's books, using librarians, teachers, and critics from around the country as reviewers. Includes both positive and negative reviews. Categorizes reviews by age levels. Also includes feature articles on children's literature, children's library services, technology, and nonprint materials. December issue includes a "Best Books" section.

Science Books and Films. **American Association for the Advancement of Science. Bimonthly.** Reviews trade, text, and reference books for students in all grades in both pure and applied sciences. Includes nonprint materials. Indicates level of expertise required to use a piece of material. Books are reviewed by specialists in the field.

Science and Children. **National Science Teachers Association. Eight times/year.** Includes a monthly column that reviews books and nonprint materials.

Selected Professional websites

American Association of School Librarians <www.ala.org/aasl>. The American Association of School Librarians is a division of the American Library Association responsible for planning, improving, and extending library media services for children and young people.

Association for Library Service to Children <www.ala.org/alsc>. The Association for Library Service to Children is the division of the American Library Association that oversees the Caldecott and Newbery awards and provides many other activities relating to children and books.

Children's Book Council <www.cbcbooks.org>. The Children's Book Council is the trade association of U.S. publishers of children's books. The Council promotes the use and enjoyment of trade books and related materials for young people and disseminates information about children's trade book publishing. This site provides links to author websites and provides bibliographies such as Notable Social Studies Trade Books for Children and Outstanding Science Books for Children.

Cooperative Children's Book Center (CCBC) <www.education.wisc.edu/ccbc>. The Cooperative Children's Book Center at the University of Wisconsin-Madison is a noncirculating examination study and research library for adults with an interest in children's and young-adult literature.

Council for Exceptional Children
<https://www.cec.sped.org/>.
The Council advocates on behalf of children with exceptionalities and oversees the Dolly Gray Awards.

International Board on Books for Young People
<http://www.ibby.org/>.
This is a nonprofit organization that represents an international network of people who are committed to bringing children and books together. The USBBY is the United States section: http://usbby.org/HomePage.asp

International Literacy Association
<www.reading.org>.
The International Literacy Association seeks to promote literacy by improving the quality of reading instruction, serving as a clearinghouse for reading research, and promoting life-long reading habits.

National Council of Teachers of English
<www.ncte.org>.
NCTE is a professional organization of educators in English Studies, Literacy, and the Language Arts. *The Council Chronicle* provides a forum for members to reflect on a variety of topics.

Young Adult Library Services Association of the American Library Association
<www.ala.org/yalsa>.
The Young Adult Library Services Association is the division of the American Library Association that oversees the Printz Award and provides many other activities relating to young adults.

Author, Illustrator, Title Index

Subject Index